THE WORLD SINCE 1945

THE WORLD SINCE 1945

T. E. VADNEY

Facts On File Publications
New York, New York ● Oxford, England

THE WORLD SINCE 1945

Library of Congress Cataloging-in-Publication Data

Vadney, Thomas E., 1939-
    The world since 1945.

    Includes index.
    1. History, Modern—1945-   . I. Title.
D840.V25   1987   909.82   87-9145
ISBN 0-8160-1815-4

Printed in the United States of America

10 9 8 7 6 5 4 3 2 1

CONTENTS

LIST OF MAPS

PREFACE

This book is a survey of recent global history, although it makes no claim to cover literally everything that has ever happened since the Second World War. To try and do so within the confines of a single volume would result in a mere list of names and dates, and leave little room for explanation. Accordingly the strategy has been to select particular cases as examples of more general trends, and to explore them in some detail. Readers may or may not agree with the choices presented here, and there are certainly many issues and regions which do not receive the attention they deserve. Yet the book examines a broad spectrum of regional and international developments, emphasizing the role of the superpowers and particularly their relations with the Third World, so that we shall have more than enough to contend with. The narrative highlights political events, and thus provides a foundation for more specialized reading in social and economic history.

Readers will note that I have allotted more space to the Western Bloc than to the Eastern. By the 1980s there were no more than thirty countries (out of approximately 170 in all) which claimed to be Marxist in some respect, and I have struck a balance accordingly. I have also given a large amount of space to developments in the Third World, because it is home to three-quarters of the world's population. Moreover, perhaps as many as 25 million people have lost their lives in wars and other conflicts in Asia, the Middle East, Africa and Latin America since 1945. The history of the Third World is thus central to any study which purports to be global in scope. In addition I frequently reach further into the past and examine events well before the Second World War, in order to provide necessary background. The strength of the historical approach is that it introduces whatever evidence is needed for understanding the issues at hand, whether it is from the same or from an earlier time. There are, of course, other ways of interpreting events besides the views in these pages, but my goal has been to emphasize the specific historical contingencies prevailing in each situation, and thus to explain a variety of different outcomes.

I have kept textual references to a minimum, and acknowledge my indebtedness to other authors in the Bibliographical Note. The quality of their work is remarkable indeed, as is the quantity. I have also benefited from the advice of colleagues throughout Canada and from the support of my home university. I wish to thank Ed Moulton, Lionel Steiman, Tim Anna, John Kendle, Henry Heller, Brian Evans, David Johnson, P. E. Prestwich, Sinh Vinh, H. E. Wilson, Fritz Lehmann, Ron Finch, Ron Harpelle, Ryan Toews, Doug Sprague and, most of all, Mark Gabbert for their assistance, and the University of Manitoba for leave to carry out research and to write.

PART I

FROM THE SECOND WORLD WAR
TO DECOLONIZATION

1

THE ORIGINS OF
THE POST-1945 WORLD

The background to global history since 1945 is to be found in the Second World War, though not simply in the defeat of Germany and Japan. More importantly for the future, the war marked the emergence of the United States and the Soviet Union as the chief arbiters of international affairs. This did not mean that their authority was beyond question or that they invariably realized their goals. But certainly the Americans and the Russians were left with more power than anyone else. By contrast the war reduced the influence of Britain and the nations of Western Europe, and in addition undermined their capacity to govern the colonial world. It thus paved the way for a rapid movement towards decolonization, and in some places (e.g. Indo-China) spurred the development of national liberation struggles and revolution.

The Second World War had other consequences as well. It marked the beginning of the nuclear age, at Hiroshima and Nagasaki. The world was a considerably more dangerous place as a result. The war also led directly to the consolidation of the Eastern or Communist Bloc. Before the outbreak of hostilities in 1939 only one country in the entire world was a satellite of the Soviet Union – the Mongolian People's Republic (MPR). Lying between the frontiers of China and Siberia, the MPR had strategic importance for the Russians, but the association of the two nations did not constitute a threat to the capitalist powers of the West or mean that communism was on its way to becoming a global force. For all practical purposes a communist bloc or group of nations did not exist, and the USSR was isolated. With Russia's entry into the Second World War, however, all this began to change, and despite American antipathy towards the expansion of communism. Accordingly it is with the war itself, and particularly the role of the USSR and the USA, that we shall begin.

THE SOVIET UNION AND
THE COMING OF WAR

The Soviet Union became one of the principals in the alliance against Germany on 22 June 1941, when Hitler's armies launched an invasion of the USSR under the code name 'Operation Barbarossa'. By then Europe had been at war for nearly two years, and Germany had established control over most of the Continent by either conquest or the threat of conquest. Despite this the Americans had not entered the war, and would not do so until December. Only the United Kingdom held out, with the help of Imperial and Commonwealth troops. The British turned back the *Luftwaffe* in the air battles over England and engaged the Germans and Italians in North Africa, where they threatened the British hold on Egypt and the Suez Canal. But the main prize was Europe, and there not a single Western army challenged the enemy. The last Allied troops had been evacuated from France in June 1940, a year before the invasion of Russia, and a British initiative in Greece had been defeated in the spring of 1941.

When the Soviets were attacked, therefore, the fortunes of the anti-German forces were at their lowest. Yet the Russians themselves were responsible for this in no small measure. In August 1939 they had signed a non-aggression pact with the Nazis. Until then they had participated in talks with the British and French about forming an anti-German coalition, but with the Nazi–Soviet Pact the Russians reversed their position and Hitler was free to do as he would. On 1 September 1939 German troops marched into Poland and launched Europe into what soon became a general war.

The Nazi–Soviet Pact came as a shock because it indicated that the Russians had been bargaining in secret with Hitler while at the same time continuing talks in Moscow with the UK and France. Soviet historians rationalize this on the grounds that the Western powers only 'made a pretence of negotiating' and that 'the British and French statesmen still secretly tried to come to terms with Germany in exchange for giving her a free hand in the East'.* Unfortunately the Western record of appeasing Hitler before 1939 lent just enough credibility to such a charge for the Russians to doubt whether they could count on London and Paris. For

---

* A. Z. Manfred (ed.), *A Short History of the World* (Moscow: 1974), II, 154–5. The spellings used in quotations and other references have been made consistent with the rest of the text.

this reason they bargained with both sides, but it was the Germans who met their terms. In a separate protocol that went beyond the non-aggression pact, Hitler and Stalin agreed that Poland and the rest of Eastern Europe would be divided into two spheres of influence, one German and the other Soviet. Hitler was thereby relieved of the possibility that the USSR might join an anti-German alliance, and was at liberty to proceed accordingly. For his part Stalin gained a modicum of security, and when the war broke out, he laid claim to parts of Poland and Finland and all of Lithuania, Latvia and Estonia. A buffer zone in Eastern Europe between the USSR and the West was thus a goal of Soviet foreign policy from the very start of the Second World War.

EAST–WEST RELATIONS
In the West, of course, the Nazi–Soviet Pact was regarded as a singular act of treachery. Yet an alliance among the United Kingdom, France and Russia would have been equally incongruous. The need to contain Hitler had created common interests between the Western powers and the USSR, but their relations had also been characterized by hostility ever since the Bolshevik Revolution of 1917. The Soviets had ended capitalist enterprise in their country, repudiated the debts of the Czarist government, and nationalized the private property of Russians and foreigners alike. The loss to the West was substantial. By 1914 foreigners held nearly half of Russia's national debt. In 1917 they owned more than one-third of its industrial investment and had major holdings in railways, banking, engineering and chemicals, and in oil, coal and other minerals, often controlling 50 per cent or more of an industry. Moreover, upon seizing power, the Soviets abandoned their allies in the First World War and made a separate peace with Germany. This was a popular decision inside Russia and helped the Bolsheviks consolidate their power at home, but Britain and France feared it would also enable the Kaiser's armies to increase their pressure on the Western Front. Adding insult to injury, the Soviets published a series of secret treaties to which the Czar had been party and which outlined the territorial ambitions of the European powers after the war. The revelations caused discord among the Allies, and culminated in demands by the United States (which had not been a signatory) that they be put aside.

What appeared to be the greatest threat to emerge from Russia, however, was the Communist International, or Comintern, founded by

Vladimir Ilyich Lenin in March 1919 as an agency of worldwide revolution. Lenin had led the Bolsheviks to power in Russia, but believed that the survival of the Soviet revolution depended upon its extension elsewhere, especially to the developed West. Precisely because capitalism was a global phenomenon, it had to be met with a global strategy. Otherwise the USSR would remain isolated and vulnerable to attack by the capitalist powers. This was no imaginary fear, as Britain, France, the United States, Japan and other countries had already intervened on the side of counter-revolutionaries operating inside Russia. The goal was to strangle Bolshevism at birth and overthrow the Soviet government. The number of foreign troops was insufficient to affect the outcome of the revolution and the Bolsheviks survived, but the resort to direct military intervention set the tone of East–West relations thereafter.

Western fears of Bolshevism, moreover, seemed to be confirmed by events elsewhere. With the end of the First World War many parts of Europe appeared to be on the verge of revolution. In Germany the radical Spartacists led uprisings in Berlin and other centres, and a short-lived communist republic was proclaimed in Bavaria in April 1919. Between March and August of the same year communists under Béla Kun formed the government of Hungary. In the early 1920s sporadic uprisings occurred again in Germany and also in Bulgaria and Estonia. Even in far off North America people did not feel safe, so that the years 1918–20 are known in US history as the 'Great Red Scare'. But by 1924 (the year of Lenin's death) the radicals invariably had been defeated, often with appalling brutality, and the forces of revolution were in retreat.

The result was a strategic and ideological crisis for the Bolsheviks, but one that Lenin's successor, Joseph Stalin, had resolved by the end of the 1920s. Equally important, his solution made the USSR even less of a threat than Westerners realized. Stalin imposed a new political line, 'Socialism in One Country', which reconciled the defeat of Bolshevism abroad with its survival in the USSR and justified placing the needs of the Soviet Union before those of revolution in the West. Given developments in Europe, Stalin believed that Russia could expect to remain the only communist country in the world for some time to come. A combination of repression and reform had stemmed the tide of revolution elsewhere on the Continent. While the Comintern persisted in its efforts to influence the course of a great civil war in China, by the end of the 1920s communists were in retreat there as well. Hence the task at hand was to protect the Soviet Union as the bastion of revolutionary communism in a hostile world. To this end the Comintern was instructed to act with greater circumspection, and to give priority to the national interests of the USSR.

With their recent taste of Bolshevism, Western leaders were not about to give much credence to the emerging Comintern line. Yet in the long run the policy of 'Socialism in One Country' turned out to be related to other developments, the effect of which was also to draw the USSR inward. First, in consolidating his personal political power, Stalin eliminated several of his opponents, including those who advocated a more active foreign policy. Chief among these was Leon Trotsky, who was exiled at the end of the 1920s and assassinated in 1940. The most outspoken proponent of world revolution was thus expelled from the ranks of Soviet policy-makers. Second, the change in Comintern policy was significant because it reflected the interests of an emergent ruling class. In time this turned out to have considerable import for East–West relations. A new elite had begun to take shape as soon as the Bolsheviks seized power in 1917. Communist party members took up posts in the army and the government. They soon constituted a vested interest in Russian society, one which enjoyed special privileges in the form of greater power, higher material rewards and higher status than the rest of the population. But all these prerogatives depended on preserving the *status quo*, and this had implications for foreign affairs. The new ruling class feared that successful revolutions abroad might raise demands inside the USSR for an improvement in the condition of the working class there, demands which could only be met at the expense of the elite. More participation by the people in decision-making, for example, would erode the authority and power of bureaucrats in both party and state. Furthermore, the promotion of global revolution risked drawing a response from the more powerful West, thereby endangering the survival of the USSR and with it the privileges of the Soviet ruling class. For a variety of reasons, then, the new leaders of the USSR were beginning to abjure adventurism in foreign affairs.

The evolution of Soviet society, however, was too gradual and too obscure to have an effect on Western policy towards the USSR. For most of the inter-war period the European powers attempted to establish a *cordon sanitaire* guarding the approaches from Russia to the West and made up of buffer states in Eastern Europe. This was the settled policy of the negotiators who gathered for the Paris Peace Conference in 1919 to draw up treaties ending the First World War. By dividing Eastern Europe into a number of competitive states, each jealously guarding its autonomy, they hoped not only to check German power but Russian as well. Finland, Estonia, Latvia, Lithuania and Poland had all been incorporated into Czarist Russia before the war, and afterwards had a stake in preventing a resurgence of Russian power. The other countries of Eastern Europe, made up of the remnants of the Austro-Hungarian Empire and of the strongly nationalistic states of the Balkans, could also be counted upon to oppose both Germany and the Soviet Union.

Besides trying to tip the balance of power their way, the Western nations ostracized the USSR. There was no Russian representative at Paris, for example, and it was not until 1934 that the Soviet Union was admitted to the League of Nations, the predecessor of the United Nations. It was only by the mid-1920s that most countries even accorded the USSR diplomatic recognition, although many had resumed limited commercial contacts before then. The United States held out the longest, and refused to recognize the Soviet government until 1933. Even then Washington acted mainly out of self-interest. The Western world was in the throes of the Great Depression, which had begun in 1929. American entrepreneurs, including the United States Chamber of Commerce, therefore decided it was time to expand trade with the USSR. They needed the business, and lobbied the administration of President Franklin Roosevelt accordingly. For his part Stalin wanted to buy foreign technology in order to spur industrialization.

Recognition was extended, but the hoped-for markets failed to materialize. The Russian economy had severe problems of its own, arising mainly from Stalin's policies of rapid industrialization and the compulsory collectivization of agriculture. Millions of Soviet citizens were sent to prison or into exile, or even executed, for resisting his Five Year Plans, and the Russian economy was thrown into chaos. It has been estimated that during the decade 1930–40 at least 6.5 million people (and possibly more than twice this number) lost their lives in Stalin's terror, including those who starved to death as the result of economic dislocation as well as those who were executed or who died in prison. Again, few Westerners had a very clear understanding of developments inside the USSR, so that Americans tended to exaggerate the potential of the Russian market. They were to be disappointed. For their part the Soviets welcomed American recognition, but they also perceived the motives of self-interest behind it, so relations remained cool.

THE GERMAN PROBLEM

The European powers, however, and not the United States dominated international politics between the two world wars. Yet the Americans certainly were a major factor in the global economy, and held a huge debt contracted by the Western Allies during the First World War. Accordingly they were involved in periodic negotiations to reschedule this debt and also to reduce Germany's reparations payments, which had been exacted by the victors at the Paris Peace Conference to make the Germans pay for the war. Washington also played an important role in disarmament and in conferences to outlaw war as an instrument of national policy. Yet it never joined the League of Nations, so that its role in global diplomacy was limited. The US would not emerge as leader of the Western Bloc until the Second World War. In the meantime the initiative was in the hands of the British and French, and for them the German problem was the principal issue of the inter-war period, even exceeding Bolshevism in importance.

Germany was weak in both economic and military terms in the 1920s, and even for a long time after Hitler assumed power in the early 1930s. Britain and France acting together might have been able to maintain order in Europe. The difficulty was that they disagreed on how to handle Germany. The issues were complex, but in effect they came down to this: France (which had been the site of most of the fighting during the First World War) favoured reprisals against Germany and placed questions of security first, whereas Britain tended to favour the reintegration of Germany into European life as quickly as possible. The British reasoned that the Germans were too important a component of the Continental economy to be cut off. In consequence, when the French occupied the Ruhr industrial region of Germany in 1923 in order to force the payment of reparations, the British questioned the merits of military action. Of course, Britain saw itself as an island fortress. Geography provided a certain measure of security, a luxury not shared by France. Furthermore, the victors had taken over Germany's merchant fleet and its colonies, while its navy had been scuttled. As a result the United Kingdom had achieved both the security and the economic reparations that France as a Continental power found more difficult to obtain. And whereas France saw the nations of Eastern Europe as a substitute for an alliance with Moscow against Berlin, Britain tended to see them as nurturing a sense of grievance among Germans, thus hindering reconciliation. Italy might have assumed a mediating role between Britain and France, because it had been on the Allied side during the war, but as the 1930s unfolded its leader, Benito Mussolini, gravitated towards Germany. Thus differences among the European powers militated against consistent policies towards Germany, and created opportunities for Hitler.

Certainly Hitler gave plenty of warning about his eventual plans to restore Germany as a great power. It was a fact that after becoming chancellor on 30 January 1933 he was prepared to back down in the face of resistance. Yet he soon discovered that the divisions between Britain and France were quite sufficient to prevent them from acting decisively. As a result the British view that Germany's legitimate interests must be recognized carried the day. The issue was how to define 'legitimate', but Hitler seized the initiative. The very year he became chancellor he announced Germany's withdrawal from the League of Nations and from the Geneva Disarmament Conference. In 1934 he backtracked by signing a non-aggression pact with Poland, a move which encouraged the British. But in the same year he provided aid to Nazis attempting to overthrow the government of Austria, though he denied responsibility when they failed. The Austrian crisis inspired a limited *rapprochement*, born of necessity, between Paris and Moscow, and France sponsored the admission of Russia to the League of Nations in September 1934.

Yet Hitler continued to test his adversaries. In March 1935 he renounced the disarmament clauses of the Versailles Treaty, introduced general conscription, and accelerated the build-up of his military forces. In reply Britain, France and for the time being Italy met at the Stresa Conference to condemn these moves and also Hitler's designs on Austria. They threatened reprisals against further indications of possible German aggression, but the effect of this was vitiated when the British signed a naval treaty with Germany in June. The treaty limited the German navy to one-third that of Britain, but allowed an equal number of submarines. It suggested that the United Kingdom still hoped to achieve reconciliation with Germany, and was a significant departure from French policy. The events of 1934–5 induced France to strengthen the Russian connection, resulting in an agreement whereby each would provide aid to the other in the event of unprovoked aggression – in other words, in the event of an attack by Germany.

Hitler's record of success, however, won the admiration of the Italians. Initially Mussolini saw Germany as his chief competitor for influence in Europe, but in time he became the Nazis' most important ally. He proceeded to apply similar tactics by invading Ethiopia in 1935, which had long been a goal of Italian imperialists. It was an easy target, and League of Nations sanctions proved ineffective. Ethiopia was conquered by the spring of 1936. The discomfiture this caused Britain and France only encouraged both dictators. On 7 March 1936 Hitler sent troops into the Rhineland, which had been demilitarized by the Versailles Treaty, and thus took over a region intended to serve as a buffer between France and Germany. This latest success drew Mussolini yet closer to the Nazis, so that what became known as the Berlin–Rome Axis began to take shape. Equally important, Hitler attracted support from many of the states of Eastern Europe. By the 1930s all the countries between Germany and Russia except Czechoslovakia were right-wing dictatorships, and their leaders were increasingly awed by Hitler's decisive rebuilding of German power. If further proof were needed, it was provided by the Spanish Civil War (1936–9). Both Germany and Italy dispatched arms and personnel to fascist rebels led by General Francisco Franco. While the Russians attempted to help radical and anarchist elements identified with the republican forces, the latter went down to defeat. Indeed, Stalin's support had been ambiguous at best, because he was more worried about the growing strength of the Nazis. A fascist Germany, after all, had the potential to threaten Russia's security much more directly than a fascist Spain. In 1938 Hitler used the threat of force to incorporate Austria into the Third Reich, and the next year the Italians took over Albania.

Throughout, Britain and France were unable to agree on how far to co-operate with the USSR as the only other major power directly affected by the likelihood of further German expansion and therefore willing to take a stand. Indeed Moscow consistently urged stronger action against Berlin, a fact which only made the signing of the Nazi–Soviet Pact of 1939 all the more tragic. But in the late 1930s events inside Russia intervened to confirm the worst fears of the Western powers as to the character of the Soviet regime. In 1936 Moscow published a new constitution which appeared to set the USSR on the road to democratic government. In August of the same year, however, the first of three major show trials began. Charges of treason leading to jail or death were levelled at leading figures of the communist party and government, including many of the 'old Bolsheviks' associated with Lenin. Stalin persecuted less important persons as well, and instituted a series of purges which effectively eliminated all those who might have challenged his authority. He even attempted to replace certain leaders of communist parties abroad. By the end of the last trial in 1938 millions of people had been affected, including important members of the Russian general staff, that is, the top military officers. Stalin's image as a ruthless dictator emerged more clearly than ever, and convinced Britain and France once again that there was little to choose between Hitler and Stalin. This turn in events also suggested that the Russian dictator was unstable and unreliable, so that the meaning of any commitment he might make could be doubted. From Stalin's perspective, of course, the West was not particularly dependable either.

Both sides' suspicions were soon to be corroborated. In the spring of 1938 Hitler began making demands that the Sudetenland, an area of Czechoslovakia containing a large German population, be placed under the protection of the Reich. The UK took the lead in proposing compromise, and at the Munich Conference of September 1938 the British prime minister, Neville Chamberlain, met with Hitler, Mussolini and Edouard Daladier of France. It was agreed that Germany might absorb the Sudetenland – hardly a compromise. The Czechs were not allowed to participate in the talks, but were simply informed of the decision. The Russians were not consulted either, and to them it looked as if Britain and France were willing to settle with Hitler at any price. The implications for their own safety were clear. For the time being London and Paris placed their faith in appeasement, for which Munich became justly famous, and the world briefly achieved what Chamberlain described as 'peace in our time'.

Any illusion that meaningful security had been established dissolved in March 1939, when Hitler completed the dismemberment of Czechoslovakia, with help from Hungary (which wished to take control of the province of Ruthenia). The result was that an entire nation disappeared from the map as the direct consequence of Hitler's ambitions. In response Britain and France began discussions with Russia concerning a co-ordinated strategy, but later in the summer so did the Germans. The outcome was the Nazi–Soviet Pact. What actually led up to a general war was Hitler's demand in the summer of 1939 that Poland return territories which had been part of Germany before the First World War. When invasion followed, on 1 September, Britain and France at last drew the line and declared war. Without the Russians, however, the Western powers lacked the means for waging an effective campaign in Eastern Europe. The facts of geography and the limits of their power determined this, and so Poland could not be defended. By the end of the month Germany took the western half of the country, and Russia occupied the rest. The next year Hitler's armies struck through Western

Europe in a *Blitzkrieg* (or 'lightning war', a surprise offensive in which air and mechanized ground forces attacked in a co-ordinated strategy). It began to look as though Stalin had made a realistic, if Machiavellian, choice.

It was doubtful, however, whether Stalin really believed that he had achieved long-term security by signing the Nazi–Soviet Pact. Hitler had always spoken of the East as the most probable direction of future German expansion. In due course, therefore, the Russians used the breathing-spell provided by the pact to accelerate the build-up of their military forces. More importantly for the future, the record of pre-war relations made it apparent that the Grand Alliance of Britain, Russia and later the United States, once formed in 1941, would be united by very little indeed, and that the same kind of manoeuvring for advantage would be likely to carry over into the war itself. This is in fact what happened, and the consequences accounted for both the Soviet Union's strategic position at the end of the war and for its continuing alienation from its Western associates. But the Grand Alliance was still in the future.

THE GERMAN SWEEP

Once Poland was divided between Germany and the Soviet Union, the Russians decided to consolidate their defences. Their first move was to demand concessions from Finland, but when these were turned down the USSR invaded. The two countries reached a settlement by March 1940. Then Moscow went on to annex Lithuania, Latvia and Estonia by the summer of the same year. Romania was forced to return former Russian territories as well. In the early stages of the war, however, the main action was in Western Europe and did not involve the USSR. After a lull through the winter of 1939–40, known as the 'Phoney War', Germany invaded Denmark and Norway on 9 April 1940, and then in May conquered the Netherlands, Belgium and Luxembourg. The Nazis entered Paris on 14 June, and the French sought an armistice on 17 June. Just before the fall of France, Italy invaded in the south. It looked like a clean sweep for the Axis powers until the German air force met its match in the 'Battle of Britain', the air war over England. By the autumn of 1940 it was apparent that the *Luftwaffe* could not control the skies. This was Hitler's first major setback. He postponed plans for an invasion of Britain ('Operation Sea-Lion') and looked to the east instead, where he could deploy his considerable advantages in land power to good effect. Before he could move against Russia (notwithstanding the Nazi–Soviet

Pact), however, Hitler had to consolidate his position in the Balkans and deal with a series of crises created by his over-ambitious ally, Mussolini.

After the Nazi triumph in Western Europe the governments of Hungary, Romania and Bulgaria joined the German bloc, albeit under threat of invasion. All three signed the Tripartite Pact, an alliance of fascist states created by Germany, Italy and Japan in September 1940. Yugoslavia, however, resisted. Hitler therefore invaded in April 1941. He also had to save the Italians from defeat in the same region. Mussolini had attacked Greece from Albania in October 1940, but encountered heavy resistance. The Greeks drove his forces back into Albania, and the British sent troops from North Africa to assist. Hitler came to the rescue, conquering Greece and Crete by the end of May 1941. With the Balkans and Greece secure, the Nazis could proceed with their plans to invade Russia. Furthermore, the diversion of British forces to Greece weakened the UK's position in North Africa. There too German troops had been dispatched to help the Italians, who hoped to expand their colonial holdings in the region. Although his forces were spread across many fronts, Hitler's successes had been rapid and substantial. He felt ready, therefore, to take on the Russians, and invaded on 22 June 1941.

THE AMERICANS
The invasion of the USSR created the Anglo-Russian alliance that might have been in 1939. As soon as Hitler moved, Prime Minister Winston Churchill of Britain promised all aid possible to Russia. The problem was that he had little to spare. According to the terms of international law the United States was still neutral, but some months later President Franklin Roosevelt of the United States declared the Soviet Union eligible for assistance under Lend Lease. Lend Lease was an American programme for sending military supplies to nations desig- nated by the president as vital to American security. The US did not enter the war just yet, and a public-opinion poll in November 1941 indicated that fewer than 35 per cent of Americans would vote to go to war if a referendum were held on the issue. Providing war *matériel* to other nations was one matter, but becoming a belligerent was quite another. In the meantime the only troops fighting the Nazis on the Continent were Soviet ones. The Germans were approaching Moscow and Leningrad by October 1941, and the Russian government had to be evacuated to Kuibyshev. But neither Moscow nor Leningrad

surrendered, and the USSR launched its first counter-offensive before the end of 1941.

Without the United States the Grand Alliance was still incomplete. Roosevelt had been alert to the implications of Nazi aggression and pressed for greater American involvement. But the public was more directly affected by domestic issues, chiefly the Great Depression. Safe in 'Fortress America', thousands of miles from the fighting in an age before jet aircraft had become operational and well before the era of the intercontinental ballistic missile, many people in the United States gave scant attention to European affairs. Even the incredible anti-Semitic campaigns of the Hitler regime, which culminated in the Holocaust and the murder of six million Jews, were insufficient to induce action. Indeed, anti-Semitism was endemic to America as well as Europe. It was hardly a German monopoly, so that the United States was not ready to fight in order to save the Jews. Of course, the mass exterminations in the gas chambers of Auschwitz, Treblinka, Belzec, Sobibor, Maidanek and other concentration camps were still in the future, though even then the Allies would effectively ignore them. Still, in the 1930s German Jews had also been subjected to persecution, and sent away to prison camps. To Americans, however, it was none of their concern.

THE FAR EAST

Developments in the Far East, not European affairs, drew the United States into the war. The two theatres were not unrelated in the sense that the conflict in Europe made it impossible for Britain, France and the Netherlands to defend their colonies in Asia, and thus provided Japanese expansionists with the opportunity of a lifetime. This affected vital American interests. While the Philippine Islands were a US colony and no doubt in some danger, the possibility that Japan would take over the rest of South-East Asia plus China was just as threatening in Washington's view. As one of the lesser colonial powers in the Far East, the United States had a long-standing policy of advocating free and open markets, not exclusive spheres of influence, but the Japanese seemed determined to establish the latter.

The 'Open Door Policy' summarized the American position. In a series of diplomatic notes prepared in 1899 and 1900 Washington had proposed that the merchants of all nations be accorded equal access to the various zones of control established by other imperial powers in China. The Americans were in no position to set up zones of their own, because they were preoccupied with the pacification of the Philippine Islands. They had taken the Philippines from Spain during the Spanish–American War of 1898, but then encountered the fierce resistance of the Filipino independence movement. A guerrilla war developed which lasted well into the twentieth century. Because the Americans were tied down in the Philippines, it was very much in their interest to suggest that the China market be opened to all merchants on an equal basis.

The United States believed that other trading nations had an interest in supporting the Open Door as well. Countries which were competitive in business had nothing to fear and perhaps much to gain. If there were no exclusive zones, then the merchants of each country would have access to all of China, not just part of it. For this reason the British in particular encouraged the American initiative. They were the leading foreign power in China, but feared the consequences of a new round of imperial expansion by Germany, Russia, Japan and France. Nevertheless self-interest was the test of the applicability of the Open Door. In theory, it became a general principle of American foreign policy. In practice, Washington promoted it mainly in areas of the world that the United States itself could not hope to dominate. Consequently, in the Philippines, the US was not especially vocal about extending the principles of the Open Door. In the case of China, however, the Open Door was consistent with American interests.

Accordingly Japan's annexation of Korea in 1910, its conquest of Manchuria in the early 1930s and its subsequent plans for establishing an exclusive 'Greater East Asia Co-Prosperity Sphere' all ran directly counter to American goals in the Far East. As an Asian power Japan was in a strong position to make good its claim to pre-eminence in the region, a claim which it compared to the US Monroe Doctrine for Latin America. In brief, the Monroe Doctrine warned non-American powers to abjure colonial aggrandizement in the Western Hemisphere, and unilaterally proclaimed a special role for the United States as protector of the area. With the German occupation of the Netherlands and France, and Hitler's threat to invade Britain, Japan had a golden opportunity to take over their colonies. All three European countries had major holdings in the Far East, and these were now vulnerable. The only problem was that events on the Chinese mainland stood in the way of a Japanese campaign in South-East Asia.

Japan had invaded the north-eastern Chinese region of Manchuria in 1931, where it set up a puppet state called Manchukuo. In 1937 Tokyo launched a full-scale invasion of the rest of the country, but established effective control only over parts of North China, the major coastal cities, and areas along the railway and river systems. The government of Chiang Kai-shek* would not capitulate, and the China campaign became more and more protracted. Equally important, in Manchuria and the north Japan was trespassing into an area of long-standing interest to the Russians. A number of clashes took place with the Soviet army. The most serious occurred at Nomonhan on the Manchurian–Mongolian frontier between May and September 1939, and resulted in a defeat of considerable strategic significance for the Japanese. They needed to settle with the USSR, especially as the signing of the Nazi–Soviet Pact eased the pressure on the Russians in Europe and might allow them to take an even stronger stand in the Far East.

On the other hand, Stalin remained wary of Hitler, and was not looking for a major war in Asia. After Japan joined the other Axis Powers in signing the Tripartite Pact in 1940, Tokyo obtained the good offices of Berlin in negotiating a settlement with Moscow. Also, tensions between the USSR and Japan lessened as the latter turned its attention to South-East Asia, away from areas on the Russian borders. For Japan, challenging Russian influence in China could wait, but moving into South-East Asia was an opportunity to be seized while it was available. For their part the Russians also required an accommodation. By the spring of 1941 German–Soviet relations were rapidly deteriorating. Stalin hardly needed a diversion in the Far East at this time. The outcome was that the Russians and the Japanese came to terms, and signed a neutrality pact on 13 April 1941.

Once Hitler invaded the Soviet Union, of course, he wanted Japan to attack Russia, the neutrality pact notwithstanding. Tokyo considered doing so, but only if the German invasion of the Soviet Union proved to be a success. When the Nazi advance slowed to a halt in the autumn of 1941, the Japanese decided to adhere to the neutrality pact. Besides, for the Japanese to open a major new front against the USSR just to help Germany would stretch their military capacity to the limit. And doing so could only come at the expense of their opportunities in South-East Asia. The Tripartite Pact only obliged Japan to assist Germany if it were attacked, not if it were the aggressor, so Tokyo was within its legal rights to stand aside. Observing the neutrality agreement proved to be a matter of self-interest for both Tokyo and Moscow, and each capital adhered to

* Except where common usage recommends the retention of Wade-Giles forms, the transliteration of Chinese names is in Pinyin.

it until the very end of the Second World War. But the pact also left the Americans as the only obstacle to Japanese ambitions in the Far East.

Washington's interest was to make sure that no single power dominated the Far East to the exclusion of other nations. It was in Tokyo's interest to challenge this. After the invasion of the Chinese mainland in 1937 Japan seized the large Chinese-controlled island of Hainan in the South China Sea in 1939. With the fall of France in 1940 it stationed troops in the north of Indo-China, which was a French colony. In the summer of 1941 the Japanese took possession of the rest of the country. Technically this had been done with the permission of the French authorities at Vichy, where the Germans allowed a puppet government to administer south-east France, but the French were in no position to resist. In the same period Japan induced Thailand to become a reluctant ally.

In the meantime Washington applied economic sanctions to dissuade Tokyo from closing the Open Door in Asia. In the autumn of 1940 it cut off the export of essential supplies of scrap metal, but this played into the hands of Japanese expansionists. South-East Asia was a vast storehouse of petroleum, rubber, tin and other vital resources, so that controlling the region seemed more urgent than ever. In the summer of 1941 the Roosevelt administration also froze all Japanese assets in the United States, and prohibited the export of oil to Japan. Washington and Tokyo attempted to negotiate in the late summer and autumn, but neither side would yield what it had come to regard as its vital interest, access for the Americans and exclusive control for the Japanese. Neither Japan nor the US would make any concessions on the central issue of these talks, the Japanese presence in China. Tokyo therefore decided to establish its claim to hegemony in Asia by force. It launched a general invasion of South-East Asia, preceded by a raid on Pearl Harbor in the Hawaiian Islands on 7 December 1941. The next day the Japanese attacked the British colonies of Hong Kong and Malaya, the US-occupied Wake Island and the Philippines, beginning thereby what for a time was an impressive string of victories.

The main Japanese assault thus was in South-East Asia, but the Pearl Harbor raid had two objectives. One was to wage psychological warfare on the American people by delivering a devastating blow to US territory. As with most attempts to break the morale of an enemy, it had precisely the opposite effect. The other objective was to destroy the US Pacific fleet, which was based at Pearl Harbor. Japanese strategists knew perfectly well that their staying power could not match that of the

Americans. Dependent on the outside world for virtually all strategic raw materials, including oil, they could not stand a protracted war. The occupation of South-East Asia would solve this problem, but the area had first to be conquered. And this still did not overcome the inferiority of Japan's domestic industries in comparison to those of the United States. Japan was simply not as developed an industrial nation. Therefore the only way it could succeed was by a dramatic blow against the American fleet, the one force that could threaten its plans for South-East Asia. The European powers were obviously no problem at this time, so only the Americans remained to be disposed of. The Pearl Harbor raid, of course, would mean war with the United States, but if it succeeded Japan would be able to take whatever it wanted in Asia and the Pacific before the Americans had a chance to retaliate.

In retrospect Pearl Harbor turned out to be a fundamental strategic blunder for Japan. It brought the United States into the war, but without crippling its military capacity. While five battleships were sunk or disabled, for example, no aircraft carriers were destroyed, these being at sea when the attack came. Yet it was a combination of air and naval power that would prove decisive in the Pacific war. Pearl Harbor was also a mistake because it had no impact at all on America's industrial might, and so did not hurt the US war effort in the long term. Furthermore, it unified the American people as no other event could. Given the state of public opinion in the US before 7 December, it was not inconceivable that the United States might have remained neutral for a while longer had Japan left American territory alone and only taken the colonies of Britain, France and Holland.

Just as significantly, the Pearl Harbor raid drew the United States into the European conflict. When the Americans declared war on Japan, the response of Hitler was to lend diplomatic support to Tokyo by issuing a declaration of war against the US, even though he was not obliged to do so under the terms of the Tripartite Pact. This decision no doubt was a mistake on his part, because the Americans might have concentrated their attention on the Far East had Germany (and Italy) not declared war. But Hitler was eager to engage the Americans. After all, they were already deeply involved with the anti-German forces, though not as belligerents. They had begun to supply material assistance under Lend Lease to the British and Soviets well before the culmination of the Pacific crisis. Thus, anything the Japanese did to harass the United States would reduce its ability to help its friends in the West. Germany did not actually plan to take part in the Asian fighting, because it was fully occupied in

Europe and North Africa, but in many ways it did gain by what was happening in the Far East. In any event, Berlin felt it had reason enough to show its support for Tokyo. This was a fatal error, however, for it meant that the US would now join Britain and the USSR as a full-fledged belligerent in the European war. The Grand Alliance was complete.

THE EUROPEAN WAR AND THE
QUESTION OF A SECOND FRONT

The Allies decided to give priority to the European theatre even though the Japanese moved with dramatic swiftness. The strategically important islands of Guam and Wake and the British colony of Hong Kong all fell in December 1941, and by the summer of 1942 Japanese troops had secured Thailand, the Malay peninsula, the Dutch East Indies and the Philippine Islands. But Japan did not represent an immediate threat to the US mainland (Pearl Harbor was as close as it ever came), whereas Germany had carried the battle to the gates of Moscow and still dominated Europe. Hence the war in the West must come first, and there the main question was how soon the British and Americans could open a Second Front on the Continent and thus relieve the Russians.

Given their relations with the Soviet Union before the war, the central problem for the Western Allies was twofold: the co-operation of the Russians was essential for victory, but the defeat of the Axis Powers would enhance the position of the USSR in the post-war world. If the West attempted to check Russia too overtly, there was the remote but none the less real possibility that the Soviets might conclude a separate peace with Germany, as they had in the First World War. Alternatively they might not be receptive to helping in the Far East after the defeat of Germany. The neutrality pact they had signed with Japan still remained in effect.

The USSR's goals were clear from the start. Shortly after the invasion of Russia in June 1941 Stalin began pressing for a formal alliance with Britain. In brief, he demanded the same kind of territorial concessions in Eastern Europe that he had obtained in the Nazi–Soviet Pact of 1939. To Westerners the request seemed brazen indeed, especially because German armies still had the offensive. But precisely because Russia's survival was at stake, Stalin insisted that the other Allies recognize his strategic interests as one of the principal war aims of the anti-German coalition. Churchill was willing to consider the matter. Spheres of influence were hardly an alien idea to the leader of the world's foremost imperial power. Moreover, Russia's role in the war meant that its interests might have to be recognized. Yet he was not keen to yield unless absolutely necessary, and no commitments were made in 1941. Delay was the wisest policy, because the possibility that the Americans might enter the war promised to strengthen the British bargaining position.

Once the United States joined the Grand Alliance, Roosevelt resisted the Russians' claims. The president was reluctant to surrender any strategic advantage to Stalin, and he did not wish to invite a political backlash from various ethnic minorities in the US who had an interest in the fate of Eastern Europe. Further, both Churchill and Roosevelt argued that a Second Front would do more for the USSR than any purely formal recognition of its interests in a treaty, though the two Western leaders did not agree exactly when such a Front would be feasible. The Russians gave in, and in May 1942 signed a treaty of alliance with Britain which was silent on territorial questions. Stalin was not pleased, but settled for what was possible. In an effort to smooth things over Roosevelt subsequently encouraged the Russians to believe that the Western Allies would open a Second Front somewhere in Europe by the end of the year. The problem, however, was to deliver, and on this Churchill and Roosevelt were in sharp disagreement.

The British argued that neither they nor the Americans were ready to invade Europe, and that the best way to take pressure off the Russians was to deal with the Axis forces in North Africa. It was true that if the Allies could bring about the surrender of Germany proper North Africa would take care of itself. But Churchill countered that a Second Front in Europe was simply not possible in 1942, and he prevailed. The result was only the first of many postponements, which convinced the Russians that they were being used by the Western Allies. Moscow wanted a cross-Channel invasion, so as to draw about forty German divisions from the Russian Front.

However much the delay may have been due to America's late entry into the war and its consequent unpreparedness, Stalin interpreted it as a sign of bad faith. Unlike the Western powers he did not have the luxury of choosing when and where to fight, and remained wary of his new-found friends. Later the British and Americans promised action for 1943, and landings took place in Sicily and Italy. As we shall see presently, the Germans very quickly blocked their advance, while the Russians remained convinced that the only Second Front that really counted was one across the English Channel. Churchill and Roosevelt finally committed themselves to invade France by the spring of 1944, prompting Stalin to observe acidly that it was about time they helped reduce 'the enormous sacrifices of the Soviet armies, compared with which the sacrifices of the Anglo-American armies are insignificant'.*

In the long run the failure to open a Second Front sooner would place considerable diplomatic leverage in Stalin's hands, but the Western Allies reasoned that there was no point in being foolhardy and attacking through France before they were ready. Dieppe showed that. This was a port city on the French coast where a frontal assault was attempted on 19 August 1942. Planned as a test of German strength and as a symbol of Western commitment to a Second Front, it was a disaster from start to finish. It probably was intended to be, in order to show the Russians that the Western Allies were not yet able to attack the Continent. Canadians were assigned the unenviable task and bore the brunt of the action. British commandos also played a role, but fewer than half of the 5,000 Canadians returned. The US provided a token force of fifty American Rangers, and the British were responsible for naval and air operations. But Dieppe was a raid, not an invasion, and in 1942 the main contribution of the West was in North Africa.

On 24 October 1942 General Bernard Montgomery and the British Eighth Army launched an attack from Egypt, while two weeks later, on 8 November, the Americans and some additional British units landed to the west at Casablanca, Oran and Algiers. Despite the best efforts of the brilliant German commander, General Erwin Rommel, the Allied forces closed in steadily. By May 1943 Axis resistance came to an end, with the loss of fifteen divisions and more than 2,000 aircraft. The African theatre was sufficiently secure to allow Churchill and Roosevelt to meet in January 1943 at Casablanca in Morocco. There they called for the 'unconditional surrender' of the Axis Powers, including Japan. Stalin was notably absent, and the other two leaders decided on an invasion of Sicily and Italy for later in the year. This, of course, meant a further delay in a cross-Channel invasion, to the consternation of Moscow. Invading Germany via Italy was too risky in the Russian view, because geography made it relatively easy for the enemy to block an advance up the Italian boot. Controlling a very short battle line would be sufficient to stop the British and Americans, and indeed this was exactly what happened. The Allies crossed over from North Africa and landed in Sicily on 10 July

---

* Cited in Gabriel Kolko, *The Politics of War: The World and United States Foreign Policy, 1943–1945* (New York: 1970), 16.

1943 and in Italy on 3 September. Stalin's predictions came true, and the Italian campaign bogged down. Rome would not be taken until June 1944, even though the Italian government surrendered when the invasion began. The Germans took over from their erstwhile Italian allies and easily sealed off the Western advance.

As far as the Russians were concerned, they had already turned the tide of the war. Moreover, they had done so before the end of the North African campaign, much less the invasion of Italy. At Stalingrad on 31 January 1943 they had captured about 100,000 Nazi troops out of an original force of 300,000. Twenty-one German divisions had participated in the siege of the city since the late summer of 1942. After the Battle of Stalingrad the Red Army began marching west, and had reconquered most of the Ukraine by the end of the year. Thus Russian historians argue that 'the crucial battles of the Second World War were fought on the Soviet–German Front'.*

The Russian interpretation is not without merit. When the Western Allies landed in Normandy on D-Day, 6 June 1944, sixty-one German divisions were operating in France and the Low Countries, while twenty-five German and four Italian divisions were in Italy. The latter belonged to a puppet government which the Nazis had set up after the Italian surrender in 1943. On the Russian Front there were 199 German divisions and sixty-three more from Romania, Hungary, Bulgaria and Finland. (The Finns had joined Germany in attacking the USSR in 1941, but were hardly pro-Nazi.) The Western landings at Normandy, however, were the greatest amphibious operation ever undertaken in history. Combined with the Russian successes on the Eastern Front, Normandy made the defeat of Hitler only a matter of time. The liberation of France and Belgium was well advanced by September 1944, and the Germans' last major counter-offensive came at the end of the year in the Ardennes Forest (the 'Battle of the Bulge'). Yet the fighting in the Ardennes was a timely reminder that the West still needed the Russian army, particularly as American strategists projected that the war in the Pacific might well last into 1946, possibly longer.

THE WAR IN ASIA AND THE PACIFIC
The Americans were charged with responsibility for the Asian theatre. Their initial successes came much earlier than expected. In May 1942

* Manfred, II, 260.

the Battle of the Coral Sea (off the island of New Guinea, north of Australia) resulted in a draw, but it was also the first time the Japanese had failed to make an advance. In June the Battle of Midway (north-west of Hawaii) was an outright defeat for the Japanese navy, which lost four aircraft carriers. By early 1943 enemy offensives in the Solomon Islands and on New Guinea were stopped, and the US began an island-hopping strategy which brought it steadily closer to Japan itself. American troops landed in the Philippines in the autumn of 1944, though the islands were not secure until well into the next year. But perhaps the two most crucial battles in 1945 were fought on the islands of Iwo Jima (February–March) and Okinawa (April–June). Iwo Jima provided an air base for bombing runs on Japan itself, while Okinawa was only 350 miles from Kyushu, the southernmost of the main Japanese islands, and therefore was a likely staging area for an eventual invasion. The US planned to invade Kyushu in November 1945 and then the largest of the Home Islands, Honshu, in March 1946. Estimates varied, but some strategists suggested that the USA might suffer a million casualties in an invasion attempt. Victory in the Pacific seemed assured, but no one doubted that a formidable task still lay ahead.

YALTA

By early 1945 the war in Europe was considerably more advanced than in the Pacific, and the imminent defeat of Germany meant it was time for the 'Big Three' (Churchill, Stalin and Roosevelt) to meet and settle accounts. At the Yalta Conference of 3–11 February 1945, held in the Russian Crimea, the Soviets bargained from a position of strength. Despite the devastation of their homeland they had consolidated their military position and occupied a large part of Eastern Europe. By the end of the month they would drive the Germans out of Poland and move to within fifty miles of Berlin. The Americans would cross the Rhine on 8 March, but at the time of Yalta it was already clear that influence in Europe was to be divided largely according to the position of the armies. Moreover, the United States wanted Russian help in defeating Japan. Small amounts of American aid to the Chinese had led to very disappointing results, so Soviet armies could serve a useful function by attacking Japanese forces in Manchuria, North China and Korea, while the Americans invaded the Home Islands.

As it turned out, the war in the Far East would come to a sudden end in the summer of 1945 when the US became the only nation in history, then or since, to use the atomic bomb in warfare. But this was several months in the future, and at Yalta the bomb could not be taken into account in calculating strategy in the Far East. Work on a nuclear weapon had only begun during the war itself, and no one could be certain when it would become operational. In the meantime this left the Russians with a strong hand to play. The USSR was not about to commit more lives and resources without something in return. At the foreign ministers' conference held in Moscow in October 1943 the Russians agreed to enter the war against Japan some time after the defeat of Germany. Later in the year, at the Teheran Conference with Churchill and Roosevelt, Stalin indicated his interest in strategic concessions in the Far East. These were defined by December 1944 as control of the Kurile Islands and southern Sakhalin Island (both immediately north of Japan), Port Arthur and Dairen on the China coast, and the Chinese Eastern and the South Manchurian Railways, plus recognition by China of the Mongolian People's Republic as an independent state (it had been part of China before 1912). The MPR, it will be recalled, was the Soviet government's first satellite. At Yalta, Churchill and Roosevelt agreed to these terms. Stalin affirmed that he would go to war against Japan no later than three months after the defeat of Germany. He also agreed to sign a treaty of friendship and alliance with the pro-Western government of China, led by Chiang Kai-shek.

Stalin fulfilled both commitments, although the Russian declaration of war against Japan only came on 8 August, exactly three months after Germany's surrender but two days after the first atomic bombing. The bomb made Soviet participation in the Far East unnecessary, and the timing of the Russians' declaration of war made it appear that they only entered at the last minute in order to share in the spoils. It was unlikely, however, that the Americans and British expected them to act any sooner, and given the US timetable for an invasion of the Home Islands, it was not necessary for them to have done so. Moreover, the Russians were not given any precise indication of US plans to deploy the bomb. The American president only informed Stalin of the bomb project in July, and then in such vague terms that he did not even use the word 'atomic'. Given their losses in Europe and the task of occupying enemy territories there, the Russians could not make a wholesale shift of their forces to the Far East, at least not immediately. The bomb put the Soviet declaration in a bad light, but in fact Stalin did exactly what he had agreed to at Yalta and as required by the original game plan – that is, by a plan that did not rely on the bomb's availability.

The Chinese did not participate in the Yalta Conference and were not consulted about concessions made in their name, but Chiang later accepted them as a small price to pay for Russia's support. China had been rent by a civil war in the late 1920s and 1930s which pitted Chiang's Nationalist Party against the Chinese Communist Party (CCP). Stalin always doubted whether the CCP could defeat the Nationalists on the battlefield. Indeed, Chiang drove the communists into the north-west of the country, though final victory remained elusive. In 1936, therefore, the Comintern urged the CCP to come to terms with the Nationalists and form a United Front. The communists did so in 1937. This would assure their survival after the severe losses of the civil war, while uniting all Chinese against the Japanese invasion. Nevertheless relations between the two factions remained tense, and it was likely the civil war would resume once the Japanese were dislodged from the Chinese mainland. The communists had expanded their base of support during the Second World War, but Stalin still doubted their capacity to win. Accordingly, in August 1945, the USSR signed a treaty with the Nationalists, the Soong–Stalin Agreement, in the expectation that they would remain at the head of the legal government of China. As in the 1930s, Stalin put ideology aside and opted for a pragmatic approach. The result was a major coup for Chiang and his Western supporters.

As has been noted, the bomb would make the Yalta arrangements for the Far Eastern war unnecessary, but at the time they were little enough to concede for Russian military help and for Soviet recognition of the Chinese Nationalists. This did not stop critics after the war from arguing that the West and particularly Roosevelt gave away too much at Yalta. Some argued that it was not necessary to entice the Russians, as sooner or later they would participate in order to share in the spoils. The USSR, however, was an ally and had acquitted itself well in the European fighting, so Western leaders knew the value of its army. Furthermore, the Yalta agreements defined the upper limits of Russian gains in the Far East. Without a specific agreement there would have been nothing to stop the USSR from entering the war against Japan on its own and attempting to seize all the territories it could. In the actual outcome, the Yalta agreements had a somewhat surprising value. Having received satisfaction at Yalta, Moscow rejected later appeals from Tokyo that the USSR remain neutral or even provide assistance, so as to allow the Japanese to bargain for better terms of surrender when the time came. In the early summer of 1945 Japan raised the possibility of substantial territorial concessions in return for Moscow's co-operation, but the Soviets were not tempted.

Three other issues dominated the Yalta talks: the status of Eastern Europe, the occupation of Germany and the creation of a new international body to replace the defunct League of Nations. Again, post-war critics notwithstanding, the Western negotiators bargained shrewdly in the face of considerable Russian advantages, and gave nothing away that the USSR was not in a position to take anyway. If the West failed to prevail on every issue, it was owing largely to the problem of the Second Front. The battlefield strategy of Britain and America saved lives for them, but it also increased Russia's bargaining power.

The Eastern European settlement was the clearest example. Russian armies had possession of the land, so the USSR determined its future. Indeed, well before the end of the war Roosevelt had accepted the likelihood of Soviet hegemony in the region. In the autumn of 1943 Archbishop Francis Spellman of New York prepared a memorandum of a conversation with the president. Roosevelt told him that 'the European people will simply have to endure' Soviet domination, and that 'the world will be divided into spheres of influence'.* The pattern was so well set that in conversations between Churchill and Stalin at Moscow in October 1944 the two leaders discussed apportioning influence in percentage terms, for example 90 per cent for Russia in Romania but 90 per cent for Britain in Greece.

Poland became the test case for what would happen in Eastern Europe, and the settlements in the rest of the area followed the precedent it set. Aside from boundary adjustments, the central issue was the make-up of a new government. The USSR insisted that the communist-dominated Lublin Committee, which it had set up in July 1944 to act as a provisional authority, form the core of the government. The West, however, supported the claims of a group of exiles who had fled to London at the beginning of the war. Stalin had broken off relations with the London Poles in April 1943, because they accused the Russians of brutally slaughtering 15,000 Polish officers in the spring of 1940 in the Katyn Forest. Most Western historians now accept that the executions did in fact take place. Further, the Soviets believed that the London government was an advance agent of Western penetration into Eastern Europe, an area too vital for Stalin to surrender. After all, Germany had

---

* Cited in Robert Gannon, *The Cardinal Spellman Story* (Garden City: 1962), 222–4.

invaded Russia through Poland twice in the twentieth century. It was not going to happen again.

Stalin shrewdly compared Soviet hegemony in Eastern Europe to Western dominance in Italy, France, Greece and (as would surely be the case once the war in the Far East was over) Japan. Because Italy had surrendered first, in September 1943 (though the Germans kept the war going there until 1945), the occupation and administration of the south provided the precedents for Stalin's position at Yalta. In vain the USSR had sought an effective role in the Italian occupation, but the Western powers resisted, and with success. They knew that indigenous support for the communist party in Italy was considerable, and might provide the Russians with influence in the West. Indeed, communist party members also played a major role in the resistance movement in France, and were a threat there as well. The other Allies did go along with Russian demands that a commission be created to oversee the Italian surrender and occupation, and that the Soviets be represented. But real authority was vested in the Allied commander, an American, and the USSR played an insignificant role. On the other hand, the Western Allies made no effort to interfere in the Russian handling of surrender terms in Eastern Europe when Soviet armies entered countries like Romania in 1944.

Because the Russians were in possession of Poland, and given the Italian and other precedents, the Allies agreed that the Lublin government would bring in 'democratic leaders from Poland itself and from Poles abroad', and would hold 'free and unfettered elections as soon as possible'.* There was little substance in these provisions, but there was hardly any more the Western Allies could do without going to war over the issue, and this simply was not an option in February 1945. Japan still had to be defeated. For their part the London Poles wanted to return and run everything as though nothing had changed since before the war. This was unrealistic in the extreme, and if Churchill and Roosevelt had attempted to back them at all costs, they would probably have obtained nothing from the Russians. The only practical alternative was to place as many London exiles as possible in the Polish government, and this was done.

Germany was somewhat different. There the armies of the Big Three would all play a role in the occupation of the country, and the Russians

---

* Cited in John Lewis Gaddis, *The United States and the Origins of the Cold War: 1941–1947* (New York: 1972), 162–3.

and the Americans would meet at the Elbe river 26 April 1945. The West was in a stronger position, and the Yalta agreements reflected this fact. Each of the Big Three was to have a zone of occupation. At the insistence of Britain and the US, France was allowed in as well. Moreover, the US successfully resisted Russian efforts to fix a reparations bill for Germany. Earlier Roosevelt had supported proposals for dismembering and de-industrializing the Reich, as a way of preventing Germany from ever again menacing Europe. By the time of Yalta, though, the Americans were moving towards the British position that the restoration of the German economy was essential to European prosperity and stability. In addition, a strong German state might someday serve as a useful check against the Soviet Union. Not surprisingly the French did not relish the prospect of a resurgent Germany, while the Russians proposed $20,000 million as a likely figure for reparations, with payment to be in the form of capital goods (machines and factories), current production and labour. Instead of agreeing to specifics at this time, however, Britain and the US only acknowledged the USSR's claims as the basis for further discussion. The details were postponed, and a commission was created to meet in Moscow and deal with the matter.

The United Nations was the fourth subject of the Yalta Conference. The Americans had proposed the basic plan at Dumbarton Oaks (in Washington, DC) in September 1944. It embodied what Roosevelt referred to as the 'Four Policemen' concept. This envisaged a special role for the US, the UK, the USSR and China in managing global affairs, and thus was designed to ensure that the UN would function more effectively than the old League of Nations. Roosevelt regarded the latter as paralysed by incessant debate. In the UN this problem would be solved by vesting the authority to act in a Security Council, with the great powers as permanent members and a limited number of others as rotating members. The Big Four would dominate. The other nations of the world could participate in a General Assembly, where they might debate to their hearts' content. All countries fighting the Axis Powers would be eligible to join.

At Yalta the Russians agreed to add France as a permanent member of the Security Council and to take only three seats in the General Assembly instead of the sixteen (to represent the several constituent republics of the USSR) they had demanded at the Dumbarton Oaks Conference. Stalin was co-operative possibly because he regarded the UN as Western-dominated anyway. Granting this, there was no point in creating a fuss over it. Nationalist China, for example, was clearly a stalking-horse for the USA, and virtually an extra vote for the Americans on the Security Council. It was simply too dependent on the United States to take an independent line. Nothing about the UN, however, would preclude the Russians from acting freely within their own sphere of influence, and therefore they could agree to participate.

What clinched the matter was that the permanent members of the Security Council were given a power of veto, and so could prevent any UN action against their interests. Critics of the Yalta accords have interpreted this as an abnegation of effective international action, but in 1945 the veto was as important to the Americans as the Russians. The United States Senate probably would not have ratified membership in the United Nations unless American sovereignty were protected. The opponents of US participation in the League of Nations had argued earlier that it seemed to have the power to commit member nations to go to war, so the State Department feared that plans for a new international security organization might founder on the same point unless the veto were in place. The veto power thus was favoured as much by Roosevelt as by Stalin.

POTSDAM

If Yalta demonstrated the relation between battlefield developments and the shape of the post-1945 world, so did the next conference of wartime leaders. This took place at Potsdam (near Berlin), from 17 July to 2 August 1945. Between Yalta and Potsdam, Hitler committed suicide (on 30 April) and the Germans surrendered (on 7 May to Eisenhower at Rheims and on 8 May to the Soviet Marshal G. K. Zhukov at Berlin). Roosevelt died of natural causes on 12 April at Warm Springs, Georgia, and was succeeded by his vice-president, Harry S. Truman, former US senator from the state of Missouri. During the Potsdam Conference, Churchill would lose a general election in Britain and be replaced as prime minister by Clement Attlee of the Labour Party. However great a wartime leader, Churchill was an arch-Conservative, and apparently regarded by the UK electorate as the wrong man for solving the domestic problems of post-war Britain. New leaders were emerging in the West, but Stalin remained in the East. Before Potsdam he showed that he regarded Yalta as giving Russia a free hand in Eastern Europe, and he reorganized the Polish government accordingly. The result was a diplomatic crisis with the British and Americans in the spring. Although they obtained minor concessions, Truman decided that it was time to be firm with the Soviets. Developments during the Potsdam Conference were to give him the opportunity.

The main issues were German reparations and the Japanese war. It was finally agreed that each victor could take reparations from its own zone, with the proviso that the USSR was entitled to an additional 10 per cent of the capital equipment removed from the Western-occupied areas, and would be eligible to buy another 15 per cent by exchanging primary commodities (such as food and coal) from its own zone. The West had an advantage in that more German industry fell within its zones than within the Soviet sphere, and was thus in a position to control what Russia received, as each power had first call on reparations from its own occupation zone. The US did not wish to see Germany stripped of everything, lest this mean American taxpayers would have to provide more relief. Besides, a draconian policy would only postpone the day when Germany once again could contribute to the European economy. Otherwise, the conference referred a number of issues, including the matter of negotiating peace treaties with Germany's satellites, to a Council of Foreign Ministers, and Stalin renewed his commitment to enter the war against Japan. Indeed, since May there had been a slow but continuous movement of Russian troops to the Far East from the European Front, and preparations for action in China and Korea were advancing.

The most important event that affected the conference, however, did not take place at Potsdam but in the American South-West, at Alamogordo in the New Mexico desert. There, on 16 July, the world's first atomic bomb was successfully detonated. With this, as Churchill wrote later, Russian help in Asia was 'not likely to be needed, and Stalin's bargaining power, which he had used with such effect upon the Americans at Yalta, was therefore gone'.* Truman's advisers were not so sanguine, because the bomb was still somewhat experimental. Moreover, it was not available in any significant numbers. The US military still thought an invasion of the Japanese Home Islands might be necessary. But it did seem to the American president that in the long run the balance of power had shifted decisively in favour of the West.

Until the Potsdam Conference neither the British nor the Americans had informed the Russians about the 'Manhattan Project' to build the bomb, even though the USSR was their principal ally. The Russians had

---

* Winston Churchill, *The Second World War*, Vol. VI: *Triumph and Tragedy* (London: 1954), 554.

their own sources, of course, and knew about it. They had calculated
their diplomatic moves in this light, realizing that the West would have
the edge in nuclear weapons for some time to come. No doubt this was
one more reason why they had taken an adamant stand on Eastern
Europe. On 24 July Truman told Stalin about the bomb, but did not go
into any details: 'I casually mentioned to Stalin that we had a new weapon
of unusual destructive force. The Russian premier showed no special
interest. All he said was that he was glad to hear it and hoped we would
make "good use of it against the Japanese".'*

The British and Americans had always assumed that the bomb would
be deployed as soon as it was ready, even though qualitatively it was
unlike any other weapon in history and someday might threaten the
survival of the human race itself. In 1945 it was difficult for policy-
makers to conceive of the difference between what thereafter would be
called 'conventional' weapons and nuclear weapons. Before proceeding,
the Allies issued the Potsdam Declaration as a veiled warning to Japan.
The atomic bomb was not mentioned in specific terms in order to
preserve the element of surprise. Instead, the Declaration simply called
upon Japan to surrender or suffer 'the utter devastation of the Japanese
homeland'. But then it went on to list several terms: the replacement of
Japan's current political leaders; occupation by Allied forces; the surrender of Japan's conquests and colonies; the disarming of its military forces
and their return home; the trial of 'war criminals'; the continuation of
Japan as an industrial nation (to permit reparations) but without the
capacity to rearm; the 'revival and strengthening of democratic tenden-
cies'; and the establishment of a 'peacefully inclined and responsible
government'. Japan was to be given access to (but not control of) sources
of raw materials abroad, to permit its economic redevelopment, and
would be allowed to participate in the global market. The Declaration
concluded with a call upon the government 'to proclaim now the
unconditional surrender of all Japanese armed forces'.†

The problem was that the Potsdam Declaration contained a huge
contradiction. It outlined terms, and thus seemed to be a modification of
the Allied call for unconditional surrender first issued at the Casablanca
Conference of 1943 and actually imposed on Germany. The effect may
have been to mislead the Japanese into thinking they had more room for

* Harry S. Truman, *Memoirs*, Vol. I: *Year of Decisions* (Garden City: 1955), 416.
† Cited in *ibid.*, 390–92.

manoeuvre and more time to bargain than was actually the case. Moreover, the Declaration omitted any guarantee of the future status of the Japanese emperor. As we shall note presently, this was an essential condition for Tokyo. By the time of the Declaration, however, Truman had already ordered the US Air Force to proceed with bombing as soon as possible after 3 August. The president designated four cities as targets: Hiroshima, Kokura, Nagasaki and Niigata, with the exact order to be determined by weather and tactical considerations. The first bomb was dropped on Hiroshima on 6 August, and a second on Nagasaki on 9 August. The Soviets declared war on the eighth, and on the tenth the Japanese notified the US of their intention to give in. The formal surrender ceremony took place on the US battleship *Missouri* in Tokyo Bay on 2 September 1945.

THE BALANCE OF POWER

Historians have debated whether Truman ordered the bombing of Japan in order to end the war quickly and perhaps obviate the need for an invasion, or to overawe the Soviets by demonstrating the power of the new weapon. Obviously he acted for both reasons, but given the entire history of East–West relations both before and during the war it should have been no surprise that the president would want to put the Russians in their place. He proceeded even though Stalin had informed the Potsdam Conference of Japan's efforts to bargain with him, a fact which suggested that Tokyo was desperate and perhaps ready to sue for peace even before the atomic bomb was used.

Truman also rejected the advice of a minority of his own experts that a more explicit warning be given about the bomb, and that concessions on the status of the emperor be offered as an additional inducement to negotiate. The Allies might allow the emperor to remain head of state. In Japanese tradition he was regarded as having the attributes of divinity, and was a symbol of the continuity of Japanese history. Assurances regarding his role in the future would be an oblique way of suggesting that the existing structure of authority might be preserved after the war, making it a bit easier for the Japanese government to yield. This would be very much to the interest of the US too, but not just in shortening the war. Japan's leaders could also be of service once the fighting was over. The Japanese political elite was strongly anti-communist, and many of Truman's advisers were certain that the US could work with these people in the years to come. Japan's rulers had as much to gain as the

Americans in preserving order and heading off the possibility that communists and other leftists might take advantage of defeat to make a bid for power. There was much more to the question of the emperor's status than met the eye, and Truman was hardly unaware of his alternatives.

None the less the president seemed determined to use the bomb, so the Russians probably were a very important factor in his decision. In any event, after the war a good many Americans quite logically valued the atomic bomb more for its long-term geopolitical significance than for its role in the Japanese war. They most likely agreed with the rather blunt view of Senator Edwin Johnson of Colorado, who believed that the US, armed 'with vision and guts and plenty of atomic bombs', was at last in a position to 'compel mankind to adopt the policy of lasting peace', or, he warned, 'be burned to a crisp'.*

In fact the US was not about to use the bomb in a war with Russia, but this was the only way it would have had an impact on Soviet policy. In 1945 the USSR was still a formidable military power, and the American capacity to build bombs was limited. Moreover, Russia was still an ally, notwithstanding stormy East–West relations during the Second World War. Its contribution to victory was beyond question, and its continued co-operation, wary though it might be, was to be valued. Most importantly, Western policy-makers believed that the economic power of the USA would create durable links between the emerging Soviet Bloc and the West. Economics might create common interests and lead to a more secure world than would a reliance on brute force. All Europe, including Russia, needed to be reconstructed, and the Japanese would need aid in the Far East. For their part the Americans needed markets and investment opportunities to maintain their domestic prosperity. After all, no one in the US looked forward to the possibility that the Great Depression of the 1930s might resume after the war. The world's needs coincided with America's needs, or so it was believed in Washington.

The Second World War thus ended the isolation of both the USSR and the USA, but left the Americans in a much better position to shape the post-war world. The increase in the Soviet Union's power and influence since before the war had certainly been considerable, but in 1945 it was still more a regional than a global power. For the time being it had to concentrate on reconstruction at home and on consolidating its control over the nations of Eastern Europe. All of the latter had opposed

* Cited in Gaddis, 245.

Russian influence in the region before the war, some even to the point of aligning with the Nazis. It would take some time for the Russians to establish effective hegemony. They followed a set of priorities according to the strategic position of a given country and the strength of local communists as a political force. Hence in Poland the Soviets moved swiftly to assert their control, but given the limits of their power proceeded more gradually in areas of lesser military importance. The Eastern Bloc did not come into existence as a cohesive unit all at once in 1945. Not until 1948 would Soviet influence reach its zenith in Eastern Europe. Even then Yugoslavia would reject the Moscow party line, and with American economic and military aid would succeed in following an independent course.

By contrast the US emerged from the war in a much stronger position. The American mainland had been immune from attack, and its people had been spared the trauma of invasion. Hardly any civilians had died, while in the Soviet Union the population had been decimated. A good deal of the Second World War had been fought within the boundaries of the USSR, and the cost in lives reflected the fact. Soviet dead probably numbered 20 million, though in the early post-war period the Russians tried to cover up the extent of their losses. They did not wish to exaggerate their weaknesses in the face of an increasingly hostile West. The other leaders of the anti-Axis alliance, Britain and the United States, suffered a million killed in all theatres of war combined: Europe, North Africa and the Far East. By itself, the US lost about 400,000 lives from all causes, on the battlefield and as the result of associated risks (such as accident and disease). As the Soviet Union played only a minor role in Asia and none in North Africa, the Russian loss of life clearly showed where the worst fighting took place.

The United States also had a monopoly on the atomic bomb, and it had the world's largest air force and navy. Its strategic position, moreover, would continue to improve in the decades to come, so that by 1982 it had established military bases in thirty-two countries, compared to thirteen for the Soviets in the same year. Only in conventional land forces did America fall behind its chief rival in the post-war period. In 1945 the USA and the USSR each had about 12 million troops under arms. By 1947 the Americans would cut back to 1.5 million, while the Russians would keep 3–4 million. Yet this was a sign of the relative weakness of the USSR, not its strength. Lacking the strategic capabilities of the Americans in overall terms, and for the time being able to establish permanent bases only in Eastern Europe and Mongolia (with a temporary presence in China and Korea), the Soviets attempted to offset their disadvantages with higher troop levels.

Finally, while the Soviets' industrial heartland had been devastated, the war had ended the Great Depression in the West and made the US more than twice as productive as before. The American gross national product rose from $90,500 million in 1939 to $211,900 million in 1945, or from $691 to $1,515 per person, and this at a time when a regulated economy kept inflation to a minimum. Whereas Russia needed to turn inward and consolidate its position, America's requirement was to move outward into the world market-place. Its prosperity was largely the product of the war, of serving as what Roosevelt was fond of calling the 'arsenal of democracy', supplying war *matériel* for itself and its allies. Thus for the United States the immediate problem of the post-war era would be to maintain and expand its existing economic strength.

In 1945 the Americans seemed to have the initiative. Even the Russians sought a huge loan from Washington, and towards the end of the war had indicated that they would like $6,000 million from the United States for reconstruction. This suggested that Washington might have considerable leverage over Moscow in the post-war world. At Yalta the Americans had acknowledged the creation of a Soviet sphere of influence in Europe, but this did not mean that they were prepared to see it expand there or elsewhere. On the contrary, the task for the future was to restrict further Russian gains, and possibly make inroads into Moscow's sphere. Because of its military and economic power the United States apparently had a good chance to shape the future. The history of the early post-war world, consequently, was in large part the story of how the Americans used their advantages, for if any single country were a global power at the end of the Second World War it was the United States not the Soviet Union. The question to ask, therefore, is why did the U S A prove incapable of stemming the growth of the Eastern Bloc after 1945?

2

THE UNITED STATES
AS A GLOBAL POWER

The problem for American policy-makers immediately after the Second World War was that the power and prosperity of the United States depended upon expansion, whereas it was in the interest of America's chief wartime allies to resist this. Once the war was over, the US wanted to turn back Russian gains in Eastern Europe (Yalta notwithstanding) and anywhere else the Soviet Union might act. But protecting its newly won sphere of influence was non-negotiable as far as Moscow was concerned. In the Western Bloc the United Kingdom and the nations of Europe did not relish being displaced by the United States as arbiters of world affairs, and they harboured doubts about American ideas for reforming the global economy. The latter were aimed at breaking up exclusive trading blocs, thus increasing opportunities for American businessmen, though possibly at the expense of Europeans. The Great Depression of the 1930s had exacerbated economic nationalism and spurred protectionism. Given the problems of post-war reconstruction, many nations in Western Europe were not yet prepared to accept freer trade and expose themselves to American competition. Therefore, while the USA had emerged from the war as the strongest country in the world, it could not rest on its laurels. Many other countries were prepared to resist its ideas, so that America's future depended upon an activist policy towards both its competitors in the Eastern Bloc and its own partners in the Western Bloc.

THE SOVIET UNION AND
EASTERN EUROPE

The USSR posed the biggest problem for the United States, yet the Americans did have an opportunity to increase their influence. The reason was that in 1945 the Soviet domination of Eastern Europe was still incomplete, and remained so for about three years after the war. In the meantime the US had its chance. There was no doubt that the Russians were determined to dominate Eastern Europe, or that the West expected this to be the outcome. The United States and Britain had agreed to as much at Yalta. But when, how and to what degree the Soviets would achieve hegemony were still open questions at the end of the Second World War. The so-called 'Iron Curtain' did not descend all at once around Eastern Europe, and had not even done so by the time Winston Churchill popularized the term in 1946. Indeed, the Iron Curtain image was a propaganda device to generate support for Western initiatives against the USSR precisely at a time when there was still an opportunity to act.

The Russian army had occupied most though not all of Eastern Europe, but the question of permanent control was more complicated than merely stationing troops. Real security required a political strategy to establish regimes which would be friendly to the USSR over the long run. The problem was that many of the pre-war governments in the region had sympathized with the Nazis, and in some places (Germany, Hungary and Romania) they had outlawed the communist party altogether. While all this prepared the communists to assume an important role in the clandestine organizations of the wartime resistance, it also inhibited the formation of mass political parties on the left. In 1942, for example, there were probably only a dozen active communist party members in Hungary. The Romanian communist party had about 900 members in early 1944, and by the autumn of the same year the Bulgarian party had about 15,000. Furthermore, all the pre-war parties of Eastern Europe had been weakened by Soviet interference. The Russian goal had been to make certain that leaders acceptable to them controlled the communist movement, but this led to heresy hunts and drove away anyone who disagreed with Moscow. Perhaps the most extreme example was the Polish communist party, which Stalin ordered dissolved in 1938 as part of a purge of alleged fascist and Trotskyite infiltrators. Added to all these problems, of course, was the universal fear of Soviet domination throughout Eastern Europe. This created a high potential for the restoration of the nationalistic and anti-socialist regimes of the pre-war period – that is, if the region were left to its own devices.

Yet, once the Russians began conquering Eastern Europe from the Nazis, there was an influx of new members into the communist parties of the region. This was still not enough to make them a majority of the electorate. Moreover, the credentials of many of these people were suspect. Those who had been unable to show their support earlier because of pre-war or Nazi oppression now came forward, but so did many former fascist collaborators who joined in order to be on the winning side. In other words, more than a few opportunists worked their way into the ranks of the party. The same thing happened in the state bureaucracy, which expanded rapidly as the government took over more and more of the economy. Given the salience of nationalism in Eastern Europe, furthermore, it remained a question of how pliable either the party loyalists or the opportunists would prove to be. A partial solution for the Russians was to reserve at least some leadership posts for exiles who had fled the Germans and spent the war years in the Soviet Union. Having survived the Nazis and Stalin's purges as well, they were a subservient but also a very small group. The basic problem remained: the communists were a minority in most East European countries right after the war. In all parts of the region non-communist political parties reasserted their right to play a role in government. Among the most important were the right-wing Smallholders Party in Hungary, the peasant-based Polish People's Party, some Christian Democrats in the Eastern zone of Germany and a variety of social democrats (on the left of the political spectrum but not sympathetic to Moscow) throughout the area.

The Soviets needed to act quickly to preserve order and to exploit Eastern Europe for their own benefit, so they had little choice but to work with what they had. Though communists took charge of key posts, it was not possible to throw out all the old officials from top to bottom and replace them with an entirely new group. The institutions of government were too complex to permit this. Even monarchy did not end immediately, though obviously Moscow tolerated it only during a period of transition. The USSR permitted King Michael of Romania, who had made a timely switch from the German to the Soviet side in 1944, to retain his throne until the end of 1947. Earlier Stalin himself had urged communists in Yugoslavia to reinstate the king as part of a general strategy of placing victory before politics and working with all anti-Nazi forces. In Bulgaria there was no incumbent actually on the throne after 1945, but for a time legal power remained vested in a regency council.

The outcome of elections held shortly after the war confirmed the difficulty of imposing hegemony. Although held under the watchful eye of Russian authorities, the communist party received only 17 per cent of the ballots in the Hungarian elections of November 1945. In Czechoslovakia, which was the one Eastern European country where a large communist movement had existed before the war, the party received 38 per cent in the elections of May 1946. Polish communists did not dare risk an election until January 1947, precisely because time was needed to take charge of the political system. Their country was particularly unsettled, at times verging on civil war. Remember, the Russians had seized eastern Poland after the Germans had invaded in 1939, and so after the war anti-Soviet feeling still ran high. Anti-communist factions resorted to violence and sabotage until the end of 1946, so that the Russian army had to be called upon to assist Polish security forces. Official figures indicated that 15,000 persons were killed. Western support for the Polish government in exile (the London Poles) exacerbated the situation and fuelled Polish nationalism.

Thus, for the first two or three years after the Second World War, the communists bought time by permitting other parties to function and by participating in coalition governments. To be sure, they insisted on taking charge of the key ministries or departments, especially those for economic planning, justice and the interior. In Eastern Europe the latter ministry controlled the police, and therefore was vital for deploying the power of the state against anti-communists and preparing the way for the eventual imposition of one-party rule. The main point, however, was that the Soviets did indeed have to prepare the way. They did not step into a situation where politically they exercised uncontested power, and this was precisely what gave the Americans an opportunity to influence the outcome. Short of war, there was no way the United States could take Eastern Europe away from the Russians, but the Americans certainly did have room for manoeuvre.

TITO

Eastern Europe was not an American sphere of influence, so indigenous forces were more important in resisting Soviet hegemony. Marshal Josip Broz Tito of Yugoslavia assumed the leading role. During the war Tito had made the communist party the principal force in the Yugoslav resistance, and by 1943 formally established a government to rule the areas under his control. This government allowed the Soviet army to enter the country in September 1944, with the stipulation that civil administration remain in its own hands. For his part Stalin expected that the Western Allies might exercise considerable influence over Yugoslavia after the war, and conceded as much to Churchill at their Moscow meeting the next month. Stalin's flexibility on Yugoslavia hardly won Tito's loyalty. In any event, the Soviet problem after 1945 was clear. Whereas in most countries the Russians found too few communists by the end of the war, the problem in Yugoslavia was that the party was too strong for Soviet tastes. It had attained power independently and was at no time under Russian control. Moreover, Tito played on the nationalist and anti-Russian traditions of the whole Balkans region, and supported various proposals for establishing a federation among Albania, Bulgaria, Czechoslovakia, Hungary, Poland, Romania, Yugoslavia and possibly even Greece. Stalin had a federation plan of his own, but as a device for diluting Yugoslavia's influence. Tito, though, had something more ambitious in mind, and saw a new association of nations as a way of reducing Eastern Europe's subservience to the USSR.

Furthermore, Tito had become a vocal critic of Soviet communism and compared it unfavourably with the Yugoslav variety. Tito was also much too popular a figure for Stalin to tolerate for very long. In addition Belgrade and Moscow disagreed over trade relations and over the Greek civil war. Tito saw the success of right-wing forces in Greece as threatening Yugoslavia's security, whereas the Russians regarded the country as firmly in the Western sphere and therefore off limits. Stalin could hardly expect the West to leave his sphere alone if he were to interfere in its areas, so to protect himself he refused to provoke the Western Bloc in Greece.

Tito's independent policies posed a direct threat to Soviet hegemony in the region, and a formal break occurred in June 1948. Stalin ordered Yugoslavia expelled from the Cominform (or Communist Information Bureau). The Cominform had been organized the year before as a means of imposing a common political line on the communist parties of Eastern Europe. With the break in Soviet–Yugoslav relations Tito was ostracized and accused of 'slanderous propaganda' against the USSR, and of being under the influence of 'counter-revolutionary Trotskyism'. More to the point, he was charged with 'pursuing an unfriendly policy towards the Soviet Union'.* Stalin moved troops to Yugoslavia's borders, cut off virtually all trade, encouraged anti-Tito elements inside the country, and launched a massive propaganda war. But Yugoslav nationalism and American aid enabled the country to withstand the Russian blockade. In trade, gains in the West offset losses in the East, and the United States provided economic aid in 1949 and military aid in 1951. The World

---

* Cited in Adam Westoby, *Communism since World War II* (New York: 1981), 69.

Bank and International Monetary Fund extended credits, and the British also concluded a trade agreement. Yugoslavia even joined the European Coal and Steel Community, one of the organizations that led to the formation of the Common Market in Western Europe some years later.

Tito remained a committed communist and never allowed the West to dictate his policies, but Yugoslavia represented a signal failure in Soviet foreign policy. Furthermore, the Yugoslav case seemed to demonstrate that the USSR could not easily succeed anywhere in the region. In countries where pro-Soviet communist parties were either non-existent or marginal the Russians were forced to work with non-communists, at least temporarily. But where communists were strong, as in Yugoslavia, they were also likely to be independent, nationalistic and hardly amenable to Soviet dictation. In either case the Soviets would need time to cement their hegemony. Again, this created opportunities for the United States.

SOVIET EXPANSIONISM AND THE WEST

Preoccupied with Eastern Europe, the Soviets were in no position to challenge the West in its sphere of influence. The Russians might seek to advance their fortunes in areas where the East–West division remained unclear, such as Iran and Turkey, but if the boundaries were not in doubt (as in Europe) Stalin respected the Western zone. This should have surprised no one. Ever since the announcement of 'Socialism in One Country' as Comintern policy Stalin had placed Russia's national interests ahead of global revolution. For example, in the 1930s he instructed the communist parties of Europe to co-operate with non-communists in Popular Front coalitions that opposed Hitler. At the time this was regarded as a help to the USSR, but it also meant ordering communists to put aside their anti-capitalist goals and work within the existing political and economic system. The Nazi–Soviet Pact of 1939 temporarily resolved the differences between Germany and Russia, and thus led to a reversal of the Popular Front strategy. It was perhaps the most extreme example of Stalin's essentially pragmatic approach. He even sacrificed communist lives for the sake of Germany's friendship. Thus, between 1939 and 1941, before the Nazis invaded Russia, Stalin returned 470 leftist exiles at the Gestapo's request. They had fled to the USSR seeking asylum, but the Germans wanted them back for prosecution as subversives. Stalin obliged. When forced into the war on the Allied side in 1941, the Soviet dictator decided to dismantle the

Communist International (in 1943) as a gesture of goodwill towards his new-found friends in the West. Although long in decline as the vanguard of world revolution, with the Grand Alliance the Comintern became totally expendable. More importantly, Stalin committed himself at Yalta to a division of the post-war world into spheres of influence. Unable to achieve mastery over the West, he hoped that by honouring a spheres approach he would head off American interference in the Eastern Bloc.

All this is not to say that there were no opportunities for the Russians to make trouble in the Western Bloc. In France and Italy the communist movement had grown rapidly after the war, partly because of its role in the resistance. In each country it was a political force to be reckoned with, especially as the pre-war political establishment was somewhat discredited, in France by its failure to stop the Nazi invasion and then its collaboration with the Vichy regime, and in Italy by its subservience to Mussolini. Communist party membership in France grew to over a million by 1946, while in Italy it rose from a meagre 5,000 in early 1943 to 1.7 million at the end of 1945. Membership in other Western European countries was also on the increase. Even during the Second World War, however, the United States and Britain were alert to the trend, and acted quickly to support as leaders strong anti-communists such as Charles de Gaulle of France and Alcide de Gasperi of Italy. Yet the problem of finding political leaders acceptable to the dominant powers in the West was simpler than for the Russians in the East, in part because Stalin chose not to risk provoking his partners in the Grand Alliance. In 1944 he had ordered communists in Western Europe to disarm (they had accumulated a store of weapons during the resistance) and to co-operate with the governments favoured by the Americans and the British. In a sense a new Popular Front strategy began to emerge, although in the face of increasing East–West hostility it lasted only a few years. Communists held cabinet posts in the French and Italian governments until 1947, helped to contain strikes, and generally worked to preserve order rather than make revolution. As the French communist leader, Maurice Thorez, said, 'We are for the revolution, tomorrow', but 'today we wish the capitalist system to function according to its own laws'.* As an exile returned from Moscow, Thorez well articulated the Russian view. Proletarian revolution could wait; the safety of the USSR could not.

The limits of Soviet power recommended that a similar stance be

* Cited in *ibid.*, 20.

adopted elsewhere as well. Thus, Stalin refused to be drawn into the Greek civil war. Tito wanted Moscow to intervene, but this was a major source of tension between the USSR and Yugoslavia and contributed to their break in relations. In China the Russians continued to recognize the Nationalist government of Chiang Kai-shek instead of the communists, despite the resumption of hostilities between the two sides. Because the northern half of Korea had been the scene of Russian military operations in the war against Japan, the Soviets were able to sponsor a communist regime there, but in other parts of the Far East they had little choice but to accept the restoration of Western power. Local communists in many Japanese-occupied areas did attempt to resist the reimposition of Western colonialism in South-East Asia after 1945, and guerrilla movements developed in the Philippines, the Dutch East Indies, Malaya and Indo-China. The Russians, however, were unable to help, and were not so foolhardy as to intervene in what at the time seemed likely to be a series of lost causes. In fact, rather than offer the guerrillas at least moral support, the communist parties of France and Holland sided with their home governments in seeking the restoration of empire. In short, there were more than a few contradictions between communist ideology and practice after the Second World War. Yet this was precisely the point. Stalin's policies were dictated more by pragmatic than by ideological considerations, and Soviet expansionism focused mainly on Eastern Europe, not the rest of the world. This could well change in the future, but in the late 1940s it meant that the United States was in a strong position to advance the fortunes of the West.

THE UNITED STATES AND
THE EASTERN BLOC

At the end of the Second World War most American policy-makers believed that the key to influencing developments in the Eastern Bloc was economic, especially because the Russians wanted US aid. Thus W. Averell Harriman, the American ambassador to Moscow, argued that Washington had a real opportunity to use 'economic assistance' to shape 'political events' and possibly limit the scope of Soviet hegemony in Eastern Europe.* Aid policy, however, required careful calculation. If the terms were too easy or credits extended too soon, the US might lose

---

* Cited in Thomas Paterson, *Soviet–American Confrontation: Postwar Reconstruction and the Origins of the Cold War* (London: 1973), 36.

the power to extract concessions from the Russians. How much to give and when to give it were vital questions.

The United States could not allow the Soviets to define the terms of any post-war assistance it might receive. The Russians attempted to do so in February 1944 by suggesting a loan of $1,000 million at 0.5 per cent interest over twenty-five years, and again in January 1945 (just before the Yalta Conference), when they raised their bid to $6,000 million. In each instance they were in a strong bargaining position. Their 1944 request came well before D-Day while they still dominated the war on the Continent, and in early 1945 the Americans still needed their help in the Far East. The US thus had every reason to stall. The Americans knew that time was on their side, for once the war was over the Russians' bargaining power would be reduced. Indeed, when Germany surrendered in May 1945, the game plan became clear. The US immediately suspended most Lend Lease aid to Russia except that earmarked for the Far Eastern theatre. The move was intended to give the Soviets notice that any future assistance, beyond that directly related to the war effort, depended on their good behaviour. The Russians had no choice but to retrench, and in late August 1945 they submitted a revised loan request of $1,000 million. Yet scaling down their demands did not really resolve the fundamental question, which was whether the Soviets would conform to American plans for the post-war world, and so the US State Department continued to delay. In February 1946 it demanded that the Russians negotiate a number of outstanding issues before talks could begin on a loan. These included the settling of Lend Lease accounts and the claims of US citizens against the Soviet government, treaties concerning trade and navigation, the future of Eastern Europe, and Russian membership in the US-dominated International Monetary Fund and International Bank for Reconstruction and Development (the World Bank). In the interim the Americans had agreed to extend a loan of $3,750 million to the British.

American policy-makers, however, were beginning to discover that their power over the USSR was in fact quite limited. The Russians were unwilling to bargain their autonomy for American money, and by the summer of 1946 the Soviet loan was dead. If anything, US demands for concessions first and loan talks afterwards drove the Russians into a shell, and for them emphasized once again the importance of making the Eastern Bloc invulnerable to manipulation by the West. Moreover, it was well within the Soviets' capacity to carry on by themselves. United States credits were not absolutely essential to their plans for reconstruction.

They would have been a help, and the Russians certainly were interested, but the USSR had alternatives. It was entitled to reparations from the Germans and also from Nazi allies in Eastern Europe. It took over German-owned industries in the same region, and required East European governments to share the ownership of other key enterprises with the USSR. This served as a way of siphoning off resources, beyond reparations, at bargain prices. Further, Stalin was quite willing to exploit his own people if necessary to achieve security against the West. They would simply have to accept a lower standard of living until the state's priorities were met. He had forced them to do so in the past, and was ready to do so again. The same was true for the people of Eastern Europe. No doubt the Russians would have exploited the region regardless of what the Americans did, but the failure to obtain a US loan hardened their approach. And as Soviet exploitation delayed Eastern Europe's recovery, it became more necessary than ever for Moscow to strengthen its political grip on the region, in order to head off the possibility of social disorder. In many respects, then, the Americans' strategy proved counter-productive to their goal of opening up the Soviet Bloc to more outside influences. The same problem was evident in trade policy. By 1947 US legislation allowed the president to require the disclosure of economic intelligence as a condition of trade. The result was that American exports to the USSR virtually ceased by the early 1950s.

CONTESTED AREAS

It was not the case, however, that the division of the world into two spheres of influence was universally accepted or always clear-cut. Although the Russians had a stake in respecting a spheres approach, the Yugoslavs saw it as a constraint on their autonomy and on their regional ambitions. Thus, when the British intervened in Greece on behalf of right-wing political forces, Marshal Tito decided to assert his independence from Soviet policy and intervene on behalf of the left. Tito had not been party to the Stalin–Churchill talks of October 1944 in Moscow, where it had been presumed that British influence in Greece would be paramount after the war. He did not feel bound by any obligations undertaken by the Russians. On the other hand, it was the USSR itself which took the initiative in challenging the East–West division in areas where it was less clear. The chief targets were Iran and Turkey. The Russians claimed an oil concession from the former and demanded a military agreement with the latter. Neither Iran nor Turkey had been the subject of the Moscow talks, so Stalin regarded them as fair game.

In Greece the Nazis had been defeated by 1944, at a time when most of the country was in the hands of the resistance. Rather than work with these forces, the British set up a government of their own choosing led by George Papandreou. The resistance was organized politically as the National Liberation Front (or EAM, from its Greek name), and its military arm was the National Popular Liberation Army (or ELAS). The problem for Britain was that EAM and ELAS included many communists, although they were not dominated by Moscow. In fact it was only in mid-1944 that a delegation of Russian military officers (ten of them) visited the headquarters of the Liberation Army. They were unimpressed, and took the view that it would not be in the interest of the USSR to support the rebels against Britain's plans for imposing a pro-Western government. The point was confirmed in October when Stalin met with Churchill and explicitly recognized the British as having primacy in the area. Even the American ambassador reported that the leaders of the EAM had 'waited in vain for Russia to support them in their revolt', although he feared eventually it would do so.*

The Greek crisis, however, developed in a context of rising East–West hostility, so Washington increasingly interpreted events as the work of the Soviets. But this was a misreading of the situation, and it turned out that the US position was based less on evidence (which was difficult to come by) than logic: if communists were taking over the resistance in Greece, then it must be the work of the USSR as leader of the Eastern Bloc. The mistake was that this credited the Russians with a greater degree of control than they actually enjoyed. They did not want to violate the Western sphere of influence at this point or at this time, yet they could not prevent their allies from doing so. The real source of such outside aid as the rebels received was Yugoslavia, which in the long term was much less of a threat to Western interests than the USSR. In addition, Albania and Bulgaria yielded to pressure from Tito, and offered sanctuary and small amounts of supplies.

War broke out between the British puppet government and the ELAS in December 1944. In February 1945 the rebels agreed to elections, but the other side resorted to violence and intimidation in order to guarantee that it would win. Its actions were no different from communist tactics against non-communist parties in places like Poland. As a result the

---

* Cited in *ibid.*, 204.

rebels withdrew their commitment to participate in the vote. The elections did take place in March 1946, but the rebels resumed full-scale warfare by May. As the United States believed that the Soviets were behind these developments, it extended economic and military aid to the government of Greece. The official regime was undoubtedly repressive, but the Americans reasoned that anything was better than a communist government. The Soviets did not match the Western aid contributions, and when the rebels proclaimed an independent government in December 1947, the USSR did not even accord it diplomatic recognition. Of course, the Russians directed a barrage of propaganda against the British-sponsored government throughout the crisis, and this no doubt confirmed the worst suspicions of the Americans. But the propaganda campaign was mainly a public-relations ploy to project an image of Russia's commitment to revolutionary change and thus to win favour with leftist movements around the world. After all, some of the latter might succeed in winning power in the years to come, particularly in colonial areas where the potential for disorder was high. Their support for the Eastern Bloc would be worth having someday. In the meantime Stalin's vulnerabilities in Europe recommended avoiding a hot war with the West in its sphere. In the end this was fatal for the EAM–ELAS, because there were limits to how far they could work with Tito, and they eventually had a falling-out. The rebels saw that Tito was really engaged in a type of regional imperialism. They hardly looked forward to the prospect of expelling the British only to be dominated by the Yugoslavs. As the Greeks became increasingly restless under his tutelage, Tito finally turned his back on them and closed his southern borders. Without a sanctuary the ELAS was cornered and defeated, though the odds of its winning even with outside help were minimal. The end came in October 1949, when EAM declared a cease-fire, and Greece was saved for the West.

In oil-rich Iran it was indeed the Soviets who acted. They did so, however, in the context of the Second World War, which in their view had given them as legitimate an interest in the region as Britain and the United States. In the 1930s Iran had been a meeting-ground for conflicting geopolitical interests. German influence rose steadily, though the United Kingdom retained control of the oil sector. Further, at various times in the past both the British and the Russians had asserted their ascendancy over the country. Following the Nazi invasion of the Soviet Union in June 1941 the UK and the USSR agreed to occupy Iran for the duration of the war and six months thereafter. The objective was to prevent the government in Teheran falling into the hands of elements sympathetic to the Nazis, and to secure the country as a line of supply from the West to Russia. Hence the British and the Soviets intervened, and the Shah abdicated in favour of his son (he in turn was overthrown many years later, in 1979). In effect they installed a pro-Allied regime, and power in Iran shifted from the Shah to the politicians in the legislature. Once the United States became part of the Grand Alliance, it too established a presence on Iranian territory. Most of the supplies going to the USSR from the West were American, and so the US dispatched military personnel and advisers to Iran in 1942. By 1945 the country was thus a likely setting for a test of East–West strength, as each of the Big Three powers had a claim to influence in the region.

In 1944 the British and Americans applied for oil concessions. The Iranian fields had been monopolized by the UK since early in the century, but the British wanted to expand. With the war the Americans were in a strong position to press their claims as well. The Iranian government especially welcomed the American request (although it did allow the British to increase their holdings). The United States represented a new power in the country, and therefore might be useful in offsetting Britain's traditional influence as well as Russia's. Not surprisingly the American bid for oil alarmed the Soviets. They feared US penetration of a country on their borders. For this reason, in both a strategic and an economic ploy, they too applied for an oil concession. Furthermore, they encouraged secessionist forces in the north of Iran as a way of pressuring Teheran to accept their demands. The real goal was not the independence of dissatisfied minorities in the north, however, but oil and security against the rising influence of the USA in the Middle East. When the Russians thought they had achieved their goals, they withdrew their support for the rebels.

The presence of Russian troops in the country gave the USSR some leverage. A 1942 treaty allowed them to remain until March 1946, but they threatened to stay longer unless they received oil. American troops departed in January, and the British military left in March. It turned out that the Soviets departed a short time later, but only when Prime Minister Qavam as-Saltaneh concluded an agreement to form a joint Soviet–Iranian oil company, subject to ratification by the *majles* (the Iranian parliament). Once the Russians had pulled out their troops, however, they had surrendered their trump card. Given their problems in Eastern Europe, they did not want to keep substantial numbers of soldiers in Iran. The result, though, was to give the Iranians the upper hand. Qavam dismissed four Tudeh Party members (i.e. Iranian communists) from his coalition cabinet in the autumn of 1946. He also moved closer to the Americans, continuing the US advisory role and obtaining military aid. The *majles* rejected the Soviet oil bid in October 1947, and there was little the USSR could do about it short of a major show of military force. Qavam thus outwitted the Russians, and events played into the hands of the Western powers.

The Russians' ability to intimidate Turkey was even less impressive. Once again, they believed that the Second World War had entitled them to an interest in the region, but given a hostile Western response and the limits of their own power they were unable to press their claims. The issue was the control of the Dardanelles, the straits between the Black Sea and the Mediterranean which provided the only access to the ports of Southern Europe and North Africa for Russian naval and merchant ships. During the Second World War Turkey had been technically neutral, but it had also been anti-Soviet and wary of the West. Accordingly it closed the Dardanelles to the Allies (including the USSR), while granting free passage to the Nazis. As a leading participant in the war against Germany, therefore, Moscow in mid-1945 demanded an agreement with Turkey on joint control of the straits. The Soviets felt this was their due by virtue of the Allied victory. Further, they demanded border revisions between the two countries, and raised the possibility of establishing a Soviet military base on Turkish territory. Washington opposed all this, suggesting instead that a United Nations agency take control of the straits and that the US be included as one of its members. Moscow noted that Washington made no offer of a similar arrangement (with Soviet participation) for international waterways under Western control, such as the Panama and Suez canals, and it could not see why the Americans should have a say in running the Dardanelles. After all, the USA was thousands of miles from Turkey, whereas the latter shared a border with Russia and affected the Soviets' regional security. In 1946 the USSR took the initiative and stationed troops adjacent to Turkish territory, but the Americans responded by sending warships to Istanbul. The Soviets were in no position to go to war over the issue, so that to resolve the matter in favour of the West the US simply needed to stage a show of force in the eastern Mediterranean. By the year's end the crisis had reached a stalemate, which in effect meant a defeat for the Russians.

Many of the facts concerning the grounds on which the Soviets based their claims in Iran and Turkey were lost in the welter of propaganda emanating from both the USA and the USSR. The same was true of Stalin's policies towards Greece. In any contest for Western public opinion, however, the Russians were bound to lose. Given the history of East–West relations before the Second World War and the unquestionably oppressive character of communist regimes in the USSR and Eastern Europe, the Soviets were vulnerable to attack. Instead of inquiring whether Russian strategic claims in the Mediterranean and Middle East were as legitimate as those of the United States and Britain, the Western media were predisposed to make the morality of communism the issue. While this was certainly worth examining, emphasizing anti-communism also served two functions, and hence was encouraged by the policy-makers. First, it deflected debate away from the material interests of the West in the same areas and bypassed the question of whether the Americans and British had any more right to be there than the Russians. Second, it drew attention away from the character of the pro-Western regimes in Greece, Iran and Turkey. Although the latter maintained a façade of parliamentary institutions, they were anything but democratic. Thus the issue of what the West was doing did not receive the same airing as the issue of communism.

In any event, the Americans had effectively defended Western interests. As in the case of aid and trade, however, their very power made the Russians all the more wary. This trend was well advanced by the time of the famous Truman Doctrine, outlined in March 1947. It was prompted by two diplomatic notes from the United Kingdom, the first asking the Americans to assume the entire British effort in sustaining the Greek government, and the second emphasizing the strategic importance of Turkey as well. The economic crisis at home was forcing Britain to withdraw from the region (indeed, the rationing of some items lasted into the 1950s). For their part the Americans had already proved willing to increase their role. In fact, they had allocated $181.5 million in economic assistance to Greece before the Truman Doctrine, while the deployment of their naval forces had made them the major factor in the Turkish crisis. Furthermore, they were interested in Iranian and also Arab oil. The British notes created a crisis in Washington, and provided an opportunity for the Truman administration to sell the American public on the need to support the administration's long-term global objectives as well. When the president went to Congress and requested $400 million in military and economic assistance for Greece and Turkey, he also took the occasion to enunciate a set of general principles for the conduct of East–West relations. He couched his address in universal terms (democracy versus totalitarianism), and offered support to any pro-Western government that feared the threat of communist subversion. Along with the Marshall Plan for West European reconstruction (we shall examine this in due course), the Truman Doctrine symbolized the increasingly hostile environment which became known as the Cold War.

THE COLD WAR AND THE BOMB

Another casualty of US–USSR tension was the control of nuclear arms. The Truman administration knew perfectly well that it was only a matter of time before the Soviets, and indeed other nations, had an atomic bomb of their own. The Americans may have had a temporary advantage in the engineering required to construct a weapon, but its scientific foundation was no secret. As it turned out, the USSR exploded its first bomb in August 1949, much sooner than some US officials had expected. This led to charges that the Russian success had to be the result of a breach of American security. Although spying did occur, it was much less important than commonly supposed and was not sufficient to explain the Soviet A-bomb. The secret of the bomb was within the reach of any nation with the requisite scientific and technical resources. For this reason, in 1946, the Truman administration proposed that the United Nations assume control of atomic energy in the future and that the atom be limited to peaceful applications only. This was the Baruch Plan, named after the American charged with presenting it to the United Nations.

The US plan called for the creation of an international authority to license and inspect nuclear installations throughout the world, and to invoke sanctions (not subject to the Security Council's veto) against any nation found to be building atomic weapons. But the plan also contained a very important reservation, and it was on this point that the proposal ultimately broke down. The United States refused to destroy its nuclear stockpile until the UN authority was fully operational, but the Soviets were unwilling to conclude an agreement as long as the US had a monopoly on the atomic bomb. The Kremlin wanted nuclear parity established first, and discussions to proceed from there. Otherwise it was in no position to bargain on an equal footing. To the Russians parity meant one of two things in 1946: either they must build a bomb of their own or the Americans must destroy their nuclear arsenal as a token of good faith.

The American reservation was presumably intended to serve as an incentive for other powers to co-operate, but it also meant that, while the USSR would have to stop work on weapons development in order to bring the plan into effect, the US would still keep its existing arsenal. This was no small point, as it would take some time to set up the international agency, to survey global nuclear resources, to approve applications for the peaceful use of atomic energy, to conduct inspections, and generally to assure the United States that no country was secretly building bombs. A period of years might pass in which the USA would possess atomic weapons, while the USSR would be obliged to remain without equivalent defences. The Soviets were therefore alarmed that the American proposal contained no deadline for when its conditions would be met, or for when American weapons would be destroyed. They were also fearful of suspending their veto power in the Security Council, because it was dominated by the Western and not the Eastern Bloc. In any dispute the US would win over the USSR. And since the United States continued to conduct above-ground atomic tests even after proposing the international control of nuclear weapons, the Russians were inclined to be sceptical of American intentions.

The Soviets had other reservations as well. They feared that the structure of the control agency itself would leave them and their allies in a minority position relative to the United States and its supporters. For the time being they did offer to accept the principle of international inspection, although only after objecting that it might serve as a cover for Western intelligence activities inside the USSR. To the Soviets, however, the entire American plan was biased in favour of the West. Accordingly they placed a counter-proposal before the United Nations calling for the immediate dismantling of all (i.e. American) nuclear weapons, with a treaty on international control to be signed afterwards. Because the Russians were not yet capable of deploying a bomb, they argued that the only way the two powers could be on an equal footing was for the US to give up its monopoly. For the Americans the problem with the Russian proposal was that it contained no guarantee for the enforcement of the weapons ban – there was nothing to assure them that the USSR would not work on a bomb in secret – so the US would not accept the Soviet plan any more than the USSR would agree to the American proposal. The real problem was that neither side trusted the other. Indeed, from the very beginning of discussions there had been a considerable body of opinion in the US Congress which did not share the Truman administration's view that international control was safer than national control, even on American terms. As East–West relations continued to deteriorate, there were many in the administration itself who began to have doubts as well. Whatever the rights and wrongs of either the American or the Russian position, however, the stalemate was such that the question of nuclear arms control would not be revived again until the mid-1950s.

THE UNITED STATES AND THE WESTERN BLOC

It was not only the Soviet Union which posed a problem for the United States in the post-war period. America's own allies represented a challenge as well. Britain in particular expected to play a major role in global affairs. While all the allies acknowledged that the Second World War had placed the United States at the head of the Western Bloc, they also had an interest in not conceding any more authority to the Americans than absolutely necessary, in order to protect their own freedom of action. Their problem, however, was much like that of the Russians. They wanted American help to rebuild, and therefore Washington hoped that in return they would go along with its ideas for the post-war world. The key to US influence in the West was the so-called 'dollar shortage'. Because of the disruption caused by the war, America's partners were not able to produce enough exports to earn the foreign exchange (i.e., dollars or other currencies negotiable in the United States) needed to purchase imports from the US. Yet it was America which had to be the principal foreign source of goods and services for reconstruction after the war. The allies would need long-term loans and short-term help with their balance of payments. Accordingly the United States took the initiative, and at the Bretton Woods Conference of July 1944 proposed the creation of the International Bank for Reconstruction and Development (the World Bank) and the International Monetary Fund.

The role of the World Bank was to make loans directly to member nations or guarantee loans made by private bankers. The last provision was a means of increasing the pool of credits available by inducing private financial institutions to make loans to countries whose current credit rating might not be sound but whose future prospects were promising. The Bank would guarantee repayment should a borrower default. Its overall goals were to 'assist in the reconstruction and development' of members, and to promote 'private foreign investment' and the 'long-range balanced growth of international trade'. The International Monetary Fund was designed to complement the work of the Bank. Its job was to 'assist in the establishment of a multilateral system of payments' in order to facilitate international trade.* This would be done by means of a reserve or pool of foreign currencies from which members might borrow to meet short-term balance of payments deficits between themselves and other nations. This would make certain that countries experiencing temporary shortages of foreign exchange for the importation of commodities would still be able to buy in world markets.

The United States provided about one-third of the seed money for both institutions and thus had about one-third of the voting power. Given that no other single country contributed as much, this was enough to control both the Bank and the Fund. In addition the headquarters of both were located in Washington, DC, and American citizens assumed the top offices in each. Because so much of the private funding which the Bank might guarantee came from Wall Street and the American banking community, the influence of US business was substantial. If a private banker were unwilling to extend a loan, then there would be nothing for the World Bank to guarantee. Borrowers thus had to pass muster with private sector bankers committed to promoting American investment and American trade. Their decisions to grant (or, just as important, to withhold) credit would have a major influence on the economic policies of other countries. The actual operations of the Bank and the Fund thus would have the effect of placing a great deal of control in New York as the world's financial centre. Just as America's role during the Second World War as the 'arsenal of democracy' had provided the economic backing for its claim to leadership of the Western allies, so too the Bank and the Fund were intended to help perpetuate its primacy in the post-war world.

Although the Bank and the IMF were designed for the West, the United States also hoped to involve Russia and Eastern Europe, in order to increase its capacity to apply economic pressure on the Soviet Bloc. In the course of negotiations over the failed Russian loan the USSR did agree to send observers to various planning sessions for the Bank and the Fund. But Moscow never applied for membership, because it was clear that both institutions were intended to promote private and not state enterprise, and that they were stalking-horses for US business interests. Poland and Czechoslovakia did join, however, and soon found them-

* Cited in *ibid.*, 149.

selves the object of US efforts to use the Bank and Fund to influence their investment and trade policies. They would not yield, and therefore were refused loans even though they were members. Hence Poland resigned in 1950 and Czechoslovakia in 1954. In the meantime the political character of Bank and Fund policy had become readily apparent when Yugoslavia (though not a member of either) was granted aid. This was part of the Western effort to support Tito against Stalin. Most IMF and Bank money, however, was destined for Western nations.

In the West the British were the chief rivals of the United States. As one of the world's greatest mercantile nations, the United Kingdom had a stake in the restoration of the global market, but not necessarily on American terms. Although it had co-sponsored the World Bank and International Monetary Fund, Britain also feared that US economic power would offset the international character of the new institutions, and that they would promote the interests of the US much more effectively than those of other members of the Western Bloc. Moreover, by 1945 the Truman administration was working on a blueprint for something called the International Trade Organization (ITO). The ITO would apply the same principles in the realm of trade that the Bank and the Fund did in the realm of finance. It was intended to provide the institutional framework for negotiations to reduce trade barriers and to promote private enterprise in the international market-place. The approach would be multilateral; that is, it would bring many countries together in a common effort to reduce tariffs and other restrictions. It thus represented a quantum leap beyond bilateral concessions between only two nations. No doubt it would be difficult to make multilateralism work, because it involved the vested interests of many nations. Moreover, protectionist sentiment was strong in the US Congress, so that the wisdom of the Truman administration's initiative was not universally accepted even in the United States. And even within the ranks of the administration there was little interest in giving up America's special economic ties to areas such as the Philippines, even though they were scheduled for independence. In theory, a general lowering of trade barriers would open up new markets for everyone, but it was a question of just how far Washington itself was willing to go with multilateralism.

The British suspected that the American idea of multilateralism was really a means for the US to gain access to markets dominated by the UK, and this at a time when their economy was still reeling from the war. Once again they feared that what appeared to be an international agency might benefit the Americans more than anyone else. The United States, after all, had the strongest economy in the West, and would be likely to outdo them in any markets opened up under the provisions of the ITO. The British thus were inclined to protect what they already had, which was substantial. They still controlled the largest empire in the world, and they retained preferential trade agreements with the associated but independent states of the British Commonwealth (Canada, Australia, New Zealand and the Union of South Africa). Agreements limiting the convertibility of currencies (such as Indian rupees to British pounds sterling but not directly to American dollars) were also in effect, and had an important impact on trade patterns. This was no small matter, because the 'sterling bloc', combined with other countries with which Britain maintained payments agreements, had accounted for about one-half of the world's imports and exports before the Second World War. While the British themselves did not monopolize all this trade, London none the less was the financial centre for a good deal of it. Obviously, the United States had a considerable interest in winning more of this business for itself.

The problem for the British (and other Western nations as well) was that their wartime losses made them vulnerable to the same kind of pressure tactics as the United States applied to the Soviets. In May 1945 Washington made cuts in Lend Lease to them as well as the Russians, and with the end of the war in August abruptly suspended aid altogether. United States legislation passed in the spring of 1945 prohibited the diversion of Lend Lease assistance for post-war reconstruction, but the British were none the less caught off guard. They were under the impression that at the Quebec Conference of September 1944 Roosevelt had committed himself to finding some way of extending reconstruction aid, and that this would be forthcoming before the end of the war under the guise of Lend Lease or in some other form. But the Truman administration decided that the immediate cessation of Lend Lease (in accordance with a strict interpretation of the law) would be a good way to shock the British into realizing that US help with reconstruction would not be an outright gift, in recognition of losses already suffered, but would be conditional on their acceptance of American policies in the post-war world.

With the suspension of Lend Lease the British were in desperate economic straits. Their wartime costs were high, and they had run up huge debts with their partners in the sterling bloc and with other countries. The result was that they were forced to seek a loan from the

United States at a time when they were not in a strong position to bargain. Yet it turned out that they were not completely without power. There were upper limits on how many concessions the Americans could demand in return for a loan without hurting the UK economy and thus themselves. The British were among America's best customers. While the Americans wanted to cut Britain down to size, they also had an interest in the revitalization of its economy. The US negotiators thus faced a delicate task in striking a balance between these two goals. As in their dealings with the Russians, the Americans were about to discover that their superior power did not guarantee that they would have their way on every point.

The loan agreement concluded in December 1945 reflected the American dilemma. Britain's request for $5,000 million to $6,000 million was scaled down to $3,750 million at nominal interest; $20,000 million of Lend Lease indebtedness was forgiven; and over $6,000 million of surplus and Lend Lease goods were sold for a token sum. Yet the financial terms were in America's own best interest. They would help restore Britain as a trading partner. Also, the terms were worth conceding if the British would yield to US leadership on the question of restructuring the global market, and this they did, up to a point. They promised to modify their currency restrictions so that members of the sterling bloc might increase their trade with the United States, and they expressed their 'full agreement on all important points' contained in the Americans' proposal for the ITO, accepting them 'as a basis for international discussion'.* But, while the currency provisions were definite, the limits of American power were evident on the more important question of a multilateral approach to trade barriers. The British had committed themselves only to further negotiations at an international conference. They went no farther because they knew perfectly well that the Americans had to grant them credit or see trade between the two countries fall off drastically. The British also knew that the ITO threatened the economic interests of too many other countries to be readily accepted, so they could afford to go along with the idea in the expectation that others would resist. As it turned out, they were correct. The ITO also ran into trouble in the US Congress. Domestic as well as international factors thus imposed constraints on US policy. The eventual outcome was that, although the administration obtained some of its goals with the signing of the General Agreement on Tariffs and

* Cited in *ibid.*, 163.

Trade at Geneva (GATT) in 1947, and although this provided a framework for multilateral talks, the ITO itself never came into being.

For the Americans the fundamental problem was that their allies were not strong enough in economic terms to give wholehearted support to the cause of multilateralism. They could all agree that in theory a mutual reduction in trade barriers by all sides would open up economic opportunities for everyone, and that this would be good for them as well as the United States. But given that they were weak and the Americans were strong, the competition for markets would hardly be fair. Before multilateralism would have a real chance, therefore, Europe's capacity to compete had to be restored and its industrial base reconstituted, but in 1947–8 this was a long way from being achieved. The World Bank and the International Monetary Fund were just beginning their operations, and their impact was yet to be felt. For example, by 1948 the Bank had approved loans totalling only $497 million to four countries. This was hardly enough to sustain European recovery. In the same year the British exhausted their $3,750 million loan, plus an additional credit of $1,250 million from Canada. And because they were running out of dollars, they decided to back out of the convertibility clauses of their agreement with the United States, thus dealing a severe blow to multilateralism. The other nations of Europe were no better off. By 1947 the United States had extended more than $9,000 million in foreign aid to Western Europe (including Britain), and the Canadians had added nearly $600 million more for other countries besides the UK, but these sums were still not enough to restore Europe's economy, as proved by the persisting dollar shortage. Europe was simply not producing enough to earn its own way in the world. In the spring of 1947 American officials estimated that US exports for the year would total about $16,000 million, but that America's trading partners would be able to come up with the cash for only half of this. Loans, credits and aid would cover the balance, but obviously this was not a permanent solution. As long as European reconstruction lagged, moreover, American efforts to generate support for the multilateral institutions which the US regarded as vital to its own prosperity would come to little. Economically weak nations would hardly be amenable to lowering tariffs and other barriers to trade. Obviously a new approach was needed.

THE MARSHALL PLAN

Because the multilateralist goals of the United States could not succeed without its allies' recovery, and because European reconstruction had made insufficient progress by 1947, the Americans decided to act. They were motivated by an additional consideration as well: the need to strengthen the West in the Cold War. In the Marshall Plan (the European Recovery Plan, or ERP) the United States found a strategy for solving the economic problems of the Western Bloc while also challenging the Eastern Bloc. From the American point of view it tied everything together.

As in the past, the approach was to give the American proposal at least the appearance of an internationally sponsored programme, but the US in fact guided it from start to finish. On 5 June 1947 the US secretary of state, George C. Marshall, called upon all the nations of Europe to make their reconstruction needs known to the United States, which then would do its best to provide the requisite aid. Marshall's offer was completely open in that it addressed all the countries of Europe, East as well as West. The British and French, as the principals on the European side, were instructed as to how to proceed, and arranged to meet with the Russians in Paris before the end of the month in order to formulate a response to the American offer. Although the Soviet foreign minister, V. M. Molotov, did go to Paris, the talks quickly broke down. This was exactly what the Americans had expected would happen. They had never intended that the Soviets receive aid (that is, unless they were willing to open up Eastern Europe, an unlikely possibility). By attaching conditions to the Marshall Plan the US hoped to manoeuvre the USSR into rejecting what seemed to be a generous offer of assistance and thus force the Soviets into taking the blame for the worsening Cold War. State Department thinking was well summarized in a report prepared under the direction of Soviet specialist George Kennan, which argued that the terms of a new approach should be such that the Soviets and their satellites 'would either exclude themselves by unwillingness to accept the proposed conditions or agree to abandon the exclusive orientation of their economies'.*

To participate, the Soviets would have had to welcome American private investment in Eastern Europe, but this was impossible from their point of view. It would strengthen the very classes most opposed to the

* Cited in *ibid.*, 210–11.

communist party, thus immensely complicating Russian efforts to establish political control over the region. In addition Soviet participation would have required a mutual exchange of economic intelligence, in order to plan the allocation of ERP funds. Again, the Russians saw this as a direct threat to their security, because such information would reveal exactly where they were vulnerable and would be of military as well as economic value to the Americans. The greatest difficulty for the USSR, however, was the British and French (and American) preference for a common, co-ordinated programme for the Continent as a whole. The Russians feared this would be a step towards the integration of the East and West European economies. Not only would this reduce the autonomy of the Soviet Bloc, but it might permanently retard the economic development of the Russian sphere as well. The risk was that the less industrially developed East might become permanently subordinated to the much more industrially advanced West, with the former specializing in mainly agricultural commodities and raw materials and the latter specializing in manufacturing and remaining the centre of technological innovation. The prospect was hardly attractive to the Soviets, and Molotov left Paris on 3 July. It took little insight to realize that the American plan had really been designed to meet Western needs. Once the Russians were gone, Britain and France convened a meeting of sixteen interested nations, and serious planning began. The first ERP funds were approved by Congress in June 1948.

In the United States support for the Marshall Plan was widespread. This was because of the Cold War and the increasingly anti-Soviet attitude of both the administration and Congress, and also because the ERP benefited the US directly. Congress provided that most of the money for the goods needed to rebuild Europe be spent in America itself, although some expenditures were permitted in Canada as well. Thus the Marshall Plan represented a huge government subsidy to American business, labour and agriculture, and played a vital role in fuelling the post-war boom in the US. In Europe the results seemed equally impressive. By the time the plan came to an end, in 1952, about $13,000 million had been appropriated. With the goods supplied by the US, industrial output in Western Europe rose to 35 per cent above pre-war levels, and agricultural output to 10 per cent above.

Yet the Marshall Plan could not claim all the credit. The outbreak of the Korean War in 1950 (see Chapter 4) also created an impetus for increased economic activity. Korea led to a general arms build-up throughout the Western world, on the assumption that the Soviets were behind the new war and that their ambitions were ultimately global in scope. The story of Korea was in fact more complicated than this, but the United States decided it was necessary to increase military expenditures not only for the Far East but for Europe as well. The result was that by 1952 possibly 80 per cent of all American aid to Western Europe was for military purposes rather than reconstruction. American prosperity thus became more and more dependent on defence production, because the United States was the world's leading supplier of weapons. Moreover, the US made purchases of strategic goods in Europe and especially in Japan, which in turn helped its allies earn dollars. The whole Western economy therefore felt the effects of increased military spending and this has to be included with the Marshall Plan in explaining the economic well-being of the United States and its partners.

Still other factors dovetailed with the Marshall Plan to account for the increase in Western prosperity. For example, well before the Korean War the United States had inaugurated a programme for stockpiling strategic raw materials. The major sources of supply were to be found in Canada but also in the colonies of Western Europe. In fact France and Belgium used Marshall Plan money to increase raw-materials production in the areas they controlled, because sales of colonial resources helped offset their balance of payments deficits with the United States. The main reason why they could take advantage of the stockpiling programme, however, was not the ERP, but because they still dominated a large part of the colonial world. Once again, the prosperity of the West depended on more than just the Marshall Plan.

Where America fell short of its target for the ERP was on the question of multilateralism. While giving out aid the United States urged the Europeans to move quickly towards integrating the Continental economy. By reducing or eliminating tariffs and quotas at national boundaries Western Europe might become an entity capable of competing with the United States, and thus be more receptive to American ideas about further reducing trade barriers. But this was more easily said than done. Europe had never been a single unit, and it would take more than American pressure to change this. Although the European Coal and Steel Community was ratified by France, West Germany, Italy, the Netherlands, Belgium and Luxembourg in 1952 and provided for the elimination of import duties and quotas on steel and coal, it took most of the decade before the European Economic Community (or Common Market) began operation in 1958. Even then it required another ten years before duties among member nations were abolished. Furthermore, the Common Market would not bring together all of Western Europe, but initially only the six members of the Coal and Steel Community. In the meantime the fundamental problem for the Americans remained the same. Their economy was still so much stronger than any of the individual nations of Europe that their allies would continue to have reservations about multilateralism for some time to come. The economic results of the Marshall Plan were mixed indeed.

The impact of the ERP on East–West relations, however, was more definite: they worsened considerably, particularly as the Marshall Plan drove the Russians even further inward. The ERP caused dissension in the Eastern Bloc, and therefore induced the Soviets to fortify their control of the region. Because the USSR was short of funds for its own reconstruction, much less that of its satellites, both Poland and Czechoslovakia expressed an interest in participating in the American programme. The Soviet Union had no choice but to stop them. Otherwise its authority in Eastern Europe would be seriously undermined. To mollify their allies the Russians devised a scheme of their own, the Molotov Plan, but it was a pale imitation of the ERP. The Molotov Plan consisted of a set of trade agreements negotiated by the USSR and its satellites between July and September 1947. It was not a co-ordinated, regional plan and by itself did little to accelerate Eastern European reconstruction. As part of the same effort the USSR also organized the Cominform in 1947, but, as we have seen, this was intended to further the political unity of the Soviet Bloc, not to provide money. In any event, the Cominform soon became entangled in the conflict between Tito and Stalin. Further action would not come until two years later, in 1949, when the USSR set up the Council for Mutual Economic Assistance (COMECON). The Council was still not an agency for providing aid, but was more like the future Common Market for Western Europe. It was intended to provide the framework for regional economic planning, but encountered considerable resistance from the satellite states. They feared COMECON would retard their development and promote that of the USSR. In brief, the Soviets were simply unable to respond effectively to the Marshall Plan, and this hardly improved East–West relations.

AMERICA AND THE ENEMY STATES

The Marshall Plan was intended to consolidate America's relations with its allies in Western Europe, while at the same time upstaging the

Soviets. Equally vital to US interests, however, was the rehabilitation of Germany and Japan. Although occupied as enemy states, they were among the world's leading industrial powers, and had the potential to make an important contribution to the prosperity and security of the West. Accordingly, both received substantial amounts of American aid. The non-Soviet zones of Germany were among the largest beneficiaries of the ERP, while Japan received help under other legislation. Despite the war the United States in some ways had more in common with them than with its erstwhile Soviet comrades. Both had a long tradition of anti-communism, so that as US–USSR relations deteriorated the Americans very quickly came to regard their former enemies as stalwart allies.

As it happened, Japan presented a much simpler problem than Germany. Whereas Hitler opted for Armageddon (a decisive last stand) and ordered his troops to fight to the death, the Japanese followed a very different course, and in the end worked to facilitate rather than obstruct surrender. Although Westerners had feared that Japan's use of kamikaze tactics in the last days of the war indicated that it would resist beyond all reason rather than give up, the reality proved quite otherwise. Also, in Japan the Americans were able to exclude the Soviet Union from any effective role in the occupation, but in Germany the country was divided among four powers. In the one case the US had complete control, while the other became an object of East–West conflict.

Japan

By the spring of 1945 the Japanese government had to face three facts. The economic base needed for carrying on the war was crippled beyond repair; there was the possibility of mass starvation in Japan itself; and the Home Islands would be virtually cut off from China and South-East Asia in the event of an American victory on Okinawa. The end of the war was clearly in sight, and the outcome for Japan would be defeat. While the cabinet remained divided on what to do next, at least until the atomic bombs started falling, the more far-sighted among Japan's businessmen and politicians realized the importance of preparing for surrender and occupation. This was particularly in the interest of the *zaibatsu* – the large, diversified holding companies that controlled the country's most important industries and financial institutions. They had close connections with the government, and were the source of the wealth and power of Japan's elite, i.e. of its upper classes. The Imperial Household itself had major holding in *zaibatsu* enterprises. Given that the economic and political elite of Japan had a great deal of property to protect, the logic of co-operating with the enemy in order to limit reprisals became increasingly persuasive in government circles.

Accordingly, by the time the government decided to notify the United States of its intention to surrender (which it did on 10 August), Japanese officials had formed some definite ideas as to how to proceed. The normally secluded Emperor Hirohito broke with tradition and played a public role in events, a fact which in itself sent a message to the Americans that Japan was prepared to co-operate. He went on the radio and urged his people not to resist any further. In addition members of the royal family visited the armies in the field, in order to invoke the authority of the emperor and thus ensure that the military obeyed the command to give up. A new government was formed to oversee the transfer of political power to the occupation forces. For the first time in history a member of the imperial family headed the cabinet, again to make certain that everything proceeded according to plan. Perhaps the most important act of the transitional government was to transfer about $10,000 million worth of assets to supporters of the regime, chiefly those linked with the *zaibatsu* and other large firms. The aim was to help key businesses and members of the political and economic elite ride out the hard times ahead, so that someday they might make a comeback. The government had considerable leeway to act because Hiroshima and Nagasaki had brought the war to an end so quickly that the Americans were not yet ready to land their occupation forces. Indeed, the formal surrender ceremony would not take place until 2 September. Meanwhile the Japanese government used its time well.

The Japanese strategy thus was to capitulate totally on the military front while taking defensive measures on the home front. But whether the government, even purged of its most outspoken militarists, would succeed in holding on to power still depended on the Americans. As it turned out, there were a number of considerations which recommended that the United States work with those who had facilitated the surrender. First and most obvious, the US was desperately short of personnel fluent in Japanese, much less knowledgeable about the details of the country's economic and political structures. There was little choice but to depend on the existing authorities. Second, the Americans did not wish to see the disintegration of Japanese society, as this would only create opportunities for the left. The profits of the *zaibatsu* had been earned by the exploitation of cheap labour, and Japanese communists or even trade unionists might use the occasion of defeat to mobilize the masses. If anything, the

United States needed to support the Japanese government and provide it with the means to maintain order. It did so, and over the next several years the commander of the occupation forces, General Douglas MacArthur, even proved willing to deploy American troops against Japanese strikers in labour disputes. The price of stability was to maintain the traditional ruling group, those in government and in the managerial ranks of business who had succeeded in preserving order in the past. Third, US goals did not require a major disruption of Japanese society, with all its attendant risks. The American interest was to prevent Japan from closing the Open Door and blocking access to the markets and resources of Asia. With Tokyo's surrender this had been accomplished. The destruction of Japan's military capacity meant that in the future it would not be able to establish an exclusive sphere of influence, and therefore would have an even greater stake in the Open Door policy than the Americans. It was no accident that the 1947 Japanese constitution, written by the occupation authorities, provided that Japan renounce war as an instrument of policy in the future. From then on there was no question about Japan's observance of the Open Door. Given that the Americans had achieved their objectives, the more immediate concern was Japan's internal stability, and in this respect repentant members of the Japanese elite could be quite helpful.

Both the US and the Japanese governments wanted order, and so a symbiotic relationship soon developed, which explains the Americans' willingness to allow the emperor to remain in office. He was the authority figure for an entire social system. His staying was a sign that the United States was not interested in undermining the power of the state or that of the elite. There would be changes, including the introduction of universal suffrage and a programme of land reform, but what did not change proved far more important.

Of course, in the United States there were calls for reprisals. The momentum of the war and the lust for vengeance assured this. American policy-makers often were divided on exactly how to strike a balance between punishment and reconciliation, so sometimes contradictory decisions were made. But the overall thrust was towards rehabilitating Japan and making it into an ally. A number of developments illustrated the trend. A programme for excluding militarists from public life was undertaken by early 1946, but was highly selective. A mere 0.29 per cent of the population in Japan was excluded after the Second World War, while in the American zone of Germany 2.5 per cent suffered this fate. In fact, the US decision not to impose direct military rule but to work through the existing governmental structures made too drastic a purge impractical. Of the over 200,000 purgees, about 80 per cent were in the army and other branches of the military and the rest were politicians, bureaucrats and business leaders. Approximately 99 per cent of persons whose past was reviewed were given a clean bill of health. High-profile figures, such as the wartime prime minister, Tōjō Hideki, were placed on trial, but even Winston Churchill objected on the grounds that by the same standards he and Roosevelt would have been executed had the Allies lost the war. In the end, while individuals were affected, the personnel of the bureaucracy, the political system and the business sector remained basically intact.

Proposals to reorganize the economic system were hardly any more effective. The *zaibatsu* were taken as the chief target, especially the 'Big Four' – Mitsui, Mitsubishi, Sumitomo and Yasuda. Reformers in the United States argued that the *zaibatsu* bore a heavy responsibility for the war and therefore should be broken up. As Japan's most powerful business enterprises they had encouraged expansionism in order to gain exclusive control of new markets and assured sources of raw materials. Furthermore, their exploitative labour policies had increased the potential for social disorder. And because their low-wage policies had placed constraints on the growth of the domestic market, Japan had been forced to emphasize exports and go in search of foreign markets. There was, according to this view, a close relationship between the structure of the domestic economy and the causes of the war. The *zaibatsu* had to go. Yet other American policy-makers feared the consequences of attempting to restructure the Japanese economy. The result might be economic chaos, thus adding to the costs of the occupation and weakening a potential ally. Moreover, because the United States accounted for over 80 per cent of the pre-war foreign investment in Japan, some Americans wondered whether their assets would be affected as well, and so were not keen about the so-called 'deconcentration' programme. For example, General Electric had invested in Toshiba, Westinghouse in Mitsubishi, Owens-Libby in Sumitomo, American Can in Mitsui and Goodrich in Furukawa. In due course the deconcentration programme was gutted. By 1948 only nine cases out of an initial list of about 1,200 had been concluded, and it was decided not to proceed any further.

Two events clinched Japan's future place in the Western Bloc. In 1949 the communists defeated Chiang Kai-shek in China and established the People's Republic. This ended Washington's hopes that the Nationalists would become a powerful ally in the Far East. And the next year, 1950, the Korean War broke out. Japan's importance as a base of operations and as a source of supply was demonstrated beyond question. The United States thus proceeded to sign a treaty of peace on 8 September 1951, despite the protests of the USSR (which was not satisfied with the terms of the treaty) and despite a commitment given during the Second World War not to make a separate peace with any of the enemy states. China objected as well, because the United States excluded it from the peace negotiations, even though it had been one of Japan's principal victims. But given that both the USSR and China were communist states, and given the outbreak of the war in Korea, the United States felt justified in going ahead. It also signed a security treaty with Japan, the anti-war provision of the 1947 constitution notwithstanding. Yet these were new times.

Germany

From the American point of view the Japanese situation was ideal. The United States had found a compliant, anti-communist ruling group, and this simplified the process of integrating the country into the Western Bloc and mobilizing its resources. Because the Soviets lacked the capacity to station an occupation force in Japan, moreover, they had been unable to make the US recognize their right to a meaningful role in policy. In fact the American government unilaterally designated Douglas MacArthur the Supreme Commander for the Allied Powers. While the USSR was given token membership on various commissions, real authority was vested in MacArthur, and he reported only to the US president. Germany, on the other hand, was quite another matter. The government had disintegrated, and the country had been divided four ways among the US, Russia, Britain and France. Though all the powers paid lip-service to the idea of reunifying the country someday, it was not in the interest of either the West or the East to see this happen if it meant Germany would join the other side.

The USSR controlled the largest single zone measured by area, but the Americans had the advantage in that the Western zones (taken together) were bigger and contained more of German industry. The eastern or Soviet reaches of the country were more agricultural. Thus, even if reunification on American terms proved impossible, the West would wind up with most of the country in its camp. As in the case of Eastern Europe generally, the United States did have an opportunity to influence developments in the Soviet zone. The key to American power was reparations. Potsdam had recognized the Russians' extraordinary contribution to the war effort by permitting them to take capital goods not only from their own zone but from the Western zones as well. Yet whether the USSR actually received what it was entitled to from the other zones depended upon the co-operation of the US, Britain and France. Further, the Americans knew that dismantling a portion of German industry and shipping it to the Soviets would hurt the country and retard its ability to contribute to European prosperity once again. Indeed, if too many reparations were taken, the costs of occupation would increase. There was, in other words, a good deal to be said for obstructing the efforts of the USSR to obtain industrial equipment from the Western zones. Doing so might make Russia agree to American terms concerning reunification. Although for a time during the Second World War Franklin Roosevelt had subscribed to a programme for deindustrializing Germany known as the Morgenthau Plan, in fact it was in the West's interest to restore the country as quickly as possible and integrate it into the Western Bloc. As in the case of Japan, there were calls for harsh reprisals, and many more individuals were affected by purges and trials for war crimes. At Nuremberg leading figures of the Nazi regime were tried by an international tribunal, with twenty-five of them sentenced to death over a two-year period. The restoration of Germany, however, soon became the settled policy of the United States, just as in the case of Japan. The United States secretary of state, James Byrnes, indicated this in a major policy address given at Stuttgart on 6 September 1946.

Byrnes announced that the Americans were determined to move ahead with reunification whether the USSR co-operated or not. In December 1946 the United States and Britain arranged a merger of their zones under the name Bizonia, and in 1948 Trizonia took form with the co-operation of France. At the same time the Americans stalled on the transfer of reparations, in the hope of forcing the USSR to conform to the decision taken at Potsdam that Germany be treated as one economic unit. In March 1946 a plan for removing capital equipment from the Western zones was announced and gave the Russians some satisfaction, although they received less than they wanted. It would have cut back German industry to about 70 per cent of its pre-war capacity, and would have completely razed a number of strategic industries, including the manufacture of synthetic oil, petrol and rubber. The plan did not set precise figures, but probably between 1,500 and 2,000 plants would have been taken apart and turned over. In time, however, the Russians shifted ground and wanted reparations taken out of current production rather than capital equipment. The US was delaying the implementation of the 1946 plan, and it was also becoming apparent that removing factories was difficult and involved a high degree of waste. The Soviets even reduced dismantling in their own zone for this reason. But the Americans would not agree to convert to current production unless the USSR made political concessions, and so relations between the two powers continued to deteriorate. By the end of the dismantling programme only 668 factories in the Western zones were completely removed, and no agreement was reached on current production. Thus the Soviets did not receive what they regarded as fair compensation for the war. The Americans, however, were disappointed as well. Manipulating reparations did not make the USSR any more pliable on the question of reunification.

The Soviets resisted American pressure because in the long run they had more to gain by opposing reunification than by conceding it in exchange for reparations. Given that the West controlled three out of the four zones of occupation, there was no opportunity for the USSR to impose a communist party on most areas of Germany. As the Russians undermined non-communist parties in their zone, so too the Western powers undermined the communist party in the rest of the country. This meant that the Soviets could hardly expect to control a reunified Germany, and hence they decided to hold on to what they already had. It was remotely possible that a single but neutral German state might have been agreed upon, but this became less and less likely as the Cold War worsened.

The issue of reunification came to a crisis over Berlin. The four occupying powers shared control of the former Nazi capital, even though it was deep inside the Soviet zone of Germany. Western access therefore was vulnerable, at least by road and rail. Accordingly, on 23 June 1948, the Soviets blockaded the land routes to the city in protest against persistent US efforts to centralize the administration of economic policy as a step towards eventual reunification. The immediate cause of the crisis was an American decision to introduce a new currency in the Western-controlled parts of the country, after a plan to reform the monetary system for all four zones had failed to be adopted because of Soviet opposition. The real issue, however, was not just the terms of currency reform but reunification; hence the blockade.

President Truman responded by ordering B–29 bombers (character-ized officially as 'atomic-capable') to the European theatre. Secretary of

State Marshall observed that the Russians would at last have to face up to the likelihood that 'the United States would really use the atomic bomb against them in the event of war'.* With the bomb in reserve, therefore, the Americans proceeded in measured steps. They made no effort to open the land links to West Berlin by force, and instead supplied the city by air for nearly a year. Millions of tons of food and other necessities were flown in, and even coal was airlifted. For their part, the Russians made no attempt to interfere with the Western airlift. They lacked superiority in the air and had no atomic capability of their own. Yet both sides claimed victory when the blockade was lifted on 12 May 1949. The US had confirmed its rights and those of its allies in Berlin, and because of the crisis could justify integrating the non-Soviet zones into the Western Bloc. For the Soviets the blockade had been quite sufficient for achieving their goal, which was simply to keep what they already had and to prevent the Americans from gaining influence over all of Germany. Given that they had no hope of dominating the whole country themselves, the Soviets' best option was to set up a separate but pliable regime in the east, and in this they succeeded. By the time the crisis came to an end, both sides had taken steps to make the division of Germany virtually permanent. The Western powers cleared the way for the establishment of the Federal Republic of Germany on 23 May 1949, while the Russians proclaimed the German Democratic Republic in their zone on 7 October 1949.

NATO AND AMERICAN LEADERSHIP

The Berlin Crisis also provided the impetus for the United States and its North Atlantic partners to establish a formal military alliance with America at the head. At first many policy-makers in Washington had reservations about entering into a permanent commitment, so that Europeans and Canadians were initially more important in promoting the idea. The US Congress in particular had reservations about so-called 'entangling' alliances. But there were countervailing arguments which recommended that the United States embrace such a policy, and in due course the Americans became staunch supporters of an Atlantic alliance. Moreover, the skeleton of an organization already existed. In 1947 Britain and France had signed a mutual defence treaty, and the

* Cited in E. P. Thompson and Dan Smith (eds), *Protest and Survive* (New York: 1981), *xx–xxi.*

next year a more inclusive arrangement, known as the Brussels Pact, had been concluded among Britain, France and the Low Countries (Belgium, Luxembourg and the Netherlands). Both agreements, however, were more the product of the Second World War than the Cold War, and were aimed at containing a resurgent Germany instead of a former ally in the form of Russia. The Berlin Blockade obviously changed the context of Western Europe's defence. While the Europeans remained wary of the Germans, they increasingly feared the USSR. At the same time the Americans were interested in promoting an anti-Soviet military agreement among their allies, though their own role in the alliance took some time to be defined. Eventually, the North Atlantic Treaty was signed in Washington on 4 April 1949 by the United States, Canada, Britain, France, Belgium, Denmark, Iceland, Italy, Norway, Portugal and the Netherlands. Greece and Turkey joined in 1952, and the Federal Republic of Germany in 1955. The signatories agreed to come to each other's aid should any of them be attacked, although NATO itself could not commit any nation to go to war and left the final decision in the hands of member countries.

When the NATO treaty was signed, American intelligence estimates indicated that the Russians were unlikely to launch an all-out war in Europe at the end of the 1940s or in the early 1950s. Indeed, future secretary of state John Foster Dulles testified before a congressional committee that he did 'not know of any responsible high official, military or civilian . . . who believes that the Soviet [Union] now plans conquest by open military aggression'.* Yet in time the United States did come to support the idea of NATO enthusiastically. The Soviets may not have been an immediate military threat globally, but it was important to keep them on the defensive. Just as important, NATO turned out to be another way of institutionalizing America's leadership of the Western Bloc. As the Marshall Plan had been designed to draw Western Europe closer to the USA, so too NATO had a similar effect.

In addition NATO might make US plans for the eventual restoration of Germany more palatable by someday merging its armies into a larger command structure. The French in particular needed reassuring, as their country had been invaded by the Germans three times since 1870. Finally, NATO would contribute to a build-up of conventional forces in

---

* Cited in Joyce and Gabriel Kolko, *The Limits of Power: The World and United States Foreign Policy, 1945–1954* (London: 1972), 499.

Western Europe. In the view of some policy-makers this was important in order to help America's allies maintain internal order in the event of subversion from within. After all, communists had scored well in recent elections, though by 1949 their drawing power was declining. Atomic weapons were hardly relevant to containing the threat of domestic political turmoil, whereas conventional armies were. In fact, one US senator, Arthur Vandenberg, noted that NATO forces were needed 'chiefly for the *practical* purpose of assuring adequate defence against internal subversion'.* NATO thus was a significant step in the consolidation of Western security, internally as well as externally.

The Russians followed suit in due course, but only by 1955 with the formation of the Warsaw Pact (officially, the Eastern European Mutual Assistance Treaty) among Albania, Bulgaria, Czechoslovakia, the German Democratic Republic, Hungary, Poland, Romania and the USSR. It turned out that an alliance system was more useful to Moscow than Washington in containing internal dissension among its partners. In fact the only time Warsaw Pact armies conducted a joint military action (apart from practice manoeuvres) was in 1968, when they intervened in Czechoslovakia to stop what the USSR regarded as unacceptable political reforms.

To summarize, the United States moved on a broad range of fronts after 1945. More than any other nation it had the capacity to act on a global scale, and it did so. Indeed, it must have been tempting for Americans to think that they should simply deploy the atomic bomb against the USSR while they still had a monopoly of nuclear weapons, and that this would resolve many of their problems in the world. Yet such a course of action would hardly have done so, for it would not have changed the ways in which the power of the West itself contributed to global instability. This was an important point, regardless of what the Russians were doing. The US and its allies were quite capable of generating problems on their own without help from the Soviets, so that global stability was likely to remain elusive. In the early post-war period this was perhaps no more clear than in the colonial world. There the West was the principal external influence. The USSR did not control a large number of colonies by comparison, and in this period its activities were confined mainly to

* Cited in *ibid.*

propaganda. The colonial world thus offered a test case for whether Western hegemony could be equated with peace and order, and so it is to this that we now turn.

3

THE THIRD WORLD:

COLONIALISM, NEO-COLONIALISM

AND REVOLUTION

The greatest challenge to the West in the Third World after 1945 was not the loss of its colonies but the threat of social revolution. Although in many cases decolonization came about sooner than expected, revolution affected the material interests of the West in even more fundamental ways. This is not to say that the European powers regarded decolonization as of little consequence, or that they all responded in the same ways. Certainly the British accepted the logic of withdrawing from India. Therefore they did not seek to prevent independence so much as to influence its terms. Other colonial powers, however, were more likely to go to war in order to delay the end of empire, e.g. the French in Indo-China and Algeria, the Dutch in the East Indies (Indonesia) or later the Portuguese in Africa. Terrible slaughter resulted on all sides, and was the price of resisting the end of the colonial era. Furthermore, the decline of colonialism caused serious problems within the Western Bloc, and strained the unity of the North Atlantic alliance. The reason was that the United States considered the coming of independence to the Third World as an opportunity to open up new markets and to increase its political influence. The Americans therefore were not unhappy to see the weakening of European imperialism.

Yet, despite the loss of their colonies and differences in their national interests, the industrialized countries of the West were still in an excellent position to influence events in the Third World, and to do so in ways which partially offset the effects of decolonization. However virulently Third World leaders might attack imperialism, they still needed the markets and investments which the former colonial powers provided. Hence most Third World countries remained part of the global capitalist system and linked to the West, regardless of their political status. In many places colonialism was superseded by neo-colonialism. Whereas the former involved direct rule by an imperial power, the latter referred to situations in which underdeveloped nations achieved political independence but remained economically dependent on the West.

Social revolution, on the other hand, represented a direct attack not only on Western political authority but on Western property, and in many ways posed a greater problem than the decline of colonialism. If the newly independent nations of the Third World refrained from expropriating Western investments and profits, and continued to allow access to their markets, resources and cheap labour, then the West could live with decolonization. But the advocates of Third World revolution proposed programmes for nationalizing foreign as well as domestic capital, and planned to move towards some form of socialism. In addition they usually identified with the Eastern rather than the Western Bloc. All this obviously endangered the economic and strategic position of the West, so that the possibility of a revolutionary movement assuming power somewhere in the Third World invariably mobilized both Americans and Europeans to defend their interests. Accordingly, much of what happened in the Third World after 1945 was affected by the threat of revolution and by Western efforts to develop counter-revolutionary strategies, either to anticipate and guide change into safe channels or to destabilize leftist regimes which did succeed in coming to power. The problem was that the very success of these efforts perpetuated the conditions which had led to social revolution in the first place, and guaranteed that the history of the Third World would be one of continuing conflict.

THE WEST AND THE THIRD WORLD

In 1945 Western Europe and the United States still claimed most of the Third World as colonies or protectorates. These included virtually all of South-East and South Asia, most of Africa, numerous strategically significant islands in the Atlantic and Pacific, and some parts of the Middle East. The West also dominated the foreign trade of Latin America, though almost the entire region had achieved political independence from Spain and Portugal in the nineteenth century. For all practical purposes most of the Third World was a Western sphere of influence. Indeed, the very term was a Western invention, and had meaning only in relation to the industrialized capitalist West as the so-called 'First World'. The same was true of the term 'Second World', i.e. Russia and the nations of Eastern Europe. Because the latter were founded on principles of economic and social organization distinct from those of the First World, they were treated as a separate global system.

The hallmark of Third World status, however, was not separation from but economic integration, on unequal terms, with the Western industrial world. Beginning in the fifteenth century, and culminating in the late nineteenth and early twentieth centuries, the West had expanded overseas and incorporated most of the world into a global market dominated by Europe and later also the United States. Among other powers only Japan stood out as a rival. Colonies were established and spheres of influence delineated, resulting in a dramatic effect on trade patterns. For example, the value of exports from British India to the United Kingdom, Western Europe and North America in 1900 was almost double the value of its exports to the rest of Asia. Because the export trade was usually dominated by foreigners, they tended to profit the most. The effect was to divert resources and the gains of cheap labour from the Third World to the West, thus retarding the development of the former.

This is not to suggest that the prosperity of the First World depended mainly on the exploitation of the Third World before 1945. On the contrary, the Western powers conducted most of their trade with each other, as they constituted the richest markets. The same was true of investment. Usually only a small percentage of the total trade and capital of an imperial nation went to its colonies. Moreover, it was not the case that every single colony or dependency in the Third World turned out to be profitable for the First World. Sometimes the cost of ruling a particular region exceeded the overall economic gains to be had. Even in such cases, however, individual private enterprises might earn profits or receive high returns on investments, inducing their owners to appeal for the continuing protection of their home governments. If these people had enough political influence, they might have their way. The imperial powers also had strategic and other motives for establishing colonies, quite apart from the profits and losses of individual businesses. Indeed strategic considerations might justify public expenditures well beyond any strictly private financial gains.

Yet the point here is not to emphasize the effects on the imperial nations, but their impact on the colonial world. In this respect, and in overall terms, the First World tended to benefit more than the Third World from their relationship, so that the unequal nature of their ties helped explain the most obvious characteristics of the latter: chronic

poverty and eventually a potential for social revolution. Colonialism may
not have entirely accounted for the wealth of the West, yet it went far to
explain the retardation of the Third World. There were certainly other
causes, including local oligarchies who collaborated with foreign capital
in order to take advantage of their own people, but the evolution of a
global market designed to serve the needs of the First World was a major
influence in the history of the Third World.

Western ideology emphasized the benefits of foreign rule and foreign
investment, and held out the promise of mutually advantageous development in the future. Yet the facts were otherwise. Although total global
production increased over time, its relative distribution became more
rather than less distorted. Historian L. S. Stavrianos estimates that the
average per person income of the Third World was possibly one-fifth
that of the First World in 1850, one-sixth in 1900, one-tenth in 1960 and
one-fourteenth in 1970. While this was the result of a variety of factors, it
was none the less the case that the West was the most important external
force affecting the pattern of Third World development, through centuries of colonialism. It was a fact that Western businesses took more
from the Third World than they put in, and that in many places they
steadily increased their rate of exploitation. This was hardly surprising,
as the purpose of Western trade and investment was to make a profit. But
this also meant that the interdependence of the two worlds was anything
but mutual.*

The role of the Third World in the war against Germany and Japan
also confirmed its importance to the West. Millions of colonials served in
the armies and labour battalions of the various belligerents. Africans
were used by the Allies to defend France, East Africa, North Africa and
the Far East (especially Burma, where they suffered their worst casualties). In addition over two million Indians served under the British in
South Asia, and were kept at the ready in case of a Japanese invasion of
India. They also saw duty in North Africa, Ethiopia, Syria, Iraq, Burma
and Malaya. The Axis powers did likewise, with the exception of
Germany, which had lost its colonies as a result of the First World War.
But the Italians and particularly the Japanese used colonial troops. In fact
Japan's anti-Western policies attracted some followers in Asia despite its

* L. S. Stavrianos, *Global Rift: The Third World Comes of Age* (New York:
  1981), 38. Also see his Introduction for a discussion of the term 'Third
  World' and the historical tendency of underdevelopment to persist and
  even worsen (in relative terms) rather than be ameliorated over time.
  Related discussions appear in chapters 2, 8, 13 and 19.

own imperial ambitions, so that it was able to call upon volunteers in Burma, Malaya, the Dutch East Indies and also from among captured Indian soldiers who were anxious to overthrow the British raj.

The economic contributions of the colonial world were equally important in winning the war. Exports from Britain's West African colonies, for example, rose more than 100 per cent between 1938 and 1946. When France was occupied by the Nazis, its equatorial colonies in Africa supported the anti-Axis forces, but the rest (i.e. in North and West Africa, as well as Madagascar) declared for Vichy and so were blockaded by Britain. Once the Allies began pushing the Germans back in North Africa, however, the pro-Vichy colonies switched sides, or were taken over by the Free French of General Charles de Gaulle, and added their productive capacity to the Allied cause. The Belgian territories of the Congo and Rwanda-Urundi played a role as well. Colonial administrators restrained wages and prices, and thus made sure that the demand for Third World labour and commodities did not drive up costs for the Allies.

It was obvious that the usefulness of the Third World to the First World would not cease with the war, and for several reasons. First, resources would be required for the reconstruction of Europe and for the Western build-up against the Russians. In particular, substitutes would be needed for the raw materials and agricultural commodities that had come from Eastern Europe in the past, but which after 1945 would be monopolized by the Soviet Bloc. Second, the control of Third World exports might help Europe meet its balance of payments problems with the United States. Third, to the extent that the West could hold on to its colonies or develop neo-colonial relationships, it might protect existing investments in the Third World and preserve opportunities for profit-making ventures in the future. And fourth, in the case of Britain and France colonialism and neo-colonialism might provide a means of asserting their status as great powers, and thus restrain American pretensions in the post-war world.

Accordingly, however the question of political independence might be resolved, the West wanted to protect its economic stake in the Third World after 1945. That it intended to do so was abundantly clear from its foreign-aid strategies. These were designed mainly to develop infrastructures such as transportation and communications links, vocational and technical schools, hospitals and clinics, or hydroelectric and irrigation projects. Such public investments were needed to create an economic environment in which private enterprise might thrive. How could modern business function without improved harbours, roads, railways, airports, communications, health facilities, electricity in abundance or water for both industry and agriculture? How could Western Europeans and Americans deal with other cultures unless native leaders were educated in Western ways of doing business, and versed in the virtues of private rather than state-owned enterprise?

Because Western businessmen stood to gain from investing in Third World mines, plantations and such manufacturing as took advantage of cheap labour, Western governments considered it in the interest of their corporate citizens to provide what was commonly called 'aid for development'. While launched amid a fanfare about helping less-developed countries, such assistance was of direct benefit to the West. By supporting infrastructural development it helped create favourable conditions for trade and for the investment of private capital. An example of such aid was the British Overseas Food Corporation. This was created after the Second World War, and was intended to raise agricultural production in Britain's African colonies, but mainly for export, not local consumption. Similarly the government of France in 1951 described its aid programme for the so-called 'French Union' (a euphemism for the French empire) as designed 'to increase agricultural and industrial production in the perspective of a European community'.* The Colombo Plan was another development project launched in the early 1950s by the white nations of the British Commonwealth. In due course they were joined by the United States, which became the largest contributor of funds. But the US had programmes of its own; Point Four was the best known of these in the early post-war period, and provided economic and technical assistance.

It should be noted that much if not most Western aid was 'tied'. In other words, it was granted on the condition that it be spent on (or tied to) goods and services purchased in the donor country. Foreign aid thus usually amounted to an indirect subsidy to Western business and labour. In the Third World itself, however, the immediate goals of specific programmes were not always realized. Yet the aid programmes were none the less important for what they revealed about Western intentions. Further, in overall terms and apart from the question of aid, the West remained the net beneficiary of private foreign investment and trade. This had considerable import. It meant that Third World status was not

* Cited in Basil Davidson, *Africa in Modern History: The Search for a New Society* (Harmondsworth: 1978), 207–8.

necessarily a transitional stage of development, one inevitably to be outgrown in time. Nor was it the result of chance – a lesser endowment of natural or human resources for example. The Third World had plenty of resources, but they were being drained away by other countries. Underdevelopment thus was a continuing condition and had identifiable causes. To a considerable extent it resulted from the specific way in which the Third World had been integrated with the First World, but this would be difficult to change.

THE SECOND WORLD WAR AND
ANTI-COLONIALISM

The most immediate factor affecting the Third World in 1945 was the war between the Allies and the Axis. Both sides relied on their colonial subjects to help with the war effort, and this spurred the growth of nationalist and sometimes revolutionary agitation in the Third World. In the Western camp military service overseas brought Africans, Indians and other Asians into contact with each other, and raised their political consciousness. Allied policy did this as well. Foremost in this respect was the Atlantic Charter, agreed to by Winston Churchill and Franklin Roosevelt in August 1941. Intended as a demonstration of growing co-operation between Britain and America at a time when the United States had not yet become a belligerent, and therefore as a warning to the Axis powers, it outlined principles of order for the post-war world. In effect it was an early attempt to list Western war aims. Chief among these was the ending of further territorial expansion at the expense of other countries, and recognition of the right of all people to choose their own form of government. The scope of the Charter was called into question a month later, however, when Churchill served notice in the British House of Commons that it applied only to the victims of Nazi aggression. Roosevelt demurred, claiming that the Charter applied everywhere, but of course this reflected America's interest in seeing the break-up of Europe's empires. In any event, and despite disagreements among the Allies as to the meaning of their own declaration, nationalists in the Third World seized upon the Charter as an opportunity to question the West's right to rule.

Japan had an even more powerful impact on the growth of anti-colonialism during the Second World War. Its brilliant military campaigns in Malaya, Burma, the Dutch East Indies and the Philippines demonstrated the capacity of a non-white people to overwhelm the imperial powers of Europe and America. Just as important, its conquests had immediate political consequences in the West. When the Dutch East Indies were occupied, for example, Queen Wilhelmina of the Netherlands announced that a new and more autonomous status would be granted to the colony after the war. The Dutch were shocked to see so many colonials collaborate with the enemy, and thus promised a better future in the hope of facilitating the restoration of the Dutch empire someday. Although independence was the last thing the Queen was willing to grant, her concessions fuelled Indonesian nationalism and hastened the day when it would come about. Events in the Chinese theatre also inspired changes in Western policy. As one way of countering Japan's presence in the country, Britain and the United States in January 1943 announced that they would surrender the special treaty rights (relating to trade, tariffs and the protection of their nationals) which they had extracted from the Chinese government a century before. In addition, the Americans pressed the British to accelerate reform in India. They also made it known that they would not look kindly upon the resumption of French rule in Indo-China.

The Far Eastern war had other consequences as well. Because the Japanese expanded so rapidly into South-East Asia, they sometimes had no choice but to call upon local leaders for help in running the occupied areas. They simply did not have the personnel to rule large parts of Asia while at the same time conducting a major war in the Pacific and another (of considerably longer duration) in China. Although more than a few opportunists went to work for Japan, collaborators were also to be found among the advocates of Third World independence. An example was Achmed Sukarno, who later became the first president of Indonesia. Moreover, Japan also had sympathizers in areas made secure by the West. Perhaps the best known of these was Subhas Chandra Bose of India. Once an important leader of the Congress Party, he turned to the Axis powers for support against the British. In 1943 he took charge of the Japanese-sponsored Provisional Government of Free India, based at Singapore.

Nationalists hardly looked forward to the imposition of Japanese hegemony, yet the situation of Japan in Asia was qualitatively different from that of Europe or America. Whatever their own ambitions, the Japanese were the only Asian people capable of challenging Western imperialism. Asian nationalists therefore viewed Japan's role in the war with considerable ambiguity, and some of them accepted administrative posts under the occupation forces. If Japan succeeded in winning the war and establishing its authority on a permanent basis, collaboration would at least mean a greater share in power than under Western rule. Not all nationalists collaborated, of course, and many went underground and fought the Japanese. In doing so they gained experience in the kind of guerrilla tactics which would be deployed against the Western powers in Indo-China, Indonesia, Malaya, Burma and the Philippines after the war. Thus, even if Japan were defeated, things would never be the same for the West.

In the meantime other events affected the future of imperialism in Asia. As the war began turning against the Japanese in late 1942 and early 1943, they decided to seek support by promising greater political if not economic independence to selected countries. Though without a great deal of practical effect, steps were taken to bestow more autonomy on Japan's puppet government in China at Nanjing and to grant independence to Burma and the Philippines. Further, there seemed to be the prospect of similar action elsewhere. In November 1943 the Japanese staged the Greater East Asia Conference in Tokyo. Resolutions were adopted which became for Japan what the Atlantic Charter had been for the West. They promised eventual recognition of the autonomy of the countries of East Asia. The conference was a thinly veiled attempt to generate enthusiasm for the war effort by giving the conquered territories a stake in the outcome. And while it was clear that Japan still intended to establish a new bloc under its leadership and based on the Greater East Asia Co-Prosperity Sphere, to some Asians this seemed no worse than the Western alternative.

Japan thus made a concerted effort to legitimize its own expansion by posing as the leader of a new pan-Asian order. Moreover, it moved beyond the world of diplomacy to exploit anti-Western feelings as well. That this was possible had been evident from the early days of the war, when in many parts of South-East Asia segments of the local population had assisted the Japanese invasion. In addition colonials serving in Western armies sometimes had deserted or refused to fight. Anti-Western sentiment was widespread in Asia, and needed only to be mobilized. In the Philippines, for example, there was a long tradition of anti-Americanism dating back to the turn of the century. The United States had seized the Philippines in 1898, and from then until about 1906 had waged war against the independence movement led by Emilio Aguinaldo. Although well before the Second World War the US had committed itself to eventual autonomy for the Philippines, and although the average American no doubt believed that his country's policies were responsive to Filipino aspirations, the history of US–Philippine relations looked different from the other side. To many Filipinos the salient fact was not that the US was prepared to grant political autonomy in the near future, but that it had blocked independence earlier. Hence, when the Japanese occupied the islands in 1941–2, they calculatedly acted to humiliate Americans in front of Filipinos. It was this that in part explained the Bataan Death March and similar instances of brutality against captured US soldiers. As it turned out, such atrocities enabled the American General Douglas MacArthur to cover up major strategic and tactical errors in his defence of the islands. The victory of the Japanese was ascribed to savagery, not superior fighting ability. The brutality was real enough, but it did not explain Japan's success. Moreover, it had political import, because reprisals against Yankees often had the effect of fanning anti-Americanism.

Perhaps Japan's most important impact, however, came at the end of the war. After having encouraged the prospect of a politically auton-omous South-East Asia, the Japanese turned around and co-operated with the Allied command in suppressing the very movements they had helped to create. Because the Second World War came to a sudden end in August 1945, the United States and Britain were unable to dispatch occupation forces to take immediate control of all Japan's conquests. For example, the British landed in Indonesia only by late September, while the Dutch imperial armies arrived in October. In the meantime the Allies requested that the Japanese stay at their posts and maintain order. They were pleased to do so. As we have seen, the Japanese had a strategy for coping with defeat, and they took advantage of any opportunity to win favour with the victors. While this proved the emptiness of Japanese propaganda about a new pan-Asian order, it also rebounded against the Western powers as well. To colonials, the willingness of the West to work with its enemy in the last days of the war revealed an equal degree of cynicism. It left little doubt that the Western nations preferred to resume their imperial careers, the rhetoric of the Atlantic Charter notwithstanding.

THE SOVIET UNION AND THE THIRD WORLD

In the early post-war period the USSR was not a major player in the colonial world. It confined its Third World activities mainly to anti-imperialist propaganda, while in practice conceding hegemony to the West. The Russians had little choice in the matter, as they were simply in

no position to extend substantial material aid to would-be revolutionaries. For example, communists in Vietnam proclaimed an independent
government in 1945 and soon became engulfed in a protracted war
against French colonial rule, but the USSR only began providing aid
some years later, in 1950. Even then the outcome would not be resolved
for a generation. No doubt the Soviets would have preferred to be more
active, for the USSR had a strategic interest in supporting anti-Western
movements of almost any kind. But for the time being the Soviets needed
to give priority to Eastern Europe, and they lacked the resources to match
Western offers of economic and military assistance to the underdeveloped countries. Moreover, they were not well positioned to act in the
Third World, because the USSR was not a major colonial power.
Although it included many non-Russian peoples within its own boundaries, it controlled nothing comparable to the worldwide British empire,
or even that of the French. This meant that the Soviets could not act as
directly as the West, or influence the terms of Third World independence to the same degree. They did retain some of their Third World
winnings from the Yalta Conference (the Kurile Islands and the southern half of Sakhalin Island), but returned the rest to the jurisdiction of
China in the 1950s.

Of course, Westerners tended to think of Soviet satellite states as
colonies. A somewhat more accurate analogy, however, was with neo-
colonial relationships in the West, though satellites were more tightly
controlled. Satellites were legally independent nations, but in most other
respects integrated with and dependent upon the USSR. Even so, the
only Russian satellites in the Third World until 1960 (when a treaty was
signed with Cuba after Fidel Castro had assumed power) were the
Mongolian People's Republic (MPR) and the Democratic People's
Republic of Korea (the DPRK or North Korea). The MPR had been in
the Soviet orbit since the 1920s. Korea had been annexed by the
Japanese in 1910, and at the end of the Second World War was divided in
half and occupied by the USSR and the USA. In 1948 the Russians set
up the DPRK in the north and made it into a full-fledged satellite (a few
weeks earlier the Americans had established the Republic of Korea in
the south). The next year, 1949, the People's Republic of China (PRC)
came into being, although the USSR could not claim credit for this. The
country was never a Russian satellite. The Chinese Revolution was the
result of a crisis arising largely from the historical impact of Western
imperialism, and owed little to Soviet subversion. As we have noted
earlier, Stalin had advised the communists to co-operate with the

pro-Western government of General Chiang Kai-shek rather than attempt to take control of the whole country. Yet after the Second World War they proceeded to defeat Chiang on their own. And while the Russians did begin providing economic and military aid to the PRC in 1950 and for a short time retained economic assets and port facilities in the country, by the end of the decade the two countries fell out, causing a major schism in the Communist Bloc.

The first post-war Soviet programmes of economic assistance for non-communist countries were inaugurated only in the mid-1950s. The same was true of military aid, with one important exception. As we shall see presently, Eastern Bloc weapons reached Israel in 1948 during its war of independence. Subsequently a small shipment of light arms was sold to Guatemala in 1954, but the first major military aid package for a non-communist country went to Egypt in 1955, with the USSR working through sales by Czechoslovakia as a front. By contrast, the Americans and their allies had provided aid from 1945 on, so the West had a considerable lead-time over the Russians in competing for the loyalty of the Third World. From the mid-1950s until 1978 Moscow committed itself to a total of $46,800 million worth of aid to the underdeveloped countries, of which $17,100 million was economic assistance and $29,700 million was military. It should be noted, however, that actual deliveries fell far short of this. Statistics for the somewhat longer period 1945–78 indicate that the US offered $94,800 million in economic aid to the Third World, and for 1950–79 about $80,100 million in military aid, including the cost of education and training for military personnel. The USSR provided military-technical training for 75,000 Third World nationals between 1954 and 1978, while 412,446 were trained between 1950 and 1979 by the USA under the Military Assistance Programme and the International Military Education and Training Programme. The Russian and US data are not strictly comparable in that they cover different periods of time and employ different definitions of aid, but they are sufficient to suggest the relative scale of the USSR's efforts as compared to the USA's. Moreover, the above statistics are from American sources, and may exaggerate Moscow's role in order to justify Washington's policies. Information from the World Bank comparing the Eastern and Western blocs as a whole confirms the difference. For example, the Bank estimated that in 1980 capital aid to the Third World from the governments of the 'centrally planned economies' (mainly Russia, Eastern Europe, China and Cuba) equalled $1,000 million, compared to $25,000 million for the industrialized capitalist nations. In sum, the USSR offered nothing equivalent to the aid programmes which the US made available in the first decade after 1945, and even later in the post-war period the Russians lagged behind.

COLONIALISM IF POSSIBLE

In 1945 the goal of the Western imperial powers was to prolong the colonial era or at least to define the terms of Third World independence. The proof was that they were sometimes willing to go to war in order to do so. Even in cases where independence was likely to prove irresistible, it might be important to invoke the colonial option temporarily. This would gain precious time to groom local leaders acceptable to the West, so that when independence was conceded power would not fall into the hands of revolutionaries. Where the evolution of a nationalist but non-communist leadership was already well advanced, the imperial nations could contemplate independence sooner rather than later, as the British did in India shortly after the Second World War. But where such leaders were unavailable in sufficient numbers or lacked political experience, as in sub-Sahara Africa, then the best policy was delay. Accordingly the British did not surrender control of their African colonies until the late 1950s and the 1960s. Different situations called for different strategies, and no one formula fit every case. And not all colonial powers agreed upon the best strategy. Compared to the British, the French were considerably less flexible. Initially their instinct was to hold on to everything, including extensive possessions in Africa and Indo-China (Vietnam, Laos and Cambodia). The result was that they became involved in a series of disastrous colonial wars. The smaller of the European imperial powers, Belgium, Holland, Portugal and Spain, were even more adamant in defending colonialism. The reason was obvious enough – they were less able to withstand the competition from foreign capital that would come with the loss of exclusive control, and therefore were less receptive to the neo-colonial solution than Britain or even France. Of the lesser colonial powers it was the Netherlands which went to war in the early post-1945 period.

The only power in the West that looked forward to Third World independence was the United States, at least in the case of non-US colonies. Having relatively few colonial possessions themselves, the Americans valued access to other nations' territories, and welcomed the end of European empire. It should be noted, however, that except for proceeding with Philippine independence the United States kept all its other possessions (Puerto Rico, the Virgin Islands, the Panama Canal Zone, American Samoa, Guam, and the future states of Hawaii and Alaska). Even in the Philippines the Americans succeeded in establishing a model neo-colonial state, so that in reality the islands were less than totally autonomous. Yet US anti-colonialism proved more than a little ambiguous in other ways as well. Although Washington had much to gain from promoting the independence of other countries' colonies, as the threat of communist revolution increased in the post-war world it decided in many instances to support European efforts to maintain control rather than risk seeing social revolutionaries come to power. Thus, while general trends were discernible in American policy, these were adapted to the specific contingencies prevailing in each Third World situation.

The task of defending colonialism nevertheless fell mainly to the Europeans in the early post-war period. That they intended to do so was indicated by their willingness to deploy military force. In the Middle East, where a series of Western protectorates had been established after the First World War, the French bombarded Damascus and attempted to maintain a presence in Syria and Lebanon despite a grant of autonomy to both during the Second World War. They were forced to withdraw their troops in 1946. Similarly, in Algeria the French brutally suppressed revolts at Guélm and at Sétif in 1945. Estimates of those killed in the disorders ranged from 8,000 to 45,000. Lesser outbreaks occurred in Tunisia and Morocco. More than a million Europeans lived in Algeria, so the French treated it as part of metropolitan France, while the other two countries were protectorates. It would not be until the 1950s that the Algerians would be able to launch a full-scale war of liberation. In Madagascar rebellion broke out in March 1947, and took the French some years to suppress. The official state of siege was lifted only in 1956. The figures are uncertain, but probably tens of thousands died (many from starvation) in the course of this little-known war. By 1948 the French were holding almost 6,000 Malagasy as political prisoners. But it was Indo-China that presented the gravest problem for France. There the threat was not merely from nationalists but from revolutionary forces led by the communist Ho Chi Minh. In November 1946 the French bombarded Haiphong in the north of Vietnam, with about 6,000 lives lost. The communists were forced out of their capital at Hanoi, and a major war began that would not be concluded until 1975. The fear of a successful communist revolution, moreover, eventually drew the United States into the conflict. Washington supplied billions of dollars in military aid for the French war effort, and after 1954 took over the direction of Vietnamese affairs itself. The Vietnam War constituted a major crisis for the West from the 1950s to the 1970s. Before it was over, millions of people were killed. It was not resolved in the early post-war period, and therefore will be detailed in later chapters.

The Netherlands also waged a dogged colonial war in the years immediately after 1945. This was against Indonesian independence. After taking the Dutch East Indies in 1942, the Japanese freed a number of nationalists from Dutch jails, gave them posts in the occupation regime, and held out the promise of eventual independence. At the end of the war these men came together with others and declared a republic under the leadership of Sukarno. Given the way Japan's conquest had discredited Dutch military power, and given that Holland had been occupied by the Germans during the Second World War, the leaders of the Indonesian Republic expected that it would be impossible for the Dutch to return. But then the Allies ordered Japan to hold the country until Western troops arrived. British and Australian forces landed at the end of September, and the Dutch followed in early October, i.e. nearly two months after Japan's effective decision to surrender. The Dutch immediately began the conquest of republican-controlled areas, but achieved only partial success. Several truces followed, and various agreements about the future of Indonesia were signed. But invariably the Dutch renewed the hostilities in order to enforce their interpretation of what had been agreed to. Despite mediation efforts by the United Nations the war dragged on until 1949, when exhaustion, and pressure from other Western powers (which had an interest in seeing exclusive Dutch control come to an end), forced the Netherlands to come to terms with the Republic. The republicans had also suffered setbacks. There were divisions among Indonesian nationalists, and the Dutch had made important military gains, though not enough to win outright. It was in the interest of both sides to settle. The Republic of the United States of Indonesia thus was established in 1949, though on Dutch terms. The latter included a commitment by the Sukarno republicans to participate in a Netherlands–Indonesia Union under the Dutch crown. This was intended to establish a special relationship between Indonesia and Holland, and to enable the Dutch to maintain their paramount influence in the region. But, once the Dutch had granted sovereignty, the Indonesians reorganized the structure of government. In 1950 they created the Republic of Indonesia and broke all ties with the Dutch crown. By then there was little the Dutch could do, as they had withdrawn their armies. Yet their effort was important, because it illustrated how far some Europeans were willing to go to defend colonialism. The problem for the Dutch was that they lacked sufficient power to do so.

INDEPENDENCE IF NECESSARY

Thus, in some parts of the Third World, the forces of nationalism were too strong to resist. In such cases the main question was whether the Western powers would become involved in protracted wars for empire, or whether they would concede that colonialism was coming to an end and withdraw. As we have noted, the probability that the imperialist nations would choose the latter option depended on whether they could identify nationalists who were willing to respect Western rights in the post-colonial world and who therefore could be entrusted with political power. Yet every situation was different, and even the neo-colonial option might require a resort to force.

British Malaya was a case in point, although it did not turn into a major problem until 1948, when a jungle war began which involved communist guerrillas. These were mainly ethnic Chinese, and during the Second World War had links to the armed wing of the Malayan Communist Party, known as the Malayan People's Anti-Japanese Army, or MPAJA. The MPAJA had played the leading role in the resistance, and for this reason received aid from the British. Japan's invasion of China had helped raise the political consciousness of the Chinese in Malaya, and in part accounted for their anti-Japanese activities. Tokyo sought the support of the ethnic Malays, and many collaborated. After the war the communists disbanded the MPAJA, expecting the British to reward them with a share in power for their role in the resistance. They were to be disappointed. Moreover, the country's ethnic divisions undercut the communists' opportunities. The Malays were in the majority, and wanted to maintain restrictions on the legal rights of non-Malays. Chinese and Indians were almost half the total population. For their part the British wanted to avoid a communist takeover, and so tended to favour the Malays. At the same time London saw the need to contain Malayan chauvinism so as to avoid ethnic conflict. The communists concluded that they were not to be allowed an effective role in any constitutional settlement. Therefore they abandoned politics, and in 1948 resorted to armed struggle. Between 1948 and 1953 the British killed or captured almost 7,000 guerrillas, and on their side suffered

1,500 dead and 2,000 wounded. Almost 500,000 squatters, mainly Chinese, were forcibly relocated into secure areas, to prevent them from aiding the guerrillas. Once the communists' defeat seemed assured, however, the United Kingdom conceded independence in 1957. The terms of independence acknowledged the rights of non-communist Chinese and other ethnic groups in an effort to achieve a modicum of ethnic peace, but they also recognized the special position of the Malays. During the negotiations in London the leaders of the new country gave assurances that Malaya would remain in the sterling area, and that British investments and the repatriation of profits would be secure. In 1963 Malaya joined other new states in the region to form Malaysia.

In the Philippines even the Americans had a problem which required a military solution. Nothwithstanding Washington's commitment to granting independence as soon as possible after the Second World War, the Hukbalahap, or Anti-Japanese People's Liberation Army, redirected its wartime guerrilla activities and after 1945 continued as a revolutionary movement. At one time the 'Huks' had control of large parts of the main island of Luzon, and ruled over 500,000 people. While they were not such a threat as to prevent the US from going through with independence in 1946, nevertheless military action was needed to deal with them. It took the new Philippine Republic (with American help) until the early 1950s before the movement was effectively crushed. The United States secured even more privileges for itself in the Philippines than the British had in Malaya, and successfully imposed a neo-colonial relationship.

Aside from the Huks, the main task for the Americans was to rehabilitate the pre-war native leadership. Many members of the Commonwealth government (as the US colonial regime was called) had collaborated with the Japanese during the Pacific War. As in the case of Japan, however, reprisals were selective, and the first president of the independent Philippine Republic, Manuel Roxas, had been a collaborator himself. Because Roxas could be counted upon to deal with the threat of communism, he received the backing of General Douglas MacArthur. The existence of an armed minority in the countryside capable of carrying on guerrilla war made the installation of anti-communist leaders urgent. In this respect the fact of collaboration did not necessarily work against the pre-war political establishment, as the Japanese were just as anti-communist as the Americans. Washington granted independence on 4 July 1946, and the new president declared a political amnesty for collaborators in January 1948.

That political independence barely affected fundamental American interests, however, was apparent from the terms negotiated by the United States as a condition for ending the colonial regime. These were embodied in the Philippine Trade Act of 1946, the Philippine Rehabilitation Act of 1946 and the Military Bases Agreement (effective March 1947). The Trade Act established quotas for key Philippine exports to the US (which protected US interests), but otherwise provided for free trade during a period of eight years, followed by a gradual introduction of protective tariffs by both sides over the next twenty-five years. This left the Philippine economy susceptible to American domination. The act pegged the peso to the US dollar, and provided that the exchange rate could not be altered without American consent. Furthermore, US nationals and corporations were given the same rights as Filipinos in developing the country's natural resources and public utilities. The Philippine Rehabilitation Act provided compensation for damages incurred during the war, but payment was made contingent upon the implementation of the Trade Act. The Military Bases Agreement allowed the United States a ninety-nine year lease on twenty-three army, navy and air force installations on Filipino soil, although the lease was shortened a few years later. The United States also agreed to provide military advisers, hardware and training, thus enabling the new government to fight the Huks and to contribute to regional security in South-East Asia.

All these agreements compromised the sovereignty of the new Philippine Republic, yet there was little the Filipinos could do but accept the American terms. Thus the United States surrendered legal control of its largest colony, while placing limits on both the economic and political autonomy of the new regime. Washington had the muscle to define future relations with its ex-colony so as to prolong American domination. Needless to say, the governments of the United Kingdom and other Western Bloc countries noted the contradiction between the American commitment to rhetorical anti-colonialism and the terms which the US imposed on the Philippines. Yet this was hardly the point, as no Western imperial power intended to give up any more than necessary in the Third World after 1945.

INDIA

As we have indicated, every situation in the post-1945 colonial world was different. In India a powerful native ruling class forced the issue of independence. The neo-colonial option was considerably less feasible, although a sufficient consensus on economic matters existed between the Indian elite and the British elite for the new government not to nationalize foreign property. About 75 per cent of all foreign capital in India at independence was British, and the United Kingdom dominated key industries (tea, jute, mining, shipping, foreign trade and banking). Yet its pre-eminence was in decline. Before the anti-Axis war India had been a debtor to the UK, but afterwards the British owed huge sums to the Indians. This meant a major shift in economic power from the imperial centre to India itself. The devastation of the British economy by the world war meant that the UK would have to reduce its global activities. And in the face of decades of nationalist agitation in India the British had no choice but to surrender their political claims. Indeed, they had been moving towards allowing some form of autonomy even before the Second World War.

London accepted the logic of events, and withdrew in 1947. Well before independence an Indian bourgeoisie had succeeded in asserting its right to participate in all except the top levels of government. It was very important for the country's future that they rather than some other social class gain a share of power, and that social revolutionaries acquire few followers. As we shall see, the Indian elite had a stake in promoting the traditional hierarchical values of Indian society, albeit within a context of social reform. Hindu–Muslim strife marred the transition to independence and resulted in terrible bloodshed, but it was no mere coincidence that many of the Indian elite advocated non-violent forms of protest. They feared that violence would lead to the emergence of new leaders who might attack their authority as well as that of the British.

The British had established control of most of the subcontinent by the early nineteenth century, but they had done so piecemeal, and they ruled the area with a minimum of their own people. British authority until 1858 remained in the hands of the East India Company, but then the crown assumed control. Like the company, the crown directly governed only about 60 per cent of India's territory. For the rest, treaties of allegiance were concluded with the princely rulers of the 550 native states which were still in existence in 1858. The result was a dual structure of authority, British provinces plus native states, with ultimate control of the whole subcontinent vested in a central government which was eventually located in New Delhi. On the eve of the First World War, before nationalism in India had become a mass phenomenon, an indigenous bureaucracy of approximately 500,000 native officials and clerks assisted a small group of only 4,000 British administrators, this at a time when the total population of India was 300 million. There were also about 70,000 British troops, although Indians also served in the army and out-numbered the British by a considerable margin.

Because Britain's presence was minimal, it sought allies among the princes, large landowners, Muslim leaders and the small number of Christians. The British mistrusted the Western-educated classes who wanted high administrative posts. Yet they needed the Indians to run the government, so the latter gained more and more posts. For their part Brahman and other upper-caste Hindus were quick to take advantage of English education, and joined the accessible ranks of the government. The attractions were a dependable source of income and a certain social status. The use of English as the language of higher education and of government also helped concentrate power in the hands of the native elite, as it was mainly the upper castes who were able to acquire the Western learning needed for a position in the civil service. In time, of course, the educated classes asserted an interest in wresting control from the British and taking full charge of all levels of government for themselves. But as members of the Indian bourgeoisie they hardly had an interest in moving towards socialism. Socialists and even communists did exist among Indian leaders, but they were a minority and served mainly to strengthen the British commitment to other nationalists.

The principal vehicle of South Asian nationalism was the Indian National Congress, founded in 1885 at Bombay City. Most of the early Congress representatives were high-caste Hindus, although for many years Muslims played an important minority role in the organization. The British governing establishment disliked the Congress, and encour-aged the formation of a separate Muslim League in 1905. In time the League became the focal point for the creation of a separate Muslim state (Pakistan). The generally middle- and upper-class composition of the League was similar to the Congress, except that initially it was dominated by the old landed aristocracy and titled nobility. But the Congress was the largest nationalist organization. Its founders all spoke English and were mainly university graduates. Lawyers, journalists, teachers and other professionals dominated, with a few well-to-do landowners, but no princes or nobles from the native states. The original objectives of the Congress were to build a sense of nationalism, to obtain representative government, and to secure more places for Indians in the colonial administration. A small number of British sympathizers partici-pated in its formation, attesting to a certain compatibility between the

Indian and foreign elites. The Congress was anything but a mass movement in its early days, nor did it regard itself as such. Instead it claimed a role as arbiter between the Indian people and the British, and shared in the paternalistic attitudes of the imperial authorities. As one Congress leader said, the members were 'the true interpreters and mediators between the masses of our countrymen and our rulers'.*

Congress members certainly had much to gain by increasing their role in government, but as an urban middle-class movement they were too few to compel the British to leave India. Somehow the Congress or another organization had to mobilize the masses of people against the British, so as to use the power of numbers to force them out. But from the perspective of the Indian elite this had to be done without losing control. Confrontation and violence might conceivably turn against them as well as Great Britain.

It was Mohandas Karamchand Gandhi who responded to the needs of the masses and thus won their support for the Congress. Gandhi came from a merchant-caste family in Western India, where his father had been chief minister of a small princely state. He obtained an English education locally, and then studied law in London. He was called to the bar in 1891. Gandhi subsequently went to South Africa, and as a result of his struggle on behalf of poor Indians against the white racist regime he learned to identify with the masses. On his return to India in 1915 he threw off his Western ways and adopted the garb of the Indian peasant. He even travelled third class. His ascetic life quickly earned him the title of Mahatma, or 'Great Soul', and made him the political guru of the Indian masses. Most importantly, he preached the power of *satyagraha*, or what might be translated as 'soul force' or change through peaceful means. He turned the Congress from an elite movement of upper-caste and English-educated Indians into a political party with widespread support. His principal tactic was non-violent resistance, specifically the boycotting (*hartal*) of British-made goods and non-co-operation with the imperial authorities. For Gandhi such forms of protest were the only practical alternatives, given that the native population was unarmed. But Gandhi did not think any other tactic was desirable either. To the Indian political elite non-violence had the virtue of being effective against the British without resorting to such radicalizing experiences as guerrilla warfare or an armed resistance movement. This did not mean the elite opposed social reform. On the contrary, reform might head off more

* Cited in Stanley Wolpert, *A New History of India* (Oxford: 1982), 259.

radical developments, and was an essential part of the Congress programme. Gandhi was particularly concerned about the status of women and of the outcasts of Indian society, the so-called 'untouchables'. Yet he also supported the traditional principles of Indian hierarchy and order.

The Second World War was the immediate event that led to Indian and also Pakistani independence. In 1939 the British viceroy proclaimed war against Germany on India's behalf, though without consulting the Indian legislative council. This was perfectly legal, but it renewed the debate on the country's political status. And for the Indians the moment was opportune. The British were wholly occupied with the European war and after 1941 with the threat from Japan. They could not afford trouble in South Asia, and had to take nationalist demands seriously. Stability in India was essential in order to fend off a possible Japanese invasion of the subcontinent. Accordingly the British acted to win the co-operation of Indian nationalists and attempted to respond to their aspirations, at least within limits. The India of the Congress Party and the Muslim League was not a hotbed of communist revolution, so the British government could afford to make concessions concerning the future. The problem was that they did not go far enough.

Throughout the war the British promised full autonomy, but not until the fighting was over. In the meantime India was to join with Britain in concentrating totally on the defeat of the Axis powers. The argument was that the victory of the West was the surest way to achieve independence, for it would head off possible Japanese expansion and thus the imposition of a new imperialism. To the Congress, of course, the old imperialism was quite enough, and they saw no legitimate reason to deny the country immediate autonomy in return for a commitment to support the war against Japan. This the British refused, and in due course the Congress Party passed its famous 'Quit India' resolution of August 1942, demanding immediate independence and threatening massive though non-violent resistance. Britain's response was unusually short-sighted: the Congress was banned and its leaders were thrown in jail, where they remained for much of the war. Altogether, about 60,000 persons were arrested by the end of the year in a wholesale stifling of dissent, and many of these were held without trial. Over 1,000 people were killed in the associated disorder, as non-violence broke down in the face of British repression.

In the meantime Britain's problems with the Congress enhanced the fortunes of the Muslim League, led by Mohammad Ali Jinnah, and eventually had an important effect on the terms of Indian independence. The League collaborated fully in the war effort. The outcome would be the creation of a separate state for the Muslims, Pakistan. (In 1971 Bangladesh would break away from Pakistan to form yet another independent state.) Jinnah co-operated with the British in order to win support for his cause, although he did offer to form a coalition with the Congress Party if it would recognize League demands. These overtures were rejected because the Congress did not want to see the country divided, but this only strengthened Jinnah's claims on the British. The result, however, exacerbated existing ethnic and religious strife between Hindus and Muslims, and left Britain in the middle once the world war was over.

The end of the war meant that it was time for the British to make good on their promises of independence. The only question was whether, or on what terms, the subcontinent would be divided. If there was any doubt about the need to settle the Indian question quickly, it was resolved by two crises: the trial of Indians who had served with Bose and the Japanese, and a mutiny in the Royal Indian Navy. The trial, in the winter of 1945–6, made Bose's officers into national heroes. They had actually fought to make India free, yet were charged with treason by foreigners. The contradiction of being loyal to both India and the British Empire was all too clear. Massive protests resulted, and the British were forced to compromise. Those convicted were given suspended sentences. The mutiny began in February 1946 at Bombay, and soon involved some members of the Indian air force and workers in the city. By the time it had run its course twenty naval bases and seventy-four ships of the fleet had been seized, amidst calls for revolution. Such outbursts confirmed the need to install the Congress as the party of order before continuing turmoil allowed radical elements to take over. The British redoubled their efforts to mediate between Jinnah on the League side and Jawaharlal Nehru on the Congress side. A Kashmiri Brahman educated at Harrow and Trinity College, Cambridge, Nehru had replaced Gandhi as the principal Congress leader. He would become the first prime minister of independent India.

Throughout 1946 the British and the Congress worked to keep India intact by promoting a plan for a unified country in which the Muslims would have regional autonomy in the areas where they were dominant. But Jinnah wanted a separate Muslim nation, and proclaimed 16 August 1946 as 'Direct Action Day'. The outcome was a series of religious riots, and some of the worst Hindu–Muslim atrocities the country was to witness. As a result of the deadlock and the violence the British, in early 1947, announced their intention to withdraw by June 1948, no matter what. They knew that they could not really control the situation, and in effect issued an ultimatum. The Congress and the League would have to settle before the British left or risk even more chaos. The imperial authorities would not be there to maintain what order they could. Neither Nehru nor Jinnah stood to gain from anarchy, and the British knew it. Lord Louis Mountbatten was dispatched as the viceroy charged with supervising the transition. He opted for creating an independent Pakistan, and for all practical purposes imposed an agreement. The new Muslim state would be carved out of north-western India and eastern Bengal (i.e. predominantly Muslim regions, though with significant Hindu minorities), while the princely states were given the option of deciding which nation to join. The British parliament quickly approved the plan, as it had the formal assent of both the League and the Congress. Also, delay might lead to further violence. On 15 August 1947 India and Pakistan became legally independent.

The immediate consequence, however, was not the end of internal strife. Instead, the violence escalated, especially in the north-west, as Muslims were driven from Hindu areas and Hindus from Muslim areas. About a million people were killed in the course of these events, while approximately 13 million terror-stricken refugees had fled from one country to the other by mid-1948. Furthermore, protracted negotiations were required before several of the large princely states joined either side. The delay disturbed India–Pakistan relations for years to come. Major conflicts, for example, developed over the border region of Kashmir. These were resolved mainly in India's favour by military force, though only after years of turmoil.

All these were problems for India and Pakistan after 1947. They both entered the British Commonwealth, though as republics rather than constitutional monarchies under the British crown. The British could be satisfied that they had achieved their objectives, a speedy retreat and (once the communal strife abated) a relatively stable Indian sub-continent. Given that they were no longer able to rule, it was in their self-interest to work with Gandhi, Nehru and Jinnah. And for the Indian and Pakistani elite it was important to come to terms quickly, lest the violence threaten the basis of their authority and not just that of the colonial regime. As it was, many died, and Gandhi himself was assassinated by a Hindu fanatic shortly after independence, on 30 January 1948.

It should be noted, in addition, that the British granted independence to Ceylon in 1948, as it was an integral part of South Asia and could hardly be denied equal treatment. In 1972 Ceylon changed from a dominion, independent but recognizing the British monarch as its own, to a republic under the traditional name Sri Lanka. There were, however, still other European powers in the region. Both the Portuguese and the French remained in South Asia after the British. Their presence dated to the sixteenth and seventeenth centuries, but they had never succeeded in establishing control on the same scale as Britain. For their part the French had few territories left in the region (less than 200 square miles in all), and turned them over to India in the early 1950s. The Portuguese retained the port cities of Goa, Daman and Diu. Because Portugal's own economy was underdeveloped compared to many other imperialist nations, it feared their competition and therefore was reluctant to surrender exclusive control of its colonies. The Portuguese stubbornly stood their ground, but in 1961 were driven out by Indian arms.

THE SPECTRE OF REVOLUTION: CHINA

In most parts of the colonial world during the 1940s and 1950s revolutionaries were a long way from assuming control of the state. The major exception was in Asia, where on 1 October 1949 communists proclaimed the People's Republic of China as the official government of the country. As in the case of India, however, the establishment of the new regime was conditioned by events that had occurred long before the Second World War. Although the Chinese Revolution had broad ramifications for the post-war world, it was the culmination of a lengthy crisis associated with the disintegration of the Manchu, or Qing, Dynasty. This was one of the great epic struggles of human history. It involved the future of a quarter of the world's population, and therefore requires our particular attention.

The Manchus had ruled China since the 1600s, but by the nineteenth century their authority was rapidly declining. They were challenged by massive peasant uprisings, the greatest of which was the Taiping Rebellion of 1850–64 that cost the lives of 20–30 million people. Other rebel leaders in the north-west, south-west and central regions also attempted to break away from the government at Beijing and to establish independent kingdoms of their own, so that the very unity of the country was at issue. But the most important factor in the decline of the Manchus was the impact of imperialism. The foreign presence was enough to disrupt the existing order, but not to create a new one in its place, so that neither colonialism nor neo-colonialism was to prevail after the Second World War. Instead a revolutionary regime succeeded in taking power and in closing China to the West.

Until the Opium War of 1839–42 the Chinese government had allowed foreign traders only limited access to the country, and restricted their activities to the southern port of Guangzhou. But then the British government took the lead in opening China to the rest of the world. It acted in defence of the right of private merchant companies to engage in the very profitable business of importing opium (produced in India) for sale to Chinese drug traffickers. When the Manchus attempted to stop this, Great Britain went to war in the name of free trade, and delivered the first of many military defeats which the Chinese were to suffer at the hands of foreigners. Major conflicts developed later with Britain and France in 1856–8 and again in 1860, with the Japanese in 1894–5 and with virtually the entire foreign contingent in 1900. In the last case a joint expeditionary force made up of troops from Britain, France, Germany, Russia, Japan and the United States, plus token forces from the Austro-Hungarian Empire, occupied much of Beijing. The foreign powers decisively put down an anti-foreign uprising known as the Boxer Rebellion. There were other conflicts as well, but in every case the outcome was humiliation for China, mounting indemnity payments, and trade and territorial concessions for the imperialist powers. Czarist Russia gained the most territory.

Foreigners never occupied the whole country, but instead established themselves at strategic points known as treaty ports. These were located on the coast and at important transportation junctions inland. They were so named because they were areas where the Chinese government had ceded part of its jurisdiction by treaty, although it did so under duress. Thus the British seized Hong Kong Island and parts of neighbouring Kowloon Peninsula, but later took a lease (effective until 1997) on other territories near by. They obtained special rights in Guangzhou and Shanghai plus many other cities by similar means. Other examples included the Germans at Qingdao and the Japanese at Harbin. Even the Americans gained rights in a treaty port, despite the Open Door Policy. In all there were probably about a hundred treaty ports. Equally important, they served as the framework for spheres of political influence and economic domination. Guangzhou to the Yangtze Valley was a mainly British zone; Yunnan and other areas north of Indo-China were French;

Manchuria was Russian and later Japanese; Shandong became German; and Fujian was under Japan's influence. In 1860 Russia acquired vast territories in northern Manchuria, and Britain and France eventually established themselves in countries on China's southern borders. This erosion of Beijing's autonomy, combined with worsening peasant unrest and the rise of powerful, regionally based leaders who challenged the authority of Beijing, ended what little claim the Manchus had as the legitimate rulers of China.

The result was the formation of several opposition groups which favoured either the imposition of constitutionally defined limits on the monarchy or the establishment of a republic. In the face of Manchu resistance to change the republican option gained support among Western-educated students and military officers in the treaty ports. In the 1890s and early 1900s several uprisings were attempted by those who wanted to establish a modern national government. The last of these revolts, inaugurated at the city of Wuchang in October 1911, led to the formation of a provisional republic under the leadership of Sun Yat-sen, although for the time being the Manchus remained in power at Beijing and had the stronger armies.

Sun, however, proved to be both resourceful and flexible. He had been educated in Honolulu, Hong Kong and Guangzhou, and for many years had worked among anti-Manchu Chinese at home and abroad. He was thoroughly familiar with Western political institutions, and for a time resided in the United States. To Sun, the adaptation of Western institutions to Chinese conditions, beginning with a republican form of government, was the first step towards ending foreign domination and solving the country's social and economic problems.

The problem was that the republicans were few in number. They were disunited as well. Except for a few poorly motivated rebel units of the regular army they had no organized forces on which to rely. Hence, they had little choice except to make a deal with the other side. The dynasty had lost its legitimacy, but this did not guarantee that the newly proclaimed republic would succeed to power. A more likely outcome was anarchy and the disintegration of the country. In late 1911, therefore, Sun opened negotiations with the man who had emerged as the key figure in the dying Manchu administration, the wily General Yuan Shikai. Yuan saw that the days of the dynasty were numbered, and so was willing to co-operate, at a price. In return for the presidency of the republic Yuan facilitated the abdication of the Manchus and provided the military backing which the new government needed. Sun knew that

Yuan had little commitment to republicanism, but stepped aside in the hope of saving China from complete chaos. If Yuan's armies could reunify the country, then reform might proceed from there.

Any expectation that Yuan would create national unity and restore China's autonomy, however, was soon to be disappointed. Whereas Sun saw republicanism, anti-imperialism and reform as the solutions to China's problems, it turned out that Yuan was more interested in founding a new dynasty, with himself as emperor. This not only alienated Sun and his faction, but also some of Yuan's own henchmen. The latter had ambitions of their own, and so the nation descended into a period of warlordism, as provincial military governors fought each other for control of men and resources. At the same time the foreign powers took advantage of Yuan's discomfiture to make additional claims for special privileges. The Japanese presented what became known as the Twenty-one Demands in 1915, the Czarist government of Russia asserted the primacy of its influence in Outer Mongolia, and the British demanded that Beijing respect their pre-eminence in Tibet (or Xizang). After Yuan's death in 1916 the situation deteriorated further. The warlords continued to fight whomever was in charge in Beijing, as well as each other. In the meantime Sun made repeated efforts to secure a base at Guangzhou, but dissension with his remaining military supporters forced him to flee to Shanghai in 1922, and the fortunes of his faction, the emerging Nationalist Party, or Guomindang, seemed to reach their lowest point.

The Chinese Communists

In the early 1920s both the regime at Beijing (headed by various successors of Yuan) and Sun's movement at Shanghai laid claim to the authority of the republic. Yet a new force was about to become a factor in the balance of power, the Chinese Communist Party (CCP). At the National University in Beijing a small group of students and professors had concluded that the relevant model for China to follow was the Russian Revolution. Obviously the republic had failed to restore either unity or autonomy. Whatever the Soviet Union might become in the future, in the years immediately following 1917 it enjoyed considerable prestige among Chinese intellectuals. The Bolsheviks had succeeded in ending the rule of the Czar and the Russian nobility, and were facing up to the danger of counter-revolution. For China the old dynastic system and the warlords represented an analogous threat. Further, the Bol-sheviks were resisting foreign intervention, a fact which suggested that the Chinese should watch developments inside Russia very closely.

The May Fourth Movement of 1919 spurred the re-emergence of Sun's Guomindang, this time with a broader base of popular support than earlier, but it also provided the catalyst for the formation of a small communist party as well. 'May Fourth' was a massive demonstration which began with 5,000 university students in Beijing and then spread to other major cities. The occasion of these events was a decision taken by the Paris Peace Conference at the end of the First World War, whereby the Allied powers permitted Japan to take over Germany's concessions in China as spoils of war, rather than allow them to revert to Beijing's control. Moreover, the Japanese revealed that in 1918 Beijing had secretly assented to their plans in return for a loan (in effect, a bribe). When the news reached China from Paris, demonstrators took to the streets on 4 May 1919 and staged marches against both the treachery of the Allies and the supine conduct of the Chinese government. More importantly, May Fourth quickly turned into a popular urban protest, to the benefit of the Guomindang. It drew in ordinary working people and shopkeepers, and demonstrated the possibility of mobilizing mass action against the regime. May Fourth also mobilized those who were dissatisfied with the republic and who looked to the guidance of Li Dazhao and Chen Duxiu, both professors at the National University. In July 1921 a small group of their supporters gathered at Shanghai to found the Chinese Communist Party. Among the earliest members was Mao Zedong, a young man of peasant background who had worked as a library clerk at the university and who would lead the communists to victory many years later.

With this, the contending forces consisted of the military regime at Beijing, Sun's Nationalist Party, the new Communist Party and several regional warlords who refused to accept any central authority. The Guomindang, however, was soon to gain the upper hand, and with Soviet help. Because the CCP had fewer than a hundred members in 1921, the Russians hoped to influence events in China by co-operating with other forces, those which seemed to have a better chance of taking over the whole country. Their policy was more pragmatic than ideological. Yet at first Moscow doubted Sun's chances. Accordingly the Soviets sent agents to Beijing, but the rulers there would not receive them. Then they tried the warlord Wu Peifu, with no better result. This left Sun, and so at last they turned to him.

Sun was receptive because neither the Western powers nor Japan would recognize him as the true heir of the republic. Instead they acknowledged the authority of Beijing, which continued to honour the treaty obligations of the Manchus. It was thus in the interests of the foreign powers to treat Beijing as the legal government of China. For this reason, when the Russians turned to Sun with offers of money and arms, he accepted. With their help he would be able to recapture Guangzhou and then march north against Beijing and the warlords. The USSR also seemed to renounce the Czar's rights in China and, for the time being, in Mongolia. The Soviets asked that in return Sun accept communists into the Nationalist Party as individual members, although there was to be no formal fusion of the two parties. Thus the interests of the CCP were protected, as it would continue to exist as a separate entity yet would have an opportunity to influence Sun. The pay-off for the Soviets was that they would establish relations with a faction more likely to take power than the CCP. The deal was completed in 1923, about forty Russian political and military advisers arrived the same year, and Guangzhou was retaken. Sun died in 1925, and over the next few years his military protégé, General Chiang Kai-shek checkmated his civilian rivals and consolidated his position as the head of the Nationalist Party. The Guomindang was fighting an all-out war for survival, so it was no surprise that a military figure should assume leadership. The Northern Expedition (first planned by Sun) was launched in 1926 to consolidate the Guomindang's control of the country. By the next year Chiang had made enough progress on the battlefield to be able to afford to turn to other matters.

Civil War

That there was a need to do so, in Chiang's view, became evident from the growing strength of the communists. Chinese Communist Party and Nationalist goals had never been entirely compatible, yet allowing communists into the Guomindang had been a small price to pay for Soviet aid. Further, by accepting the communists Sun, and later especially Chiang, had hoped to keep an eye on their activities and prevent them from becoming a competing centre of power. This was easier said than done. While the CCP had only 500 members in 1924, these increased to about 20,000 by 1925 and 58,000 at the beginning of 1927. In addition communists began to assume important offices in the Nationalist Party itself, and played a major role in efforts to organize among workers in Guangzhou and Shanghai and peasants in the provinces of Hunan and Guangdong. In the latter the organizing campaign was so successful that membership in the peasant associations reached

500,000 in 1925, and rose to perhaps two million by 1927. The new organizations enabled Chiang to consolidate his base of operations, and thus helped clear the way for the Northern Expedition. Yet their mass character also endangered Chiang's ability to control their activities.

The May Thirtieth Movement of 1925 was a case in point. This began as a localized strike in Shanghai but quickly spread to other centres and became the spur to further mass organization. Initially a protest against foreign exploitation of Chinese workers, May Thirtieth soon turned on domestically owned enterprises as well. Working conditions in Chinese factories were no better than in foreign-run factories, so the protests could hardly fail to spread. This had serious implications for Chiang. Popular support was needed for the campaign against Beijing and the warlords, but the forces unleashed by May Thirtieth threatened to move away from the task of national unification in favour of social objectives. Moreover, the crowds began attacking the business interests and property of some of the most important backers of the Nationalist cause. These included the army's financial patrons: the absentee landlords and the small banking, commercial and industrial elite in the cities. These people wanted order, and supported the Guomindang in the belief that Chiang had the best chance of achieving it. They did not want a social revolution which would increase the power of the lower classes. Yet the urban workers' movement and the peasant associations continued to grow over the next two years, as did the CCP. The Soviets advised the Chinese communists to strike a lower profile in order to preserve the alliance with the Guomindang. They remained convinced that in any contest for power the Nationalists would win. But the communists had already become too strong to suit Chiang, so he determined to break up the alliance himself.

In April 1927, after he had consolidated his base in the Yangtze heartland, Chiang began a wholesale liquidation of the CCP, starting at Shanghai and moving on to Nanjing, Fuzhou, Guangzhou and other centres. It was the beginning of a three-year purge known as the 'White Terror'. Suspected communists and communist-sympathizers were shot on sight, and party cells were broken up. The loss of life numbered in the hundreds of thousands. Fewer than 10,000 CCP members were left when it was all over. They were scattered into the countryside, and were cut off from their Soviet advisers. Accordingly, new leaders emerged. They responded pragmatically to the loss of their urban bases, and proceeded to develop a rural guerrilla movement. This was the beginning of the Red Army. Their chief political strategist was Mao Zedong. He did not become chairman of the reorganized Communist Party until January 1935, however, and then only after factional infighting and interference by the Comintern.

In the meantime, and despite their victories over the warlords and the CCP, the Nationalists were in the unenviable position of not being able to achieve any immediate improvement in China's condition. Hence the communists still had appeal, and might be able to rebuild. In the countryside all the landlord–peasant grievances that had enabled them to win support in the past still prevailed. If anything, social conditions had worsened. And in the cities commerce was disturbed by the new Nationalist–CCP civil war, so that along with the worldwide economic depression that began in 1929 there was little basis for economic growth. Further, because the Guomindang had subdued some of the warlords not by conquering them but by making them allies and finding a place for them in Nationalist ranks, they remained a constant source of trouble. It was hardly any surprise that Chiang continued to rely on authoritarian methods of rule. His government did gain the recognition of the foreign powers, but none of them surrendered any treaty ports or other concessions. Indeed, beginning with the takeover of Manchuria in 1931, Japan dramatically expanded its territorial claims.

At the end of 1927 Mao had led the remnants of a defeated communist force to the border areas of the provinces of Hunan and Jiangxi. Like certain peasant leaders before him, he set about building an army and extending his regional control. From the beginning he sent political cadres or organizers among the peasantry to improve social conditions. The goal was to provide immediate, concrete gains and thus win the loyalty of the people. In addition, the cadres recruited for the Red Army, as it was essential to provide security for those who supported Mao and the Communist Party. After all, such people risked Guomindang reprisals and had to be protected if the CCP were to be a credible political force. The recruitment campaigns also helped build up the strength to march against Chiang. By 1931 the communists had secured control of the southern half of Jiangxi province and established the Chinese Soviet Republic. The choice of name, however, did not indicate a direct link to the USSR. 'Soviet' was used in a generic sense to announce the formation of a revolutionary government. Mao's new republic encompassed perhaps 15,000 square miles and three million people. In addition there were about twelve other pockets of communist control in different parts of China. These included perhaps six million people. Most important, in the light of the 1927 Shanghai Massacre, the Red Army took shape, and rose to 300,000 troops.

Chiang could hardly fail to take notice of these developments. He therefore launched a series of campaigns against the communists, and the Jiangxi Republic fell in 1934. There then followed a year of mobile warfare along a circuitous route nearly 7,000 miles in length. This became known as the 'Long March', and by October 1935 brought Mao and his remaining forces to Shaanxi province to the north-west, where a new capital was established at Yanan. Of the 100,000 troops that began the march with Mao, it is variously estimated that between 8,000 and 30,000 survived. But Mao's forces had reached the last rural sanctuary under communist control, so in 1936 Chiang made new preparations to attack.

In the meantime the CCP issued a call for an end to the civil war and total concentration on the threat from Japan. It was clear that the Japanese were contemplating an all-out invasion. In addition to Manchuria they had already attacked Inner Mongolia (or Nei Monggol) and Shanghai, and had also established their authority in the province of Hebei. Therefore the communist call for united action against the foreign aggressor was popular indeed. Most importantly, the Nationalist army operating in the Yanan area, and based at Xian in Shaanxi, regarded Mao's plea as a more plausible course of action than Chiang's vendetta against the communists. Made up mainly of Manchurians who wished to liberate their home region from the rule of a Japanese puppet government, they in effect mutinied against Guomindang orders. When Chiang visited the Xian army to reassert his authority in December 1936, he was taken prisoner instead.

At this point the CCP shrewdly intervened in order to secure a compromise. With Mao's principal adviser, Zhou Enlai, acting as mediator, the communists agreed to use their good offices to secure Chiang's release if he would call off the civil war. In addition they offered to accept Guomindang leadership of an anti-Japanese war, and to place their forces under Nationalist direction, though communist armies would keep their own commanders and would remain separate entities. Yanan would not claim independence, but the communists did require that it be given regional autonomy. Chiang yielded and the deal was made, but apparently it was never put in writing. For the time being the civil war came to an end, and the communists gained the breathing spell needed to recover after the Long March. Again they had shown themselves to be flexible and willing to compromise with the more powerful Nationalists.

The Impact of Japan and the Second World War

Once the Japanese had proceeded to launch their general invasion of China in July 1937, however, a new situation began to unfold. What transpired was really two wars. The Nationalist forces suffered repeated defeats, and retreated to the west and south-west. But Chiang never considered surrendering, and instead began to play a waiting game. He hoped that a Japanese–Western conflict would develop in due course, and that the Americans would defeat Japan and thereby save China. After 1939 and his main territorial losses, therefore, Chiang's strategy was to sit it out until such an eventuality developed. In the meantime, his armies would operate defensively.

The communists fought a different war. Known by the Nationalist designation as the Eighth Route Army, their forces relied mainly on guerrilla tactics and operated in northern China. As well, the CCP sent cadres to organize underground resistance in the Japanese-occupied provinces. The Nationalists might have attempted to do the same, but Chiang's strategy was to wait. Thus the communist presence in the occupied areas served only to enhance the credibility of the CCP as compared to the Guomindang. The communists were often successful, because the Japanese simply did not have the capacity to establish effective rule in the rural hinterland. They made forays into the country-side, but it was in the great cities and along the major transportation routes that their authority was most secure. After Pearl Harbor, more-over, the China theatre assumed secondary importance in Tokyo's strategic planning, so that it became easier for the communists to increase their gains. This was to have a telling impact on events after 1945.

Further, the potential for internal conflict remained. Chiang had never really wanted to co-operate with the CCP, despite the Xian truce. This became abundantly clear in 1941, when the communist New Fourth Army moved south into Guomindang territory. Chiang ordered it to return northward. In accordance with the Xian understanding the communists obeyed. But then Nationalist forces attacked them as they were crossing the Yangtze River, and inflicted heavy losses. It turned out, however, that there was not to be a renewal of the civil war just yet. After all, the Japanese still had to be defeated. This was hardly the time for a major diversion. Instead Chiang backed off, harbouring his troops and confining his campaign against the CCP to a blockade of supplies destined for Yanan. For their part the communists did not retaliate, even after the Yangtze River incident. Fighting the Guomindang would weaken them, and permit the Japanese to make gains in the north, i.e. in areas where the CCP enjoyed considerable success and was gaining local control. Both Mao and Chiang were looking to the future. Overt Guomindang–CCP conflict therefore remained low-keyed for the rest of the Second World War.

To 1949

The conflict was none the less fundamental, and all-out civil war was likely after Japan's surrender in 1945. There was a faint hope, however, that fighting might be averted. The United States in particular did not wish to see a renewal of the conflict, as it had more important priorities elsewhere. The Americans therefore used their good offices to secure a permanent settlement. Furthermore, they were not sanguine about influencing the outcome in China should civil war break out again. A compromise was to be recommended, rather than risk losing everything. A new war in China might also worsen relations with the USSR, which for the time being recognized the pro-Western Guomindang. President Harry Truman thus sent General George C. Marshall, his future secretary of state, on a mission to China in the hope of mediating a lasting agreement. Both sides co-operated initially rather than take the blame for being the first to renew the hostilities.

The negotiators met in the Guomindang wartime capital, Chongqing. Chiang required virtually total submission from the CCP, whereas the latter regarded the communist role in the anti-Japanese war as entitling it to a real share of power in a reconstituted China. In brief, Chiang demanded that the communists lay down their arms and surrender the areas they controlled. He was willing to recognize them as a political party, but refused to form a coalition government with them. The communists proposed the merger of the Guomindang and CCP armies, and a role for both sides in a new government. Chiang was asking Mao to disband and submit, whereas Mao was asking Chiang to surrender exclusive control of the one force that kept him in power, the Nationalist army. Neither the Guomindang nor the CCP would yield, with the result that the Marshall mission failed and civil war broke out again in 1946. The Americans made what for them was the obvious choice. Chiang offered the hope of a pro-Western China, and so the US supplied him with arms, advisers and money. In fact, even during the Marshall mission aid had continued to flow to the Nationalists, so that the CCP accurately perceived the United States as less than a neutral arbitrator.

Manchuria became the focal point of the new war. The Russians had liberated the region from Japan, and after looting its industrial plant formally turned control over to the Guomindang. At the end of the Second World War the Americans also began airlifting Nationalist troops to strategic points in the north, but the CCP started moving forces overland from North China into Manchuria as well. As elsewhere, the communists took charge of the countryside, and established a political and not merely a military presence, so that the problem for Chiang was to open a land route from the south to the north and especially to Manchuria. Despite an army four times the size of the CCP's he failed to do so by the end of 1947. This meant that the rural areas would not be his, and that supplying Guomindang troops in the north would be virtually impossible. From both a political and a tactical standpoint, therefore, this was the beginning of the end. In the autumn of 1948 the communists went on the offensive in the north, and began taking and holding even the cities. By the year's end the CCP held Manchuria and was advancing south. Beijing surrendered in January 1949, and Nationalist resistance disintegrated thereafter.

With the fall of Beijing the communists sent emissaries south to offer terms, and some negotiations did take place. Even at this point the CCP preferred to make a deal. Mao hoped that a negotiated settlement, which might include the integration of the Guomindang into a new government, would win immediate diplomatic recognition for the new regime. But the talks broke down, and so the communists crossed the Yangtze River into the south. There was only token resistance, and Chiang Kai-shek fled to the island of Taiwan.

From the perspective of global history, the significance of the communist victory can be gauged by the hostility of the United States. The Americans did not recognize the new government until 1 January 1979. In international law diplomatic recognition does not imply approval of a regime, but is only a legal acknowledgement that it exercises effective authority within its national boundaries. It is required before ambassadors, trade representatives and other officials are exchanged between two countries, and its import is more practical than ideological. Nevertheless, the United States refused to deal with the People's Republic, and instead for almost thirty years maintained the fiction that Chiang's regime on Taiwan was the government of all China. Further, the

Americans successfully blocked China's participation in the United Nations until 1971.

In sum, it had proved impossible for the West to determine the outcome in China. The situation was simply too chaotic. Moreover, this was essentially the legacy of Western imperialism, not the result of Soviet subversion, and therefore had implications for the status of Western interests in other parts of the Third World. Yet there was still Chiang. Although unable to enforce his authority on the mainland, he established a Guomindang government on Taiwan and continued to be the object of especially American favour. Over the years the United States provided massive foreign aid. Chiang symbolized the US determination to deny the outcome of the civil war, and so the Americans wanted to assure that his regime succeeded. In the long run, however, Taiwan became more important for its economic than its strategic value. Chiang guaranteed investors a pool of cheap but skilled labour by outlawing independent trade unions and opposition political parties, muzzling the press, and jailing opponents of his rule. The result was to attract substantial amounts of foreign capital. Over the next several decades Taiwan experienced a high rate of economic growth, while in the rest of China a great struggle began over the future of the revolution (see Chapters 4 and 9).

THE ARAB–ISRAELI CRISIS
Although neo-colonialism was one solution to the decline of Western influence in the Third World, the outcome in China suggested that its success could not always be guaranteed. Yet after the Second World War the West did succeed in maintaining a vital interest in a very special kind of experiment. This was in the Middle East, where Israel was established as an independent state on 14 May 1948. Israel was a special case because independence was the work of a returning population that over the centuries had been driven from the region and then persecuted wherever it sought refuge. The return of the Jews of the Diaspora (or dispersal) began largely as the result of Russian and other European persecution in the late nineteenth century, and accelerated with the rise of fascism in the 1920s and 1930s, especially in Germany but elsewhere as well. The result was the formation of a largely Europeanized Jewish community in what was then called Palestine, and the eventual achievement of autonomy from Britain. The British had governed the area under League of Nations authorization. But independence came at the

cost of expelling an Arab population that had been in the majority before the Second World War. Hence the aspirations of the Palestinian Arabs for autonomy were blocked, and they took the place of the Jews as a people without a national homeland. A new refugee population was created, and became a major source of instability in the post-war world.

The movement to restore Palestine to the Jews was called Zionism, and was more the product of events in nineteenth-century Europe than the Middle East. Anti-Semitism was rampant on the Continent, but in the late 1800s was worst in Russia, including parts of Poland and areas populated by Lithuanians and Ukrainians (which were under Czarist rule). Great *pogroms*, or massacres, took place, and left tens of thousands dead. In most parts of Europe, though, the Jews saw an improvement in their legal status while still suffering discrimination socially. Even in Western European countries like France, where the Jews had made significant gains, toleration remained fragile. The Dreyfus case was a notable example at the turn of the century, and involved a conspiracy in the French army to disgrace and imprison one of its Jewish officers. Yet for most Jews the best response was still to work for change within their own countries. There was no Jewish nation state to offer a haven, and assimilation into mainstream European society was therefore the choice of the majority. It was a minority that looked to the alternative, i.e. the establishment of a Jewish homeland, preferably in the Middle East but possibly elsewhere if need be. These people doubted whether assimilation would work, whether it would ever result in full acceptance into European life. In addition they were inspired by the religious idea of a return to Zion. The growth of nationalism in the nineteenth century also influenced their thinking. In an age which saw the unification of Italy and Germany (before the mid nineteenth century they had been composed of a number of separate states), the idea of forming a distinctly Jewish nation was consistent with trends in Europe itself. The eventual outcome was the founding of the World Zionist Organization in 1897 to work for the creation of a Jewish homeland.

Whether such a project would ever succeed, however, depended on more than just good will or humanitarianism. The problem was that before Jews could claim a homeland in the Middle East they needed to settle a sizeable population there. A tiny Jewish community did exist in Palestine and began to expand slowly with the arrival of new immigrants, but by the end of the First World War the Arabs still constituted 70 per cent of the population. There were only about 56,000 Jews in a few dozen settlements. For the Zionists to achieve their goal, Jewish colonization would need the protection of one of the great powers, and given the realities of global diplomacy, such a sponsor would have to gain something concrete for its trouble. Supporting the Jews could turn into a costly adventure, so there had to be an offsetting reward. Such a contingency developed, however, with the First World War.

The war brought about the conditions in which Britain acquired an interest in supporting the Zionist cause, though as simply one aspect of its overall policy in the Middle East. Support for the Jews became a practical possibility when Turkey entered the world war on the side of Germany, and the Allies made the partition of the Turkish empire one of their war aims. The Turks still ruled most of the area from Persia (Iran) to the Mediterranean. When they entered the war, their empire became fair game for attack. The Allies proceeded to do so by fomenting rebellion among Turkey's subject peoples. Britain and France encouraged Arab leaders to break away from the control of Istanbul, Britain in particular leading them to believe that it would support their independence after the war. The British officer T. E. Lawrence (the famous 'Lawrence of Arabia') played a vital role in creating this impression. Yet at the same time Britain was party to secret treaties for dividing the Middle East among the Allied powers after the world war, and it was these agreements which represented its real intentions. When this became clear, and Britain and France acted to take over the region at the end of the hostilities in Europe, the Arabs resisted. Accordingly the new League of Nations established a system of mandates, whereby the foreign powers were to maintain their presence while overseeing a period of transition to self-government. The British acquired mandates for Palestine (where long-term foreign control was expected), Transjordan (later called Jordan) and Iraq, while the French did the same in Syria and Lebanon.

It was during the First World War that the British decided to support the Zionist cause, and in November 1917 issued a policy statement to this effect known as the Balfour Declaration. There was a humanitarian dimension to the decision, but it was mainly motivated by strategic considerations. Recognizing Zionism might strengthen the support of Jews in the United States for the Allied war effort, and thus help consolidate public opinion in America. Because Russia had fought alongside the Allies yet was rabidly anti-Semitic, many US Jews had been less than enthusiastic about the war before the Czar's abdication earlier in the year. The mistake of the British cabinet, however, was to exaggerate the influence of American Jews, so that the practical effect of the Declaration was difficult to gauge. British policy also reflected the changing situation in Russia itself, where the people were weary of war. The Declaration was intended to appeal to Jewish revolutionaries, in the rather desperate hope that they might argue against making a separate peace with Germany. But the British had again misread the realities. Most Jewish revolutionaries were against Zionism, and believed (mistakenly as it turned out) that a new regime in Russia would liberate them as well as other oppressed groups. In their view Russia should leave the war and begin the construction of a new society.

The British statement, however, had still other motives. It was intended to pre-empt the possibility of a similar declaration by Germany. The Germans too saw some propaganda value in such a policy. Another goal was to head off French claims to part of Palestine. Although partners in the world war, Britain and France had conflicting interests in some parts of the Middle East. In addition the British hoped that the Zionists might contribute to the economic development of Palestine, and in this way serve as a stabilizing influence in the region. Most Jewish immigrants came from more-developed countries. They had much to offer. As the number of immigrants increased, Arab hostility to the Jews would escalate, but in 1917 the cost of supporting Zionism did not seem unreasonable to the British, while there were possibly many benefits to be had. Besides, the British were not proposing to establish an all-Jewish nation state in the Middle East, a difficult undertaking indeed, but only to support the right of Jews to return to their traditional homeland and to live there. The Balfour Declaration in no way precluded the claims of the Arabs.

Thus, after the war, the principles of the Balfour Declaration were incorporated into a League of Nations mandate for Palestine. Separate mandates were established for other areas as well, because both Britain and France had an interest in preventing Arab unity. Many competing Arab states would work to their advantage. In effect the approach was one of divide and rule. The Arabs saw the mandate system as a betrayal of Britain's wartime commitment to independence, which it was. They wanted full and immediate freedom, but for the time being the great powers had their way. The mandate for Palestine therefore acknowledged the historical roots of the Jewish people in the country and supported their right to establish communities in Palestine. It did not promise an exclusively Jewish state, but it did direct the British to support Jewish immigration to the Middle East. In recognition of Jewish rights

Hebrew was made one of the official languages of Palestine, along with Arabic and English.

Britain's commitment to Zionism, however, waned as its interests in the Middle East changed and as the friendship of the Arabs became more important. This was hardly surprising, because the Balfour Declaration had been motivated by strategic considerations in the first place. At the start Jewish migration to Palestine increased slowly. The number of arrivals averaged only 10,000 per year in the 1920s, and in 1927–8 more people left than entered. But arrivals rose substantially in the 1930s, with the persecution of Jews in Germany and other parts of Central and Eastern Europe. Arab opposition to additional Jewish immigration thus also rose – the Arabs were afraid of becoming a minority in what had been their land for a thousand years. At the same time the discovery of more and more Middle Eastern oil and the events leading up to the Second World War meant that Britain and the other Western powers wanted the support of the Arab countries. In view of the British and French record in the region after the First World War, many Arabs were inclined to be cool towards the West. In Palestine, therefore, London gradually began to appreciate the advantages of limiting Jewish immigration. The problem was that Britain curtailed its support for the Zionists at the very time anti-Semitism in Europe was worsening and when the Jews most needed a haven.

The first signs of trouble occurred early enough, at the beginning of the 1920s when Arabs rioted against Jewish immigration. The immediate outcome was the Churchill White Paper, an interpretation of Britain's League mandate. (A White Paper is simply a government report on current or projected policy.) This reiterated that a homeland for the Jews did not mean the establishment of a Jewish nation state or otherwise forcing all the residents of Palestine to adopt Jewish nationality. British policy was to protect the development of the existing Jewish community as a right (not a privilege) of the Jews, but not to abrogate the rights of the Arabs. The goals of the White Paper were to calm Arab opinion, and to prevent the Jews from nurturing unrealistic expectations. Arab–Jewish relations thereafter remained quiet for most of the 1920s, but then new attacks on the Jews broke out in 1929. These led to the first suggestions that Jewish immigration be restricted. Trouble worsened in the 1930s, and led to considerable vacillation on the part of the British government. This was the result of attempting to reconcile the irreconcilable interests of Arabs and Jews. Initially London veered towards dividing Palestine into an Arab state, a Jewish state and a British buffer zone. The Arabs, of course, opposed this on the grounds that all of Palestine had been theirs until the Jews had begun to return in significant numbers, with the outcome that the British were persuaded to backtrack, and to decide against partition. Accordingly they convened a conference of Arabs and Jews in London to discuss the future, but this became stalemated. Therefore the British acted unilaterally and issued the White Paper of 1939. This recommended that Britain surrender its mandate within ten years to an independent state, provided that Jewish rights were given protection permanently in a constitution. Jewish immigration would be limited to 75,000 people during the next five years. Thereafter it would depend on the approval of the Arabs. These provisions would make the Jews about one-third of the total population of Palestine.

The 1939 White Paper steeled the resolve of the Zionists. Until then they had been prepared to accept a gradualist approach. But the practical effect of the new British policy was to freeze the size of the Jewish community in Palestine, thus precluding the possibility of its becoming a majority of the population and enjoying the security that would go with such a status. It was at this point that the Zionists changed their strategy. No longer would they be satisfied with a homeland within another state, but would work for a new Jewish nation in the full legal sense. The world war prevented substantial immigration during the early 1940s, but in 1945 the issue was immediately joined.

Palestine was a magnet for survivors of the Holocaust, although many went to other countries as well. The post-war situation, however, was complicated by Washington's increasing interest. Although it had attempted to develop a stake in oil after the First World War, the US had not been the dominant Western player in Middle Eastern politics. After the Second World War, however, Britain's disastrous economic problems at home required reducing its global commitments, and Washington became more of a factor in the region. The Jewish community in the United States supported the goal of a Zionist state, partly because many other Americans preferred to see Jewish refugees go to the Middle East rather than land on their shores. There was little chance that the US would admit large numbers of Jews, and it had not done so during the 1930s or the Second World War. American domestic politics thus began to have an impact on developments. The Truman administration pressed the United Kingdom to allow more immigration to Palestine, but would not go so far as to answer Britain's call for a US role in maintaining regional order. For their part the British chose to protect their relations with the Arabs over those with the Zionists. They opposed further Jewish immigration beyond the limits suggested in the 1939 White Paper. This reflected the long-term evolution of their policy since the 1930s. The Jews therefore resorted to terrorism, the Arabs took reprisals, and the British were caught in the middle. Soon Palestine was engulfed in a virtual state of war.

The UK finally gave up trying to settle the Palestine question, and placed it before the United Nations in April 1947. By the year's end the General Assembly adopted a resolution in favour of partitioning the country into separate Jewish and Arab states. This was largely the result of lobbying efforts by the Truman administration (though the US State Department resisted the president's policy). Truman's stand was much influenced by domestic political considerations. He was facing a tough fight for re-election in the coming year, and needed every vote he could attract. For the Jews of Palestine, however, the UN decision was a major victory. The General Assembly had acknowledged the legitimacy of a Jewish state, while the Arabs were being asked to surrender lands they regarded as already theirs. Accordingly December 1947 marked the beginning of a much larger war. Because the UK was determined to withdraw, the battle was mainly between Jews and Arabs, though the British could hardly escape unscathed. The Arabs achieved some early successes, especially where they were defending territory. The Jews had the more difficult task of taking land and cities. As the fighting worsened, the UN considered forming a military force to carry out the partition policy. In addition Truman came under pressure to send American troops, but he was not keen to do so. Rather than risk becoming entangled any further the president shifted ground in accordance with advice from the State Department. In March 1948 the Americans suggested a UN Trusteeship for a unified Palestine instead of partition. The effect of this was to quicken the effort of the Jews in the war. They needed to seize and hold more territory and thus force the issue of partition, lest the international community support some alternative plan. If they held the land, it would be difficult to avoid creating two states. The steady withdrawal of British troops cleared the way for new offensives, and the timely arrival of Eastern Bloc arms (from Czechoslovakia) helped turn the tide. The Russians supported partition because they had an interest in seeing the decline of British influence in the Middle East. The Jews began scoring gains, so that the course of battle and not the UN promised to determine the fate of Palestine. When the remaining British left in May 1948, the Jews declared independence as the state of Israel on the fourteenth of the same month. Truman immediately abandoned the idea of a UN trusteeship and recognized the new country. So did the Russians.

Upon Israel's declaration of independence, Egypt, Transjordan, Syria, Lebanon and Iraq intervened. Yet they were not united, and failed even to co-ordinate their battlefield strategies. Different Arab nations sought to impose different solutions, in the hope of either annexing territory or at least dominating any new Arab state that might possibly emerge. Earlier Western policies of creating competing states in the Middle East (under the mandate system) and of encouraging particularism worked to the advantage of the Israelis. There was no Arab unity, and the Israelis succeeded in expanding well beyond the territory originally reserved for a Jewish state under the UN partition plan. By early 1949 Egypt gave up the battle and signed an armistice. Facing the prospect of fighting on by themselves, the other intervening countries followed suit within the next several months.

Israel thus succeeded in establishing its right to exist, though it would have to defend this right many more times in the future. The Arab–Israeli war of 1947–9 was simply the first of a series. On the other side, the Arabs of Palestine lost a homeland. They were unable to establish an autonomous state of their own. Instead, the armistice agreements between Israel and the intervening Arab nations provided that Transjordan (renamed Jordan at this point) and Egypt should divide the territories of Palestine that the Israelis had not conquered. About 700,000 Palestinian Arabs thus became refugees in Jordan, Egypt (in the Gaza Strip), Syria and Lebanon. This left roughly 150,000 Arabs who remained behind in Israel. Further, because no Arab nation accepted the outcome as permanent (until Egypt accorded diplomatic recognition in 1980), Israel remained surrounded by hostile neighbours.

The 1940s thus witnessed dramatic changes in the Third World. Yet except in China and the few areas under Soviet domination the influence of the Western powers was hardly eliminated, whether it took the form of a few more years of colonialism (as in much of Africa) or developed into new-colonialism (as in the Philippines). India launched a more independent course of development, but even before the Second World War the British had expected to withdraw in the foreseeable future. The different outcomes simply showed that the capacity of the Western powers to shape events in the Third World varied considerably. It depended on the contingencies prevailing in each situation. There often was no way to

achieve stability, because the interests at stake were inherently contradictory. In Palestine, for example, the needs of Arab and Jew proved
irreconcilable, and the same seemed to be true of First World–Third
World relations in general. Nevertheless, compared to the Soviet Union,
the West was still the more important external force in the Third World.
The USSR simply had few opportunities to influence developments,
and for the time being gave *de facto* recognition to the supremacy of
Western interests. Until 1949 it pursued such a course even in China,
one of the very few places where Third World revolutionaries actually
took control as the effective government. This meant, however, that
anti-imperialism and Third World revolution were emerging in a context
not of Soviet expansionism but of Western influence. The question for
the future, accordingly, was whether this would change, and whether the
1950s would represent a new phase in the history of both the Third
World and East–West relations. The outbreak of a new war in Korea on
25 June 1950 brought client states of the USA and the USSR into a
direct military confrontation for the first time, and possibly offered an
answer.

4

ASIA IN CRISIS

The 1950s turned out not to represent a sharp break with the recent past, but instead saw the development of existing trends. This meant that the United States remained a more powerful actor on the global stage than the Soviet Union, though many Americans were not so sure and tended to blame all their troubles on a communist conspiracy to take over the world. For their part the Russians still saw themselves as the victims of capitalist encirclement. Actually, neither of the so-called 'superpowers' was any closer to prevailing over the other. Just as important, they were no nearer to mastering affairs within their own spheres. Both the USA and the USSR were powerful, and one more so than the other, but neither was invincible. While students of the Cold War often speak of a bipolar world (i.e. a world dominated by two leading powers) in describing the late 1940s and the 1950s, the United States and the Soviet Union did not literally decide everything. We have already seen plenty of evidence of this fact. To affect global affairs it was not necessary for other nations to be superpowers themselves. Countries which the Americans and Russians might regard as somewhat peripheral to the main interests of the Western and Eastern blocs were quite capable of creating crises on their own, and of acting in response to local rather than global challenges. It was impossible for either superpower to dictate all that its allies did, and there were some countries, especially in the Third World, which attempted to remain neutral and therefore independent of either bloc. Furthermore, the 1950s saw major rifts in both camps, so that by the end of the decade it was clear that the Russians could not speak for the Chinese and that the Americans could not speak for the French, to cite only two examples. Neither bloc was a monolith. The superpowers thus could find themselves drawn into a crisis precipitated by another country, and at a time or in a place they might not have chosen themselves. Such was the case in the Far East.

THE FAR EAST AND KOREA

At the beginning of 1950 Western policy-makers thought a Far Eastern crisis was most likely to develop over Taiwan or Indo-China. Although the communists had established the People's Republic of China (PRC) in 1949, Chiang Kai-shek threatened to return and renew the civil war. Mao Zedong therefore concentrated his troops on the mainland opposite Taiwan. As it turned out, neither side invaded the other, although at the time no one could be certain what might happen. The communist regime was anxious to consolidate its power inside China proper, and this had implications for Taiwan as well. At the end of the civil war China south of the Yangtze River had fallen into the hands of the Red Army virtually without a fight, except for several important pockets of resistance, so the communist party needed to establish its authority in what had once been the Guomindang's stronghold. Everyone who had sympathized with Chiang could hardly flee to Taiwan, and most Nationalists had no choice but to remain behind. Nor did the communists necessarily want them to leave. Some of the Guomindang's staunchest supporters had expertise in industry, banking and commerce. Despite their past loyalties they and their managerial skills would be needed in the new China. The trouble was these same people were a likely source of internal subversion as long as Chiang threatened to return. It was therefore an open question whether the communists would attack Taiwan in an effort to end the Nationalists' influence once and for all, and so China-watchers in the West kept a close eye on developments.

Indo-China was even more dangerous, because a full-scale colonial war was already in progress. France had been fighting the Vietminh (or League for the Independence of Vietnam) since late 1946. By the end of the decade the French effort was foundering, so the United States began providing aid. After all, the Vietminh were not merely nationalists but communists, and so had to be defeated. As early as September 1948 the American ambassador to Paris indicated that the US was willing to see the French spend some Marshall Plan money in Indo-China, and in May 1949 the US State Department raised the possibility of arms aid as well. Consultations took place in Saigon between American and French military officers in December 1949, and on 8 May 1950 (only weeks before the outbreak of a new war in Korea) Secretary of State Dean Acheson announced that the US would provide the French with military assistance, though not combat troops. American advisers arrived in Indo-China on 2 August 1950. There were ten of them, and their job was to supervise the utilization of US aid.

Yet it was neither Taiwan nor Indo-China which developed into a major crisis for the United States in 1950. Instead, American forces were committed to a war in Korea, and US troops went into full-scale battle for the first time since the surrender of the Axis Powers. The Korean conflict was important because to Westerners it seemed to be a clear-cut case of communist aggression, and a sign of Soviet expansionism rather than the result of problems in Korea itself. After all, North Korea (the Democratic People's Republic of Korea, or DPRK) was a Russian satellite, and South Korea (the Republic of Korea, or ROK) was an American satellite. Further, there was no disputing that on 25 June 1950 the North moved first and attacked the South. Even so, at the time conclusions about the Soviet role were more conjecture than fact. In the absence of direct evidence either to confirm or to deny that the USSR rather than the North Koreans had planned the attack, the Americans simply assumed the worst. Moreover, the ideological climate in the United States was such that they did so despite evidence to the contrary. For example, while Korea had been occupied by the USSR and the USA after the Second World War, the Soviets had withdrawn their forces in December 1948. (The Americans left six months later in June 1949.) More importantly, when the war broke out, the USSR failed to appear at the United Nations in order to veto American resolutions branding the North as the aggressor and calling upon UN members to provide assistance to the South, including troops. Since January 1950 the Soviets had been boycotting the United Nations over its failure to seat the delegates of the PRC rather than Taiwan as the representatives of all China. They did not return in time to stop action against one of their own satellites. Recent evidence indicates that the North Koreans consulted Moscow about their plans early in 1950, but apparently the Russians had given no commitment to save Pyongyang if it ran into trouble. Indeed, it appears that Stalin urged caution, though he had much to gain if the North succeeded. Whatever the exact Soviet role, however, Taiwan and Indo-China had primed the Americans to act. The US intervened with air and naval power within forty-eight hours, and on 30 June President Truman authorized the deployment of American ground forces.

The Origins of the War

The source of the conflict would have been clearer had Westerners looked at events of before June 1950. The policy-makers were familiar with the facts, but they had little to gain by drawing attention to the recent past, as this might have led to criticism of their policies. Hence the media and the public in the United States remained uncertain about the long-term origins of the war. For the most part they tended to date the beginning of the crisis from the invasion, with the result that it certainly did appear to be a simple act of aggression by one country against another. While this was helpful in generating support for the American war effort, the facts were much more complicated.

The context of the Korean War was defined mainly by Japan's annexation of the country in 1910, after several decades of struggle with China and particularly Czarist Russia for influence in the region. The Japanese exploited the country for all it was worth, and the result was that spontaneous uprisings occurred all over the peninsula when defeat forced them to withdraw at the end of the Second World War. Japan's impact was most evident in how it developed Korea to serve mainly Japanese needs. Thus, while rice production increased by approximately 50 per cent between 1912 and 1933, the amount of rice exported went up seventeen times. Not surprisingly consumption in Korea itself declined dramatically. The south was mainly agricultural, while the north was also exploited for its mines and hydroelectric power, so that Korea was by no means an industrial backwater. In 1945 the country's railway system was comparable to China's (excluding Manchuria), and before the war it was the site of one of the largest petrochemical plants in the world. Korean industry, however, was tightly integrated with that of Japan. Virtually all foreign trade was with either the Home Islands or Japanese-controlled Manchuria. In addition Koreans became subject to a military draft for service in Japan's armies during the 1940s, and a system of conscript labour which involved about 2.5 million Koreans was also introduced. Another two million Koreans worked in Japan itself, and at least 1.5 million were employed in Manchuria. Not surprisingly, anti-Japanese guerrilla activity developed inside Korea even before the Second World War, as did tenant revolts and labour strife. Communists and other leftists tended to dominate these struggles. Koreans across the border in Manchuria also joined various guerrilla forces, and it was from among these that emerged the future leader of the DPRK, Kim Il Sung. Needless to say, it required ample police powers to enforce Japanese rule. Political activity was severely restricted, and the police regularly used torture. As the Sino-Japanese crisis deepened towards the end of the 1930s, Japan attempted to complete the process of integration and resorted to policies of cultural repression. After 1938 the Japanese forbade the use of the Korean language in schools and newspapers. Koreans were also required to renounce their original family names and to adopt Japanese names instead.

Accordingly the dissolution of Japanese authority in August 1945 resulted in the formation of the Committee for the Preparation of Korean Independence (CPKI) by a coalition of nationalist leaders. The CPKI initially was encouraged by the Japanese in the hope that by so doing they would head off Korean reprisals and thus facilitate their own withdrawal. The CPKI, however, was in no sense dominated by the Japanese, and as events took a radical turn they soon came to oppose it. Although the precise data are uncertain, it appears that by the end of August there were at least 145 CPKI branches throughout Korea. In addition hundreds of 'Red Peasant Unions' and labour organizations took shape. As with the CPKI, these organizing activities were occasioned by Japan's sudden surrender, but their origins were indigenous and based on pre-war and wartime anti-Japanese resistance movements. Communists and other leftists played a prominent role, but the new organizations brought together people of many different political persuasions. Within a short time, on 6 September, the Korean People's Republic (KPR) was set up by a united front of both nationalist and communist activists, largely to make sure that an independent government was in place before the occupying powers imposed a provisional regime of their own. The Koreans feared such a regime would be subservient to foreign interests. At the same time the various branches of the CPKI reconstituted themselves into local authorities called 'People's Committees', and these spread throughout the peninsula. Again, the total numbers are uncertain, but it is known that in the southern half of the country People's Committees soon operated in about 50 per cent of all counties.

Thus, because of Japan's impact on Korea, proposals for radical change enjoyed widespread support among the people at the end of the Second World War, and provided an opportunity for Korean communists and leftists to increase their following. But not all Koreans welcomed these developments. There was a right wing in the country's political life, although it was probably a minority of the population in 1945. For example, in the same month that the KPR was established, the

Korean Democratic Party was founded with the backing of important landlord and entrepreneurial interests. It could be compared in character to the Guomindang in China, and was to become the strongest of several right-wing parties and factions in South Korea during the American occupation. The Korean Democrats and others like them feared the direction Korean politics were taking at the end of the war, so there was a high potential for political conflict in the country.

Yet it was not up to the Koreans to decide their future all by themselves. As the result of wartime agreements among the Allied Powers the country was occupied by the Russians north of the thirty-eighth parallel and by the Americans to the south. This presumably was a temporary expedient to fill the power vacuum left by Japan's defeat, and it was expected that Korea would be reunited in due course. It was the United States that wanted Korea divided, because Soviet troops had already entered the northern reaches of the country by August 1945, i.e. just as the Japanese served notice of their intention to surrender. It was apparent that American forces would not be able to land for some weeks, and that Russian troops could easily occupy the entire peninsula. In effect all of Korea would be lost to the USSR by default. Rather than have this happen, the US decided that a deal should be made to divide responsibility for the region. Much to the Americans' surprise, Moscow proved agreeable. Korea was hardly a top priority for the Russians, and they had more important places to deploy their military power. In the meantime the American authorities ordered the Japanese commander in Korea to 'maintain order and preserve the machinery of government' until the US Army arrived in the south.* It did so on 8 September. The decision to divide Korea thus represented a net gain for the United States.

Once the war was over, however, it was the US not the USSR that faced the most serious problem. Given the revolutionary potential of the People's Committees, the Americans considered them an obstacle to the integration of Korea into the Western Bloc. The Committees had popular support and espoused socialist goals. For example, they and the various peasant unions authorized the seizure of farmland owned by Japanese and Korean landlords, and proceeded to redistribute it in their own programmes of land reform. Moreover, the Committee's leaders had assumed power as a result of the war and would be difficult to control.

---

* Cited in Joyce and Gabriel Kolko, *The Limits of Power: The World and United States Foreign Policy, 1945–1954* (London: 1972), 280.

The Committee leadership was not part of the pre-war political establishment, and hence did not have a vested interest in the *status quo*. Many of them did not favour private enterprise, and approved the takeover of factories and land by workers and peasants. The spectre of communism loomed. Accordingly the Americans moved to disband the Korean People's Republic, the People's Committees and their affiliated unions, but given the long history of anti-Japanese resistance in Korea this was easier said than done. As a result, a guerrilla war developed in the southern zone of Korea by 1947.

In the north the Soviet Union found itself in a different situation. Its task was to guide rather than reverse existing trends. Soviet interests were basically compatible with those of the People's Committees, so that the USSR turned to them as the basis of local government and as the foundation for a provisional communist regime north of the thirty-eighth parallel. This enabled the Russians to remain in the background, at least compared to the Americans. For example, while the US set up a military government for the south, the Soviets did not need to do so in the north. Their position was somewhat analogous to that of the American occupation authorities in Japan between 1945 and 1950. None of this is to say that Koreans in the Russian zone were free to do whatever they pleased. The Soviet presence guaranteed that any new government in the north would be communist, just as the Americans were determined that the south would be non-communist. In short, conditions inside Korea at the end of the Second World War facilitated the establishment of a pro-Soviet regime in one half of the country while complicating the creation of a pro-American regime in the other half. By early 1946 the USSR had installed Kim Il Sung as chairman of the North Korean Interim People's Committee, i.e. the central communist government. Kim proved a durable figure, and would remain in power for well over a generation.

The northern government immediately instituted a series of reforms designed to enhance the credibility of the communists. These began in the spring and summer of 1946, and stood in marked contrast to developments in the south. The most important was land reform. It has been estimated that 76 per cent of peasant households benefited. And while individual titles were not transferable, none of this land was collectivized before the Korean War. In the south the Americans cancelled the land reforms of the People's Committees. After all, these had involved the seizure and redistribution of private property by revolutionaries who claimed to exercise the power of the state. If foreign investment were to be secure in the future, the United States could hardly afford to concede the legitimacy of such acts of confiscation – a very important principle was at stake. The conflict between the People's Committees and the US was thus fundamental. In addition the northern regime nationalized large-scale industry, banking and commerce (though the small-business sector was left in private hands). Other reforms included the establishment of standards of work and sexual equality, some of which had not yet been introduced even in industrialized Western countries. For example, a new labour law proclaimed the principle of equal pay for equal work and allowed seventy-seven days' maternity leave. There was also a campaign to overcome illiteracy. Of course, the communist government in Korea was anything but democratic. But what so many Westerners failed to understand was that the emergent South Korean regime was hardly democratic either. It therefore was not to be presumed that the American-sponsored regime was regarded more favourably by Koreans than the Russian-sponsored regime.

In the south several nationalist but also pro-Western leaders offered themselves to the Americans as candidates for a Korean-based provisional government, but it was the ageing Syngman Rhee (he was seventy in 1945) who won the favour of the United States. A long-time resident of the United States, during the Second World War he had claimed to represent a government-in-exile (the Korean Provisional Government) established in China at the Guomindang capital of Chongqing. Rhee was thus well known to the Americans, and though not the leader of the Chongqing faction, none the less eventually emerged as the US choice in the post-war period. His supporters were similar to Chiang Kai-shek's Nationalists, and Rhee personally was a virulent anti-communist. In February 1946 the American military government appointed a so-called 'Representative Democratic Council' to begin taking over local control. The Council was made up of right-wing politicians, and Rhee was installed as its head. At the same time the US decided that elections should be held for a provisional legislature. Later a US officer recalled that, 'while the State Department expected Military Government to continue operating behind a façade of neutrality, the Americans were expected to make every effort to secure a rightist victory'.* Action was needed because US intelligence estimated that the left would win in any fair contest.

All this was done without the agreement of the USSR as the other

* Cited in *ibid.*, 292.

occupying power in Korea, but neither Russia nor the United States was interested in seeing the peninsula reunited except on its own terms. The USSR had also chosen February 1946 to install Kim Il Sung, so the Americans and Russians established the bases of separate governments at about the same time. Meetings between the USA and the USSR to discuss reunification did take place in 1946 and again in 1947, but the situation was much like that of Germany at the same point in its history. Meanwhile a series of strikes and demonstrations in the south during the autumn of 1946 attested to the strength of the left. In one incident police killed forty-one strikers, and later the military courts sentenced several protestors to death and imprisoned hundreds more. It was clear that the United States would have to act forcefully to demobilize the supporters of the People's Committees and the Korean People's Republic. It proceeded to do so, and by 1947 had driven the left underground.

The stalemate with the Soviet Union over the future of Korea induced the United States to propose that the two countries place the matter before the United Nations. The Russians opposed this, and wanted the occupying powers simply to withdraw. They believed that without the protection of the Americans the right wing would be defeated in the south, and a government compatible with their interests would emerge. The Americans would hardly accept this, and proposed that a special commission be created to supervise separate elections in each zone. After this the country would be reunified. In the meantime the occupying powers would remain in place. The US knew this would assure a communist victory in the north, but by remaining on the scene it expected to guarantee a right-wing victory in the south. Because more people lived in the American zone (seventeen million) than in the Soviet zone (nine million), the outcome would be a pro-Western majority in any new government. American influence at the United Nations carried the day, but the Russians refused to co-operate in a scheme that would leave their side in a minority position. Therefore UN-supervised elections took place only in the south, on 10 May 1948, and predictably the result was a victory for the Rhee faction. Hundreds of people were killed and thousands arrested in the rioting and other violence which preceded the voting. Later, on 25 August, the communists held their own elections in the north for a Supreme People's Council. Not surprisingly Kim was confirmed in power. The formal inauguration of the new South Korean government took place on 15 August 1948, and of the new North Korean government on 9 September 1948. By the next year both the Americans and the Russians had withdrawn their occupation forces in the apparent belief that the Korean situation was sufficiently stable.

In the south, however, politics remained in a state of turmoil, and trouble came from both poles of the political spectrum. Rhee and others on the right were not satisfied with the outcome, because the American decision to hold elections without Russian co-operation meant that the country would probably remain permanently divided. The right wing in the south wanted all of Korea, as did the communists in the north, for which reason Rhee pressed the Americans for more arms aid, but the US gave him only enough for defensive purposes. Washington feared that anything more would result in Rhee's striking north in a war to reunify the whole peninsula under his rule. The Russians followed a similar approach with the North Koreans, although in 1949–50 both super-powers increased their military contributions. Each attempted to meet and offset the increases of the other. The United States and the Soviet Union seemed to want a balance so as to avoid a crisis in the region. The problem was they could not always control the Koreans. In 1949 Pyongyang began recalling tens of thousands of troops from China, where they had been fighting as part of the Red Army in the civil war.

The southern left still presented a challenge as well. Rhee continued the US policy of excluding supporters of the People's Committees from politics. Barred from participating in the official political system, communists and others resorted to force, and by 1947–8 a guerrilla war was under way in the south. Nothing equivalent developed in the north, and while Westerners attributed this to the repressiveness of the DPRK regime, there was more to it than this. The North Korean government was not democratic, but its reforms seem to have won it a good deal of support. The DPRK's formula for stability was indeed a rigid political system, but also social change. Moreover, in South Korea Rhee too resorted to repression, but in the absence of fundamental reform he found it difficult to establish a stable political order. Guerrilla activities were particularly strong on the island of Cheju off the southern tip of the Korean peninsula and in the mountainous central zones of the ROK, i.e. in areas once controlled by the People's Committees. The government claimed to have killed almost 20,000 rebels in frontier areas, though Pyongyang asserted that there were some 90,000 guerrillas operating inside Rhee's territory in 1949. These included mainly southerners but also northerners. In all, over 100,000 people had been killed after the Second World War as the result of guerrilla war, peasant uprisings, labour conflict and engagements along the thirty-eighth parallel and for all practical purposes the southern left had been defeated by early 1950.

Yet South Korea did not enter a period of stability. Rhee's repression alienated even many on the right. Not every right-winger was a supporter of the president's administration, but the opposition was divided. Rhee took advantage of this and ruled as a dictator, despite the existence of a national assembly. Thus, while the regime displayed the trappings of a democracy, the assembly was stymied and power was centralized in Rhee's hands. He used his authority to close opposition newspapers and to arrest and apparently torture members of the assembly itself. One estimate is that in September 1949 the government was holding about 36,000 political prisoners. No one seemed immune, so that many on the political right were fearful for their safety. The degree of anti-government feeling was perhaps most clearly indicated when Rhee himself proposed to postpone elections scheduled for May 1950. But the Americans objected that this would only worsen the political turmoil, and insisted that Rhee go through with them.

Officials in the United States were not pleased with Rhee's conduct, yet they were not prepared to abandon him and continued to supply economic and military aid. At least he was a good anti-communist. Moreover, the US commander in the Pacific, General Douglas MacArthur, had developed close ties with the South Korean president. Each man cultivated the other's ego, and the general saw the president as an ally in pressing Washington to give higher priority to Asian affairs, i.e. to MacArthur's jurisdiction. MacArthur also interpreted Korean developments in moral terms, and forgave many of Rhee's abuses of power on the grounds that anti-communism represented a higher morality than the Korean's political methods. Yet these methods contributed to Rhee's poor showing in the 1950 elections, despite efforts to rig the outcome. His party received a minority of seats in the national assembly, but because of a divided opposition remained in power. In June the North Koreans sent delegates south to meet with various opposition groups and to propose Korea-wide elections followed by reunification. They hoped to take advantage of the anti-Rhee feeling evident in the May elections. But Rhee ordered their arrest, and countered by proposing that there be UN-supervised elections only in the north. Those elected would then be admitted to the South Korean assembly, where they would be a minority.

Thus, by the early summer of 1950, each side felt it had more reason than ever to strike at the other. For Rhee, there was the danger that Northern efforts to conspire with his political opponents might be effective. A war would permit him to solve the problem of the North once and for all. In such an event the Americans would have little choice but to support him – they could hardly abandon an ally. For Kim, the instability in the South was both a danger and an opportunity. The danger was that Rhee would launch a war against the North, and indeed the South Korean president was explicit about his intention to do so sooner or later. The opportunity was that the political uncertainty following the May elections might permit an easy Northern victory. Kim's decision to send delegates south to talk to the opposition indicated he was willing to try and take advantage of the situation. Moreover, earlier in the year he had visited Moscow and requested more military aid, though the Russians were unwilling to commit troops to Korea. On the other hand, it must have been tempting for them to hope Kim might succeed, and it turned out that he made the first move. North Korean forces attacked in the vicinity of the South Korean capital, Seoul, on 25 June 1950.

In due course a debate developed as to whether the United States itself had invited the attack. In January 1950 Secretary of State Dean Acheson had made a speech which seemed to imply that South Korea was outside the US defence perimeter for the Far East. The limits of American power required that Washington give higher priority to the defence of some allies (such as Japan) than to others. Hence historians speculated that the speech encouraged the North to move against the South in the expectation that the Americans would not respond. What the secretary in fact said, however, was that the United States by itself could not be expected to protect every one of its allies in the entire world. In the event of a crisis the people on the scene, assisted by the collective security mechanisms of the United Nations, would have to assume the responsibility for defending certain regions. In other words, it might be up to America's allies to help protect more of the Western sphere. At no time did Acheson suggest that Korea was expendable. He had prepared his speech carefully during a period of several days, so that it was unlikely his observations were made offhand or without forethought. On the contrary, a speech calling upon America's allies for a larger role in Western defences had to be phrased carefully, lest it encourage adventurism on the part of Rhee (and also Chiang on Taiwan). The note of ambiguity in Acheson's comments was perhaps calculated with this in mind. When all is said and done, however, it is a mistake to exaggerate the impact of a single speech. Other US policy statements on Korea during the spring of 1950 suggested a continuing commitment. In fact, as late as 18 June the future secretary of state, John Foster Dulles, gave a speech in the South

Korean National Assembly which had been approved by Washington and which pledged America's support: 'You are not alone. You will never be alone so long as you continue to play worthily your part in the great design of human freedom.'*

Because the North struck first, many accounts of the Korean War begin with the invasion itself and treat this as the cause of the war. For Westerners this has the advantage of placing the entire blame on the other side. Yet, as we have seen, the origins of the crisis were complex, so that a number of issues merit our consideration. For example, how much did the turmoil in the South contribute to Pyongyang's decision, tempting it to act while Rhee was in difficulty and lest he strike first? To what extent did US support for the dictatorial Rhee contribute to the turmoil, and thus to the chain of events that led to war? Also consider the American role in suppressing the South Korean left after the Second World War. What of the Russians? Their policy was equally supportive of Kim, though he had fewer political problems at home than Rhee. Whereas the strength of the left created difficulties for the Americans in the south, it helped the Russians in the north. Any explanation of the war therefore must take account of the balance of political power inside each of the Koreas. And what about the impact of the Cold War? The determination of each superpower to support its side contributed to the emergence of two Koreas, and helped set the scene for one or the other to try and reunify the country on its terms. No doubt additional questions might be raised, yet, whatever we may conclude about the origins of the war, it is apparent that the story of Korea depends on how we interpret the events before June 1950. The explanation that the cause of the conflict was the invasion of the twenty-fifth will not suffice.

The Course of the War

Although uncertain whether the Russians were behind events, the Americans intervened with air and naval power within two days, and on 30 June President Truman authorized the dispatch of ground forces. The United States had obtained a resolution from the United Nations on 27 June calling upon members to assist South Korea, and Truman used this as the basis of his authority. The American Congress was never asked to declare war, and legally (though not as a practical matter) US troops were under the command of the UN. Several Western nations contributed token forces as well, though the US fielded half of the

* Cited in *ibid.*, 577.

ground troops and the ROK provided most of the rest. Nearly all air and sea engagements were the responsibility of the United States. At first the battle went badly for the South, but on 15 September General Mac-Arthur staged a landing at Inchon, near Seoul, which placed him in a position to invade the North. At the same time (i.e. still in September) Truman gave permission for MacArthur to operate above the thirty-eighth parallel as soon as the general judged it was tactically advantageous, unless the Russians or Chinese intervened in the meantime. It was the South Koreans, however, who crossed the border first, on 1 October 1950. Shortly thereafter the United States went to the UN, and on 7 October won its approval for conquering the North and reunifying the peninsula. American forces moved into the DPRK the same day, as the US had orchestrated the UN vote to coincide with its plans to invade the North, and MacArthur began a rapid advance towards the Korea–China border.

All this was a significant departure from the Truman administration's 'containment' policy. This had been formulated in 1947 by George Kennan of the State Department's Policy Planning Staff, and presumably had become the settled policy of the US government by 1950. The virtue of containment was that it suggested a way of challenging the Soviets while minimizing the risk of a Third World War. It meant blocking the expansion of the East but not attempting to roll back its borders. Kennan believed it might work because he predicted that eventually the internal stresses of the Soviet system would lead to its collapse. Time, he argued, was on the side of the West, and someday the USSR would self-destruct. Containment was not a retreat, however, from the overall goal of making inroads into the Communist Bloc by means other than war, e.g. foreign aid. This meant that the Americans were providing financial and military assistance to Tito in Yugoslavia at the very time containment became a catchword for administration policy. Containment was therefore not an abandonment of the essentially activist approach of the United States since 1945, and related only to means, not ends.

It hardly needs to be pointed out that Kennan's image of an inherently flawed Soviet empire was not entirely consistent with the administration doctrine that the Western Bloc was menaced by a powerful, worldwide communist conspiracy. Yet containment was a useful theory for marshalling public opinion behind Truman's policies. It promised a stout defence of the West against Soviet expansionism, yet abjured military aggression against communist countries and hence made it a bit easier for Americans to live with the prospect of a protracted East–West struggle. Korea, though, did define the limits of containment. Means turned out to be less important than ends. When Truman was presented with a rare opportunity to advance into the Communist Bloc by military means, he proceeded to do so and ordered the invasion of a Soviet satellite state.

The US president soon regretted his decision. He no doubt thought he was free to act because by September it was clear that the Russians had no intention of intervening with troops. Indeed, during the summer the Russians (and also the British) had made suggestions for negotiations not only on the Korean crisis but also on the status of China and Taiwan. India had made a similar proposal as well, and both the USSR and the PRC responded favourably. The US, however, rejected all these ideas (as well as another Russian plan presented at the United Nations on 2 October), and offered no alternatives of its own. Truman felt he could win, and the Russians evidently were not keen for a fight. Why compromise? Further, General MacArthur reported his view that it was unlikely the Chinese would enter the fray. Virtually all authorities then and later agreed that China had not instigated the invasion of 25 June and that a crisis in Korea was against its interests. It needed to concentrate on rebuilding after its long civil war and on resolving the Taiwan question. Yet it turned out that the Chinese were not about to permit the United States to march troops up to their border with North Korea, MacArthur notwithstanding. They may not have started the war, but they had a vital interest in its outcome. Accordingly, before the UN gave its approval for crossing the thirty-eighth parallel, the Chinese issued a warning that they would intervene if the DPRK were invaded. The Americans thought that China was bluffing, but they soon found out differently. The first contact with Chinese troops was made in late October, and by November they were encountered in massive numbers. After having taken almost all of North Korea in the weeks before, MacArthur's forces reeled under the onslaught, so that by the spring of 1951 the war had settled down to a stalemate at about the original boundary between North and South. There it would remain until an armistice was signed in 1953.

Once the PRC had intervened, it became evident to Truman that it was time to return to a policy of containment. China's entry raised the possibility of a general war in Asia, something quite beyond the capabilities of the Americans to fight. After all, China was the world's most populous nation. Its manpower far exceeded that of the US, so that the latter could hardly expect to outlast the Chinese in an Asian land war. Of course, there was always the atomic bomb. MacArthur repeatedly suggested that it be used, and on 30 November 1950 Truman himself admitted at a press conference that he had always regarded this as an option. His statement immediately brought the British prime minister, Clement Attlee, to Washington on a mission to urge restraint. Attlee's arguments eventually proved persuasive, and he had the backing of the French as well. The North Atlantic allies did not want to see a wider conflict in Asia, as this could only work to the advantage of the USSR. It would draw the US away from the European theatre, but it was the latter which was the first priority of both NATO and the Soviets.

Truman understood all this, and so shifted course early in the new year. MacArthur, however, disagreed and pressed for a war against China if necessary to win in Korea. Besides raising the possibility of the bomb, he wanted to transport some of Chiang Kai-shek's troops to Korea, an action that the Chinese Communists no doubt would have regarded as provocative and as a major escalation of the conflict. The general attempted to take the initiative in defining US foreign policy on a number of occasions. Tension developed between MacArthur on the one hand and Truman and the Joint Chiefs of Staff on the other, and eventually the president fired his Pacific commander for what amounted to insubordination.

With this the Korean crisis began to cool down, and by July 1951 truce talks were under way. It was the prospect that a military solution could no longer be imposed after China's intervention that finally brought the Americans to the peace table. In essence, the eventual armistice of 1953 returned to a two-Koreas policy, with a new border following the battlelines near the thirty-eighth parallel. The UN forces suffered over 94,000 dead, plus hundreds of thousands wounded. About 34,000 Americans were killed in battle, with an additional 21,000 dying from other causes (accident or disease). There were over 113,000 wounded. This equalled approximately half the US losses in the First World War. It was likely that South Korean civilian deaths numbered at least a million, with the number for the DPRK considerably higher. The communists probably suffered more than 1.5 million military casualties. The total number of Americans under arms throughout the world (and including Korea) between 1950 and 1953 approached six million. Though sometimes described as a 'limited' or 'brush-fire' war, as distinct from a world war, the Korean crisis was only small-scale in comparison to what would have happened had atomic bombs been used.

By any other standard it was a major conflict. But perhaps most alarming was that a negotiated settlement was not seriously pursued until China's intervention. It was true that North Korea had initiated the crisis of 25 June, and though it acted for very complex reasons, this hardly placed the United States in a mood to talk. It was also the case that in the summer of 1950 the Americans were losing on the battlefield, and thus in a poor position to bargain. Yet once the tables were turned, at Inchon, the temptation of a total victory by military means proved too much for Truman to resist. MacArthur encouraged an aggressive stance, but ultimately it was the president and his security advisers who made the decision to cross the thirty-eighth parallel. Their choice should have come as no surprise, however, as it was consistent with US policies towards other regions where the West faced challenges, whether from the USSR or from local revolutionaries.

VIETNAM

There was a growing sentiment in the Truman administration, well before the outbreak of the Korean War, that America's military capabilities should be expanded. Besides committing aid to the French in Indo-China, the US National Security Council in April 1950 finalized a classified policy paper designated NSC–68 which recommended more than tripling current American military expenditures, i.e. to about the levels of the Second World War when the United States was fully mobilized. With the outbreak of a hot war in Korea this followed as a matter of course. A little earlier, in January 1950, the administration had also announced its decision to build a hydrogen bomb. This was a direct answer to the Soviets' successful testing of a nuclear device in 1949, but it was also an important step in escalating the arms race. It suggested that the US was no more prepared to concede parity on atomic weapons to the USSR than it had been when the Baruch Plan was proposed in 1946. Yet this meant that as long as the Americans were ahead the Russians were not about to let up either, so that prospects for controlling the arms race remained bleak.

There were still more developments in the spring of 1950. Discussions were under way in administration circles concerning German rearmament, a very sensitive issue for America's European allies. After all, Hitler had been defeated only five years earlier. With the Korean War the Americans had to deploy more of their military resources in Asia, and so regarded Germany's ability to contribute to European defence as a matter of some urgency. The US did increase its troop levels in Europe later in the year, but it also raised the matter of rearming West Germany. The French, however, insisted that any such scheme would have to be worked out within the framework of an integrated force. They wanted authority over German troops vested in a joint Allied command. The Americans were agreeable, so as to appease those who feared a resurgent Germany, and thus succeeded in initiating negotiations to this end.

The Korean War resulted in other measures as well. In the summer of 1950 the United States decided to give extensive military aid to Chiang Kai-shek, and instituted reconnaissance flights over the Chinese mainland. It was also true that the US stationed the Seventh Fleet in the waters between Taiwan and the mainland, in order to prevent Chiang from taking advantage of the crisis in Korea to strike at the People's Republic and thereby draw the US into a war to retake the country. Yet the US still regarded the Nationalist regime on Taiwan as an important ally, and the possibility of calling upon Chiang to provide troops for other theatres of war remained a live issue for several years to come. As we shall see in due course, some administration officials recommended that the Nationalists help the French during the 1954 Indo-China crisis. Hence, the movement of the Seventh Fleet has to be seen in a wider context, and of course it must be remembered that the long-term objective was to protect Chiang. It sent a clear message to the Chinese communists not to try anything.

It was Indo-China, however, that proved to be a more trying test of American resolve, although before 1954 the US role was to support France. Like Korea, Indo-China was the scene of a major war, and one that in the mid-1960s would be escalated even further. Since the late nineteenth century the French had administered Indo-China as five distinct entities. Laos and Cambodia were kingdoms under the protection of France, while the area known as Vietnam was divided into Tonkin, Annam and Cochin China. Tonkin was in the north and included the Red River Delta and the cities of Hanoi and Haiphong. Its legal status was that of a French protectorate. The same was true of Annam, where the Vietnamese emperor was allowed to maintain his court at the city of Hué. Geographically it included the central areas of Vietnam. In the south was Cochin China, mainly the Mekong River delta and the site of the 'Paris of the Orient', Saigon. Cochin China was the least developed part of Vietnam when the French arrived, and so was made an outright colony with no pretence as to protectorate status. Of all areas of Indo-China it was in Vietnam where historically the French had the greatest impact and where resistance was strongest after the Second World War.

The origins of the Indo-China (or mainly the Vietnam) War were to be found in France's efforts to reimpose its colonial rule after 1945. Although Japan controlled the region during the Second World War, France was the main colonial power in the area. In fact, until March 1945 the region was administered by officials of the Vichy regime on Japan's behalf, so that the French retained a presence even after they had submitted to the Japanese. Traditionally China also had territorial ambitions in the country, mainly around the Red River Delta. The Delta area had been a Chinese colony until the tenth century AD. It was in effect the original Vietnamese state. After repulsing a major Chinese effort to repossess the region in the fifteenth century, the Vietnamese began to expand southward. By the sixteenth century they had moved into Annam, and by the seventeenth had reached the sparsely settled Mekong River Delta. These developments brought the Vietnamese into conflict with Siam (Thailand), which was competing for ascendancy over Laos and Cambodia. Indo-China thus became afflicted by a long history of territorial rivalry, a fact which was to continue to disturb the region even in the twentieth century.

Yet Vietnam itself became divided in the process of expansion. It did not develop southward as a single entity. As the northerners of the Red River Delta began moving south, they found it difficult to maintain control over their more distant territories. Moreover, oppressive rule often resulted in rebellion. In the seventeenth century, accordingly, the Trinh warlord family seized power in the Red River Delta, while the Nguyen warlords took the coast of Annam. It was the Nguyen kingdom that continued to expand and reached the Mekong River Delta. Thus there were two Vietnamese dynasties, and differences between northerners and southerners began to develop. These were not as great as those between Vietnamese and Laotians or Cambodians, nor did they constitute the basis of ethnic or cultural divisions. The older Red River region reflected its past links to China and was the more developed area. By contrast the south was more of a frontier region, with less cohesive social structures. Also, geography linked the Mekong River Delta more to Cambodia and Laos than to Tonkin or Annam.

Vietnam eventually did become politically unified. After a rebellion against their rule in the late eighteenth century the Nguyens reconquered their kingdom and went on to take the north as well, so that by the early nineteenth century the Nguyen emperor, Gia Long, had united all of Vietnam under one dynasty for the first time in history. The problem was that Catholic missionaries from France had already arrived on the scene, and turned out to be the advance agents of Western imperialism.

The French

It was imperial competition which alerted France to the importance of Vietnam. French economic interests in China proper were concentrated in the area north of Indo-China. Moving into Vietnam, Cambodia and Laos therefore made sense from a strategic point of view. It would prevent some other colonial power from seizing control of a region adjacent to the French sphere of influence in China. Of course, Vietnam had value in its own right, though the French hoped its river systems might be used to tap markets in South China. The north had mineral wealth and the south had considerable agricultural potential. For this reason, in the mid nineteenth century, the French took the Mekong Delta, i.e. the least developed and least settled part of Vietnam. The navigability of the Mekong proved limited, however, so French merchants looked north to the Red River. In 1873, and without authorization from the government of France, the adventurer François Garnier attacked Hanoi and proclaimed it open to French merchants. Given the high stakes, it was not long before the French government acted as well.

In the early 1880s Paris ordered its military to seize the Red River Delta and to bombard the imperial capital at Hué. This was done under the pretext of protecting French missionaries from persecution. In the face of their earlier losses in the south, and given their military weakness, the Nguyens were soon forced to yield, and the French then went on to assert suzerainty over Laos and Cambodia. In Vietnam they installed their own protégé on the throne at Hué, and established Tonkin and Annam as protectorates in addition to their colony in the south, Cochin China. This remained the administrative structure of Vietnam until the Second World War. The stability that existed up to the Japanese occupation in 1940–41, however, was the result of French power. All the regional rivalries in Indo-China and in Vietnam itself which had characterized the pre-colonial past remained just below the surface. If anything, the French exacerbated these, because their entire administrative structure was based on the principle of divide and rule. It was to their advantage to encourage differences, in order to head off the development of an effective nationalism capable of challenging French colonialism.

Thus, under France, the unified state of Vietnam disappeared, and foreigners went on to remake another Third World country so as to serve the needs of the First World. Plantations and mines were developed according to the geography and resources of each area. Transportation and other infrastructures were built, financed by taxes on the Vietnamese. International trade was restricted to French markets, so that the Indo-Chinese peoples could not bargain for better terms elsewhere. Taxes were made payable in money, not in kind, thus forcing peasants to produce a surplus for distant markets rather than continue a largely subsistence economy. Alternatively they might go to work on French plantations or in French mines. They had to do so in order to earn the hard currency needed to pay the tax collector. The colonial regime also assumed a monopoly on the sale of salt, alcohol and opium, and then proceeded to impose exorbitant prices. The pattern was similar to colonial regimes elsewhere. In short, there was a connection between the impoverishment of the Indo-Chinese and the French economic stake in South-East Asia. While many other features of Vietnamese life underwent change, these will suffice to illustrate the French impact.

Vietnamese Nationalism

The result, of course, was resistance, but given the fragmentation of Vietnamese political life this took time to develop. Nationalism certainly meant being anti-French, but it was quite another matter to organize the makings of a coherent nationalist movement to provide an alternative to colonialism. The French easily broke up a variety of nationalist organizations in the 1920s and 1930s, but one proved more difficult to deal with. This was led by Ho Chi Minh, who was to become the nemesis of both the French and the Americans until his death in 1969. Ho had been born in Annam in 1890, the son of a provincial mandarin or government official. But rather than follow in his father's footsteps he first became a school teacher and then emerged as a leading proponent of Vietnamese autonomy. By 1918 he had gone to France and the imperial capital, and during the Paris Peace Conference lobbied on behalf of Indo-China's independence, though obviously without effect. He also wrote for socialist newspapers, and was among the founding members of the French Communist Party in 1920. He then spent a few years in Moscow in the early 1920s, before being sent by the Comintern to Guangzhou as one of its advisers to the Guomindang and the Chinese Communist Party. At the same time, in Vietnam itself, nationalist agitation by radical students resulted in a crackdown by the French authorities. Ho therefore organized the Thanh Nien (or Youth) Party among those who had fled to

Hong Kong. This became one of the forerunners of the Indo-Chinese Communist Party (ICP). There were revolutionary parties in Vietnam itself, of course, but because of the need to operate clandestinely they were isolated from each other. By 1930, however, Ho drew a number of communist organizations together at Hong Kong to form the ICP. It was the Comintern that decided one party should be organized for all Indo-China rather than only Vietnam, but given the regional rivalries that had existed historically in the area separate parties in Vietnam, Laos and Cambodia would emerge eventually.

In 1930 a premature anti-colonial uprising resulted in the elimination of the main non-communist nationalist organization in Vietnam. The French did not seem to realize that suppressing moderates only helped clear the way for revolutionaries. Events, though, did not turn immediately in Ho's favour. The ICP had begun to achieve some successes in organizing workers and peasants, and even formed local governing bodies (called 'soviets') in some villages. The ICP's strength was concentrated mainly in the province of Nghe Thinh, located in the central coastal region of Vietnam. Not surprisingly the colonial authorities brought these activities to a quick end. Fortunately for him, Ho was in Hong Kong when the French struck, and though arrested by the British as a subversive, he was soon released and went back to Moscow in the mid-1930s. Ho reappeared in Vietnam in 1940, when he attempted to organize new uprisings, but without success. He therefore fled again, this time to South China.

It was the Second World War which provided Ho and his colleagues with their chance. In the spring of 1941 they organized the League for the Independence of Vietnam, the Vietminh, among exiles in South China, but it was not until 1945 that events broke their way. In the meantime Ho's forces engaged in anti-Japanese guerrilla activities in Vietnam and thus legitimized their claim to be the only effective nationalist alternative after the war. Vietminh operations were limited to the north, and paradoxically depended on support from one of Chiang Kai-shek's warlords. The Chinese had an interest in aiding anyone who resisted Japan, and of course they hoped to establish their hegemony over Indo-China in the future. But after the war the more important fact proved to be that Ho had developed an independent nationalist movement in the north, while other Vietnamese leaders tended to collaborate with the French and Japanese.

It was Japan's sudden surrender which provided Ho with the opportunity to step into what had become a power vacuum and set up the only effective Vietnamese government. In March 1945 the Japanese had ended the French administration of Indo-China and proceeded to establish a formally independent government for Vietnam, with the current emperor, Bao Dai, at its head. At the moment of Japan's defeat, therefore, the French were temporarily out of the way, while Bao Dai's government was a Japanese creation and of dubious legitimacy. Furthermore, as elsewhere in Asia, Allied occupation forces were unable to land immediately, so when 1,000 Vietminh marched into Hanoi in mid-August they encountered no resistance, and on 2 September 1945 Ho proclaimed the Democratic Republic of Vietnam (DRV). Just before this Bao Dai had abdicated and offered to serve the new regime, though not for long. Soon the former emperor retired to Hong Kong and then Europe (a few years later the French would bring him back to head a puppet government in the south). Ho was thus in the advantageous position of having few other Vietnamese claimants to oppose him. With Bao Dai out of power he became the leader of the only indigenous government in Vietnam. Ho's problem was not that other domestic nationalists were able to contest his claim to power but that the French would return and outgun the new regime in a military confrontation.

The Return of the French
In the immediate context of 1945 it was the British who were responsible for occupying the south of Vietnam on behalf of the victorious Allies. This had been agreed to at the Potsdam Conference, though the United Kingdom could ill afford to become mired down in Indo-China. The British arrived on 12 September, confined their presence to Cochin China, and proceeded to release the French officials jailed in March by Japan. They also drove the Vietminh out of Saigon, even though the latter were willing to postpone full independence and accept a five- to ten-year period of transition. In other words, the British prepared the way for the arrival of a French expeditionary force in October. The UK wanted to withdraw just as soon as possible.

For the time being France was able to establish itself only in the south, because Potsdam had provided that the Chinese Nationalists should represent the Allies in the north. Given their problems at home, the Chinese did not become deeply involved in running their part of Vietnam. Until well into the next year, 1946, Ho was able to carry on, and he consolidated his government at Hanoi. The Chinese did withdraw in 1946, however, and Ho attempted to come to terms with the French. His main goal was to avoid war, as his political authority was well established in the north, and a military contest was the one thing that could hurt him. Ho came to an agreement in March with the French commander in Vietnam concerning the independence and territorial integrity of the DRV and its right to maintain an army, but all within the French Union. During the course of these discussions he allowed French troops to return to Tonkin. Yet any plans about the future of Vietnam required the approval of Paris. Ho went to France, but negotiations became protracted as the French reconsidered their interests. The post-war governments at Paris included communist ministers, and presumably these people would be friendly to the Vietminh cause. Instead they followed Stalin's policy of observing the Western sphere of influence where its boundaries were clearly drawn, and supported the imperial ambitions of their non-communist colleagues. Moreover, as these events unfolded, a new colonial government (the Republic of Cochin China) was taking shape in the south of Vietnam at the instigation of French settlers and also the French high commissioner in Indo-China. The outcome was virtually inevitable. The Paris talks between the DRV and France broke down, and another colonial war began. In November 1946 the first major clash occurred with the French bombardment of Haiphong. A full-scale war began the next month, when the Vietminh attempted to take French military positions in Tonkin. By the time an armistice was signed in 1954 French forces had suffered 92,000 killed, 114,000 wounded and over 20,000 missing. In addition, the US had supplied a total of $2,900 million in military aid and by 1954 was bearing 80 per cent of the costs of the war.

The main problem for France was that Ho's forces had considerable support among the population, especially in the north. The proof of this was to be found not only in the eventual failure of the French war effort but in the failure of its political strategy as well. The puppet government, the Republic of Cochin China, was installed at Saigon. As it was not an autonomous entity, it could hardly appeal to Vietnamese nationalists and draw them away from the DRV. In 1949, therefore, the French organized a new and formally independent regime known as the State of Vietnam, and this absorbed Cochin China. The French hoped that the new government might rally nationalists around a pro-Western regime and constitute the foundation for a neo-colonial solution to the Vietnam conundrum. It restored the principle of a united Vietnam, in theory if not in reality (Ho controlled much of the north), and presumably reversed the imperial policy of divide and rule. The lack of real independence was clear in that the French wanted all of what it called the 'Associated

States' of Indo-China (Vietnam, Laos and Cambodia) to remain in the French Union. Also, Paris installed its own choice, Bao Dai, as head of the new Vietnamese state. Full sovereignty thus remained as elusive as ever.

Dien Bien Phu and the Americans

The end for the French came in the spring of 1954 at the Battle of Dien Bien Phu, in Tonkin, deep inside Vietminh territory. Dien Bien Phu was a fortified area at the bottom of a valley about nine miles long and six miles wide. Its strategic value was limited, and it was simply intended to serve as a threat against Vietminh operations in Laos. Yet, because the French did not control the surrounding countryside, Dien Bien Phu was not particularly well suited to its task, especially as the French command never intended it to become the centre of a major campaign. Indeed, the overall strategy for Indo-China (code named the Navarre Plan) did not call for major offensives before the autumn of 1954 at the earliest. But Dien Bien Phu was a particularly tempting target for the Vietminh, and they chose to move much sooner, attacking on 13 March 1954. Given Dien Bien Phu's location behind enemy lines, the French strategy had been to supply the base by air, not to maintain links by land. The Vietminh thus simply moved into the hills surrounding the valley, and laid siege. The intensity of their attack soon made it impossible for airplanes to land, so that supplies could only be parachuted in.

The result was a major crisis for the French. Dien Bien Phu was likely to prove indefensible, and so within a week General Paul Ely of the French General Staff for National Defence flew to Washington to warn the Americans and to ask what the US might be prepared to offer in the way of help. The importance of Dien Bien Phu was more than a matter of strategy or tactics. In France there was widespread dissatisfaction with a war that had gone on for eight years without resolution. No French government could expect to maintain a majority in the National Assembly, and thus stay in power, unless it could find a way out of the morass very soon. Consequently the prospect of a negotiated settlement became more and more likely as the chances for a military victory receded. Dien Bien Phu brought the issue into clear focus, and for the French public symbolized the frustrations of years of fighting. Yet the future of Vietnam was of concern to the United States as well, and for the Americans Dien Bien Phu raised the question of whether the West could defend its sphere of influence. Thus, as Ely crossed the Atlantic from Paris, US policy pointed in only one direction: America must persuade the French government to stay in Vietnam and fight, despite public opinion in France itself and even if it meant increasing the US commitment to providing support for the war effort.

The danger that the French would withdraw was particularly acute in the spring of 1954, as an international conference to discuss Far Eastern affairs had been scheduled to meet at Geneva in April. This eventually brought together representatives of the US, France, the United Kingdom, the USSR, the PRC, Laos, Cambodia, and both the Vietminh and the State of Vietnam. The risk was that the French would use the occasion to compromise with the Vietminh. But many members of the highest councils of US policy-making still believed that a military victory was possible, and were not in a mood to see France sacrifice Western interests in South-East Asia. Indeed, the Americans had agreed to attend the Geneva Conference under extreme pressure not only from France but from Britain as well. The British saw signs of increasing flexibility on the Soviet side in the period since the death of Stalin (in March 1953), and they favoured normalizing the West's relations with the People's Republic of China. The UK did not want to see the US drawn into a protracted war in the Far East, thus diverting American attention away from Europe. After all, Washington had just extricated itself from Korea. The need to discuss outstanding issues concerning Korea and to deal with the future of Indo-China, the British believed, offered an opportunity for a general resolution of East–West tensions in Asia.

The Americans, of course, did not wish to sit down at the same negotiating table with the representatives of the PRC, lest this imply some form of official recognition of the communist regime in China. They finally accepted a compromise in which the People's Republic would not be one of the conveners of the Geneva Conference but would none the less be allowed to participate. The US was explicit in insisting that this did not mean diplomatic recognition. Moreover, the Americans were not prepared to trade away any Western interests. It was one thing to have them agree to attend the Geneva Conference, but it would be quite another to make them compromise with the representatives of Ho Chi Minh or Mao Zedong.

The reality was that the impending opening of the Geneva Conference only made the Americans more interested in a military solution, so the arrival of General Ely in Washington on 20 March came at a crucial moment. If the French were in a strong military position in the spring of 1954, this would obviate the need to make concessions to the other side.

The opening of the Vietminh campaign against Dien Bien Phu in March, just weeks before Geneva, thus was unfortunate for the Americans as well as the French. It represented a major crisis for US policy, and led the administration of President Dwight Eisenhower to consider a massive increase in the American role in Vietnam. Eisenhower had been the Allied commander at Normandy, and had been elected president of the United States in 1952. As we shall see, his foreign policies were generally consistent with those of his predecessor, Harry Truman.

As we have noted, US aid to the French had begun in 1950, and was part of the American response not only to events in Indo-China, but to the possible threat from the PRC as well. In the specific situation of Dien Bien Phu in 1954 the Americans continued to regard the PRC as their principal enemy. The Chinese did supply military advisers to the Vietminh and assisted in the training of troops, and although it is impossible to estimate their exact numbers, it is certain that they were few. No authority would argue that they determined the outcome of the Vietnam War. There is some evidence that Chinese did fight along side the Vietminh, but again their numbers were insignificant. More important was material aid from both Russia and China, though in the case of the latter war goods were often sold rather than given to Hanoi. This assistance, however, began only about the same time the United States initiated its aid programme to the French. The reason for the delay in outside aid for the Vietminh (recall that the war had begun in 1946) was not mysterious. China was engulfed in its own civil war until 1949 and in no position to supply arms. And for their part the Soviets continued to regard Indo-China as part of the Western sphere. They had other priorities. The Russian policy became untenable, however, when the PRC accorded diplomatic recognition to Ho Chi Minh in January 1950. The Chinese thus showed that they were prepared to increase their influence in the region once they were in a position to do so. But this threatened the Soviets' standing as leader of the Eastern Bloc, so within a matter of weeks they too recognized the Hanoi government. Until then they had not exchanged ambassadors, but the Chinese initiative forced them to abjure their hands-off policy. Thereafter both China and the USSR provided the Vietminh with assistance. Even so, in 1954 John Foster Dulles, Eisenhower's secretary of state, acknowledged that American aid to France was ten times the amount Ho's allies supplied to him.

United States assistance thus began soon after the Chinese and Russians had recognized the Democratic Republic of Vietnam, and far exceeded their efforts. Furthermore, it involved more than just money and arms. As early as January 1953 US Air Force personnel were sent to Vietnam to overhaul various types of aircraft. The first unit to go was a detachment of the Twenty-Fourth Air Depot Wing from Clark Air Base in the Philippines. The French were desperately short of qualified technicians to service their US-supplied aircraft, and so had requested a loan of personnel. They also needed pilots to fly transports. These were supplied by contracting out employees of the Civil Air Transport. The CAT was a presumably civilian airline organized in 1946, but had been bought into by the US Central Intelligence Agency and was performing missions for the CIA in many parts of the world. Pilots from the CAT made their first foray into a combat zone, over Laos, on 8 May 1953, and a year later they found themselves flying supplies into Dien Bien Phu.

Given the degree of past American involvement it was hardly surprising that the crisis of 1954 led US policy-makers to discuss additional measures. Therefore, in April and May 1954, the US Air Force transported about 1,000 French paratroopers from Europe to Vietnam. At the same time American ships (designated 'Task Force 70' and including aircraft carriers) were sent to patrol the Gulf of Tonkin and show the flag. In addition a number of other measures were considered (though not adopted) which showed how vital Vietnam was to the Eisenhower administration. These included the possibility of blockading the coast of mainland China and even engaging the PRC militarily; deploying Chiang Kai-shek's troops; conducting covert operations in the PRC; assuming direct responsibility for the training of Vietnamese troops; intervening with air and naval power to rescue Dien Bien Phu itself; and even using American ground troops or the atomic bomb. The seriousness of the 1954 Vietnam crisis is not to be underestimated, and the above options were considered by the National Security Council, the Joint Chiefs of Staff and other top advisers to Eisenhower. Some evidence exists to suggest that Secretary of State Dulles may have made an offer directly to the French foreign minister, Georges Bidault, to deploy nuclear weapons.

None of these contingencies materialized, mainly because of reservations among the majority of the Joint Chiefs of Staff, members of the US Congressional leadership, and the British and even the French. The reasons were clear enough. Direct US intervention, especially if action were taken against China, risked a general war in Asia at a time when America's allies still regarded the Soviet threat in Europe as more important. Moreover, using atomic weapons might well lead to retaliation by the USSR and thus a Third World War. The British were particularly convinced of the last point, and Eisenhower had come to much the same conclusion by the time the Geneva Conference opened. And the French, of course, noted that using atomic bombs at Dien Bien Phu would wipe out their forces as well as those of the enemy. Therefore, because the Western powers were unable to co-ordinate a military solution, the wisest strategy at Geneva from the American point of view was to stand pat and agree to nothing. Dien Bien Phu fell during the course of the conference, on 7 May 1954, and the next day the diplomats turned from discussing Korea to Indo-China.

The Geneva Conference

The actual scenario at Geneva, of course, was not entirely up to the Americans to orchestrate. A domestic political crisis in France had the effect of quickening events considerably. On 12 June the government of Prime Minister Joseph Laniel lost an important vote in the National Assembly and fell from power. On 16 June Pierre Mendès-France formed a new cabinet. Because of increasing opposition to the Vietnam War in France itself, especially after Dien Bien Phu, the new premier pledged to end the war within thirty days or resign. Developments were thus coalescing to assure some sort of a settlement.

Moreover, it was not only the French who wanted the Geneva Conference to succeed by coming to specific agreements about Indo-China. The Chinese, for example, also had a considerable stake in the outcome. It would vitally affect their own security, and the conference itself was a form of recognition for the PRC's status as a great power, American legalisms distinguishing conveners and participants notwithstanding. China thus worked to win the co-operation of Hanoi in achieving a settlement.

The Russians did likewise, as they did not wish to be distracted from European matters by a major crisis in Asia. They hoped as well that, once France was extricated from Indo-China and thus less dependent on the Americans for assistance, it might pursue a more independent policy within the Western Bloc. The result could limit America's capacity to speak on behalf of Europe. The French might even torpedo such ventures as German rearmament, and indeed, after Geneva the National Assembly voted against the proposed European Defence Community, i.e. the plan for an integrated Continental military force including Germans. Later in the year the French did yield to renewed pressure for a German rearmament scheme within the framework of NATO and with guarantees concerning the deployment of Germany's military forces. But the French were tired of being directed by the Americans, and were indeed interested in becoming more independent of the US, for which reason Mendès-France secretly initiated a programme to develop a nuclear capability for France, as one way of asserting his country's status as a great power. The Soviets were on the mark when they viewed Geneva as an opportunity to make trouble in the Atlantic Alliance.

For their part the British did not want to see the Indo-China war turn into a general conflict in Asia. On the contrary, they were the leading proponents of the idea that Geneva offered an opportunity to settle a number of outstanding issues in the Far East. Therefore they opposed any action which might provoke the People's Republic of China, lest it intervene militarily in the Indo-China war. The British were particularly worried by the US secretary of state, John Foster Dulles. He still seemed to be searching for a military solution, so that they wondered whether the nuclear option really had been put aside. The problem from their point of view was that the French had lost their territory and been defeated, but this still did not justify risking a Third World War or becoming bogged down in another Asian land war.

It was the United States that saw little to gain from a settlement, because Ho in effect had won. And as far as the risk of a general war in Asia was concerned, some policy-makers reasoned that China would never again be as weak as it was then. According to this argument, it was doubtful whether the PRC would respond if the US intervened directly in Vietnam. There was no time like the present to challenge the communists. The main problem at Geneva, though, was that the West had little bargaining power because of Dien Bien Phu. Consequently the Americans refused to agree to anything.

Nevertheless, two sets of documents were presented to the Geneva Conference on 20–21 July. The first consisted of armistice agreements and declarations concerning Vietnam, Cambodia and Laos, though the terms of the Vietnamese settlement were obviously the most important. The 'Agreement on the Cessation of Hostilities in Vietnam' declared a cease-fire and also proscribed foreign military operations in the area. In addition it temporarily divided the country in half, 'pending the general elections which will bring about the unification of Vietnam'. French troops were to withdraw from the north, while the Vietminh agreed to withdraw from the south, with a demilitarized zone in-between. The

Vietminh agreed, even though they controlled about two-thirds of the country, except for major cities in the south. Although victorious, Ho's forces were exhausted, so Hanoi was prepared to compromise and give up territory. The Vietnamese were also under pressure from the PRC and the USSR to settle with the West. But the most important reason for agreeing to the terms of the armistice was that Ho expected to win any election, so that eventually all of Vietnam would be reunited under his rule. Only the relevant belligerent powers signed the armistice agreements.

The second document was the 'Final Declaration'. It was intended to sum up the understanding of the other participants at the conference. The Declaration confirmed the armistice terms for all three parts of Indo-China. In the case of Vietnam it observed that 'general elections shall be held in July 1956'. It also specified that representatives from each side would consult about the arrangements, beginning in July 1955. Neither the armistice nor the Final Declaration assumed two Vietnams, north and south, but treated the country as a unity. Moreover, France was to administer the south during the truce, not its puppet government at Saigon. The Vietminh were not pleased that the ultimate settlement was to be delayed two years, but the prospect of elections meant they could accept the agreement. After all, Ho was the best known nationalist leader in Vietnam and head of the only government not tainted by collaboration with the French. He would do well in any poll. Indeed, Eisenhower and Dulles believed that even in a fair contest Ho would probably win.

The problem for the Vietminh was that at the end of the conference none of the participants signed the Final Declaration, mainly because of American opposition. Washington was adamant, and without its support the Declaration had little value. The Americans believed that signing might imply diplomatic recognition for Beijing and Hanoi. It would also commit them to support elections. The effect of this might well be to lose Vietnam for the West. The Final Declaration only confirmed Washington's earlier opinion that the Western Bloc would have little bargaining power at Geneva, and so the United States rejected the political settlement negotiated by the other powers. Instead it issued a separate statement distancing itself from the Final Declaration while pledging to seek 'unity through free elections supervised by the United Nations'. The US also asserted 'its traditional position that peoples are entitled to determine their own future and that it will not join in an arrangement which would hinder this'. The meaning of the American statement was that the US reserved to itself the right to decide whether the 1956 election would be fair, and (as it turned out) whether it should take place at all.*

It was clear that the Americans were opposed to a settlement. Even so, Ho observed the terms of the armistice. After all, the armistice agreement made explicit reference to elections, and France was the relevant power in Vietnam, not the United States. Surely the French would accept elections as part of the plan for extricating themselves from Indo-China. What the Vietminh leader did not anticipate, however, was that the French would withdraw before the elections. This left the Saigon government as the sole authority in the south, but, like the United States, it had not agreed to anything at Geneva. Saigon had signed neither the armistice nor the Final Declaration. Moreover, during the Geneva Conference Bao Dai (then in France) turned the Vietnamese government over to Ngo Dinh Diem. Diem soon became the hope of the Americans, and by the end of 1954 they had redirected their programme of aid to the Saigon government. But Diem had every interest in preventing elections. He could hardly expect to win, as Ho was far better known and had a popular base of support. In due course, therefore, Diem came out against holding a vote, and the Americans supported him. The US announced its decision in June 1955. The Americans argued that any elections held in the north would not be fair to Diem, though, if South Korean precedents held, Ho could not expect a fair shake in the south either. The US had thus found a surrogate for the French, but the outcome was the failure of the Geneva settlement and a gradual renewal of the war. A North Vietnam and a South Vietnam emerged largely as the result of the American refusal to accept the French defeat in 1954. While there was a period of relative calm in the late 1950s as each side regrouped, the world had not heard the last of the Vietnam War.

SEATO

The United States and its allies also developed a co-ordinated approach to the South-East Asian region generally. This took the form of the

---

* The armistice agreements, the Final Declaration and the statement of American policy may be found in US, Department of State, *American Foreign Policy, 1950–1955: Basic Documents* (Washington, DC: 1957), I, 750–88.

South-East Asia Treaty Organization (SEATO), agreed to at Manila in September 1954. SEATO was intended to be a mutual defence pact for the area similar to NATO for the North Atlantic countries. In the event of aggression the signatories would aid each other, though whether any specific country went to war would depend on its own constitutional processes; joint action was not automatic. Vietnam, Laos and Cambodia were not invited to become members, because the armistice at Geneva prohibited further foreign military involvement in Indo-China, but SEATO extended its protection to them in a special protocol. This violated the spirit of the Indo-China armistice, but so did US aid to Saigon. That SEATO was really a Western scheme to preserve the *status quo* in South-East Asia and thus protect Western interests, however, was evident from its original membership. There were only three Asian powers: the Philippines, Pakistan and Thailand. The rest were the United States, Britain, France and the English-speaking South Pacific countries of Australia and New Zealand. While SEATO never developed into an Asian equivalent of NATO, in 1954 its formation was important as a sign of how the United States saw the future. The Americans were not going to abandon their interests in the Far East. As it turned out, neither were the Soviets. And while North Korea and North Vietnam continued to require Russian aid and diplomatic support, China was the great windfall for the Eastern Bloc.

THE PEOPLE'S REPUBLIC OF CHINA

The problem for the Soviet Union was that China had the potential to become a great power, and thus would be difficult to control. The Chinese had won the civil war on their own, and though after 1949 the PRC needed economic and military assistance from the USSR, Beijing was unwilling to accept Soviet political domination. Accordingly, at no time was the Russian presence in China equivalent to that of the Americans in South Korea or the French in Vietnam or even Laos and Cambodia. The Russians never controlled China's government or economy. Moreover, within a decade the internal dynamics of Chinese political life were to have a devastating impact on the unity of the Eastern Bloc, and led to a virtually complete break between the USSR and the PRC.

Although the communists faced a monumental task in constructing a new order in China, controlling rural base areas during the civil war had given them considerable experience in governing. Large parts of the country had come under their rule well before 1949. Moreover, they administered these territories with the same sense of pragmatism as had guided their relations with the Guomindang, and this too worked to their advantage. Even in areas under exclusive Chinese Communist Party control the strategy after 1937 was to build a united front, called the 'New Democracy', of all those willing to co-operate with the emerging regime, regardless of their class interests or political past. This was done even though it meant postponing some of the more radical goals of the CCP. For example, land reform (redistributing the property of the rich to the poor) would have been very popular with the dispossessed masses, but it also would have disrupted the economy and inspired resistance among the gentry and the so-called 'rich' and 'middle' peasantry at a time when the CCP could ill afford such distractions. Until the late 1940s, therefore, land reform was instituted only on a very limited scale. Party policy varied from one place to another, and depended on local conditions, i.e. on the degree of mass support for the communists and the strength of the opposition. Even as victory neared, however, the CCP remained committed to the united front, on the grounds that the help of all Chinese would be needed in the task of reconstruction. It happened that in many instances the local population took things into their own hands and seized the land of their enemies. Vigilantes took reprisals, sometimes with the encouragement of CCP cadres, but the official strategy was still to move cautiously and to prepare the way for change by propaganda, persuasion and peer pressure.

On the international front the Chinese had an important advantage in that they were not completely isolated, as the Bolsheviks had been in 1917. The Soviet Union accorded diplomatic recognition on 2 October 1949, and the other nations of Eastern Europe followed suit within two months. Many Western countries did likewise, pressure from the United States notwithstanding. Accordingly, by 1968, a total of fifty-one countries recognized the People's Republic, although sixty-five others still supported the Nationalists on Taiwan. The USSR, of course, was the only significant source of material support from the outside world. Whatever the Soviets' disagreements about the correct strategy for the civil war, there was no doubt that the USSR would provide aid and protection for the PRC. And while diplomatic recognition by selected Western powers was important, Russian support assured that countries such as the United States would be circumspect about intervening on behalf of counter-revolutionaries, as had happened in the Soviet Union earlier.

Yet there was much to be done: the country had to be made secure against both internal and external subversion; a formal system of government had to be devised; and the greatest problem of all, China's economic backwardness, had to be solved. The first job of the new rulers, however, was to clear out the last remnants of organized Guomindang resistance on the mainland. On 1 October 1949 Nationalist armies and their warlord allies still operated inside China proper, mainly in the west and south. The last of these were defeated when Xinjiang province fell in March 1950. The large island of Hainan was taken the next month, and by autumn Tibet was conquered. In 1951 the latter was officially incorporated into the PRC, though resistance to Chinese rule remained a live issue for decades to come. Because Tibet had been part of China before the 1911–12 revolution, however, the communists as well as the Nationalists regarded it as rightfully theirs. The Chinese also had claims against the Soviets over territories taken by the Czars and dating from the seventeenth century, but obviously these would have to wait for the time being. As tensions developed between the USSR and the PRC later, however, the Chinese would threaten force over the territorial question. A major military confrontation would take place along the Ussuri River in 1969. But this was in the future. In the early days of the People's Republic a more urgent strategic question was the status of Taiwan. Evidence exists to suggest that the PRC was planning an invasion, perhaps for the summer of 1950, but the outbreak of war in Korea precluded this. As we have noted, the Americans moved the Seventh Fleet to the Straits of Taiwan and extended military aid to Chiang Kai-shek, making the Nationalist regime a *de facto* protectorate of the United States.

It thus should have been no surprise that the PRC remained under army rule until 1954. The country was divided into six military districts, and the Red Army took charge of civil administration. In the meantime the foundation for civilian rule was established on the basis of what Mao described as a 'people's democratic dictatorship'. This harked back to the New Democracy of earlier days. In other words, a socialist state was not declared immediately, but instead the CCP instituted a provisional government of national unity. This was based on a coalition of four classes: the poor peasantry; the urban workers or proletariat; the petty bourgeoisie, or small shopowners and self-employed craftsmen; and the 'national' bourgeoisie, i.e. those businessmen who were willing to co-operate with the new regime. The last was a particularly important group, as it had experience in managing factories, banks, trading companies and generally all the types of enterprises to be found in the most modern sector of the economy. The term 'national' was applied to entrepreneurs who had broken their ties to the Guomindang and to foreign capital, and who had not fled the country. Their co-operation would be needed after 1949, and the hope was that they would remain and contribute their wealth and expertise to China's economic reconstruction.

Of course, the wealthiest members of the business class, described by Mao as the 'bureaucratic' bourgeoisie because of their links to the Nationalist government and their ability to mobilize public power on behalf of their private interests, had already departed for Taiwan, Hong Kong or the United States. In fact the principal financial patrons of the Guomindang, the Soong and Kung families, absconded with a goodly portion of the Nationalist treasury and took up residence in the USA, so the communists nationalized their properties and those of others who fled, and thereby came into possession of some of the most important and most technologically advanced enterprises in the country. Yet the new regime did not immediately take over the enterprises of those businessmen who remained behind. There was no mistaking the ultimate goal of the new rulers, but they were prepared to make temporary concessions to the private sector. It was more clearly in the interest of the other members of Mao's class alliance to support the new regime, as traditionally they were the most oppressed members of Chinese society and had much to gain by supporting the CCP. But a pragmatic approach characterized Mao's policies in the early years of the PRC, despite his reputation in the West as a fanatic.

The structure of the new government thus reflected the coalition strategy. Besides the CCP about a dozen non-communist political parties were invited to participate in the People's Political Consultative Conference, which met in Beijing in September 1949. It was this body which approved a new structure of government and appointed Mao as chairman of the Republic or head of state. It was in effect a constitutional convention, and promulgated an Organic Law to govern the country until the adoption of a formal constitution and the establishment of the National People's Congress in 1954. In the meantime the Government Administrative Council (later called the State Council) became the nation's executive branch. It immediately began to build the bureaucratic agencies needed to take over from the Red Army, and it undertook the job of reconstruction. The army continued its administrative duties, however, during 1949–54. Non-communists were given eleven of the twenty-four ministries in the government, and three of six vice-chairmanships set up to assist Mao. Much of this was tokenism, of course, and the communists remained firmly in control, but it also reflected a desire to unify the country after the long civil war. After all, the CCP had won, and did not have to make any concessions. That it did so was significant.

What provided the link between civil and military administration was the Chinese Communist Party. Important state and army positions were held mainly by CCP members; thus Mao was head of the party as well as the state, and the same pattern was duplicated throughout the political system. In 1949 the CCP was run by a central committee of forty-four members, an inner group of fourteen called the Politburo (or Political Bureau) and at the very centre a Politburo Standing Committee of five headed by Mao. In brief, the party became the actual centre of state power.

The authority of the communists, of course, rested on their victory in the civil war and on their broad base of popular support. But not everyone had sided with them. While the new leaders of China were prepared to make temporary concessions to those who would accept the outcome of the civil war and acknowledge the right of the CCP to rule, the threat of internal subversion remained. Those who did not submit paid the price, and the result was a reign of terror, mainly in the period from 1949 to 1952. Given that most of the bureaucratic bourgeoisie had fled, it was the gentry in the countryside who became the main object of attention. A variety of security agencies were established in the government, the army and the party. Mass meetings were called to sentence the more prominent subversives to death or prison, while others were handled by the normal judicial agencies or the secret police. Action against counter-revolutionaries had taken place before as well as after 1949, and seemed to be the unavoidable consequence of civil war and revolution, but the government gave official sanction to such events in its decree of 21 February 1951 entitled 'Regulations Regarding the Punishment of Counter-Revolutionaries'. Many people also lost their lives when new village leaders took the law into their own hands, and settled old scores against the gentry and rich peasants. Indeed, much of the violence was associated with a new programme of land reform inaugurated in 1950, so that many instances of mass action were influenced by material gain as well as the fear of subversion. It has been estimated that perhaps two million people lost their lives as the result of state-sanctioned and vigilante activity in the first three years of communist rule. Thereafter the terror subsided.

What seemed to have influenced the severity of the repression was the outbreak of the Korean War. While violence had occurred before then, it did not equal what was to follow. The American role in Korea meant that the most powerful nation in the world was fighting on the very borders of the People's Republic, and doing so less than a year after the establishment of the new regime. To the communists US intervention in China itself seemed a real possibility. The American decision to extend aid to the French in Indo-China and to Chiang Kai-shek on Taiwan seemed to confirm the point, as did the presence of the US Seventh Fleet in the Straits of Taiwan. The Americans permitted Guomindang agents and commandos to slip across the Straits and land on the China coast. In the United States the pro-Nationalist 'China Lobby' called for 'unleashing' Chiang to attack the mainland. All this made Beijing very sensitive to the threat of counter-revolution at home. At the same time it made the opponents of the regime more recalcitrant, in the expectation that Korea might lead to a US intervention in China and possibly a Guomindang restoration. Beijing thus stepped up its hunt for subversives. And because it regarded the gentry as a bastion of reaction, it also speeded up its programme of land reform – hence the reign of terror.

Such events were hardly unknown in the annals of world history. Indeed, what happened in the People's Republic after 1949 recalled the White Terror launched by Chiang Kai-shek against the communists in the late 1920s. Moralizing about the rights or wrongs of these developments was beside the point, because the historical situation did not offer a choice between terror and non-violence. The only question was whether reprisals would be taken by victorious revolutionaries or victorious counter-revolutionaries. And given the regime's fear of an imminent American attack, the events of 1949–52 become even more understandable. This is in no way to excuse what happened, just as Chiang's repression on Taiwan could not be dismissed. In both cases the gap between rhetoric and reality, between promises of a peaceful and prosperous order and the fact of repression, was glaring enough. Westerners tended to condemn the communists and overlook the Nationalists' equally chequered record, but such judgements were coloured more by Western political preferences than historical perspective. Considering the fundamental economic and social changes the CCP proposed to introduce, it was remarkable that the period of revolutionary disorder did not last longer.

Reconstruction

China's economic problems also imposed severe constraints on the new regime. Not only did the economy have to be rebuilt after a generation of civil war, modern technology had to be introduced in both city and country. The immediate need was simply to increase productivity. Without this the CCP would not be able to resolve the age-old problems of poverty and inequality, and would probably be no more secure in power than its predecessors. Productivity had to rise before the promises of socialism could be honoured, as the latter depended on achieving a level of output such as to make a better life available to all rather than only the few. The strategy to accomplish this was twofold: 'national capitalism' in the urban sector and land reform in the countryside. Both were preparatory to the introduction of the First Five Year Plan (FFYP) in 1953 and the official beginning of a socialist phase.

National capitalism directly reflected Mao's emphasis on the need for unity and for mobilizing the national bourgeoisie on behalf of the new China. Thus the early urban economy was a mix of privately owned and state-owned enterprises. The government sector was created mainly out of the assets of the bureaucratic bourgeoisie and the holdings of foreigners, which were confiscated by the state. But there was no interference with the small shopkeepers or with independent handicraft manufacturers, of which there were over a million. Most importantly, the national bourgeoisie was allowed to keep its industrial and commercial establishments, i.e. the factories and other businesses which operated much as any capitalist enterprise in the West. In fact this sector grew. During the first four years of the new regime the number of private industrial enterprises rose from about 120,000 to 150,000. The number of employees in such firms increased from 1.6 million to over 2.2 million. In all, the private sector produced well more than one-third of the country's industrial output during this period. Private enterprise was of course highly regulated. The state, trade unions and local workers' councils all infringed on management prerogatives, and the government's power to allocate supplies and raw materials gave it the ultimate control of industry. Yet owners were allowed to keep their profits, and this enabled the government to win their co-operation in mobilizing the country's resources and labour power.

The government was candid that its ultimate goal was to take over ownership of the private sector, and that the national capitalist phase was temporary. It culminated in 1952–3. Thereafter, with the introduction of the First Five Year Plan, the state began to nationalize all private businesses of any significance. In many cases it proceeded by temporarily reorganizing them into jointly owned enterprises, with the participation of both the government and the national bourgeoisie. The state assumed first a majority interest and later complete control, though frequently former owners were left in place as salaried employees to manage the firm. They were also paid dividends of 5 per cent on their remaining shares. For all practical purposes the process of taking over the assets of the national bourgeoisie was complete by 1956. It has been estimated, however, that about 250,000 former owners were still receiving dividends in the mid 1960s. The petty bourgeoisie was unaffected by all this, because the government expected that its small shops and its hand methods of production would soon disappear anyway. Presumably, the large state-owned manufacturing and distributing companies would simply out-compete the shop and handicraft sector.

The Agrarian Reform Law, proclaimed in June 1950, governed developments in the countryside. There the goal was not only to revive production but to demobilize the gentry as a political force. Thus, as we have noted, the gentry became the focus of the post-1949 reign of terror. The political as distinct from economic rationale behind land reform was to break up the gentry, and also the rich peasantry, as the classes most likely to support subversive activity. After all, these people owned the most land, and hardly wished to surrender their privileged position in Chinese society. Yet, unless they were forced to do so, the CCP could not fulfil its promise to give land to the landless. Sooner or later the regime would have to move against the gentry and the rich peasants, and once victory over the Guomindang had been achieved, the time had come to act.

In strictly economic terms the hope was that a nation of small property-owners would be more productive than the 70 per cent of the rural population who formerly made up the poor peasantry. The latter consisted of landless labourers, tenant farmers and peasant-owners whose holdings were so small that they did not provide a living. Above them were the middle peasants, about 20 per cent of the people in the countryside. These owned just enough land to earn a living without having to seek additional employment. They were therefore regarded as a somewhat privileged group by Chinese standards. Then came the rich peasants, about 6 per cent. Unlike the gentry at the very pinnacle, they worked their own land but also had enough to rent out and to hire to other people. The real rural elite, however, was the gentry. This was essentially a landlord class, though often with investments in small industrial or commercial enterprises. By responding to the needs of the majority of the rural population the CCP hoped to remove its political opponents and to provide the poor peasantry with the incentive to produce more. Presumably land reform would accomplish both objectives, though, as with national capitalism, the communists were candid in describing this as a transitional stage. They saw the creation of large collective farms someday as the best way to raise productivity.

In the meantime the government took control of about 117 million acres of arable land, which was distributed to approximately 300 million peasants. The average holding was probably about one-third of an acre, though the actual size of individual properties varied considerably from region to region. Moreover, they varied according to a person's past as a landlord or as a rich, middle or poor peasant. Land reform did not result in perfect equality by any means. Also, it created many small economic units whose owners were still too poor to afford farm machinery, chemical fertilizers or other types of modern agricultural technology. Productivity did rise slightly with land reform, but the regime probably gained more in political than economic terms.

Thus, in contrast to what happened in the cities, a fundamental social change occurred immediately after 1949 in the countryside. But this change was not specifically socialist in nature. The 1950 Agrarian Reform Law made most peasants into private landowners, and therefore constituted a bourgeois or capitalist stage of development. In this respect land reform was comparable to national capitalism in the urban areas, in that the regime regarded it as only a half-way house to public ownership.

The Transition to Socialism
While national capitalism and land reform had restored productivity to the best levels of the civil war period by 1952, the Beijing government could not afford to pause. Reconstruction was not the same as development, and while it might prepare the way for socialism, the regime believed that the introduction of the latter would result in even more impressive gains. State ownership would facilitate the consolidation of small businesses and farms into larger and more efficient units. This would create enterprises large enough to afford investment in modern technology. It would also achieve economies of scale, i.e. the savings that result from integrating several formerly separate steps in the production process. Accordingly, in 1953 the People's Republic inaugurated its

First Five Year Plan, and announced the beginning of the transition to socialism.

Before looking at the events of the next few years, however, it is important to appreciate that China under Mao was not the same as Russia under Stalin. Despite the apparent domination of one man, at least as perceived in the West, the CCP had a core of capable leaders with varying political and economic views. Two main groups, known as the 'Maoists' and the 'modernizers', eventually emerged. The latter were led by Liu Shaoqi and Deng Xiaoping. Yet in the 1950s and even the 1960s neither side seemed strong enough to purge the other completely. Each faction waxed or waned as different members of the top state and party organs changed sides in response to the success or failure of current policy. Moreover, the factions were only just emerging in the 1950s, and so were quite unstable. Hence, there was a continuing struggle for control of the state and party, and the balance of power was often close. In the early years of the People's Republic, Westerners failed to realize this and assumed that Mao was completely in charge, but in time the reality became clearer.

The First Five Year Plan
The issue that separated the two factions was the expansion of the central planning agencies associated with the First Five Year Plan. The FFYP accelerated the country's development and maximized the growth of a largely urban-based technical and managerial elite. This was because the FFYP gave priority to industrialization over agricultural development. While Mao accepted the need for rapid economic growth and initially supported the Five Year Plan, he soon became more critical and attacked its emphasis on industrial development at the expense of rural development. The reason for this was simple. The principal base of Mao's support was to be found in the countryside. It was there that the civil war had been fought and won, and it was there that Mao had built a loyal following among officials of the government, the army and the party. But the bureaucrats and planners associated with the urban industrialization programmes of the FFYP and so favoured by Liu and Deng were a distinct group, and thus a competing centre of power. As they increased in strength and took over more and more policy-making functions, they became a threat to Mao's authority. By seeking to redirect the initial emphasis of the FFYP from urban to rural development, the Maoist group hoped to protect its base of support and hence its influence in the government.

From Mao's point of view the First Five Year Plan raised another problem as well. This was the degree of Soviet influence in China. In a series of aid agreements signed in 1950, 1953, 1954 and 1956 the USSR provided China with technical assistance and limited financial help. Russian money accounted for only 3 per cent of total state investment under the FFYP, but it was Soviet technology which the PRC valued most. The Russians agreed to assist in the construction of 156 major industrial projects. These were to serve as the core of modern industry in China, and throughout the 1950s thousands of Soviet and East European scientists and engineers served in the PRC. The problem was that the Soviet model of development had political implications for the emerging Maoist faction. Of the total capital invested under the FFYP almost 90 per cent went to heavy industry and associated transport, energy and urban infrastructures, while less than 10 per cent went to agriculture.

The Russians argued that such a course of development was necessary to build a strong defence industry in China, thereby protecting the new regime against a possible American intervention. But they also assumed from their own experience that emphasizing heavy industry would make the regime more secure at home by expanding the size of the urban proletariat. In the 1920s and 1930s Stalin had encountered massive opposition from the Russian peasantry, and so Soviet advisers in China saw the development of the urban sector as a counterbalance to rural resistance. After all, land reform had created a class of small capitalist property-holders in the countryside, and the Russians interpreted this as an obstacle to eventual collectivization. They failed to credit Mao's view that Chinese conditions were different, and that in the case of the PRC the peasantry was the most revolutionary class. In any event, the Soviets controlled the technology that the Chinese needed, and so the Russian approach had to be considered.

Yet, despite the priorities of the FFYP and the preferences of the USSR, the collectivization of agriculture could not be completely neglected. After all, productivity in the farm sector barely kept pace with the increase in population, and food shortages were common. The small peasant holdings cultivated by traditional methods of farming were simply not productive enough. They would have to be consolidated into larger, more efficient units. The government consequently decided to press ahead with collectivization sooner than originally planned, though the official state policy was to proceed cautiously and by stages. First, mutual-aid teams of six or more households were encouraged to help each other work their individual farms, though each retained title to its own land and kept all the profits therefrom. In due course lower-stage co-operatives involving perhaps as many as thirty families were formed. Their holdings were farmed collectively, but each household still owned its particular plot of land. The third and final step was the higher-stage co-operative, ranging in size from 100 to 300 households. These were similar to Russian collective farms. It was at this point that all holdings were pooled and the private ownership of land came to an end, except that small private plots were retained for family consumption or for producing something extra for sale.

Once begun, however, co-operativization moved ahead much more quickly than anyone had thought possible. This played into Mao's hands, and placed him in a better position to speak out against his political opponents. Co-operativization seemed to have the support of most of the countryside. There was little violence associated with the change, in marked contrast to the introduction of land reform earlier. By the autumn of 1956 possibly 90 per cent of the rural population had been organized into 485,000 higher-stage co-operatives or collective farms. Those remaining were persuaded or pressured into joining collectives by early 1957.

It turned out that the speed and success of the collectivization campaign was the result of three factors. First, the earlier programmes of land reform had effectively demobilized the classes most opposed to change. Second, although land reform had created a new class of small owners, this group had not had time to coalesce into a vested interest capable of resisting the state. Third, because land reform had not in itself ended rural poverty, this new class was still open to change. It was therefore possible for CCP organizers or cadres to persuade many peasant landowners that they would be better off by pooling their resources with those of others in an effort to create larger and more efficient agricultural enterprises.

The Hundred Flowers

The success of collectivization confirmed Mao's confidence in the peasant masses as his most loyal supporters, and led him to conclude that there was no time like the present to move against the advocates of Soviet-style development. He denounced them as an incipient capitalist class more concerned with personal advancement than the good of society as a whole. They were at odds, he said, with the aspirations of the peasantry, most of whom gained by the levelling trends developing in the countryside. Of course, dismantling some of the central planning agencies of the FFYP would not turn more power over to the people at large but to the local officialdom. On the whole, the latter could be counted upon to support Mao in any showdown with the faction forming around Liu Shaoqi. Over the next several years the political debate focused on the problem of bureaucracy as such, but in fact the real struggle was over who would control the bureaucracy, the Maoists or Liu and the modernizers. Indeed, as a practical matter the former were as much a bureaucratic elite as the latter.

Mao's initial move was to launch what became known as the Hundred Flowers campaign in 1956. The name came from an ancient Confucian saying, 'Let a hundred flowers blossom, let a hundred schools of thought contend.'* We should not be misled, however, by the formal language. Such rhetoric had a clear political purpose. Mao's goal was to attack an opposing faction in the CCP which threatened to crowd him out of power. He attempted this by calling upon the country's intelligentsia (i.e. the academic and professional community) to evaluate the FFYP, and particularly the problem of elitism, in the expectation that criticism would discredit his enemies. Given the strength of his opponents in the party and the government, however, the campaign did not really gain momentum until the spring of 1957. Then the torrent of criticism, much of it against communism *per se*, was such that even Mao became alarmed. Accordingly he brought the campaign to a quick and ignominious end.

Mao turned on the critics. He had drawn them out in the first place as part of his political strategy, but by the summer was attacking them as subversives. In the West this was usually interpreted as a betrayal of the worst kind, yet it was more complicated than this. Intellectual freedom had never been a well-established tradition in China. When Mao called for criticism, he was not identifying with a Western ideal (indeed, in the West itself practice did not always match theory). Perhaps this was a flaw in his view of the world, but it certainly reflected Chinese conditions. His goal was to purify the party and the state, and he therefore expected critics to stay within the boundaries of the CCP's official ideology. His opponents most likely shared this view, though they might interpret party ideology differently. In any event, the campaign had come up with enough evidence to discredit many of Mao's opponents. As a result perhaps a million party members were punished. Penalties ranged from reprimand to probation to expulsion from the CCP.

* Cited in Maurice Meisner, *Mao's China and After: A History of the People's Republic* (London: 1986), 177.

The Great Leap Forward

The rising fortunes of the Maoists resulted in the quiet abandonment of the Second Five Year Plan and the announcement of the Great Leap Forward (GLF) in 1958. The Great Leap was not a departure from the goal of industrialization, but a scheme to achieve the simultaneous development of both country and city, and at an accelerated pace. China thus revised the Soviet model in a fundamental way, with the result that the Russians feared the PRC was heading for trouble. They began to wonder whether it was worth committing money and technical assistance to a regime which they increasingly believed was bent on self-destruction. They also had an interest in keeping China dependent on Soviet technology, and thereby amenable to Russian influence. But the Maoists believed that abandoning the Second Five Year Plan was the best way to preserve their power inside China itself, and acted accordingly.

The Great Leap Forward was officially a programme to increase productivity in both country and city while at the same time reducing the importance of the new bureaucrats who had administered the FFYP. Central planning agencies were scaled down in size, and more control was placed in the hands of local officials, particularly Maoists. The institution most identified with the Leap, however, was the commune. While a few urban communes were organized around factories or neighbourhoods, the majority were to be found in the countryside. These carried collectivization to its logical conclusion by consolidating higher-stage co-operatives into units about the size of a township or county. They also established thousands of small industrial enterprises. Given that China was capital-poor but rich in labour, the idea was to develop as much industry as possible in the countryside, i.e. where 80 per cent of the people were.

Yet the commune was not the result of an elaborate blueprint of the type that had guided the FFYP. After all, the origins of the Great Leap Forward were more political than economic. Communes were the work of Maoist cadres in the countryside, and evolved in response to the announcement of the GLF and the decision to give higher priority to rural development. The first experiments with communization began in Henan province in April 1958, and the CCP Central Committee ratified the movement only five months later, on 29 August. In the meantime communes had spread like wildfire. By the end of the year almost all parts of the country were affected. Hundreds of thousands of higher-stage co-operatives were regrouped into 24,000 communes. They ranged in size from 5,000 to 100,000 people, but on average contained about 30,000. They varied considerably in their commitment to communism, with some simply representing a new form of the county and others abolishing all private property. The family unit was not dissolved (despite Western reports to this effect), though common nurseries for children and common mess halls existed in many places. And while experiments in establishing iron and steel foundries on the communes failed, efforts to operate other industries were quite successful in the long run. The object was to take advantage of local resources, and thus commune enterprises in food processing, the manufacture and repair of agricultural implements and light consumer goods, the production of chemical fertilizers, and even small mining and oil refining ventures achieved an excellent record. Communes also undertook public-works projects, such as irrigation systems and hydroelectric installations. In this respect, at least, the Chinese model of development turned out to have considerable relevance for Third World countries, although it was attacked by Soviets and Westerners alike. It was a form of labour-intensive rather than capital-intensive development, and thus addressed the hope of most Third World nations that someday they might break their dependency on foreign investment. After all, investors wanted profits for themselves, and took wealth out of the Third World.

The Restoration of the 'Bureaucrats'

But all was not sweetness and light. Communization seems to have been the result of mass enthusiasm in the countryside, driven by the prospect that large-scale organization and diversification would increase productivity and bring immediate benefits to commune members. Communization, however, also meant a wholesale reorganization of the entire rural economy, and chaos soon resulted. The change was simply too much too fast. Further, some of the worst natural disasters in recent Chinese history plagued the Great Leap after 1958: typhoons, floods, droughts and pestilence. These came at precisely the wrong moment for Mao, and helped make it possible for his opponents to argue that something was wrong with the Leap itself. It hardly needs to be pointed out, of course, that the FFYP planners and bureaucrats were adversely affected by the Leap, so they coalesced against Mao as their putative leader.

The counter-attack began as early as December 1958. The CCP Central Committee met at Wuhan to discuss the first signs of trouble with the GLF. Greater local autonomy was making the co-ordination of the national economy more problematical. Some co-operatives were resisting communization. Local authorities were having a difficult time managing large-scale undertakings. Fiscal accountability was inadequate. Finally, food shortages were developing. While the party united behind the GLF as a matter of form, a slow-down was put into effect. Moreover, Mao's opponents on the Central Committee were strong enough for him to be induced to resign as chairman of the People's Republic. Yet the balance of power apparently was such that Mao still had important allies within the leadership, and he retained his most crucial position as head of the CCP. In April 1959 Liu Shaoqi became Mao's successor as head of state. His right hand man, Deng Xiaoping, had been secretary-general of the Communist Party since the mid-1950s, and was thus able to keep a close watch on the party leader. Though the struggle for power continued to see-saw back and forth, and though the Maoists scored some important victories over the advocates of Soviet-style development later in the year, Mao's faction went into decline until the mid 1960s and the Cultural Revolution (see Chapter 9). In the meantime Liu oversaw a retrenchment reminiscent of the First Five Year Plan, although the system of communes was not dismantled.

The Sino-Soviet Split

The Great Leap Forward had another purpose besides undermining Mao Zedong's political opponents. This was to limit the degree of Soviet influence in China. On this Liu and Mao tended to agree, so that we must take note once again that politics in China were considerably more fluid than in Russia under Stalin. Indeed, Liu's reservations about the GLF emerged mainly after it had run into trouble. And as we have seen, Mao's relations with Stalin during the civil war had been anything but close. All Chinese leaders were wary of becoming too dependent on the Soviets.

Events well before the GLF provided the first occasion for the public expression of differences between the two leading communist powers. In 1956 political turmoil developed in Poland and Hungary, and in the latter case resulted in the intervention of Russian troops (see Chapter 5). All this followed within months the meeting of the Twentieth Congress of the Soviet Communist Party, where the new leader of the USSR, Nikita Khrushchev, had denounced Stalin's rule as oppressive and even criminal (Stalin had died in 1953). But, while the Chinese supported the use of troops in Hungary, they rejected Khrushchev's attack on Stalin. Instead they argued that the difficulties of communism in Eastern

Europe were to be attributed to the problem of Soviet hegemony. The crisis went beyond the crimes of one man, and the Chinese even defended Stalin as a great if sometimes misguided revolutionary leader. In particular they blamed 1956 on the Soviet Union's unwillingness to respect the autonomy of other communist countries and on its brutal exploitation of Eastern Europe after the Second World War. The leaders of the PRC were not about to allow the same thing to happen to them. Yet Sino-Soviet differences remained muted for the time being, as both nations had much to gain by being allies. In 1957 the USSR even agreed to provide the PRC with technical assistance for constructing atomic weapons.

The Great Leap Forward, however, resulted in a renewal of the debate. Sometimes this exchange became rather theoretical, but we should not be misled by the terms of the discourse. As we have seen, choices concerning economic development had political consequences inside China itself, and they also determined the extent to which the PRC would remain dependent on the USSR for aid and protection. The rising ascendancy of the Maoists in 1956–8 meant a decline of Russian influence in China, and so the Russians became increasingly vocal in their criticisms of the GLF. The Chinese answered in kind, and raised a number of other issues as well, mainly in the sphere of foreign relations.

In particular the Chinese feared Khrushchev's efforts to woo the West. The Russian interest was to contain the arms race, because the USSR still lacked the money and resources to keep up with the Americans. An accommodation with the USA would ease the pressure on the Soviet economy. Also, as a country that had lost tens of millions of people in war, Russia's stake in arms control was more than a matter of debating points. In due course Khrushchev's efforts came to naught, but in the meantime the PRC attacked all talk of 'peaceful coexistence'. China had little to gain from a *rapprochement*, however tenuous, between the USA and the USSR – the Chinese continued to regard the Americans as an imminent threat to the survival of the PRC. And in the late 1950s there seemed to be concrete evidence that the Russians were prepared to sacrifice Chinese interests for their own purposes. The USSR provided little diplomatic support for the PRC in times of crisis.

In 1958 the Chinese communists bombarded the islands of Quemoy and Matsu off the Chinese mainland. They were responding to a build-up of Nationalist troops on the islands, but the USSR kept in the background until the Chinese agreed to discuss the issue informally (to avoid the question of diplomatic recognition) with the USA. Then the Russians offered vocal support, but their earlier inaction had already signalled to the Americans that they had no intention of endangering the possibility of peaceful coexistence. Similarly the USSR provided arms aid to India even as it connived to support an uprising in 1959 in Tibet. This was led by the Dalai Lama's supporters in Lhasa (the capital) and by eastern tribesmen. The Dalai Lama, who based his authority on divine right and ruled over a virtually feudal system in central Tibet that involved a form of serfdom, had been allowed to remain in power when the Chinese took over in 1950. But, when the rebellion failed, he fled the country (apparently with CIA help). Guomindang agents had also been active in Tibet. In addition the Chinese had border disputes with India itself, and these broke out into a short war in the Himalayan Mountains in the fall of 1962. The Chinese won, in the sense that they were able to maintain their incursions across borders defined by the British and retained by India after 1947. Meanwhile Russian friendship for India continued.

By the time of the 1962 Himalayan War, however, the most important single event of the Sino-Soviet Split had already taken place. In the summer of 1959 Khrushchev unilaterally cancelled his earlier agreement to supply the PRC with nuclear-weapons technology. Yet there was more to come. By 1960 Chinese attacks on peaceful coexistence became ever more vociferous. By then much of the debate took the form of defending the tiny country of Albania against Soviet hegemony, but the leaders of the communist world were in no doubt about the real dispute. Hence, in July, Khrushchev recalled all Soviet scientists and technicians who were working in the PRC. They even took their blueprints with them, and for all practical purposes the Sino-Soviet break was complete. It seemed that the East was in as much disarray as the West.

5

THE ALLIANCES

In effect the old policy of 'Socialism in One Country' governed the Soviet Union's relations with China. This meant that the national interests of the USSR took precedence over the needs of its allies. Developments in Eastern Europe during the 1950s served only to confirm the point. There the Russians were in a much stronger position to influence events, yet it remained to be seen whether long-term stability could be achieved. Years of Soviet occupation and exploitation had exacerbated the threat of resistance and rebellion, and major crises (some resulting in military intervention or the threat of it) were to erupt in East Germany, Poland, Hungary and Albania. Moreover, the danger from the West, particularly the spectre of a rearmed and resurgent Germany, continued to haunt Soviet strategic thinking, so that for the Russians the worst-case scenario was the possibility of a conjunction between internal and external crises.

It was not only the Soviets, however, who feared the consequences of disunity among their European allies, but the Americans as well, although they never had to resort to armed force to restore discipline. To US policy-makers such methods may have seemed necessary to maintain American influence in the Third World, i.e. in areas on the peripheries of the West's developed centres. But unlike the USSR in Eastern Europe the USA never found itself fighting in the very heartland of the Western Bloc. This did not mean that America's partners accepted its leadership without question. Indeed, some advocates of the Common Market looked forward to the day when Western Europe might emerge as a 'Third Force', independent of both the United States and the Soviet Union and holding the balance of power between them. But this was not very likely in the foreseeable future, and in the meantime several issues created tensions between America and its allies. Chief among these was German rearmament, with France leading the opposition. Europe's stake in the Third World also brought it into conflict with the USA, particularly in the Middle East. In sum, the trend towards European integration and Atlantic unity was offset by centrifugal forces, so that the hope of community remained elusive for the West as well as for the East. It turned out, however, that the communists, not the Western powers, faced the most severe threats from within.

THE SATELLITES AFTER 1945

In Eastern Europe the successive crises of the 1950s were the direct outcome of the political and economic system imposed by the Russians after the Second World War. The particulars varied from country to country, but, in brief, Soviet hegemony led to the nationalization of private enterprise and the establishment of one-party rule, including the installation of national leaders dependent on the USSR to remain in power and therefore subservient to its interests. Further, it meant integrating the economy of Eastern Europe with that of the Soviet Union, so as to offset weaknesses in Russian industry and agriculture. The plan was for each of the satellites to produce what the USSR needed, and to emphasize specialities where each had a comparative advantage, i.e. where it was particularly well-endowed in resources or efficient in production relative to other members of the Eastern Bloc; thus Poland would mine coal and build steel ships, as it excelled in these industries. Yet the goal was not to promote balanced development within each country or even within the bloc as a whole, but to complement the development of the USSR. In the West the nearest equivalent was the relationship between the First World and the Third World, and the Russians had something similar in mind for their allies in Eastern Europe.

Hence, throughout the region, Soviet puppets introduced programmes for accelerating industrialization, particularly in the basic or 'heavy' industries (such as iron and steel) essential for expanding the defence and manufacturing sectors. They also acted to collectivize agriculture, mainly by imposing high taxes on private farmers and fixing the price of produce at low levels. The goal was the same as in the Soviet Union earlier, to force people off the land and into the cities, where they might serve as a labour pool for the new industries. And consolidating many small-holdings into a few large agricultural enterprises would increase efficiency, though as it turned out this worked better in theory than in practice.

All these programmes were modelled on Soviet-style five-year plans, and were administered by a complex of central planning agencies, setting national goals and allocating resources and labour accordingly. Furthermore, the whole system was backed up by an array of social and ideological controls, lest dissenters mobilize the people against the often harsh demands of the regime. The rationale was that post-war reconstruction required sacrifices by all, and that discipline in the short term would mean a better way of life in the long term. Accordingly, independent labour unions were not permitted, and those organized by the state were dominated by communist party members. Government censorship of the press, education, and even cultural and artistic expression completed the circle. In the USSR itself, for example, it was illegal for a citizen to own a private printing press, and 'socialist realism' lauded the virtues of sacrifice and discipline in literature, the cinema and the theatre. Even science was affected, and in the field of genetics Trofim Lysenko touted the possibility of moulding a new Soviet man. Andrei Zhdanov, Stalin's chief ideologue and the organizer of the Cominform, enforced the campaign of conformity until his death in 1948, but it extended into the early 1950s. Further, it was imposed on the rest of Eastern Europe, where the dimension of Russian nationalism was not likely to win very much support.

Yet the system did achieve results. By the end of 1947 many Soviet industries had attained pre-war levels of production, though the performance of the agricultural sector would remain dismal for decades to come. It should be pointed out, however, that the Russian labour force was augmented by about two million German prisoners of war. (France and Britain also put German soldiers to work in industry and agriculture, but only for a short time after the war.) None the less, the comeback by Soviet industry was impressive, even allowing for the unreliability of statistical data from the Eastern Bloc. Moreover, the satellites were not far behind, despite their subservience to Russia. For example, it appears that in Czechoslovakia and East Germany industrial production had doubled pre-war levels by 1955, while in Poland it was possibly four to five times as great. In the 1960s such dramatic rates of growth would slow down, and of course the figures were less impressive if one remembers that Eastern Europe was not highly industrialized before the Second World War. Post-war industrialization started at a very low point, and this places the doubling or even quadrupling of earlier records in a different light. Also, many of the gains were the result of simply adding more labour rather than increasing its efficiency. Augmenting the number of workers produced impressive results in opening mines and developing heavy industry, i.e. in activities where the labour force did not have to be highly educated to perform the tasks demanded of it. But at later stages of economic development the quality rather than the quantity of labour would be more important, and then growth rates would decline.

Perhaps the most important reason for the gains recorded throughout the Eastern Bloc was simply the exploitation of labour. In 1955 real income was only 8 per cent above pre-war levels in Czechoslovakia, and 9 per cent in East Germany, while it was actually down by 20 per cent in Poland. The paradox of Eastern Europe therefore was that workers seemed to suffer even as overall industrial output increased, whereas in the West workers tended to prosper in boom times and suffered most during an economic slowdown or depression. This was because in the East the central planners diverted profits from the consumer and agricultural sectors, so that gains in industry came at the expense of a higher standard of living for the general population. Obviously such sacrifices could not be required indefinitely, especially because there had been terrible losses of life during the Second World War – for example, six million civilians (half of them Jews) in Poland alone.

The industrialization of Eastern Europe also took place in a context of direct Soviet exploitation. In the Russian view this was justified as a form of reparations. East Germany, of course, had been part of the Reich itself, and consequently could expect harsh treatment. But the USSR also believed that reprisals were warranted in the case of Nazi satellites such as Hungary and Bulgaria, and even Romania (though it had not joined in the German invasion of Russia). For the other countries of the region, such as Poland, the Russians justified the unequal trade relations which they dictated as the price of liberation from the Nazis.

Whatever the rationale, the USSR imposed its will through a variety of devices. One of the most important was the mixed company, i.e. an enterprise in which control was shared by the Soviets with the local state. Not surprisingly such arrangements were invariably unfair, because most of the investment funds came from the satellite states and not the USSR – the Russians were better at sharing in the profits than the costs. In addition, these and other businesses were the victims of discriminatory trade relations between the Russians and their presumed comrades in Eastern Europe, whereby the Soviets insisted on the right to make purchases at prices below those prevailing on world markets and sometimes paid less than the cost of production. Poland, for example, was required to sell coal at prices which barely covered the cost of transport, and this at a time when there was a strong demand for its output in

Sweden and Denmark. Similarly the Yugoslavs later claimed to have exported molybdenum to Russia at perhaps one-tenth the cost of production. The satellites had little choice in all this. The Soviets feared Western competition for the trade of Eastern Europe, and so did not allow the satellites to resume their pre-war patterns of trade. Indeed they interpreted American interest in the region as a plot to divert its resources, so that the Communist Bloc might remain underdeveloped relative to the West. While economic need motivated Soviet policy, then, so did the USSR's strategy in the Cold War.

As we have noted, Stalin's plans depended on the existence of pliable national leaders throughout the region. The Red Army, of course, was the ultimate guarantor of East European loyalty. It remained as an occupation force everywhere except Yugoslavia and Albania, until the establishment of the Warsaw Pact in 1955 provided a new legal foundation for stationing Soviet troops in Eastern Europe. Technically the pact was a regional military alliance on the model of the North Atlantic Treaty Organization of 1949. Yet the USSR could hardly afford to resort to military force every time a problem arose, though it was prepared to do so if need be. Instead its principal method for guaranteeing the loyalty of its puppets was the political purge.

Errant leaders paid with their lives, so that executions and mysterious disappearances were an integral feature of what became known as 'Stalinism'. Tito's break with Russia in 1948 marked the resumption of a 1930s-style reign of terror. The very methods which had been deployed so effectively against non-communist political parties between 1945 and 1948 in Eastern Europe were soon turned on suspect communists as well. The victims often included those who had played a role in the anti-Nazi resistance and who thus had popular support in their own countries. In other words, they tended to be nationalists like Tito. The survivors, on the other hand, were Moscow loyalists, and included some who had spent the war years in Russia. Leaders with an independent political base seemed to be most feared by Stalin. Accordingly, as the Yugoslav crisis developed, the heresy hunts began. In Poland the general secretary of the communist party and vice-premier, Wladislaw Gomulka, was placed under arrest, as were a number of cabinet ministers. The foreign minister of Hungary, Laszlo Rajk, was executed, and the minister of the interior, Janos Kadar, was jailed and also tortured. The acting prime minister of Bulgaria, Traichko Kostov, was sentenced to death, and ten communist ministers were purged from the government, as were six members of the party politburo. In Albania the Yugoslav sympathizer Kochi Xoxe was yet another victim. In Czechoslovakia the general secretary of the communist party, Rudolf Slansky, and ten cabinet ministers were given death sentences in 1952 after show trials which were openly anti-Semitic. Anti-Semitism was to be mobilized many times in the future against alleged enemies of the state in Russia and the satellites. The purges affected lesser officials as well, though for them the penalty was less likely to be death. Imprisonment, expulsion from the party or the loss of a government job was the more usual fate, but large numbers of people were affected in one way or another throughout Eastern Europe.

THE END OF THE STALIN ERA

Obviously something had to give, and well before 1953 and the first signs of overt resistance (in East Berlin) some members of the Soviet politburo had come to appreciate the need for change. The death of Stalin on 5 March 1953 gave them their chance. For some time several of their number had argued in favour of a 'new course' – in other words, concessions to raise the standard of living and to win the minds and hearts of people throughout the Communist Bloc. Yet even after 1953 Soviet policy vacillated between reform and retrenchment. The failure to define a coherent programme of action in the face of impending rebellion in the satellite states was the result of a leadership crisis inside the USSR itself, as a struggle for power developed among Stalin's heirs.

The problem, though, went much deeper than simply the question of leadership. More to the point, none of the reforms which even the moderates were prepared to concede went so far as to alter the undemocratic character of the East European order, and so the legitimacy of communist rule was still in question. The governments of the region were to remain under the control of a communist ruling elite whose authority was based on its monopoly of state power and whose interests were not always compatible with those of the people at large. Nor did the prospect of change imply an end to Soviet domination. The USSR was not going to allow any of the satellites to jeopardize the unity and security of the Communist Bloc *vis-à-vis* the West, as Tito had done. Accordingly, while the 1950s were a time of fitful reform throughout Eastern Europe, the potential for trouble by no means disappeared.

Furthermore, it was hardly in the interest of every Eastern Bloc politician to support change. Certainly, hard-line Stalinists in both the USSR and the satellites were not about to accept the new course without a fight. Change would threaten their tenure in office, and there would possibly be reprisals for the purges of the past. More moderate leaders therefore faced dogged opposition from many of their colleagues at the very top of the communist hierarchy. There were also reservations among the rank-and-file bureaucrats. These numbered in the millions, and they too had a vested interest in the *status quo*. For them the material gains of government jobs were perhaps the main consideration, and they tended to resist changes which might imperil their privileges. It was not so much that they resorted to open resistance or insubordination but that they simply failed to respond. Inertia was to undo many a reform ordered from the top, i.e. when the moderates were in the ascendancy. For the ordinary communist functionary much was at stake. Not only did the administrative and managerial officialdom enjoy higher salaries than the average working person, its members had access to perquisites of many kinds (e.g. better housing and special shops which stocked a wider variety of goods, including imports, than were available to the general population). Most importantly, they were able to obtain the best educational opportunities for their offspring. This meant their children stood a better chance of becoming officials themselves, thus placing the bureaucracy in a position to perpetuate itself as a class.

After 1945, therefore, a new ruling class took form in Eastern Europe, just as had happened in Russia earlier. Such an outcome was inherent in any system where the state owned and managed the major enterprises. But the whole process was accelerated in the satellites because many pre-war officials joined the communist party when the Nazis were defeated, hoping to refurbish their past and protect themselves against reprisals and material deprivation. The arrest and trial of Nazi sympathizers in the East was much less thorough than in Western Europe, as the communists desperately needed the old officialdom to run the post-war state. Obviously these people were hardly committed revolutionaries. They simply speeded up the process whereby the communist party became a new interest group in Eastern European society.

To the Russians and the national communist leaders whom they kept in power the opportunism of many new communist party members was not entirely a disadvantage. It meant that many of the new people could be counted upon to identify with the party rather than the people, in the realization that their jobs and personal safety depended upon obedience to the organization. This reduced the risk of opposition from within the party and the state, a matter of no little importance. The bureaucracy would be asked to make heavy demands on the population, demands which would be unpopular. Hence the need was for discipline, not ideological purity.

Some sense of the size of this group can be gleaned from statistics on the distribution of income. Information is not available for the USSR, but experts at the World Bank have reconstructed data for most of the countries of Eastern Europe, based on about twenty years of communist hegemony (i.e. on figures mainly for the middle and late 1960s). Such data must be used with caution, because income is defined differently from country to country. Further, the statistics may exaggerate the degree of inequality, in that high levels of social services and benefits (for example, free medical care, free university education for those who qualify, subsidized housing and subsidized food prices) are available throughout the Eastern Bloc. But Montek Ahluwalia suggests the following profile. It appears that in Poland the poorest quintile (or lowest one-fifth) of the population received 9.8 per cent of all income, whereas the richest quintile (the top one-fifth of income recipients) received 36 per cent. The comparable poles for Bulgaria were 9.8 and 35 per cent; for Czechoslovakia, 12 and 31 per cent; for Hungary, 8.5 and 33.5 per cent; and for Yugoslavia 6.5 and 41.5 per cent. In short, there was a group at the top, and it was materially better off than other classes. In absolute terms its wealth did not compare with that of the richest classes in the West, but it was a privileged elite.*

The rank-and-file bureaucracy, however, was more than simply a centre of privilege. It also constituted a brake on productivity, and so reduced the capacity of the system to raise the standard of living over the long term. It thus severely constrained the possibility of containing popular discontent and heading off resistance to communist rule. For example, rather than risk being caught short and unable to fulfil their production quotas, managers tended to argue for lower targets than they were sometimes capable of achieving. The result was a serious under-utilization of plant and equipment. Output did rise, and impressively so, but the potential gain was probably higher than actually realized. In addition the bureaucrats' tendency to protect themselves led to considerable waste. Managers requested more inputs (raw materials, energy, components, labour) than they really needed, and proceeded to hoard any extra they did receive. Similarly they preferred to stick to

* Montek Ahluwalia, 'Inequality, Poverty and Development', *Journal of Development Economics*, 3 (1976), 307–42.

tried-and-true ways rather than attempt innovation. After all, introducing new methods involved a degree of risk, and disturbed existing bureaucratic routines. The result was that outmoded designs and techniques would remain in use long after they had been abandoned in the West. And given that rising output was the test of success under the quota system, quantity was too often placed ahead of quality. Each country's economic plan always demanded more and more, whether or not more meant better. Of course, party leaders throughout the region took advantage of their control of the media to identify the interests of the people with those of the state and its managers, but time soon showed the magnitude of their failure.

THE SUCCESSION

Perhaps the most remarkable feature of Eastern European history after 1945 was that mass resistance did not break out any sooner than it did. With the demise of Stalin, however, this was about to change. By the early summer of 1953 demonstrations and strikes were occurring throughout the region. Moreover, they coincided with a succession crisis inside the Kremlin itself.

Shortly after Stalin's death a system of collective leadership was announced in Moscow. This, of course, simply masked the beginnings of a power struggle that would last several years. In the West Georgi Malenkov was generally regarded as the heir apparent. Only fifty-one, he immediately took Stalin's place, becoming head of the Council of Ministers (in effect, the prime minister) and general secretary of the communist party. In other words, he assumed the two most important political positions in the country, the top government post and the top party post. The problem was that potential rivals still remained ensconced in the inner councils of both state and party, and they had a vested interest in undermining Malenkov's power. Otherwise they might be excluded from a real share in governing, just as in Stalin's time. They had nothing to gain by allowing one of their number to amass as much power as the old dictator. Within nine days of Malenkov's assumption of office, therefore, they ganged up and forced him to surrender his position as party secretary, though he was allowed to remain prime minister.

A more savage fate awaited Lavrenti Beria. As head of the secret police he was in charge of the terror apparatus which Stalin had deployed with such effect, but this also meant that every other member of the collective leadership, including Malenkov, wanted to eliminate him from power. Moreover, there was considerable support for limiting the activities of the police, at least in so far as they threatened the top officials. After all, the people who exercised authority were invariably the first victims of a purge, and so Stalin's successors had much to gain by destroying Beria and his secret operations. The troubles in Eastern Europe soon provided an excuse, and in June 1953 Beria was arrested on trumped up charges of subverting communist rule in East Germany and acting as a foreign agent for the West. In December he was found guilty, though not allowed to be present at his own trial, and sent before a firing squad.

Thereafter the struggle for the Kremlin leadership became a bit more civilized. Malenkov's successor as party secretary was Nikita Khrushchev, who assumed the post in September 1953. Khrushchev's great talent was as an organizer, and he exploited his new position for all it was worth. He used the first secretary's considerable patronage powers to appoint his supporters to key offices throughout the communist hierarchy, and in a very short time managed to create his own political machine inside the party. Khrushchev mastered the art of factional politics as well. In the post-Stalin era it proved increasingly important for Soviet leaders to bargain with each other for mutual support. While this was in no sense a democratic process, nevertheless a considerable amount of give-and-take did occur in the highest councils of state and party. But this again created opportunities for Khrushchev, as he was adept at playing one group against another. Sometimes, therefore, Khrushchev veered towards Malenkov and others who favoured the new course. At other times he sought the favour of old Stalin loyalists such as V. M. Molotov (the foreign minister who had negotiated the Nazi–Soviet Pact of 1939) and members of the military.

Khrushchev turned out to be a reformer not a Stalinist, but meanwhile he played both ends against the middle. By February 1955 he was able to manoeuvre Malenkov out of his job as government head, and became the most powerful political figure in the USSR. He had to fend off a challenge from Malenkov, Molotov and others in 1957, but he won and by March 1958 became head of the Council of Ministers. Thus he succeeded where Malenkov had failed, and controlled both the top state and the top party jobs. In the meantime Malenkov had been sent to Siberia to begin a new career as the manager of a hydroelectric station, but at least he was not executed. Molotov lost his job as foreign minister and became ambassador to Outer Mongolia. In 1961 he was expelled from the Soviet communist party, but lived to see the day when he would be readmitted, in 1984.

The problem with all this manoeuvring was that it had repercussions in Eastern Europe. The Russians continued to interfere in the politics of the region, in order to install puppets who would follow the lead of whatever faction happened to control the Kremlin. Each satellite had its Stalinist faction, of course, and these people resisted any change. They had a considerable stake in vindicating the policies of the past. Otherwise it would mean the end of their position and power. But the moderate factions took advantage of the power struggle in the Kremlin to seek allies for their side. With the possible exception of Hungary in 1956, however, few communist leaders were interested in democracy. The debate was over the best means of perpetuating communist rule, and hence the position of the bureaucracy. That this was insufficient to safeguard communist authority soon became apparent.

THE SPECTRE OF REVOLUTION

On 16 June 1953, just about three months after the death of Stalin, demonstrators marched on the East German government in Berlin, and demanded that its leaders appear and answer for their policies. The issue was the imposition of new work norms, in particular a government directive threatening the construction trades with a one-third reduction wages if productivity did not rise by at least 10 per cent. Given that the state owned and operated the nation's industries, what began as an economic protest soon turned into a political protest, with demonstrators demanding free elections and the withdrawal of Russian occupation forces.

The origins of the 1953 crisis, however, were more complex than just economic exploitation or even Soviet domination. In fact, before Stalin's demise, the USSR had urged the East German regime to introduce reforms. The problem was that the country's leaders did not think it in their own interest to do so. The head of the East German communist party was Walter Ulbricht, a hard-line Stalinist who had spent the Nazi era in Russia and returned to take over the country at the end of the Second World War. He was one of the most loyal of Stalin's Eastern European lieutenants, but he was also threatened by divided counsels among the top Soviet leadership.

In the period of stalemate on the German question after the Berlin blockade some Russian policy-makers began to consider new ways to prevent the rearmament of West Germany and its admission to NATO. As we shall see presently, this was a sore point with the French as well, and a source of division within the Western Bloc. But in the early 1950s the Russians seemed to hold out the possibility of some sort of a deal on Germany. The USSR apparently was willing to consider reunification on the condition that the country join neither the Western nor the Eastern Bloc – in other words, that it be neutral. Because West Germany was more industrially developed than East Germany, the Russians had much to gain by neutralizing it diplomatically and thus preventing it from becoming a full-fledged member of the Western alliance. The Soviets had no hope of controlling all of Germany themselves, so the next best bet was to prevent the West from incorporating it. This was exactly the agreement to be concluded on Austria in 1955. But Germany was more important strategically, and hence a less likely object of compromise.

For Ulbricht the problem was that reunification would require free elections if the West were ever to accept the Russian idea. Given the unpopularity of his government, he would probably make a poor show- ing. Moreover, the Federal Republic was considerably more populous than the German Democratic Republic, and would be able to outvote the communists, even if the latter enjoyed 100 per cent support in the eastern part of the country. While the Russians might be willing to sacrifice East Germany in order to achieve greater security for themselves, Ulbricht faced the prospect of being forced out of power. The likely outcome would be to make the communists just another opposition party in a reunited German state. The Soviet strategy proceeded far enough for Stalin himself to propose the scheme to the Western powers in March 1952. Both the United States and West Germany understood the Russians' objective, however, and so rejected the proposal outright. Moreover, because Soviet policy vacillated, it was not certain whether the plan was to be taken seriously. Though revived later in the decade by both sides, it never gained enough support to succeed.

In the early 1950s, however, Ulbricht was considerably less sure of the eventual outcome, and he resolved to pursue an independent course. He wanted to keep control of the GDR for himself, and so in 1952 decided to accelerate the country's industrial development. He would make East Germany too valuable for the Russians to sacrifice. No doubt Ulbricht was able to act as he did because of divisions in the Kremlin; there were disagreements on the USSR's German policy even before the death of Stalin and the ensuing leadership crisis, which gave the German leader room for manoeuvre. He refused Russian advice to ease up in the spring of 1953, and pressed ahead despite the risk of popular resistance. The difficulty was that Ulbricht's decision to increase the pace of development, and thus the exploitation of labour, led directly to the events of June.

Within a day of the first marches in East Berlin disturbances spread to several other cities, including Leipzig, Jena, Magdeburg and Dresden. A protest of national proportions quickly developed, and literally hundreds of thousands of people joined in. But the whole affair was spontaneous, which meant it was also not very well organized. There was no central direction, and the strikers' demonstrations were not co-ordinated for maximum effect. Nevertheless it required Soviet power to save the Ulbricht government, and on 17 June the Russians intervened with troops and tanks. They had little difficulty in bringing the demonstrators to heel within a few days, though at the cost of dozens killed or executed and thousands arrested. Moreover, there were signs of trouble elsewhere. In June the city of Pilsen in Czechoslovakia had been the scene of anti-government riots, and strikes occurred in Hungary and Romania. In July trouble broke out at the Vorkuta labour camps in Siberia, i.e. in the USSR itself. Perhaps 25,000 prisoners stopped work.

The events of 1953 obviously recommended a change in policy on the part of both Russian and Eastern European leaders. The result was to help anti-Stalinists in the satellites win greater recognition. The outcome was dramatic. Victims of the post-1948 purges found themselves released from jail and even restored to office. For those who had been executed, of course, it was too late, but some of them were dug up from their graves and reburied, this time with full state honours. Among the living, important leaders made a comeback. Thus, in Hungary, the Soviets ordered the dominant Stalinist faction to make room for Imre Nagy, a moderate. Nagy had been demoted (though not jailed) in the country's 1949 purge, but as a result of Soviet influence was made prime minister in June 1953. The Stalinists, however, were allowed to retain control of the communist party, and it turned out that they were not willing to accept second place for long. Eighteen months later, when Kremlin factionalism left Nagy without Soviet support, he was turned out of office and then expelled from the party. Yet Nagy's reforms could hardly be taken back, and it remained to be seen whether his successors could reassert their authority. Later, in October 1955, Wladislaw Gomulka was set free in Poland. He had been dismissed as head of the communist party in 1948 and was subsequently placed in 'protective custody'. But with new men in the Kremlin and the clear need for moderate leaders capable of mollifying popular discontent in Poland itself, his fortunes began to rise. By the summer of 1956 he was readmitted to the party, and quickly moved back to centre stage. So did Nagy, though, as we shall see, with less fortunate results for him personally.

Even in the USSR reform was in the air. Thousands of prisoners were released from the labour camps as the result of amnesty decrees issued in 1953, 1955, 1956 and 1957 (although persons charged with political crimes generally had to wait until the early 1960s). In the arts the demand for political content and for rigid conformity to the party line was relaxed. Ilya Ehrenburg's novel *The Thaw* provided an apt title for this phase of Russian history. More resources were also allocated to agriculture and consumer goods, and some Russian leaders talked of a limited *rapprochement* with the West. In the face of the mounting crisis in Eastern Europe the USSR could hardly compete with the United States in defence spending. Yet there were other considerations working against *rapprochement*, so that although an East–West summit conference was held in July 1955 at Geneva the results proved disappointing. The rearmament of West Germany (which had been in the works since 1950) and its admission to NATO a few months before the conference (in May) constituted a major obstacle to improved relations. Indeed, the German question had provided the main impetus behind the signing of the Warsaw Pact, also in May. At Geneva, therefore, no progress was made on the German question. The same was true of the other issue which dominated the talks, nuclear disarmament. The Russians proposed an outright ban on atomic weapons, though with no means of enforcement, while the Americans suggested a system of aerial or 'Open Skies' inspection as a first step. Eisenhower thought some form of inspection essential to guarantee any agreement, while Khrushchev believed inspection would simply serve as a cover for US intelligence activities over the USSR. In consequence the 'spirit of Geneva' proved ephemeral indeed.

DE-STALINIZATION

Yet the most serious crises of the Eastern Bloc were still to come, in 1956. In a surprise move calculated to place his opponents on the defensive Nikita Khrushchev went before the Twentieth Congress of the Soviet communist party on 25 February and delivered his famous 'secret' speech denouncing Stalin as a pathological criminal. Speaking at midnight to a closed session of the congress, he also implied that all

unreconstructed Stalinists were guilty as well (no matter that Khrushchev himself had been one of the late dictator's trusted lieutenants).
Despite the mystery surrounding its delivery, the speech was never
intended to remain secret. Otherwise it would not achieve its objective of
intimidating Khrushchev's opponents. The idea of delivering it to a
closed session was no doubt intended to heighten curiosity about what
the party secretary would say, and thus guarantee that the contents would
be leaked. After all, there were more than 1,400 party officials present
from all over the Soviet Union, so the attack on Stalin did not remain
quiet for very long. And though never published in the USSR, copies of
the speech were made available to party members and to foreign
communist parties for study. In due course the US Central Intelligence
Agency obtained the text. It was released by the State Department, and
appeared in the Western press by June 1956. Five years later the
Twenty-Second Congress voted to remove Stalin's body from the
mausoleum on Red Square in Moscow,where it had been preserved and
placed on display beside the body of Lenin. The remains were then
reinterred by the walls of the Kremlin, a considerably less distinguished
resting-place.

For the satellites 'de-Stalinization' seemed to hold out the possibility
of greater autonomy. Khrushchev's speech implied that the Russians
were prepared to admit they were not infallible, and that perhaps there
was room for differences within the Eastern Bloc. More significantly,
this seemed to be confirmed by the Kremlin's efforts to patch up its
relations with Yugoslavia. In 1955 Khrushchev had visited Belgrade,
where he publicly expressed regret for Stalin's break with Tito. A
number of economic agreements were concluded subsequently. Then,
in April 1956, the Cominform was dissolved, eliminating a major source
of irritation between the two countries. In June of the same year,
therefore, Tito arrived in Moscow amid much ceremony for a state visit.
The problem for the countries of Eastern Europe, however, was to gauge
just how far the Russians were prepared to go. The answer would be
crystal clear before the year was out.

Poland
On 28 June 1956, in Poznan, one of Poland's major industrial centres,
locomotive workers went on strike against government-imposed wage
cuts. As in East Berlin three years earlier, the protest quickly gained
momentum, turning into a city-wide general strike and moving on to
political objectives. The Polish army proved quite capable of restoring

order in a few days, though with fifty-three killed and 300 injured (according to official estimates). It was time for a change in leadership, so in July Nikolai Bulganin and Georgi Zhukov arrived in Warsaw from Moscow. Both were allies of Khrushchev at this time, Bulganin as chairman of the Council of Ministers and Zhukov as defence minister. The outcome of this comradely consultation was a compromise whereby Wladislaw Gomulka would be readmitted to the party and restored to membership on the Central Committee. Because the Russians feared the possibility of further trouble, they were prepared to tolerate a moderate like Gomulka. But, as they were anxious to avoid any erosion of communist authority, they also left the Stalinists in the majority – there was only the appearance, not the substance, of change. The result was predictable: continuing discontent among the people. This only strengthened the moderates, and over the next several months they argued that there had to be still more change if the political situation were to be stabilized. By autumn, therefore, it seemed virtually certain that Gomulka would be appointed general secretary of the Polish communist party.

Never bashful about intervening in satellite politics, the Soviets stepped in again. The Poles were invited to consult in Moscow, but declined. Accordingly Khrushchev, Molotov and other top Russian officials decided to fly to Warsaw, unannounced and uninvited, on 19 October. At the same time Russian troops were placed on alert around the Polish capital in an undisguised threat of military intervention. The USSR, however, had overplayed its hand. The deployment of Russian troops only galvanized Gomulka and the Polish Central Committee, so that when they met with Khrushchev and company it became clear that the Poles were prepared to meet force with force. Indeed, demonstrators had taken to the streets in a show of support for the government and in protest against the presence of Soviet troops in the country. The prospect looked messy, to say the least, yet a solution was at hand. The Russians retreated once Gomulka convinced them that he would pre-serve bureaucratic rule and that Poland would remain a loyal member of the Warsaw Pact. For the Soviets the real issue all along had been whether developments in Poland would endanger communist party hegemony, and hence the unity of the Eastern Bloc.

Although the crisis of the Eastern Bloc was real enough, the Soviet intervention in Poland reflected more than a little paranoia. Indeed, it had led Khrushchev to misjudge the Polish situation very badly. What the Russians had failed to realize, at least initially, was that Gomulka had no intention of undermining one-party rule or the Warsaw Pact. He certainly wanted changes inside Poland itself, but his reformism was calculated to preserve communist power in Poland, not to establish a new order. The forms of democracy were strengthened and there were economic concessions, but within two years Gomulka was openly warning against the dangers of 'revisionism'. Moreover, he also saw the alliance with Russia as a useful check on Germany. As long as the GDR remained part of a Soviet defence structure, German reunification would be impossible. A resurgent Germany would never again threaten Poland or the rest of the Continent, or so he hoped. In time the Russians therefore came to regard Gomulka as a faithful ally.

Hungary

The outcome in Hungary was very different. There the unity of the Warsaw Pact and the future of one-party rule were likewise at issue. After the downfall of Nagy and the restoration of the Stalinists in 1955 continuing agitation among workers, students and intellectuals suggested that it was time for another shake-up. In July 1956 Anastas Mikoyan, the Soviet deputy prime minister, was sent to Budapest with orders to reorganize the communist party leadership. But the Russians were not interested in fundamental change in Hungary any more than in Poland, and so they simply replaced one Stalinist regime with another. The new man in charge was Erno Gero, general secretary of the communist party. As in Poland, though, the lack of any real change meant that the country remained in a potentially explosive situation. This became very clear when hundreds of thousands of people turned out for a state funeral on 6 October 1956 to honour victims of the late 1940s purges. Then came the crisis in Poland, with the spectre of Russian military intervention. It will be recalled that Soviet troops moved into position around Warsaw on 19 October. Despite efforts to censor the news, word of these developments spread, and on 23 October students in Budapest marched in a show of solidarity with Poland. Security guards opened fire, and Gero called on the Russians to impose order. Early the next day Soviet tanks took up position in Budapest. The Central Committee declared martial law, but also decided it might be wise to restore Nagy as prime minister.

In the meantime Russian troops became involved in the street fighting. To the alarm of party leaders in both Moscow and Budapest, there were instances of fraternization between Soviet soldiers and Hungarian citizens, though the presence of Soviet troops of course caused the trouble to spread. Workers walked off the job, and quickly took over from the students in the vanguard of the fighting. Indeed, the enthusiasm of the latter was flagging. Although members of the intelligentsia (students, teachers, professionals) had played a leading role in formulating the grievances of the people against the regime, they were also a privileged sector of society, so the working class soon became the real centre of resistance. It was the ordinary people who would man the front lines in the days ahead. They began seizing guns from armaments factories, from the police and from Hungarian soldiers. In fact some of the latter defected to the demonstrators' side, and were soon organized under the leadership of Colonel Pal Maleter.

The by now customary contingent of Soviet officials duly arrived in the Hungarian capital. In an effort to cool the situation Nagy was installed as prime minister, and Janos Kadar replaced Gero as general secretary of the communist party. Kadar had been purged earlier, but then rehabilitated in 1955. The problem was that, although head of the government once again, Nagy was not really capable of taking charge. He had been pushed along by events, and had not sought the leadership. He was soon to find himself in an untenable position *vis-à-vis* the Russians, unlike Gomulka in Poland.

While Nagy's appointment helped reduce the level of violence, the political situation remained volatile. Workers were occupying public buildings and setting up 'revolutionary councils' throughout the land. In other words, new political forces independent of both party and state were coming into being. The risk was that they might well present themselves as an alternative to communist rule, something the Soviets were not about to tolerate. On the other hand, they could hardly be ignored either, and the Russians' cautious approach in Poland suggested to Nagy that perhaps he could make concessions. The problem was that he went much farther than Gomulka.

On 30 October Nagy went on national radio and announced 'the abrogation of the one-party system and the formation of a government based on the democratic co-operation among the coalition parties of 1945'. He also announced the beginning of talks with the USSR 'about the withdrawal of Soviet troops from Hungary'. Kadar then spoke, fully supporting both decisions and condemning the Stalinists as agents of 'despotism and national enslavement'.* The new government came into

* Cited in Julius Braunthal, *History of the International*, Vol. 3: *1943–1968* (Boulder, Col.: 1980), 420.

existence on 1 November 1956. It included representatives of the communist party, the social democrats, peasants' and farmers' parties, and also Pal Maleter (to speak for the revolutionary councils and for the dissident troops).

As these events unfolded, the Russians sent a new delegation to Budapest, on 30 October. At the same time Soviet troops were pulled out of the city, and it seemed that some sort of compromise might be possible. The result was to lull the Hungarians into a false sense of security, and the next day fresh contingents of Russian troops began arriving in the country. Nagy protested, but he was none the less reassured by the USSR's apparent willingness to negotiate. The Hungarian government mistakenly assumed that it still had the initiative, so Nagy served notice that he intended to withdraw Hungary from the Warsaw Pact and declare neutrality. A message was dispatched to Dag Hammarskjöld, the secretary-general of the United Nations, asking that 'the question of Hungary's neutrality' be placed on the agenda of the General Assembly. Therefore, on the night of 3 November, Russian troops surrounded Budapest and at dawn the next day opened fire. As they did, Nagy broadcast news of the attack on Hungarian radio, accusing the Soviets of 'overthrowing the legal democratic government of Hungary', and vowing not to surrender. But within the hour Janos Kadar came forward and announced that he had formed a new government. Although presumably one of Nagy's staunchest supporters, Kadar had dropped out of sight a few days before, but now showed up in Soviet-controlled territory. The mission of the new government was to fight 'the counter-revolutionary threat'.*

What can only be described as open warfare broke out between street fighters and Russian tanks. The Soviets did not want a repeat of the fraternization that had occurred a few weeks earlier, and so sent tanks (rather than foot soldiers) against civilians, even though this meant using excessive firepower. In two weeks of pitched battle several thousand people were killed and many more injured. Probably 200,000 persons fled to the West during the course of the crisis. Nagy took sanctuary in the Yugoslav embassy, but on 22 November was lured out and arrested by the Russians after Kadar had issued a letter of safe conduct. Apparently the Soviets were not prepared to respect the authority of even their own puppet (although it is possible that Kadar had co-operated in the ruse). Nagy was taken to Romania, and in 1958 tried for treason and executed.

* Cited in *ibid.*, 422–3.

By the end of November the fighting had died down, but it required several more months of negotiations with the revolutionary councils and with strikers before order was restored completely. This was because the formation of a Central Workers' Council in Budapest on 14 November had in effect created a national headquarters for the resisters. It was sufficiently powerful for even the Russians to treat its leaders gingerly, and only in December were the first arrests made (inspiring a forty-eight hour general strike). It was not until November 1957 that the Kadar government felt secure enough to abolish all local councils. But, however long it might take to reconsolidate the government's position, the preponderance of power was on its side. Petrol bombs were not all that effective against tanks, though the Western press published photographs of the exceptions. More importantly, the government and the Russians had staying power. They controlled the food supply and the job market, and literally starved out the last of the resisters. Hungary was saved for one-party rule and the Warsaw Pact.

The events of 1956, however, were more than simply the result of Soviet imperialism. This certainly was a principal consideration, and the one most historians emphasize. But in the case of both Poland and Hungary national leaders were found to do the Soviets' bidding. Therefore Gomulka, Kadar and those who joined their governments were perhaps as responsible for the outcome as the Russians. Both Poland and Hungary were examples of how the bureaucratic dynamic might prevail, as local communists, not just the Soviets, sought to preserve their monopoly on state power. In short, internal as well as external forces militated against change, but this also meant that the stability of the post-1956 order would be fragile indeed.

Albania

Albania was the smallest of the Soviets' Eastern European allies, yet its size belied its importance in the affairs of the communist world. As we have already observed (Chapter 4), it became a factor in the Sino-Soviet dispute, at least on the ideological level. The conflict between the USSR and Albania, however, had its own origins, quite apart from the Chinese connection, being the result of Khrushchev's *rapprochement* with Tito. As long as the USSR and Yugoslavia were at loggerheads, the Albanians could count on the Soviets to protect them from Tito's territorial ambitions. But when the Russians and the Yugoslavs made up, Albania's security was threatened.

Albania had gained its independence from Turkey only in 1912, but after the First World War was forced to become a satellite of Italy. In 1939 Mussolini invaded, thus ending any pretence of Albanian autonomy. During the Second World War the communists under Enver Hoxha played a leading role in the anti-Axis resistance, only to fall under the sway of the Yugoslavs. Help from Tito was essential to the Albanian resistance, and he therefore expected to have a say in the future of the country. Albania and Yugoslavia were the only two countries in Eastern Europe to defeat the Nazis without the help of the Soviet army.

The result was that the influence of nationalists like Hoxha declined, and Yugoslav sympathizers took charge of the Albanian communist party. After the war this was reflected in a series of treaties between the two countries which co-ordinated their respective economic plans, standardized their monetary systems, established a common price system and a customs union, and generally integrated the two economies. There were even proposals to merge their military forces, but the growth in Yugoslav influence culminated in the suggestion, in April 1948, by Yugoslavia's chief partisan in Albania, Kochi Xoxe, that the two countries be united into a single state. What saved Albania was Tito's expulsion from the Cominform in June of the same year. With Russia's support the Albanian communist party was purged of Yugoslav influences, and in effect the USSR guaranteed the country's independence. The Soviets provided economic aid and technical assistance, and Albania became a member of COMECON and later the Warsaw Pact. Thus a nationalist but still communist leadership took charge in Albania, and Enver Hoxha returned to the ascendancy.

The Khrushchev–Tito reconciliation changed everything. Moreover, it did so at a time when the Chinese were beginning to assert their independence from Soviet influence, so the Albanians henceforth looked to Mao Zedong for protection. However theoretical (and, to outsiders, bizarre) the rhetoric of the Sino-Soviet split and Albania's role in it may have seemed, the issues were concrete indeed. To sum up, Balkan nationalism contributed to yet another fracture in the unity of the East.

THE ATLANTIC ALLIANCE
The threat of internal subversion also seemed real to many people in the developed nations of the West. The communist countries by no means had a monopoly on fear in the 1950s. Politicians such as the American senator Joseph McCarthy built careers on their exploits as Red-hunters.

McCarthy was hardly the first to do so in the post-1945 world, however, and well before 'McCarthyism' became a household word in the United States, President Harry Truman had instituted a programme of loyalty checks on government employees. In addition, espionage operations were uncovered in the United States and Canada, although only a very few people went to jail or were executed for spying. Developments in the West thus were not comparable to the purges in the East.

In retrospect it appears that Western Europe and North America faced few threats from within, at least compared to the Soviet Bloc. But this is not how everyone saw it in the early 1950s. The Berlin Blockade, the Soviet nuclear bomb, the communist victory in China and especially the outbreak of a hot war in Korea all suggested that vigilance was very much in order. Later some historians would question whether these events were in fact signs of Russian expansionism. The argument is that they were defensive in nature, designed to preserve the USSR's existing sphere of influence, or in some cases (China and Korea) not the result of Russian actions. While this glosses over Moscow's interest in extending its influence (e.g. through the Comintern earlier), it does reflect the limits of Soviet power in the 1940s and early 1950s. At the time, however, many people saw these events as concrete signs of a global communist conspiracy. In the realm of policy (as distinct from public opinion) it was the Korean War which led to a general review of Western defence strategy, and induced Washington to raise the question of West Germany's rearmament. This turned out to be a source of considerable disharmony within the Atlantic Alliance.

The United States regarded the reintegration of Germany into European life as essential. As we have seen, projects such as the Morgenthau Plan were quickly abandoned after the Second World War, and the Western occupation forces soon ended the dismantling of German industry. Even such reprisals as were taken had little long-term effect: for instance, the Allied occupation authorities broke up the I. G. Farben conglomerate, but its successor companies prospered. I. G. Farben was the manufacturer of Zyklon-B, the gas used to murder millions of Jews during the Holocaust. Similarly the Allies required Friedrich Flick to sell his holdings in coal and steel, but, as he was permitted to keep the proceeds from the sale, he simply reinvested in the automobile industry. The International Military Tribunal at Nuremberg sentenced Alfred Krupp of the famous arms manufacturing family to twelve years in prison. It also ordered the confiscation of all his wealth. Yet in 1951 the US high commissioner in West Germany allowed him to go free. His property was returned as well. The Cold War turned old enemies into new friends in a fairly short time. And, as in the case of Japan, a number of US companies (e.g. General Motors, Chicago Pneumatic Tool, International Harvester and others) had invested in German industry before the Second World War, and they too wished to see the country integrated into the Western Bloc. Indeed, when the war broke out in 1939, some American industrialists had worried about violating their patent agreements with German companies, lest breaking such contracts endanger future business.

Germany's military and intelligence resources were also of value to the Western Allies, and were another reason for rehabilitating the former enemy. German scientists and military officers were interrogated on weapons development and rocketry, and key figures such as Werner von Braun (developer of the V–2 rocket) were whisked away to the United States, though large numbers were also taken by the Russians. Formerly director of German missile research at Peenemünde, von Braun many years later played a leading role in the American programme to land a man on the moon. Of equal interest to the West were Germany's intelligence agents. After the war known Nazis were recruited and protected by the US army. One of the most infamous was Klaus Barbie, chief of the Gestapo in the French city of Lyons. The French resistance blamed Barbie for the execution of 4,000 people and the deportation (to concentration camps) of another 7,500. He was well enough protected, however, to elude justice for almost forty years. Another example was Reinhard Gehlen, who had been in charge of Nazi spy activities behind Soviet lines. American authorities arranged for his transfer to the United States in August 1945, disguised as a US general. After careful bargaining with American officials he was allowed back to Germany, where he organized espionage against the USSR. In due course Gehlen took charge of West German intelligence operations. The evidence suggests that hundreds of Nazi officials were secretly brought to the United States, and that some were even provided with US citizenship as part of a cover-up. Apparently the US president was not kept informed of these operations.

From the very beginning of the post-war era, therefore, Western policy towards Germany was more than a little ambiguous. As the Berlin Blockade provided the catalyst for the establishment of separate German states, so too the Korean War suggested, at least to American policy-makers, the necessity of West Germany's rearmament.

EUROPEAN INTEGRATION AND GERMAN REARMAMENT

What helped make the rearming of the Federal Republic politically feasible was its integration into a West European economic community. Presumably, a German state dependent on the other countries of the region for its prosperity would not again threaten its neighbours. The Americans had always favoured as much economic integration in Western Europe as possible, even though this might mean creating a powerful rival in the global market-place. But, as we saw in Chapter 2, this also assured that the Continent would be a strong trading partner, a customer for the United States as well as a competitor. And just as important, European recovery was needed to support the North Atlantic Treaty Organization. If Europeans were prosperous, they could contribute more to the defence of the Western Bloc. Accordingly the United States had made a lowering of trade barriers among its European partners a condition of Marshall Plan aid.

Yet the United States could go only so far in forcing economic integration. Because it needed to restore its trading partners in order to assure its own prosperity, the Europeans knew that reconstruction aid would be forthcoming regardless of how much, or how little, progress was made on integration. American bargaining power was thus too limited to result in an immediate diminution of rivalries in Europe. A permanent agency for economic co-operation, however, did emerge from the Marshall Plan. The Organization of European Economic Co-operation (OEEC) was established to co-ordinate American aid, and after the conclusion of the Marshall Plan continued to work for a freer flow of trade. But although the OEEC was expanded in 1960 to include the United States and Canada (and in 1964 Japan) and became the Organization for Economic Co-operation and Development (OECD), it did not evolve into a customs union or a common market. Nor did another institution, the Council of Europe. This was created in 1948 as a forum for exchanging ideas on European problems, but had no independent powers of its own. Some people thought of it as a first step towards the founding of a 'United States of Europe' and thus the basis for eventual political unity, but this proved ephemeral.

As it turned out, Western European economic integration was to have humbler origins. Some supporters of integration, such as Jean Monnet, believed that a step-by-step approach had a better chance of succeeding than more grandiose schemes. Monnet was in charge of national economic planning in France after 1945, and thus very much involved in devising practical means for restoring international trade. He appreciated, for example, the utility of economic co-operation for guaranteeing French access to German coal and coke. For West Germany, of course, such co-operation was the first step towards its acceptance back into the family of nations. Indeed, it gave the country some bargaining power with the Western Allies. Other nations stood to gain as well, so Monnet's proposals for French–German economic co-operation were soon expanded to include Italy, the Netherlands, Belgium and Luxembourg. This was the impetus behind the founding of the European Coal and Steel Community (ECSC). It came into operation in 1952, and because coal and steel constituted about one-quarter of the member nations' trade, was an important precedent for further integration. Furthermore, the 1950s were a period of general prosperity in Western Europe, and the good times were ascribed in part to the ECSC. It helped make the case for additional experimentation. The ultimate outcome would be the formation of the Common Market, or European Economic Community (EEC), established by the 1957 Treaty of Rome.

As we have noted, the outbreak of the Korean War made West Germany's rearmament very likely. A German contribution to the defence of Western Europe would ease the burden on the United States, so Washington suggested the restoration of the Federal Republic as a military power, albeit with safeguards. The problem was that many Europeans, and particularly the French, simply did not trust the Germans. But for Monnet, who had many friends in the United States and who believed in the American mission to lead the West, the trend towards economic co-operation pointed the way. The same approach might be applied in the military sphere: merge the forces of the Federal Republic into a larger entity, where the rest of Europe could keep an eye on them. Therefore, when the US secretary of state, Dean Acheson, raised the question of West German rearmament in September 1950, Monnet urged the French government to support the Americans, but by proposing the establishment of an all-European army. This would not be a coalition of national forces, as the Americans seemed to have in mind, but an altogether new military force. The idea was to organize troop units from many different countries into one army, and to place them under a common command. Further, the new force would be financed by a common budget. In this way the Federal Republic might contribute to Europe's defence without raising the spectre of German militarism.

The French government adopted the idea as its own, and the premier, René Pleven, proposed it to the other allies on 24 October 1950.

The United States was certain that the Pleven Plan was a delaying tactic, because anti-German feeling still ran high in France. Was Pleven simply trying to kill the whole idea of rearming West Germany by suggesting a scheme which would affect the sovereignty of all the European allies and thus lessen the chance that they would approve the plan? After all, every country in Western Europe would have to place some of its troops under a common command. Or was the French government really trying to head off opposition to German rearmament by adopting Monnet's suggestion? Whatever their suspicions, the Americans accepted the Pleven Plan in principle as the only way of dealing with the French fear of a resurgent Germany. Also, at this time, the Americans were anxious to humour Paris because of the Indo-China war. One reason many of the French objected to a rearmed Germany was because they were bogged down in Asia. Their commitments elsewhere left them militarily weak in Europe, so they were reluctant to ratify any scheme that restored outright autonomy to West Germany on military matters. If responding to French sensibilities was necessary to have Germany rearmed, then the Americans would do so.

Accordingly a treaty to implement the Pleven Plan, officially the European Defence Community, or EDC, was signed in the spring of 1952. But it still had to be ratified by the home governments of the various participating countries. As we have already seen, the EDC soon became entangled in the negotiations to bring the French war in Indo-China to an end. The Russians used their good offices to press the Vietminh to compromise at the 1954 Geneva Conference, and the French National Assembly defeated the EDC scheme in August of the same year, which suited the Russian interest in blocking or at least delaying West German rearmament.

The defeat of the EDC, however, proved irrelevant in the face of the Americans' determination to proceed with German rearmament. It was immediately apparent that Washington was prepared to act with or without the co-operation of France, and that recalcitrance would not prevent the US from realizing its goal. The French government there-fore concluded that a compromise was in its own best interest, so that it might at least influence the terms of German rearmament. Also, the British lent their support by promising to maintain their troops on the Continent as a counter to German influence in the North Atlantic Treaty

Organization, while Konrad Adenauer agreed to a ban on the manufacture of nuclear weapons by his country. These proved to be the kind of firm guarantees that the French were looking for. They were still not keen, but by October 1954 Paris accepted a plan for the admission of the Federal Republic to NATO. The Western Allies of the Second World War thus ended their official occupation of Germany, and the former enemy entered the Atlantic Alliance in 1955.

The ultimate outcome of French resistance was that no exclusively European military structure emerged. Instead NATO remained the principal line of defence, but this was dominated by the Americans. Washington had yielded to the Pleven Plan only to mollify France, yet it was French vacillation which left NATO as the only alternative. Moreover, the outcome suggested that the likelihood of European integration on other fronts was limited. As we have noted, the Treaty of Rome would establish the Common Market, but there was virtually no movement towards political unity, towards a United States of Europe. Indeed, Britain refused to join even the Common Market, and when it changed its mind in the early 1960s, its application for admission was rejected by Charles de Gaulle of France.

COMPETITION IN THE THIRD WORLD: IRAN

Another source of disunity in the Atlantic Alliance was competition between the United States and Europe in the Third World. By the 1950s, of course, there was nothing new about this, but the decade witnessed some notable examples, such as in the Middle East, where the decline of British influence dramatically enhanced American opportunities in the oil industry. Moreover, the US government was quite willing to assist in the process, so that a good deal of the success of American businessmen was due to a timely deployment of diplomatic power and sometimes covert aid to friendly local leaders. It would be inaccurate, however, to see the history of the Third World as entirely the story of contending external forces. Third World leaders acted in response to internal pressures as well. The economically underdeveloped countries were hardly inert or passive, and rivalries among the imperial powers sometimes enabled local leaders to play one outsider against another. The outcome, however, was not necessarily greater autonomy for the Third World, but often only the replacement of one source of foreign hegemony by another.

Iran (Persia) under the Qajar and then the Pahlavi dynasties was a case in point. It had long been the site of rivalry between Russia and the United Kingdom. The Czars had territorial ambitions in the immediate area, while Britain's stake in India recommended that it bring neighbouring countries under its influence. During most of the nineteenth and early twentieth centuries Britain and Russia divided the country into spheres of influence. From the mid nineteenth century on they enjoyed extra-territorial rights (i.e. immunity from Iranian law) and won tariff concessions. The latter caused major dislocations in the Iranian economy, because foreign factory-made goods could be sold in Iran for less than locally produced goods manufactured by handicraft methods. Both powers also exacted special economic concessions. These involved allowing foreign monopolies over the production, sale or export of specific commodities; the basis of the UK's later domination of the Iranian petroleum industry was thereby established in 1901, when British interests obtained oil rights in all of the country except for five provinces in the north. The British and the Russians sometimes encouraged the separatist ambitions of local leaders, just to keep the Qajar shahs off balance. On the whole, however, it was in the interest of outsiders to support Teheran precisely because it was weak and therefore pliable.

The Iranian business class, or *bazaar*, protested the granting of concessions, but it was only towards the end of the nineteenth century that such protests turned into a mass movement and that Iranian nationalists became effectively organized. The population, after all, was mainly rural and nomadic, and hence dispersed. It was difficult to mobilize national as opposed to regional identities against foreign inroads. For most people Islam was a more immediate influence in their lives than nationalism. The *ulama*, or clergy, did not play the principal role in the early nationalist protests, but as defenders of Iranian tradition they often sided with the *bazaaris* and other opponents of the regime. (It was not until the late twentieth century that they took charge of the anti-government movement.) In 1890, however, the first major anti-foreign protests succeeded. The Shah granted a concession over the marketing and sale of tobacco to British interests. The result was the most broadly based nationalist protest to date, and a boycott of tobacco products throughout the country. The tobacco interests included landowners, farmers, exporters and merchants. Many people's livelihood depended on tobacco, and therefore a broad movement emerged. The upshot was that the Shah withdrew the concession in 1892, thus marking the start of an effective nationalist opposition that would soon lead to efforts to limit the Shah's power and establish a constitutional monarchy.

The outcome was the 'Constitutional Revolution' and the creation of a representative assembly called the *majles* in 1906. Guild and later landlord and other wealthy interests dominated the new legislature, with many *ulama* elected as members. The assembly wrote a constitution, which the Shah and his successor reluctantly accepted. This reduced the power of the Shah, and required *majles* approval for all important decisions, including foreign concessions. Within a few years, however, the imperial powers effectively destroyed the power of the *majles*. In 1907 Britain and Czarist Russia agreed to a treaty which formally divided Iran into spheres of influence. Teheran fell within the Russians' zone, and the Shah moved against the *majles* with their support. Despite occasional setbacks along the way, Russian military intervention eventually brought the Constitutional Revolution to an end in 1911. Although *majleses* continued to be elected from 1914 on, Iran remained under foreign hegemony. It required little insight on the part of the outsiders to see that they could not afford to allow nationalists and constitutionalists to exercise power in Teheran. Their goal was a puppet government with authority concentrated in the hands of a weak Shah. The First World War further eroded Iran's autonomy. Because Turkey and Germany were allies, the Middle East was caught up in the conflict. The Turks sent troops into Iran, and the Germans organized tribal uprisings against the British. Both Russia and Britain stationed more troops in Iran, and occupied most of the country by the autumn of 1917. But with the Bolshevik Revolution of the same year the Russians gave up most of their rights in the country, and the British emerged as the main foreign power in the region.

The United Kingdom hoped to consolidate its influence by establishing a protectorate. This took the form of the Anglo-Persian Treaty of 1919. The result was a new wave of nationalist resistance in Iran, and in some areas outright rebellion. Despite continued British pressure, the *majles* never ratified the treaty, and a coup brought a new government to power in 1921. Because Britain's plans for imposing a protectorate were proving impractical, over the next few years the UK reluctantly accepted the establishment of an effective Iranian government. The strong man in the new regime was not the prime minister but the minister of war, Reza Khan. He was the commander of the only modern military force in the country, the Cossack Brigade (organized in the nineteenth century with Russian help). He proceeded to suppress the separatist forces, thus reducing the opportunities for the British to make trouble. He favoured a republic, not to achieve popular rule but to end the power of the Qajars and create a strong, modern state. In the face of landlord and *ulama* resistance to change, however, Reza Khan instead launched the Pahlavi dynasty in 1925, with himself as Shah. The *ulama* in particular feared the erosion of Islamic traditions likely to follow from the creation of a republic, and sought a pledge that Reza Khan would respect Islamic law. He agreed, and a constituent assembly confirmed the new dynasty at the end of the year. It was the son (Mohammad Reza) of this Shah who was allowed to assume power when the British and Russians invaded the country at the beginning of the Second World War (see Chapter 2).

Reza Khan was not a social reformer in the sense of improving the lot of the common people, but built up the power of the central government, particularly the military and the government bureaucracy. He assumed control of the country, moving against tribal autonomy and disarming the nomads. He also imposed new legal codes modelled on Western principles, thus undermining religious law and custom (just as the *ulama* had feared). He took charge of tariff policy, and negotiated new trade agreements with the Western powers. Educational reform followed Western models, with the upper and middle classes as the main participants. Reform even extended to the role of women, and they were allowed to attend the new Teheran University, founded in 1935. Many of the changes followed those of the famous reformer Ataturk in Turkey. Reza Khan did not, however, institute land reform.

The rising power of the new Shah adversely affected British fortunes, yet did not end Western influences. The Shah's efforts to offset the UK created opportunities for others. New investors arrived, with the Germans in the lead. The British, however, still monopolized the oil industry, and there was growing pressure for obtaining a better deal for Iran. In 1932 the Shah cancelled the Anglo-Persian Oil Company concession, and negotiated a new settlement. Yet falling demand (because of the 1929 Depression) and the need for foreign expertise in the oil fields limited his bargaining power. He concluded a new arrangement in which the area of British operations was reduced, but the term of the agreement was extended from 1961 (as originally negotiated) to 1993. It was quite possible that the oil fields would be depleted by then (though this later turned out not to be the case). While the royalties paid to Iran for its oil rose, the Shah was still not satisfied.

Thus the Germans made considerable headway. By 1939–41, they dominated about half of Iran's foreign trade, while Nazi agents established themselves in the country in case of war. With Hitler's invasion of Russia in 1941 Germany hoped to use Iran as a base for operations against the USSR (which bordered Iran in the north). Thus, as we have seen, the British and Russians intervened in order to force the Shah to abdicate and secure Iran for the anti-Axis bloc. They restored cabinet government as a way of reducing the power of an unfriendly Shah. It was also the case that the Shah's successor was young and inexperienced, and this too contributed to a shift of political power to the *majles*. Otherwise the British and the Russians both promoted political movements which would protect their differing interests, with Moscow supporting the new Tudeh (or 'masses') Party and London anti-leftist groups such as the National Will Party. The British exercised the most influence over the southern tribal areas, while the presence of Russian troops in the north encouraged separatists there. During the war the Americans also provided financial and military advisers to Teheran, foreshadowing a growing US interest in the region. As we have noted (Chapter 2), however, at the end of the war the Iranians blocked Russian demands for an oil concession, while the Americans had only begun to lay the basis for future claims. The British thus remained the most important outside influence. Accordingly they were at the centre of the crises of the 1950s.

The Iranians were particularly unhappy because in other countries of the Middle East the Americans were offering a 50–50 share of profits between themselves and the host governments. In Iran the government did not even have the right to inspect the books of the British concession, by then renamed the Anglo-Iranian Oil Company (AIOC). Oil revenues were paid in pounds sterling, but the amount was fixed. Because oil prices rose about threefold between 1933 and the 1950s, Iranian revenues declined as a percentage of the total earnings. The net profits of the AIOC between 1945 and 1950 were almost three times the royalties paid Iran, and this after allowing for depreciation and British taxes. The inflation of the pound also hurt Iran's real income. Further, Iranians were not being trained for managerial or skilled positions in the oil fields.

The Plot to Restore the Shah

In the face of rising anti-British agitation the terms of the 1933 oil agreement had to be changed, and the AIOC acknowledged this. Talks were opened with Teheran in 1947, and while the government concluded a new arrangement, it failed to satisfy the *majles*. Consequently

elections for a new assembly brought a coalition of more radical nationalists to power, and in March 1951 the *majles* voted in favour of nationalizing the oil industry. Popular demonstrations indicated widespread
support for such action. The outspoken Mohammad Mosaddeq then
became prime minister, against the wishes of the Shah. During this
period the Tudeh Party, declared illegal by a previous right-wing
government, was permitted to operate openly. Mosaddeq looked to the
United States for support against Britain, but the Americans were
suspicious of the prime minister. He was too friendly with the Tudeh,
and repeatedly threatened to seek Soviet aid if Washington did not help.

In the Western press Mosaddeq was more and more portrayed as a
wild fanatic and perhaps a closet communist. At best he was seen as
unstable, at worst a Russian stooge. In Iran, though, he enjoyed a good
deal of support. The Shah attempted to dismiss him in 1952, but popular
demonstrations brought about his return. It thus seemed that real
changes were in the offing, a fact which alarmed Britain and the United
States. The Shah and his prime minister repeatedly came into conflict,
particularly over Mosaddeq's effort to take charge of the army. The
effort failed, a fact of major import for Mosaddeq's survival in the future.
Thus, in 1953, when the Americans proposed a coup against Mosaddeq,
the Shah was receptive. British intelligence probably was the first to
suggest the idea, though it would have no direct part in the actual plot.
Instead the scheme was taken up by the US Central Intelligence Agency.
Washington regarded Iranian nationalization as a dangerous precedent.
Besides, no doubt a grateful Shah would allow American oil companies a
share of Iranian production, once Mosaddeq was overthrown. The goal,
therefore, was to depose the prime minister and increase the power of the
Shah at the expense of the *majles*.

Before the coup the US had supported an AIOC-sponsored boycott
of Iranian oil on world markets, and the loss of revenue hurt Mosaddeq's
government badly. By late 1952 and early 1953, therefore, the time to
strike was opportune, because Iran was in financial distress. This might
erode support for the fiery nationalist. Kermit Roosevelt of the CIA, son
of former US president Theodore Roosevelt, went to Iran and set the
conspiracy in motion. The plan was for the Shah to dismiss Mosaddeq as
prime minister, and to install General Fazlollah Zahedi, who had collaborated with the Nazis during the Second World War. But Mosaddeq
found out about the plot, with the result that the Shah fled first to
Baghdad and then to Rome. Large anti-Shah demonstrations then
followed, with the Tudeh in the vanguard, but the CIA was also secretly

financing demonstrations against Mosaddeq's government. The prime minister feared that further violence by his partisans would cost the government support, and that he was losing control of events. He therefore called out the army, but it was a right-wing stronghold. Moreover, calling out the army caused dissension between the prime minister and the Tudeh, and hurt their efforts to resist the CIA–Shah coup. Instead of protecting Mosaddeq's supporters, the army moved against the crowds of Tudeh members and other anti-Shah forces. Mosaddeq was overthrown and jailed. The coup had not gone exactly according to plan, but the result was the same. It restored the Shah as the centre of power in Iran, and one now linked closely to the Americans. They would continue to nurture the growth of his power in the coming years. The restoration of the Shah's authority and the subordination of the *majles* was the real point of the anti-Mosaddeq coup.

About a year later, in the summer of 1954, a new oil agreement was concluded. The nationalized Iranian oil company continued in existence, but henceforth it was to produce and market oil through a new international consortium. The old AIOC (renamed British Petroleum, or BP) was to handle 40 per cent of the business, while five large American companies each received an 8 per cent share (Standard Oil of New Jersey, Standard Oil of California, Gulf, Texas Oil and Socony-Mobil). The balance went to Dutch and French interests, and later the American companies shared the spoils with some of their smaller US competitors. In other words, whereas the Americans before the crisis did not control the main stake, afterwards they had a share equal to that of the British. Moreover, a secret accord among consortium members limited Iranian petroleum production, in order to control the Shah's revenues and keep him subservient to Western interests.

For the Americans, sponsorship of the 1953 coup had paid off handsomely. It brought them a giant step closer to displacing the United Kingdom as the dominant neo-colonial power in the country. The problem was that continued outside domination only postponed the day when Iran would explode in a fury of anti-Western and anti-American revolution. In the meantime the Shah instituted what became one of the world's most repressive dictatorships, aided and abetted by the CIA. The United States placed access to Iranian oil and the need to keep Iran in the Western Bloc ahead of all other considerations, including fundamental human rights, and the result was to rebound against it in the future. And while the British were grateful for having survived the Mosaddeq threat, they also knew that once again they had been pushed aside by American power. Clearly the pre-eminence of Europe and Britain as global forces was fading. And it was not just the overthrow of Mosaddeq which showed this. The Suez Crisis of 1956 also served to drive the point home, but not before shattering the unity of the Western Bloc.

THE RUSSIANS AND THE THIRD WORLD

The Soviet Union, however, was also implicated in the Suez Crisis. By the mid-1950s the Russians were launching their first large-scale programmes of military and economic assistance designed to win friends and influence people in the non-communist Third World. No longer were their efforts to be confined principally to propaganda, with material support reserved mainly for nations which were already communist (e.g. North Korea and China) or for movements which were actively engaged in anti-colonial and revolutionary warfare and which had formed *de facto* governments (e.g. the Vietminh). As we have already noted (Chapter 3), before the mid-1950s the USSR had little material assistance to spare for Third World revolutionaries who did not already control the state, and hardly any for non-communist countries. Thus the USSR did not provide aid to Ho Chi Minh until four years after the war with the French had begun, while outside the communist world arms aid for Israel (in 1948) was the exception which proved the rule. Yet, once the Russians had recovered from the devastation of the Second World War, this began to change. The result was to make the West's relations with its colonies and former colonies considerably more complicated than in the past, and to contribute to dissension within the Western Bloc itself. Western Europeans came to feel that sometimes the United States was a bit too ready to sacrifice their colonial interests in order to win the support of the Third World in the East–West struggle.

Of course, it was virtually inevitable that sooner or later the Russians would attempt to increase their influence in the Third World. Such a policy would contribute to the security of the USSR, and hence was in its national interest. And although Russia was the largest country on earth by area and therefore rich in a variety of natural resources, it still needed its share of strategic raw materials from the Third World, just as the United States or any other developed nation. No country is literally self-sufficient in every respect. Further, trade with the Third World promised to help the Russians solve their balance of payments problems, so that markets were of interest as well. For example, much later (in the

1970s), when a considerable amount of business had resumed with Western Europe and North America, the Russians would use income earned from a favourable balance with the Third World to offset deficits arising from their unfavourable balance with the developed nations of the West. The Russian interest in earning foreign exchange was the result of its need to import foreign technology, such as sophisticated machinery or computers. Doing so required currencies negotiable in the developed West, and these could be obtained through trade with the Third World. After all, most of the latter were within the Western orbit, even though many were willing to trade with Russia. In sum, the USSR had a good many reasons for cultivating nations outside the Communist Bloc. Some of these reasons, moreover, were not so different from those of the West in the same regions. Furthermore, the Soviet balance of payments dilemma testified to the supremacy of the global capitalist market, for the Russians had to play the game of international trade largely by capitalist rules. Sometimes they made bartering arrangements with Third World countries, or set up jointly owned enterprises, but on many occasions it was very much in the Russian interest to receive payment in Western currencies.

The main motive for wooing the underdeveloped nations in the 1950s, however, was strategic. Stalin's basic approach to diplomacy had been to delineate a Soviet and an American sphere of influence, mainly in Europe, and in the immediate post-1945 period to concede actual control of the colonial world to the West. At the time this was a realistic reading of the Russians' capacity to act globally. But, as Soviet power grew, it became possible to challenge the pre-eminence of the West in areas the latter traditionally had dominated. The opportunities were only compounded by the decline of colonialism. Furthermore, changes in military technology (in the 1950s these included the first practical steps towards the development of intercontinental ballistic missiles) made the whole concept of spheres or buffer zones less relevant, and this reduced the likelihood that the Soviets would respect the boundaries of the old spheres. Outside Europe the latter were never very clear anyway. In the Russian view the Americans had already violated the territorial integrity of the Communist Bloc by crossing the thirty-eighth parallel in Korea. For its part, of course, the United States defined the communists as the aggressors.

As a result the mid-1950s saw the Russians launch a series of aid initiatives in the Third World. These were still not on the scale of the Western effort, but they did show the USSR's rising capacity to act as a world power. They concluded long-term arrangements to provide economic and technical assistance to India in 1955, and Khrushchev and Bulganin visited the country in a calculated display of interest in Third World problems. The next year they extended additional technical aid and provided credits equal to US $126 million. At about the same time the Russians courted the favour of Burma, and agreed to build medical, tourist, sports and educational facilities. The USSR made $100 million worth of aid available to Indonesia in 1957, and included military assistance. Another $250 million was extended three years later, again with large quantities of modern weaponry. The Soviets even committed themselves to building a nuclear power plant in the country, but subsequently a right-wing coup against the Indonesian government brought Soviet aid to a speedy end (see Chapter 9). Extending loans or technical and military assistance did not guarantee the loyalty of a would-be client, as both the USSR and the USA were to learn many times over.

In the 1950s, however, it was the Russians' role in the Middle East, particularly in Egypt, that most directly challenged Western hegemony. A larger Soviet presence would affect vital Western interests. Cairo was virtually a British protectorate; Arab oil was vital to Western prosperity; and the future of Israel was of special concern to many people in Europe and America.

Suez

In the specific area of the Middle East, obviously, Soviet power was not the only factor affecting the situation. The West played a much larger role. The British (still the principal foreign power in the region) retained major economic stakes, chiefly in oil and (with the French) in the Suez Canal, while the Americans were very interested in expanding their stake as well. The United Kingdom also had a small but none the less important military presence (for example, its troops were stationed in Jordan, Iraq and Egypt). In addition, the British were committed to providing arms to a number of Arab states. British aid was a token of the Western determination to maintain friendship with the Arabs as well as Israel, and thus retain access to their oil. Another strategic consideration was the US goal of drawing the Arabs into some sort of a regional defensive alliance (perhaps similar to NATO) to offset the influence of the USSR, so that the East–West struggle was a factor in the Middle East. The problem was that Western interests ran headlong into Arab nationalism. For the time being the most important example was Egypt

(Iran was in a separate category, as its people were not Arab but Persian, and on many questions were at odds with the Arabs). In 1952 Egyptian military officers staged a nationalist revolution which resulted in the installation of a government committed to expelling Britain from its garrisons along the Suez Canal. And then there was the question of Israel's right to exist as an independent state, a problem exacerbated by its identification with the West, i.e. with the powers that for so long had dominated the Middle East and that had alienated Arab nationalists.

For their part the Israelis had some reason for optimism after the 1948 war. They had received support from both the USA and the USSR, including diplomatic recognition, so the prospect that the future of Israel might somehow be insulated from the Cold War seemed at least possible if not probable. It certainly was worth the effort to cultivate both sides. The Russian interest in supporting Israeli independence had been to see Britain expelled as the traditional hegemonic power in Palestine and environs. And there were other reasons for the Israelis to be hopeful. After all, various Arab belligerents in the 1948 war had negotiated armistice agreements with Israel, so that perhaps these could serve as the basis of a permanent settlement. Any reason for optimism about relations with either the Soviets or the Arabs, however, soon disappeared.

Israel had much to gain by keeping the Russians friendly. It did not want Moscow to interfere with the movement of Jewish immigrants from Eastern Europe. It also hoped to win the Kremlin's permission for Jews to leave the USSR itself. Yet Israel still wanted the support of the Jewish community in the United States – American Jews had contributed generously to the Israeli cause. Washington might also be a source of economic and possibly military aid. Indeed, as it became clear that the Arabs were not going to sign a permanent treaty of peace, the question of military aid took on considerable importance, especially because the British were shipping weapons to a number of Arab nations in the region. It will be recalled that in administering Palestine the UK tended to be more pro-Arab than pro-Jewish before vacating its mandate over the area in 1948. Therefore, in 1950, the government of Israel made a formal request to buy arms from the United States. For the time being the US held back lest it escalate the Middle Eastern arms race. Even so, Israel's American connections served only to alienate the Russians. The USSR would gain little if it turned out that the Israelis had expelled the British from Palestine only to fall under the sway of the Americans. Besides, it was perfectly clear to the USSR that there was more to be gained by cultivating the Arabs. They were the majority in the Middle East; they had oil; and they were restless under Western tutelage.

The Soviet commitment to Israel had been dubious anyway. It was the result of a tactical manoeuvre to undercut British influence in the area, and not of a long-term commitment to the Jewish cause. Historically, in Eastern Europe and Russia itself anti-Semitism had been as virulent as in Nazi Germany. The Slansky trial in Czechoslovakia, or the 1953 'doctors' plot' in Russia (when a number of Soviet physicians, including several Jews, were falsely accused of conspiring to murder top USSR leaders), were simply among the most recent examples. But it was the East–West conflict that was the immediate cause of the reversion in Soviet attitudes.

Great-power competition for the loyalty of the Arabs was virtually inevitable. The British were committed to providing arms, but in the 1950s it was the Americans who did the most to raise the stakes. However supportive of Israel, they also wanted to persuade the Arab nations to stand by the USA in the Cold War. In 1951, therefore, the United States, Britain, France and Turkey suggested forming a Middle Eastern Defence Command, though it was the Americans who were really behind the scheme. Egypt was first on the list of potential recruits, as it was the site of the Suez Canal and therefore of paramount strategic importance to Western shipping and oil interests. But the Egyptian government, itself facing trouble at home, dared not accept the idea. Egyptian nationalists asked why their country should be a stalking-horse for the United States in the Cold War, when for them the main task at hand was to end Western and particularly British domination. The Americans persisted, however, and by early 1954 oversaw the signing of a mutual defence treaty between Turkey and Pakistan. Both countries were drawn into the plan by US promises of economic and military assistance. The next year Washington lured Iraq into the alliance by the same means. Hence, the name Baghdad Pact (formally the Central Treaty Organization) was applied to the emerging alliance. Later in the same year, 1955, Britain and then Iran also joined. It appeared that the American goal of creating an anti-Soviet bloc in the Middle East was working. The US itself did not become a member of the Baghdad Pact, as it still hoped to attract the Egyptians, and the last thing Washington wanted to do was to leave the impression that the pact was US-dominated. Few people were fooled, of course, and so the question of constructing a regional alliance linked to the West was a major source of contention among the Arabs themselves. The participation of Iran complicated the issue further.

Not surprisingly the Russians did not look kindly on these developments. Neither did the Israelis. After all, America was arming many nations which were sworn enemies of the Jewish cause. The risk was that guns intended to defend the Middle East against possible Soviet penetration might be turned on Israel. And to the British it was perfectly clear that the Americans wanted to dominate what had once been their sphere. The United Kingdom also blamed the US for introducing the Cold War into the Middle East, fearing that such a course would only destabilize the region further. The Russians were doing their part to make inroads too, but until 1955 the Soviet role did not involve arms aid. American plans for the Baghdad Pact, though, were likely to provoke the USSR into counter-measures.

It was the 1952 Egyptian Revolution which offered the USSR an opportunity to improve its strategic position *vis-à-vis* the Arabs. The revolution was not the result of Soviet subversion, however; nor were communists the driving force behind the new government. Instead it was led by the military, first under the titular leadership of General Mohammad Neguib and then (from 1954) under the real strong man of the revolution, Colonel Gamal Abdel Nasser, and was more nationalist than anything else in character. The goal was to rid the country of a government which was both corrupt and subservient to foreign interests.

Although Egypt had been part of the Ottoman Empire in the nineteenth century and thus fell under the authority of the sultan of Turkey, British troops occupied the country in 1881–2. Their mission was to preserve the government of the Khedive, the sultan's viceroy, precisely because it was weak and therefore pliable. The Khedive had contracted huge foreign debts, and as a result had been forced to allow outsiders to administer the country's finances. Accordingly, when nationalists in the army staged a rebellion in an attempt to overthrow the government and end foreign domination, the British intervened. They did not take over the country directly, however, and only proclaimed Egypt a formal protectorate during the First World War. Indeed, they promised to withdraw their forces as soon as the Egyptian government was capable of maintaining order, and reiterated this pledge a total of sixty-six times between the 1880s and the early 1920s. Although the protectorate legally came to an end in 1922, the British were not really ready to concede that the Egyptians could run their own affairs. Only in 1930 did Egypt regain full autonomy over its finances. Even then British

influence remained paramount. In 1936, for example, the United Kingdom negotiated the right to keep a garrison of 10,000 troops in the canal
zone for a further period of twenty years. And when King Farouk
hesitated to appoint a pro-Allied prime minister at the beginning of the
Second World War, the British threatened to overthrow his government.
His palace encircled by foreign troops, the king yielded. By the 1950s
and the rise of Nasser, however, Britain's days in Egypt were numbered.

The revolution had grave implications for Israel, because the Americans thought it more urgent than ever to cultivate the Egyptians. The
US did not want Nasser and company to turn to the USSR for aid and
sustenance. As with the Baghdad Pact, however, American policy
towards Egypt had the potential to threaten Israel's security. In the early
1950s the Israelis found their requests for US help being turned aside,
while Washington was clearly prepared to offer substantial assistance to
Cairo. Moreover, the Americans placed pressure on Britain to accom-
modate Egyptian demands for full sovereignty over the Suez Canal.
Under the 1936 treaty the British were obliged to remove their troops by
1956, but Nasser wanted them out as soon as possible. Of course, this
also meant that British forces would no longer serve as a buffer between
the Arab world and Israel's southern flank. An agreement on the UK's
departure from the Suez Canal was concluded by Nasser in the summer
of 1954, though it did allow the British to return should Turkey or the
Arab League (Egypt, Syria, Lebanon, Jordan, Saudi Arabia, Yemen,
Iraq and Libya) be attacked by any outside country except Israel (e.g. the
USSR). Given America's sympathy for Egypt in the negotiations, US
policy-makers expected that Nasser would now be willing to join the
Baghdad Pact. This would consolidate the anti-Soviet alliance in the
Middle East, and presumably Nasser's involvement in a pro-Western
alliance would also lessen the Arab threat to Israel, allowing Jewish
objections to US policy to be put aside. But the Americans were to be
bitterly disappointed – Nasser would remain aloof despite their hopes.
Moreover, it seemed to the Israelis that their interests were being
countered at every turn, and that in the event of a crisis perhaps they
should be prepared to take things into their own hands.

What spoiled the American plan to woo Nasser was that the United
States was attempting to create an alliance among nations of diverse and
conflicting interests. The Americans hoped to overcome these by alerting the Arabs to the communist threat, but traditional rivalries in the
region proved more powerful. United States aid to Iraq as a member of
the Baghdad Pact enabled the Iraqis to bid for leadership of the Arab

world, a role coveted by the Egyptians. Accordingly Nasser decided to outflank the Americans and the Iraqis by courting the Russians. The result was an agreement, announced in September 1955, to sell cotton to the Eastern Bloc in return for Czechoslovak arms, though the deal was really with the USSR. Nasser's interest in undermining the Baghdad Pact played right into Soviet hands. The USSR projected itself as the friend of Arab nationalism against the Western imperial powers, while Nasser emerged as the only Arab leader apparently capable of standing up to the West. And Russian guns meant Egypt was in a position to advance the cause of the Palestinian Arabs against Israel.

To the Israelis there seemed to be only one thing to do. The United States should counter the rising influence of the Soviet Union in Egypt by providing Israel with the means to defend itself. The result would be to redeem the credibility of the US as a nation willing and able to defend its interests in the Middle East. Instead both the Americans and the British adopted a policy of appeasement, and agreed to provide funding for the Aswan Dam, one of the world's largest irrigation and hydroelectric programmes and Nasser's pet project. Even the French swallowed their pride and sought to patch up relations with Egypt. They had been badly hurt by Nasser's aid to anti-colonial rebels in Algeria, but none the less joined the Western campaign of appeasement. In effect the West chose to try outbidding the Soviets for Nasser's co-operation. The Israelis were far less sanguine that Egypt could be bought. In the meantime the number of incidents along the frontier between Israel and the Arab world began to increase.

In point of fact, time was on the Israeli side, because Nasser remained implacable. He was determined to play East against West, which finally forced the United States, Britain and France to consider reprisals. In the spring of 1956, accordingly, the French began to sell arms to Israel. The Israelis still wanted American weapons, though, not only to add to their arsenal but to signal to Nasser that the USA was prepared to come to their defence. In other words, the political impact of receiving American arms would be far greater than French help, however welcome the latter. The breakthrough for the Jews occurred when it became known that the United States was agreeable to allowing France to divert weapons earmarked for NATO to Israel. The significance of this was just about the same as if the Americans themselves had provided the arms. Nasser's response was to taunt the Americans by withdrawing diplomatic recognition from Chiang Kai-shek's regime on Taiwan and shifting it to the People's Republic. Egypt's policy towards China, of course, made no difference to developments in Asia, but was intended to send a message to the Americans that Nasser was not about to be intimidated. But neither was the USA. Under growing pressure from Britain, France and, in the Middle East, Turkey and Iraq, as well as the US Congress, John Foster Dulles withdrew American financial support for the Aswan Dam in July.

Nasser's response was to nationalize the Suez Canal (it was owned by French and British interests). Since the Americans had withdrawn their commitment of aid, he would use its revenue to build the Aswan Dam. The result was panic in London and Paris, because Europe's shipping and a considerable amount of its oil supply were now subject to the whim of a person increasingly portrayed as a madman. The Western press described Nasser as a new Hitler, impossible to please, and drew dubious analogies with the events that had led to the Second World War. The message was clear: it was time to remember Munich, and put aside any thought of further appeasement.

Not surprisingly Nasser was a hero in the Arab world. He had not taken leave of his senses. Both Syria and Jordan became virtual Egyptian satellites. What determined the developments of the next few months, however, was that Europe's material interests were in conflict with Egyptian nationalism. The same was true of Israel's needs, particularly its quest for security in a hostile Arab world. For this reason, in the summer and autumn of 1956, Britain, France and Israel conspired to initiate a war against Egypt. The rationale was that a pre-emptive strike was justified on the grounds that Nasser was clearly planning to strangle Europe's oil lifeline and to attack Israel. The conspiracy was kept secret from the United States, and the Americans would be taken by surprise when the plot began to unfold. The result was another fracture in the Western alliance, but Washington's earlier wooing of Nasser had shaken the confidence of its closest allies. The latter believed that the time had come for them to take charge and to make the hard decisions that the US seemed unwilling to face. If, as they believed, this meant resorting to force, so be it. Moreover, with the Russians distracted by events in Poland and Hungary, there was little likelihood that the USSR would interfere in the Middle East.

As planned, the Israelis moved first. They invaded Egypt, specifically the Sinai Peninsula, on 29 October. It was prearranged that the British and French would then intervene in the name of restoring order, though the real purpose was to secure the canal and to destroy Egypt's capacity to threaten Israel. British and French aircraft bombed military targets in

Egypt on 30 October. On 5 November paratroopers landed, followed by an amphibious force the day after, but they failed to take the canal. Instead the waterway was severely damaged in the fighting, so that it would remain closed to navigation for years to come.

Whatever their own mistakes in the past, the Americans considered a hot war in the Middle East to be the worst possible outcome. War would surely play into the hands of the Soviets and fuel Arab nationalism. The Americans therefore went to the United Nations and obtained resolutions calling for an end to the fighting and the withdrawal of all foreign forces. Given that the canal was now closed, the US was in a strong position to manipulate the world oil market, particularly supplies from Venezuela, and thus had the means to compel the Europeans to withdraw. It was also clear that the Americans were prepared to undermine the value of the pound and the franc on world money markets. Britain and France therefore were forced to desist immediately. For their part the Russians threatened to intervene with force unless Britain and France withdrew, but the conspirators' projection that the USSR would not be able to act proved correct. The USA placed its forces on alert in case the Russians were to do something, but in fact there was little likelihood of this. The Soviets had their hands full in Eastern Europe, and Russian troops opened fire in Budapest the day before the British and French landed in Egypt. Universally condemned, and having failed to protect the canal from damage, Britain and France agreed to a cease-fire on 6 November. They also agreed to withdraw their troops, as did the Israelis. The Europeans left by the end of the year, and Israel's forces departed in February 1957.

The Suez Crisis left the Western Bloc in disarray. Britain, France and Israel had been prepared to risk the wrath of the United States, calculating that it would be worth it if they were to succeed. Success in this situation had to be defined as a quick and dramatic strike, one designed to catch the Egyptians off guard. The need was to take the canal before they could react. Otherwise there was the chance that it would be damaged and blocked, which was exactly what happened. But the whole business was badly managed on the European side, and the decision to intervene after Israel had struck first proved fatal. By the time Britain and France moved, the element of surprise was lost. Thus the Egyptian campaign, while demonstrating once again Israel's military prowess, definitively ended European claims to hegemony in the region. Their armed forces had proved incapable of taking charge, leaving the USA as the uncontested representative of Western interests in the Middle East.

The Europeans, though, could not help but be a bit cynical about what they saw as America's overly pious condemnation of their actions. Had not the US itself applied a type of force in Iran against Mosaddeq? What was the difference between 1953 and 1956? Moreover, in 1958 the USA would land troops in Lebanon (see Chapter 11), again suggesting a double standard. The Americans were quite prepared to use military force where it served their interests.

No party to the conflict emerged unscathed. The invasion drove Nasser into the arms of Khrushchev as the only possible source of outside aid, and enabled the USSR to score propaganda points against the Western aggressors. On the other hand, the USSR's inability to affect the immediate outcome also tarnished its reputation as a reliable supporter of the Arab cause. And in the long run it turned out that the Egyptians were unwilling to accept Russian domination any more than Western, so that many years later (in 1976) Cairo would abrogate a Soviet–Egyptian friendship treaty (signed in 1971). The USSR thus would have little to show for a considerable material and diplomatic investment. Finally, while Israel had once again proved its worth as a military power, the war also negated the possibility of a negotiated peace with the Arab world for years to come. But perhaps no other outcome was possible.

6

DECOLONIZATION IN AFRICA

Whatever the impact of Soviet aid in winning the loyalty of non-communist countries in the 1950s, the Third World was still mainly under the influence of the West. Indeed, such was to be the case for the foreseeable future. Yet, as we have seen, the Western presence spurred the growth of nationalist and revolutionary movements, and did so quite independently of what the Russians were up to. In some ways the West was its own worst enemy. The repercussions, moreover, could spread well beyond the Third World. Perhaps the best example was the terrible colonial war which the French fought in Algeria from 1954 to 1962, and which eventuated in the fall of the Fourth Republic (the successor to Vichy) in France itself.

THE MAGHRIB
Unlike the British after the Second World War, the French were determined to retain direct control of their colonies in Africa, and did not regard neo-colonialism as an attractive option. This was particularly the case in the Maghrib (Algeria, Tunisia and Morocco), where there were large settler populations, i.e. permanent residents whose origins were European and who wished to remain linked to France. The French term for these people was *colons*. In 1945 more than a million of them lived in Algeria, about 300,000 in Morocco and 250,000 in Tunisia. It was thus Algeria where the French stake was greatest, and this was reflected in its legal status as a *département*, or province, of France itself. Morocco and Tunisia were formally protectorates, an important distinction. Protectorate status meant that in law the French regarded each as an independent country, though under their guardianship. But no such pretence was maintained in the case of Algeria. Moreover, pro-French extremists there were determined to maintain the *status quo*, and were not averse to

employing assassination against African proponents of independence, north or south of the Sahara. In the past, promises of political equality between metropolitan France and its overseas possessions had per-suaded some native colonials to opt for assimilation rather than inde-pendence. In the post-war period, however, as it became evident that such pledges were really a cover for a permanent French presence, the assimilationist alternative became less and less attractive to local leaders. Also, events in Egypt influenced the Maghrib, both before and after the 1952 coup by reformist military officers, and the war in Indo-China weakened the capacity of the French to deal with challenges elsewhere until their withdrawal from South-East Asia in 1954.

It turned out that Tunisia and Morocco moved more easily to independence than Algeria – perhaps the smaller settler population was one reason – but this is not to say that the French conceded autonomy without a fight. When the Bey, or ruler, of Tunis added his support to the independence cause in the late 1940s, the French responded with increasing repression. In 1952 they banned the chief pro-independence political movement, the *Néo-Destour*, and threw its leaders in jail. This was done even though the *Néo-Destour* brought together members of Tunisia's professional and petty bourgeois classes, some educated in France itself, who wanted independence so that they could take charge of their own country – that is, they wanted a political not a social revolution. The French, however, were not prepared to concede anything, at least for the time being. The result was a guerrilla war which within two years required 70,000 French troops to be sent to the country. Yet this development had a dual impact. On the one hand it strengthened the bargaining power of *Néo-Destour* leaders like Habib Bourguiba (though in prison, he none the less spoke for the movement), but on the other threatened their ability to control the independence movement. The guerrillas in the hills had their own commanders, and represented peasant interests as opposed to those of the native elite. Hence Bour-guiba wanted to settle with the French before he lost control. The French too had much to gain by dealing with him rather than more radical forces. It had taken a small war to move the French to this point, but eventually they did come around to the neo-colonial option in Tunisia. Accordingly, in 1954, they released Bourguiba from prison, lifted the ban on the *Néo-Destour*, and offered amnesty to the guerrillas. In 1955 the French proceeded to grant internal autonomy. This in turn contributed to a division in the *Neo-Déstour* between those who favoured emphasizing social change and moderates like Bourguiba who wanted independence but not an internal revolution. Thus having divided the nationalist forces and steeled the moderates against the threat of more radical elements, France granted independence to Bourguiba and his faction in 1956.

Much the same story unfolded in Morocco. There too the local elite joined forces with other groups in the population and formed what was known as the *Istiqlal*, in late 1943. Again the French moved from a policy of repression to one of accepting leaders who might not threaten their most vital interests. Because the Sultan Mohammad V served as a rallying point for resistance, the French deposed him in 1953. But instead of ending anti-French activity the result was to intensify it. Peasant fighting forces began operating in the countryside, just as Paris faced a worsening crisis in Algeria and disaster in Indo-China. At the same time it was on the verge of accepting complete independence for Tunisia. The French therefore decided to yield. They could not afford to become engaged in yet another major war. The sultan returned, and independence followed in 1956, just a few weeks before Tunisia acquired full autonomy.

The War in Algeria

It was perhaps a little easier for France to accept change in Tunisia and Morocco because the European population was much smaller than in Algeria. Remember that in the latter there were about a million people who were European (French, Spanish and Italian) by descent and culture. Many of these had been born in North Africa and regarded it as their permanent home. While some had been schooled in France and attended university there, most planned to continue living in Algeria. All Europeans were hardly wealthy, yet even the impoverished wanted to maintain the French connection – it was the main thing that gave them a social advantage over indigenous Algerians. Therefore most people of European descent, rich or poor, tended to accept both the validity and the workability of the assimilationist solution for integrating the Arabs into metropolitan France. Most native Algerians, however, did not. The result was a crisis that led to the fall of the Fourth Republic in France itself and raised the spectre of a right-wing *coup d'état.*

As in other parts of the colonial world, the anti-Axis war spurred the development of nationalist sentiment. For a time Algeria was under the control of the Vichy government, but when the Allies landed in 1942 the Free French took charge. While they wanted to end the Nazi occupation of Europe, it was clear that the liberators were not prepared to vacate

North Africa once the war was over, though they did promise reform. And French Algerians were prepared to concede even less. Indeed, many of them had sympathized with Vichy, and identified with a government determined to save what it could of the old order, including the French empire. The Germans, after all, had allowed Vichy to continue administering North Africa until the Allied invasion. As we have already noted (Chapter 3), violence broke out between the French and the Arabs at the end of the Second World War. But for nearly a decade France was able to preserve the *status quo*.

Events took a new direction, however, when a small group of Algerian nationalists under the leadership of Ahmed Ben Bella concluded that force was the only way to end French rule. They began to organize in secret as the *Front de Libération Nationale* (FLN), and in the autumn of 1954 launched an armed uprising. By 1956 the fighting had spread throughout the north of the country, with Algerian women playing a major role. Before the crisis was over, the French army in Algeria would grow to 500,000 troops, and this within a few years of the débâcle at Dien Bien Phu. Moreover, the French government was forced to send conscripts to Algeria, something it had never done in the case of Indo-China. As a result the war affected many in France who were not enthusiastic supporters of empire, and widespread dissatisfaction with the war in North Africa developed by the late 1950s. France had freed itself from one military disaster only to become embroiled in another. As late as 1958 probably a majority of French citizens still favoured protecting the interests of the *colons* whatever the price. But others considered that it was a lost cause, so that French politics tended to become polarized, and France itself entered upon a particularly unstable period in its history.

While civilians dominated the events of the late 1950s and early 1960s, the French officer corps played a key role as well. The problem was that the army had grown apart from the rest of society, and came to see itself as called to a special mission to save the honour of France. In effect this meant violating the normally well-respected boundary between civilian and military rule. Discredited by defeat in the Second World War and Indo-China, and having been forced to stand by as independence was conceded to Tunisia and Morocco, the officer corps was anxious to vindicate the credibility of the military. Some of its members regarded a possible compromise in Algeria as the last straw, something which absolutely had to be resisted. Algeria was one of the few places left where the army could prove its mettle. Many officers tended to doubt the ability of civilians to make the difficult decision to impose a military solution on the colonial problem. Before the Algerian crisis was over, some of them concluded that the only thing to do was to overthrow the government of France and establish a new regime. Among the people of France, though, there seemed to be little support for such an extreme course of action. For example, while some of the conspirators looked to General Charles de Gaulle to provide the Fourth Republic with strong leadership, a public opinion poll in 1958 showed that only 13 per cent of the French population favoured his return to politics. It should be noted that the general did not actually participate in or encourage the army plot that was about to unfold, though he would take advantage of the crisis to assume power on his own terms.

The moment of truth came in the spring of 1958. A new premier, Pierre Pflimlin, assumed power after a month of uncertainty over the formation of a new coalition government in the French National Assembly. In effect there had been a period of interregnum in Paris, while the politicians pieced together a new cabinet. But this only encouraged the conspirators to take things into their own hands, especially as there were rumours that the new premier was prepared to negotiate an end to the Algerian war, a policy which could only culminate in the French surrendering control. A negotiated settlement would in effect mean another ignominious defeat for the army. Therefore, on 13 May 1958, the conspirators instigated a mass demonstration in Algiers against the new government, in the hope of intimidating the National Assembly and forcing it to reject the new cabinet. Violence broke out, government buildings were sacked, and a Committee of Public Safety led by General Jacques Massu assumed political power.

De Gaulle and the Fifth Republic

In France the possibility of civil war seemed imminent, as extremists considered launching a paratroop attack on Paris and other centres. But pro-Gaullists among the conspirators and in France itself preferred a peaceful settlement, and saw the crisis as an opportunity to make de Gaulle premier. De Gaulle himself assumed an ambiguous posture. He was willing to serve the country but disclaimed any interest in a *coup d'état*. It was clear, however, that he favoured a new constitutional order, as the general also made it known that he would not participate in the political *status quo* or assume office via the procedures of the Fourth Republic. De Gaulle secretly and skilfully bargained with the leaders of the National Assembly, and suggested that without him civil war was the likely fate of France. Further, the Gaullists gained the support of members of the Committee of Public Safety in Algiers and recognized the authority of one of its supporters, General Raoul Salan, over the country. Events quickened when pro-Gaullists staged a coup and took over Corsica (French since 1768) on 24 May. In the face of renewed rumours of an impending paratroop attack on Paris, Pflimlin resigned in favour of de Gaulle. For his part de Gaulle agreed to become premier in accordance with existing constitutional practice, despite his earlier reservations. On 1 June he went to the National Assembly, where he was installed in office. For all practical purposes the Fourth Republic was dead, and France was about to restructure its government, investing the president with much stronger executive powers than in the past. The Assembly adjourned after giving de Gaulle complete authority to rule for six months and instructing him to prepare a new constitution. The latter was to be ratified by a popular referendum.

Yet de Gaulle proved to be no dictator, as some of the army extremists in Algeria may have hoped. He did favour a heavy dose of executive power, but to guarantee that the new Fifth Republic would always be capable of acting, no matter how factionalized the politics of the National Assembly. And while de Gaulle introduced constraints on the democratic process, he was hardly interested in abolishing it altogether. For example, the president would no longer be elected by the National Assembly, but by an electoral college of 80,000 members who in turn were selected mainly by local governments. Similarly he restricted the Assembly's right to turn out a cabinet. But parliamentary government continued, and the constitutional reforms were less drastic than many had expected. The new constitution was approved in a referendum held in the autumn. It turned out that de Gaulle did favour a stronger republic, but a republic none the less. Moreover, he recognized the limits of French colonial power.

The proof of this was soon to come. Upon assuming power de Gaulle began to work secretly for a compromise solution in Algeria, though without immediate results. Both the rebels (i.e. the indigenous Algerians) and the *colons* were adamant. The fighting continued, and on 19 September 1958 the rebels announced the formation of a provisional government. French extremists attempted another military coup in Algiers (January 1960), but it soon came to naught. When peace talks between Paris and the Arabs finally were agreed to in 1961, however, events again took a dangerous turn. General Salan and General Maurice Challe set up the *Organisation de l'Armée secrète*, or OAS, and proceeded to stage an uprising in April. But in the face of what was clearly becoming a lost cause, most of the army rank and file remained loyal, whatever the generals might want to do. This final crisis rallied the nation around de Gaulle, and the OAS plot fell apart. Talks therefore began with the Algerian Arabs in May, as planned. Yet the extremists had not made their final play, and at this point resorted to indiscriminate terrorism, including attacks in Paris itself. Nevertheless, both the Arabs and de Gaulle knew that France had been exhausted by the struggle. Negotiations continued despite OAS provocations, and peace was agreed to at the French resort of Evian in 1962. Paris formally proclaimed Algeria free on 3 July.

Independent Algeria

More than 250,000 Algerians had been killed in the course of the struggle, with the last-gasp effort of the OAS responsible for possibly 12,000 casualties. This made Algeria the site of one of the worst of the post-1945 colonial wars, and the effect was to drive the country in a more radical direction than Tunisia or Morocco. Of necessity, peasant forces provided the backbone of the rebel army, though the FLN leadership tended to be petty bourgeois or middle class. The latter had experience in politics and had much to gain by displacing the French. Some members of the leadership advocated social revolution, but others were more nationalists than anything else. The latter appreciated the need to mobilize the masses in order to wage an anti-colonial war and expel the French, but their commitment to social change was not as great as that of the revolutionaries. None the less, given the magnitude of the military struggle in Algeria as compared to elsewhere in North Africa, the peasantry assumed considerable importance in the outcome. Hence it was likely that the leaders of the new regime would respond to its aspirations, particularly for land reform. This would come at the cost of the *colons*, whose property would be expropriated.

Accordingly, to many students of politics at the time, it seemed that the new Algerian government might assume a socialist cast, in marked contrast to the more clearly neo-colonial outcome in the rest of the Maghrib. In fact, Ben Bella, who was elected first president of Algeria in 1963, did legalize the expropriation of most foreign-owned land and hundreds of business enterprises, most of which had been abandoned by the French. About 800,000 *colons* fled the country and became refugees in France. For the time being Algerian landlords did not lose their property, so a good deal of land was still concentrated in the hands of the few. But in June 1965 Ben Bella would fall victim to a military coup by his one-time ally Houari Boumédienne, and the so-called Algerian 'revolution' took a new turn. While Boumédienne set up an authoritarian regime, he also propagated a populist and anti-imperialist ideology, and carried out various programmes of reform. Beginning in 1971, additional land was redistributed from among the holdings of major Algerian owners, though much still remained under their control. Further, between 1968 and 1974 Boumédienne nationalized what was left of foreign-owned enterprises. Yet he did compromise and permit foreign investment. It was just that the latter had to be via mixed corporations, with the Algerian government holding at least 51 per cent of the shares. The balance could be held by private capital. Thus companies such as Getty Petroleum, El Paso Natural Gas, Elf and *Compagnie Française des Pétroles* were able to defend their stake in the Algerian energy sector, and it seemed probable that the country would remain closely tied to the West. Algeria achieved much greater economic independence from the First World than most countries in the Third World, but it was also clear that Boumédienne represented a compromise and that French influences (cultural and economic) remained strong. Consequently France gradually, if begrudgingly, accepted the outcome.

SOUTH OF THE SAHARA

British West Africa

South of the Sahara, Britain and France were the major colonial powers, though Belgium and Portugal also held vast territories. Of the two leaders it was the British who moved more readily towards decolonization and neo-colonial forms of influence. Their colonies in West Africa (Gold Coast, Gambia, Nigeria and Sierra Leone) provided the model for change throughout the region, much to the dismay of the more recalcitrant French. In point of fact London was not particularly eager to surrender its colonies, but it was realistic. It also helped that there were very few whites in these territories, so the settler factor was less telling than for the French in the Maghrib. Further, by offering membership in the British Commonwealth to the newly independent nations of Africa, perhaps London might perpetuate its influence. Most importantly, the British were reasonably confident that economic power would be sufficient to preserve their influence in sub-Sahara Africa. They had created the largest empire in the world, and it would be difficult for their former colonies to alter existing patterns of trade. Links had developed between businessmen and politicians in the United Kingdom and their counterparts in Africa, and these people had an interest in preserving such connections for their mutual profit. Because Britain had more economic power than France and other imperial nations, it moved with greater self-assurance towards neo-colonial forms of influence. This was perhaps the most important reason for the difference in how each colonial power approached the question of decolonization.

Outsiders might make inroads into Britain's former colonies once they became independent (e.g. by offering better terms of trade and investment), but this by no means meant it was impossible for the United Kingdom to defend its interests. It should be remembered that, despite its own economic problems in the early post-war period, the UK was still one of the most competitive industrial countries in the world. Russia and Continental Europe lay in ruins, and in the Far East Japan was occupied until 1952, leaving the British well off in at least relative terms. Within a short time, of course, other countries would challenge Britain's position in the world market-place (e.g. West Germany), but London could expect to play an important role in the affairs of its former possessions even after decolonization, for which reason the Colonial Office could afford to take a more conciliatory approach than the *Quai d'Orsay*. In West Africa, the Gold Coast (or Ghana) was the first black African country to achieve independence in the post-1945 period, and so will receive our particular attention. Other colonies were just as important and arguably more so, but in 1957 Ghana became an independent dominion within the British Commonwealth and then in 1960 a republic.

What most affected the transition in Ghana and elsewhere was the small size of the native political class. It was an elite, and though it had a stake in independence did not necessarily want to share power with other groups in African society. The more important businessmen were dependent on foreign markets and thus vulnerable to British influence, but some of them did help organize the anti-colonial opposition. They hoped thereby to gain a greater say in the economic life of their country. Yet it was the professionals who tended to take the lead in Gold Coast political life, and perhaps were most visible. By the end of the 1940s, however, there were only 32 journalists, 38 medical doctors, 114 lawyers and 435 clergy out of a total population of 4.5 million. In addition, teachers and civil servants (generally restricted by the British to the second ranks of the government bureaucracy) played an important part. Even so, Basil Davidson estimates that 'fewer than a thousand' persons made up the anti-imperialist leadership in the Gold Coast. (In relative terms the native elite was even smaller in some other colonies. At about the same period, for example, Nigeria had only 150 lawyers, 160 doctors and 786 clergy for a much larger population of forty million.)*

Although all the Western powers cultivated their reputations for providing educational opportunities to Third World peoples, the reality was that advanced education was available only to a tiny elite. In 1939 there were just 400 Africans (from Britain's tropical colonies) attending universities in the UK, and sixteen years later, in 1955, the number had risen only to 3,000. Of course, there were a small number of institutions of higher education in Africa itself, and greater numbers of people attended these. But the idea that the colonial powers established pro-grammes of mass education is simply untrue. Higher education in particular (including the status and jobs it brought) remained the privilege of the few even after the Second World War. The politically active and the educated tended to be the same group, and were the *crème de la crème* of African society. Obviously many of these people could be counted upon to work for a peaceful transfer of power, so as to perpetuate their own ascendancy after independence.

Many members of the political class therefore opposed imperialism, because foreign control stood in the way of their assuming full power as the rulers of their own countries. And because of their desire to retain their position in society, they tended to be reformers, not revolutionaries, when it came to social issues. They had much to lose if the power of the lower classes were to increase, so it was usually the case that they stood for change only up to a point. There were exceptions, but in the 1940s and 1950s these people served only to prove the rule. One such was Kwame Nkrumah, who had studied in the United States and after the Second World War moved in radical and anti-imperialist circles in London. He was particularly influenced by the West Indian socialist C. R. L. James. Once back home, however, he and many other African leftists turned out to be less radical than they seemed when abroad, as they came to appreciate that Britain intended to compromise. From their point of view a small measure of confrontation followed by a large measure of co-operation might be the best course of action.

Thus the situation was not quite the same as in the Maghrib or India, in that the radicals were even less of a threat to the majority of moderate

* Basil Davidson, *Africa in Modern History: The Search for a New Society* (Harmondsworth: 1978), 223.

independence leaders. Of course, the latter reluctantly conceded that mass action might play an important role in persuading the British to leave; strikes and demonstrations would bring the pressure of numbers to bear on the few British administrators and soldiers stationed in the country. That the moderates hoped to dominate any new political order, however, was apparent in that they acted to create mass political parties only after the Second World War, not earlier. In other words, they did not rush to embrace the people, but proceeded cautiously and in a manner calculated to preserve their monopoly of political leadership. It was also relevant, of course, that the imperial powers discouraged mass organizing activity before and during the war, particularly in the case of labour unions and strikes. Later, as independence came within sight, the moderates called upon more radical leaders like Nkrumah for help in organizing the masses, though it was still their clear intention to remain in charge of events.

As old hands at the colonial (and neo-colonial) game, the British understood the interests of the local elite very well. They also saw a need to develop the political skills of the indigenous leadership, though on terms acceptable to the UK. In 1947 the more important merchants and crop-brokers, the professionals and certain tribal chiefs formed the United Gold Coast Convention (UGCC). In Nkrumah's words, the UGCC was intended to resolve 'the problem of reconciling the leadership of the intelligentsia with the broad mass of the people'.* The problem was that the backers of the UGCC were not adept at organizing mass political action. This was where Nkrumah came in. The UGCC invited him to return from the UK and begin the task of mobilizing the population of Gold Coast colony against the British. Nkrumah was dubious about associating with the UGCC lest he be co-opted politically, but he decided to chance it.

Nkrumah's organizing activities were highly successful, but by the next year, 1948, they resulted in violent demonstrations and the arrest of the most important leaders of the Convention. Nkrumah seemed to believe that violence could be a useful means of increasing the pressure on the British, but his UGCC colleagues feared it might eventuate in social revolution. And they certainly did not like being packed off to jail. The British shrewdly responded by making concessions, and set up a committee of Africans under Sir Henley Coussey to write a new

---

* Cited in Roland Oliver and Anthony Atmore, *Africa since 1800* (Cambridge: 1972), 228.

constitution for the colony. They invited all the important UGCC leaders except Nkrumah to participate, and thus tried to isolate the leading radical from the majority moderates. But while this exacerbated the growing split between Nkrumah and his UGCC colleagues, it also served to identify him as the real leader of the anti-British opposition. The image of the United Gold Coast Convention was seriously compromised, with the result that, when in June 1949 Nkrumah formed the Convention People's Party, or CPP, popular support shifted from the UGCC to him. He had become a highly visible figure, and thus was able to take many of the rank and file away from the UGCC while also attracting new followers. In this respect his exclusion from the Coussey Committee worked to his advantage.

The strength of the new party was demonstrated by a general strike in 1950, and then by its victory in a general election held under the new colonial constitution in 1951. Preferring to avoid further strife, and seeing who had the support of the people, the British executed a timely retreat and called upon Nkrumah to form the government, and promised to move the country towards full independence. For his part Nkrumah was not so radical as to risk what had been gained by pressing for an immediate grant of autonomy. In the end, the deal he made with the British was probably not very different than what other Ghanaian leaders would have concluded had the UGCC inherited power. When in 1957 the British governor congratulated Nkrumah on realizing his goal, Nkrumah responded, 'You have contributed a great deal towards this; in fact I might not have succeeded without your help and co-operation. This is a very happy day for us both!'* The governor agreed.

While there were important differences in the independence struggle in the rest of British West Africa, the overall pattern had much in common with Ghana. The British knew when to give in, and the result was to see friendly leaders safely installed in power. The UK thus avoided open warfare in West Africa, though not the violence associated with strikes and other forms of protest. In Nigeria tribal and regional divisions were particularly vexing and therefore complicated the transition. It was difficult to reconcile differences among the Hausa-speaking and Muslim north, the Yoruba-speaking west and the Ibo-speaking east, even within a federal rather than unitary form of organization. Moreover, throughout Africa the boundaries of the new nation states were more the

---

* Cited in *ibid.*, 230.

result of European imperial control than a reflection of divisions established by the indigenous population. For most of the population local and
ethnic rather than nationalist loyalties took priority. Nation-building was
thus a delicate business indeed. On the whole, however, London moved
towards the neo-colonial solution more easily than most other imperial
powers, although the story was somewhat different in British East Africa.
The reason was the settler factor. Considerable numbers of whites had
settled in Kenya and Rhodesia, and had carved vast plantations out of
native lands, so that the end of colonialism was more difficult to manage.
Even so, London gave up the fight a bit sooner than Paris.

British East Africa

The white settler population was not distributed evenly throughout East
Africa, however, and some areas experienced a less difficult transition to
independence than others. There were comparatively few British permanently resident in Uganda and Tanganyika (the latter united with
Zanzibar to form Tanzania in 1964), or in the specially administered
territories to the far south: Swaziland, Basutoland (Lesotho) and
Bechuanaland (Botswana). Whites from the Union of South Africa
(which had become an independent state in 1910 and was no longer
under the authority of the Colonial Office) owned a significant amount of
property in Swaziland, however, and London maintained a lively interest
in their well-being.

The countries where the most trouble occurred were Kenya and
Southern Rhodesia. They both had important white settler populations,
but the native political establishment was considerably less numerous
and less experienced in the art of politics than in West Africa. Among
other reasons, this was because the settler population had used its
influence on the colonial government to deny sufficient funding for
native secondary and post-secondary education. The result was an even
smaller native elite, which meant there was a risk that political activists
from the lower ranks of East African society might take over the
independence struggle. But leaders with close ties to the people were
often radical on social issues, wanting, for example, to take back native
lands expropriated by the foreigners. It was thus more urgent than ever
for the British to identify leaders whom they could entrust with power.

In Kenya the British preference was for what was called a 'multiracial'
constitution, i.e. one which would provide the white minority enough
seats in a legislative assembly to guarantee its control of the political
process for at least the next generation. The principle of one person, one

vote (or majority rule) was not acceptable because blacks outnumbered whites. After the Second World War, however, events moved too quickly to make such a solution feasible. The main source of opposition came from the Kikuyu people, and took the form of the famous Mau Mau Rebellion. The Kikuyu were a large population group which the expansion of settler plantations had forced into a land area much too small to support their numbers. Many went to Nairobi and other towns seeking a livelihood, but instead found unemployment and poverty. The goal of the rebellion was to restore native lands which had been occupied by outsiders. In 1951 the Kikuyu began a campaign of terror against the whites, mainly attacking farms on the frontier of settler territory. Atrocities were committed on both sides. Although he denied the charge, the Kikuyu leader Jomo Kenyatta was jailed for fomenting rebellion, but his arrest did not stem the violence.

Indeed, it would turn out that Kenyatta had much more in common with Nkrumah than with the guerrillas in the highlands. Throughout the 1930s and the Second World War he had studied and worked in Britain, and in 1938 published a book in the field of African anthropology. He thus had considerable standing as an intellectual, and upon returning to Nairobi in 1946 his fame enabled him to assume a position of leadership in the independence struggle. When the Mau Mau took to battle, however, Kenyatta denounced terrorism, but this did not save him from British reprisals. In 1953 he was sentenced to a term of hard labour. Though released in 1959, he was required to reside in a remote part of the country. He did not regain total freedom until 1961, by which time events had forced the British to adopt a new policy. Before the Mau Mau were defeated in 1956, however, the British imprisoned about 90,000 Kikuyu captives (confining them in what some authorities have described as concentration camps), and moved well over a million Kikuyu and also Embu civilians into secured village areas. In all, perhaps 10,000 people were killed, including about a hundred British, though the estimates of casualties vary widely. The heavy losses on the African side were largely the result of reprisals taken by the insurgents against Kikuyu accused of collaborating with the British. In the end, the military superiority of the UK resulted in defeat for the Mau Mau, and by 1956 the rebellion was broken. But Kenyatta remained in jail.

Nevertheless the uprising did accelerate independence and majority rule. By forcing the British to reconsider the feasibility of imposing a multiracial constitution, the Mau Mau had made their point. In the short run they were defeated, but the whole country could not be administered as an armed camp for ever. The UK had committed about 50,000 troops and police to Kenya. While the settlers wanted them to remain, London could not afford to keep them there on a long-term basis. Furthermore, given developments in the rest of Africa, independence had to come sooner or later – the only issue was the terms on which it would be granted. With the outbreak of rebellion in 1951 white settler recalcitrance had led to open warfare, but there was a way out. Despite the charges laid against Kenyatta in 1953, he was indeed a moderate. And it was increasingly apparent that he had not been the driving force behind the Mau Mau. Therefore, as the British concluded that African rule would have to be accepted, they decided that perhaps Kenyatta was the right person to assume power after all. They permitted him to stand for election to the colonial legislative council in 1961, and when independence was conceded, in 1963, he became head of the new government. The result was thus a compromise, though one achieved at a high price for Africans and British alike. Not surprisingly, given the caution of the new leadership, the disparities between the masses and the elite (including blacks and the whites who remained) were not about to disappear. Although farms formerly owned by white settlers were redistributed and Africans took over more and more European jobs, data on income distribution show that the bottom 20 per cent of the population received 3.8 per cent of income in the late 1960s, whereas the top 20 per cent received 68 per cent of all income. In 1979 there were still 50,000 Europeans and 60,000 Asians in the country, out of a total population of over fifteen million.

The conflict in Kenya had ramifications elsewhere as well. It helped convince the British that the whites in Africa would have to forego multiracialism and accept black majority rule. In Tanganyika this was facilitated by Julius Nyerere. Also, there were comparatively few white settlers in the country, and this eased matters. But, like Nkrumah and other nationalist leaders, Nyerere was hardly a typical African. He had studied at Edinburgh and then gone on to organize a mass political party in his home country, the Tanganyika African National Union. He mobilized large numbers of people behind the independence movement and thus took up a position of power *vis-à-vis* the UK. Although he was consistently more radical in politics than black leaders in many other British colonies, he was still moderate enough for the British to work with. He preached a variety of Christian socialism which seemed to offer some protection to whites. Nyerere opposed a multiracial constitution, but also made it abundantly clear that whites need not fear black majority rule. And, as in the Gold Coast, the British governor, Sir Richard Turnbull, worked closely with Nyerere. Independence was granted in December 1961. Uganda followed shortly after (in 1962), on terms very similar to those in Kenya and Tanganyika. A major crisis, however, developed to the south, and particularly in Southern Rhodesia.

Southern Rhodesia had been part of an experiment in the early 1950s to impose multiracialism as a way of protecting the white minority. In 1953 the Central African Federation had been formed among Nyasaland, Northern Rhodesia and Southern Rhodesia. It was the last of these which was the main centre of settler resistance to majority rule, as the number of whites in the first two was considerably smaller. In 1923 (at a time when there were only about 34,000 whites in the country) London had granted Southern Rhodesia status as a self-governing British colony, though blacks had no say in the political system there or in the other British territories of the region. In the 1930s some whites in Nyasaland and Northern Rhodesia became interested in amalgamating with Southern Rhodesia. The idea was for the whites of the region to unite in an effort to preserve their political position. As the whites of the first two territories were an even smaller minority than those of the third, they wanted to pool their strength. Furthermore, amalgamation would create a more viable economic unit by reserving the whole region for future development by whites rather than possibly losing the two colonies with the fewest British settlers. The Second World War intervened to prevent any action on colonial questions, but with the continent-wide movement towards independence after 1945 whites in the three colonies believed that it was time to proceed.

For the British Colonial Office a system of multiracial power-sharing with the whites in control but with blacks participating might serve as the first step towards the creation of a moderate native ruling class, one that in time could be trusted with more and more power. Multiracialism looked better than the white supremacist policies of Rhodesia's neighbour, the Union of South Africa. London believed South Africa's commitment to a policy of strict segregation between blacks and whites in all spheres of life (called *apartheid*) could only lead to disorder and possibly guerrilla war. The British certainly knew that most white Southern Rhodesians saw the federation as a way of preserving white supremacy and that black Africans opposed it for precisely this reason. But it was hoped that the economic benefits of unification would mitigate the political problems and help create the kind of black bourgeoisie that would have a common interest with the whites.

It did not work out. While economic growth was impressive, so were the disparities between blacks and whites. Whereas the annual income of black wage-earners averaged less than £90 in 1961, white wage-earners received almost fourteen times as much. Equally important, the settler population showed no interest in sharing more political power with the indigenous peoples, and this at a time when independence was gaining ground throughout the rest of Africa. As one apologist of white Southern Rhodesia put it in 1956, 'Political control must remain in the hands of civilized people, which for the foreseeable future means the Europeans.'* Not surprisingly, by the end of the 1950s strikes and demonstrations began to occur, so that a state of emergency was declared in Southern Rhodesia and Nyasaland. This permitted the colonial authorities to arrest and detain African nationalists without trial.

By this time, however, black resistance to the Federation and events elsewhere had persuaded the Colonial Office that multiracialism would not work. A series of British government investigations had concluded that the experiment in power-sharing had only provided a camouflage for subordinating the majority to the minority. By the early 1960s, therefore, London permitted Nyasaland and Northern Rhodesia to part company with Southern Rhodesia. From its point of view this would be better than seeing something equivalent to the Mau Mau develop. On 6 July 1964 Nyasaland became the independent state of Malawi, and on 24 October of the same year Northern Rhodesia became Zambia.

From this point on the whites of Southern Rhodesia began referring to their country (which in legal terms remained a British colony) as simply Rhodesia. The failure of the federation created an opportunity for white supremacists to take virtually complete charge of politics, so that negotiations with the UK over independence were likely to fail. After two years of talks the government of Rhodesian prime minister Ian Smith issued its Unilateral Declaration of Independence (UDI) on 11 November 1965, citing ringing phrases from the American Declaration of Independence in justification for its course. But it was the *de facto* policy of the Smith government that the 250,000 whites should continue to govern the four million blacks of the country for an indefinite period, so further efforts at negotiation failed. In 1970 Rhodesia broke all legal ties to the British crown, and proclaimed itself a republic. Britain was in no position to use military force in the situation, and the result was to disrupt its relations with the black nations of Africa. The solution to the majority rule

* Cited in *ibid.*, 266.

question was not to come for many more years, and only after a long guerrilla war. The country would finally attain autonomy as Zimbabwe in 1980, but this was far in the future.

The French Colonies

Developments in the British colonies south of the Sahara were to have a considerable impact on the nearby territories of France. The effect was to increase the pressure for independence in the face of French resistance. Relatively few Europeans were permanently resident in the eight federated colonies of French West Africa: Dahomey, French Guinea, French Sudan, Ivory Coast, Mauritania, Niger, Senegal and Upper Volta. The same was true of the island of Madagascar (off the eastern coast of the continent) and the four federated colonies of French Equatorial Africa: Chad, Gabon, Middle Congo (which became the Congo Republic in 1960) and Ubangi-Shari (the future Central African Republic). The role of the settlers was thus not at all comparable to their role in Algeria, and, in the context of the wars in Indo-China (see Chapter 4) and Algeria, Paris was less able to resort to full-scale war in West and Equatorial Africa. On the other hand, it was less necessary. This was in large part because it found more co-operative local leaders than in other places, though their numbers were very small. As elsewhere, the native elite wanted political change but were not interested in sacrificing their economic and social position.

As we have already noted, the island of Madagascar was the scene of a colonial war in the late 1940s. The use of force was more successful there (from the French point of view) than in North Africa, so that in due course Paris was able to subdue the island. By June 1960 events had evolved to the point where acceptable (subservient) leaders were installed in power and formal independence conceded. In 1972, however, a military coup resulted in a new government and turned the island towards more radical change. Elsewhere in French Africa the neo-colonial solution of indirect influence seemed more effective, however reluctantly France moved to such a policy.

The reorganization of the French empire into the 'French Union' after the Second World War represented an important if tentative gain for all the colonies, but especially for West and Equatorial Africa. On paper, at least, the Union constituted the first step towards a more equal relationship between metropolitan France and its dependencies. In the case of sub-Saharan Africa some of the worst abuses of colonialism, such as forced labour, came to an end. The post-war constitution of France provided important advances, though full independence would come only with the Fifth Republic of de Gaulle. But the Fourth did establish territorial assemblies (with very few powers) to deal with local issues, and admitted about twenty black African representatives to the French National Assembly.

However limited, the right to participate in governance had consequences. New political organizations were formed, such as the *Parti Démocratique de la Côte d'Ivoire*, led by Félix Houphouët-Boigny. Even more important, the possibility of uniting the colonies for concerted action appeared in 1946, when representatives from the various West African and Equatorial territories came together and established the *Rassemblement Démocratique Africain* (RDA). At the very same time the imperial policy of assimilating colonials via the French Union provided an additional opportunity to present the colonial case in Paris. Participation in the Union meant that African colonials had the right to send delegates to the National Assembly. There they became part of the complex coalition politics which afflicted the Fourth Republic. Initially the RDA allied itself with the communists in the Assembly because they supported anti-imperialism (in theory if not always in practice). But when the communists were forced out of the French cabinet in 1947, the Africans faced the liability of being associated with an opposition rather than a government party. Their influence was thus less than before. Accordingly, in 1951, Houphouët-Boigny broke the RDA's link to the communists in return for a government commitment to internal autonomy for the territories. In due course he joined the government and became a cabinet minister. In effect he was prepared to compromise with the French in order to gain something rather than hold out for everything. The latter meant risking conflict with France, possibly war, and this in turn might provide social revolutionaries with an opportunity to seize power. As a wealthy planter in the Ivory Coast, Houphouët-Boigny stood to inherit the leadership of the country once internal autonomy was granted. He was therefore prepared to settle for concrete gains in the present rather than a less certain outcome in the future, and so were many other members of his class in the rest of French Africa.

During the next several years, however, an alternative began to emerge. This came from somewhat more radical elements in the RDA who wanted to build on the colonial federations which the French had established and which provided a degree of administrative unity for the eight territories of West Africa and the four colonies of French Equatorial Africa. The idea was to create two centres of power rather than twelve. By standing together, the African colonies might improve their chances of dealing with France from a position of greater strength, whether inside or outside the French Union. Paris, of course, preferred to deal with one colony at a time and thus did not favour bestowing autonomy on the federations, however much they may have been an administrative convenience in the past. 'Divide and rule' seemed to be its maxim for the future. Houphouët-Boigny and others like him did not welcome federation either. It threatened their deal with the French, and they preferred to assume the leadership of their own countries rather than merge their interests in a larger entity. From the vantage point of the political elite it might be better to have twelve presidents instead of only two. So, with such powerful interests arrayed against it, the federation plan had little chance of succeeding. In 1956 the government of metropolitan France proposed an enabling act to permit the gradual introduction of internal autonomy in the black African colonies, but as twelve distinct entities. External affairs, finance, and the police and the military would remain in imperial hands.

The fall of the Fourth Republic in 1958 quickened events considerably. The continuing war in Algeria (combined with defeat in Indo-China) meant that Paris would have to follow the neo-colonial route. There simply was no other choice. Accordingly the task at hand was to shape the terms of disengagement so as to preserve as much French influence as possible. This required supporting moderates like Houphouët-Boigny. De Gaulle therefore offered a new deal to the territories, but with a catch. Each colony was given the option of either remaining associated with France (in what would be henceforth referred to not as the French Union but the 'French Community') or becoming totally independent. French aid, however, would be suspended in the latter eventuality. Given that none of the colonies could really afford to give up such assistance, all but one, Guinea, voted to become part of the French Community.

Yet blackmail could not work indefinitely, and the pressure for full autonomy continued to grow. Moreover, given enough time, the French became confident of their ability to dominate a fragmented black Africa even without the Community, and reversed their earlier insistence on some sort of a formal political tie to the territories. Economic and military assistance, trade, credit and investment were obviously effective substitutes for direct rule. The main point was to keep the colonies divided. After granting autonomy to the associated states of the French Community, this proved quite feasible. The reason was that, once installed in power, the leaders of the new governments acquired a vested interest in retaining office. Most of them were like Houphouët-Boigny, and did not wish to surrender their newly won power to some other authority. Hence the French found it easy to head off any further talk of a united African front. Having prevented this, Paris could afford to concede full autonomy, even outside the French Community. And so it was done, in 1960.

THE OTHER EMPIRES

While we have not discussed the fate of every British and French colony in Africa, none the less we can discern a pattern. How readily London and Paris moved away from colonialism and towards neo-colonialism depended on whether reliable local leaders could be identified. The goal was to facilitate the perpetuation of Western influence, but by indirect (i.e. economic) means. Yet the transition was hardly easy or smooth. The French were more reluctant to rely on economic influence alone than the British, at least initially, and the presence of large settler populations in some colonies (e.g. Algeria and Rhodesia) created crises which delayed independence.

Moreover, there were no guarantees of continuing hegemony in the future, and many newly independent states in Africa would prove susceptible to Soviet or Chinese communist influence, though often under the policy of non-alignment (i.e. not taking sides in the East–West struggle). Tanzania, for example, was to forge links to the People's Republic of China and also Cuba (the latter acting as a Soviet surrogate), while still maintaining ties to Britain and the Commonwealth. In time military coups would also occur in a number of African countries, and undo the political settlements worked out by Britain and France. Still, the mere fact of a *coup d'état* did not inevitably mean that the new leaders would be anti-Western. Some were, and some were not. Indeed, military or other dictators were often quite prepared to deal with the West. Even schemes for nationalizing foreign-owned enterprise did not completely upset British–French calculations. African countries still had to conduct international trade in a market dominated by the old imperial powers. The overriding fact from the Western point of view was that, regardless of the political coloration of any particular regime, Africa on the whole remained dependent on the First World. Not all the colonial powers, though, followed the British–French example. On the contrary, the Belgians and the Portuguese seemed determined to hold out against all odds, as we shall see in due course. The old Italian empire, however, posed a simpler problem.

Italy lost control of all its colonies in Africa as a result of its defeat in the Second World War, with one exception: it was allowed to hold a trusteeship over its former colony of Somalia from 1950 until 1960, mainly because no other power was willing to assume responsibility for the territory. At the end of this period the country joined British Somalia and became independent. But in Libya and Ethiopia (both of which had become Italian colonies only in the twentieth century) the anti-Axis Allies refused Italy any role in setting the terms of independence. Moreover, they allowed Emperor Haile Selassie of Ethiopia to retake the former Italian colony of Eritrea and keep the Ogaden, a largely desert area in the eastern reaches of his kingdom. Eritrea had indeed once been part of Ethiopia, but centuries before. In the 1500s it had been occupied by the Turks, followed in the nineteenth century by the Egyptians and then the Italians. The Ogaden was populated mainly by Somalis, so that the new state of Somalia also had an interest in the region. Consequently, in the 1970s, Ethiopian control would lead to secessionist movements and war in both areas.

Of more immediate concern at the time of decolonization was that Libya, Ethiopia and Somalia remain under Western influence, and for the time being they did. In 1969, however, a military coup brought Colonel Moammar Gadhafi to power in Libya, and in 1974 another military regime was formed in Ethiopia, with Colonel Mengistu Haile Mariam eventually emerging as leader. Both assumed a pronounced anti-Western stance. For a time in the 1970s the strategic situation was complicated by Somali military action against Ethiopia, over the Ogaden. Moreover, Somalia received Soviet arms aid, and in return for its assistance the USSR proposed to build naval and missile facilities in the country. Gadhafi also looked to the USSR for assistance, and after the USSR and Somalia had a falling out, so did Ethiopia. Yet Soviet subversion was not the principal cause of the changes occurring in any of these countries. The reasons were much more fundamental and long term than Russian manoeuvring, but the USSR certainly did take advantage of developments to increase its influence in Africa. For the Soviets the problem was that rising influence in some countries was offset by declining influence in others, so that the net gain for the Soviet Union was dubious. Witness the switch from Somalia to Ethiopia. But again, all this was some way in the future.

The Congo

For the West in the 1950s and early 1960s far more problematical was the future of the Belgian Congo. Belgium, of course, had been a victim of Nazi aggression and was occupied during the Second World War. But it was also on the Allied side. There was no doubt that the Western powers would permit it to regain control of one of the largest colonies in central Africa. In the context of the 1950s and 1960s, however, and owing to pressure from other nations, it was difficult for the Belgians to resist the continent-wide movement to independence. They had certainly intended to do so, but in 1959 unrest among the Africans boiled over into strikes, rioting, looting and other disorders. Particularly worrisome to the Belgians was the sacking of European businesses, schools and homes which took place in the capital of Léopoldville, but law and order broke down throughout the country. As elsewhere, the political crisis was compounded by tribal divisions among Africans themselves, so that there seemed to be few native leaders available who were capable of keeping the entire country unified. The one with the broadest base of national support proved to be Patrice Lumumba, but he turned out to be too radical for Western tastes.

The problem for Brussels, however, was not just the unity of an independent Congo, but that there were very few Africans skilled in running a Western-style political system. As with the other imperial powers, this was the result of its own deliberate policies, which had kept blacks from gaining such experience. Advanced education was not available in the Congo until 1954, and virtually no Congolese were educated at European universities. As one Belgian expert pointed out in 1956, 'The formation of an elite and of responsible, directing cadres is a generation behind the British and French territories.'* Europeans, for example, made up almost half of the Congo's civil service on the eve of independence. Africans filled only the lower-level positions. Not one had a posting in the top civil service rank. As the agitation for autonomy mounted, the Belgians thus found themselves without even the tiny native ruling class that was to be found in places such as West Africa and that might be depended upon to respect their interests. Amazingly, though, Belgium decided to grant independence to the Congo by the early 1960s, ready or not.

---

* Cited in *ibid.*, 252.

No doubt Brussels was shocked into action by the riots in Léopold-ville. This created a sense of imminent disaster unless it gave way on the question of political autonomy. But there was more to the decision than this. Resisting would be likely to lead to a guerrilla war of some sort, perhaps drawing the Africans together despite their tribal divisions and resulting in a united front of Congolese against Belgians. It might be wise to accept the end of empire before the situation deteriorated any further. And there was an even more important consideration. Given that Brussels had failed to groom a native elite, there was no option but to exploit the political inexperience and tribal divisions of the Congolese as best it could. Precisely because the African leaders were ill-prepared to take over from the colonial authorities, they would have a difficult time establishing effective control of the economy, and would have to depend on Belgian business and mining interests for advice and support. And, of course, the Belgian government would be prepared to extend its assist-ance as well. In other words, once decolonization became unavoidable, the strategy seems to have been to rush the Congo towards inde-pendence as quickly as possible, so that the new leaders would have to accept outside help. This would be neo-colonialism on the cheap, without the trouble of grooming a native elite on the British–French model. Given Belgium's failure to nurture such a group, though, there was not much else to do but hope for the best. The problem was that the strategy worked only after a period of violence and civil war.

The colonial regime came to an end on 30 June 1960, but the immediate result was the disintegration of the country and mob action against Europeans, including a mutiny of the black rank and file in the army, or *Force Publique*, which was still officered by whites. Brussels therefore ordered paratroopers into action to protect the roughly 90,000 Belgians still in the country, and the new Congo government was immediately confronted with a reassertion of imperial power. At the same time the province of Katanga seceded, and South Kasai followed suit a short time later. Katanga was of greater interest to the West, because it was rich in copper, uranium, cobalt, gold, diamonds and other minerals. It was led by Moise Tshombe, who had the backing of Belgian copper interests and who came from one of the few wealthy African families in the country. The government of Léopoldville regarded him as the agent of the principal foreign mining company, the *Union Minière*.

On 12–13 July the national government, headed by Patrice Lumumba as prime minister and his rival Joseph Kasavubu as president, asked for United Nations assistance in bringing the secessionists to heel, and the Security Council authorized the creation of a UN military force (including contingents from Ghana, Nigeria and Ethiopia) to intervene. The Council also called upon Belgium to remove its troops. The problem was that the UN forces seemed interested in conducting only a holding action to preserve the *status quo*. Their intervention did not result in the reunification of the country. Lumumba suspected that this reflected the Belgian and also the growing US interest in Katanga. The province would be extremely vulnerable to outside influences if it succeeded in separating from the rest of the country, and therefore Lumumba believed that powers such as the United States were not really interested in seeing the UN reunify the country, at least not on his terms.

Accordingly Lumumba asked the Soviet Union and its allies to provide assistance. This discredited him in Western capitals, and in September President Kasavubu and Joseph-Désiré Mobutu (head of the armed forces and later known as Mobutu Sese Seko) ordered his dismissal as prime minister. In reality the pro-Western military man, Mobutu, became the chief power in Léopoldville. There was little opportunity, accordingly, for the USSR to intervene in Congolese developments with any effect, though it was more than willing to try. Nevertheless the Americans still regarded Lumumba as a threat. He was the most popular political leader in the country, and his influence was not to be discounted too soon. Indeed, in the autumn, the Lumumba ally Antoine Gizenga succeeded in establishing a pro-Soviet regime at Stanleyville. But Moscow's hopes for expanding its influence in Africa soon suffered a major setback. Early in 1961 the Léopoldville government turned Lumumba over to his arch-enemies in Katanga, and there he was murdered.

It was alleged that the US Central Intelligence Agency played a role in Lumumba's demise, and a subsequent American probe into the Agency's activities found that there was indeed a plan to assassinate him. Moreover, while it could not be proved that the scheme had the approval of the president himself, the investigation did find that 'the Director of Central Intelligence, Allen Dulles, authorized an assassination plot'. Further, 'the plot proceeded to the point that lethal substances and instruments specifically intended for use in an assassination were delivered by the CIA to the Congo Station.' Events, however, outstripped any covert American activity, so that although 'there is no evidence that the assassination operation was terminated before Lumumba's death', none the less the CIA had no part in his murder.* The reality was that rivalries in the Congo itself were quite enough to doom Lumumba. In any event it was certainly in the interest of the United States to see him removed.

Despite Lumumba's suspicion that the US favoured a strategy of divide and rule, by 1961 American policy-makers were beginning to fear the consequences of continued disunity. They were concerned lest it jeopardize the mining sector and create more opportunities for the Soviets, and so began to press Tshombe to end the secession. With the troublesome Lumumba gone and the Americans offering their good offices in negotiations with the leader of Katanga, the UN proceeded to bring Katanga back into the Congo by a combination of diplomacy and (more importantly) military force, though its troops did not establish effective control of the province until 1963. Yet with the departure of the UN contingent the political uncertainty continued, and for a time even Moise Tshombe was rehabilitated and headed the national government. After all, his province was essential to the Congo economy, and he still had many supporters. His co-operation was to be valued. And from the Western point of view he was politically safe. The US in particular appreciated his outspoken anti-Sovietism, and he was well regarded by right-wing activists in the United States, such as the John Birch Society. But it was Mobutu who eventually emerged as national president, after a military coup in 1965. Early the next year he assumed all legislative powers. The Congo, henceforth Zaïre, continued into the 1980s under his rule. He wanted foreign investment and professed anti-communism, so business interests in the West considered him a friendly leader. This remained the case even though the government liquidated the *Union Minière* in 1966. For the Western allies, however, the more salient fact was that Léopoldville (renamed Kinshasa) remained firmly within the Western orbit. Still, it was also clear that the Belgian policy of neglect had placed the neo-colonial solution in jeopardy, and had created an opportunity for the Soviets to interfere. It was an experience no Western capital wished to see repeated.

---

* US Senate, 94th Congress, 1st Session, *Alleged Assassination Plots Involving Foreign Leaders*, Report No. 94–465 (Washington, DC: 20 November 1975), 13, 19, 51–2.

THE FUTURE

Yet it would happen again, in the Portuguese colonies of Mozambique, Angola and Guinea-Bissau. Despite the lessons of the recent past, Portugal remained adamant on the colonial question, with the result that the opposition became more and more radicalized and turned to armed struggle. Too weak economically to make the neo-colonial solution work, and fearful of the outside competition that would come with independence, it hoped to maintain exclusive control by force. The longer the crisis lasted, however, the more time social revolutionaries had to consolidate their hold on the country. By the mid-1970s Portuguese rule in Africa came to an end in military defeat, though only after an army coup in Lisbon itself. This, however, was some years away (see Chapter 12).

In the meantime the white settlers of the Union of South Africa could hardly fail to take notice of events elsewhere on the continent. After all, they constituted only 18 per cent of the total Union population, and had much to fear from the rising tide of black nationalism. Although South Africa was one of the independent nations of the British Commonwealth and therefore shared in British parliamentary traditions, only the whites had full political or even civil rights. In effect blacks (or Bantu) were treated as aliens in their own country. Long before the Second World War the whites had used their virtual monopoly of political power to designate specific areas as reserves for the African population, and for all practical purposes ruled these territories as internal colonies. In time the native reserves came to constitute about 13 per cent of South Africa's territory, even though blacks were 70 per cent of the population. By the late 1940s the reserve strategy seemed to be a permanent fixture of South African life, and the foundation for what South Africans came to call *apartheid*; i.e. the 'separate development' of the ethnically diverse peoples of the region.

By the late 1950s and the 1960s, however, and under the pressure of decolonization elsewhere, whites began considering the merits of converting the reserves into legally independent homelands, or 'Bantustans' (Bantu states), though still within the borders of the Union itself and only after many years of apprenticeship in the art of government. The hope was to fend off criticism of apartheid from abroad and to co-opt enough native chiefs into the scheme to keep the blacks divided and thus off balance politically. Giving the chiefs a vested interest in governance might contribute to both goals. But, for the whites, what clinched the matter was the way independence would affect black claims to a share of political power in the Union. Bantustan independence would mean that the citizenship of black people would be determined by their tribal origins. They would not be citizens of the Union of South Africa but only of their Bantustans. Hence white power in South Africa proper would be safe, as blacks would literally be foreigners anywhere but in their official homelands.

The transition from the reserve to the Bantustan system, however, was only beginning to gain momentum in the late 1950s and early 1960s, and the first homeland to advance to *de jure* if not *de facto* independence (Transkei) would not do so until 1976. Accordingly we shall save the story of South Africa for later, particularly because the 1970s crisis in Portugal's colonies as well as the situation in Rhodesia helped bring the Bantustan strategy to maturation. What needs to be noted at this point is that decolonization did have an impact on the Union of South Africa even though it was an independent nation. Yet there is more to be said about the Third World in the 1950s. Indeed, in Latin America the United States was discovering that trouble could develop even in regions where the neo-colonial solution had a long history.

PART II

THE POST-MISSILE CRISIS ERA

7

A NEO-COLONIAL WORLD:

LATIN AMERICA

Political independence combined with continuing economic dependence were the hallmarks of Latin American history well before the post-1945 rush to decolonization. Although conquered by Spain and Portugal in the sixteenth century, most of the region had succeeded in establishing its legal autonomy by the 1820s. Yet the legacy of the colonial past was not easily exorcised. The conquest of the Indian empires of Latin America, particularly the Aztecs and Incas, had reduced them to Third World status. Their entire social order was integrated into a trans-Atlantic market and restructured to serve the needs of outsiders. Vast territories were organized as vice-royalties (or colonial kingdoms) subject to Madrid and Lisbon. Further, the coming of the *conquistadores* resulted in a demographic disaster, mainly as the result of the introduction of European diseases and of efforts to enslave the native population. In Mexico, for example, the number of Indians declined from perhaps as many as 25 million in 1519 to somewhat over one million in 1605; in Peru it fell from a likely peak of seven million to just under two million by 1580. Black slaves from Africa helped make up the loss, and in due course Spanish law recognized certain communally owned Indian lands as inalienable. But the decimation of the Indian population was bleak testimony to the impact of Europe. Of course, so was the trade in African slaves.

Latin America's Third World status was also linked to the situation of Spain and Portugal as dependencies (and thus underdeveloped areas) of Western Europe. The voyages of discovery and the appropriation of the wealth of the New World meant that both powers could prosper without developing, i.e. without building the kind of diversified and eventually industrialized society of which England was the model. Instead, Spain and Portugal simply looted the Americas, thus setting the latter on a course of export-oriented growth rather than diversified development.

For the Spanish the central plateau of Mexico and the mountainous empire of the Incas offered a rich storehouse of precious metals, chiefly silver, which could be taken home and spent on imports from other parts of Europe. Mining therefore became the leading economic sector in the Spanish empire, with haciendas established mainly to supply food for port towns and mining operations and not for a global market. The hacienda also represented a form of status for the non-industrial elite of the New World, as it was modelled on the virtually self-sufficient landed estate of feudal times. But this also reflected the pre-industrial orientation of the conquerers, and limited the possibility of development in the New World. It stood in marked contrast to the Thirteen Colonies of Britain in North America, where complex, diversified economies evolved. These carried on a lively export trade with the mother country, and Britain certainly intended that they remain subordinate to its interests. But the British colonies engaged in intercolonial trade as well, and by 1776 had established a complex commercial network, run by colonials and reaching even into the Caribbean. Diversification also meant that they were firmly on the road to eventual industrialization.

THE NEO-COLONIAL ERA

Independence did come to Latin America, though events in Europe more than in the Americas provided the immediate occasion for the break. The Napoleonic wars overwhelmed Spain and Portugal, and eroded their authority in the New World. Yet the establishment of autonomous states in the early nineteenth century proved to be more of a political than a social revolution. The Latin American wars of independence were mainly a series of intramural disputes between competing elites in the New and Old Worlds, each of which wanted to control the region on its own terms. Although at various points in the independence struggle popular discontent manifested itself and new leaders came forward (particularly from among the military), the poverty of the masses remained essentially unchanged. Moreover, independence did nothing to alter the unequal economic relations between Europe and Latin America which were at the root of the area's impoverishment in the first place. Britain quickly displaced Spain as Latin America's most important trading partner, but in most other respects the latter's role in the global market underwent little change. Thus diversified development (as distinct from mere quantitative growth) remained retarded, and as a consequence many of the social problems inherited from the colonial past persisted. These were to have a significant impact on the course of Latin American politics in the future. As elsewhere, economic under-development would affect the potential for social revolution.

Yet the precise nature of Latin America's dependency varied over time. After 1850 the region entered upon a period of rapid economic growth, fuelled mainly by the industrial revolution in Europe and North America. The result was the evolution of a much larger export–import sector than in the past, with Latin America serving as a source of raw materials and as a market for the manufactures of the industrialized world. The growing urban populations of the developed world also created a demand for imported foodstuffs from the region. The effect was a dramatic increase in Latin America's shipments of primary commodities such as copper, zinc, tin, guano and nitrate fertilizers, wool, rubber, tobacco, coffee, sugar, beef, hides, bananas and grain. At the same time governments began to develop the infrastructures needed to sustain an export economy: ports, canals and railways. The problem was that foreigners provided most of the money for these facilities, so that the region was soon deeply in debt. Outsiders were also the source of investment capital for the expansion of agriculture and establishment of mining enterprises and small industries, and though in many countries the indigenous elite played a large role, a high percentage of foreign ownership typified the commercial and industrial sectors. Industrializ-ation, however, was on a very modest scale, and did not alter the region's dependency on the export of primary commodities. By 1929 the most industrially developed country was Argentina, where industry accounted for 23 per cent of total national production. Then came Mexico at just over 14 per cent, followed by Brazil at about 12 per cent, Chile at 8 per cent, and Colombia at 6 per cent. Accordingly most manufactures still had to be imported.

There were other problems. In countries with a significant indigenous population governments opened up Indian lands to exploitation by entrepreneurs, even though in many cases such lands had long been recognized as the communal property of the native peoples. The idea was to make more land available for commercial agriculture, and also to create a labour surplus. Land once used for subsistence farming, i.e. for local consumption, was thus converted to production for export. Dispos-sessing the Indians also enhanced the profitability of the export sector, as their numbers swelled the labour market, a fact which kept wages depressed. Thus, in 1881–2, the ruling oligarchy of El Salvador issued a set of decrees declaring private rather than communal property-holding as the only legal form of land tenure, in effect abolishing common lands. In this way the peasantry lost control of vast tracts of the country's land over the next several decades. Without formal title there was nothing they could do to prevent developers from staking a claim to what in law were defined as vacant areas. All this spurred the growth of commercial agriculture in El Salvador, but obviously it also exacerbated the poverty of the population and widened the gap between rich and poor. The timing and rate of change varied from place to place, but in some of the less economically developed areas of Central America the process of dispossession continued well into the twentieth century, even into the 1950s and 1960s.

The expansion of the export–import economy of the late nineteenth and early twentieth centuries resulted in other social changes as well, and had an important impact on politics. In the most industrially developed countries the urbanized middle sectors of society began to increase in size. In Argentina, for example, half the people were classified as urban by the First World War, and in Buenos Aires the middle class was approaching one-third of the city's population. The establishment of small and often foreign-owned industries in Argentina, Brazil and Chile also spurred the growth of the industrial working class, especially after the turn of the century. Distinct from workers pursuing traditional handicrafts, this class began to form trade unions and mutual aid societies, and laid the groundwork for becoming a political force in the future. For the time being, however, the degree of industrial labour organization remained low, as most manufacturing activity still took place in small shops rather than the huge factories associated with industrialization in the First World. It was not until after the Great Depression of 1929 that the working classes exerted a significant impact on Latin American politics.

In the meantime the oligarchies of some countries reformed the political system and opened it up to new groups. Argentina may serve as an example. In the face of rising demands for broader political rights (even the middle class was effectively excluded from politics), the national government in 1912 bestowed the vote on all males over eighteen. Yet this was really a transitional stratagem. While the expansion of the electorate did promise to enhance the political influence of the masses someday, it did not make the labour vote the determining factor in Argentinian politics right away. The immediate impact of electoral reform was to draw together the middle and upper sectors of society. The extension of the franchise to its members meant that the middle class acquired enough of a stake in the existing order to make it an ally of the oligarchy. A system of co-optation began to evolve, whereby the upper classes combined with the middle classes to offset the political power of the lower classes. Of course, in the long run electoral reform might co-opt workers into the existing political system as well. It did offer workers the prospect of a share in power, and so might defuse the appeal of anarchism, syndicalism and other revolutionary ideologies. Such ideas were gaining in popularity at the turn of the century, largely among Italian and other European immigrants. But by creating an alliance of the upper and middle classes the immediate effect of electoral reform was to manage and direct the demand for change, at least for the time being.

It should be emphasized, however, that although the reformist model also evolved in Chile and some other countries there was nothing inevitable about it. Elsewhere politics often took a different course. Perhaps the clearest example was Mexico, where from 1876 to 1911 Porfirio Diaz ruled as dictator despite the institutional forms of republicanism. Although Diaz used his monopoly of power to promote economic development, the benefits were not widely dispersed among the population. The eventual outcome was the Mexican Revolution, and a very different history than Argentina or Chile. And even in the latter countries governments often resorted to police powers to limit the scope of labour and middle-class politics, and the military sometimes acted to install leaders of its own choosing. There was no single pattern of politics evolving consistently through time for all of Latin America, and the experience of each country was different.

The 1930s Depression, however, once again altered the terms of Latin America's integration into the global market and thus had an impact on politics. The value of its exports fell by half, wiping out the income needed to buy imported manufactures. There was no choice but to concentrate on internal development. The result later came to be described by analysts as 'import-substitution industrialization', or ISI. In the 1930s it was mainly those countries which already had an industrial base which followed the ISI pattern. The loss of income from exports provided a type of tariff protection and thus helped ISI along, as Latin Americans lacked the foreign exchange to maintain their normal purchases of imported manufactures. Instead, more of the region's raw materials were utilized at home, at least in some countries. Just as important, the outcome provided jobs and promised to keep the urban labour force from falling prey to radical politics, though the landed oligarchy still feared the consequences of working-class political power.

Indeed, the political system was severely tested by the Depression, and in the years after 1929 military coups took place in Argentina, Brazil, Chile, Nicaragua, Guatemala, El Salvador, Honduras and Cuba, among others.

The state sometimes took a leading role in ISI because foreign investment had dried up and because local entrepreneurs lacked the capital necessary to revive the economy. Accordingly, besides raising tariffs (depending on the country, not all followed the same policies) to protect such industry as did exist and investing in infrastructures, governments also made direct investments in industrial undertakings, such as steel in Chile and Brazil or petroleum in Argentina and Mexico (where foreign oil companies were also expropriated). A large role for government in business thus became a normal state of affairs in the region, as publicly owned development corporations assumed responsibility for industrial investment. Perhaps the most famous of these was Chile's CORFO, or *Corporación de Fomento de la Producción*.

There were, of course, political consequences. The process of ISI meant a further expansion of the urban working classes, though the impact of this varied from one country to another. In Chile a competitive party system survived despite the intervention of the military. By the late 1930s and early 1940s a popular-front government was in power, and included even socialists and communists. It did not remain united for long, but it was an important precedent in Chilean politics. In Argentina a type of populist politics (based on a coalition of urban labour and other social groups) emerged by the mid-1940s under the charismatic leadership of Juan Perón. For the first time the mobilization of the urban working class became a major factor in the country's political life, though only with the toleration of the army. The latter hoped to find someone to manage the masses, and accepted Perón as long as he did so. The politics of personalism evolved in Brazil as well, under Getúlio Vargas from the 1930s to 1954.

Events in Europe in the 1930s and 1940s also had an impact on the situation, but the European influence suggested channelling popular aspirations in favour of a hierarchical not an egalitarian order. This was the era of Hitler and Mussolini. Many people in Latin America admired their decisive leadership, particularly the way they had restored prosperity to their countries. Further, the fascists of Europe had evolved a corporatist model of politics, i.e. one which appeared to allocate political influence by functional group (e.g. labour and capital) rather than simply by numbers. In this way, presumably, classes with contradictory interests might share power according to their role in society, accepting the fact that some were more important than others and therefore should have a larger say in policy. Not surprisingly some members of the Latin American elite thought corporatism might be the key to political stability in their part of the world as well.

The problem with the emergent populist movements was that they attempted to reconcile contradictory class interests – specifically, to satisfy popular demands without threatening the power of the oligarchy. The hope was that ISI and the earnings produced by rising exports during and after the Second World War would help increase wages and make it possible for government to provide more social benefits for the working classes, thus winning their loyalty. While charismatic leaders might succeed as long as the economy prospered, the faltering of world demand for Latin American commodities at the end of the 1940s, combined with the inflation consequent on high levels of government spending, doomed populism as a long-term policy. By the 1950s economists, and the military, were preaching restraint, and charisma in politics increasingly gave way to even more overt authoritarianism. The problem was that in the long run ISI did not work. It did not occur on such a scale as to reduce the region's vulnerability to the global market, and Latin America remained dependent on exports rather than internal development as the mainstay of its prosperity. The regional economy was as a result still susceptible to global cycles of boom and bust, and politics reflected this fact.

There were a number of reasons why ISI proved inadequate. First, while the governments of the region could raise capital more easily than the private sector, they still did not have enough to achieve a level of industrialization comparable to that of the First World. Second, the technology for industrialization still had to be imported, so that Latin America remained financially indebted to Europe and the United States. Third, the deployment of advanced technology meant that fewer jobs were created than expected. Imported technology was capital-intensive precisely because it came from the most industrially developed countries of the world, and was not well suited to solving Latin America's unemployment problems. And fourth, the amount of demand for manufactures in any single country or even region of Latin America was insufficient to sustain a high level of industrial activity without access to world markets. But it was the precipitate decline of the global market in the 1930s that had accounted for the economic crisis in the first place. Moreover, the Depression brought a wave of economic nationalism, so that the nations of the world, including some in Latin America, raised their tariffs in an effort to protect their own industries from outside competition. In the face of the Depression, however, ISI was the only strategy available, so many countries attempted to make it work. Such success as ISI did seem to achieve was really the result of the Second World War and the post-war boom in the First World. This is not to say that ISI made no contribution to regional prosperity, but only that it was not enough to bring about economic and hence political stability.

The result was that by the 1950s and 1960s governments were moving back to a foreign-financed export–import economy, usually at the behest of military regimes. It often took repressive governments to accomplish the retreat from ISI. Economic stagnation translated into political unrest among the working classes, both urban and rural, so that the army moved to demobilize popular political parties. Indeed, leftist guerrilla movements had begun to appear in many places by the 1960s and 1970s, giving the military authorities another reason to act. Once in power the latter attempted to stimulate the economy by attracting multinational corporations. But the multinationals only found the region attractive in so far as they could take advantage of cheap labour and raw materials, so that the cycle of dependency was renewed. Repression by the host governments created a favourable investment for foreign capital by abolishing or restricting the right to form labour unions, setting low wages, demobilizing political opposition even at the cost of a free press and free speech, and otherwise clearing the way for highly exploitative labour relations. In sum, Latin America's dependency had come full circle, and the result was likely to be continuing social and political turmoil.

ARGENTINA AND JUAN PERÓN

Argentina was perhaps the clearest example of some of the above trends, particularly the new mass politics represented by populism. (Remember that populism in Latin America was urban-based and associated with the rise of industry and the expansion of the city working class, in contrast to the experience of the United States where it was a rural and even anti-urban movement.) As in many other countries, the 1929 Depression served as the catalyst for an army coup (in 1930), and a provisional military government was established, headed by General José Uriburu. But the events of 1930 were more than a seizure of power by the officer corps, and in fact the army was not in the habit of turning out governments (it had not done so since the 1860s). Although they took the initiative, the officers had the support of the cattle and wheat barons and even some factions of the middle and working classes. There was little doubt, however, that the army's closest allies were the cattle and wheat oligarchy which had dominated politics before the First World War. Since then, and as the result of legislation extending the franchise, putatively middle-class parties had been in power. After the 1930 coup, however, the army's hope was that the old oligarchy might take control of the political system once again, and serve as a bastion against the political forces unleashed by the rise of industry. Elections in late 1931 restored the legal niceties of civilian rule, though the military banned the candidate of the chief opposition party and thus guaranteed the victory of one of its own, General Agustín Justo.

With the decline of the export sector, however, Argentinian entrepreneurs had few options but to increase their stake in industry. This was less the result of a coherent economic plan on the part of the government than the outcome of the Depression. The economic crash devastated the market for Argentina's traditional exports. Moreover, the members of the British Commonwealth closed ranks in the face of the Great Depression, and at the Ottawa Conference of 1932 agreed to establish a system of 'imperial preferences'. This simply meant that they would trade as much as possible among themselves, to the exclusion of outsiders. Canada, Australia and New Zealand thus threatened to take over Argentina's role as one of the major suppliers of beef, lamb, wool and grain to the United Kingdom. Buenos Aires responded by allowing British manufacturers free access to its domestic market if the UK would continue to buy Argentina's primary commodities. In other words, the Argentinians bargained to be exempted from the application of imperial preferences. This saved the country from the worst effects of the Depression, though at the cost of leaving its industrial sector open to foreign competition. Yet it turned out not to make a great deal of difference, because Argentina simply could not afford to buy foreign-made products. The effect of the 1930s Depression was to provide virtually the same protection as tariffs for some of the country's infant industries. Industrialization thus advanced despite and not because of government policy. It was ISI by default.

In reality, though, the army and the cattle-and-wheat oligarchy hoped to preserve the old export–import economy, because such a pattern of growth would head off the expansion of working-class power associated with industrialization. In the absence of any alternatives available to the private sector, however, the country's industry did experience modest growth. Furthermore, by the late 1930s it was about 60 per cent owned by Argentinian rather than foreign capital. But it was the resumption of massive exports during the Second World War, not domestic manufacturing, that brought the country out of the Depression. Once again the world needed Argentina's primary commodities. The problem was that such industrialization as already had occurred proved quite sufficient to exacerbate the social changes which so worried the old elite. The industrial workforce grew from 500,000 in the mid-1930s to about two million by the late 1940s. Although enterprises of fewer than a hundred employees were still the norm, many of these people worked in large factories.

The governments of the 1930s and early 1940s thus remained in power less as the result of a coherent economic plan than a combination of coalition politics and rigged elections. The army and the oligarchy had much to fear from the political consequences of the expansion of industry, so that even the 1940s promise of prosperity did not lead to a democratic opening. Indeed, from 1931 on only the forms not the substance of competitive politics had been observed, and while a later president, Roberto Ortiz, did seem amenable to free elections for a brief interlude beginning in 1938, not even these were conceded after 1940. Illness forced Ortiz out of office, and his vice-president, Ramón Castillo, proceeded to suspend the national congress, despite (or more likely because of) the rising numbers of city workers. The rise of industry also created a new entrepreneurial elite, which was another threat to the power of the traditional political authorities. In effect the 1930s and early 1940s witnessed the last hurrah of the old cattle-and-wheat oligarchy. With the help of the army they proposed to dominate politics and to exclude the new groups created by urban-industrial development.

Yet the demographic trends associated with industry were bound to have an impact on politics sooner or later, and the potential for disorder remained high. The only thing the civilian leaders did, however, was to manipulate the political system in favour of the existing ruling groups. This could not work for ever, and the lack of real participation simply heightened the demands of the middle and working classes for a share in political power, not the tokenism of the past. What good was it to have universal manhood suffrage if the state moved against opposition parties and labour organizations, and outlawed their candidates for office? Thus the pressure for change was increasing. At the same time the generals hovered in the background, growing ever more restless and wondering whether the civilian politicians could ever achieve order. Further, the outbreak of the Second World War encouraged the military's ultra-nationalism. The army's pro-Axis sympathies (Argentina did not declare war on Germany and Japan until 1945) reinforced its sense of mission, as many officers believed that Hitler and Mussolini were models to be emulated. The argument was that in Argentina as in Europe decisive leadership was needed to save the country from class war and the threat of Bolshevism. Anti-Semitism was rife, and during the war years Jews and other minorities were the victims of both vigilante and official violence. Increasingly the generals came to regard themselves as once again called upon to rule directly rather than through civilian inter-mediaries. These views were shared by more junior officers as well, particularly a new military brotherhood organized in 1942–3 and known as the *Grupo de Oficiales Unidos*, or GOU, the Group of United Officers.

The result was another military coup, on 4 June 1943. A new government, first under General Pedro Ramírez and later General Edelmiro Farrell, assumed office. But the 1943 coup only confirmed the army's aspiration for power, not its readiness to find a new political formula for ruling the country. Initially there was no change in either domestic or foreign policy. However alarmed the officers may have been at the threat of political instability under civilian rule, it turned out that few of them had any better ideas about how to manage the new political classes that had been forming over the last several decades. But one among their number did. This was Juan Perón. Before the coup he had been under Farrell's command, and when the latter was appointed war minister in the Ramírez government, he brought Perón along to fill the number two post. It was a lucky break for Perón, an undistinguished colonel in the Argentinian army but one of the GOU's founding members. He had had a secondary role in the army coups of both 1930 and 1943, but with Farrell's patronage was poised for greater things. Because of past failures to produce political order, Perón opted to mobilize rather than resist the masses. He therefore inaugurated a new era in Argentian politics.

Perón served the 1943 Ramírez government as under-secretary of the War Department and as labour secretary, neither of which were major postings at the time but which he used to good advantage. This was possible because his immediate superior (Farrell) was not politically adept and therefore depended on him to an unusual degree. The War Department placed Perón in a position to influence appointments in the army and thus to increase his personal following among the officer corps.

And the Labour Department provided an opportunity to cultivate the masses, mainly by intervening in strikes to win settlements favourable to the working class and by co-opting the trade union leadership. Indeed, Perón promoted the expansion of labour organization as a way of furthering his own political ambitions, and hundreds of thousands of new members joined at the encouragement of the labour secretary. At Perón's prodding, the military government also improved health and retirement benefits for the working class, and provided for job security, workplace inspections, and paid vacations and holidays. By the time Farrell took over the presidency in 1944, Perón was well on his way to becoming the most important man in the government, and thus added the vice-presidency and the top position in the war ministry to his roster of offices. Earlier, in November 1943, the Labour Department had been given a much higher priority, and social security was officially added to the secretary's responsibilities. Perón made certain that the public understood that the advances in social welfare were his doing.

Perón saw the necessity of a new political strategy, one that would satisfy the masses, if stability were ever to be more than a mere chimera. The people could not be ignored any longer. He soon overshadowed the president, who was really a caretaker ruler acting on behalf of the army. A charismatic figure, at ease with the common folk, Perón was also a demagogue, and he proved quite willing to use force and terror against his enemies. But most recent governments had been capable of the latter, so that what distinguished Perón was his talent for drawing the masses behind the kind of strong leadership the army favoured. The problem was that the crowd could only be pleased as long as the economy remained strong. It took prosperity to provide the government and the private sector with the tax revenues and profits to finance benefits for labour and the middle classes.

Yet in 1945 Perón was still not president, and in fact his popularity with the masses was initially a cause of alarm among the officer corps. Most of the army still feared the consequences of democracy, and did not understand that Perón was less a democrat than a rabble-rouser and a master of mob rule. He would run the people, not be run by them. Accordingly, on 9 October, an army garrison forced Perón to resign and imprisoned him in what amounted to yet another coup. Farrell was left in office, but this time the outcome was more than the military bargained for. At the bidding of Perón's political lieutenants crowds of union members and others took to the streets of Buenos Aires in such numbers that the generals concluded that it was too dangerous to risk a confrontation. Disunity in army ranks on how to handle the crisis also recommended caution, and no doubt helped Perón. His mistress, Eva Duarte, played a vital role in events. An actress and singer of dubious talent, she none the less was a forceful and (as would become more apparent in time) demagogic personality, and she steeled Perón's resolve to wait out the crisis rather than go into exile. Soon she would marry Perón and become his partner in ruling the country. Unsure of its ability to control the crowds and unwilling to risk civil war, the army backed down and freed Perón on 17 October. What started out as an attempt to eliminate him from power only proved the success of his earlier measures for cultivating the masses, and left him as the front runner for the presidential election of 1946. In sum, the army's intervention boomeranged.

What followed was almost anti-climactic. Perón won the election, though not by an overwhelming majority. He received 54 per cent of the popular vote, though his supporters achieved a stronger showing in the national congress. But once in office he relied on the post-war boom to consolidate his power. Accumulated credits from wartime sales also helped. Argentina had exported to both sides, Axis and Allied, during the Second World War, and made huge profits by charging what the market would bear. But the conflict had also reduced the flow of imports. Both the state and business therefore had accumulated reserves which Perón could draw upon, at least for a while. The good times lasted until about 1950. Meanwhile the government embarked upon a new programme of industrialization. The idea was to expand the domestic market, which would be a gain for Argentinian entrepreneurs, labour and the urban middle class, i.e. for Perón's principal supporters. Government policy offered considerably less to the rural sector, as the day of the cattle-and-wheat oligarchy had passed. Of course, industrial development required importing foreign technology, machines and energy supplies, so the country's reserves were quickly depleted. Government-dictated wage increases and social benefits had the same effect, however politically profitable for Perón. In 1947 Perón issued a symbolic declaration of economic independence from foreign domination, and the next year the government bought control of the country's railways (which had been mainly British-owned) and assumed ownership of most of the banking, insurance, shipping, grain elevator and communications sectors. More importantly, it promoted a state agency to take over the marketing of the country's key exports (still mainly primary commodities) and the purchase of imports, and to guide the reallocation of resources from the rural to the urban sectors. This was the IAPI or *Instituto Argentino de Producción e Intercambio*.

While *Peronistas* cultivated an image of social progress, they also backed this up with a heavy dose of repression. The strategy was to trade social welfare for civil liberties. For example, Eva Perón established a philanthropic foundation to distribute assistance in her name, and for all practical purposes she guided Labour Department policy. But corruption afflicted the whole system, including the IAPI. A new constitution gave the vote to women in 1949, and the president's wife took charge of managing the new bloc of votes. The *Partido Peronista Feminino* was established to complement the *Partido Peronista*. For critics of the regime, on the other hand, there were the *descamisados*. These were gangs much like Mussolini's Black Shirts or Hitler's Brown Shirts, and were deployed by the *Peronista* Party to discipline the regime's enemies. The methods were the same as in the Nazi era: beatings, destruction of property and other forms of terrorism. The legal authorities helped by the opportune use of their powers of arrest. Even opposition members of the congress were intimidated and imprisoned. In 1951 Perón suggested that his wife run as his vice-presidential candidate in the coming elections, but the army (not surprisingly the stronghold of Argentinian *machismo*) vetoed this. She died of cancer the next year at the age of thirty-three. Her value to the regime was perhaps nowhere more apparent than in scattered but vocal demands that the Roman Catholic Church canonize her as a saint. It was not to be.

The storm clouds were on the horizon well before Eva Perón's death. By the early 1950s exports fell drastically, as European agriculture recovered in the years after the Second World War. Shipments of meat, for example, fell to about one-third of pre-war levels. The result was a decline in income for both the public and the private sectors. Further, the country's accumulated reserves were exhausted by the cost of repatriating foreign-owned enterprises and by the regime's social-welfare measures. Yet the industrialization programme still depended on importing foreign technology, because Argentina did not have a highly developed research and development sector or a machine tool industry. In the face of declining revenues, therefore, the government adopted a policy of fiscal restraint, but this meant a slowdown in public investment. More and more the government turned to the *descamisados* to silence its critics. It imposed censorship on the press, including the famous opposition newspapers *La Nación* and *La Prensa*, and in contrast to 1946 rigged the 1952 presidential election. The opposition did run a candidate, but government control of the media limited his access to the electorate, and thugs disrupted his public appearances. Perón won 65 per cent of the ballots cast, and it may well be that he was still popular enough to be the genuine choice of the people. After all, he still promised them a great deal, and projected an anti-establishment image. Yet the regime's interference in the election showed Perón's increasing sense of insecurity.

Indeed, once he was confirmed in office, the country's economic problems induced Perón to reverse his government's commitment to economic independence. The result was a fundamental shift in policy. Perón invited foreign capital back into the country, and when Milton Eisenhower (brother of the US president) visited Buenos Aires in 1953, he was fêted as the advance agent of Yankee money. Equally important, Perón informed labour that it was time to freeze wages and social benefits. Perhaps most interesting, though, was the president's attack on the Catholic Church. Perón had built his political career on his talent for wooing the masses, yet in 1954 he began a campaign against an institution which enjoyed the loyalty of most of his followers. He took steps to legalize divorce and prostitution, dismissed clerics from the education system, and ordered his congress to revoke the status of the church as the country's established religion. Popular demonstrations against these attacks resulted only in police and *descamisado* violence against church property and the clergy itself. In June 1955 Pope Pius XII issued a decree of excommunication against all government officials who acted against the clergy. Perón seems to have been reacting to the efforts of a few churchmen to penetrate the labour movement and to promote a reform party (the *Partido Demócrata Christiano*). But his response was out of proportion to the threat and turned out to be a major political blunder. At last he gave the opposition an issue to rally the masses, as most Argentinians were Catholics.

The key actor in the events of the next few months, however, was the army. The country's economic and political troubles provided the rationale, and the attack on the church provided the context in which the military could act with some confidence that a *coup d'état* would be accepted by enough of the population. The military had never entirely welcomed Perón's ascendancy (remember October 1945), and it was apparent the president was slipping. For the officers to remain loyal meant tying their fortunes to a falling star. Their sense of survival was too keen for this. The end came in September, beginning with a series of army revolts in the provinces and then spreading to Buenos Aires. The military was far more united than in 1945, and so the *descamisados* were no match. The navy threatened to bombard the city, and overflights by the air force spread panic among the population. By the twenty-first the capital was occupied, and Perón quietly went into exile.

Yet Perón had mobilized important forces in Argentinian society, and these did not disappear. As in the past, the generals were better at diagnosing the disease than prescribing a cure. The problem for the future was to find some way of co-opting the *Peronistas* into a movement acceptable to the army, and this became the central preoccupation of government, whether military or civilian, over the next decades. Most of the post-1955 regimes were run by soldiers, as the army intervened whenever it appeared that the few civilian presidents were making too many concessions to Perón's followers. The outcome was steadily worsening political polarization, so that by the early 1970s small urban guerrilla movements began to appear, and Argentinian politics seemed to be on the brink of civil war and possibly social revolution. This persuaded even the army that perhaps it was time for Perón's return to power, after eighteen years of exile. But this is a story for the future.

THE UNITED STATES AND
HEMISPHERIC SECURITY

Thus the eventual failure of populism drove Argentina back into the arms of outside investors and renewed its dependency on the First World. The army reimposed a regimen of foreign-led economic growth, and in effect restored the export–import economy of the past. For the officer corps, economic recovery was more important than democracy, and it proved capable of enforcing a solution, at least for the balance of the 1950s and the 1960s. The same was not true throughout the Western Hemisphere, and to the United States the danger seemed acute in Central America and the Caribbean. There local leaders welcomed foreign capital, but failed to preserve the stability essential for a favourable investment climate. Moreover, the region was of immediate strategic importance to the USA, simply because it was close to home and because of the Panama Canal. There was also the need to protect 'our' raw materials (as the State Department's chief Soviet specialist, George Kennan, undiplomatically put it) and to prevent the USSR from exploiting the possibility of social revolution on the very borders of the USA.*

* Cited in Walter LaFeber, *Inevitable Revolutions: The United States in Central America* (London: 1983), 107.

The United States therefore became more deeply entangled in the internal affairs of Central America and the Caribbean than in the rest of the Western Hemisphere. Indeed, this had been the case before as well as after 1945. The United States sent troops to Cuba during its war for independence from Spain in 1898, but then imposed a protectorate which lasted until 1934. This included the right to control the country's foreign policy and to intervene in its internal affairs. In fact, Washington forced the Cubans to confirm these rights in their constitution. Troops were stationed in the country from 1898 to 1902 and from 1906 to 1909, and returned for brief episodes in 1917 and 1922. The US formally surrendered its privileges in 1934, but retained a naval base at Guantánamo Bay and was able to keep watch over Cuba and indeed the entire Caribbean region. But Cuba was only the beginning.

In 1903 the United States used the threat of force to separate Panama from Colombia, because the latter had resisted plans for an isthmian canal across what was then its territory. The US in effect created the country of Panama so that it could proceed with its plans. Panama became a *de facto* US protectorate, and remained so until 1936. The surrender of the Canal Zone, however, was not conceded until much later, with the ratification of the Panama Canal Treaties in 1978. These provided that Washington would transfer complete authority to Panama, but only by the year 2000. Even then the US retained the right to intervene to defend the Canal should it ever be endangered.

Yet the list did not end there. The Dominican Republic was a United States protectorate from 1905 to 1940, including a period of military occupation between 1916 and 1924. Washington also acted as guardian over Nicaragua from 1911 to 1933, and marines occupied the country in 1909–10, 1912–25 and, after a short break, 1926–33. The troops were withdrawn only when Nicaragua established its own National Guard (under Anastasio Somoza García), which for the next four and a half decades proved capable of preserving a regime which Washington continued to support despite its dictatorial character. Similarly US troops left Haiti in 1934, though Washington retained the right to supervise the country's finances until 1941. The 1911 Mexican Revolution also caused a crisis in US–Latin American relations. Marines occupied Vera Cruz in 1914, and in 1916 President Woodrow Wilson ordered General John ('Black Jack') Pershing to cross the border and track down the famous Pancho Villa, leader of one of the contending factions in the Mexican revolution. Villa had crossed the US–Mexican border, but Wilson's real objective was to influence the policies of the revolutionary government. Pershing's forces soon grew to over 10,000 troops and penetrated more than 300 miles into Mexican territory. The Mexican president, Venustiano Carranza, feared that the USA might be planning to establish a permanent presence, and there was a real danger of all-out war between the two nations. Before the crisis was over, Wilson called up the National Guard and dispatched 100,000 troops to protect the US border. Deepening US involvement in the First World War, however, compelled Washington to reconsider its priorities, and Pershing's expedition was ordered home without having captured Villa. The last US troops withdrew by February 1917. Wilson did not have a great deal to show for his interference, and in the 1920s the State Department began having second thoughts about the effectiveness of direct intervention. This view gained more and more credence throughout the decade. There was never unanimity, but because US relations with Central America, the Caribbean and Mexico remained troubled the advocates of a new approach gained a hearing. The eventual result was the 'Good Neighbour Policy', formally announced by President Franklin Roosevelt in 1933. In sum, this committed the United States to surrender its self-proclaimed right to take unilateral military action in the Western Hemisphere.

Yet there was less to the Good Neighbour Policy than met the eye. Roosevelt made much ado about the new approach, as though the USA deserved special credit for seeking non-military solutions to its problems with nearby countries. In fact, the Good Neighbour Policy did not represent a hands-off strategy, but a greater emphasis on economic rather than military leverage. Besides, direct intervention fomented anti-Yankee resentment, and so the State Department increasingly viewed such tactics as counter-productive.

Moreover, while the above concerns were uppermost in the minds of policy-makers during the late 1920s and the 1930s, in the long run it turned out that the military option had not really been abandoned. It simply assumed new forms. For example, US Marines would not be needed so often if Washington were to provide training and weapons to indigenous military forces. These could act as surrogates in place of US troops, because the new armies were controlled by governments dependent on Washington for aid and trade. The precedent for this was Somoza's National Guard in Nicaragua, which had been organized in the 1930s, but the main impact of the policy came in the 1950s and after.

While billions of dollars were spent on hardware after the Second World War, training was every bit as important in upgrading the capabilities of the military in Latin America, and the scale of US activity was considerable. Almost 83,000 military personnel from twenty-one Latin American countries were processed between 1950 and 1979 under the US International Military Education and Training Programme and the Military Assistance Programme, and many of these people later went on to assume positions of political leadership in their home countries. One of the most important training-centres was the School of the Americas in the Panama Canal Zone. In addition, foreign personnel attended, among others, the US Army Infantry School in Fort Benning, Georgia; the Army Military Police School at Fort Gordon, Georgia; the Army Intelligence School at Fort Huachuca, Arizona; the Army Institute for Military Assistance, or the so-called 'Green Beret' school, at Fort Bragg, North Carolina; the Naval Amphibious School in Coronado, California; the Naval War College in Newport, Rhode Island; and the Naval Guided Missile School in Dam Neck, Virginia. The main point of this training effort was not to assist the US in its global or hemispheric operations, but to enable local armies to head off internal threats from social revolutionaries. Much of the training therefore concentrated on counter-insurgency and anti-guerrilla tactics, the hope being that the local military could take care of its own domestic problems so that US intervention would not be necessary.

There were other qualifications to the Good Neighbour Policy, though again these emerged most clearly after the Second World War. At Rio de Janeiro in August 1947 the United States renewed the interventionist option, but as a multilateral undertaking in unison with countries it would help arm. The new approach resulted in the signing of the Inter-American Treaty for Reciprocal Assistance (the Rio Pact). This was simply a hemispheric defensive alliance. From Washington's point of view perhaps the most important feature of the Rio Pact was that it took advantage of provisions in the United Nations Charter (Articles 51–3) which allowed regional associations to act independently of the UN in emergencies. The real import of the new alliance, therefore, was to create a system which the United States hoped to dominate, though within a structure of shared power. American businessmen and members of the US Congress did not relish the prospect of UN interference so close to home. After all, the Soviets had representation in the United Nations, so this was a sufficient reason for limiting its authority in the Western Hemisphere.

More important than the Rio Pact, as it turned out, was the Organization of American States, founded at Bogotá in 1948. The OAS was supposed to regularize the process of hemispheric consultation by providing a framework for discussion, and to complement the military alliance created at Rio. As with the Rio treaty, however, the effect was to exempt the Americas from UN interference and thus protect the claim of the United States to a special role in the region, though again within a framework of multilateral rather than unilateral action. Article 15 of the OAS charter provided that 'no State or group of States has the right to intervene, directly or indirectly, for any reason whatever, in the internal or external affairs of any other State', and thus seemed to provide international sanction for the Good Neighbour Policy. But the import of Article 15 was vitiated by another clause which allowed for action to be 'adopted for the maintenance of peace and security in accordance with existing treaties', such as the Rio Pact.

That the United States regarded the latter as the operative clause in case of internal or external subversion soon became clear in State Department interpretations of the OAS charter. Briefly, US policy-makers concluded that 'the doctrine of nonintervention never did proscribe the assumption by the organized community of a legitimate concern with any circumstances that threatened the common welfare'.* Intervention was still acceptable as long as it was the work of the group and not just one nation acting alone. Because Washington was determined to dominate the OAS, however, many other American nations regarded its interpretation as a distinction without a difference. The question of intervention thus remained a live issue in the years to come, as the nations south of the Rio Grande resisted or vitiated repeated US schemes for OAS action on Cuba, the Dominican Republic and Nicaragua. The mere creation of a new multilateral organization did not banish the spectre of US hegemony, and USA–Latin American relations remained disturbed. Indeed, the future would show that, if Washington could not have its way on multilateral action, it was prepared to abandon the Good Neighbour Policy and resort to unilateral action, though preferably by indirect means. A crisis in Guatemala proved this soon enough.

COUNTER-REVOLUTION: GUATEMALA
On 15 May 1954, 2,000 tons of small arms and ammunition arrived in Guatemala from the Eastern Bloc, thus setting the scene for a US-

* Cited in *ibid.*, 93–4.

sponsored *coup d'état* against the government of Jacobo Arbenz the same year. The weaponry had been manufactured in Czechoslovakia and shipped from the port of Szczecin in Poland on a vessel chartered by a Swedish company from a British company. Most importantly, it was Guatemala which had been looking for an arms deal, not the USSR, so that the sale was not part of a concerted Soviet plan to intervene in Central America (though the East no doubt was willing to take advantage of an opportunity to cause trouble in the heart of the Western sphere). In fact, the USSR did not even have an embassy in the country, though it had accorded diplomatic recognition to a new Guatemalan government in 1945. Guatemala was in the market because the United States and its allies had refused to sell it arms since 1948. The decision to buy from Eastern Europe was apparently a last resort. Indeed, Arbenz and his predecessor, Juan José Arévalo, had attempted to make purchases in Western Europe, Mexico, Cuba and Argentina before turning to the East, but all sales were blocked by the USA. The United States was unhappy with developments in Guatemala, and withheld military aid and even sales as a way of pressing the government to make changes. Then the introduction of Czech arms into the region provided the excuse for a direct blow against the regime.

Far more was at issue than the arrival of the first shipment of communist-made weapons purchased by a Central American government, as United States–Guatemalan relations had been deteriorating ever since the end of the Second World War. In point of fact the 1954 coup had less to do with any Soviet threat than with the fate of US property. It was hardly in the interest of the United States government, however, to publicize this, and the media failed to note the omission. Far better to blame the Russians than to see the region's problems as the product of unequal economic relations between the First World and the Third World. The latter would imply that the crisis was of the West's own making. Many people in the United States therefore saw 1954 as an isolated event rather than as one chapter in a long series of US–Central American confrontations.

The Guatemalan crisis really began a decade earlier, with the overthrow of the dictatorship of Jorge Ubico and the holding of free elections in 1944. The victor was Juan José Arévalo, an exiled author and teacher who had returned from Argentina to run for the presidency. The problem was that the preceding years of dictatorship had prevented the formation of a stable party system, so that the restoration of democracy saw the emergence of a myriad of political factions. No single party was capable of ruling alone. Arévalo ran on a platform he characterized as 'spiritual socialism', and relied on a fluid coalition of various leftists, including communists. The new president, however, was not a communist himself. Neither he nor his successor, Arbenz, proposed nationalizing the entire economy, but only key sectors, and therefore represented a middle ground between a totally collectivized and a totally privatized system. Arévalo proscribed the communist party as such, though it regrouped under various names and sometimes in competing organizations. Communists were even deported during his administration. But Arévalo also defended the right of all citizens who stayed within the law to enjoy full civil rights, and so individual communists and their sympathizers soon played a large role in events. The communists' advantage was that they had a coherent programme to offer, in contrast to some other movements. The disarray of the political system thus placed the left in a strong position to influence policy, especially as Arévalo's own platform was not very specific. Given the legacy of repression and exploitation under Ubico, however, the left would most likely have been strong no matter who led the government, and therefore the United States became alarmed at the direction of Guatemala's politics.

To red-hunters in the United States the proof of the country's communization came soon enough. For example, the Law of Forced Rental required large landowners to lease uncultivated properties to peasants at nominal rates, raising the spectre of more radical land reform sometime in the future. In addition, the government introduced social security, established a central bank, and permitted unions to organize and to go on strike. Communist labour leaders were particularly successful in negotiating wage increases, and they dominated the *Confederación General de Trabajadores de Guatemala*, a coalition of labour organizations. By the 1950s the urban labour movement had become the principal base of communist influence over the government.

Elections were held in 1950, but the State Department found little encouragement in the outcome. The new president was Jacobo Arbenz, an army man and defence minister in the previous cabinet. In the complex manoeuvring over the succession during the preceding year Arbenz had emerged as the candidate of the left. His chief rival for the presidency had been Francisco Javier Arana, head of the armed forces and the most influential right-winger in the government. As Arana's star rose, however, the left closed ranks behind Arbenz. Then, on 18 July 1949, Arana was assassinated in an ambush outside Guatemala City. The new president therefore came to power under a cloud of suspicion that he had engineered the removal of the candidate of the right. This had the effect of further polarizing Guatemalan politics.

Yet there was a great deal of support in Guatemala for the type of programmes proposed by Arbenz. They seemed to be what the majority of people wanted, though not the oligarchy, so that it is too simple to explain the new president's policies as simply the pet projects of a few leftist king-makers. After all, at the peak of its power in 1954 the Guatemalan communist party had only 4,000 members, this in a country of five million. Even the national congress of fifty-six members included only four communist representatives, and none held cabinet positions. And as would become obvious at the time of the 1954 coup, the communists did not control the army, which in the end proved to be the most important centre of power. The main source of communist strength was in the union sector. The president's policies, however, were not the result of overwhelming communist control, but reflected popular demands for change in response to hundreds of years of exploitation. This did mean that in the Guatemalan case communists and non-communists supported many of the same policies, making it possible for Washington to condemn virtually any supporter of the government as a red. For his part Arbenz assessed the domestic political situation, and increased the pace of reform. His mistake was to underestimate the international repercussions. He harassed US businesses and allowed the communist party to operate in the open, so that within a few months of his inauguration Arbenz found himself in Washington's disfavour.

It was the land question which proved to be the test case. This brought Arbenz into conflict with the local oligarchy but also the United Fruit Company, the largest US enterprise in Central America and a symbol of Yankee imperialism. With major investments in banana production, transportation, communications and electric utilities, United Fruit was Guatemala's biggest employer (over 10,000 workers). It was also the country's principal landowner. In fact, it monopolized vast tracts which were left untilled. The idea was to deny competitors access to fertile lands, but this also blocked alternative uses, especially to grow food crops and to relieve peasant demands for land reform.

On 17 June 1952 the Arbenz government promulgated the Agrarian Reform Law. This was a popular measure considering that only 2 per cent of the total population held title to about 72 per cent of agricultural land. Since the fall of Ubico, however, the formation of peasant unions had progressed to the point where the *Confederación Nacional Campesina de Guatemala* (CNCG) was established in 1950. This was a federation of *campesino*, or peasant, organizations, and at its height claimed 400,000 members. The CNCG leadership was independent of the communist movement, but none the less formed an increasingly close alliance with it. The peasants and also Arbenz needed the communists' political support on the land question, while for their part the communists saw the CNCG as an ally in attacking the oligarchy. Once again communists had an important say in developments, yet were not the sole or even the main impetus behind them. The pressure for land reform had far more to do with the monopoly power exercised by United Fruit and the local elite.

The 1952 law was aimed at large plantation owners, whether Guatemalan or foreign, and provided for the expropriation of holdings which were not under cultivation. Plantations in full production were exempt. Compensation was to be in the form of government bonds, but with a catch. The value of the land was fixed on the basis of the owners' current tax assessments. As these tended to underestimate the real worth of their property, owners soon found that compensation would be considerably less than they wanted. One of the hardest hit was United Fruit, and the next year the government moved to expropriate 234,000 acres of unused lands owned by the company. Compensation was set at $630,000, but the State Department demanded almost $16,000,000. And because United Fruit held title to hundreds of thousands of acres more, it was clearly vulnerable to additional losses. Indeed, in 1954 the government prepared to take another 173,000 acres in a second expropriation. In all, the government took approximately 1.5 million acres from about 1,000 plantations around the country. Further, peasants were given the right to participate in the administration of the programme, so that the CNCG grew in political importance. And while communists played a large role in these events, the *campesino* unions did not fall under outright communist control.

The United States government could hardly fail to take notice of events, especially since the former law firm of the secretary of state, John Foster Dulles, had represented United Fruit. Furthermore, the head of the Central Intelligence Agency, Allen Dulles, had been a member of the company's board of trustees. This is not to say that the events of 1954 were designed exclusively to save United Fruit. But it is to say that the Eisenhower administration probably shared the company's perspective, and found cause for alarm in its treatment at the hands of Arbenz. It was simply the focal point in a larger dispute over the treatment of private property. The outcome might influence events elsewhere in Central America, so Washington was not about to let it pass.

Accordingly, in the late summer of 1953, the Eisenhower administration decided to act. The plan was to stage a coup against Arbenz, and to replace him with Colonel Carlos Castillo Armas. The CIA arranged to train a small force of Guatemalans in neighbouring Honduras (on United Fruit properties). In effect the US launched a conspiracy to overthrow the legally constituted government of Guatemala, though it did attempt to gain the sanction of international law. In March 1954, at the Caracas meeting of the OAS, John Foster Dulles presented a resolution condemning communism in the Western Hemisphere and calling for 'appropriate action in accordance with existing treaties'. A number of Latin American nations regarded this as simply an excuse for US intervention. In rebuttal Dulles pledged his belief 'that there is not a single American state which would practise intervention against another American state'.* Given the CIA's activities, of course, such a statement was at variance with the facts. The resolution passed, but with Mexico and Argentina abstaining and with Guatemala opposed. Yet even many of those who voted with the United States did so in the expectation that the US would provide much needed economic assistance as a *quid pro quo* in exchange for their political support, and later they expressed reservations. A Somoza might offer enthusiastic endorsement, but it was clear that the OAS did not regard the Guatemalan crisis in quite the same light as Washington, and that the passage of the Dulles resolution was virtually meaningless as an endorsement of United States policy.

In Washington's view legalities were less important than property rights and hemispheric security, and the delivery of communist-made weapons in May provided the excuse to invoke the Caracas resolution. The outcome was a move back to unilateral intervention, though behind the mask of indigenous forces. Castillo Armas and a few hundred supporters crossed into Guatemala from Honduras on 18 June 1954, but made little headway. The CIA provided radio services designed to confuse the Guatemalan people into believing that the invaders were marching on the capital city, but the hoped-for popular uprising against Arbenz failed to materialize. This left Castillo Armas in considerable danger, and when two of his aircraft were shot down President Eisenhower approved the transfer of two P-51 fighter bombers to third parties, who then were to assist Armas. The dictators Anastasio Somoza of Nicaragua and Rafael Trujillo of the Dominican Republic also

---

* Cited in Cole Blasier, *The Hovering Giant: US Responses to Revolutionary Change in Latin America* (London: 1976), 167–8.

helped. The aircraft were used to cause panic among the population by strafing and bombing population centres.

The outbreak of fighting, of course, placed the Guatemalan army in a position to determine the outcome. Would the officers stand by the country's president? Before the coup Arbenz had considered setting up a people's militia, but the officer corps feared the consequences of creating a competing military force and therefore opposed the idea. Indeed, for some time the army had entertained reservations about several other policies of the president, so in the face of a crisis the military turned on Arbenz and the game was up. He had no choice but to resign and clear the way for Castillo Armas. John Foster Dulles went on US television to explain how little Guatemala had headed off 'the evil purpose of the Kremlin to destroy the inter-American system', though obviously the real threat to US interests came from within the hemisphere.*

Castillo Armas cancelled land reform and restored the property of the United Fruit Company and other large landowners, forcing peasant families to vacate their newly won farms. In addition he welcomed back foreign investors, rescinded the labour laws of Arévalo and Arbenz, and executed hundreds of their supporters. He established literacy qualifications for voting, thus effectively eliminating the peasantry from a role in politics. United Fruit did contribute 100,000 acres to a government resettlement programme and agreed to pay higher taxes, but the defeat of democracy would only lead to turmoil in the future. Indeed, within three years Castillo Armas himself fell to an assassin. Perhaps the United States would have learned to live with an Arbenz if it had known what lay ahead. The Guatemalan coup meant the effective end of the Good Neighbour Policy, though it is doubtful whether it ever had any substance. The United States reclaimed the right to intervene unilaterally, and thus assumed the burden of arbitrating the crises to come. For the short term, however, the 'Colossus of the North' seemed to be having its way in Central America. The same could not be said for the rest of the Caribbean basin, and in Cuba the United States was to encounter its most serious challenge.

REVOLUTION: CUBA

The Guatemalan operation was a great success for the United States, or so it was thought in the 1950s. More importantly, the outcome shaped

* Cited in LaFeber, 124.

Washington's responses to other crises as well. The catch was that Guatemala also contained lessons for revolutionaries. When the US attempted to pursue a similar strategy in Cuba a few years later, the other side was better prepared. The fall of Arbenz had a major influence on Fidel Castro, who provided much of the leadership and inspiration behind the Cuban Revolution of 1959. Moreover, one of his chief collaborators was Ernesto Ché Guevara, an Argentinian who had finished a medical degree but then travelled throughout Latin America and met with radicals and revolutionaries in several countries. He reached Guatemala early in 1954, where he witnessed the coup later in the year. Although he played no important part in events, the experience crystallized his commitment to revolutionary action. He fled to Mexico and in due course joined Castro. Castro had studied law and been active among radical political groups at the University of Havana, and subsequently led an ill-fated attack on the government of dictator Fulgencio Batista. But instead of toppling the regime, Castro found himself in prison and then exile. By the time Guevara and Castro joined forces in Mexico, the latter was planning his return to Cuba.

For Castro and Guevara the lesson of Guatemala was very clear indeed. The Eisenhower administration had succeeded in overthrowing a popular revolution mainly because the officer corps defected. Therefore, the first thing Castro did when he assumed power in Cuba was to dismantle the army of the old regime and replace it with a new organization of his own. Unlike Arbenz he made certain that the revolutionaries controlled the military. The result was to make it considerably more difficult for the United States to act against the Cuban Revolution.

To policy-makers in the United States, Cuba hardly seemed the most likely candidate for a revolution. Economically it was better off than many nations in Latin America. Literacy rates, educational opportunities, the general level of health and wages also compared favourably. As elsewhere, though, the ownership of land was highly concentrated, income inequality was severe, and much of the workforce depended on seasonal labour. About 80 per cent of the country's export earnings came from sugar, with the United States buying 50 per cent of the total crop during the 1950s. The US paid higher than world prices, though purchases were strictly controlled under a quota system dividing its market among several sources of supply. The price scale really had the effect of providing a small subsidy to US manufacturers, because high sugar prices meant that Cuba could import more from the USA. Also, many of the sugar companies in Cuba were owned by US citizens, who wanted a guaranteed return. For its part Havana granted tariff concessions on US-manufactured goods. The system therefore made sense from Washington's point of view. The rest of the sugar crop was less profitable for Cuba. Over-production kept world prices depressed. In fact the instability in world markets induced US investors to sell many of their sugar plantations and mills to Cubans, so that, while almost 80 per cent of production was foreign-owned on the eve of the Second World War, it was down to 40 per cent by the time Castro came to power. More US dollars wound up in other types of investment than sugar. Still, Cuba received more investment from the United States than most other Latin American countries. The problem was that its well-being depended too much on a single crop and on trade and investment from a single source, the United States. But, perhaps most important, the country had been ruled by Fulgencio Batista for twenty-five years, and had degenerated into dictatorship, repression, racketeering and gangsterism.

Batista came to power several months after widespread uprisings and strikes had broken out against the dictatorship of Gerardo Machado in 1933. In the aftermath he co-operated with a leftist junta which briefly assumed authority. Only a sergeant in the Cuban army, Batista turned out to have his own political ambitions and a keen sense of how to realize them. The junta needed the support of the military, and so looked not to Machado's officers but to Batista as the presumed representative of the enlisted men. He was appointed colonel and placed in charge of the army, which soon became his personal power base. The new colonel was no radical, however, and staged a coup in January 1934. Moreover, he acted with Washington's encouragement. Franklin Roosevelt had ordered the US Navy to take up positions off Cuba's shores. While the United States had not threatened intervention against Machado, it was another matter when the spectre of socialism was at hand. Batista became the strong man of Cuba for the next quarter of a century, usually ruling through puppets but sometimes assuming office himself. Though early Batista governments instituted various reforms (including wage and social legislation, public works and better education), by the end the result was hardly any better than under Machado. In 1952 turmoil in both the economy and politics induced Batista to suspend the constitution and to rule directly as dictator. It was at this point that Castro and also a variety of other opposition forces became a factor in events, though without the support of Cuba's communists.

Moscow dominated the communist party of Cuba, virtually neutralizing it as a revolutionary force. This was the result of the popular front strategy before the Second World War. A major factor in the Cuban labour movement, the communists agreed to support the pro-Batista government in 1938, and except for a minor break after the signing of the Nazi–Soviet Pact of 1939 continued to co-operate until the Cold War era. In return Batista allowed them to operate as a legal political party, eventually operating under the name *Partido Socialista Popular*. The deal revealed the communists' opportunism, a trait which would be exhibited again and again. In 1942 two communists joined the cabinet. After the war the party continued to follow Moscow's lead, but the USSR had in effect conceded countries like Cuba to the West. And the Cold War meant that there was no chance that the popular-front strategy could last. In due course the communists were driven underground. But, given the marginal role of Cuba in Soviet foreign policy, Moscow's directives did not change, so that the real anti-Batista opposition was left to other forces. When Castro finally did come to power, he was not indebted to the communists for his success.

To Castro, and others who had emerged from the milieu of radical university politics, Batista's dictatorship left no alternative except a resort to armed force. The official political system was simply not open to opponents of the regime. Moreover, the revolutionaries would have to rely on a dramatic strike (i.e. on arms alone), because the mass of the population had yet to be mobilized. Perhaps such a move would be the first step towards inciting a popular uprising. Therefore, on 26 July 1953, Castro led a contingent of perhaps 165 would-be revolutionaries against the Moncada Barracks in Santiago de Cuba, but was taken prisoner. His tiny group of radicals hardly seemed a threat to the life of the regime, however, and in 1955 he was freed in a general amnesty. This was a capital error on Batista's part, because Castro went to Mexico and began building a new force. In December 1956 he returned with about eighty men and landed on the Cuban coast, only to be met by Batista's army. A dozen survivors escaped to the Sierra Maestra Mountains, including Castro and Guevara. There they regrouped. They also established links to other anti-Batista forces. Castro was not yet the undisputed leader of the opposition (particularly for the urban resistance), but his dramatic forays from the hills and the legend of 26 July soon made him the best-known resistance figure. The spreading rural and urban guerrilla war left Batista in desperate straits, and the brutality of his response was such as to alienate his closest allies at home and abroad. The United

States prohibited the shipment of arms to Cuba in March 1958. It turned out, however, that the US had something else in mind besides a Castroite victory.

By the summer of 1958 Castro's 26 July Movement had joined forces with several other opposition groups. Though Cuba's communists established tentative contacts with Castro early in the year, they still held aloof. More importantly, the emerging coalition included representatives of business, professional and middle-class interests. The problem for Batista was that all classes in Cuba, not just the dispossessed, were coalescing against him. The middle and upper layers of society were not threatened so much by economic exploitation as by the political system. Batista's terror endangered the lives of all his opponents, and his dictatorship denied business and the intelligentsia a role in determining policy. With the alienation of these people, Batista's days were numbered, so that for Washington the question was no longer whether Batista could survive but who would be his successor.

Accordingly, early in December 1958, the United States suggested privately to Batista that he step down in favour of a military junta, which would then offer concessions to the opposition. The idea was to deny the fruits of victory to the other side, especially the revolutionaries, but Batista refused to co-operate. Yet it proved impossible for his government to hold out. At the end of the month he fled the country. Only then did he name a military officer as his successor. The army had been the foundation of his power, and so a leader drawn from its ranks could be trusted to arbitrate among the contending forces. Castro understood this all too well, though in reality Batista's army was falling apart and there was little chance that the ploy could succeed. Nevertheless, when the revolutionary forces marched into Havana on 1 January 1959 and a new government was established, Castro and Ché Guevara immediately took charge of the army. Until late 1958 the 26 July Movement consisted of just a few hundred guerrillas. Batista's forces were considerably more numerous. Hence the need to act. Otherwise the government reflected its origins as a coalition of anti-Batista forces, and José Miró Cardona (representing the professional and business reformers) assumed the role of prime minister, though not for long. Castro's armed revolutionaries and not the middle class held the preponderance of power. Consequently within a few weeks Miró Cardona resigned, and Castro took his place. Though hardly pleased, Washington recognized the new government. After all, at that time it still represented a broad coalition of forces, so there might be the opportunity to limit Castro's influence.

The Revolution in Action

Even with the departure of some middle-class representatives from the coalition, the first months of 1959 (until May) witnessed only the typical reforms of a newly installed nationalist regime: the state-decreed reduction of rents and utilities rates, the takeover of the US-owned Cuban Telephone Company, and the trial and subsequent execution or imprisonment of hundreds of *Batistianos* charged with torture and other atrocities. While individuals were singled out for specific crimes, there was no immediate attack on important property-owners as a class or on the government bureaucracy as such, though it and the regular army were purged of the more notorious members of the preceding government. There was not even a wholesale seizure of foreign-owned enterprises. The new government initially promised to abide by the Constitution of 1940, but in February legislative and executive power was vested in the cabinet and elections postponed indefinitely. It was at this point that Castro took over as prime minister. He travelled to the United States in April amidst talk of possible aid and credits, but made no attempt to conclude an agreeement. His idea was to avoid any appearance of selling out to Washington.

For its part the Soviet Union took a guarded approach to Cuba, and did not send an ambassador right away. Batista had broken off diplomatic relations with Moscow in 1952, and although the USSR recognized the new government in January 1959, it was not until June that Ché Guevara established contact with the Russians. A Tass correspondent took up a permanent posting in Cuba by the end of the year, and Soviet deputy premier Anastas Mikoyan signed the first of several aid and trade agreements with Havana in February 1960. Yet the formal restoration of full diplomatic relations did not occur until May 1960. For some time Castro seemed more of a reforming nationalist than a social revolutionary, so that the State Department decided to be patient.

Yet the United States was about to discover that it would be very difficult to reach an accommodation with Havana. The trial of the *Batistianos* raised tensions right away. The victims included some of Washington's more dependable Cuban allies. Had they continued to play a part in the country's politics, they could have been relied upon to offset revolutionaries in the regime. But perhaps the problem with the most potential for disturbing US–Cuban relations in the future was that Castro did not have a detailed plan of action when he came to power, only a set of general principles, such as land reform and a Cuba independent of US control. The specifics of implementing his programme were unclear, and he therefore reacted to events as they unfolded. Given the inherent conflict between his aspirations and the US goal of protecting its stake in the country, the tendency was for tensions to escalate, as one *ad hoc* response led to another.

From the first, Castro was predisposed to expect trouble with the United States, perhaps another Guatemala-style intervention. He was also keenly aware of the danger of internal subversion. The threat of disunity at home persuaded him to move against other political factions, though for the time being the old Cuban communist party remained a minor factor in developments. As Castro began attacking the interests of the anti-Batista middle classes, however, large numbers of them joined the exodus of *Batistianos* to Miami and other US destinations. While this no doubt helped the regime consolidate its power at home, it also created a community of counter-revolutionary exiles who proceeded to launch armed forays against their homeland. Throughout 1959 Washington's official policy was to prevent the US mainland from being used as a base for activities against a government which it recognized. But as US–Cuban relations worsened, the Central Intelligence Agency began recruiting among the exiles, and moreover did so no later than December 1959. Castro did not identify openly with socialism until early 1961, and did not declare himself to be a Marxist–Leninist until December of the same year. The State Department, though, had come to this conclusion well before then.

In May 1959 Havana proclaimed the Agrarian Reform Law. It was a half-way measure in that it limited the size of holdings but did not nationalize all land. It thus restricted single farms to about 1,000 acres and grazing operations to 3,300 acres. Any holdings in excess of these limits were to be expropriated. It applied to Cuban as well as foreign-owned property, and so was not a specifically anti-US act. The State Department therefore did not protest the principle of land reform, especially as Havana acknowledged the right of compensation (though the exact terms remained a subject of dispute). On another issue, however, it took a hard line and resisted Castro's efforts to buy arms. He first approached sellers in the United States and Western Europe, but Washington refused to permit sales and pressed its allies to do the same. Accordingly, in March 1960, Castro warned that he would buy wherever he could, meaning Eastern Europe. Besides embargoing arms, the US also considered disciplining Cuba by cutting the sugar quota, though the Eisenhower administration took no action in 1959.

To the Bay of Pigs

Events quickened with the arrival in Havana of Soviet first deputy premier Anastas Mikoyan in February 1960. The Russians saw a chance to take advantage of the situation, and signed agreements committing the USSR to buy Cuban sugar for five years and providing $100 million in credit. (Earlier the USSR had purchased small quantities of Cuban sugar from Batista as well.) East Germany and Poland also purchased Cuban sugar in due course, though Moscow became the mainstay of the Cuban economy. A month after Mikoyan's visit Castro accused the United States of sabotaging a shipment of French munitions that had arrived in Havana Harbour. It was no mere coincidence, therefore, that on 17 March 1960 President Eisenhower formally ordered the CIA to 'organize the training of Cuban exiles, mainly in Guatemala, against a possible future day when they might return to their homeland'.* Thus the United States began contemplating a resort to military force, but with the help of surrogates acting on its behalf. On 28 March Castro repudiated the Rio Pact, and the first shipment of Eastern Bloc arms arrived some months later. In the spring and early summer he also nationalized a major US-owned mining company and the four principal US-owned hotels in Havana. Yet the question of compensation remained open, suggesting that the Cuban government did not intend a clean break with the United States.

The problem was that other matters agitated US–Cuban relations, and precluded compromise. Soviet oil became a key test. Cuba's principal source of energy was imported petroleum, but Western suppliers were under pressure from the United States to cut sales. Accordingly Castro turned to the Soviets as an alternate source of supply. When the Cuban branches of Texaco and Esso (along with Shell, an Anglo-Dutch company) refused to accept Russian oil for refining, however, Castro interpreted this as a direct affront to Cuban sovereignty. He therefore nationalized the offending companies, which in fact had acted upon advice from the US State Department, whereupon on 6 July 1960, the Eisenhower Administration cut the sugar quota (it would be effectively ended once and for all in December). Havana's response came with the nationalization of twenty-six US companies in August, all US-owned banks in September and finally another 166 enterprises in October.

* Dwight Eisenhower, *The White House Years: Waging Peace, 1956–1961* (Garden City: 1965), 533.

It was up to the US to make the next move, and on 19 October the administration imposed a trade embargo on Cuba, exempting only medical supplies and certain foods. This simply drove Castro closer to the Soviets, and as his dependency increased he began placing old-line communists in prominent posts throughout the government. The summer of 1960 marked the turning-point of communist influence on the Cuban revolution. The paradox was that Cuban communists had expressed doubts about the nationalizations of August to October, fearing additional reprisals from Washington. It is likely that this reflected the tentative nature of the Soviet commitment to Havana up to this point. But soon the failure of US plans to topple Castro by force opened up new opportunities for the USSR, and drew Moscow into its most dangerous adventure since the end of the Second World War. In the meantime a new president assumed office in the United States, John F. Kennedy.

Although before his election Kennedy was not informed of secret contingency plans for an invasion of Cuba by exiles, he had taken a strong stand against Castro during the 1960 presidential campaign. He therefore approved of Eisenhower's decision to break diplomatic relations with Havana on 3 January 1961. And once he assumed office later in the month, everything conspired to force an early decision on invading. There was the sheer momentum of a project that had been afoot for nearly a year. Vested interests, particularly in the CIA, were eager to improve on the record of Guatemala. The US Joint Chiefs of Staff and the president's top civilian advisers seemed prepared to go along with the idea. The president of Guatemala wanted the exiles out of his country as soon as possible. And Kennedy needed to back up the tough stance he had taken during the campaign. Perhaps most important, he insisted that no US troops be directly involved in the landing, though Americans might provide air cover and intelligence. This had the effect of making it easier to decide in favour of the enterprise. If something went wrong, it would be possible to deny everything. Kennedy therefore approved on the condition that the exiles understood that they were mainly on their own. Their leaders, however, were convinced that the CIA would not allow the venture to fail, so apparently the precise terms of US support were not clear to all those involved. In any event, Kennedy gave the go-ahead.

The landing took place at the Bay of Pigs on 17 April 1961, and was a disaster from start to finish. There were only 1,400 invaders. The hope was that news of their arrival would inspire an uprising inside Cuba and precipitate the fall of the government in Havana. But this was wishful thinking. The Cuban Revolution, particularly land reform, was popular at home if not in Washington, and every US action against Castro simply increased his support. The Cuban army met the invaders on the beach, and there was no uprising. Further, it was immediately apparent that the United States was behind the plan and that it was not an independent initiative by exiles. There was no covering up Washington's complicity. And, more than any other event, the Bay of Pigs served to tempt the Russians into establishing a larger presence in Cuba, though they never signed a formal military alliance with Castro which would commit them to any specific action.

The Missile Crisis

The Soviets decided to install nuclear missiles in Cuba, and caught the US State Department with its guard down. In the aftermath of the Bay of Pigs, Khrushchev had given assurances to Kennedy that although the USSR was prepared to defend Cuba against another attack it did not plan to establish military bases of its own on the island. In fact this was consistent with Soviet practice generally. Heretofore the USSR had refrained from locating offensive nuclear missiles in other countries, not even in Eastern Europe. Moreover, the Russians had adhered to this policy despite the American decision to place nuclear weapons in Western Europe and Turkey. Only in the 1980s would Moscow deploy medium-range missiles in the countries of the Warsaw Pact. The Soviet Union had thus been more circumspect than the United States about basing nuclear weapons on foreign soil, but then Cuba proved to be a dangerous exception.

In July 1962, more than a year after the Bay of Pigs, US spy planes detected an increase in Soviet shipments to Cuba. On 29 August the first surface-to-air missiles (SAMs) were sighted, yet these were clearly defensive not offensive. In other words, they were designed to shoot down incoming aircraft. They did not have enough range to reach any other country and thus initiate a war. As a result of the Bay of Pigs, Havana wanted to upgrade its defences, and Washington was prepared to tolerate this. But, just to be on the safe side, in September Kennedy requested that the US Congress authorize him to place as many as 150,000 reserve troops on active duty. Further, he increased the number of spy flights over Cuba. On 3 October Congress urged the White House to stop 'by whatever means may be necessary, including the use of arms, the creation in Cuba of a foreign military base that endangered United

States security'.* All these steps were taken before there was any definite sign of a Soviet offensive capability in the Western Hemisphere, so that there were no grounds for misunderstanding the US position. On 14 October, however, aerial photographs revealed an offensive missile base under construction. Two days later the White House set up an executive committee (known as 'Ex Com') to advise the president on what to do next.

The fear was that Moscow planned a test of US resolve in the wake of the Bay of Pigs. From the Soviet point of view there were a number of outstanding issues which might be pressed. Khrushchev had been agitating on the Berlin question for some time, and wanted to end the West's right to occupy part of the city, a right dating back to the Second World War. After all, Berlin was in the heart of the Eastern Bloc and hence something of a Trojan Horse. The USSR had nothing like it in the West. The Western zones of occupation were also an escape route for refugees from communism, and 152,000 people from the East took advantage of a porous border in 1960. The escape rate kept rising the next year (the peak occurred on 6 August, when 2,305 people crossed from East to West Berlin), so on 13 August 1961 the East Germans began building the Berlin Wall to seal off the border. Another live issue for the Russians was the presence of US Jupiter missiles in Turkey and Italy, though because the Jupiters were fast becoming obsolete a more telling threat came from plans to deploy Polaris nuclear submarines in the Eastern Mediterranean. There was also the chance that Moscow's aim was to achieve a major strategic coup in the Western Hemisphere and undermine the Monroe Doctrine, though improving its position in the East–West conflict was more likely to be the main consideration.

Ex Com reviewed these and other issues, searching for a link to developments in Cuba. After all, Castro offered the Russians an opportunity to challenge the US advantage in air power, missiles and nuclear weaponry, an advantage which had prevailed consistently since the Second World War and which still existed. While Kennedy had scored political points in the 1960 US presidential campaign by making much of Western weaknesses, the Soviets so far had been unable to catch up. Kennedy's so-called 'missile gap' was really in the East not the West, notwithstanding his campaign rhetoric. By mid-1961 the United States had deployed considerably more than a thousand tactical and intercon-

* Cited in George Ball, *The Past Has Another Pattern: Memoirs* (London: 1982), 291.

tinental bombers, 48 Polaris missiles, 40 intercontinental ballistic missiles (ICBMs), and about 100 intermediate range missiles (based in Europe) aimed at the Soviet Union. The Soviets' intermediate bombers and missiles, of course, could threaten Western Europe but not the continental United States, whereas for Washington the same type of weapons (based in Europe) could strike at the very heartland of the Soviet Union. Geography seemed to be on Washington's side. The USSR had fewer than 200 intercontinental bombers and possibly just four (and probably no more than ten) ICBMs capable of a direct attack on the USA. Moreover, US intelligence had successfully probed Soviet weaknesses. Until 1960, and the shooting down of a U–2 spy plane piloted by Gary Powers, the United States had conducted a series of reconnaissance flights over Soviet territory. Khrushchev therefore needed to restore the credibility of the Russian nuclear threat and to do so quickly. Cuba provided a ready solution. Bases close to North America would do the job, because short-range and medium-range missiles then could reach the USA itself.

Both sides maintained secrecy for the time being. Moscow needed to complete the construction of its offensive missile sites before it would be in a position to threaten the US, while Washington needed to calculate a response. Yet Kennedy did face a time limit. He had to make the first move, so as to confront the Russians before their missiles were armed and ready to fire. Otherwise, the USA itself would be likely to be hit in any military confrontation over Cuba or any other issue. Ex Com therefore quickly divided into two groups. One favoured the 'Fast Track', i.e. a surprise air raid on the missile sites, with an invasion as a possible sequel. The other favoured the 'Slow Track', a naval blockade on the shipment of military equipment to Cuba. The problem with the first was that it was irrevocable and would force a Soviet response, possibly precipitating a world war. Kennedy thus chose the second, in order to give the Russians time to retreat. There was still the risk that a Soviet ship might try to run the blockade or that Khrushchev might strike at US missiles in Turkey, but at least the Slow Track did not predetermine the outcome to the same extent. None the less, by 18 October the US Department of Defence began deploying aircraft and troops in case orders were issued for bombing and invading the island. The next day the press started asking questions about troop movements. Obviously the time was fast approaching when Kennedy would have to make the crisis public. Organizing for possible military action was simply too massive an operation to hide for very long.

On 22 October 1962 the president went on US television and announced that a blockade would go into effect in two days' time. Nineteen US naval vessels moved into position off Cuba, and twelve of the twenty-five Russian ships travelling to Cuba either halted in mid-ocean or altered course. On 25 October, and with the advice of the United States, the secretary-general of the United Nations, U Thant, called on the Russians to cancel all ship movements for the time being. He also asked Kennedy to avoid a confrontation. The hope was that this would head off an encounter between Soviet and US vessels, and buy time for diplomacy. By the next day both Kennedy and Khrushchev had replied affirmatively. From Washington's point of view, however, the blockade was not really working. It was supposed to halt preparation of the missile sites, yet despite the suspension of Russian ship movements construction continued. If the installations became operational, then Kennedy's position would be virtually untenable. An attempt to destroy the missiles would mean that the Soviets might fire them against the continental USA. On the other hand, it was debatable whether Moscow was prepared to risk a war with the United States over Cuba. Still, Ex Com was uncertain, and therefore reconsidered whether it should recommend an air strike before the missile sites were finished.

Then an apparent breakthrough occurred on 26 October with the arrival of a rambling message from Khrushchev. The Soviet chairman had apparently composed it himself. In a roundabout way he proposed that the USSR remove its missiles permanently in exchange for an end to the blockade and a pledge by the USA not to invade Cuba in the future. The next day, however, Radio Moscow broadcast another missive in Khrushchev's name. This was considerably more formal and probably the work of the Soviet equivalent of Ex Com. It raised the price of Soviet withdrawal to include the removal of Jupiters from Turkey. United States intelligence also reported that one Russian ship had resumed a course for Cuba and that construction on the missile sites was continuing. Further, a U–2 spy plane had just been shot down over Cuba by a surface-to-air missile. It began to seem as though Khrushchev's first message was a diversionary tactic, so the US Joint Chiefs of Staff recommended an air strike by no later than 30 October. Yet Kennedy resisted precipitate action. He ordered the Jupiters in Turkey disarmed, and followed a suggestion that he reply only to Khrushchev's first message and ignore the second. At the same time the Soviet ambassador in Washington was informally told that the US was likely soon to remove its Jupiters from Turkey and Italy, but not as part of a deal over Cuba.

Submarines armed with Polaris missiles were to be deployed in the Mediterranean in 1963. On the other side, the Russians also showed a capacity to compromise, however belatedly, in that they decided to overlook the president's failure to concede anything openly on the Jupiters, even though the Russian demand had been made in public. On 28 October the USSR offered to cease construction of the missile bases in return for a US pledge not to invade Cuba. Further, it agreed to allow United Nations representatives to verify the dismantling, though Castro refused to co-operate on the last point. Kennedy accepted right away, and the immediate crisis was over.

The Aftermath

The missile crisis thus represented a defeat and a victory for both sides. The Russians had failed to gain a strategic advantage against the West, a plus for the USA, while Washington was forced to pledge that it would not invade Cuba, a gain for the Eastern Bloc. It was a fact, however, that some officials in Washington continued to devise ways of toppling Castro, but by covert means. United States Congressional investigations later discovered evidence that CIA operatives had arranged possibly eight assassination attempts against Castro, though the Cuban leader claimed the actual number was much greater. On other fronts, though, Washington and Moscow agreed to set up a direct communications system (the 'hot line') between the two capitals, to assure the rapid interchange of information and views in the event of another major crisis. In addition talks (already in progress) were pressed forward on a treaty partially banning the testing of nuclear weapons. For the first time since Hiroshima both sides (along with Britain) proved willing to sign an agreement limiting the testing of atomic weapons. They did so on 5 August 1963.

The treaty proscribed tests in the atmosphere or under water, but did allow underground testing. Between 1963 and 1965 over ninety countries added their signatures. The People's Republic of China and France refused to sign, but the treaty was at least a first step towards arms control. For the PRC, Khrushchev's retreat in Cuba confirmed its analysis that the USSR had ceased to be a revolutionary state and was unwilling to challenge the United States as the greatest single threat to the Eastern Bloc. Beijing's view was understandable considering the US role in the Korean war and given Washington's contingency plans against China in the early 1950s. The Chinese therefore opted to continue developing nuclear weapons, and exploded their first atomic bomb in 1964. For the president of France, Charles de Gaulle, Kennedy's preference not to consult with but only to inform his allies during the missile crisis suggested that the Atlantic Alliance was not really a partnership of equals but an instrument for arrogating all authority to Washington. While he supported Kennedy's handling of the crisis itself, he also concluded that it was time for France and Europe to pursue a more independent course.

The idea of Europe as a Third Force was hardly new, nor was de Gaulle's well-known sensitivity to slights against the prestige of France. Long before Cuba he wondered whether the USA might sacrifice Europe in the event of an East–West crisis. Upon assuming leadership of the Fifth Republic he had proposed a tripartite directorate of Paris, London and Washington to determine Western policy. His objective was to offset the special relationship between Britain and the United States, and (given that France was not then a nuclear power) to gain a veto over any decision to use atomic weapons. Washington and London failed to respond with concessions, and so de Gaulle withdrew the French Mediterranean fleet from NATO's command in March 1959. He also resisted US requests to station nuclear weapons on French soil. Of even more significance for American authority, he accelerated plans for the so-called '*force de frappe*'. This was a small nuclear arsenal just capable of threatening Russian cities. The theory was that it would not take many bombs to make the Russians wary of Paris. It was thus possible for France to resume its former place in global affairs. Kennedy hoped to prevent this by proposing the formation of the Multilateral Force, or MLF, in which the control of nuclear weapons in Europe would be shared. The catch was that Washington would provide the weapons only if the MLF were integrated with US defences, so it was apparent Kennedy did not intend to surrender ultimate control. The real purpose of the scheme, to head off the development of national nuclear deterrents independent of US control, was much too transparent. Then the missile crisis shook de Gaulle's confidence in Kennedy all the more (it had never been very great), and confirmed Paris in pursuing its own course. In January 1963 de Gaulle vetoed British plans to enter the Common Market on the grounds that the UK's close ties to the United States would simply make it a stalking-horse for Washington in Europe. Paradoxically he acted just after Washington had backed out of commitments to supply Britain with the Skybolt missile. The British had counted on the Skybolt as the basis for their own nuclear-strike capacity, and though Kennedy agreed to provide Polaris submarines instead, the result was a crisis in Anglo-American relations. Kennedy made the mistake, however, of not offering the same deal to de Gaulle, who thus remained convinced of American perfidy. Eventually, in 1966, de Gaulle withdrew all French forces from the NATO command structure.

The missile crisis also had important ramifications for revolutionary change throughout Latin America. For an interlude of about five or six years at most Castro followed a course more independent of Moscow precisely because the crisis revealed Khrushchev to be unreliable or at least incompetent. Castro's chief goal was to survive the depredations of the United States, so clearly demonstrated at the Bay of Pigs, but also to avoid becoming a pawn of the Russians in the East–West struggle. After all, Cuba's immediate need was to consolidate the revolution at home and to achieve hemispheric security, not to resolve the Soviet Union's strategic problems. Yet in the missile crisis Havana had been drawn into East–West issues and used by the USSR. In the aftermath there was little choice for Castro except to rely on the USSR for aid and arms, but even before the events of 1962 he had come to the conclusion that perhaps Cuba should seek safety in an alternative approach as well. Havana should become a centre of international revolutionary activity. If the cause of social revolution could be advanced in the rest of Latin America, the regional hegemony of the USA would be compromised and Cuba would no longer be surrounded by hostile states beholden to Washington. Maybe this would be a better way to achieve security for the Cuban Revolution than relying exclusively on the Russians. Thus, even before the missile crisis, Castro and Ché Guevara were making plans to export the Cuban Revolution, but the events of 1962 emphasized the importance of proceeding with urgency.

The tactic was to promote guerrilla warfare, whether by communist or non-communist revolutionaries. Ideological purity was less important than the task of overthrowing right-wing, pro-American governments, so Cuba was prepared to work with a variety of movements in the region. In Havana's view Bolivia, Venezuela, Colombia, Paraguay, Honduras, Guatemala and Haiti seemed ripe for change, especially in light of the less-than-impressive results being achieved by Kennedy's Alliance for Progress. This was a programme of aid for development, and though the USA provided the major part of the funding (other powers in the Americas provided the rest), the amounts were hardly sufficient to the need. Further, the Alliance tended to bolster existing governments (which was Washington's intent), and thus had a dubious impact on reform. Yet exporting revolution proved more difficult for Havana than expected. Ché Guevara resigned from the Cuban cabinet in 1965 in order to carry the new strategy to the mountains of Bolivia. The idea was not to wait for a specific set of conditions that presumably predisposed a nation to revolution. In Cuba events had moved rapidly, suggesting that the guerrillas themselves could create the right conditions. Besides, the masses of people were too oppressed to develop a vision of a new society or to mobilize without the leadership of outsiders more experienced in social reconstruction. Guevara's approach thus was to launch a guerrilla war first, with the result that the people would be drawn into the struggle. As in Mao's China, the struggle itself would force the population to choose sides. And because the majority of Third World peoples were impoverished, their choice would undermine the old order. But in the autumn of 1967 the Bolivian army captured and executed Guevara.

Even before Guevara's death, however, it had become evident that the strategy was flawed, as the peasants of Latin America did not immediately rally to the cause. His analysis was indeed based on the Cuban experience, but it overlooked some of the factors which explained the rapid and easy victory there (easy by comparison with other settings, for example, Vietnam). Not least in explaining the success of the 26 July Movement was the attitude of the United States. While hardly welcoming Castro, Washington had abandoned Batista. There was no military intervention on his behalf, something that could not always be counted upon. Also, the situation under Batista brought together a variety of interests and classes, so that it was not exclusively a peasant revolution. The multi-class coalition also meant that the Castroites had strength in the cities, a distinct advantage in challenging power at the centre. Ché was unable to duplicate this in the mountains of South America. In Cuba the coalition held together until well after Batista's flight, and helps explain Castro's success.

Perhaps the most important factor constraining the Cuban initiative, however, was its isolation internationally and hence its unavoidable dependency on a single patron, the Soviet Union. In the long run, economics once again forced Castro to become more receptive to Moscow's ideas about the possibilities in Latin America. Mismanagement at home (notably the shortfall in the 1965–70 sugar quota), plus the US trade embargo (which by 1962 was supported by all the nations of Latin America except Mexico), translated into a permanent deficit in Cuba's balance of trade. The Russians doubted that a large-scale challenge to US hegemony in the Western Hemisphere could succeed at this time. They did not want to provoke Washington again, and feared that Castro's internationalism might do precisely this. Moscow was not about to give generously to Castro unless he accepted the party line. Havana's recognition of this was symbolized by its support of the Warsaw Pact invasion of Czechoslovakia in 1968 (see Chapter 10), so that by the end of the 1960s the Cuban initiative was in retreat. Only in the 1970s would it be revived, but under very different circumstances and at Moscow's explicit direction. Then the USSR would rely on Havana to act as its surrogate in Africa, i.e. in an area where direct intervention was not practical for the Russians. If Cuba were to send troops to an area in turmoil, it would be considerably less provocative than if the USSR were to do so. But this only illustrated Cuba's dependency on the Soviet Union. Moreover, Cuba's later activities in Africa stood in stark contrast to its low profile in Latin America. Even so, the Cuban Revolution did result in an improved standard of living for the average citizen, and a marked reduction in the economic and social inequalities of earlier times. Castro may not have succeeded abroad, but at home he continued to enjoy widespread support.

The results of Washington's Cuban policy were thus quite different from the outcome in Guatemala. Hence, in April 1965, when supporters of the reformist Juan Bosch launched an armed uprising in the Dominican Republic, Kennedy's successor, Lyndon Johnson, moved quickly and, in contrast to Guatemala and Cuba, by direct US military action. Bosch had been elected in the wake of the assassination of Rafael Trujillo (dictator from 1931 to 1961), but then was overthrown by rightist forces in 1963. Yet the US did not see fit then to intervene to protect him as the constitutional president of the country. The possibility that the left-leaning Bosch might return to power in 1965, however, induced Johnson to dispatch a contingent of US marines which eventually rose to 25,000 personnel.

Most world capitals regarded Washington's response as an over-reaction, and it certainly banished the ghost of the Good Neighbour Policy once and for all. Johnson did not consult the Organization of American States before acting, thereby violating an explicit treaty obligation of the United States. But the US president justified his action on the grounds that the Dominican situation could provide another opportunity for communism. This was a gross exaggeration of the politics of Juan Bosch. Nevertheless the next month Washington applied pressure and obtained the approval of a divided OAS for a peacekeeping force of troops from the United States and Brazil (Brazil was under military rule, but in the 1960s was one of the largest beneficiaries of US aid in the world). This force supervised elections in June 1966. Not surprisingly the result was a victory for the anti-Bosch forces, and so the troops left in the autumn. The new president, Joaquín Balaguer, introduced a regime of token reform backed up by firm rule if not outright authoritarianism. Balaguer was a former associate of Trujillo, yet his election did bring political stability to the country. From a regional perspective the whole episode was symptomatic of the US determination to prevent another Cuba. The only question was what means were most effective. Economic warfare and indirect intervention had failed in Cuba, and had tempted the Russians into a crisis which threatened a Third World War. While the Dominican affair came on too quickly for Johnson to do anything but act directly, the issue remained as to the most effective defence against the spread of social revolution in the Western Hemisphere. Few in Washington questioned the right of the USA to intervene, only how best to do it. Accordingly the potential for conflict remained high.

8

THE WARS IN INDO-CHINA

Castro had provided the Soviet Union with an opportunity to establish a presence in the Western Hemisphere. Yet the United States and its European allies still exercised more power in the Third World than the USSR. Moreover, they were determined to keep it that way, as events in Indo-China were to show once again. Of course, the Russians had a propaganda and political strategy for the Third World, and provided aid and advisers to selected (not all) social revolutionaries. Compared to the West, however, the USSR was more artful in avoiding direct military action outside Europe in the period after 1945. Moscow undertook its first full-scale war in the Third World only in 1979, in Afghanistan (see Chapter 12), though earlier it had engaged in border clashes with China and in the 1970s it used Cuba as a surrogate in Africa. As we have observed, the Russians were far more likely to go on the march in Eastern Europe. For the Western powers it was different. They had sent their armies to South–East Asia, Africa and Latin America decades before the USSR ventured into Afghanistan or asked Havana for help elsewhere. Recall the Dutch East Indies, British Malaya, Korea, Algeria, Kenya, the Belgian Congo, the Dominican Republic and French Indo-China, to mention only the most important engagements. Moreover, there were still crises to come, and these would ensnare the armies of Europe and America. Accordingly we must hold to our course and continue tracking the role of the West as the principal external influence in the Third World.

Some historians have argued that the failure of the United States to neutralize the Cuban Revolution resulted in a reassessment of Washington's policy towards the Third World generally. Indeed it did. But the question was whether the new approaches would stand the test of time, or whether the USA would fall back on the policies of the past as a last resort. Presumably, after Cuba the Kennedy and Johnson administrations opted for a greater emphasis on counter-insurgency, i.e. on covert operations against revolutionaries combined with efforts to generate popular support for governments friendly to the USA. The strategy involved not only military but also social and economic programmes. The idea was to offset communist promises to introduce land reform, to humble the rich and the powerful, and to end foreign domination. The Bay of Pigs suggested that the US had a great deal to learn, and that failing to do so only invited Soviet interference. Hence the new emphasis.

Yet it turned out that Washington had hardly abjured the use of direct military force, and in the long run this proved more significant than the techniques of counter-insurgency. Certainly the Dominican crisis showed that the military option was always available, but Indo-China revealed just how far the Americans were willing to go. Paradoxically, South Vietnam was to have been a showplace for counter-insurgency. Instead it became a stark contradiction, and by the time the war was over millions of American military personnel had seen duty in Vietnam. Some even saw action in Cambodia, although there and in Laos US clients did most of the fighting on the ground. The wars in Indo-China thus were among the most important encounters between the First World and the Third World in the post-1945 era.

DIEM

As the French began withdrawing from Indo-China in 1954–5, the immediate problem for the United States was to establish a stable anti-communist government in South Vietnam. Yet Washington could not identify too closely with a new regime at Saigon lest this destroy the credibility of its nationalist credentials. A pro-Western government could hardly deflect communist charges of being a front for foreign domination if the French were expelled only to be replaced by the Americans. Moreover, the Eisenhower administration pretty well had to support whichever local leader emerged from the morass of Vietnamese politics, because the political system in the south was in total disarray. Both the French and the Vietminh had acted to eliminate non-communist nationalists, the first in order to retain Indo-China as a colony, and the second in order to intimidate competitors. There was no clear front-runner on the non-communist side, no one with the acclamation of a Ho Chi Minh. Thus Bao Dai's new prime minister, Ngo Dinh Diem, assumed power more as the result of promoting his own claims than of popular demand. The consequence was that Diem faced a monumental task in creating support for the Saigon government, a task complicated by his sectarian and autocratic habits.*

Diem was born in 1901 of a Catholic family that had once acted as high officials at the Vietnamese royal court in Hué. As a youth he considered becoming a priest, but rejected this for an administrative career instead. He won immediate advancement, and was soon appointed a provincial chief. In 1933 he joined the cabinet of the young emperor, Bao Dai, but landed in trouble. He resigned over the unwillingness of Paris to increase the powers of the Vietnamese government, and thereafter retreated into obscurity, though subject to French surveillance.

During the Second World War the Vichy French were allowed to remain in Indo-China and administer the region on behalf of Tokyo. Whereas elsewhere some nationalists collaborated with the Japanese against the Western colonial powers (in the hope of gaining concessions), in Vietnam it was the French who became the chief collaborators. This meant that the only course open to determined patriots was guerrilla warfare, but Diem stood aside. The consequence was that he failed to establish his nationalist credentials among the masses, as Ho Chi Minh did, and instead remained in obscurity. Indeed, Diem would never overcome his disinclination to mix with the common people. He always demanded the obeisance due one born to rule, and conducted himself as more the mandarin than the popular hero. Even so, Diem was too independent for the Japanese. In the last days of the Pacific war, when they jailed the French and turned authority over to a formally independent regime, they did not choose Diem to join the new government. Instead they found more pliable nationalists to entrust with power. And because Diem was an outspoken anti-communist he found no favour with the Vietminh either. As a matter of fact, in 1945 the communists took him captive and exiled him to an obscure village in the north, though he was released in 1946. Thereafter Diem continued his modest efforts to attract a following, but with no success. Nevertheless the Vietminh regretted having freed him, and in the late 1940s plotted his assassination. Accordingly, in 1950, Diem left for the United States

* The outline of facts concerning the course of the wars in Indo-China mainly follows Stanley Karnow, *Vietnam: A History* (Harmondsworth: 1984). On matters of interpretation, however, Karnow's overall perspective differs from the position taken here, and offers readers an alternative point of view.

and the safety of exile. Discretion seemed to be the better part of valour.

Unknown outside Vietnam, Diem took advantage of his sojourn in America to promote his cause. Although he went into retreat at a Roman Catholic seminary run by the Maryknoll Fathers, an order of missionaries, it turned out that Diem was interested in more than just personal renewal. He succeeded in obtaining introductions to important Americans, including the future president, John F. Kennedy (then a member of the US Senate and also a Catholic), and Francis Cardinal Spellman, and cultivated his standing as a representative of Vietnamese nationalism. This was hardly enough to win the official support of Washington, but it did help prepare the way for the future. In the meantime the Eisenhower administration still backed the French. In 1953, therefore, Diem took up residence at a monastery in Belgium, which also became a base for political activity. With the help of a brother living in Paris he became known among Vietnamese exiles in France, so that when Bao Dai (who had left South-East Asia for the Riviera) needed a new prime minister the next year Diem found himself in the right place at the right time. It was the Geneva Conference which gave Diem his chance.

The outcome of the conference meant that the French would no longer be available to support the Saigon government, so Bao Dai needed a new foreign sponsor. Diem seemed to have connections in the United States, and might be useful in attracting American support. Also, another of Diem's brothers, Ngo Dinh Nhu, had formed a political coalition in Vietnam which might serve as the foundation for a new government in the aftermath of Geneva. For Bao Dai, therefore, Diem might be the key to survival. Actually Diem had yet to gain any influence in Washington, and it was mainly Catholics who supported the political ambitions of the Ngo Dinh clan, but the reality was less important than what Bao Dai believed or (more accurately) imagined. In any case the emperor appointed Diem prime minister on 18 June 1954, and a week later Diem flew to Saigon. A small crowd of a few hundred people welcomed him back, and Diem entered the city virtually unnoticed. The task at hand, quite clearly, was to make good his claim to power. Bao Dai's endorsement was not enough.

Despite doubts about Diem's capacity to rule, the United States soon committed an initial instalment of $300 million in assistance to the new regime. John Foster Dulles considered aid the best way to stabilize the country. Vietnam was in chaos, with army generals, armed factions such as the Binh Xuyen (numbering perhaps 40,000 and deeply implicated in organized crime and terrorism) and even various religious sects defying the authority of Saigon. For the Americans the problem was that they needed Diem as much as he needed them, so that the prime minister was in effect able to blackmail them into giving money. This also meant that aid never gave Washington as much say in events as the prime minister's relatives. Diem surrounded himself with friends and relations, to the virtual exclusion of other political groups in the country. He thus never achieved a coalition of all nationalist forces, and instead seemed bent upon establishing a new dynasty. Though Diem was not personally corrupt himself (indeed, he was even ascetic at times), his government was rent through with corruption and crime. It seemed that government benefited mainly the prime minister's clients, so there was little chance that the regime could achieve a broad base of support. And in the realm of policy Diem alienated the masses of the people. For example, when the Vietminh controlled part of the south before Geneva, they instituted a programme of free land reform, but once he came to power Diem demanded that peasants pay for such properties as were made available. United States experts provided advice on the agrarian question, but Diem ignored most of their ideas, engaging in mainly token gestures. He considered it more important to have the backing of the leading families of the south, so he usually sided with the large landowners. At the end of the decade Saigon tried to establish *agrovilles*, or what the Americans later called 'strategic hamlets' when they attempted the same thing beginning in 1962. The plan was to move peasants into defensible villages away from the communist guerrillas, but of course the result was to uproot communities and create ill-will towards Saigon. Further, the *agroville* residents were often forced to work without pay. Diem seemed oblivious to the consequences, probably because he saw the communist threat as mainly a question of military security and not as a social and political problem. To the average Vietnamese, though, the Saigon government appeared little different from the French.

Still, the regime lasted for nine years, until 1963. Diem gained a foothold for a number of reasons. He was persistent and had more than a little courage. He faced up to the threat of an army coup in the early days of his government, and succeeded in defeating independent factions that had taken up arms. All this involved a heavy dose of military force, but Diem was successful. By the spring of 1955, for example, the Binh Xuyen had been defeated as the result of a small-scale war which Diem unleashed in and around Saigon itself. He also attacked rebellious religious sects such as the Hoa Hao and Cao Dai. And though Diem would not be particularly receptive to Washington's advice over the long run, in 1954–5 an American did play an important part in consolidating the regime – Colonel Edward Lansdale.

Lansdale had worked for the predecessor of the Central Intelligence Agency, the Office of Strategic Services, during the Second World War, and later with the Philippine government against the Hukbalahap. He helped Diem move against adversaries in the south, and assisted in staging a referendum in late 1955 to depose Bao Dai and end the monarchy, with Diem declaring the Republic of Vietnam and succeeding as president. Diem's forces threatened and intimidated voters, so that he received more than 98 per cent of the votes. The outcome was hardly more credible than an election in the one-party states of Eastern Europe. In addition Lansdale established the Saigon Military Mission and received funding from the Central Intelligence Agency. And he helped organize covert activities against Hanoi. The strategy was to gather teams of South Vietnamese commandos for training at American bases in the Philippine Islands, with the US navy landing them along the Northern coast so that they might attack the Vietminh on their home ground. Directed by another American agent, Major Lucien Conein, these teams gathered intelligence, engaged in sabotage, and generally tried to foment discontent against Hanoi. Except for spreading alarm among Catholics already fleeing to the south, they were not particularly successful, so that it would be a mistake to credit Lansdale and Conein with the survival of the Saigon government. Yet these activities were important for another reason. Although secret at the time, they clearly show that the USA was violating its pledge to observe the spirit of the Geneva Accords (a pledge given even though Washington had not signed them). The point was that the American initiative had not begun after a period of patient waiting for a political settlement to take place in Indo-China itself, but was attempted from the very start. Indeed, Lansdale had arrived in Vietnam just before Diem's return in the early summer of 1954. This was also well before the end of the Geneva Conference itself. In a sense the Americans landed first, and it certainly looked as though Washington had no intention of giving Geneva a chance.

There was another reason why Diem succeeded in establishing his authority. In accordance with the terms of Geneva, Ho had ordered about 100,000 Vietminh to retreat to the north, though some were directed to stay behind and work among the people. This made it considerably easier for Saigon to secure its military position in the

Mekong Delta in 1955–6. In fact, just about all the remaining Vietminh in the area were driven out. Thus, when Diem decided not to go through with the elections scheduled for 1956 to reunify the country, Ho had little in the way of military leverage. It turned out that he had little diplomatic leverage either, as the Soviet Union and China were unwilling to make an issue of the election. Beijing feared that adventurism in Vietnam might draw the Americans into another war on their borders. The memory of Korea was still fresh, and the People's Republic needed time to consolidate its internal affairs without foreign distractions. For its part Moscow was facing rebellion in Eastern Europe. Both capitals had more pressing priorities than Indo-China. Perhaps the clearest sign of this came in 1957, when Moscow proposed the admission of both Hanoi and Saigon to the United Nations, which would have meant the recognition of north and south as separate nations.

Ho had other problems as well. In the aftermath of the Geneva Conference almost one million refugees, many of them Catholics, fled the north. Not only were these people a loss to the northern economy, but by moving south they provided Diem with some claim to popular support, albeit very limited. On the other hand, the departure of the Catholics also helped Ho, by reducing the likelihood of sectarian opposition of the type Diem faced from Buddhists and smaller groups such as the Cao Dai. Still, the northern regime faced economic problems, which revolved around land reform, that proved just as divisive.

The communists divided the entire northern population into five categories, with landlords at one pole and peasants at the other. Although large estates of the sort found in the Mekong Delta were not numerous in the north, the regime seemed determined to root out anyone who could possibly be smeared as a member of the gentry. Cadres made egregious errors in classifying people, and as in China earlier land reform provided an occasion for settling old scores. Vigilantes perpetrated a good many crimes in the name of punishing alleged capitalists. It is not known exactly how many people were killed, but certainly they numbered in the thousands. For many more thousands punishment meant a term in the labour camps. The result was rebellion. In the province of Nghe Thinh, Ho's birthplace, an uprising occurred in November 1956. Hanoi responded with force, and perhaps 6,000 peasants were either killed or exiled from their native region. Ho very quickly retreated, however, because it was clear that the implementation of land reform, not the policy itself but the way it was being administered, had hurt the country.

But then it became the turn of the cadres to suffer reprisals, as villagers took revenge. The new regime was off to a very bad start, so Ho could not focus completely on events in the south. Rice shortages and sabotage by departing refugees compounded his problems. Ho personally confessed error in the handling of land reform. Like Diem, he needed time to consolidate his power at home. He also needed a new strategy in the south.

With the breakdown of the Geneva Accords, Ho ordered the southern guerrillas, known as the Vietcong, to organize new fighting units. He did so in October 1957. And two years later the Vietminh undertook major improvements to the so-called Ho Chi Minh Trail. This was a primitive network of paths and roads through the jungles of Laos and Cambodia, and the principal supply route to the south. Yet these measures were still precautionary, as Hanoi had not recovered sufficiently from the war with the French and from its own internal problems to launch an all-out war just yet. Diem had made important gains against the guerrillas in the south, however, and some Vietcong launched attacks despite orders from Ho to bide their time. Accordingly, by 1959, Hanoi agreed to permit limited strikes. The result was a significant increase in the number of government officials killed in the south. In 1961, 2,600 of them fell victim to the Vietcong. Although these acts were best described as terrorism, some experts on Vietnam have noted that the communists tended to be selective rather than indiscriminate in the use of force, at least by comparison with the South Vietnamese military – official representatives of the Saigon government were favourite Vietcong targets. But the Saigon army more often bombarded whole villages and whole groups, injuring innocent and enemy alike. The United States had supplied Diem's troops with modern arms, including artillery, whereas once Ho had withdrawn his regular army forces from the south, in accordance with Geneva, the communist guerrillas relied mainly on their rifles and bayonets.

For Diem the question was whether he could win given the domestic turmoil also developing in the south. Diem's repressive tactics and the corruption of his clique were beginning to catch up with him. In 1960 he clamped down on dissident journalists, students and other opinion leaders. They were arrested, and the government closed opposition newspapers as well. In November a small number of disaffected army officers ordered their troops to attack the presidential palace. Badly organized, they were soon defeated, and Diem used the occasion to imprison still more critics of the regime. And there was more trouble to come. At the end of the year Hanoi organized the National Liberation Front (NLF) in the south. Though it was communist-dominated, the idea was to unify a variety of anti-Saigon forces on Diem's home ground. It also provided a cover for northern operations below the demilitarized zone (which were proscribed by the Geneva Accords), because the NLF claimed to be an indigenous movement. The same month, the US ambassador wondered whether the time had come for Washington to support an 'alternative leadership' in Saigon.*

LAOS

For the time being, however, Washington remained committed to Diem. He was still the only leader available. Although intrigue was rife among his generals, their own in-fighting prevented any one of them from emerging as the undisputed leader of a coup, while the politicians who opposed him were also in disarray. Given that the Americans were in no mood to yield on the future of South Vietnam, they would have to make do with Diem. After John F. Kennedy assumed the presidency in January 1961, he did prove agreeable to an East–West compromise on Laos (negotiated at Geneva) which pledged both sides to respect its neutrality, but he refused the same deal for Vietnam. Hanoi was willing, but Kennedy suspected that neutrality would simply serve as a smoke-screen for a Vietminh takeover in the south, and he was not about to compromise there. Also, from the American point of view there were considerable differences between the two countries.

Whereas the United States was well placed to support Diem, the danger of a communist military victory in Laos was more immediate, so that in this case neutrality seemed the lesser evil. In October 1945 nationalist forces had declared independence but were easily crushed by the French and driven from the capital, Vientiane, in April 1946. Thereafter various resistance movements (including communists using the name 'Pathet Lao') received aid from the Vietminh and the Indo-Chinese Communist Party, and struggled against the French. By 1954 the Pathet Lao controlled a small amount of territory in the north-east of the country, but Laotian nationalism profited mainly from the defeat of the French at Dien Bien Phu. The result of the Vietminh victory in neighbouring Vietnam was autonomy for all three regions of Indo-China. After the Geneva Conference of 1954, however, a civil war

* Cited in *ibid.*, 235.

developed in Laos between pro-Western forces (backed by American aid and advisers) on one side and a combination of neutralists and communists on the other (with aid from the Vietnamese and later some from the Chinese and Soviets). In 1956 the government in Vientiane and the Pathet Lao signed an armistice, and the next year they formed a coalition and then held elections in 1958. But this compromise broke under American pressure, and the civil war resumed.

By the early 1960s, however, it appeared that the Pathet Lao and the neutralists just might win. Kennedy therefore decided to negotiate at Geneva. Besides, there was nothing to prevent the United States from operating covertly inside Laos even after agreeing to its formal neutrality and accepting a coalition government. This was exactly what happened. The terms of the Geneva agreements on Laos were negotiated in 1961 and 1962, but almost immediately afterwards the CIA went ahead and persuaded Meo hill tribes to harass the communists. The complex tribal and ethnic divisions of Laos made it easy to set one group against another. Soon a general war resumed, so that in 1963 the pro-communist members of the coalition cabinet withdrew. The Geneva compromise was finished. The next year American B-52s secretly began bombing Laotian targets, mainly to attack the movement of Vietminh supplies through Laos down the Ho Chi Minh Trail to South Vietnam. Thus, in the 1960s, the policy of the United States was to give lip service to Laotian neutrality while secretly conducting a holding action against the Pathet Lao. At this point Washington still saw South Vietnam as the main prize. If it held, communism in the rest of Indo-China might be contained.

MANAGING THE CRISIS

The problem was to avoid losing control of events. Kennedy had other priorities besides a jungle war in Indo-China. The task, therefore, was to show the enemy that America was determined to support Saigon, on the theory that once Hanoi understood this it would settle for half, rather than all, of Vietnam. Success required persistence. The new administration commissioned the Pentagon, the RAND Corporation and other agencies to conduct study after study in the hope of calculating the precise level of support needed. Both Kennedy and his successor, Lyndon Johnson, chaired long discussions among cabinet members and other advisers before launching new initiatives. While unexpected results sometimes developed from carefully considered decisions, none the less they thoroughly aired each option before making the final choice. There was nothing accidental or haphazard about how they proceeded. In fact, they relied heavily on persons expert in the analysis of statistics and other data, the archetype being Robert McNamara, secretary of defence – that is, until 1968 when he became disenchanted with the war and was forced to resign.

One of Kennedy's first choices in the spring of 1961 was to raise the number of US advisers in Vietnam to almost 800. This contravened the Geneva injunction against any increase in foreign military contingents (as did later decisions which eventuated in the stationing of about 16,200 personnel in the country by the time of Kennedy's death in 1963). Lyndon Johnson, the vice-president, visited South Vietnam a month after the Bay of Pigs débâcle, and returned to report that if the country fell Americans would soon be pushed back to the Pacific coast of the United States itself. But such extravagant rhetoric only increased Diem's belief that Washington could not do without him, and made him more difficult to influence.

Other presidential emissaries subsequently travelled to South-East Asia, all with essentially the same result. In public the American visitors brimmed over with optimism, but their reports to the president usually told a different story. The pace of the war was increasing, and Diem was failing either to contain the Vietminh or to placate the domestic turmoil. Indeed things were so bad that in the autumn of 1961, after a tour of inspection on behalf of Kennedy, General Maxwell Taylor suggested that 8,000 American combat troops be sent to Vietnam, admitting that they might be only the first of a much larger force. But it was the general's view that Hanoi would not match the American escalation, or that, if it did, bombing North Vietnamese territory would solve the problem. Again the theory seemed to be that, if the United States could hold on long enough, the enemy would tire and retreat. The Joint Chiefs, along with Defence Secretary McNamara, agreed, except that they suggested intervening with 200,000 men, this in the autumn of 1961. But Kennedy was inclined to take a less hawkish position for a while longer. He decided against combat troops but did increase American aid (including helicopters and more advisers) to Diem's own forces. Moreover, he allowed US pilots to fly combat missions, though under the guise of training Vietnamese, these flights starting from Bienhoa airfield in South Vietnam. All this was done secretly, as it clearly contravened the US commitment to respect the Geneva Accords. Soon American helicopters were providing air support for Vietnamese troops, delivering them to battle areas and firing on the enemy. Yet to the American press Kennedy unequivocally denied that US personnel were involved in combat, as he knew the electorate would be split over a hot war in Asia. Kennedy had been elected in 1960 by a very narrow margin of the popular vote, and did not wish to endanger his delicate hold on power. Furthermore, he was in a weak position *vis-à-vis* Congress, and needed to take a middle ground so as to satisfy both hawks and doves. In effect he was trying to have it both ways: fight a war, but not cause any alarm about it.

The difficulty was that the Vietminh, like Kennedy, also believed that the key to victory was to outlast the enemy. And in the early 1960s they had reason to believe that their patience would be rewarded, as the domestic turmoil in the south continued to worsen. In February 1962 two South Vietnamese air force pilots staged a bombing run on the presidential palace and for a moment seemed to threaten the life of the regime, but their motives turned out to be more personal than political. They did not instigate a general uprising. A far more significant source of opposition came from the Buddhists, whose protests became an issue for Washington both because they were a vocal minority within the total population and because Diem's response shook the confidence of the Americans in his government. If Diem could not keep the peace in Saigon, how was he going to conduct a successful campaign in the countryside?

THE BUDDHISTS

The Buddhists became the focal point of opposition to the Diem regime. They had often been subject to persecution, and the early emperors had regarded them as a threat to their rule. After all, the political system reflected Vietnam's links to China, and it was Confucianism, not Buddhism, which provided the ideological underpinnings of imperial authority. Later the French proselytized in the hope that converts to Catholicism would result in a degree of assimilation and thus make foreign rule more secure. The Catholic Church in Vietnam eventually became the largest single owner of land under the French, and Diem's eldest brother, Ngo Dinh Thuc, became archbishop of Hué. Along with another brother, Ngo Dinh Nhu, Thuc exerted considerable influence over Diem. For all practical purposes both brothers shared power with him, and Madame Nhu acted as the country's 'first lady' for the bachelor Diem. In sum, a Catholic oligarchy had emerged to rule the country, and the Buddhists were vulnerable. Yet the events that soon transpired were not simply or even primarily a religious conflict, but followed from Diem's authoritarianism.

The initial clash came in May 1963, when thousands of Buddhists in Hué gathered to protest at a prohibition against raising the Buddhist flag (Catholics in the same city had recently been permitted to fly the papal banner). The authorities sent armoured vehicles against the demonstrators, panic ensued, and nine people were killed. Diem accused the Buddhists of being communist sympathizers, when in fact most of them were quite the opposite politically, though they had no love for the regime. The outcome was predictable: more demonstrations against Saigon, while troops repeatedly went into action against the crowds. The Buddhists therefore launched a concerted anti-government campaign notable for its careful planning. They organized rallies by Buddhist clergy and laymen around the country, lobbied friends in the army and in the government administration, held briefings for the domestic and particularly the foreign media, and generally took a professional approach to managing news and opinion. The US embassy also protested at the treatment of the Buddhists, but to no effect. Washington believed that Saigon was worsening an already difficult situation. For a long time the State Department had been urging Diem to open up the political system and allow broader participation. At one point the embassy even suggested that Diem might lose America's backing, a possibility that the Nhus and Diem had suspected well before the Buddhists took to the streets. Distrust was rising in both Washington and Saigon.

An event soon occurred, however, that in due course broke the tie between Washington and Diem. On 11 June 1963, and with help from other Buddhist clergy, the monk Thich Quang Duc set himself on fire in the middle of a crossroads in Saigon. Sitting immobile, he was consumed by the flames. The Buddhists had alerted foreign reporters and prepared press releases explaining that Quang Duc's self-imposed martyrdom was a protest against Diem's persecution. Newspapers and television around the world carried pictures of the sight. The Buddhists intended it to be a spectacle, the more shocking the better, in order to turn American opinion against Saigon. Other monks immolated themselves in the following months, as did an American, in New York City's Times Square. This made it very difficult for Washington to talk about defending freedom in South Vietnam, especially as Madame Nhu grabbed headlines with brutal comments about the Buddhist 'barbecue'.*

* Cited in *ibid.*, 281.

Moreover, she accused the United States of secretly promoting the protests, in order to force Diem out of power. Yet the worst was still to come. On 21 August Diem ordered forces loyal to him to attack Buddhist temples in Hué, Saigon and other cities. Over a thousand clergy and activists were arrested, with many injured and others simply unaccounted for. In Hué monks and nuns resisted Diem's soldiers for eight hours before surrendering. The result was a new wave of demonstrations against the regime, and not just by Buddhists. Diem's foreign minister resigned in protest, as did his ambassador to Washington (Madame Nhu's father). On 22 August the new US ambassador to Saigon, Henry Cabot Lodge, arrived in Vietnam. Very quickly he concluded that Diem had to go.

THE ASSASSINATION

Diem suspected Lodge from the first. He was well aware that Saigon was rife with schemes to overthrow the government, and that the Americans were implicated. Indeed, Lucien Conein had returned to Vietnam in 1962, presumably as an adviser to the country's interior department. But his real mission was to keep track of the web of plots and counterplots that seemed to be the substance of Vietnamese politics in this period. By the summer of 1963 Conein had become the contact man between the American embassy and a group of generals conspiring to overthrow Diem. The generals had not made any moves so far, however, and would not do so until they were in a position to estimate Washington's attitude with some assurance. The essential point was whether the USA would recognize and assist any new government they might form. It is fair to say that Washington had the power to make or break Diem. Unless it gave the word, the generals would not act.

Kennedy personally had been aware of the generals' scheming since June, but gave no commitment of American support. With the attack on the Buddhists of 21 August, however, the policy-makers in Washington considered what to do next. Far from united, they none the less edged towards action. In a much argued about decision, on 24 August they instructed Lodge to press Diem to reform, chiefly by removing his brother Nhu. The Americans regarded Nhu as the evil genius behind the events of recent months. They also suspected (correctly, as it turned out) that he was negotiating on the sly with the Vietminh, either to compromise with them in the hope of retaining power should the Americans abandon Diem, or to panic the US into currying his favour lest he sell out to the North. Perhaps the most controversial aspect of Washington's decision, however, was to allow Lodge to inform the generals that, unless Diem removed Nhu, the USA might be prepared to countenance a coup. At the end of the month (29 August) Lodge cabled Kennedy urging him to end US aid to Diem. This, of course, would be precisely the kind of sign the generals were waiting for – it would imply Washington's support for a new government. Indeed, by then Lodge had concluded that 'we are launched on a course from which there is no respectable turning back: the overthrow of the Diem government'.*

The coup, however, did not take place for several more weeks. Conein maintained contact with the Vietnamese generals, but they hesitated until certain of American approval. The US, of course, played no direct part in the conspiracy, but always operated in the background, Kennedy insisting on avoiding any actions 'that might tend to identify the United States too closely'. On the other hand, the president's position (inspired by Lodge and conveyed to the generals by Conein) was that 'we also do not wish to leave the impression that the United States would thwart a change of government'.† After weeks of uncertainty everything seemed to be coming together at the end of October, though not before Kennedy had second thoughts. Fearing another Bay of Pigs bungle, he met with the National Security Council on 29 October. The outcome was an order to Lodge counselling delay. The ambassador resisted the idea, and the president ultimately left it up to his judgement. But Lodge was eager to give the generals the go-ahead.

On 1 November 1963 the conspirators finally made their move, but so did Nhu and Diem, who had found out about the generals' plot and therefore planned a pre-emptive coup for the same day. The idea was to have forces loyal to Diem stage a phoney uprising and declare a revolutionary government. Other loyal forces then would promptly and efficiently restore order, allowing the Ngo brothers to return in triumph and showing the Americans that only they could manage the confused state of affairs in Saigon. The flaw was that Diem had unwittingly chosen one of the chief conspirators on the side of the dissident generals to oversee the military side of his counter-coup. By the time Diem and Nhu discovered their error, it was too late. Captured in the early hours of the next day, they were shot to death. At no time was it the intention of Kennedy, Lodge or any other US official that Diem and his brother be

* Cited in *ibid.*, 289.
† Cited in *ibid.*, 295.

killed, and Kennedy in particular was deeply disturbed by news of the event. The US goal was a change of government, not murder. On the other hand, the idea of a coup had been discussed by the president's advisers for months, and it is difficult to escape the conclusion that the policy-makers were aware of the risks associated with the overthrow of any government, much less one in the conspiratorial world of Saigon. As in Cuba, Washington's main concern had been not whether the US had the right to affect the situation but whether the generals' plans would work.

THE AMERICANIZATION OF THE WAR

The Americans had encouraged a coup in the hope that a new government might placate the non-communist opposition in the south and thus be able to concentrate on the war against the Vietcong. They were to be bitterly disappointed. The generals were soon feuding among themselves, and over the next year they reorganized the government seven times. In other words, the coup did nothing to resolve the political situation inside South Vietnam, and the war effort continued to flounder. Paradoxically the communists in Hanoi were no more certain than the Americans as to the eventual outcome. The fall of Diem forced them to re-evaluate their entire strategy, which they did in December 1963. To Ho Chi Minh and company Diem's removal suggested that Washington was positioning itself for a protracted battle. Until then the communists had been persuaded that guerrilla warfare was sufficient to win – the internal turmoil in the South had crippled Saigon's war effort, so that the Vietcong were able to operate with telling effect. Then the overthrow of Diem indicated that the Americans were determined to sustain the Saigon regime. The communists concluded that there was even a possibility that the US might commit combat troops. Accordingly Hanoi decided to send North Vietnamese regular forces (these had been withdrawn after the Geneva Accords) into the South, and did so well before Washington opted to do the same for Saigon. In Ho's view Vietcong guerrillas could no longer do the job alone. In 1964 about 10,000 North Vietnamese troops entered South Vietnam, mainly via the Ho Chi Minh Trail through Laos and Cambodia, and in 1967 at least 20,000 arrived each month. In the ensuing years of war, however, the communists denied that they were deploying regulars in the South, so as to appear to be observing the terms of Geneva.

Although Ho moved first, he was correct in assuming that the

Americans would eventually introduce their own combat troops into South Vietnam, though this did not happen just yet. Still, events seemed to draw the United States ever closer to such a commitment. The assassination of John F. Kennedy three weeks after the death of Diem had placed Lyndon Johnson in the White House. The new president, a big man from Texas, was determined to stand firm. Johnson's forte, however, had been domestic politics. Inexperienced in the world of international relations, he accepted the simple verities of the Cold War. He also faced an election the next year, and feared that abandoning Vietnam would damage his chances of winning the presidency in his own right. Americans were not used to losing wars, and in 1964 the opposition Republican Party nominated an outspoken hawk, Senator Barry Goldwater, to run against him. As in Vietnam, so too in the United States domestic politics were to have consequences for foreign policy.

The result was that the Johnson administration began considering how to increase its assistance to Saigon, lest the military situation deteriorate before the election. The number of non-combatant advisers had already been increased several times, but if Saigon could not manage the war then perhaps the Americans would have to move from advice to action. In March 1964, just as North Vietnamese regulars began infiltrating the South via the Ho Chi Minh Trail, Johnson ordered Ambassador Lodge to signal Saigon that the US was prepared to countenance South Vietnamese raids into Laos to attack the Vietcong and the Vietminh. Hanoi was violating the 1961 Geneva agreement guaranteeing Laotian neutrality, so Washington felt justified in supporting Saigon. Johnson also increased the number of US reconnaissance flights over Laos and prepared contingency plans for possible operations in Cambodia. Perhaps the most important indication of US determination, however, was that targets in North Vietnam itself were being identified in case orders were given to conduct air strikes against the communist regime. These might include Hanoi and its nearby port of Haiphong, railways, industries, anti-aircraft installations and military training facilities. Of course, bombing the North would represent a major change in US policy. While so-called 'advisers' had often accompanied South Vietnamese on combat missions, officially the US was not directly involved in the fighting. Air strikes would be the kind of commitment which would seem to require the co-operation of the US Congress. In American constitutional law only Congress had the power to declare war, not the president acting alone.

The problem in Congress was that many members of the Senate and the House of Representatives had reservations about widening the war in South-East Asia. The majority supported the president's policies, but there were doubters. Indeed, a few of Johnson's closest advisers, such as Under-Secretary of State George Ball, also counselled caution. The source of their concern was not whether it was desirable to stop North Vietnam but whether it could be done. South Vietnam was in such turmoil that perhaps an American effort to intervene would simply be a waste of lives and money. Even the most optimistic of the president's advisers agreed that saving Saigon would require a major commitment of American resources. Therefore, before the president did much more for Saigon, he needed to be certain of Congressional support.

In February 1964 one of the more hawkish members of the administration, Walt Rostow, broached the idea of obtaining a joint resolution of both houses of Congress authorizing the president to do whatever was necessary to defend South Vietnam. The next month, in the course of recommending specific military actions against the North, Assistant Defence Secretary William Bundy suggested the same thing. It might require some powerful lobbying by the White House, but the president's advisers thought that some form of Congressional permission was necessary. And, bearing in mind the presidential election later in the year, a joint resolution might avoid incurring the political costs that a formal declaration of war would exact. Public-opinion polls did indicate that Americans wanted to fight communism in Indo-China, but it was also clear that an actual war would not be popular with everyone. A joint resolution thus would bestow the powers Johnson needed without a formal declaration of war. In addition, if such a resolution were to pass by large (i.e. bipartisan) majorities, Vietnam might not become an issue in the presidential campaign. Both Democrats and Republicans would be on record as having supported the same policy. Such unanimity, however, was likely to be obtainable only in the event of a crisis. Timing would be very important, so Bundy and others prepared a draft resolution by the end of May, just to be ready. It authorized the president to deploy US military power to defend any South-East Asian nation against the threat of communism, whether from external or internal sources. For the time being Johnson chose not to rush into anything, but the opportunity to place such a resolution before Congress presented itself some months later.

In the meantime Johnson opened secret contacts with Hanoi in an effort to reach what he considered a compromise. Acting through J. Blair Seaborn, the senior Canadian member of the International Control

Commission (the ICC had been set up to supervise the Geneva Accords), he offered economic assistance and diplomatic recognition in return for ending the war. He threatened otherwise to order the US Air Force and Navy to strike the North itself. Hanoi responded by demanding that the Americans leave Vietnam before any deals were concluded – to the communists the US had no right to be in the country in the first place. They also required that Vietcong be allowed to participate in a coalition government in the South, a proposal that Washington felt would doom its allies in Saigon. The result was a stalemate, and the diplomatic feint failed. Each side considered that the other was demanding virtual surrender. Thus a direct US military role moved another step closer, and the draft Congressional resolution assumed increasing importance.

TONKIN

Throughout the spring and summer of 1964 the Pentagon had been perfecting contingency plans for a possible attack on the Vietminh's home ground. Clandestine operations inside North Vietnam were an important part of these preparations. Covert activities using South Vietnamese volunteers but with American training and support had been going on since the mid-1950s, though only on an intermittent basis. But early in 1964 Johnson approved a more concerted though still secret effort. The principal objective was to trigger newly emplaced radar and anti-aircraft installations, supplied by the Russians, along North Vietnam's coast. It would therefore be useful to have commandos test North Vietnam's coastal defences, so that US naval vessels could then pinpoint their location and gauge their state of readiness. They could also map the coast and take photographs. The Pentagon wanted this information to plan for possible military action. By June, it had selected ninety-four targets in North Vietnam, and had ordered the US Navy to have its aircraft carriers ready to launch bombing missions. There were even contingency plans for a joint American and South Vietnamese amphibious invasion of the North. At the time, and even years after, Defence Secretary McNamara publicly denied that any such plans were in the works.

A secret mission designed to trigger North Vietnam's coastal radar was scheduled for March, but was cancelled because of weather conditions and also to allow the South Vietnamese time to complete their preparations. Actual operations therefore did not begin until July, when the destroyer *Maddox* was dispatched to the Gulf of Tonkin. The *Maddox* had instructions to operate at least eight miles off the coast and four miles from any North Vietnamese islands. United States naval authorities apparently thought that Hanoi was observing a three-mile limit for its territorial waters. Some time before, however, China had adopted a twelve-mile limit, as did other countries around the world, so that it was not at all certain that North Vietnam and the USA agreed on the definition of international waters. In any event the *Maddox* co-ordinated its activities with South Vietnamese squads operating along the northern coast. It was an incident arising from these operations that provided Johnson with the kind of crisis he needed in order to go to Congress and seek a joint resolution, i.e. what his acting attorney-general defined as the 'functional equivalent of a declaration of war'.*

On 31 July 1964 four South Vietnamese patrol boats attacked two Northern islands (but did not actually land) while the *Maddox* conducted electronic surveillance. The resulting intelligence was relayed to an American base in the Philippine Islands and thence to the CIA in Washington. Hanoi protested to the International Control Commission, but the ICC had no power to do anything and could only note the incident for the record. Then, on the morning of 2 August, the *Maddox* picked up Northern messages suggesting that some sort of enemy response was in the offing. The ship's commander cabled his superiors suggesting that the *Maddox*'s mission be aborted, but he was overruled. When three North Vietnamese patrol boats attacked later in the day, they found the destroyer primed for action. A twenty-minute engagement ensued. The carrier *Ticonderoga*, farther out at sea, sent fighter planes to assist, so that one Northern boat was sunk and the other two disabled. The captain of the *Maddox* believed he was in international waters at the time of the attack, though earlier in the day he had passed within ten miles of the Red River Delta and thus Haiphong, probably the most sensitive point along the coast.

Although the news services reported the attack, Lyndon Johnson held back. The presidential campaign was starting up, and he did not wish to be rushed into a decision which might imply he was trigger-happy. Wanting instead to saddle Goldwater with the warmonger label, Johnson assumed a statesmanlike stance: he decided that there would be no reprisals for the time being. Besides, it would not do to have the press and Congress begin to ask too many questions, lest it be discovered that the

* Cited in *ibid.*, 362.

Maddox was co-operating in attacks upon a country with which the United States officially was not at war. The Navy's real mission would remain a secret, as otherwise the administration could not portray the attack as unprovoked. On the other hand, the USA would not retreat either. The president directed the *Maddox* to continue its patrols, and sent a diplomatic note to Hanoi warning against any further provocations. As a precaution, the Pentagon ordered additional ships and aircraft to South-East Asia and prepared to deploy ground forces, while the State Department readied the joint resolution for presentation to Congress in case anything else happened – which it did.

On 4 August a second incident was reported, though it turned out that no one was really sure what it was all about or whether it had even taken place. The naval command had ordered the *Maddox* and another destroyer, the *C. Turner Joy*, to sail up to the limits set earlier (eight miles off the coast and four miles off islands) in order to assert US rights on the high seas. In effect the idea was to press North Vietnam to recognize a US definition of international waters. More boatloads of South Vietnamese commandos were also sent to the scene. The *Maddox* was able to intercept Northern communications, and knew that the communists associated the South Vietnamese activity with the presence of American ships in the Gulf of Tonkin. Hence there was the danger of another attack. The commander of the *Maddox* once again proposed aborting the mission, but once again was overruled. It seemed as if his superior officers wanted to provoke an incident. On the night of the fourth, with storms upsetting their sonar and radar, the two destroyers began firing at what they thought were North Vietnamese patrol boats. Subsequent debriefings, however, indicated that no one, either crew members or pilots providing air support, was sure of actually having sighted any enemy boats in the darkness. The captain of the *Maddox* reported that weather conditions may have led to a malfunction of the radar. Yet the same day, and without firm confirmation that a second attack had actually occurred, Johnson decided to act. He was for peace, but he could not afford to allow Goldwater to charge that he was pusillanimous. While US aircraft bombed an oil depot and four patrol boat bases in the north, Johnson went on television to announce that a definite attack had taken place and that US aircraft were responding. And within a few days the president won his resolution from Congress, with only two dissenting votes in the Senate and none in the House. The public also rallied round the flag – polls indicated 85 per cent support for administration policy.

In a strict sense Johnson had not conspired to manufacture the second Gulf of Tonkin incident, but his government had co-operated with South Vietnamese raids on Northern territory and thus committed a virtual act of war before the communist attack on the *Maddox*. Yet the administration denied outright that it had been engaged in hostile acts. In congressional hearings before the passing of the Tonkin resolution, McNamara disputed charges of US complicity in South Vietnamese attacks against the North: 'Our navy played absolutely no part in, was not associated with, was not aware of, any South Vietnamese actions, if there were any . . . This is a fact.'* Further, there was nothing uncalculated about administration policy. The White House, the Pentagon, the CIA and the State Department acted in concert, so a vast array of documentary evidence exists to suggest that the United States was being deliberately provocative, whatever the rights and wrongs of Hanoi's conduct. Washington was obviously no innocent victim of aggression.

ESCALATION

The decision to seek a military solution was perhaps clearest in the failure of renewed efforts to begin some sort of negotiations between Washington and Hanoi. Seaborn continued to try even after the Gulf of Tonkin incident, but with no results. The secretary-general of the United Nations, U Thant of Burma, also wanted to organize talks. So did Nikita Khrushchev. The Russians saw the war as threatening their need for peaceful co-existence in the aftermath of the Missile Crisis. Furthermore, they wanted to limit Hanoi's seemingly endless demands for more aid. U Thant thus succeeded in persuading the Soviets to act as intermediaries to the Vietminh. The latter had to be receptive up to a point, as the Soviet Union was their main source of modern weaponry and its word had to be taken seriously. The Chinese were an alternative source of supply, but lagged behind in the development of the type of sophisticated weapons needed to meet the Americans head on. Besides, the Vietnamese still regarded China as harbouring imperial ambitions of its own *vis-à-vis* South-East Asia. Khrushchev therefore had some, albeit limited, leverage over Hanoi. As an inducement to negotiate he accepted Vietminh requests for more assistance with the proviso that they look into the matter of talks. U Thant received indications from Hanoi in September that it was willing to proceed in some fashion, but

* Cited in *ibid.*, 375.

officials in the Johnson administration (apparently without informing the president) decided not to pursue the matter.

By 1964 the guerrillas, organized as the People's Revolutionary Army (PRA), may have numbered 170,000, while for the first time entire units of Vietminh regulars were beginning to arrive from the North. Hanoi co-ordinated both the PRA and its regulars through a mobile head-quarters variously located in the South and over the border in Laos and Cambodia, the Central Office for South Vietnam (COSVN). By com-parison, the South's war effort was faltering, impeded by yet more conspiring in Saigon. Only the next year, in June 1965, did a stable military government emerge under Air Vice-Marshal Nguyen Cao Ky. In the face of American pressure to produce at least the façade of democracy, it permitted the election of a constitutional assembly in 1966. A constitution was ready by March 1967, and voting for a legislature and for the presidency took place in the autumn. General Nguyen Van Thieu won the latter, but the new regime was far from democratic. The generals went through the elections mainly to please the Americans, and while ten civilian candidates were allowed to run against Thieu, they did not have a chance of winning. Indeed, some were arrested afterwards.

In 1964, however, the political future of Saigon was far from being settled, and the more immediate problem was military: how to boost the war effort. Accordingly, armed with the Gulf of Tonkin Resolution, the US administration proceeded to take over the conduct of the war. Johnson did not act immediately, because he did not wish to alarm the voters before the presidential election in the autumn. He therefore refused to respond to the Vietcong's first major attack on a US base. On 1 November, just days before the election in the United States, about a hundred guerrillas raided an air field at Bienhoa, just north of Saigon. They destroyed six B–57 bombers on the ground, damaged several others, and killed five Americans and two South Vietnamese. Johnson held back, but in December his advisers recommended a gradual escalation of the conflict. He therefore authorized the covert bombing of communist supply lines in Laos, and approved additional raids by South Vietnamese commandos along the Northern coast. At the same time the Vietcong launched a series of synchronized attacks throughout the South, again with telling effect. When they raided the outpost of Pleiku in February 1965, killing eight Americans, Johnson ordered the bomb-ing of North Vietnam itself in retaliation, and this soon became the fixed policy of the United States. Regular air raids on the North would not be cancelled until three years later, though there were occasional brief pauses in an effort to attract the enemy to the conference table. Soviet prime minister Aleksei Kosygin was in Hanoi in February to discuss aid for the North and also to urge compromise, but the American bombings persuaded the Russians to give Hanoi what it needed without further ado. It is possible that the Vietminh planned Pleiku in the hope of provoking American reprisals while Kosygin was in town.

However great the faith of American generals in air power, more than bombing would be required to hold the country. On 22 February 1965 the American commander in Vietnam, General William Westmoreland, requested ground troops to help protect the big US air base at Danang on the South Vietnamese coast. Johnson agreed, and the first US combat soldiers to land in Asia since the Korean War waded ashore on 8 March. There were 3,500 of them, the advance agents of a force that would grow to well over half a million in the next three and a half years. The official explanation was that Saigon had requested the troops, but in fact it had not even been informed beforehand, much less having appealed for help. The South Vietnamese generals had been wary of such a development, on the grounds that the presence of US troops would reduce Washington's dependency on them. But the die was cast, and the war had reached an important turning-point.

In a speech delivered at Johns Hopkins University on 7 April 1965 Johnson offered a programme of massive economic aid to the North if it would leave the South, but these terms had already been rejected by Hanoi the previous autumn. The communists refused again the very next day. There was another peace initiative in May (including a bombing pause) and on a number of subsequent occasions. The latter were kept private and involved a variety of people as go-betweens. The communists objected that Washington kept insisting they leave the South, which they regarded as part of a single Vietnam. Hanoi was adamant that the Vietcong be allowed to participate in a new and formally neutral coalition government in Saigon, and that there be a permanent cessation of the bombing and the withdrawal of the Americans before talks. Again they argued that the United States had no right to be in Vietnam in the first place. Johnson tried another bombing pause from Christmas 1965 through to January 1966, but with the same outcome. From Washington's point of view the failure of the peace initiatives justified escalating the war – it could claim to have done everything possible to reach a settlement. In fact some students of the period think that perhaps this was the purpose of Johnson's offers to begin with – having been spurned, the administration could proceed to apply force. Dean Rusk,

Johnson's secretary of state, summed up the problem: 'The prospect of large-scale reinforcements in men and defence budget increases for the next eighteen-month period requires solid preparation of the American public. A crucial element will be a clear demonstration that we have explored fully every alternative but that the aggressor has left us no choice.'*

TET

However carefully the White House calculated each escalation over the next years, the generals in the field always seemed to need more troops. While North Vietnamese regulars operated in the South and played an increasingly important part in Hanoi's strategy, the guerrilla war was the biggest problem for the United States. American troops often did very well against Vietminh regulars, but some experts estimated that the Americans needed to outnumber guerrillas ten to one just to hold their own. The guerrillas lived off the land and disappeared among the people, waiting to emerge and strike when an opportunity presented itself. This was possible because they were native to the country, and because many villagers supported the communists and protected them. Foreign in race, culture and language, the Americans were much more exposed. Their technological virtuosity also meant that they waged a very different type of warfare requiring massive logistical support. In 1967 about 100 pounds of supplies per day were being delivered for each American in the country. Yet the results were sometimes difficult to measure, as the guerrillas were still able to strike almost anywhere. No one was secure, whether on a 'search-and-destroy' mission or in a Saigon office.

The difficulty of measuring results and the constant tension of knowing the enemy could be anywhere contributed to the demoralization of many American troops. This manifested itself in the use of drugs. In 1971 Pentagon studies suggested that perhaps 30 per cent of US troops had tried hard drugs such as opium and heroin, while over half had smoked marijuana, and there was evidence that important members of the Saigon government were involved in trafficking. While Washington hoped to wear down the communists by a strategy of attrition, the fact was that the Americans were more vulnerable in a prolonged war. This point applied to the home front as well, where a growing anti-war movement was spreading, especially among draft age university students. In fact two more Americans followed the example of the Buddhists and

* Cited in *ibid.*, 483.

in November 1965 burned themselves to death as a protest against the war. The immolations took place at the Pentagon and at the United Nations. By the autumn of 1967 opinion polls indicated that more Americans thought the war was a mistake than supported it. Yet the paradox was that the majority did not favour withdrawing. Most Americans seemed to believe the war should be prosecuted to victory once the commitment was made, right or wrong.

The problem was that a military solution proved as elusive for the Americans as for the South Vietnamese. Moreover, the political situation in the South went from bad to worse. A virtual civil war broke out in the spring of 1966, after Nguyen Cao Ky (the prime minister) and Lyndon Johnson had conferred in Honolulu. Returning home with the firm backing of the American president, Ky stalled on the question of returning the country to civilian rule. The election of a constitutional convention had not yet taken place. An alliance of Buddhists and dissident officers therefore started a rebellion, taking control of the important cities of Danang and Hué and staging anti-American as well as anti-Ky demonstrations in Saigon and many other centres. Government forces retook Danang in May and Hué in June, exacting brutal reprisals, so that the Buddhists were no longer a political force in the country. But the civil war in the South left many Americans wondering just what they were fighting for. Elections did take place in due course, but it had taken a small civil war to force the military government to agree. The turmoil meant that the United States had to assume an ever larger responsibility for the war against the communists. And it was on the battlefield that the United States was to receive its greatest shock.

In the autumn of 1967 the communists attacked at several points in the central highlands of Vietnam and also in the border areas of Laos and Cambodia. In other words, they initiated a campaign in the hinterland, away from the major towns and cities, with a major battle developing at Khesanh. Khesanh was important not in itself but only because the communists chose to make it so. They sent 40,000 troops to the scene, and the United States reinforced the base and conducted some of the heaviest bombing of the war against enemy forces. Probably 10,000 Vietminh were killed compared to about 500 Americans. But Khesanh and other battles were a feint, designed to draw US and South Vietnamese troops away from more important targets, particularly the cities. The autumn campaign, in other words, was simply the prelude to a more dramatic strike early the next year, the Tet offensive.

Tet was the Vietnamese lunar New Year, and the communists had pledged to observe a truce during the celebrations. But on 31 January 1968 the Vietminh and Vietcong attacked Saigon and a hundred other cities and towns in the South, and more than matched the South's record for brutality. They even broke into the compound of the US embassy. Parts of Saigon were held for a short time, and Hué for twenty-five days. When it was all over, the communists were defeated, in the sense that they did not take and hold their targets, though they still controlled much of the countryside. Further, Hanoi had hoped that Tet would inspire an uprising in the South and result in the toppling of General Thieu's government, but it did not come to pass (by then Thieu was the new president). Yet an uprising was more a hope than a definite expectation, and the communists could be satisfied that they had sent a major shock wave through Vietnam and also the United States.

For months the US command had been sending optimistic reports to the White House, and Westmoreland even described Tet as a sign of desperation on the communists' part, one last effort to win. In the immediate aftermath he saw no need to request more troops (by the time of Tet there were about 500,000 US personnel in the country), but others reacted differently. The US Joint Chiefs of Staff (JCS) and in particular their chairman, General Earle Wheeler, saw the Tet offensive as an opportunity to call up some of the home reserves. These were troops who normally trained in the United States itself and were not subject to duty abroad except in an emergency. The JCS wanted to deploy them in order to make up for the depletion of the regular military. Vietnam had absorbed equipment but also personnel from US bases around the world, so that the Pentagon doubted its capacity to meet America's global commitments. A crisis in Vietnam might force the issue, and induce the president to do as they wished. General Wheeler thus prevailed upon General Westmoreland to request additional help, with the total figure set at 206,000 more troops. Only about 108,000 of these, however, were recommended for immediate deployment in the Indo-China theatre, with the rest slated for duty later or for bases elsewhere. To convince the president, though, Wheeler had to play down Westmoreland's initially optimistic reports from the field. But this was a dangerous game in the world of Pentagon–White House relations. Raising 206,000 troops would definitely mean calling up the reserves, and there would be a high political price to pay for Lyndon Johnson. Further, the generals admitted that they could not guarantee that even this would be enough to achieve military victory. Yet the Pentagon was recommending that the US mobilize for virtually total war, and this in an election year. The war had already exacerbated the rate of inflation, and taxes would have to be increased. It was a fact that opinion polls taken during the Tet crisis indicated that the American public favoured a stronger military response, but it was also the case that Johnson's standing with the people was plummeting. Americans wanted to win, but the president seemed incapable of delivering. The scene was set for a dramatic turnabout in the course of the war.

Perhaps more important than public opinion or even the anti-war movement in influencing Johnson was the disillusionment of his closest advisers, including some like McNamara who had once confidently predicted victory. (Indeed, Johnson had arranged the defence secretary's resignation, to be effective from February 1968, and appointed Clark Clifford – a known administration loyalist – in his place.) This is not to say that everyone was of like mind, but key figures did begin to change the president's thinking. The media as well tended to be much more critical of the possibilities in Vietnam than the public at large. By 10 March the story of the troop request had leaked to the press. And two days later the anti-war senator, Eugene McCarthy of Minnesota, won twenty of twenty-four delegates to the Democratic Party nominating convention in the New Hampshire primary (primaries are votes held by political parties in some US states to select delegates for presidential nominating conventions). On 16 March Robert Kennedy, senator from New York and brother of the slain president, entered the race. It was clear Johnson was in for a fight over the nomination.

Yet Tet itself had already moved the president to reconsider his position. Well before New Hampshire he had ordered Clifford to gather a study group to consider the troop request and indeed the whole course of the war. Clifford had long advocated a firm stand, but in the spring of 1968 concluded that the war could not be won except at a cost disproportionate to whatever might be gained. The impact on Johnson was devastating. It was time to make a definitive gesture towards negotiations. On 31 March 1968 he went on American television and announced the suspension of all bombing north of the nineteenth parallel. This would free most of North Vietnam from the air threat and confine the bombing to enemy strongholds in the South. Further, he was rejecting the Pentagon's request for more troops, except for token reinforcements. And to the surprise of virtually everyone he announced that he would not run for the presidency again. Johnson had become the target of the anti-war movement, and wished to save the country from further divisiveness. (Indeed, in Madison, Wisconsin, anti-war graffiti read 'Where is Lee Harvey Oswald now that we need him?' Oswald was the alleged assassin of John F. Kennedy.) Hanoi, disappointed that the costly Tet campaign had not led to a general uprising against Saigon, responded favourably. The first peace talks opened in Paris on 10 May, though there was no sign of progress until the autumn.

NIXON

Johnson's withdrawal from the presidential race, however, did not remove him as an influence on events. His goal was to assure the nomination of a successor who would continue his basic approach. Though Tet had forced him to negotiate, he fully intended to bargain for the autonomy of South Vietnam as a separate, pro-Western political entity. He would resist Hanoi's demand that a coalition government including the Vietcong be formed, and that this government be neutral. To the president both proposals were just the first steps towards a communist takeover in the South. Johnson therefore confided to his closest allies that he would accept a call from the Democratic Party to run again, despite his *de facto* resignation of 31 March. But this was simply not on the cards, so his vice-president, Hubert Humphrey, became the administration candidate. In June an assassin murdered Robert Kennedy, thereby removing the most popular anti-war candidate from the Democratic race. The other top runner was McCarthy. Johnson's problem was that Humphrey favoured still more compromise on Vietnam as a way of heading off the McCarthy forces, so the president was not always the most enthusiastic booster of his own vice-president. Humphrey won the nomination of his party at its Chicago convention in the summer of 1968, but after yielding to the president's demand that he make no substantive concessions to the doves. Then the administration mobilized all its power on behalf of his candidacy.

The convention was rocked by what official reports later described as a 'police riot' against anti-war demonstrators outside in the streets. Despite provocation by the authorities, in the long run the rioting hurt the anti-war cause by identifying it with radicals and extremists. Of course, this played into the hands of Johnson (and, as it would turn out, his successor), who was unwilling to go any farther in compromising on the war. Agents from the US military and the CIA infiltrated the crowds, looking for alleged subversives and possibly acting as *agents provocateurs*. The CIA role was clearly illegal, as its mandate prohibited operations inside the United States. Its job was to engage in covert activities against

threats abroad. But as the war dragged on, the White House tolerated
more and more violations of the law, even as it condemned law-breaking
by anti-war activists. And when the convention was all over, many
political pundits were still of the opinion that Johnson would have
preferred a hawkish Republican to a doveish Democrat as the next leader
of the USA. Who won the Republican Party nomination thus became
a very important question, for the president still had doubts about
Humphrey.

The nominee turned out to be Richard Nixon, Eisenhower's vice-
president from 1953 to 1961 and a supporter of Barry Goldwater in the
1964 campaign. The Republican convention was a sedate affair compared to the Democratic, and Nixon won the nomination on the first
ballot. Yet winning the election was another matter because of George
Wallace, governor of Alabama and the candidate of the American
Independent Party. Wallace was on the political right of American
politics. He competed with Nixon in drawing Democratic votes away
from Humphrey in the Southern states, especially after Humphrey broke
with Johnson's policy in late September and came out in favour of a total
end to the bombing (the 31 March exemption applied to most but not all
the North). Hanoi played to Humphrey by offering to admit Saigon
(along with the Vietcong) to the Paris negotiations in return for an
unconditional end to the air war. Johnson co-operated rather than leave
office as a warmonger, and on 31 October ended all bombing of North
Vietnam. But the shift was too late to help Humphrey, and Nixon won by
a margin of less than 1 per cent of the popular vote.

With a new president in Washington, the Paris talks stalled once more.
After all, Nixon had campaigned on a platform of 'peace with honour',
i.e. winding down America's combat role on the ground (not in the air),
while building up the South Vietnamese army so that it could take over
the fighting. Once 'Vietnamization' was completed, the Americans could
go home while the war continued. Nixon thus talked of peace for the
United States and won the votes of some doves, while saving America's
honour by not abandoning Saigon, thereby keeping the hawks happy.
The communists had been at war since 1946, however, so that whatever
happened in Paris they planned to continue fighting at the same time.
They expected the worst from Nixon. It came soon enough. In March
1969 Nixon decided to bomb communist sanctuaries in Cambodia,
which was presumably neutral territory. And there was more to come. It
seemed that the inauguration of a new president meant that the White
House was going to have to learn about Hanoi's resilience all over again.

THE WAR IN CAMBODIA

Nixon's campaign promise to reduce the number of US combat troops in Vietnam eroded America's bargaining power at the Paris peace talks. Why should Hanoi make concessions when the United States was publicly committed to reducing its presence in Indo-China? Yet the president had little choice but to make good on his promises, and in June, at a meeting with President Thieu on Midway Island, he announced the first withdrawal, 25,000 troops, with others to follow. On the other hand, Nixon had no intention of abandoning Saigon. Vietnamization would build up Thieu's army and offset the departure of US ground forces, thus gradually confining the American role to the air war in the South. Furthermore, there was nothing to prevent the president from renewing the bombing of the North. But it was Nixon's decision to bomb Cambodia that represented perhaps the most important development during his first year of office, 1969. The president decided to widen the Indo-China conflict by attacking communist sanctuaries across the border. The hope was that this might ease the military pressure on Saigon to the point where it could handle more of the fighting on the ground. The bombing would also serve notice to the negotiators at Paris that the USA was prepared to back diplomacy with force.

Vietminh operations in Cambodia had long been a provocation to the Americans. Phnom Penh was supposed to be neutral, yet in the mid-1960s its leader, Prince Norodom Sihanouk, tolerated communist bases on his territory. Moreover, he allowed the Vietminh to use the port of Sihanoukville (a considerable distance from the border with Vietnam) and to move supplies from there to sanctuaries inland. The prince was not pro-communist, but by closing his eyes to North Vietnamese violations of his sovereignty he hoped to prevent the war from engulfing his country. Also, by conniving with Hanoi Sihanouk hoped to restrain Vietminh support for indigenous communists inside Cambodia, though the latter were comparatively few in number and had established the Communist Party of Kampuchea (or Cambodia) only in 1960. It had been preceded by the Khmer Issarak (i.e. Cambodian Independence) movement founded in 1940, the Khmer People's Party and an associated provisional government formed in 1951, and other groups, none of which was as powerful as the Vietminh in Vietnam. Still, Hanoi had provided aid and advice to Cambodian opposition forces in the past, so that domestic politics influenced Sihanouk's calculations. On the other hand, he also took the precaution of cultivating China. Beijing might temper Hanoi's designs on Cambodia and possibly serve as a diplomatic counterweight to the rising influence of America in South-East Asia.

By the late 1960s, however, the Cambodian strategy was breaking down. The Cultural Revolution (see Chapter 9) caused Beijing to turn inward as the People's Republic became immersed in political turmoil, so that it could not play the role of Cambodia's protector. And the North Vietnamese build-up meant that Cambodia was being drawn deeper and deeper into the war. Well before Tet, General Westmoreland recommended ground attacks across the border. The risk to Cambodia was such that as early as December 1967 Sihanouk began to lean towards the US side, by making it known that he was prepared to allow the Americans the right of hot pursuit into his territory. South Vietnamese sabotage and intelligence teams were already secretly operating in Cambodia, sometimes accompanied by American advisers, but these activities were on a small scale compared to what was about to come. Sihanouk hoped the right of hot pursuit might head off some of Westmoreland's more grandiose schemes and also place the North Vietnamese on notice. The prince feared what a communist victory in Vietnam might mean for the future independence of his country. But Johnson hesitated, and then Tet turned him against further escalation.

By 1969 there was a new president in the White House, and he viewed the Cambodian question differently. Rather than send in ground troops just yet, however, Nixon preferred to rely on air power. This would allow him to attack the sanctuaries without disturbing his plans for bringing American combat forces home. He ordered the bombing to begin in March. It was originally planned to be short-term, but in fact continued off and on for several years. It was also supposed to be secret, so that Sihanouk (who apparently assented to Nixon's decision but was still legally neutral) would not have to protest in public. Secrecy also meant that the US Congress would not object to an action which some authorities believed would require a declaration of war. Similarly, secrecy would head off the anti-war demonstrators. It was very difficult, however, to keep such a vast undertaking quiet for long, and the story leaked to *The New York Times* and appeared in the press by May. The response of Nixon and his national security adviser, Henry Kissinger, was to arrange the wire-tapping of several reporters and government officials in an effort to plug the leak. This was the first of many activities of questionable legality that would lead to the president's resignation a few years later, on 9 August 1974.

For Cambodia the worst was yet to come. After a year of bombing, the

B–52s still had not solved the problem of the sanctuaries. If anything, the air raids forced the Vietminh and Vietcong to retreat deeper and deeper into Cambodian territory. Further, Hanoi reacted to Sihanouk's turn-about by arming the Cambodian communists, known as the Khmer Rouge. They had launched a new uprising against Phnom Penh in 1968, and with outside help began to make some headway. The regular Cambodian army therefore wanted Sihanouk to ask for American aid in order to contain the Vietnamese and to destroy the Khmer Rouge, while the prince still hoped that diplomacy might do the job. The army became increasingly disaffected, and in March 1970 decided that Sihanouk's usefulness had come to an end. General Lon Nol, who was also the prime minister, staged a right-wing coup. There were allegations of CIA involvement, and though no clear evidence of this has emerged, Washington did welcome the change. It immediately made arrange-ments to provide assistance to Lon Nol. Sihanouk found haven in Beijing, and announced that he was joining forces with the Khmer Rouge against the military government in Phnom Penh.

In 1969 and early 1970, however, the significance of the Khmer Rouge was not yet clear. The Nixon administration had announced several more troop withdrawals, so that the dispatch of American combat forces to Cambodia did not seem very likely. Moreover, in July 1969 the president had enunciated what became known as the Nixon Doctrine. This served notice that the United States was willing to provide its allies with assistance, but that it could not do all the fighting or provide all the troops. The message was that the beneficiaries of US aid would have to help themselves, and that America planned to reduce its self-appointed role as global gendarme. And in February 1970 Nixon's national security adviser, Henry Kissinger, opened secret talks in Paris with Le Duc Tho, who had played a leading role in directing Vietminh operations in South Vietnam. The idea was to negotiate outside the framework of the official talks (which were still going on in the same city) and away from the glare of publicity. Not only did this prevent leaks, but it enabled the Americans to bargain for their own interests and to place Saigon's needs in the background. For the Vietminh, secrecy meant they could bypass the Vietcong, who often disagreed with their Northern sponsors. Another sign that the American role in the war was winding down came on 20 April, when Nixon committed the administration to bringing home another 150,000 troops. But then he turned around and surprised everyone.

On 30 April 1970 the president appeared on American television to announce that a force of US and South Vietnamese soldiers was at that very moment crossing into Cambodia from Vietnam. Their goal was to destroy communist sanctuaries and to find COSVN, the field headquarters for the communist war effort. The troops were backed by B–52s. The administration described the undertaking as an 'incursion', but in fact it was an outright invasion of a country with which the United States was not at war. The result once again was to widen the Indo-China conflict, although the Americans began withdrawing in June. Yet they had failed to destroy COSVN or drive the communists out of Cambodia. Thus their immediate goal was not achieved.

More importantly, the invasion and particularly the continuing bombing devastated Cambodian society. Over the next few years possibly half the rural population abandoned the countryside in the hope of escaping the air raids against Vietminh sanctuaries. The number of persons living in Phnom Penh rose from about 600,000 to over two million between 1970 and 1975. The capital and other cities were filled with people who had abandoned their homes and their crops. As a result widespread starvation ensued. And the bombing had a brutalizing impact on the Khmer Rouge. Their plans for the future of Cambodia have never been clearly understood, and indeed it was really Vietnam that made them into an important fighting force, but for Hanoi's strategic ends and not so much for some revolutionary mission in Cambodia itself. To Westerners they seemed to come from nowhere, and it could be questioned whether they would ever have had an important role in the war without Hanoi's backing. Whatever the Khmer Rouge stood for in the long run, however, in the short term their main concern was to fight the pro-American Lon Nol government and all who collaborated with it. The problem was that the more punishment they withstood, the more paranoid they became. They began to suspect everyone, friend and foe alike, and so resorted to terror as a means of social control. In due course Khmer Rouge atrocities would attain genocidal proportions (see Chapter 12), but the Americans had unwittingly contributed to the disaster as well. William Shawcross, one of the most astute students of the crisis, argues that Washington's policies, particularly in 1969–70, were very important in creating the conditions in which the Khmer Rouge emerged.* The bombing and

---

* William Shawcross, *Sideshow: Kissinger, Nixon and the Destruction of Cambodia* (London: 1979), and *The Quality of Mercy: Cambodia, Holocaust and Modern Conscience* (New York: 1984). See also Laura Summers, 'Democratic Kampuchea', in Bogdan Szajkowski (ed.), *Marxist Governments: A World Survey* (London: 1981), II, 409–42.

invasion uprooted the rural population and spurred the Khmer Rouge's urge for revenge against alleged Lon Nol collaborators. The bombing would finally end in August 1973, well after the removal of US combat troops from the country and only at the insistence of the US Congress, but the consequences for Cambodia were to endure long after. We shall have occasion to return to the Cambodian tragedy.

PROTEST

The invasion also activated the anti-war movement in the United States as never before. The broadening of the war contradicted Nixon's plans for bringing the troops home, and seemed to portend a major reversal of policy. The outcome was death and bloodshed in America itself. On 4 May 1970 members of the National Guard (the US home reserve) shot four students dead during demonstrations at Kent State University in Ohio. Student strikes closed down over 400 universities and colleges throughout the country, while about 100,000 people turned out for a mass rally in Washington, DC. They surrounded the White House. A spokesman for the Nixon administration reacted to the Kent State killings by warning that violent dissent had provoked the tragedy, in effect blaming the victims. The president also ordered still more spying on critics of his war policy, and again these activities were of doubtful legality. More and more it seemed that the president regarded himself as above the law.

Protests even developed in the armed forces, and took a variety of forms, some violent. Anti-war troops (often reluctant draftees) occasionally carried out 'fragging' attacks against pro-war officers. These involved maiming or killing with fragmentation grenades (while on patrol, for instance). The intention was to let pro-war commanders in the field know that their men were not keen to risk their lives for a government as corrupt as General Thieu's. There were 222 incidents in 1971. The stress of fighting a guerrilla war, where the enemy was hidden among the population, also led to atrocities against the very people the Americans claimed to be helping. The most famous incident was at the small village of Mylai, where in March 1968 American soldiers murdered about 175–200 innocent civilians believed to be harbouring guerrillas, but there were other cases as well. Escape was another way to deal with the stresses of war, and the use of narcotics in Vietnam was phenomenal, as we have noted earlier. Desertion was very common too, reaching 89,000 cases in 1971. Outside the military another way for anti-war youths to protest against the war was to avoid the draft by fleeing the country. Most went to Canada, but Sweden, France and Holland were also favourite destinations. The United States government normally regarded the status of political refugee as an honourable one, but not in this case. Estimates of the number of refugees varied between 50,000 and 100,000. It was not until 1977 that President Jimmy Carter issued pardons to about 10,000 still living outside the United States, but not all chose to return home. Many did not believe that they had committed a crime requiring pardon. Even on military bases in the USA itself anti-war soldiers published over fifty underground newspapers, such as *About Face*, *Fed Up* and *Last Harass*. Enrolments in officer training programmes on US campuses declined by considerably more than 50 per cent between 1966 and 1973. Indeed, the programmes were eliminated altogether at over forty colleges and universities.

PEACE FOR AMERICA

The invasion of Cambodia, however, was hardly the Americans' last hurrah. The massive protests guaranteed that US troops would leave the country, though only after a decent interval. The administration did not want to give the appearance of yielding to street demonstrators. More importantly Nixon and Kissinger still believed that the timely application of force was necessary to spur the secret talks in Paris. For their part the communists responded to the Cambodian war by increasing their activities in Laos. Accordingly, in February 1971, the Americans and their South Vietnamese allies launched an invasion of the country, despite protests by its prime minister, Prince Souvanna Phouma. Furthermore, the invasion violated the 1961 Geneva agreement to respect the neutrality of Laos. Of course, the communists had already violated this pledge, so the United States and South Vietnam felt justified in doing so as well. The American role was limited to providing air support, and no US ground troops were involved. Hence, while anti-war protests took place again in the United States, they were not as widespread or as violent as the year before. In April the administration announced that another 100,000 troops were to be repatriated, and this also helped contain the anti-war movement. Yet Washington was still at war; it had simply made the fighting less visible to the average American.

Moreover, there were still major problems. The Laotian operation was a test of Vietnamization, but the Saigon army eventually abandoned the campaign. Despite American press releases reporting great successes, there was reason to wonder about the future. The Americans were withdrawing from the fighting on the ground, so that the security of South-East Asia increasingly depended on Saigon's performance. By the next year there would be only 70,000 American troops in South Vietnam, of which just 6,000 were for combat rather than logistical or other forms of support. In 1972 Saigon had about one million troops of its own. Even so, when the communists launched a new campaign in March 1972, both the Americans and the South Vietnamese once again were shocked by the capacity of the Vietminh and Vietcong to carry the battle into the South. Perhaps 120,000 North Vietnamese regulars attacked, along with tens of thousands of Vietcong. The USA responded by renewing the bombing of the North, including Hanoi and Haiphong, and mining the country's ports and harbours as well.

The Southern forces outnumbered the Vietminh, yet Saigon's troops were none the less thinly spread. The communists were attacking across a broad front, and gained ground in the Mekong Delta. On the other hand, Saigon was not defeated either, so that as the campaign ground to a halt by June after another costly but inconclusive effort, Hanoi had reason to pause and reconsider its situation. However impressive the communist attack, it was not enough to bring the fighting to a definitive resolution. Victory remained elusive, much as after Tet two years before. Perhaps it was time for the North to try and achieve its objectives at the bargaining table. There was another consideration as well. President Nixon made trips to both China and Russia in 1972. It was clear to Hanoi that its patrons were prepared to place their national interests ahead of the Vietminh's. In the early 1970s both Beijing and Moscow wanted to improve their relations with Washington, and therefore pressed Hanoi to make concessions in Paris. As Hanoi's only sources of aid, they had some power to persuade.

A combination of battlefield developments and Eastern Bloc politicking thus cleared the way for some serious negotiating. The secret talks between Le Duc Tho and Henry Kissinger resumed in the summer of 1972, and by October, just before the November presidential election in the US, the basis of an agreement seemed near. There was to be a cease-fire between the United States and North Vietnam, with no reference to the war between Hanoi and Saigon. United States troops would withdraw, and American prisoners of war would be repatriated. All political problems concerning the future of South Vietnam were to be left to the Vietnamese themselves. The breakthrough was possible because Kissinger withdrew America's longstanding objection to the presence of Vietminh troops in the South, while Le Duc Tho no longer insisted that Thieu be replaced by a coalition government including the Vietcong. In effect the Americans were bailing out regardless of the cost, so the North could afford to concede that Thieu might remain. For Hanoi the main point was to be rid of the Americans. Once they were gone, the Vietminh could deal with Thieu.

Yet the end did not come quite so soon. The problem was that the United States had bargained in secret and only for itself, and had reckoned without Thieu. Once informed, he objected strongly to the Paris Accords and insisted that they be amended to guarantee continued American support for his government. Without a commitment from the United States, Thieu knew that his chances of survival were slight. He thus made his objections public, embarrassing the administration and forcing Nixon on the defensive. In effect he accused the president of abandoning a faithful ally. Nixon was not about to give the appearance of surrendering to Hanoi, and so instructed Kissinger to seek additional concessions. But the North refused to co-operate. To the Vietminh it seemed that the Americans were reneging on a definite commitment, and further talks were broken off. Nixon therefore concluded that once more the enemy had to be forced into submission. He ordered the bombing of the North in December, mainly around the Hanoi–Haiphong area. In fact it was the most intensive series of air raids in the entire war. The communists fired perhaps 1,200 surface-to-air missiles, and the Americans lost fifteen B–52s, plus eleven other aircraft. Worse, it turned out that the whole campaign was probably unnecessary. By the end of the month Hanoi indicated that it was willing to renew the talks, which seemed to suggest that the bombing had forced it back to the bargaining table. Yet, when a final settlement was reached, it conformed to the same terms as before. Therefore it was not Hanoi that had modified its position. The difference was that in January the Americans were prepared to tell Thieu he had no choice in the matter – they were leaving. The US and North Vietnam initialled an agreement on 23 January 1973 and staged a formal signing on 27 January. The next month the war in Laos came to a conclusion with the establishment of a communist-dominated coalition government, but there was no end to the fighting in Cambodia. In fact the Nixon administration continued the air war until August, and the Khmer Rouge continued to fight Lon Nol thereafter.

The Paris Accords enabled the United States to withdraw its ground forces from Vietnam, but left the determination of the country's political future to Hanoi and Saigon. The result was that the war was hardly over. Neither was the US role, though it was indirect and no longer included combat troops. The Americans were still conducting air raids against the Vietminh and their Khmer Rouge allies in Cambodia (neither Laos nor Cambodia were part of the Hanoi–Washington agreement). Furthermore, under the terms of the Paris Accords they were allowed to resupply their South Vietnamese allies, though only on the basis of replacing existing equipment and not increasing the total amount of aid. In other words, the Accords limited how much military hardware the United States could provide, although the Pentagon had prepared for this contingency. The previous autumn Washington had ordered a massive transfer of equipment to Saigon in a last great rush to provide South Vietnam with everything it needed before the signing of the Paris agreement. Over a frantic six-week period the US stripped $2,000 million worth of supplies from its own bases and those of its closest Asian allies (South Korea, Taiwan and the Philippines) for shipment to South Vietnam. As a result Saigon acquired the world's fourth biggest air force, and presented a formidable military threat. If it could not win with this, could it ever win? The problem of Vietnam, however, had never been strictly military. Instead the question was also whether Saigon could win the 'hearts and minds' of the people (one of Lyndon Johnson's favourite phrases), and in this respect the record of the past was not promising. The proof was soon to come. By the beginning of 1975 the South was collapsing before a new Northern offensive, and the communists marched into Saigon (henceforth Ho Chi Minh City) on 30 April 1975. A short time before, on 17 April, the Khmer Rouge had taken Phnom Penh, while in Laos the coalition of 1973 gave way to an outright communist government by the end of the year.

RECRIMINATIONS

America's worst nightmare, the fall of Indo-China, was coming true. Soon bitter recriminations echoed throughout the land, as Americans attempted to understand what had gone wrong. How had they become trapped in a 'no-win situation'? One explanation seemed to be 'escalation', the process whereby the US had increased its commitment bit by bit and without a full appreciation of the long-term consequences. According to this theory there never had been a clear-cut decision to fight a major war, much less to pay the price necessary to win. Not even the authors of the Gulf of Tonkin resolution foresaw that someday the United States would station over 500,000 military personnel in Vietnam, and that even this would not be enough. Instead there had been a series of little decisions, few determinative in themselves but gradually adding up to a major investment of power and credibility. Eventually Washington woke up to find itself facing a choice between surrender or all-out mobilization, and perhaps even tactical nuclear war. Of course, the escalation theory did more than suggest how America had become involved – it also salved the conscience of a nation. It portrayed Vietnam as a mistake, a case of losing control. It thus was not the deliberate act of an imperial power seeking to impose its will on another country, as some of the critics contended; rather, America had the very best of intentions, but something went wrong.

While this scenario had the advantage of absolving anyone of responsibility, it did not quite fit the facts. Presidents rarely acted without consultation or study. Advisers debated the issues at length and in detail (though administration dissenters did tend to find themselves isolated and either resigned or were forced out). They may not have been able to foretell the future, but the war was hardly fought in a fit of absent-mindedness, and each new escalation was the subject of an agonizing reappraisal. A more likely explanation of US policy was that the White House, regardless of who was president, believed Vietnam was vital to American security. The United States kept sending more and more troops to South Vietnam for the simple reason that it wished to keep the country in the Western Bloc. This was entirely consistent with the American approach to other regions. The point is not that the Vietnam war was an aberration or an accident, but that it was in line with US policy ever since 1945.

To Washington, Vietnam's importance derived from its location on the West's defensive perimeter. While the French may have derived wealth from the country, this was not the Americans' main interest. Indo-China did possess natural resources of many kinds, but these were hardly enough to offset the cost of fighting the war and supporting Saigon. Nor was America's interest altruistic. There was certainly a great deal of rhetoric about bringing democracy to South Vietnam, but the reality was quite different. Even after drafting a constitution in 1966–7, the Saigon government was composed of an oligarchy operating behind a façade of representative institutions. Yet Washington supported it through thick and thin, and even when it proved resistant to American efforts at reform. When all was said and done, it was Indo-China's strategic value that was the main point, not the interests of the people who lived in the region, and it was this that explained the successive decisions to escalate.

Vietnam, Cambodia and Laos were as a consequence the site of American's biggest war after 1945. The Pentagon dropped three times the tonnage of bombs on North Vietnam as in all theatres of the Second World War combined: Europe, Africa and the Pacific. About three million US personnel served in the region, and during the same period American forces throughout the world (and including Indo-China) rose to over 50 per cent of the levels of 1941–6, at a total of 8,744,000. Approximately 58,000 Americans were dead or missing in action. Another 153,000 were hospitalized, though the total sustaining wounds of all types (major and minor) was over 300,000. Estimates calculated to err on the low rather than the high side suggest that, from the time the US assumed a combat role on the ground, over 220,000 South Vietnamese soldiers were killed, and possibly 650,000 to 1,000,000 Vietcong and Vietminh. Civilian deaths in North and South may have ranged about 400,000, but in all likelihood were much higher. Among the dead were also 4,407 military personnel from South Korea, 469 from Australia and New Zealand, and 351 from Thailand. (Most US allies, however, were unwilling to participate.) Many of the statistics are uncertain, so that a final reckoning may never be possible. Casualties as distinct from deaths were still higher, with low estimates for South Vietnamese civilians standing at one million between 1965 and 1974. Some authorities place losses of all kinds at much higher levels. In Cambodia hundreds of thousands if not millions died from the foreign and civil war as well as the famine which raged throughout the 1970s and which was exacerbated by Nixon's decision to start bombing the country in 1969. One estimate is 500,000 to 1,000,000 dead between 1969 and 1975, with perhaps an equal number for 1975–9, but more about this later. The war in Laos was less intense, but there too internecine conflicts and the US bombing took a heavy toll. In monetary terms, the Indo-China wars probably cost the Americans about $150,000 million. The commitment of resources also had a major impact on the US and world economies, contributing to inflation and the recession of the 1970s.

Despite the level of violence there were those in the United States who believed it had not been enough. In fact, within a few years the public debate ceased to be dominated by the critics of the war or even by those who sought to mitigate the blame. Many of the student demonstrators abandoned the problem once the troops came home and conscription ended, while the media moved on to other issues. Not all dissenters were silent, of course, and Congress did maintain a certain scepticism about US adventures abroad, a scepticism which persisted into the early 1980s. Still, the right wing increasingly took charge of the discussion, a fact which reflected a trend in American political life generally. These people blamed pusillanimous politicians in the United States itself for losing the war. 'Stab-in-the-back' theories began to emerge, so described because they were reminiscent of the Germans' sense of betrayal after the First World War, a phenomenon which contributed to the rise of Hitler. With enough determination, asserted the radical right, the war could have been won. Evidently many Americans persisted in seeing the Indo-China conflict as essentially a military problem, one that could be resolved with the application of sufficient force. This was a simplistic view which overlooked the social and political causes of the war and its origins in a hundred years of foreign (Western, not Soviet) domination. What this meant for America's response to future crises elsewhere remained to be seen, but Indo-China offered no easy lessons.

9

ASIA'S GREAT POWERS

France and the United States devastated Indo-Chinese society. Little wonder that revolution and mayhem convulsed the region. Yet Indo-China was also a *mélange* of peoples and cultures, and for centuries they had competed for territory and influence. This too affected the course of developments after 1945, though it is a matter we shall examine again in more detail later, when we consider Vietnam's invasion of Cambodia in 1978–9. In the present context the point to remember is that Indo-China and the rest of the Third World have their own histories. However appropriate it is to emphasize the impact of outside forces in Vietnam, there was the internal dynamic as well. In the 1960s and 1970s, however, perhaps the autonomous dimension of Third World history was more apparent elsewhere. Paradoxically, just as the United States escalated the destruction in Vietnam, Laos and Cambodia, the People's Republic of China turned inward. A rather different scenario might have been expected, though admittedly the Chinese had always been wary of direct military intervention on behalf of their comrades in North Vietnam. Yet in 1966 Beijing entered upon the Cultural Revolution and for all practical purposes turned its back on the rest of the world. To Mao Zedong events in China were far more important than what was happening in Vietnam, despite the apparent threat of American expansionism.

THE CULTURAL REVOLUTION

Mao, it will be recalled, was no longer chairman of the People's Republic after the Great Leap Forward (GLF), having been replaced by Liu Shaoqi. He still headed the Chinese Communist Party, though Liu was first vice-chairman and the organizational apparatus was in the hands of Deng Xiaoping as secretary-general. Both Liu and Deng were to the right of Mao politically, and were largely able to circumscribe Mao's freedom of action. On the other hand, Mao was not completely without power, and ultimately this proved to be the more telling point. Although the government and party were backing away from the goals of the GLF, the People's Liberation Army was still a bastion of Maoist support. Lin Biao had become defence minister in 1959, and also took charge of the communist party's Military Affairs Committee. He was the country's most important military leader, and he also seemed to be Mao's most dependable ally. Another factor favouring Mao was his prestige – he was China's founding father, a leader of immense popularity, and neither Liu nor others on the right had much to gain by deposing him outright; on the contrary, they hoped to invoke his name to justify the new course, and so wanted him in their ranks. The Liuists also valued stability and order. To remove Mao would cause serious conflict in the party and in the country, so once having taken over most (though not all) of the key posts in government and party, Liu and company preferred to leave him be.

What enabled Mao Zedong to reassert his supremacy, however, was Liu's policy of retrenchment. It played into Mao's hands by threatening to revive trends which undermined social and material equality. There were still plenty of poor people in China, and they had a considerable stake in the Great Leap's promise of a better life. Remember, for them equality meant an advance in their standard of living. Liu's policies quickly restored economic growth, but the distribution of the country's wealth remained an issue, as we shall see presently. This made it possible for Mao to play on the people's grievances and use them against the state and the party, or, more precisely, against certain people in the state and the party. Although Mao would call for a 'cultural revolution' to remedy China's ills, the grievances he exploited and the solutions he proposed were concrete and not merely a matter of ideology. In fact his answer ultimately was to create a new movement outside the framework of the communist party, which normally was the principal vehicle of political expression in the country. Mao proceeded in this fashion because the party was largely in the hands of his political enemies. In effect he temporarily established a separate base of support, mobilizing the masses directly and motivating them to attack his opponents. They did so in more literal terms than Mao intended. Before it was over, the country teetered on the brink of civil war.

The Cultural Revolution thus was the outcome of Liu's policies and the opportunities they created for Mao to make a comeback. The dismantling of the Great Leap Forward was reviving the economy by the early 1960s, but it also had social consequences which Mao seized upon to criticize Liu and the communist party itself. Although Mao later condemned him as a 'capitalist roader', Liu in fact did not propose the restoration of capitalism. The disagreements between Liu and Mao had to do with means and personnel more than goals. Under Liu agriculture still received priority over industry in the allocation of resources, the principle of government ownership prevailed in large-scale industrial and commercial enterprises, and the country remained closed to foreign investors. None the less Liu's policies did make a difference. For the right wing of the Chinese Communist Party increasing production was more important than either social equality or democratic participation. Accordingly the government moved back to highly centralized economic planning and restored the bureaucracy to its former position of authority. The result was to reduce the power of the communes to make their own decisions, making them submit to more direction from Beijing. Unemployed urban workers were also ordered to the rural areas, whether they liked it or not. In both agriculture and industry material incentives (in the form of bonuses and prizes) were emphasized to motivate greater output. Wage differentials (the GLF had not eliminated these) assured that greater rewards went to administrators, managers, technical experts and other professionals. Differentials also applied to industrial workers, and denoted varying levels of skill, just as in Western countries. In the country privately cultivated farm plots were once again encouraged, and went hand in hand with the expansion of private markets for the sale of produce. Some authorities estimate that in the mid-1960s perhaps as much as one-third of peasant income came from private rather than collectivized production and sales. In industry the Liuists also favoured the large-scale enterprises of the urban factory sector over the less efficient operations of the communes, thus denying rural areas a potentially important source of economic growth. Educators restored formal qualifications for admission to advanced studies, which meant the offspring of urban, business and bureaucratic classes once again were over-represented in the universities – the children of peasants and workers simply were not as well prepared to pass the entrance examinations.

None of these developments was politically neutral. Private plots, free markets and material incentives all contributed to social inequality in both town and country, because not everyone was well placed to take advantage of them. Some people did better than others. Moreover, the principal beneficiaries of Liu's programme were those who already possessed certain privileges: for example, they might be better educated than the average person, or they might have more resources or entrepreneurial skills. In the countryside this sometimes reflected their former status as rich or middle peasants. Alternatively they might simply possess the physical strength to work harder than other people. Whatever their advantages, certain persons were more productive, and this showed in their rising incomes. In sum, the effects of the Liu administration were to raise the spectre of a new class of rich peasants in the countryside, an elite of the skilled among workers in the cities and a restored bureaucracy in party and managerial ranks. The social trends associated with the Russian model and the First Five Year Plan began to reappear, and many people felt threatened. It seemed to them that once again a new bourgeoisie was emerging, based not on the ownership of private property, as in a capitalist society, but on income, social status and access to higher education. Minority urban interests were benefiting at the expense of the peasant majority. Here was Mao's chance. Of course, those who did benefit from Liu's policies constituted a vested interest which would oppose the Maoists, so that the scene was set for a confrontation.

Mao, however, was not in control of the government or the party, so that his problem was to find a way to implement his ideas. Of course, the party let him make speeches and offer policy papers – he was entitled to a certain obeisance, but the organization was not about to regard his suggestions as binding. The Liuist tactic was to accept Mao's ideas in principle and then sabotage them in practice. None the less this did mean that Mao had an opportunity to gain a hearing. As early as September 1962 he proposed what eventually became known as the Socialist Education Movement (SEM). Its formal goal was to revive the people's commitment to collectivism, which for Mao meant educating the masses against the social implications of Liu's policies. Because the class struggle persisted even in post-revolutionary societies, concerted action was needed to resist allegedly counter-revolutionary trends. Most importantly Mao suggested the means for implementing change: it should be done by the people acting directly, not by the party. Liu agreed with all this as a matter of theory, and so the central committee of the communist party went along with the SEM. But little of immediate consequence came of the programme. Ringing endorsements of Mao's ideas were followed by directives which had the effect of vitiating them.

Mao had not survived decades of war and revolution only to be stopped by Liu. He was nothing if not persistent. And he was not without resources, even in the early 1960s. Lin Biao promoted Mao's ideas in the People's Liberation Army (PLA). Though the hierarchical and increasingly professionalized structure of the PLA meant it was potentially as vulnerable to bureaucracy as any other institution, its roots were still in the peasantry, i.e. among the people who were the backbone of Maoist strength. Lin purged Liuists from the officer corps and instituted a campaign to indoctrinate the rank and file, and civilians as well. In the mid-1960s the army published a handbook entitled *Quotations from Chairman Mao*. The 'little red book' soon became the bible of the coming Cultural Revolution, and within three years almost a billion copies were printed.

Still, the army remained answerable to the civilian authorities and was not an independent force in Chinese society. This meant that the party remained the most important political institution in the country, even more important that the state itself. Change depended on either controlling it or somehow finding a way around it. The importance of the army indoctrination campaign was not that it was intended to prepare for a military takeover, but that it contributed to the so-called 'cult' of Mao, i.e. the adulation of Mao personally. The promotion of the cult was no accident, but a deliberate tactic to induce the uncritical acceptance of Mao's political proposals. The Maoists were making a bid to mobilize public opinion. The effect was not so very different from the way Germans had rallied behind Hitler or Argentinians behind Perón. Somehow the country's problems could be solved by a great leader. Mao later would acknowledge the dangers of dictatorship inherent in such tactics, but at the time he accepted the cult as one way of undermining the authority of the Liuists. It would be especially helpful for inspiring what Mao called his 'revolutionary successors', i.e. the youth of the country. These people presumably were open to change and uncorrupted by the past, or so the theory went. Mao even warned against tainting them with too much education, lest they become elitist and counter-revolutionary. After all, many schools were in the hands of the Liuists, so Mao worried that 'there is too much studying going on, and this is exceedingly harmful'.*

The fact remained, however, that the communist party was in charge of running the Socialist Education Movement. Not surprisingly the SEM floundered, so that something else had to be tried. And there was

* Cited in Maurice Meisner, *Mao's China and After: A History of the People's Republic* (London: 1986), 298–9.

another reason for urgency, this one personal. Mao was in his seventies, and therefore needed to deal with the Liuists before ill-health and age forced him into retirement. He had Parkinson's disease and may have had a minor stroke in 1964. He had better act while he could. In January 1965 the party approved another of his apparently innocent schemes, a 'cultural revolution'. The term suggested a renewed educational campaign, but once again the Maoists' goal was to undermine the power of Liu. The Cultural Revolution would not be fought exclusively on the ideological front. The central committee appointed a so-called 'Five-Man Group' to supervise it, but this time Mao was not about to let the party sabotage his plans.

About mid-1965 Mao left Beijing (i.e. Liu's stronghold) for Shanghai, home of the country's largest industrial working class and perhaps the most politically radical city in China, and worked from there to drum up support. In the autumn his partisans launched a press campaign against anti-Maoist satire in the theatre and in literature. To foreigners the ensuing debate seemed esoteric indeed, yet this was the beginning of the greatest power struggle in the history of the People's Republic. Events moved from talk to action in the spring of 1966. Liu seemed oblivious to the growth of Maoist support, and left on an official visit to Pakistan and Afghanistan at the end of March. This proved to be a tactical error on his part. In April, and with Liu still away, the People's Liberation Army declared its allegiance to Mao and the Cultural Revolution. The Maoists then instituted what soon turned into a general purge of the communist party in Beijing, thus preparing the way for Mao's return to the capital. Having the protection of the army was invaluable, though the events of 1966 did not constitute a military coup. The army was still under the control of the political leaders, though mainly the Maoists, not the other way round, and it may have been that the tradition of civilian control explained why Liu and company were caught off guard. Although the PLA was headed by the Maoist Lin Biao, the Liuists may not have expected it to intervene so directly in politics. But it did, and events quickened in May and June. In addition Mao's supporters took over the principal newspaper in the country, the *People's Daily*, and also the Beijing municipal government. The Maoists, backed up by the PLA, thus seized effective control of the national capital. Still, this did not automatically translate into control of the rest of the country. In many provinces and cities the Liuists held out, and soon there was widespread violence.

Events moved very swiftly, so swiftly in fact as to surprise even the

Maoists. Once having seized the organs of propaganda and the central administration in Beijing, Mao's next move was to mobilize Chinese youth. The coming rebellion was not entirely spontaneous. Mao's closest associates (including his wife, Jiang Qing) organized as the Cultural Revolution Group, and urged their supporters to attack the Liuists. At the end of May, Maoist students at the University of Beijing had put up big character posters attacking the university's administration, and events moved from there. By mid-June final examinations had been postponed, and the whole educational system was in chaos. The emergence of the 'Red Guards', however, was the most significant development of mid-1966. Composed largely of middle-school and university students, these were to become the shock troops of the anti-Liu crusade. Along with the PLA they constituted the link between the cult of Mao and the Cultural Revolution, because they gave their allegiance to Mao personally rather than to the institution of the communist party. The Red Guards were an entirely new creation, and in contrast to the army existed completely outside party control. The risk was that they might become an independent force of their own. For the time being, though, Mao apparently did not sense the danger, and on 5 August he issued a large character poster calling upon the Red Guards to 'bombard the headquarters', i.e. attack the institutional communist party, the party of Liu.* Mao meant this figuratively, but the Guards took it literally. They even succeeded in making Liu Shaoqi recant his alleged mistakes. Despite his public admission of error he was placed under house arrest and disappeared from public view in the autumn. His protégé Deng Xiaoping also fell from power.

Mao theorized that it was the masses, and particularly uncorrupted youth, who had to act, because the party could not be relied upon to reform itself. He ordered the PLA to expedite Red Guard activity, which in effect meant providing the Guards with food, lodging, and free passage on the railway system and other means of transportation. The universities and middle schools did not reopen in the autumn, and by the end of the year possibly eleven million Guards had flocked to Beijing. At huge rallies they paid homage to Chairman Mao. He urged them to travel throughout the country, and to shake up the existing party and government apparatus. Soon the Guards were engaging in mob action, physically attacking officials and others, and parading them through the streets wearing dunce's caps. Anything linked to the past or to the West

* Cited in *ibid.*, 338.

was likely to be destroyed, including museums, books and works of art. People lost their lives in the ensuing violence, and very soon the turmoil affected production. Moreover, the Cultural Revolution was spreading to the working classes of the most modern urban centres, which had the potential to push events even farther than Mao had intended. The urban proletariat had a much clearer sense of what it wanted in the way of reform than the Guards, who seemed better at destroying the past than constructing the future. Large numbers of the industrial workforce, on the other hand, took advantage of the breakdown of law and order to abandon the state-sponsored trade unions and to form new organizations of their own. These in turn began proposing programmes for building a new order, including some concrete ideas as to how the emerging working-class organizations might participate in governance. The problem was that this threatened the possibility of a Maoist restoration, and soon Mao began to turn away from his own revolution.

The Shanghai People's Commune

The main centre of working-class agitation was Shanghai, China's most industrialized and largest city, but events there were duplicated on a lesser scale in other urban centres. Shanghai had been the bastion of communist party power in the 1920s, and the site of the great strikes of the period. It was there that Chiang Kai-shek unleashed the White Terror. By the 1960s, however, probably more important than the city's radical past was the structure of its economy. It contained the largest factories in the country, and was home to an articulate industrial proletariat. The working class was by no means united, and beginning in the autumn of 1966 divided into several competing organizations. Yet these also had a great deal in common, and it turned out that this was the more important point.

Although students initiated the Cultural Revolution in Shanghai as in other cities, by autumn the initiative passed to the working class. The more radical activists tended to be those who were poorly paid or who lacked job security. There were several categories of employees in the industrial sector, with differential pay scales according to the level of skill. Not everyone was equal, despite the promises of 1949. As on the communes, a system of material incentives and bonuses had led to further distinctions. There was also a large number of temporary workers who were employed on a contract or on a seasonal basis, with many of them migrating from communes in the neighbouring countryside. Some were even day labourers. These people constituted a semi-proletariat, and did not fully share in the urban system of welfare, health and education, or in the other amenities of city life. Among their number were workers who earlier had been forced to leave the city and work on communes, but who had returned to vent their grievances. They had little in common with the lucky ones who had permanent jobs or valuable skills, and so the workers of Shanghai formed a number of organizations which reflected their differing needs. Although this meant that some groups were more and others less radical, there was also much on which they could agree, and the turmoil caused by the Cultural Revolution was just the catalyst they needed to achieve unity.

Even high-status workers supported Mao's campaign against the bureaucracy as authoritarian and corrupt. The state-sanctioned trade unions were especially unpopular, because they represented the interests of the state more than those of the population. To many people the unions were simply instruments for controlling the workers, both to mute potential opposition and to increase output. The Cultural Revolution created an opportunity for the urban working class to set up its own organizations. These soon attacked the party and took over the administration of the city and the supervision of production. Their model was the Paris Commune of 1871, the revolutionary body which had seized control of the capital of France following the Franco-Prussian War and run the city for about two months. (It should not be confused with the communes of the Great Leap Forward.) The Commune thus was an example of proletarian and democratic action and something to be emulated. For a brief moment at the end of 1966 and early in 1967 it seemed as though Shanghai might actually achieve self-rule. After a period of uncertainty the Maoists in Beijing gave their blessing, and the workers' organizations proceeded to restore order and start up the wheels of industry.

In February 1967 Beijing permitted the proclamation of the Shanghai People's Commune. Yet the establishment of the Commune occurred at the very moment Mao began to fear that Red Guard violence and confrontation with workers and peasants threatened civil war. Developments may have been settling down in Shanghai, but elsewhere there was no end to the turmoil. The Liuist bureaucracy still held out in many places, and while the Maoists were generally gaining the upper hand, the old guard seemed to have considerable staying-power. Perhaps it was time for reconciliation. Besides, there was another and equally compelling problem. In Shanghai the people seemed poised to take over power directly. The Commune did not owe its existence to Mao, but represented a new force in Chinese politics based on the working class itself. It was difficult to predict where this might end. Accordingly, even as Mao approved the formation of the Shanghai Commune, he moved to limit its autonomy. He did so by usurping the right to appoint the Commune's leaders, rather than allowing them to be elected democratically. Indeed, the Shanghai Commune lasted only nineteen days before a 'revolutionary committee' took its place. This was a new organizational form that had been taking shape at the city of Harbin and other places where the PLA had played a large role in attacking the Liuists. The committees were distinguished by a tripartite division of authority which included the new mass organizations that had emerged spontaneously in the last several months, the remnants of the battered communist party and (most importantly) representatives of the People's Liberation Army. The PLA soon assumed the job of Maoist enforcer, bringing both the masses and the party into line. As in the appointment of the leaders of the Shanghai Commune, the Maoist leadership arrogated to itself the right to proclaim the establishment of the revolutionary committees. In the context of the formal goals of the Cultural Revolution the so-called revolutionary committees were counter-revolutionary.

The army played the dominant role in the revolutionary committees, but even it was not completely reliable. Lin Biao was in charge, yet the PLA itself was by then divided between right and left. Events therefore did not immediately stabilize upon the formation of committees. Sometimes military commanders took different sides in the factional fighting that persisted throughout the spring and summer of 1967. Probably the worst incident occurred at Wuhan in July, when army factions mutinied against orders from Beijing. And in many places the population responded by criticizing and attacking the PLA. Mobs seized weapons from army depots. Even *matériel* bound for Vietnam was fair game. Anarchy loomed by August, but finally in September the turmoil began to subside. Mao, the Cultural Revolution Group, the central committee of the party, the State Council or cabinet and the Military Affairs Committee of the PLA all joined forces to issue directives empowering the army to restore peace. This was about as authoritative as any order could be under the circumstances, though sporadic incidents of violence continued well into 1968.

Too large a role for the army, however, was no more attractive to the Maoist camp than the Shanghai Commune. For the most part the PLA had remained loyal to Mao, but anything was possible in the turmoil of the late 1960s. At this time the need was to restore the communist party, purged of recalcitrants and firmly under the control of Maoists, to its former position of authority. This had been Mao's ultimate goal all along, and it was also one the premier, Zhou Enlai, had been promoting even during the Cultural Revolution. Throughout the history of the People's Republic, Zhou had been a voice of moderation, though he was also a close ally of Mao. In the autumn of 1967 Mao instituted what became the definitive purge of the party, but one calculated to accelerate its rehabilitation. Bureaucrats in need of reform were not simply hounded out of office but were sent to May Seventh Cadre Schools in the country (so called because the first one opened on 7 May 1968). There they combined manual labour with a programme of re-education. After six months to two years they returned to their former jobs, though sometimes in a different district, and at the end of 1970 Premier Zhou Enlai indicated that about 95 per cent of them had been restored to good standing.

The party's authority was assured in other ways as well. The PLA broke up any Red Guard units which refused to disband, and students returned to school by order of the party. Even so it would be a long time before the educational system recovered. In the mid-1970s, there were only a third as many university students as on the eve of the Cultural Revolution. Most importantly, the revolutionary committees became the basis for a new party organization. Finally, the question of leadership was settled once and for all, or so it seemed. Liu Shaoqi was expelled from the party in October 1968, and removed as chairman of the People's Republic. Thousands of others were accused of crimes and condemned as 'ultra-left' extremists, for having gone too far and resorted to violence against the old party. And at its Ninth Congress, convened in April 1969, the communist party guaranteed the continuity of leadership by providing for the succession. It confirmed Lin Biao as first vice-chairman of the communist party (earlier Mao had designated Lin to replace Liu in this post), and took the remarkable step of writing Lin's name into the party constitution as Mao's eventual successor.

The Fall of Lin

Naming Lin Biao as successor masked a host of unresolved issues. An opposition quickly took form within the ranks of the Maoists and questioned why the Liuists should be so easily and so quickly rehabilitated. In fact Lin was among those who opposed returning power to so many of the old bureaucrats, whether or not they had completed a programme of re-education at the May Seventh Schools. He thus moved into opposition against Mao, who foresaw civil war if a reconciliation were not effected. The scene was set for a new struggle. This time it was to be fought out according to the old rules of the game, i.e. within the councils of the communist party. It did not involve the masses of people or even the rank and file bureacracy – as in the days before the Cultural Revolution, the matter would be settled in secret, and the world would learn of the outcome only after it was all over.

Besides the leadership of the party, foreign policy also became a source of contention. In August 1968 the Soviet Union and its Warsaw Pact allies invaded Czechoslovakia and overthrew the government of Alexander Dubcek (see Chapter 10). The Russians justified this in the light of the 'Brezhnev Doctrine', whereby Moscow assumed the right to intervene in the affairs of any communist country which posed a threat to the security of the bloc as a whole. Events in Czechoslovakia seemed to be leading to another anti-bureaucratic explosion of the kind that had occurred in Eastern Europe in 1956, so the Soviets acted. The implications for China's sovereignty were clear enough, especially in the context of the long-standing Sino-Soviet split. Further, it was known that the USSR had installed nuclear missiles in Siberia for use against China in the event of war. This was by no means a remote possibility – border incidents took place with increasing frequency in the late 1960s and, as we have noted earlier, culminated in fighting along the Ussuri River in 1969. The Russians stationed about a million troops on the Sino-Soviet border, and the Chinese answered with probably an equal number. The Czechoslovak precedent, combined with the direct threat to the Chinese border, therefore inspired Mao and Zhou Enlai to develop a new foreign policy. In Chinese demonology the Soviets replaced the Americans as the most dangerous hegemonic power.

China's new foreign policy consequently required a *rapprochement* with the United States and an acceptance of the principle of peaceful co-existence with the capitalist world. In effect the latter meant that China would ally itself with almost any government which assumed an anti-Soviet stance. In due course the People's Republic established diplomatic relations with the government of Francisco Franco in Spain (still a hold-over from the fascist era of the 1930s), a military government in Greece and a dictatorship under Augusto Pinochet in Chile. Pinochet had overthrown his socialist predecessor in a 1973 *coup d'état*, so the contradiction in Chinese policy was particularly glaring. But the Pinochet affair was still to come. The most important developments in the early 1970s related to a reconciliation with the United States, despite the war in Vietnam. In July 1971 the US secretary of state, Henry Kissinger, secretly travelled to Beijing, where he arranged for a visit by the president, Richard Nixon, the next year. The first step had been taken to normalize relations between Washington and Beijing. Shortly thereafter, in September 1971, Lin Biao disappeared from sight, never to be heard from again. As Lin had opposed the restoration of the old party bureaucrats, so too he opposed *rapprochement* with Washington.

It was a year later that the story of Lin began to reach the outside world, though there were rumours concerning his disappearance before then. The presumably definitive account came from Zhou Enlai, who let it be known that Lin had been killed while attempting to flee to the Soviet Union on 13 September 1971. Lin had allegedly conspired to overthrow the government and to assassinate Mao Zedong, but the plot had fallen through. He fled, only for his airplane to crash in Mongolia. Despite Zhou's explanation the event remained shrouded in mystery, and of course this account came from one of Lin's arch enemies. It could hardly be taken as the last word.

It was just as likely that Mao had conspired to undo Lin as that Lin had moved against Mao. The outcome of the Cultural Revolution eventually placed them on opposite sides. The naming of Lin as Mao's heir at the Ninth Party Congress had taken place before their differences were entirely clear. Yet the first signs of the split had appeared at the Congress itself. Lin had proposed that the Cultural Revolution Group remain a permanent part of the communist party. The Group had been Mao's top advisory body in the campaign against Liu. But at the end of 1969 it was dismantled in accordance with Mao's wishes and as part of his programme of reconciliation. Lin's views did not prevail. The next year, in August 1970, an open confrontation between the two took place at another party meeting in Lushan. Lin proposed naming a new head of the Republic, as the post had been left vacant since the removal of Liu Shaoqi. Mao wanted to abolish the office altogether, lest Lin be the person named. Also, leaving the post vacant would strengthen the hand of Zhou Enlai. As premier he was in charge of the government administration, and Mao did not wish to compromise Zhou's control of day-to-day power. After all, Zhou was Mao's right-hand man. Lin's proposal was rejected. At the same meeting in Lushan, Lin also proposed that Mao be given special recognition in the party constitution. His idea was to give new life to the anti-bureaucratic and hence anti-Liuist principles that Mao had once so strongly advocated and that Lin still favoured.

Again, this was rejected. Yet Mao had other reasons for worrying about Lin – he was without doubt the most popular leader in China after Mao himself, and so might have a base of support in the country. Even more important, Lin was head of the army, and there was the risk that he was contemplating a military coup. On the other hand, Zhou's testimony that Lin actually attempted such a coup was fantastic. Lin had only to wait until Mao passed from the scene – Mao was old and in poor health, and within a few years (in fact by about 1973) was no longer active in the everyday affairs of the party. Lin had already been named successor as party head, so the smart strategy was simply to wait. He did not need a coup. Indeed, it is this fact which suggests that it may have been the Maoists and not Lin who did the plotting.

The Return of Deng

Thus, by the post-Cultural Revolution era, the meaning of Maoism had undergone a considerable metamorphosis. No doubt the events of the middle and late 1960s had reduced official corruption, and the revolutionary committees certainly had the potential to allow the people a larger say in affairs, both on the rural commune and in the factory. Yet it was also clear that the Cultural Revolution had not changed the fundamental social relations which had existed before the mid-1960s – in other words, it did not eliminate the class structure or alter the distribution of power, wealth and status among different groups in the population. In the countryside, for example, earnings were still calculated according to a system of workpoints instead of need. And the local communist parties tended to displace the revolutionary committees in decision-making. In the cities salary differentials remained. Temporary and contract labour still existed, while new trade unions organized the regular workforce. There was a general return to managerial control in factories, so that the principle of direct control by the workers yielded to the need for central planning. Managers consulted their employees more, but they also retained ultimate authority. Finally, the Cultural Revolution did not result in the establishment of democratic institutions in place of the authority of the communist party. On the contrary, the main outcome was the restoration of the party, but under Maoist control.

The ultimate test of the metamorphosis was still the leadership. Who actually was in charge? The question became particularly pressing as Mao's health declined. The formal end of the Cultural Revolution had not completely resolved the question of which faction was dominant. Yet a solution was in the making. In the early 1970s perhaps the most dramatic sign of things to come was the rehabilitation of Deng Xiaoping, the old Liuist. What facilitated the restoration of Deng was Mao's semi-retirement and also the support of Zhou Enlai. Deng and Zhou had been friends since their student days in Paris in the 1920s. They were also pragmatists. Zhou was committed to ending the internecine conflict of the last decade. Turmoil at home had weakened China in the wider world, and this in the face of the Soviet threat. It was time to institute what Zhou called the 'Four Modernizations', a concerted effort to develop agriculture, industry, science and defence. Economics should take priority over politics. This was precisely the view of Deng and his mentor, Liu Shaoqi. (Liu had died in prison sometime before.) In 1973, therefore, Zhou (with Mao's acquiescence) moved to restore Deng. Over the next two years Deng was re-elected to the party politburo, named the most senior of twelve vice-premiers, and made army chief of staff.

In effect Deng moved to next in line to succeed Zhou, and such a comeback would have been impossible without the latter's support. Zhou relied on him more and more, so that by the last year of Zhou's life Deng took over many of the duties of the premiership. Zhou was dying of cancer, and he wanted someone to perpetuate the policy of orderly development, especially because the leaders of the old Cultural Revolution Group (soon dubbed by their enemies the 'Gang of Four') were still around. Moreover, they had considerable influence over the ailing Mao. Indeed, their leader was Mao's wife, Jiang Qing. She and the other members of the Gang (Zhang Chunqiao, Yao Wenyuan and Wang Hongwen) had enough backing to win places on the innermost councils of the communist party at its August 1973 congress. And at the National People's Congress of 1975 Zhang became second vice-premier (one notch below Deng in seniority) and army political commissar. The struggle for control was not over yet.

The issue was joined when Zhou Enlai died on 8 January 1976. Caught between two contending factions, and suffering from the effects of a stroke, Mao used his influence to deny Deng the premiership. He supported a compromise candidate who did not completely satisfy either the left or the right. A relatively junior member of the government, Hua Guofeng, became premier with Mao's blessing. Hua was the minister of public security and sixth vice-premier, and had played a secondary role in the Cultural Revolution. Deng went into hiding, not to reappear in public until the next year. He found protection thanks to the minister of defence, who also identified with the pragmatic policies of Zhou. The problem for the Gang of Four, however, was that the founding father would not survive much longer to lend his authority to their faction. By June, Mao was no longer able to receive visitors. He died on 9 September 1976 at eighty-two years of age.

Mao's death cleared the way for a last power struggle between the radical anti-Liuists and the rehabilitated leadership. The supporters of Deng allied themselves with Hua and in October succeeded in purging the radicals from the top councils of the party and government. The Gang of Four were arrested, including Jiang Qing. They were charged with plotting to overthrow the government, although (as in the case of Lin Biao's demise) the evidence of their activities came exclusively from their enemies. Whatever the specifics, and however close China may have come to a *coup d'état* (by the Gang), it was clear that a major power struggle had been brought to a resolution. The outcome was that Hua Guofeng succeeded Mao as party chairman while remaining premier, and by the summer of 1977 Deng re-emerged as a member of the party politburo, vice-chairman of the party central committee, first deputy premier of the State Council, vice-chairman of the Military Commission and head of the PLA. The rehabilitation of Deng was part of an all-party settlement once the Gang of Four had been deposed. No doubt Deng could have assumed the premiership, but he chose instead to remain the first deputy premier.

In reality Deng had a much stronger base of support than Hua, and was the more important figure in the new scheme of things. But rather than become premier, Deng preferred to restore other leaders who had been demoted during the Cultural Revolution. He also introduced some new blood into the top ranks of party and state. It was the ascendancy of the group, not one man, which would perpetuate his policies and guard against a Maoist resurgence in the future. Thus Hu Yaobang took over the communist party secretariat at the beginning of 1980. Another sign of Deng's rising influence came on 17 May, when a national memorial service was held in honour of Liu Shaoqi. Later in the year, Hua finally acknowledged the new situation and resigned from the premiership. Deng's ally Zhao Ziyang became the new premier, while Deng and some other elder statesmen resigned as vice-premiers on account of age. But Deng and many of the others retained their party posts, which in the context of policy-making were the more important offices. The Dengists did permit Hua to remain titular party chairman, though Hu Yaobang exercised real authority.

For China the restoration of Deng meant that bureaucratic rule remained entrenched. And for the rest of the world it meant that peaceful coexistence and *rapprochement* with the United States continued as the mainstays of Chinese foreign policy in the 1980s. Finally, for the Gang of Four it was simply the end. They went on trial between November 1980 and January 1981, charged with attempting to overthrow the government after Mao's demise, and also with ordering the torture and execution of thousands of party members during the Cultural Revolution. A special court sentenced Jiang Qing and Zhang Chunqiao to death (though the executions were stayed), while their confederates were given jail sentences. Because Hua Guofeng had served as minister of public security during the Cultural Revolution, the trial provided the Dengists with an opportunity to hasten his resignation as party chairman, Hu Yaobang taking his place later in 1981. Still, Hua had not been one of the central figures in the Cultural Revolution, and he had sided with Deng in arresting the Gang of Four, so he suffered demotion, not prosecution, and became the sixth-ranking vice-chairman of the communist party. The trial of the Gang also represented a key moment in the demystification of the cult of Mao, a process which Deng had already begun. After all, the Gang of Four were among Mao's closest comrades, and his reputation suffered accordingly.

The Post-Mao Era

The new order witnessed some dramatic reversals of Maoist policy, as was evident by the early 1980s. In the countryside, for example, a system of 'household responsibility' came into effect after 1979 and undermined the production teams and brigades established during the Great Leap Forward. Instead of working the fields collectively, families and households could sign contracts to cultivate a portion of commune land almost as if it were their own. They agreed to take individual responsibility for meeting a quota specified by the government. The incentive was that any surplus above the quota became the property of the household not the commune. This surplus could be either consumed or sold in private markets for a profit. The term of the original contracts was between one and three years, but later this was increased to fifteen years in order to make them more attractive. Given the vacillation of public policy in the past, peasants wanted some assurance that the government would not change its mind and revoke the new system. Only then were they prepared to invest labour and money in developing contract lands. In addition, the Dengists increased the amount of land designated as privately cultivated plots. Whereas these once constituted only 5–10 per cent of all cultivated land, they rose now to 15 per cent. None of the changes involved the restoration of private land-holding as such, but some peasants prospered more than others. In fact the more successful were even allowed to hire labourers, though under strict government control and only on a very limited basis. The government also permitted them to take on additional jobs, and to buy such items as trucks in the expectation that they would increase their earnings.

Not surprisingly the reforms witnessed the beginnings of a new class of rich peasants, with an exceptional few earning twenty to thirty times more than the average income. Deng admitted that the strategy was 'to make some people rich first so as to lead all the people to wealth' in the long term,* but reform also contributed to rising agricultural productivity, perhaps as much as 36 per cent between 1978 and 1983. On the other hand, there were some adverse social consequences, with the peasantry becoming polarized between richer and poorer. In some instances the latter even resorted to stealing the crops of the more successful contract farmers. Rural unemployment threatened to become a problem, as some people (once protected by the commune and sharing in its profits) found it difficult to compete. The cities provided no safety valve, because there too reforms in industry resulted in lay-offs as inefficient plants were phased out. The state planners also allowed managers to deploy some profits at their own discretion: for example, to offer bonuses to workers or to invest in new technology. The changes were relative, and managers did not have the same degree of discretion as their Western counterparts. But increasingly the primary test of success became productivity, not the well-being of workers in an allegedly workers' state. The government even allowed the opening of small privately owned businesses, particularly in the service sector. Inns, restaurants and tailor's shops were typical, and the number of employees who could be hired was limited. The state did not reintroduce large-scale private enterprise, but the scope allowed small business was another sign of the Dengist concern for results more than means.

The new order was notable in other sectors as well, education being a prime example. Between 1978 and 1983 the government sent about 18,500 students abroad in a crash programme to acquire the expertise for refurbishing the country's universities and for modernizing industry and defence. Thousands of others paid their own way, so that another

* Cited in Donald Zagoria, 'China's Quiet Revolution', *Foreign Affairs*, 62 (Spring 1984), 883.

managerial elite was clearly in the process of formation. The state also expanded the educational system by establishing new institutions of higher learning. Shanghai may serve as an example. In the early 1970s the city had sixteen colleges and universities; by the early 1980s this figure exceeded fifty. China even looked for foreign investment, in order to acquire the modern technology that only outsiders could provide. In 1983 there were about a hundred joint ventures contracted with foreign enterprises, and though the Chinese retained overall control, this was even so a far cry from the Maoist creed of self-reliance. In addition Beijing designated special economic zones where foreign firms established capitalist enclaves and produced goods mainly for export. The foreign enterprises were required to pay taxes and abide by Chinese law, so that the system was not a restoration of the treaty ports of the distant past. Perhaps the most important example of such a zone was Shenzhen, near Hong Kong. For the Chinese the purpose in allowing these zones was to utilize their surplus labour and earn foreign exchange, and again to facilitate the transfer of technology. The economic zones were industrial models for Chinese engineers and planners. At the same time direct trade with the West increased significantly: US–China trade rose from $1,100 million in 1978 to $4,500 million in 1983, with comparable increases for trade with Japan and Western Europe.

In sum, the Cultural Revolution was over. On the other hand, the reforms of Deng adversely affected important groups in the population, from poor peasants unable to compete to bureaucrats who saw their sinecures endangered by the demand for efficiency. Whether rising prosperity can overcome the opposition of those threatened by change remains to be seen, so it is difficult to gauge the long-term future of Chinese politics.

JAPAN REDIVIVUS

Unlike China, Japan quickly resumed a major role in the Far East after the Second World War, though as part of an American sphere of influence. Within a generation Tokyo established what amounted to a neo-colonial presence in many parts of Asia, and also became the second largest trading partner of the United States (Canada was the biggest). The 1951 peace treaty prohibited Japan from resuming control of its former empire, but it soon became one of the most important commercial powers in the Far East. In the 1950s Tokyo established diplomatic and economic relations with its one-time colony of Taiwan and with most of the countries of the former East Asia Co-Prosperity Sphere. There was no settlement with South Korea, however, until the 1960s. Similarly Tokyo did not exchange ambassadors with Beijing until 1972, although a considerable unofficial trade had begun before then.

On the home front Japan's recovery was frequently characterized as nothing short of a 'miracle'. By the mid-1950s production had returned to pre-war levels, and grew from there. Per person income rose from less than US $150 in 1951 to more than $2,000 in 1972, which meant that the Japanese had moved ahead of the British. The gross national product rose from US $1,300 million in 1946 to almost $300,000 million in 1972 to over $1,000,000 million in 1982. To many outsiders the reasons for Japan's success seemed somewhat mysterious, mainly because they were ill-informed about the facts. Foreigners tended to ascribe the country's rapid recovery to the Japanese character, or to traditions of hard work, loyalty and respect for authority. These were real enough, because both the business and the governmental elite deliberately cultivated such values as a means of social control, and the educational system and the censoring of textbooks played an important role in this respect. Yet there were other reasons for Japan's rise from the ashes.

Behind the 'Miracle'

In the late 1940s and early 1950s Japan's resurgence was the result of three factors, as we have noted (see Chapter 2). First, the Americans feared the possibility of social revolution in the wake of defeat, and this recommended restoring the old order, purged of outright militarists, as quickly as possible. Second, the deepening Cold War (particularly the establishment of the People's Republic of China in 1949 and the outbreak of the Korean War in 1950) confirmed Washington's need for a reliable partner in Asia, which meant the United States had much to gain by helping its former enemy. Of course, the United States occupied Japan from 1945 until 1952, when the peace treaty came into effect, but permanent occupation would have diverted US troops from more important duties elsewhere, so that the need was to make Japan a contributing member of the Western alliance. Third, the old ruling class (not always the same individuals but leaders with close ties to the *zaibatsu* and other businesses) stuck together and eventually made a comeback. They soon reconstituted the government–business partnership which had made Japan a great power in the first place.

Needless to say, all three elements were related. By the end of the

1940s Washington's desire for a firmly anti-communist ally in the Far East reaffirmed the importance of supporting the type of Japanese leaders who had proven their ability to run the country in the past and who once again might make Japan a major player in the Far East, this time under American tutelage. Tokyo's contribution was to provide a base for US military operations in Asia and to produce war *matériel* and otherwise support American foreign policy. If Japan were to assume such a role, however, it needed to rebuild its domestic economy. This in turn required finding markets and raw materials, and the most likely sources were in the same parts of Asia which Tokyo once had conquered. A significant trade also developed with the United States, particularly in agricultural commodities and technology. Again, this was because Washington considered it important for Japan to prosper and become strong. In a sense Washington was breeding a competitor, but in the view of American planners in the 1950s, and even later, the Cold War was more important than economics.

American aid ($2,000 million between 1947 and 1952) played a large role in Japan's recovery, as did US insistence on a programme of economic restraint initiated in the late 1940s and designed to control inflation and especially to limit wage demands. Yet more important for the long term was the export boom driven by US procurements during the Korean War: the Americans spent approximately $4,000 million on Japanese goods and services. The biggest gains, however, came in the 1960s and after, once Tokyo had made peace with its former enemies in South-East Asia. The resumption of relations had been delayed by the question of reparations – countries invaded by Japan wanted compensation, and it took some time for specific terms to be agreed upon and for the Japanese to take advantage of the economic opportunity this offered.

Because reparations were mostly in the form of goods and services, they actually served as a stimulus for Japanese industry. It turned out that they too contributed to the restoration of Japan as a great power. Indeed, there was so much competition among businessmen in Japan for contracts that they resorted to bribery and kickbacks to obtain favourable treatment from the politicians, and Tokyo was rocked by a series of scandals as a result. Reparations also helped re-establish former patterns of trade, with South-East Asia serving as a source of raw materials. The region also became important as a market, with many nations in the area running huge deficits in their balance of trade with Japan. Japan made treaties of peace and consented to reparations with Burma in 1954, the

Philippines in 1956 and Indonesia in 1958. Trade with China also resumed, though Tokyo's recognition of Taiwan meant that Beijing would not restore diplomatic relations until the 1970s. Reparations were also a sticking-point, in that China wanted much more than the other countries of Asia. The Chinese thought this only just, because Japan had occupied their territories for a considerably longer time. Even so, unofficial trade resumed, and by 1964 exceeded that with Taiwan. Tokyo had signed a treaty of peace with Taiwan earlier (in 1952), although this was motivated by politics as much as economics – Washington wanted support for its policy of ostracizing Beijing, and pressing its allies to recognize Taipei was one way to do this.

Eventually Japan also developed a highly favourable balance of trade with the United States, its biggest customer. The Americans purchased 31 per cent of all Japanese exports in 1970 and about 26 per cent in 1982, so that the Japanese in fact were becoming less dependent on US markets (though only in relative, not absolute terms). Still, Japan's trade surplus exceeded US $12,000 million in 1982. Furthermore, the Americans tended to export large amounts of raw materials and to import manufactures (automobiles, electronic goods, iron, steel, ships). The irony was that, although Westerners had an image of Japan as unusually dependent on exports compared to other industrial countries, the facts showed quite the opposite. Calculated as a percentage of gross national product, Japan's exports were less than 10 per cent of all goods and services produced in 1970, compared to nearly 17 per cent for the United Kingdom and 19 per cent for West Germany. This remained the case, and in 1982 the figure was 13 per cent for Japan compared to about 20 per cent for many West European countries. Japan's weak point was raw materials, particularly oil. It imported far more from the Middle East and countries such as Indonesia than it exported. Even so, it had become the second largest economy in the non-communist world, after the United States.

Inside Japan itself the government played a very important part in the post-war resurgence. Through the Ministry of Finance, the Ministry of International Trade and Industry (popularly known as MITI) and the Economic Planning Agency it co-ordinated the private sector, promoted growth areas, and generally provided assistance in the form of economic research and guidance. The government guaranteed bank credit for private sector expansion, so that a much higher proportion of the financing of industry came from credit rather than shareholders or corporate revenues than in the West. This gave the Bank of Japan, the country's central bank, considerable influence over private-sector development, and no doubt accelerated the rate of expansion beyond what it might otherwise have been. The government also provided subsidies and geared the taxation system to the needs of business. Rather than invest in science and technology as much as other developed countries, however, the Japanese preferred to make licensing arrangements with industries elsewhere. Despite their eventual reputation for a high level of technical virtuosity they often built upon imported technology. This, of course, resulted in important savings while at the same time enabling the country to regain its competitiveness very quickly.

Tokyo also protected its home market with tariffs and other types of controls, including bureaucratic regulations which made it difficult for foreigners to sell in Japan. The country's very success, however, eventually undermined the rationale of protectionism. Tokyo could hardly claim that it was merely protecting infant industries until they became competitive. Moreover, tariffs and other obstacles to the free flow of goods into Japan risked reprisals from its trading partners. By the 1970s there was little choice but to relent, though on a token basis. Yet outsiders found it very difficult to compete in Japanese markets for other reasons. For example, their goods often failed to meet Japanese standards of quality, or they had higher labour costs. In the late 1970s and the 1980s, accordingly, the United States and Western Europe were erecting barriers of their own. Examples were quotas on the importing of Japanese automobiles, or requirements that goods contain a specific percentage of domestic content produced in the country where they were being sold. Still, there seemed to be a limit on how far such measures went, as Japan's customers also had a stake in reducing barriers to trade. Further, in the case of the United States, the Korean and Vietnam wars inspired Washington to press for increases in Tokyo's defence spending, the anti-war provisions of the Japanese constitution notwithstanding. It was thus important to keep the Japanese friendly, so they might increase their standby forces in case of an East–West crisis. These considerations meant that with a few exceptions (note the Nixon 'shocks' below), negotiation rather than direct reprisals tended to be the way of accommodating an economically powerful Japan within the Western Bloc during the 1970s and 1980s.

Government–business co-operation was not the only factor behind Japan's prosperity. Labour-management relations were also very important, though in ways not always well understood in the West. Private-sector managers divided the working class into the more privileged and the less privileged, and thereby helped control the cost and mobility of labour. At the top were the so-called 'lifetime', or permanent, employees, a status obtainable after a probationary period of several years. The rest were divided further into various categories of 'temporary' employees, who did not have long-term job security and received lower rates of pay. None the less, the overall result was to nurture employee loyalty to the enterprise. Lifetime employees had a proven record of conformism, while temporary workers behaved themselves in the hope of earning permanent job security. Obviously the system helped make workers pliable to the demands of management, because permanent status had to be earned. The lifetime system, however, was characteristic of only certain industries, the largest corporations, government employment (public enterprises included) and the universities. Still, even big industries might maintain a significant temporary force: about 19 per cent of all employees in the automobile industry were temporary by 1957, as were 52 per cent in one car company in 1961.

Within the lifetime system, wages varied according to years of service, starting low, peaking as workers reached their forties, and falling thereafter. The potential labour militancy of younger workers was defused by the promise of job security and a predictably rising salary, while older (and thus presumably less productive) workers received a declining salary at a time of life when they were not likely to change jobs (especially as they needed to protect their company retirement benefits). At the same time, by maintaining a pool of temporary workers, management retained the flexibility it needed to dismiss employees in times of recession. Also, large firms tended to purchase many components from the extensive small-business sector, where the availability and terms of lifetime employment were more restricted and where wages were lower. The lifetime system was by no means universal, and the links between large business and small business therefore contributed to the profits of the former. As did women. Women were about a third of all employed workers in 1972, and nearly 60 per cent of the workers in factories (of all types). Women's wages, however, averaged less than half those of men. Although most people's pay increased substantially as the economy boomed and as labour shortages developed, the distinction between lifetime and temporary employment remained, and was an important component in Japan's economic success.

Another factor in the Japanese resurgence was the country's stable politics. A multiplicity of political parties had emerged right after the Second World War, but by 1947 these coalesced into three major organizations, the Socialists on the left and two groups known as the Liberal Party and the Democratic Party. In Japan, as elsewhere, the names of parties did not always clearly reflect their politics, and the latter two were on the political right. More importantly, the two right-wing parties were to hold the preponderance of power in the post-war era, and merged as the Liberal Democratic Party (LDP) in 1955. (Remember that in Japan the right supported government intervention and central-ization, but on behalf of business, so that it did not stand for the same things as in many Western countries where it often opposed a large government role in the private sector.) The Democrats and Socialists formed a coalition in 1947–8, but this was the only time the left had a role in governing the country. The coalition was short-lived because neither side was prepared to compromise its programme beyond a certain point. The Socialists wanted change, while the Democrats (and Liberals) stood for the *status quo*. The American occupation authorities opposed the left too, and this also militated against compromise. In addition a split developed in the Socialist Party over the question of how far to collaborate with the Democrats, again weakening the left.

The breakdown of the coalition brought Yoshida Shigeru to power. He was head of the Liberal Party and had served as prime minister immediately after the war. He was acceptable to the occupation auth-orities, because he had pressed for negotiations to end the Pacific war rather than risk defeat and a possible revolutionary situation at home. Yoshida won an outright majority in the election of 1948, and remained as prime minister until 1954. It was he who facilitated the end of American occupation and the signing of the peace treaty, mainly by accepting the Security Treaty of 1951 and co-operating with US foreign policy. And it was Yoshida who presided over Japan's first post-war boom, during the Korean crisis. The Yoshida years also witnessed the rehabilitation of many former leaders, but as allies rather than enemies of the United States.

Yoshida thus reconsolidated the old order, albeit in a more democratic form as required by the Americans. Despite cycles of recession the overall prosperity of the post-war period contributed to the electoral success of the LDP after 1955, and it formed the government from the mid-1950s through to the 1980s, though on one occasion without an absolute majority in the Diet (the Japanese parliament). In a loose interpretation of the anti-war clause of the Japanese constitution, Yoshida and his LDP successors rebuilt the country's defensive and police forces, thus gaining the favour of the United States. There were even proposals to revise the constitution in this respect, and to upgrade the legal status of the emperor (under the 1947 constitution sovereignty resided in the people, not the emperor). Given the need to submit constitutional amendments to a popular referendum, however, the LDP did not press the matter of constitutional reform. Anti-war sentiment remained strong, and the people were committed to the more democratic politics of the 1947 constitution. But the LDP's proposals for constitutional change were nevertheless important for revealing its elitist preferences. As a result there was perhaps more left–right discord in the 1950s over these and other issues than at any other time in the post-occupation period. It came to a head in the proposal to revise the Security Treaty with the United States in 1960. The new treaty resulted in massive anti-American demonstrations, sometimes involving 100,000 marchers. Though Tokyo's prior consent was required, the treaty still allowed the Americans to launch military operations from their bases in Japan. It also raised the possibility of allowing US nuclear weapons on Japanese territory. The last provision was a particularly sensitive issue, but the treaty was ratified in due course, thanks to the power of the LDP in the Diet. It reaffirmed the US–Japan military alliance, and in the 1960s another economic boom mollified the opposition.

The Nixon 'Shocks'

As Japanese exports flooded the world, the United States moved to reduce its trade deficit. In 1971, and without prior consultation with America's allies, Richard Nixon imposed a 10 per cent surcharge on all imports into the USA. He also floated the American dollar. Japan was the principal target of the new policy (though West Germany and other countries also posed a problem for Washington), the idea being to force Tokyo to revalue the yen and lower its trade barriers. Yet part of the Americans' difficulty was inflation at home, some of which arose from deficit spending because of the Vietnam War. Inflation raised the prices of US exports and made them less competitive in foreign markets. The problem thus was largely American in origin, and not just Japan's fault. Still, the Japanese had little choice except to adjust the value of the yen, which made it a little easier for high-priced US goods to compete and made Japanese exports dearer in the United States. That the Americans had missed the mark in blaming their problems so heavily on the Japanese, however, became evident as Japan's trade surplus continued to rise throughout the rest of the decade.

The American decision to court the People's Republic of China also took Tokyo by surprise. Indeed, the shifts in US policy became known as the Nixon 'shocks'. Many leaders favoured improved relations with China, but resented Washington's repeated failures to consult its allies before launching major new initiatives. Some Japanese businesses had already agreed to abide by China's terms for engaging in trade with the PRC, which proscribed trading with or investing in Taiwan and South Korea. The Chinese terms also prohibited the selling of arms to the USA for the Vietnam war, or undertaking joint ventures with or becoming subsidiaries of American firms. The political left in Japan also had an interest in recognizing China, and supported the government. Still, the US policy changes came suddenly and without prior warning. In July 1971 Washington announced that Henry Kissinger had just returned from a secret visit to Beijing, and that Nixon would visit the Chinese capital the next year. Given the progress of American withdrawal from Vietnam, the Japanese wondered whether the announcement foreshadowed a US retreat into isolationism. Were the Americans making peace with China in order to reduce their role in Asia generally, and what did this mean for Japan's security?

The Nixon shocks appeared to be a rebuff to Japan and damaged the political standing of Prime Minister Sato Eisaku, who had been a firm advocate of closer ties with Taiwan. In an effort to assuage Japanese pride the American president did meet with Sato before going to China in February 1972. But Sato had to fly to the United States – Nixon did not travel to Japan. Nevertheless the president sought to patch up relations by fixing a date for the return of Okinawa to Tokyo's jurisdiction, and by promising not to make any commitments in Beijing which would threaten Japanese interests. Despite this Sato resigned in July, to be succeeded by Tanaka Kakuei.

Sato had taken the blame for Washington's apparent insensitivity to Japanese interests, so Tanaka had a good deal of political support at home for a more independent policy. In August 1972 he requested an audience with Zhou Enlai. The Chinese agreed and suggested a visit in September. Their response was far more receptive than Tokyo had anticipated, so events moved swiftly. The Chinese interest was to acquire another ally in their anti-Soviet campaign (recall that this was why they had sought improved relations with the USA). Another consideration was that Japan might serve as a source of new technology for the 'Four Modernizations' programme. Before Tanaka's arrival, therefore, Zhou let it be known informally that China was even willing to deal with Japanese companies which did business with Taiwan. In addition he offered to set aside the question of war reparations, and to acquiesce in the Japan–US Security Treaty. The latter, of course, had been anti-communist in intent. Tanaka first met with Nixon in Hawaii, to inform the president of his plans, where he also agreed to increase Japan's importation of US goods. Tribute paid, he flew to the People's Republic a few weeks later. The outcome was that Tokyo issued a formal apology for acts of war against China, and recognized Beijing as the only legal government of the country, though Zhou did not insist that Japan break its relations with Taiwan. None the less, Taipei took reprisals of its own, and severed diplomatic relations with Tokyo. Taiwan needed Japanese trade and investment, however, so that informal links continued. In fact trade between the two countries increased after 1972.

To sum up, a good deal of Japanese history after 1945 was linked to the opportunities and later the challenges arising from its association with the United States. The Americans supported a rehabilitated ruling elite and thus helped preserve the institutions which had created a disciplined and stable workforce in the past and which did so again after the war. And they accepted Japan's needs for markets and raw materials in South-East Asia and then China if Tokyo were to be a reliable partner. The result was the restoration of Japan as a great power, but, as the Nixon shocks suggested, within bounds agreeable to the United States.

THE 'MIRACLE' IN SOUTH KOREA

Westerners also cited South Korea as a case study of capitalist develop-ment and a model of Third World industrialization. American aid and troops provided security, but it was Japan which eventually played a major role in the country's rapid industrial growth in the 1970s. Anti-Japanese sentiment, due to the legacy of Japanese colonialism, delayed the complete restoration of relations until 1965, but then the Vietnam War intervened. Washington wanted Japanese recognition and develop-ment aid for Seoul as a way of relieving America of some responsibility for the country, and therefore used its influence to encourage a recon-ciliation. Just as in the case of Japan itself, the Americans regarded a healthy Korean economy as the best way to avoid internal turmoil and to prevent another crisis in the Far East. The Vietnam War was draining the United States, so Japan could serve a useful role by providing aid and investment funds to South Korea. As a gesture towards restoring diplomatic relations Tokyo came up with $300 million in economic assistance for South Korea and a similar amount in loans. More was to follow. Japanese aid was also an indirect reward for Korea as a country which was willing to provide troops for Vietnam, unlike most of America's allies. Given the constitutional limitations on Japan's defences, and the strength of anti-war sentiment in the country, Tokyo could hardly send military personnel to fight in Vietnam. Nor did the Americans expect the Japanese to do so. By helping make Seoul strong, on the other hand, Tokyo did contribute to American strategy. Of course, the Japanese also managed their investments and trade so as to create a favourable balance for themselves.

Japan thus played a major role in the rise of South Korea as an industrializing Third World country. For Tokyo, Korea was attractive because geography made it a logical place to expand. Even more important was the favourable climate of investment, though outsiders often ascribed this mainly to the achievements of private enterprise and underestimated the role of the South Korean state. From the mid-1960s on Seoul courted foreign capital, and offered incentives in the form of tax and other concessions. The state invested heavily in the infrastructures vital to an export-led economy, such as port facilities. Of particular note was the establishment of 'industrial estates', or special economic zones, where most and sometimes all duties and taxes were waived in order to attract foreign enterprises. Examples included the Masan Free Export Zone and the zones at Pukpyong and Asan Bay. The government also took effective steps to contain labour militancy. The cost of labour thus remained low compared to other Third World countries, even for skilled workers. Income inequality, however, was not as extreme as in many countries following similar strategies, and in the major cities a significant middle class had developed by the 1970s.

The problem was that South Korea had remained a right-wing dictatorship after the end of the 1950–53 war, and therefore was afflicted by continuing political turmoil. Repression simply bred opposition. After the war the South had remained under the rule of Syngman Rhee, who did little to reform the conditions that had led to a virtual civil war before 1950. The regime remained corrupt, autocratic and supernationalistic. In April 1960 major student riots erupted in Seoul and led to Rhee's resignation as president, but this simply resulted in a contest between the national legislature and the forces of order as represented by the army. The assembly attempted to reduce the powers of the presidency and establish a strong parliamentary system, but in the face of continuing factionalism and new demonstrations a military junta led by Major-General Park Chung-Hee took over in May 1961. He dissolved the national assembly, imposed press censorship, banned student demonstrations, and proscribed all political activity. Park resigned from the army in August 1963, and assumed the presidency after holding elections in October and November and thereby bestowing a gloss of legitimacy on the regime. Yet for all practical purposes Seoul remained in the hands of a military government, and former army officers took charge of most important civilian posts.

Over the next few years an opposition coalition formed around the New Democratic Party, and in 1971 its presidential candidate, Kim Dae-Jung, almost defeated Park. Perhaps concluding that his victory was too close for comfort (and facing other problems as well, both economic and from North Korea), Park suspended the constitution the next year and dismissed the national assembly. He then proclaimed the Revitalizing Reform Constitution, which allowed him to rule by decree but which also established a National Conference for Unification (NCU). This was a type of electoral college, and to no one's surprise it duly proceeded to select Park as the new president. A new national assembly was elected in February 1973, and included members of the New Democratic Party, but the government also reserved a bloc of seats to be selected by the NCU, thereby guaranteeing that Park would control a majority of seats in the new legislature. His economic policies did create prosperity for some, though it tended to be concentrated in Seoul and Pusan (by the 1980s about one-third of the population would live in these two cities) and other urban centres. Rural poverty remained endemic, and, in the face of continuing corruption and the suppression of civil rights, so did political turmoil – Kim Dae-Jung, for example, travelled abroad voicing opposition to the regime, but agents of the Korean Central Intelligence Agency (KCIA) therefore kidnapped him in Tokyo and brought him back to Seoul under arrest.

Neither Tokyo nor Washington could dissuade Park from his campaign of repression, as South Korea's role in Western defences muted the impact of their criticisms. Indeed, both the United States and Japan continued to provide aid and to invest even as one crisis followed another. For his part Park continued to rely on emergency decrees, justifying the suspension of political rights in the name of national security. Yet repression only bred more opposition, so that the security of the regime did not really increase. Accordingly, by the end of the 1970s, Park began to relent, and released a number of political prisoners (including Kim) in December 1978 and May 1979, reducing as well the jail terms of others. More prisoners were freed in the summer, but opposition demonstrations continued. Then a new crisis occurred when the head of the KCIA shot and killed President Park on 26 October 1979.

In the ensuing power struggle General Chun Doo-Hwan emerged as the new strong man, assuming temporary control of the KCIA and arresting Kim Dae-Jung and other opposition leaders along the way. After resigning from the military in August 1980, Chun was inaugurated as president in September, while Kim was condemned to death later the same month (the sentence was subsequently commuted to life imprisonment). An attempt was made to regularize the new order by proclaiming another new constitution in 1981, and Chun was inaugurated all over again. In the face of persisting domestic turmoil and international protest at the repression of human rights the president granted an amnesty to almost 3,000 political prisoners in March 1982. The government also reduced Kim Dae-Jung's sentence to twenty years, and finally decided to release him in December. In due course other political prisoners were freed as well, and allowed to participate in politics again. The catch was that Chun's power of arrest remained, and was invoked frequently, as the annual reports of the human rights lobby Amnesty International attested. Chun's strategy evidently was to improve the country's image in the West, while managing the political situation at home. As before, South Korea's strategic location on the perimeter of Western defences and its favourable climate of investment placed a limit on just how critical Western Bloc capitals were likely to be. Indeed, Japanese prime minister Nakasone Yasuhiro and US president Ronald Reagan each visited Seoul in 1983, enhancing thereby the regime's claim to legitimacy. To summarize, the story of the South Korean 'miracle' involved more than economics. The role of a frequently repressive state, acting to impose its definition of order, was also important.

A COMPARISON

The situation was not so different in North Korea. There too an authoritarian regime held sway, with the ageing Kim Il Sung surviving as leader into the 1980s. Assisted by Russian and Chinese aid, the North none the less worked towards autonomy in economic development and foreign policy in the period after the Korean War. Its aim was to minimize the country's dependency on any outside power, not even other communist countries. Neither of Kim's communist patrons wanted to see a renewal of the Korean crisis, while Kim himself wanted to pursue an independent policy *vis-à-vis* the South. Self-reliance (or *juche*) became the official ideology of the North Korean communist party, although the regime did expand its relations with the West in the early 1970s. Pyongyang apparently wanted to buy more advanced technology than was available in the Eastern Bloc, and this at a time when Western banks were offering credit on relatively easy terms. Kim gave priority to heavy industry and defence, and the result was to restore North Korea as one of the most industrialized of Third World countries. By 1970 industry may have accounted for 65 per cent of the country's national income, and in 1975 the urban areas probably accounted for 65–70 per cent of the total population. North Korea's vast mineral wealth provided a solid foundation for economic development. As unfriendly an agency as the American CIA produced intelligence reports which confirmed the record of growth.

By the end of the 1970s Pyongyang experienced difficulty in meeting its debt payments to the West, but preferred to default rather than cut back on its social programmes. Compared to the turmoil in the South, on the other hand, Pyongyang's politics were dull indeed. Although there were internal rivalries within the communist party, including the mysterious disappearances of competing leaders, Kim remained firmly in charge. He imposed a cult of personality as omnipresent as anything created by Mao or Stalin, and designated his son, Kim Jong Il, to succeed him. The regime manipulated information with incredible effectiveness, even prohibiting its citizens from listening to foreign (especially South Korean) radio. The army also provided a means for controlling the population, with the majority of young people serving for from two to five years. Kim thus achieved the kind of stability that eluded Park and Chun, mainly by being a more effective dictator. To conclude, both Koreas (not just the South) experienced exceptionally high rates of industrial growth, but in a context of authoritarian politics.

THE COUP IN INDONESIA

There was a direct connection between the role of the state and foreign investment in Indonesia as well. The world's fifth largest country by population (155 million in 1982) and rich in oil, natural gas, minerals, timber, fisheries and other resources, Indonesia had tremendous potential, but a low level of investment constrained its economic development in the immediate post-independence period. The nationalist policies of Achmed Sukarno (see Chapter 3) resulted in the expulsion of most

Dutch and Eurasian bureaucrats from government service and the takeover of Dutch-owned businesses, while domestic investment was simply not adequate to develop the country. Nor were such funds as came from the United States. It was not until a right-wing coup in 1965 that Jakarta aggressively courted foreign (mainly American and Japanese) capital. As in the case of South Korea, however, economic growth depended on more than just outside investment. It was also founded on the policies of a *de facto* military government, one prepared to deploy repression against its own people in order to create a favourable investment climate.

The events of 1965 thus constituted a turning-point in recent Indonesian history, yet few in the West understood the reasons for the army coup against Sukarno and instead saw it as the response to an alleged communist takeover. It was indeed the case that the Indonesian Communist Party had at least three million members and was a significant political force. It was the third largest communist party in the world (after the Soviet and Chinese parties), and the largest outside the communist bloc. It also played a dominant role in the union movement and in other organizations, membership of which totalled possibly twenty million. Until the coup the communists were a powerful force whose support Sukarno needed, and Western analysts feared what this might mean for the future of South-East Asia.

Indonesia's foreign policies certainly seemed to reflect communist influences, at least in the view of Washington and other Western capitals. What particularly worried them was Sukarno's ties with the Chinese. It was also relevant that the Indonesian communist party favoured Beijing in the Sino-Soviet dispute. Yet Sukarno's policies made strategic sense for Indonesia, so that to see him as a tool of domestic communists or the People's Republic was too simple. Although formally a non-aligned power, Indonesia had moved into China's orbit largely because of British plans for establishing the Malaysian Federation. These plans were finalized in 1963, and thenceforth Indonesia was stridently pro-Chinese. Neither Jakarta nor Beijing wanted a new neighbour which might continue to serve as a base for Western power in the region, and therefore Sukarno had an interest in cultivating China as a counterbalance. And the Chinese wanted Third World clients like Indonesia which would take their side against the Russians. There were territorial and ethnic considerations as well. The British decided to include their colonies on the large island of Borneo (Sarawak and Sabah) in the new Malaysia, but most of the rest of Borneo was Indonesian territory. The potential for conflict was obvious, as was evident when Sukarno applauded an uprising in the British protectorate of Brunei (also on Borneo). Still, it was not the case that he was being run by his country's communists. On the contrary, he hoped to run them, and his foreign policy followed a nationalist and not just a pro-communist strategy. Yet this was not very clear to political seers in the West.

Besides the communist party, the army was the most cohesive political force in the country. Sukarno lasted only as long as he was able to play one against the other. The threat of an army purge (perhaps similar to Chiang Kai-shek's White Terror in China) tended to keep the communists in line, while the military feared the possibility of a popular uprising and civil war should they move against the left prematurely. Sukarno's survival was also linked to his outspoken nationalism, which helped direct the communists into safe channels, i.e. away from promoting social revolution at home. Anti-imperialism was a potent way to rally their support, given the history of Dutch imperialism in the region, and Sukarno exploited every opportunity. Of course, this alarmed the Western capitals which were the object of his attacks. They did not appreciate the almost counter-revolutionary value of anti-imperialism in the context of Indonesia's politics. Sukarno also mobilized nationalism on behalf of his regime when he took over Irian Jaya from the Dutch in 1963. (Irian Jaya was the western half of the island of New Guinea; Australia controlled the eastern half until it became independent as Papua New Guinea in September 1975.) He did essentially the same thing when he played on fears of Malaysia.

There were other factors in Sukarno's political survival as well. He was an effective demagogue, and ran a strongly personalist regime. In addition the complex religious, cultural, ethnic and regional differences of a nation composed of 13,000 islands played into his hands. Although separatism was a constant threat to national unity, the country's divisions also made it difficult for a concerted opposition to form. For example, the Muslims were a major political constituency, yet no one party succeeded in winning an absolute majority in the legislature from 1949 to 1957, at which time Sukarno ended parliamentary democracy and launched what he called 'Guided Democracy'. He assumed extraordinary executive powers, and an appointed assembly replaced the elected parliament. All this happened in the context of considerable political turmoil, with Sukarno nationalizing Dutch property in December 1957 and defeating an abortive right-wing coup on Sumatra in February 1958.

Guided Democracy was hardly a gain for the left, however, because it allowed little scope for the communist party to mobilize its support as an independent political force. (Remember that the legislature was appointed.) Indeed, Sukarno instituted a policy called *Nasakom*, i.e. the strategy of unifying different groups into one grand political movement. The aim was to co-opt all political forces, including the communists, into a personalist coalition. Sukarno thus appointed communists to his cabinet, but on his terms, not theirs. Still, to many Westerners, their participation gave Sukarno's government a leftist gloss and made him vulnerable to the charge of being soft on communism, as did Sukarno's acceptance of Russian aid. The Soviet Union competed with China for the loyalty of Third World clients, and courted Indonesia even after Sukarno gravitated towards Beijing.

Yet Washington too had an opportunity to influence the situation, also by means of aid. The Indonesian army was anxious to have American help, and given his need to reconcile the military as well as the communists, Sukarno acquiesced. The most important US aid consisted of training for some 4,000 officers (including members of the general staff) of the Indonesian army. A Pentagon official later testified that the purpose in extending assistance was not to boost Sukarno's government but 'to preserve a liaison of sorts with the military of the country which in effect turned out to be one of the conclusive elements in the overthrow of that regime'.* This proved more significant than Chinese political support or Russian hardware. Washington was not satisfied with Indonesia's formal neutralism, however, and it preferred to see a government in power which was prepared to choose the Western side. This became particularly important as the Vietnam conflict deepened in the 1960s, and as the Americans began thinking of the countries of South-East Asia as 'front line' states in the battle against communism.

Sukarno's Indonesia thus was authoritarian, anti-imperialist and vocally nationalist. The government included communists yet was not itself communist, but in the eyes of the Americans it was playing a dangerous game. Many (though not all) officers of the Indonesian army agreed, especially as the post-independence economy remained sluggish. The departure of European businessmen and civil servants also left the government bureaucracy in disarray, and corruption was widespread, although the army itself was deeply implicated in the latter. And then

---

* Cited in Noam Chomsky and Edward Herman, *The Political Economy of Human Rights*, Vol. I: *The Washington Connection and Third World Fascism* (Montreal: 1979), 154.

there was Sukarno's relationship with the communist party and the People's Republic of China.

The army's chance came in the autumn of 1965. In the early hours of 1 October there was an abortive coup which the military blamed on the communist party, though the latter's role was unclear and experts subsequently doubted the official explanation. In any event, it was the excuse the officer corps needed to step in and save the country. Indeed, it was quite possible that they had concocted the alleged communist takeover in the first place, to justify seizing power. There were, furthermore, charges of American complicity in support of the army. (The precise US role remains in dispute, but Washington welcomed the change.) The outcome was that General T. N. J. Suharto established a military government, though Sukarno remained as a figurehead until March 1967 (he died in 1970). The People's Consultative Assembly elected Suharto president, and he was inaugurated in March 1968.

More revealing of the tenor of the 'New Order', as Suharto called his regime, was a bloody purge of communists and communist sympathizers. Most authorities agree that at least 500,000 people were murdered, including victims of personal vendettas executed on false charges of subversive activity. Some years later a member of the military government confirmed this estimate. Other authorities have suggested 700,000 to over a million as probably closer to the mark. According to Amnesty International, the official figure for those arrested was 750,000, and many of these (perhaps 50,000 to 100,000) were still in prison in the late 1970s. But Western capitals did little to protest. After all, Indonesia was moving into the Western sphere, so atrocities that might have been condemned if perpetrated by communists assumed a different value when committed by friends. Suharto's assumption of power brought an immediate reorientation of Indonesia's foreign policy. Soviet aid ended, and relations with China were broken. While Indonesia remained formally neutral, it did join the Association of South-East Asian Nations, a regional organization which sometimes took its cue from American policy.

The New Order represented a change in the sense that authoritarian rule now proceeded in the form of a brutal military dictatorship instead of the compulsory coalition represented by Sukarno's *Nasakom*. Suharto ended a programme of land reform instituted in 1960 and proscribed both trade unions and peasant associations. The latter policy was particularly important to his campaign to attract foreign capital, with Japan and the United States as the most important investors. Jakarta also established relations with Malaysia as another gesture to the West. In 1967 the government enacted the Foreign Investment Law to entice outside money with tax incentives and other concessions. Not surprisingly there were charges that Suharto and members of his army clique profited personally, mainly from kickbacks, bribes and the granting of franchises by foreign corporations: for example, a company associated with Suharto represented Volkswagen (whose headquarters are in West Germany), while a general owned the agency for Mitsubishi (the Japanese *zaibatsu*). In 1977 the US Securities and Exchange Commission complained of demands for pay-offs from American and other foreign companies. Foreign aid was also diverted into private pockets.

Despite an influx of foreign money, however, the results did not approach the type of highly diversified development characteristic of the industrial countries of the West. There was significant quantitative growth in sectors which were important for serving the needs of First World countries, particularly oil and mining, but Indonesia itself remained a Third World country. Further, the state-owned oil company, Pertamina, was victimized by the shady financial dealings of its own officials, and corruption affected other industries as well. By 1981 Indonesia's foreign debt passed the $20,000 million mark, and in 1982 its balance of payments deficit was $2,500 million. The ending of restrictions on imports and tight money policies at home hurt many Indonesian businesses, even in light industries which they had formerly dominated: textiles, batik, cigarettes, beverages and foodstuffs.

In addition there seemed to be no change in how the benefits of growth were distributed, so that a small elite continued to monopolize wealth as well as power. Obviously the two were related. Political turmoil therefore remained endemic, particularly at election time. General elections for the national legislature were held in July 1971 and thereafter, with victory invariably going to government-supported coalitions. The People's Consultative Assembly therefore continued to re-elect Suharto as president. But there was still plenty of trouble for the regime. Small bands of guerrillas were active on Irian Jaya and the large island province of Kalimantan (on Borneo) in the 1970s. Student riots in late 1977 and early 1978 resulted in a ban against newspapers and against student political activity. Other examples of political repression abounded throughout the post-1965 period. In response to foreign and domestic pressure the government released most of the estimated 100,000 political prisoners it held in the late 1970s, though many were either sent to remote islands (and effectively barred from political life) or subsequently placed under house arrest. Many of these people had been held without trial since the 1965 coup. Despite elections, it would be difficult to characterize the regime as other than authoritarian. In 1982 the New Order was reaffirmed when the legislature gave formal recognition to the 'double function' of the army in defence but also in social and economic affairs.

East Timor and Irian Jaya

After the coup Indonesia was not a major player in the diplomacy of the Far East, despite its importance as a source of raw materials and as a market. It was indeed a military power of some note, thanks to US aid, but Indonesia deployed its arms mainly to expand into nearby territories and to resist separatist forces. Guns were also important for controlling the political opposition, as is apparent from the discussion above. In the 1970s Suharto seized East Timor and put down a rebellion in Irian Jaya. Despite the appalling brutality of both actions, US-based media virtually ignored what was happening. Again, this no doubt was because Suharto, unlike Sukarno, was on the Western side.

Portugal and Holland had divided the island of Timor (some hundreds of miles east of Java) during the colonial period, with Indonesia falling heir to the western half when the Dutch left in 1949. The end of Portuguese rule in 1975, however, led to a civil war in East Timor between a small pro-Portuguese elite and a reformist independence movement known as FRETILIN (*Frente Revolucionária de Timor-Leste Independente*). Washington condemned the latter as Marxist, but this was a considerable exaggeration. Neither faction wanted East Timor to be absorbed into Indonesia, though it was soon apparent that FRETILIN had the most popular support. FRETILIN might very well have succeeded in establishing the country's independence, as it had defeated the opposition by September, but Suharto's troops initiated border incursions immediately, and then launched a full-fledged invasion on 7 December 1975. United States president Gerald Ford and secretary of state Henry Kissinger had visited Jakarta the day before, and it seems likely they had some idea of what was about to happen. Indeed, there was enough intelligence available for Australia to have removed its citizens, and US press reports indicated an invasion was imminent. In the ensuing war possibly 100,000 people were killed (or as much as one-sixth of the total population), with perhaps another 300,000 people interned in detention camps. This was out of a population estimated by the United

Nations to be 720,000 in 1978 but found to be only 555,000 in the Indonesian census of 1980. Whatever the exact numbers, there was agreement among the experts that the country had experienced a devastating depopulation as a direct result of the Indonesian invasion. The US apparently continued to deliver military hardware to Indonesia's army during the war, despite claims to the contrary. In July 1976 Indonesia incorporated East Timor formally and made it a province, but FRETILIN guerrillas continued fighting and controlled some territory, though in the next years their cause seemed to be doomed.

The loss of life was not so great in Irian Jaya, though in two years of fighting it approached at least 9,000. In 1977 the Free Papua Movement staged an uprising in the hope of breaking away from Indonesian rule and unifying with neighbouring Papua New Guinea. Suharto's military campaigns to suppress the independence movement raised the possibility that Indonesia might keep on marching and expand into Papua New Guinea, but in December 1979 the two countries agreed on a border. It would take some time, however, for Papua New Guinea to feel safe. Once again, all these deeds would have been likely to receive more publicity in the United States had they been perpetrated by a communist government.

A NOTE ON SOUTH ASIA

With a population approaching 700 million by the early 1980s, and often described in the Western media as the 'world's largest democracy', India was perhaps one of the most troubled as well. Independence did not lead to a major redistribution of wealth (though there was land reform), so serious social problems persisted. Moreover, the preponderance of political power remained in the hands of an English-speaking elite. With the exception of the royalty of the princely states and landlords whose estates were broken up, the same social groups as had emerged under the British remained influential. New classes of rich peasants also attained considerable political importance, as did Indian capitalist classes in both the small and the large business sectors. But corruption and favouritism in government continued, just as in many other countries.

This is not to imply that little changed in India after independence. On the contrary, Nehru abolished the legally inferior caste of the 'untouchables' and oversaw the legislation of monogamy, divorce and equal rights for women to inherit property. He created a secular state in a society deeply divided along religious lines. He contained (albeit imperfectly) the violence of the religious-communalist factions which had contributed to sectarian conflict and thus to Gandhi's assassination in 1948. Yet in other respects the post-independence government did not accelerate the pace of social reform. India, of course, had always been a hierarchical society. For example, the government still concentrated its educational resources at the university level, so that, while the professional and bureaucratic classes benefited, the overall level of literacy, especially in the villages, remained low. Only 25 per cent of the rural population could read and write by as late as 1980. And abolishing untouchability required more support from the national government than just passing a law, so probably 100 million people in this class still lived much as before. A series of five-year economic plans increased industrial production by 50 per cent in the 1950s, but to the relative neglect of the countryside, where most of the people lived. Nehru did institute land reform – the problem was that there were just too many people for the proportion of landless to be diminished by much. Yet later, especially in the 1970s, there was a 'green revolution', and India achieved agricultural self-sufficiency. In many years it even exported wheat, though crop failures sometimes necessitated purchases abroad – for example, in the early 1980s. It also made considerable strides in technological development, including nuclear power. By the 1980s India was one of the fifteen most important economies in the world, as measured by gross national product, and was one of the ten largest industrial economies. On the other hand, the per person GNP in 1982 was only US $260, one of the lowest in the world, and the distribution of wealth remained a major problem. Indian democracy also exhibited more than a few anomalies: the emergence of a virtual Congress dynasty was the clearest example. On the other hand, what Western democracies were free of anomalies, particularly the link between social position and access to political power?

Many of the country's difficulties were due to the lack of a unified political opposition. Personal, regional and religious rivalries divided those who might have offered an alternative or won a larger role for other social classes. Of course, the Congress enjoyed the advantage of having expelled the British, and so profited from the political capital this feat earned. Nationalism cemented divisions which other parties found more difficult to overcome, not that the Congress was immune to disunity or the ambitions of competing leaders. The result was not a one-party system, but certainly one-party hegemony in New Delhi. Constant territorial disputes with Pakistan and the 1962 border war with China also steeled the party. Nehru's death in May 1964 saw the accession of Lal Bahadur Shastri as the choice of the party bosses and as a compromise to head off the more independent Morarji Desai. Shastri proved his leadership during a three weeks' war with Pakistan (over Kashmir) in August–September 1965, but his sudden death in January 1966 resulted in the restoration of the direct Nehru line. Nehru's daughter, Mrs Indira Gandhi, became prime minister. She had been educated in Switzerland and the UK, and was also one of the Congress Party members imprisoned by the British during the Second World War. She thus had the connections and the credentials appropriate for a leading role in politics.

Indira Gandhi proved to be more independent than the Congress Party bosses counted on. Indeed, she remade the party, resulting in the secession of some of its most important leaders, including Desai. She also moved India closer to the Soviet Union, because her father's goal of a Third World non-aligned bloc (aloof from either Moscow or Washington) had broken down in the face of China's hostility to India. Presumably New Delhi and Beijing should have taken the lead together, and seemed on the verge of doing so some years earlier at the first conference of non-aligned nations held in Bandung (Indonesia) in 1955. The 1962 border war between the People's Republic and India precluded cooperation with Beijing, so Mrs Gandhi's policy was neutrality but with a Russian bias. In the 1960s India's need was for a counterbalance to check China, and the USSR was in the best position to provide this. United States military aid to Pakistan also drove India towards Russia. Another crisis (and opportunity) in India's foreign relations came with the breakaway of the eastern wing of Pakistan from the western part of the country. The grievances of the eastern section of Pakistan were longstanding – it had a much lower per person income, but produced most of Pakistan's exports, and yet was dominated politically by the less populous western wing. The result was a bid for separation, and in March 1971 the independent Bangladesh Republic came into being. India provided sanctuary and assistance to the Bangladeshi guerrilla forces. Islamabad sent the army to quell the rebellion, and probably ten million refugees fled to India. At the end of the year India intervened directly to assure the defeat of Pakistan's army. Obviously two governments in place of the one Pakistani state was to New Delhi's strategic advantage. On the other hand, India's detonation of a nuclear device in May 1974 was a destabilizing factor in the region. India showed it had the capacity to build an atomic bomb. The sale of Western nuclear reactor technology (particularly by Canada) had accelerated the development of New Delhi's atomic programme, and the Indian test only served to motivate Pakistan to consider acquiring the same kind of capability.

Still, India had problems enough at home, so that victory over Pakistan was not enough to assure Mrs Gandhi's tenure in office. Her high-handed rule created opportunities for the opposition to coalesce, and the new Janata Front (led by former Congress leader Desai) took shape in the mid-1970s. Further, Mrs Gandhi's critics charged her with election fraud, and in June 1975 the Allahabad high court found her guilty. The court also declared her ineligible to hold public office for the next six years. She responded by invoking a 'State of Internal Emergency', in effect suspending constitutional government. She arrested several hundred opposition leaders and proscribed most political organizations, on both the right and the left. She undermined the independence of the courts, froze wages, and banned strikes. The police abused their powers and resorted to torture, with lower-caste Indians tending to be the most vulnerable victims. Mrs Gandhi also took over elected governments in the provinces of Tamil Nadu (Madras) and Gujarat, and imposed presidential rule upon them.

The Emergency lasted two years, until it seemed safe to call a general election for March 1977. It was necessary to end the crisis and to quiet criticism, which even came from within the Congress Party. No doubt Mrs Gandhi also thought that the people would re-elect her as the paragon of law and order. Another consideration was the succession. She was grooming her son Sanjay for a political career, so it was worth affirming the legitimacy of a political system that had served the Congress dynasty well in the past. The election result, however, was a victory for the Janata coalition, though it turned out to be only a temporary setback for the Congress Party. The Janata was united more by opposition to Mrs Gandhi than anything else, and while it restored full political democracy, it provided weak and indecisive government. A Commission of Inquiry and court action threated Mrs Gandhi's political future, but the incompetence of the Janata quickly restored it. Before Desai lost his majority and resigned in July 1979, he had even resorted to preventative detention because of continuing unrest and despite his mandate to undo the abuses of Mrs Gandhi's Emergency. The outcome was a massive victory for Mrs Gandhi in the 1980 elections. The failings of the Janata permitted her victory as the representative of order and as a recognized all-India leader. Yet internal peace was never achieved, and Hindu–Sikh religious clashes were a factor in her assassination on 31 October 1984. As Sanjay had been killed in an airplane accident in 1980, his elder brother, Rajiv, became the new prime minister. Taking advantage of the remorse over the assassination, he immediately called an election, winning an unprecedented landslide (401 out of 508 seats in the lower house of the parliament) and assuring the perpetuation of Congress power.

Although it is difficult to encapsulate the complexities of the South Asian subcontinent in a few pages, there was coherence in the history of India. More successfully than many Third World countries it achieved an impressive record of industrial and agricultural growth, though foreign investment remained important and the government usually observed the strictures of the International Monetary Fund. The big problem was the distribution of the benefits of growth among classes. In the early 1980s India's most important export–import partner was the Soviet Union, followed closely by the United States and then the United Kingdom. India also imported heavily from Saudi Arabia, Japan, Iran, Iraq and West Germany, while exporting comparatively little to them in return. In the realm of diplomacy India adhered to a policy of non-alignment. In the 1980s its main foreign problems were still regional, particularly the prospect of Pakistan's building an atomic bomb and continuing high levels of US aid to the dictatorship of General Mohammad Zia ul-Haq.

Pressing problems also persisted in political and social affairs. On these the history of the post-1947 period was not notable for fundamental change. Even the Emergency failed to bring forward a new political alliance, and the Congress dynasty returned to power. Communal strife also continued, with major disturbances in the early 1980s in Assam and other states over the problem of immigrants from Bangladesh. Thousands died as a result. India also had a vital interest in the fate of Tamil-speaking Hindus in Sri Lanka. Tamil separatism gained momentum in a country where 70 per cent of the population was Buddhist and spoke Sinhala. In the 1980s Tamil terrorism resulted in terrible violence and army reprisals, with over 400 deaths in the summer of 1983. Sikh–Hindu unrest troubled India itself, mainly in the Punjab. A minority of Sikhs wanted an independent state of their own, 'Kalistan'. The Indian army attacked Sikh radicals in their holy shrine of the Golden Temple at Amritsar in June 1984, with hundreds killed. Indira Gandhi's assassins were Sikhs, and after her death in October Hindu mobs exacted reprisals. Over 2,000 people were killed in the ensuing violence. In sum, while India had experienced considerable economic development since independence, communal, separatist and political problems endured.

10

THE DEVELOPED CENTRES

The crises of the late 1960s and after were hardly limited to Asia or the Third World. Changes of equal import and drama affected the developed centres. Particularly significant for the West was the rightward shift in American politics, while in Eastern Europe there were challenges to the hegemony of the communist party. Internal crises also affected the countries of Western Europe, as waves of student and worker strikes spread across the Continent in 1968, i.e. the very same year that the Warsaw Pact ended controversial reforms in Czechoslovakia by invading. In the East, however, it turned out that Poland was to experience the most turmoil (mainly in the 1970s and early 1980s), so that the Soviet Bloc was witness to a series of continuing crises. In short, there were some major changes in the internal dynamics of the developed world. It was not just China that went through a 'cultural revolution'.

AMERICA LEFT AND RIGHT

Between 1945 and the 1970s domestic politics in the United States generally followed the path marked out by Franklin Roosevelt's 'New Deal'. Although originating as a *mélange* of economic and social programmes during the Depression of the 1930s, in time the New Deal model assumed a definite pattern. It marked important changes in American life: the rise of big government, the emergence of organized labour as a major force in politics and the economy, a limited commitment to the welfare state and minority rights, and (particularly after the Second World War) an acceptance of deficit spending to stimulate the economy. The trend was confirmed by the election of a succession of Democratic Party presidents: Roosevelt (1932, 1936, 1940, 1944), Harry Truman (1948), John Kennedy (1960) and Lyndon Johnson

(1964). Only Dwight Eisenhower's victories as a Republican in 1952 and 1956 interrupted the Democrats' reign. Yet Eisenhower's importance was that he did not challenge the basic principles of the New Deal. No doubt this was a significant factor in his election. The New Deal model thus seemed to represent a broad consensus likely to prevail for some time to come, or so many experts thought.

Then the election of Richard Nixon in 1968 and 1972 signalled the beginnings of a rightward drift in domestic politics, though the change had to be understood in its specifically American context. It is also important to note that Nixon's foreign policies departed from the prescriptions of the right wing, so that his was a transitional administration and did not represent the total triumph of the right. He was also confronted by a Congress dominated by Democrats. The point here, however, is that the swing to the right hardly meant that US politics were ever very far to the left, at least compared to other countries around the world. The range of political alternatives in the United States was much narrower than in Western Europe – no socialist has ever been elected president of the USA. Eugene Debs came closest: in 1920 he won just over 900,000 out of a total of more than 26 million ballots, or 3.4 per cent of the total.

In the United States the political alternative to the pre-Depression world was the welfare state, not socialism. Even then it was a very circumscribed welfare state. For example, the American model did not guarantee all its citizens universal health care, something taken for granted in most countries of the developed world after 1945. Instead of being treated as a basic human right, health remained a market-place commodity. This meant that the best services went to the highest bidder. The result was that health and geriatric costs in the United States kept rising, and by the 1980s absorbed more of the gross national product (at about 10 per cent) than any other country in the developed Western Bloc (including Japan). The cost of private medicine was mitigated by the efforts of trade unions to win the inclusion of health insurance in labour contracts, but union membership declined from 26 per cent of the private workforce to 16 per cent during the 1970s. Many people remained outside the union-negotiated safety net, and had to purchase health insurance from private companies. With the poorest 40 per cent of the US population receiving only 13.9 per cent of all money income in 1970 (which was hardly much improvement from the 13.6 per cent earned in 1950), large numbers of people could not afford adequate coverage. The Johnson Administration launched a 'War on Poverty', but it soon fell victim to other spending priorities, particularly Vietnam. Despite accusations of overspending and bureaucratic waste, appropriations for the programme were not even 1 per cent of the gross national product between 1964 and 1967 (i.e. at its peak). It was not the revolutionary reallocation of funds that its critics claimed, so the rightward drift of the 1970s and 1980s was relative indeed.

Still, the United States as a whole prospered after the Second World War, so that it was easy for middle- and upper-class Americans to ignore the problem of poverty. Those who shared in the burgeoning economy did not need the welfare state. These people, however, did benefit from subsidies of various kinds: for education, highway construction, government-guaranteed home loans, old-age pensions and the like. But as long as they did not go on the dole, they rarely perceived the extent to which their prosperity was subsidized by taxes. The problem was that the post-war boom resulted from very specific conditions.

'Fordism'

Economic experts appreciated that there was a vital connection between mass production and mass consumption. In other words, if the expansion of industry were accompanied by the expansion of a well-paid working class, this would contribute to the buying power needed to keep the wheels of industry turning. The need was to make the worker into a consumer of what he produced. This is sometimes called the 'Fordist' formula, because of its identification with the US automobile magnate Henry Ford. In the real world, however, prosperity depended on more than this, because managers often preferred to keep wages low in order to drive profits up. Theory and reality were not the same. Therefore it was very special conditions prevailing at the end of the Second World War which prepared the way for a post-war boom, and prosperity was more the result of these than just managerial strategy. Wartime shortages meant there was a pent-up demand for consumer goods, plus the savings to buy them with. More important for the long term, the rise of organized labour and the spread of collective bargaining meant that more workers than in the past were able to gain wage increases and thus become major consumers, which helped expand the domestic market. Although unskilled persons remained outside the post-war regime of prosperity, for many others the boom offered an opportunity to rise into the ranks of the middle class.

Still other factors figured in American economic success. Defence spending helped subsidize the private economy, particularly after the outbreak of the Korean War. Though successive governments of the United States were ideologically committed to private rather than public enterprise, the US economy was actually one of the most heavily subsidized in the world. The Pentagon committed massive amounts of funding for research, and provided a guaranteed market for industry. American contributions to the reconstruction of Europe (e.g. the Marshall Plan) and Japan had a similar effect, as it was a condition of aid that much of the money be spent on goods and services from the United States. Assisting in the rebuilding of other economies also restored them as markets for US production. The problem was that strong demand encouraged inflation, as workers sought higher wage settlements in order to share in the prosperity, and as the competition for materials and services drove prices up. Then the Vietnam war led to huge budgetary deficits and more inflation, and in the 1970s the cost of energy (particularly oil) sky-rocketed with the 1973 Arab–Israeli War (see Chapter 11). These two events came to symbolize the end of the post-war boom. Soon it was evident that the hard times of the 1970s were more than a short-lived recession, and the purchasing power of the average family declined 8.5 per cent between 1976 and 1980.

It turned out that there was more to the 1970s downswing than Vietnam and oil prices. The demand for key categories of durable consumer goods also fell off, which meant trouble for management and labour in a number of vital industries. For example, the automobile market in Western Europe and in North America expanded at about 12–13 per cent each year in the 1960s, but increases of only 2–3 per cent prevailed in the early 1980s. Another problem was the distribution of income among classes. Given that in the US this changed very little during the post-1945 period, the lower 40 per cent of earners did not help sustain expansion. In fact, there were pressures moving in the opposite direction, and these threatened to increase the already large pockets of poverty in America. Perhaps one of the most important was 'out-sourcing', i.e. the manufacture of components or goods abroad in cheap-labour markets for assembly or sale in the United States. The effect was to export jobs, and thus consumer buying power. The 1970s recession encouraged employers to mobilize against unions, using the threat of unemployment to demand concessions from labour in the form of wage-cuts and a reduction of fringe benefits. Perhaps the best example was the Chrysler Corporation. On the verge of bankruptcy it obtained major concessions from labour, and these were as important as government guarantees for loans in reviving the company's fortunes.

Labour-saving technological changes (e.g. the use of robots) also increased the power of management over labour. Indeed, this was precisely the goal of much innovation in the workplace. The effect was to force many working people from the goods-producing sector into the service industries, but these were generally low-paying. By the 1980s the McDonald's fast-food chain had more employees than the steel-making industry. In the period 1966–81 the number of new jobs in the tertiary sector (mainly health care, business services and fast-food services) increased ten times over that in the goods-producing sector.

While all these developments resulted in savings for industry, they also threatened the purchasing power of the American working class. Hamburger-makers did not earn as much as steel workers, nor did they spend as much. The result was not universal poverty, but the persistence of extremes. On the top side, the managerial elite increased in numbers, as industries became more management-intensive. By the 1980s, 9 per cent of earners in California had annual incomes of more than $50,000. This group maintained expensive tastes and high levels of consumption. On the bottom side, American goods-producing workers sometimes found themselves competing with Third World labour or forced into low-paying service industries. The result was to endanger the Fordist formula of the past: prosperity based on mass consumption. The question was whether the ossification of the rich–poor dichotomy would brake overall growth even more. It was not to be assumed that it would. Instead the extremes might persist, but with continued if slow growth. Indeed, the early 1980s trend was for the affluent to sustain the expansion of the low-wage service sector.

Politically the 1970s downswing tended to make the middle and upper classes more determined than ever to protect their material interests. The spread of poverty threatened to create pressure for more welfare measures and thus higher taxes. This was met by 'Proposition 13' in California (approved in 1978) and similar measures elsewhere. These imposed strict limits on income or property taxes in nineteen states, and were the clearest evidence of a middle- and upper-class tax revolt. The Nixon administration began to cut back on the kinds of programmes associated with Lyndon Johnson's war on poverty. A movement to remove government restrictions on business operations ('deregulation') gained momentum in the belief that private enterprise alone could overcome the recession. The argument was that business needed to be freed from government interference in order to do so. This also meant cutting taxes. The idea was that the promise of high profits would induce business and the rich to invest. This meant encouraging those who were already well off. The 1970s–1980s swing to the political right was therefore directly linked to the waning of the post-1945 boom.

Civil Rights

Another test of the US political climate was civil rights, particularly for Afro-Americans. In 1957 Congress passed the first civil-rights bill since 1875. It initiated steps to ensure that all people enjoyed the right to vote regardless of their race, but resistance in the Southern states required further intervention by both the president and Congress. As the civil-rights movement gained momentum (with mass demonstrations, marches and sit-ins), additional legislation was enacted in 1960, 1964, 1965 and 1968. The 1968 law provided that racial minorities should be accorded equal access to housing by 1970. While the denial of rights was not comparable to *apartheid* in the Republic of South Africa, the race question remained sensitive. It had deep roots in the past, and plagued American life throughout the twentieth century. For example, 126 Negroes had been lynched between 1933 (the first year of the New Deal) and 1964. There were eight victims in 1955, the worst year for lynchings after the Second World War.

It took more than laws to bring about racial equality. The evidence for this was to be found in the cities of the North and West. There the voting rights of racial minorities had been relatively secure for much of the twentieth century, but unemployment among blacks and also Hispanics was commonly double to quadruple that of whites, depending on region, gender and age. Residential segregation corralled racial minorities into huge ghettos. These were a feature of virtually every sizeable city in the United States. It was in the ghettos that moderate black leaders such as Martin Luther King lost ground to more outspoken black nationalists, such as Malcolm X of the Black Muslims, Huey Newton of the Black Panthers, and Stokely Carmichael and H. Rap Brown of the Student Non-Violent Coordinating Committee (SNCC). The more radical leaders moved away from the goal of desegregation to advocate black separatism, and some urged Afro-Americans to take up arms.

Terrible race riots scarred the middle and late 1960s, so that Americans began to fear the arrival of the 'long, hot summer', the season when most of the trouble occurred. The Watts district of Los Angeles saw thirty-four people killed and about 1,000 buildings burned during riots in 1965. Major trouble occurred again in 1966 in Cleveland, San Francisco and Chicago. Riots occurred in dozens of other cities as well.

The ghettos of Newark exploded in 1967, but the bloodiest rioting occurred at Detroit, where thirty-eight people died. About 14,000 police and military personnel were mobilized to restore order. Even tanks were sent into the streets. The loss of property in Detroit was about $500 million, mainly as the result of arson and looting. The assassination of Martin Luther King in April 1968 sparked rioting in more than a hundred cities, with the greatest trouble in the nation's capital, Washington, DC. Fifty people died throughout the country and over 20,000 were arrested at the time of the King riots. The groups most affected by unemployment, teenagers and young adults, usually took the lead. The violence tended to be contained within the ghettos themselves, and rarely spilled over into white residential districts. Most of those killed were Afro-Americans. Even in their moment of anguish they did not manage to escape the ghetto.

The Anti-War Movement

The anti-war movement also exacerbated the divisions in America and polarized politics. The intensity of the protest rose in step with the rise in the number of casualties in Vietnam and with the drafting of the university age population. The protests had deeper roots than the war, however, and were in part linked to the rise of the 'multiversity', the large university attempting to service the research and job-training demands of business and government as well as the often different demands of students. The result was the rapid growth of huge, impersonal institutions. Many American state universities doubled in size in the 1960s, and it was not unusual for single campuses to have 30,000 to 40,000 students. The civil-rights movement also spurred student activism.

The first major disruptions occurred at the University of California in Berkeley in the autumn of 1964, i.e. several months before the first US combat troops marched ashore at Danang in March 1965. The protests were initially aimed at the impersonality and conformity of the multiversity, and coalesced into the Free Speech Movement. Violence ensued and buildings were occupied. The most radical campus group in this period was Students for a Democratic Society (SDS), founded by students from the University of Michigan in 1960. On the other side were the Young Americans for Freedom (YAF), also founded in 1960, which mobilized right-wing opinion on campuses. It was the radicals who drew the headlines, however, for as the war in Vietnam escalated so did the demonstrations and the violence. By 1968 the US Secret Service was warning the president to restrict his travels, because the demonstrators posed a threat to his life. Student support for Senator Eugene McCarthy's race for the Democratic Party presidential nomination was so strong that his campaign was dubbed the 'children's crusade'. The worst protests, however, occurred at the time of the Cambodian invasion in the spring of 1970. Student strikes occurred on almost 450 campuses, and, as we have noted (Chapter 8), the Ohio National Guard killed four students and wounded eleven others at Kent State University on 4 May 1970.

The resulting grief did not bring the nation together, as construction workers in New York City (the 'hard hats') went on sometimes violent marches a few days later to support the war. Public-opinion surveys shortly reported that a majority of Americans held the student side responsible for the killings. The view seemed to be that the demonstrators had provoked the troops, and therefore received what they deserved. The Nixon White House inspired an 'Honour America Day' to counter the anti-war movement, when about 250,000 people gathered in Washington for a rally which included evangelist Billy Graham and comedian Bob Hope. In 1971, when anti-war demonstrators threatened to block rush-hour traffic in Washington, DC, police and troops responded by arresting 12,000 people. Many were detained for a few days and then released without being charged, a violation of the basic principle of *habeas corpus*. Between the ghetto riots in the cities and the anti-war demonstrations many people in the United States were ready for a dose of what they called 'law and order'. The newly found assertiveness of feminists and gays (homosexuals) only compounded the backlash.

The 'Sunbelt'

Perhaps the most important demographic trend favouring the political right was the growth of the 'Sunbelt', i.e. the states of the South and South-West. During the 1970s the population of the South increased by 21 per cent and the West by 24 per cent, while the North-East (or 'Snowbelt') grew by only 1 per cent. The Snowbelt was the site of the heavy or 'smokestack' industries (i.e. the ones most affected by industrial decline). The Sunbelt thrived on defence, aerospace and other high-technology industries, and tended to be the home base of the most anti-union businesses. The latter also opposed government intervention in the economy, but did favour high levels of defence spending. In the troubled North-East the ideology of unfettered free enterprise and self-reliance seemed less persuasive to many people.

Setbacks Abroad

Foreign affairs also contributed to the resurgence of the right in the 1970s. Defeat seemed to meet American policy on every front, encouraging a sense of beleaguerment – the whole world seemed to be against the USA. Ethiopia witnessed a revolution in 1974, which then took the country over to the Eastern Bloc. Vietnam, Cambodia and Laos all fell to communist revolutionaries in the mid-1970s. In the same period Portugal's colonies broke away from colonial rule: Guinea-Bissau, Mozambique, Cape Verde, São Tomé and Angola. The Shah of Iran fled his country in 1979, to be replaced by the outspokenly anti-American Ayatollah Ruhollah Khomaini. In March 1979 the tiny island of Grenada experienced a revolution under the New Jewel Movement of Maurice Bishop, which Washington feared might provide the Russians with a jumping-off point to the Latin American mainland. Later in the same year the pro-US Somoza dictatorship fell in Nicaragua. A left-wing coup took place in Afghanistan in April 1978, and the Russians dispatched troops to the country in December 1979 in support of a puppet government there. In the autumn of 1979 most of the staff of the American embassy in Teheran were taken hostage, not to be released until early 1981. Perhaps most threatening of all, the Russians were gaining parity in the realm of rockets and nuclear arms, and though they remained behind in some categories of weapons, they were ahead in others. For most of the period after 1945 the United States had enjoyed superiority, and it was not comforting to see this advantage disappear. The Russians suffered equally devastating setbacks in the same period, particularly Beijing's *rapprochement* with Washington and a series of crises in Czechoslovakia and Poland. And despite Moscow's successes in the arms race, the Russian economy was hardly competitive. World Bank sources estimated that by 1979 the per person gross national product of the USSR was only US $4,110 compared to $10,630 for each resident of the USA. Other authorities suggested that the total GNP of the Warsaw Pact was about only one-third that of the OECD countries. Still, these were not the best of times for Americans.

The Rise of the Militant Right

Events at home and abroad thus coalesced to provide the foundation for a gradual swing to the right in US politics. Indeed, many Americans concluded that laxity on the home front had to be ended so as to create the unity needed to meet the external threat. The rise of a militant right, however, had been in the works for some time. In 1964, for example, the right took charge of the Republican Party, though its presidential candidate (Senator Barry Goldwater of Arizona) went down to a disastrous defeat. The difference in the 1970s was that the political environment was ripe for a right-wing resurgence. This was particularly apparent on the organizational level. Besides earlier right-wing groups, such as the John Birch Society and the YAF, new groups began to appear. The most important were the political action committees, or PACs. They arose in part because of the 1974 Federal Election Campaign Act, which was an example of the unanticipated consequences of reform. The Act limited the campaign contributions of individuals to political parties, in an effort to reduce the influence of the rich on politics. Instead the law was circumvented by the formation of single-issue groups, which raised money for very specific causes and then campaigned for sympathetic candidates. As these groups were not political parties, they did not have to observe spending limits.

More importantly the PACs won the support of voters who might have been alienated by the tendency of political parties to compromise on issues. In the United States parties preferred to avoid controversy because the president was elected by a national constituency. A candidate had to please a very large number of voters (from different classes and different parts of the country) in order to win. The leader of the party with a majority in Congress did not automatically become the chief executive officer, as in a parliamentary system. When Americans went to the polls, they elected senators by state and members of the House of Representatives by district, but they all participated in electing the president (though the Constitution required that an Electoral College meet to confirm the popular choice).

For the right wing in the United States, therefore, the key to the success of the PACs was their single-issue orientation. Different groups addressed a host of controversial issues which political parties usually soft-pedalled: abortion, the equal-rights amendment recognizing the equality of women in the Constitution (it was defeated in 1982), prayer in the schools of the public educational system, Creationism (or the teaching of the biblical account of the origins of the universe in school science courses), capital punishment, the right of individuals to carry arms, the racial integration of public education and gay rights. In a nation where some authorities claimed that possibly 40 million people were 'born-again' or fundamentalist Christians, such matters were capable of mobilizing large numbers of people. For example, in 1977 the recording star Anita Bryant led an anti-gay crusade in Miami, Florida. The leader of the Moral Majority, Reverend Jerry Falwell, mobilized religion in the service of right-wing politics. Earlier, in 1969, Accuracy in Media had been founded as a press lobby for the militant right, while Joseph Coors (of Coors Beer fame) provided money to help found the Heritage Foundation in 1973. There were many other examples, and the terms 'new right' and 'militant right' became current by the late 1970s.

Politics: Nixon to Reagan

Still, the transition did not occur overnight. While the Republican Richard Nixon was elected in 1968 and 1972 and proved adept at exploiting many of the above trends, the Democrats continued to elect majorities to the US Congress (indeed, they controlled both houses of the legislature for most of the post-1945 period). It was only with the victory of Ronald Reagan in 1980 that a conservative president had a working majority in the national legislature. This was because the Republicans won a majority of Senate seats for the first time in almost three decades, while conservatives from both parties in the House of Representatives often co-operated (though technically it remained in the hands of the Democrats). The effect was to shift the balance of power away from the old New Deal consensus. As a result, in large measure, of the attacks of the PACs, fourteen notably liberal members of the Senate and fifty members of the House of Representatives failed to win re-election.

Both Nixon and Reagan favoured slowing down on matters such as racial desegregation. Indeed, the hallmark of the Nixon administration was the so-called 'Southern Strategy' to lure whites away from the Democratic Party, using the race question. This had particular appeal in the states of the South, once a Democratic stronghold, but it also worked in Northern cities where the courts had required the bussing of students from one neighbourhood to another to achieve racial integration. Both Nixon and Reagan emphasized preparedness in national defence, and wanted greater scope for private enterprise in the economy. Both favoured cutbacks in social programmes, though of the two Nixon projected an image of greater caution. On virtually all points Reagan was farther to the right than Nixon. This was particularly the case in foreign policy. For example, Nixon buried the shibboleths of the past and visited the People's Republic of China in 1972, preparing the way for eventual diplomatic recognition. He thus achieved an important coup for the US, playing on the Sino-Soviet split and maintaining the balance of global power in favour of the West. Reagan, on the other hand, attacked Russia as the 'evil empire', and broadcast the rhetoric of a new Cold War. Nixon's pragmatism gave way to a more ideological and more rigid style in American diplomacy.

The administrations of Gerald Ford and Jimmy Carter intervened between Nixon and Reagan, but it was the latter two who defined the shape of American politics in the 1970s and 1980s. Indeed, both Ford and Carter came to power only as the result of Nixon's resignation on 9 August 1974 over the Watergate scandal, when the president was caught in a cover-up of Republican efforts to burgle the Democratic National Committee's headquarters during the 1972 election. As vice-president, Ford was next in the line of succession. He served out the balance of Nixon's term, and then lost to the Democrat Carter in the 1976 election. Watergate had resulted in a backlash against the Republicans, and paved the way for Carter's victory. But the backlash proved temporary. The end of the decade marked the return of the right to the White House, stronger than ever, and the United States seemed poised on the verge of a new political era. Some political seers called it the 'Reagan Revolution'. On the other hand, the persisting crisis of social inequality and the new president's hawkish foreign policies were likely to mobilize opposition political forces, so that the prospects for the future were uncertain indeed.

THE CONTRADICTIONS OF POST-REVOLUTIONARY SOCIETY

For the Soviet Union the late 1960s and 1970s revealed systemic weaknesses worse than anything in the United States. Indeed, experts popularized the term 'post-revolutionary' to describe the USSR and other Eastern Bloc countries, the intention being to suggest that such societies fell somewhere between capitalism and socialism. The state rather than a class of private entrepreneurs owned the means of production, and so the system was not capitalist. Yet the societies of Eastern Europe were not democratic, so the population did not really have control in what were supposed to be workers' states. Presumably, transferring power from a small class of property-owners to the people at large was the point of socialist revolution, but the reality departed from the theory. A bureaucratic ruling class controlled the economy and politics.

Certainly by the 1960s and 1970s the average person was much better off in a material sense than in pre-communist times. Subsidized housing and food, free university for those who qualified, universal health care and virtually guaranteed employment (thanks to economic planning) were the norm. On the other hand, declining rates of growth meant that the overall standard of living did not come close to that of the most developed countries of Western Europe or North America. In fact they were nearer the standards of Spain or Greece, not the United States or West Germany. In 1979 the gross national product per person in Japan was more than double that of Russia (US \$8,810 to US \$4,110), and in the United Kingdom it was higher by half (at US \$6,320). Still, the social subsidies we have just noted mitigated the degree of inequality among classes in the East. Moreover, for the people of the Soviet Bloc the comparison was relative not only to the West but to the past, and it was a fact that economic conditions had improved.

The undemocratic nature of the Eastern Bloc states was the clearest departure from the theory of workers' control. There were plenty of elections, but all within the framework of the communist party or parties allied to it. It remained illegal to form independent political parties, and there was no press independent of the state. In other words, the basic pre-requisites for free expression were absent. Indeed, in Russia typewriters had to be registered, and later (in the 1980s) the private ownership of personal computers was simply not allowed. The control of political activity and of information thus departed from a democratic model.

In the USSR and the countries of Eastern Europe, however, the repression of the Stalin years (involving millions of people) eased considerably after the dictator's death. The bureaucracy itself wanted to see this happen, and the reason for this was simple. As we have already seen (Chapter 5), bureaucrats in both state and party were usually among the first victims of a purge. They had much to gain from a truce, and once Stalin was gone the trend was away from the kind of ruthless repression synonymous with his name. Fred Halliday indicates that for the late 1970s estimates of the number of Russians in jail at any single time because of their political activities ranged from 2,000 to 10,000. The US Central Intelligence Agency favoured the latter figure for the early 1980s. In 1981 Amnesty International reported that over 400 people had been disciplined for political activity in the period since 1975, and that at least a hundred of these were incarcerated in psychiatric hospitals. Others were simply sent to prison.*

---

* Fred Halliday, *The Making of the Second Cold War* (London: 1983), 140 and Note 7.

While the numbers of political prisoners declined dramatically compared to the Stalin era, developments followed a contradictory course,
because the bureaucracy was unwilling to surrender control. Political
offences no longer seemed to result in execution, as under Stalin, but the
condemnation of dissidents as demented was hardly suggestive of an
open society. The psychiatric ward or *psykhushka* was no empty threat.
Opposing the government thus involved taking risks, and the dissident
movement remained very small. One estimate for the early 1980s was
that the total number of publicly active dissidents in the USSR was only
about 1,000. Khrushchev had given considerable scope to such people,
beginning with the publication of Alexander Solzhenitsyn's *One Day
in the Life of Ivan Denisovich* in 1962, but the dissident writers Andrei
Sinyavsky and Yuli Daniel went on trial just four years later, as
did many people who protested against the Warsaw Pact invasion of
Czechoslovakia in 1968. Repression against dissidents worsened in the
1970s. The government sent Alexander Solzhenitsyn into foreign exile
(1974), while the dissident scientist Andrei Sakharov was sentenced to
internal exile at Gorky (1980). A similar fate awaited others as well.
Although about 250,000 Russian Jews were allowed to emigrate in the
1970s, they were subjected to delays and provocation. Many were
refused exit permits, and over two million remained behind (though
large numbers accepted assimilation with varying degrees of commitment, and no longer reported their origins as Jewish). In 1978 the
government prosecuted the Jewish dissident Anatoly Shcharansky as an
agent of the CIA, though he was released and allowed to go to Israel in
1986. The state of political expression consequently did not compare
well with conditions in the developed Western nations. While overt
repression declined in comparison to Stalin's time, there was no
democratic opening.

The People

The Russia of Khrushchev, Brezhnev and their successors was changing
in other ways as well. It was no longer a peasant society, but instead the
home of an increasingly urbanized and well-educated population. As of
1979, only 25 per cent of the Russian workforce was engaged in
agriculture. Compared to the United States this was a very large
proportion of the population (in the US about 4 per cent worked the
land), but in comparison with the past in Russia it was a major change.
Two-thirds of the total population had been rural on the eve of the
Second World War. The figure stood at 57 per cent at the time of Stalin's

death in 1953, but was down to 38 per cent by 1979. In the 1970s the number of rural people decreased by almost seven million while the urban population rose by nearly 28 million. It was in the cities, of course, that educational facilities and industry were concentrated. Of the four million secondary-school graduates in 1978, almost 625,000 entered university as full-time students, with many more going to technical institutes or taking up part-time and correspondence studies. Such people were indispensable to the development of a technologically sophisticated society. As was skilled labour – by 1977, 73 per cent of workers had some education beyond elementary school, in contrast to a mere 8 per cent just before the Second World War. Even so, a falling birth rate portended a decline in the labour supply. It was hence important for the state to harbour its human resources. The repressive measures of the past, arrest or exile to labour camps where only primitive work was undertaken, were not well-suited to the new times and to a society requiring an educated and technically skilled workforce. Repression was simply too wasteful, and would not help productivity.

The changes in Russian society, however, did not lead to some kind of millennium. This was because the bureaucracy resisted any diminution of its authority and privileges. An elaborate structure of labour unions existed, but workers did not have the right to strike, although sometimes they did so anyway. On the other hand, the state guaranteed virtually full employment. In a planned economy this was quite feasible. Yet full employment was a double-edged sword, since it legitimized the state's claim to authority, but also reduced the coercive power of management over labour – without the threat of the sack, how could management extract more from labour and thus raise productivity? Underemployment (highly trained people working at low-skill jobs) was a problem as well, and placed another drag on productivity. It meant the country was not receiving full value from its investment in education and technical training. Low productivity also meant that material incentives were in short supply, particularly automobiles and other expensive consumer goods. In other words, while the quality of labour was improving, other factors worked against productivity. Hence the dilemma: the productivity problem required that more be extracted from labour, but in a system of guaranteed employment and insufficient material incentives how was it possible to make people work harder?

The consequences of raising this question did not appear first in the Soviet Union, because it had the most rigid bureaucratic system in the Eastern Bloc. Other countries in the region were less effectively controlled, so the opposition was sharper elsewhere. The burden of Russian hegemony served to mobilize their people against the state as well. Czechoslovakia and then Poland became the sites of the gravest crises. The circumstances of each were different, and so must be examined in turn.

Czechoslovakia

By the 1960s the best thinking in the Eastern Bloc was that the problem of declining rates of growth might be solved by decentralizing economic decision-making and by providing more incentives to the working class. Neither of these ideas was completely new, and had been foreshadowed in the period of de-Stalinization beginning in the mid-1950s. The first involved increasing the flexibility of enterprise managers at the expense of the central planners. Furthermore, profits more than the fulfilment of quotas was to be the measure of performance in what became known as 'market socialism'. The second required giving priority to light industry and the production of consumer goods. The contradiction was that more power to management (e.g. in hiring and firing or wages) had to come at the expense of labour. The idea of reform, after all, was to produce more with the existing pool of workers. This meant giving Eastern Bloc managers at least some of the coercive powers over labour enjoyed by their counterparts in the West.

Needless to say, reform had the most support among some enterprise managers, academic economists and middle-level planners, as they all stood to gain in a redistribution of authority. Political appointees and the party bureaucracy were likely to lose decision-making power, and so many in these groups were less keen. The same was true of managers who ran older, less efficient plants and who could not compete with more modern operations. The result was a struggle to control the course of reform in most of the countries of Eastern Europe. In consequence many exceptions were made to protect special interests, and practice departed from theory, which was true in the Soviet Union as well. This meant that the impact of such reforms as were attempted was limited. Furthermore, the whole idea of economic reform was ultimately to preserve the authority of the communist party. It was a debate over means, nothing more.

Therefore in 1968, when reform led to popular demands for political change in Czechoslovakia, the Warsaw Pact decided to intervene. It proved impossible to reform the locus of economic decision-making without raising questions about decision-making in general. There was the risk that the one-party system might be threatened, and this became a source of concern to the other capitals of Eastern Europe. Just what happened?

In Czechoslovakia the impetus for reform came from the top policy-makers, those with a national perspective and therefore most concerned about declining rates of growth. Czechoslovakia's national income actually fell in 1962–3, so market socialism gained a hearing in Prague. By 1966 the government of Antonin Novotny had taken the first steps towards decentralization, instituting a system of profit accountability and giving priority to consumer goods. Yet Novotny was not an enthusiastic supporter of reform, and his decision was half-hearted at best. He was an organization man and not interested in eroding the power of the existing bureaucracy. The result was that by the next year student demonstrators took the lead in protesting at the government's half-way measures. More than symbolic gestures were needed. This accelerated the debate inside the party central committee, and by January 1968 the reform faction was strong enough to install a new party chairman, Alexander Dubcek.

While the student demonstrations certainly spurred the central committee to act, the change was not the result of a great public debate, but was fought out in the inner councils of party and state in the usual way. The replacement of Novotny in all likelihood came as a surprise to most citizens. Moreover, he had a role in selecting his successor, Dubcek, suggesting that Czechoslovakia was hardly on the verge of a major upheaval. Dubcek was a compromise candidate, the boss of the Slovak party machine and a party loyalist. No doubt Novotny intended that the new party leader should strike a balance between the demand for reform and the interests of the communist party bureaucracy. Furthermore, Novotny retained the presidency of the country.

Yet events did not stop there. Once the new leadership was in place, the next task was to define the specific content of reform. As discussion proceeded, it became evident that the ascension of Dubcek marked an important shift in the balance of political power. It favoured those who wanted wider debate and an easing of censorship. How, except through a free exchange of ideas, could an effective programme of reform be worked out? Recalcitrant leaders like Novotny became increasingly isolated. Further changes in personnel followed in March and April, with General Ludvik Svoboda taking over the presidency. The party approved an 'Action Programme' in April 1968 amidst widespread debate in the press and other media, and among politicians and intellectuals. At this point, however, working-class support was ambiguous, because labour feared that more managerial autonomy would threaten wages and job security. Scattered independent trade unions did organize and even went on strike, but most working people were not yet in the vanguard of economic reform.

From the perspective of other capitals in Eastern Europe, however, the most significant feature of the Czech reforms was the degree of debate and discussion. They doubted Dubcek's ability to maintain control, and feared the consequences for the communist party's monopoly of political power. At no time did Dubcek legalize independent political parties, though he did widen the scope for the various non-communist parties which were part of the National Front (i.e. the blanket organization which co-opted the political organizations dating back to the early post-Second World War period). Political activists did make an unsuccessful bid to form a new social democratic party, however, so that the public clamour for democracy was spreading. Opinion polls in July and August showed that Czechs definitely wanted socialism too, and by huge majorities, but to the Warsaw Pact capitals allowing polls seemed threatening in itself. Such precedents could be contagious. As early as February 1968, for example, the Polish Writers Union expressed support for the Czech reforms, and demonstrators later called for a 'Polish Dubcek'. In Czechoslovakia itself most newspapers published 'The Two Thousand Words' in June. This was a manifesto issued by writers and intellectuals, and advocated democratic reforms while promising support for the government in the event of Russian intervention.

Overt opposition from the countries of the Eastern Bloc first took the form of a propaganda campaign condemning developments in Czechoslovakia. In July, however, the leaders of the USSR and its allies issued the 'Warsaw Letter'. Romania abstained, yet it was Bucharest which inadvertently provided the litmus test of exactly what Moscow was prepared to tolerate. The Romanians pursued independent policies in the 1960s and after, dramatically increasing their trade with the West and sometimes even refusing to participate in Warsaw Pact military manoeuvres. The Romanian leader, Nicolae Ceausescu, however, maintained a tight rein on internal dissent. Given that communist party hegemony was not in danger, Moscow was prepared to tolerate Bucharest's limited deviation on other matters (though Romania never attempted to leave the Warsaw Pact, as Hungary did in 1956).

The Warsaw Letter called for the preservation of one-party rule. Dubcek's answer was to affirm his commitment to this essential principle, and also Prague's loyalty to the Warsaw Pact. But in addition he asserted the right of Czechoslovakia to manage its own affairs without outside interference. The problem was that Dubcek's response did not entirely satisfy his neighbours. For its part Prague remained circumspect, because the armies of the Warsaw Pact were engaged in exercises on Czech soil. Later in July a meeting at Cierna between the Russians and Dubcek eased Moscow's concerns somewhat, and the 'Bratislava Declaration' of 3 August seemed to indicate that a reconciliation of sorts had indeed taken place. This was intended to postpone any further moves towards a democratic opening. But when Dubcek welcomed the very independent Ceausescu to Prague for an official visit, and more importantly Tito of Yugoslavia, the other Pact members began to wonder just what kind of a commitment they had received from the Czech party head. Proposed new bylaws for the Czech communist party also seemed to allow scope for independent political factions.

On 20 August 1968, 500,000 Warsaw Pact troops invaded Czechoslovakia. Why continue to bargain with Dubeck when there was a very simple solution available? Also, the Russians could rest assured that there would be no interference from the West, because the United States was bogged down in Vietnam and the North Atlantic Treaty Organization was hardly prepared to act. It was just two years since de Gaulle had withdrawn France's military forces from NATO. In marked contrast to events in Hungary a dozen years before, Prague ordered the people not to resist with force. As a consequence there was no war as such. In effect the Russians and their allies occupied Czechoslovakia in order to preserve the undiluted hegemony of the communist party. Dubcek and other leaders were arrested and taken to Moscow, where they were forced to accept the end of Czech democratization. Then they were allowed to return to Prague. A communist party congress did meet in secret during the crisis, a remarkable feat considering that there were over 1,000 delegates in attendance. It did not order the army or the people to resist, though it did proclaim that Czechoslovakia's sovereignty had been violated. The congress concluded that there was no point in fighting the kind of losing battle which had occurred in 1956 in Hungary. In short, the end of the Czech experiment came quickly. It defined the limits of national autonomy in no uncertain terms, and confirmed that one-party rule, not democracy, was the test of orthodoxy.

There were some demonstrations later in the year, but Gustav Husak replaced Dubcek as head of the communist party in April 1969. The party expelled Dubcek altogether in 1970. During the course of the

Czech crisis Moscow announced what soon became known as the 'Brezhnev Doctrine', whereby the Russians proclaimed that they might intervene fraternally to protect their allies from the threat of counter-revolution. The message was clear, so that events in neighbouring Poland took a different course as Warsaw approached the problem of slow economic growth in the next decade.

Poland

The events of 1968 marked out the bounds of autonomy for the bureaucracies of Eastern Europe, and did so in unambiguous terms. Economic reform came second to the preservation of one-party rule. The problem was that the end of the Czech crisis did not mean the end of the region's economic troubles. The need for change remained as urgent as ever. Moreover, the success of reform still depended upon the co-operation of the working class. Labour, not management, would have to make the greatest personal sacrifices in order to raise productivity. These might entail lower wages to achieve higher profits, which then could be used for new investment and growth. Sacrifice usually involved sterner work norms, such as the speed-up and lower piece rates. It might also mean a reduction of state subsidies for food and other necessities. Subsidies strained the national budget in most Eastern Bloc countries, but consumers had come to regard them as a right. Reducing them would have the effect of increasing prices and thus eroding the standard of living.

The state wanted to achieve savings, but the result was to shift the burden of sacrifice on to the working class itself. Such changes were likely to inspire resistance. While Prague's capitulation brought the Czech experiment to an anti-climactic end, subsequent developments in Poland proceeded much farther. The bureaucracy's worst fears were confirmed with the formation of Solidarity in 1980, the first independent trade union recognized by the state in the history of the Eastern Bloc. How was it that the working class obtained such power over the bureaucracy, at least temporarily?

Solidarity did not spring into being simply as the result of what happened in 1980. Its formation was the culmination of more than a decade of crisis, and was rooted in the kinds of productivity problems which existed throughout the Eastern Bloc and which invariably seemed to raise questions about the political system. Indeed, in the spring of 1968, just as reformers in the Czech communist party were gaining the ascendancy, the government of Wladislaw Gomulka (in power since

1956) was also debating the need for economic reform. A particular target was the shipbuilding industry located in Gdansk and other Baltic ports. Shipbuilding was a major source of foreign exchange, because most of its output was sold abroad (mainly to the USSR). It was therefore a prime target for various schemes to increase productivity.

However important economic reform, Gomulka was not interested in political reform. When student demonstrations broke out at Warsaw University in March 1968, they were brutally repressed. No doubt influenced by events in Czechoslovakia, the Warsaw demonstrators were notably anti-Russian. University students were a privileged group in Polish society, however, and the government was able to exploit working-class resentments to prevent the demonstrations from spreading. It even recruited workers to help the police deal with the students. The government also resorted to anti-Semitism, an old tradition in Eastern Europe. In effect Jews were made scapegoats for the country's problems. From the government's point of view this was far safer than allowing demonstrators to blame the Russians. In 1968–9 most of Poland's remaining Jewish community of possibly 30,000 people was forced to leave. (Before the Second World War and the Holocaust the Jewish population had numbered 3.5 million.) Also, scapegoating might provide a convenient distraction from the rigours of the economic reforms soon to come. The government thus exploited the divisions within Polish society, and for the time being was successful.

The next round took place in December 1970, when the government announced major price increases. Beef went up by almost 20 per cent. There were similar increases on other food items, with ersatz coffee representing an extreme at double the old price. At the same time the price of some manufactured goods was reduced. Warsaw hoped to shift consumption patterns away from food and towards other kinds of purchases, in order to ease the strain on the much troubled farm sector. As part of his programme of concessions after 1956 Gomulka had halted the collectivization of agriculture. About 75 per cent of Polish farms were still privately owned, though in the government's view they were also inefficient. State subsidies kept food prices in line for consumers, but in 1970 Warsaw decided that this was too expensive to continue, so Gomulka cut the price of television sets and other luxuries and raised the price of food. The problem was that more than half the budget of the average working-class household went on the latter.

The price increases had been announced on a Sunday (13 December), in a vain effort to mute any protests. At the same time the government increased the salaries of the police and revised the wage structure for other categories of workers, though unfavourably in the latter case. The result was a wave of strikes on Monday, beginning in the Gdansk shipyards. The demonstrations spread rapidly to other cities. Violence ensued on a scale not seen since the invasion of Hungary in 1956. People were killed, and the communist party headquarters in Gdansk was burned down. Besides Gdansk, Szczecin and Gdynia (shipbuilding), Lodz (textiles) and Nova Nuta (steel) witnessed major trouble. By the time the crisis was over, official estimates placed the number of dead at forty-five and the injured at 1,165. The unofficial estimates were that hundreds died (with thousands more injured), and these were probably the more accurate figures.

Almost from the start workers' committees began to organize, and immediately turned from workplace issues to political questions, which was precisely what the communist party hierarchy wanted to avoid. Gomulka had lost control of the situation. It was time for a new leader, and Edward Gierek took over on 20 December. The government promised to freeze food prices for two years (though at the new levels), and to provide extra assistance to low-income families. But Gierek did not concede anything else, and in January more trouble occurred at Szczecin and Gdansk. The situation was so serious that Gierek took the extraordinary step of meeting in person with angry workers in both cities. The session at Szczecin lasted nine hours. The outcome was a truce, as some workers favoured allowing the new government a chance to prove itself. Hence it took another strike, this time at Lodz, before Gierek finally agreed to a roll-back in prices. He did so on 15 February 1971, thanks to a timely infusion of economic aid from the Soviet Union. More importantly, the government could see that divisions were appearing in the strikers' ranks, and that it might be wise to take advantage of them. Given the strikes of the preceding three months, many workers were in desperate financial straits. It was therefore difficult for the strike committees to maintain unity, as many in their ranks needed to go back to work and collect a pay-cheque. If concessions would speed up the disbanding of the workers' committees, then the government was pleased to oblige.

Working-class action had brought down the Gomulka government and forced Gierek to make concessions, but it had not resulted in a new structure of authority. In other words, the communist party still monopolized decision-making, and no permanent working-class organizations survived the events of 1970–71. Still, the matter was bound to arise again, because the country's economic problems persisted. Sooner or later Gierek would have to reopen the questions that had led to Gomulka's downfall.

Five years passed before the government made its next move. Several reasons allowed it to postpone the day of reckoning as long as it did. First, there was Soviet aid. Second, the Western banking community offered easy credit, and this enabled the government to finance the expansion of the industrial sector and the purchase of new technology. In other words, Gierek found a way to increase productivity without demanding sacrifices from the working class. Third, while new markets were difficult to find, the markets for Poland's traditional exports (especially coal) were strong in the early 1970s. The result was that the country seemed to be prospering. Official estimates were that real wages increased by 40 per cent during the period 1970–75.

Yet the gloss of prosperity proved thin indeed. Rising incomes went mainly on increased consumption of food. Because the government subsidized the farm sector, the rising demand for food strained the national budget. Both food and fodder had to be imported. There were other problems as well. By 1973–4 the Western economy entered a period of protracted recession, so that the markets for Poland's exports began to weaken. At the same time the prices of Western imports kept rising, as did the cost of servicing the country's international debts. (In 1973 indebtedness to the West was only $2,500 million, but this would rise to $11,000 million by 1976.) In sum, Gierek could no longer postpone what were likely to be some very unpopular measures.

In June 1976 the government announced a new round of price increases. Rises in the cost of meat were to be around 60 per cent, and estimates were that the total effect of this and other increases would have been to raise the cost of living by about 16 per cent. Instantly strikes spread throughout the country, in fact so rapidly that the government withdrew the increases within a day. A new crisis on the scale of 1970–71 might result in renewed efforts to create working-class organizations, and Gierek was not prepared to risk this. It was not entirely up to him, however, and in September 1976 a group of dissident intellectuals organized to defend workers against official reprisals for the strikes of June, and to publicize government abuses of power. In 1977 the original committee was expanded and assumed a more general mandate to protect all of society. It represented precisely the kind of alliance of workers and other classes which the government had successfully prevented up to this point.

The Roman Catholic Church also sided with the victims of re-pression, and this too made a difference. Of necessity the church had come to terms with the communist government after the Second World War, but this also meant that it had survived. While the church had to accept restrictions on its pastoral role, it was one of the few institutions in Poland whose authority did not derive from the state. It thus became a rallying point for strikers and others who opposed government policy. However much the church may have compromised in the past, by the 1970s it was in a unique position to speak up for the victims, although it could not provide them with sanctuary in any strict sense. Still, the role of the church meant that the opponents of the regime had a little more scope in Poland than elsewhere in Eastern Europe.

The 1976 truce could not last. By 1980 Poland's debt to the West was over $17,000 million, so that it required most of the country's export earnings just to keep up with the interest. The cost of subsidizing the agricultural sector was as high as ever, and the sluggish economy in the West continued to wreak havoc on Gierek's export strategy. The government needed to do something, and this time it needed to succeed. On 1 July 1980 a seemingly inevitable announcement decreed new price increases. Meat went up by 100 per cent. Strikes began, with the Gdansk shipyards in the vanguard. This time the government's strategy was different. Rather than roll back prices, it negotiated pay increases factory by factory that ranged between 10 and 15 per cent. The idea was to keep the workers divided, and to concede local settlements before strike committees had a chance to co-ordinate city-wide or regional responses. While pay increases would mitigate the impact of the price increases, they would not cancel out the overall effect in the long run. Just as importantly, by settling quickly on pay, the government might keep the strike committees from raising political questions.

The only problem for the government was that its strategy did not work. The 1970 and 1976 crises meant that Poland's working class had considerable political experience. Their leaders were beginning to appreciate the importance of a co-ordinated effort, particularly the need to create regional and then national networks of strike committees.

At first it did not appear that the government would be able to defend its monopoly of political power. On 14 August a sit-down strike began at the Lenin Shipyards in Gdansk, where a storm had been gathering for several weeks. The next day the Russians announced Warsaw Pact manoeuvres for East Germany and the Baltic region. At the Lenin Shipyards the Polish government attempted to manage the situation by offering substantial pay increases but no union recognition. In other words, it attempted the same tactic that had worked elsewhere. Initially the leader of the Lenin Shipyard strikers, Lech Walesa, was reluctantly prepared to accept the offer. But he soon encountered the objections of the various inter-factory strike committees then in the process of formation. Their representatives saw the need for unity in the face of the government strategy of divide and rule. Walesa therefore backed away from a settlement. On 17 August the church staged a Mass at the gates of the Lenin Shipyards, while the bishop of Gdansk sent medals of the Polish pope, John Paul II, to the strike committee. This was the kind of symbolic act that gave pause to the state officials.

As events gained momentum, Walesa emerged as leader of the newly formed Gdansk inter-factory strike committee as well as the representative of the Lenin Shipyards. Soon there were about 1,000 delegates in the organization. Walesa thus spoke for the union movement in the entire region. Another wave of strikes spread along the Baltic coast, and inter-factory committees began to take form in Szczecin and elsewhere. By 21 August the deputy prime minister, Mieczyslaw Jagielski, took over as the government negotiator, but the strikers would not compromise. During the next week the prime minister, Edward Babiuch, was dismissed, though Gierek survived as party head for the time being. The strikers clearly were gaining the initiative.

The key to the strikers' new-found power was unity. Individual strike committees were no longer settling on their own, but were joining together to form inter-factory committees. This gave them the power to close down the country's economy, so that it became possible to hold out for some sort of national or at least regional agreement. The result was a dramatic increase in the power of the working class, and on 31 August 1980 the government finally assented to the Gdansk Accords. These recognized the workers' right to form an independent union, the right to strike, better working conditions, no work on Saturdays, permission for the church to broadcast Masses on the radio, less censorship and an easing of political controls of other kinds. Agreements followed with other strikers elsewhere, and in mid-September the government conceded that the same terms would apply throughout the country.

Solidarity

Because the government could not postpone action on the country's economic problems any longer, it was forced to deal with the new unions, which on 22 September united under the name Solidarity (*Solidarnosc*). It understood the revolutionary implications of doing so and therefore proceeded with caution, a fact which no doubt kept the Russians at bay. If the Polish communist party could find a way to recoup its losses, then Moscow would leave well enough alone. The Russians recognized the depth of the crisis, and that it would be a delicate task to restore the old order. They also knew the depth of Polish nationalism, and that military intervention would be a violent affair indeed. Furthermore, in the short run, intervention would do little to alleviate the country's economic problems. It would be much less costly to let Poles deal with Poles. Besides, the Soviet Union was entangled in a war in Afghanistan. Moscow did not relish the possibility of fighting on two fronts. The danger of Russian intervention was not to be discounted completely, however, and seemed imminent in December when Moscow ordered additional military exercises. This placed limits on what the unionists could hope to accomplish. In fact it was in the interest of Poland's workers to co-operate with the government once they had gained recognition, precisely in order to prevent Russian interference. This, of course, was a plus for Warsaw in dealing with Solidarity, and the government continued to arrest selected union activists and to provoke confrontations in various factories (for example, over lengthening the working week). It needed to show that it was still in charge.

Moscow's preference to avoid intervention thus was a vote of confidence in the leadership of the Polish communist party. Although the party was divided, the Russians were betting that its leaders understood the lessons of 1968 and Czechoslovakia. On 5 September bad health provided an excuse for the removal of Gierek. Stanislaw Kania took over as party head, and in February 1981 the defence minister, General Wojciech Jaruzelski, became prime minister. Both were acceptable to Moscow, and there were regular consultations between the two capitals.

Once again, however, the country's problems did not go away just because new leaders took charge. When the government resisted demands for the establishment of a Rural Solidarity for farmers, serious trouble broke out at Rzeszow in January and February and at Bydgoszcz in March. Students wanted a union also. Another round of Warsaw Pact manoeuvres began in March, and again it seemed as if the Russians might act. The situation cooled when Walesa agreed to suspend a general strike scheduled for 31 March in support of Rural Solidarity. The decision to retreat caused a rift within Solidarity itself, as many other leaders opposed Walesa's willingness to compromise. Later in the spring, however, the supreme court did officially register Rural Solidarity as a legal organization.

Meanwhile the disruption of the past several months meant that there were shortages of raw materials, which in turn led to factory closures, unemployment and also shortages of essential consumer goods. Exports fell off, so Poland could not pay for imports of food and fodder, and this contributed to shortages of the most common foodstuffs. The result was still more agitation, as people protested. By the summer the economic situation was out of control, and the national income had fallen to about 75 per cent of the 1978 level. The government was under a great deal of pressure, and in the background were the ever-present Russians.

Accordingly the government decided on a new approach to Solidarity. The workers would have to be persuaded that they must help save the economy. It was important to achieve this through negotiation, however, because approximately one-third of communist party members were also members of Solidarity. In other words, there was a delicate balance of power in the communist party itself, so that it would be best to avoid brutal repression. That the party was drifting dangerously, however, became evident at its congress in July. Kania was confirmed as head, but by means of a secret ballot. Such a practice was hardly the Eastern Bloc norm, and it suggested that Poland might go the way of Czechoslovakia. The Russians watched with increasing apprehension.

The government wanted the workers to make more sacrifices, and therefore needed the support of Solidarity. By the autumn of 1981 the union's members probably numbered eight million or more (out of a total population of 35 million). In return for their co-operation Solidarity insisted on a say in management. The union leadership favoured co-operating with the government because the economy was in serious trouble, but the risk, of course, was that they would become mere collaborators, subordinating their demands to those of the state. At its first national congress in September and October, Solidarity agreed to a managerial role in principle, with the specifics subject to further negotiation, but the union was badly split. The more radical delegates wanted a national referendum to choose between Solidarity's management proposals and those of the government, but the Solidarity executive voted to forgo this. In effect the leadership was more inclined to compromise with the government than many of the delegates. As a result some of the latter criticized Solidarity itself for failing to follow democratic procedures, but the compromisers feared that the regime might take reprisals unless they co-operated. The congress confirmed Walesa as the leader of Solidarity, though by only 55 per cent of the vote.

In the meantime Solidarity and the government engaged in negotiations. Yet the government was more and more inclined to take a hard line on the management question, and early in October announced price increases on food and also tobacco, though it agreed to a roll-back while talks continued. If this were not bad enough, Walesa faced a new leader at the head of the communist party. For months the Russians had wanted to be rid of Kania, and finally in October he resigned. General Jaruzelski took over as party head, while continuing as prime minister and minister of defence. Although Jaruzelski was identified with the moderates, it was also the case that the drift towards democracy evident at the communist party congress of July had come to an end. No party congress voted him into office. With the church acting as mediator, Jaruzelski and Walesa staged a summit meeting on 4 November 1981. A few days later the government proposed a council, or 'Front of National Accord', but with only one out of seven seats reserved for Solidarity. Walesa wanted much more, including a larger role in economic policy, access to the media and more democratic government. The general was not about to allow an independent union to assume any real power, and so further talks between the government and Solidarity became stalemated by the end of November. Any other outcome would have been revolutionary, and would have threatened the leading role of the communist party. No doubt it also would have invited Russian intervention.

Worker and student strikes had escalated throughout the autumn. Early in December, Rural Solidarity proposed a merger with Solidarity and with the student organizations. By this time there were student strikes at seventy out of 104 universities and institutes throughout the country, as well as major new strikes in industry. On 2 December the police raided the Warsaw firefighters' training school, which 300 cadets had occupied since late November. Because the firefighters were part of the public service, much like the police themselves, the authorities regarded the occupation of their academy as a sign of Solidarity inroads into the agencies of law and order. Five days later Warsaw radio accused Walesa and others of advocating the overthrow of the government during private Solidarity meetings. On 12 December the national leaders of Solidarity (but without Walesa's endorsement) called for a national day of protest for 17 December. They also wanted to stage a national vote in the new year on the future of Jaruzelski, the communist party, the principle of free elections and military relations with the USSR.

Jaruzelski therefore had little choice except to bring Solidarity to an end, as it was directly challenging the authority of the one-party state. He proclaimed martial law on 13 December 1981, and established an Army Council of National Salvation to run the country. Yet it was not so much a military coup as a party coup, because Jaruzelski definitely acted to save the latter – a coup was necessary if the communist party was to remain in control and if Russian intervention was to be avoided. And by attacking Solidarity itself, Jaruzelski attacked the only vehicle for mobilizing concerted working-class action. With this, the Polish experiment came to a remarkably speedy denouement. The Russians did not have to intervene, because it turned out that Poles (or some of them) would do what was necessary themselves. How long they could continue to do so remained to be seen.

DÉTENTE

Whatever the ultimate outcome in Eastern Europe, the internal crises of the Soviet Bloc had implications for Russian–American relations throughout the 1970s. Long before the rise of Solidarity it was evident that Moscow needed to concentrate on problems within its own camp, and some sort of accommodation, or *détente*, with the West would help it do so. An accommodation would enable the Russians to shift resources from East–West priorities to the needs of their allies. Washington might condemn Soviet hegemony in Eastern Europe, while the Russians accused the West of interference, yet behind the rhetoric were other considerations, and these gave the Russians a tangible interest in *détente*.

The arms race was of particular importance. Keeping up with the Americans was expensive for the Russians. Indeed some policy-makers in the United States argued that the practical effect of the arms race was to undermine the economy of the other side, and that this was a more telling rationale for defence spending than the idea that there was an immediate danger of war between the superpowers. The Soviet Union supported a comparable military establishment with a gross national product normally less than half that of the United States. In any contest of economies the Eastern Bloc was clearly at a disadvantage. Moscow faced another pressing consideration as well: the *rapprochement* between Washington and Beijing, which had a direct impact on Soviet security in the Far East – by the early 1980s more Russian divisions (forty-four) were stationed on the frontier with China than on the frontier with the North Atlantic Treaty countries (thirty-one divisions).

Equally important, Moscow's interest in *détente* rose at a time when the militant right in the USA had not yet elected a fully committed president or achieved a working majority in Congress. During the administrations of Richard Nixon, Gerald Ford and Jimmy Carter (i.e. throughout the 1970s), Washington too seemed interested in an accommodation, at least on some issues. As the Vietnam war drew to a close, Nixon in particular opted for an increasingly pragmatic approach in foreign policy, despite his preference for the right wing on many domestic issues, the most important sign of change being his visit to China in 1972. Ford and Carter also supported *détente*, and Congress exercised a moderating influence on US foreign policy as well. The defeat in Vietnam suggested that there were limits to American power. Many legislators also believed that the president's role as commander-in-chief of the armed forces needed to be checked. As it was, the White House had the practical power to involve the country in war, and to do so without consulting Congress. The president could create situations in which the Senate and the House of Representatives could only rubber-stamp a presidential decision after the fact, even though constitutionally only Congress had the right to declare war.

There was talk of a new 'isolationism' in US foreign policy, as Congress intervened in areas of policy normally reserved for the White House. After the Cambodian invasion of 1970 the Cooper–Church amendment prohibited any further combat role for US troops in that country. In 1971 there were various resolutions calling for withdrawal from Vietnam, and after the departure of American ground forces from the area, in 1973, Congress ordered the ending of all US bombing in Indo-China by 15 August, much against the wishes of the Nixon administration. In 1974 Congress took steps to limit the powers of the Central Intelligence Agency, and in 1976 it refused to support covert CIA activity in Angola, where Russian aid helped revolutionaries to victory. All in all, the United States as well as Russia seemed to be ready for a new approach to foreign policy, so *détente* had perhaps a chance of success.

Further, developments elsewhere seemed to reinforce the trend. Beginning in the late 1960s, the foreign minister and then chancellor of West Germany, Willy Brandt, promoted *Ostpolitik*, or the 'eastern policy'. In effect this meant accepting the division of Europe (and Germany) imposed at the Yalta conference. If this led to better relations with the East, it might also prevent war on the Continent and thus contribute to Western security. West Germany would be on the front lines of any European conflict, and therefore had a particular interest in dealing with the question of Continental security. Although Charles de Gaulle had attempted to assume the leadership in improving Europe's relations with Russia earlier in the 1960s, it was Brandt who achieved more in the way of practical results. The likely reason for this was that the Russians feared a resurgent Germany more than a resurgent France. If Brandt were willing to accept Yalta and abjure German reunification, then Moscow could afford closer relations with Bonn. The Russians and their allies also wanted to buy Western technology in the hope that this would help solve some of the economic problems of the Eastern Bloc. More East–West trade might do the same. Moscow thus had much to gain from *rapprochement*, and therefore proved receptive to Brandt's initiatives.

The invasion of Czechoslovakia in 1968 slowed but did not stop the Brandt initiative. Western Europe was hardly immune from internal crises of its own, and these too were part of the context of *Ostpolitik*. Even as reform gained momentum in Prague in the spring of 1968, student demonstrations portended major trouble in France. Protests against an outdated curriculum and arbitrary regulations began at the University of Nanterre, and soon spread to Paris. Violence ensued at the Sorbonne and on the Left Bank. Before this there had been serious trouble at universities in Italy and Germany. In Paris the brutality of the police response won working-class support, as workers wanted more say in management. They identified with student protests against the West's own version of a bureaucratic-managerial ruling class. On 13 May 1968 a general strike brought Paris to a halt, and 300,000 demonstrators went on the march. Within a few days perhaps ten million people were involved in strikes. The government of Charles de Gaulle mobilized support in the provinces and among the middle class and weathered the storm, but the mass participation of the French population in anti-government strikes showed that there were problems in the West. And de Gaulle did decide to resign the next year. In 1968–9 it was difficult to predict where all this would lead.

The spectre of disorder thus existed in both East and West, and each side needed to look to its own affairs. As a result the West's revulsion at the invasion of Czechoslovakia did not prove fatal to Brandt's *Ostpolitik*, and he pressed on. The quest for Continental security was the overriding consideration: in 1969 Brandt signed the Nuclear Non-Proliferation Treaty (see below), thereby easing Russian (and also French) fears that Bonn might attempt to revise the post-Second World War agreements prohibiting it from building an atomic bomb, and the next year he negotiated non-agression pacts with Russia and also Poland. Both treaties explicitly recognized the existing political boundaries in Europe. West Germany refused to go so far as to accord formal diplomatic recognition to East Germany, but in 1972 the two countries did sign a treaty which regularized their relations on other matters. Earlier (in 1971) the occupying powers of the Second World War had also come to terms on the status of Berlin. East Germany had hoped to control the West's right of access to the city, but the agreement protected the rights of the occupying powers and also West Germany's particular interest in Berlin. In 1973 Bonn settled accounts with Czechoslovakia and officially recognized the return of the Sudetenland, in effect abjuring the Munich Agreement of 1938. The same year the United Nations granted membership to the two Germanies as separate countries. In 1975 the Helsinki Conference on European Security ratified the trend by confirming the existing political boundaries on the Continent, and the USSR gave its support to human-rights guarantees. The result was to recognize the political *status quo*, in the hope that this would lead to greater security, and that the growth of trade would reinforce the political settlement. It was doubtful whether policy-makers in the West expected the human-rights provisions to be effective, though they were a useful prod for attacking the USSR's record in this respect. But in reality Helsinki had more to do with politics and security.

THE ARMS RACE

On the other hand, there were developments which ran contrary to the above trends. Besides the gradually rising strength of the political right wing in the United States, the arms race was one of the most important. It hardly needs emphasizing that for most of the post-1945 era both East and West had enough nuclear weapons to destroy the world several times over. Still, the race to garner more and more warheads and missiles was not somehow made irrelevant by this fact. The race itself was an important element in East–West relations, as each side attempted to outdo the other. It was one way in which they competed.

For most of the post-1945 period, however, the US enjoyed the overall advantage. By the end of 1952 (i.e. only three years after the USSR tested its first atomic device) it had an arsenal of about 1,000 atomic weapons and had just detonated the world's first full-scale hydrogen bomb. America's special relationship with Britain was also a factor in the balance of power, because the UK joined the nuclear club the same year. None of Russia's Eastern European allies was remotely capable of equalling this feat, and by the time China did so (in 1964) Moscow and Beijing had gone their separate ways. The balance shifted even more in the West's favour when France became a nuclear power in 1960.

Throughout the post-Second World War period the United States also had the advantage of front-line bases in Europe, so that well before the advent of the intercontinental ballistic missile (ICBM) Washington could threaten the Eastern Bloc with nuclear weapons. Indeed it did so for the first time in 1948, when it moved B–29 bombers to airstrips in the UK during the Berlin crisis. While not actually armed with atomic bombs, they could be made ready on short notice, and this was the message Washington wanted Moscow to receive. At the time the Soviet Union had not succeeded in testing a bomb of its own. Furthermore, no Russian aircraft had enough range to strike directly at the United States, nor did the Soviet Union have any bases near North America which might have served as the equivalent of US bases in Western Europe. On the other hand, the USSR maintained a considerable advantage in conventional land forces. While the Russians might not have been able to attack the continental USA, they could occupy Western Europe and in this way give pause to any American plan to attack the USSR or its satellites. The Russians exploded a nuclear device in August 1949, but their atomic arsenal did not compare with that of the United States for many years to come.

In the early years of the arms race, therefore, the USSR needed to build more bombs and to develop a delivery system capable of reaching North America. It proceeded to do both. The Russians stockpiled atomic bombs, and they exploded what was apparently their first hydrogen weapon in 1953. By the mid-1950s, ten years after the Second World War, they had finally developed their first long-range bomber which could reach the US mainland. Yet the Americans were still ahead; their arsenal far exceeded the number of Soviet aircraft and bombs. At the end of the 1950s Washington also began installing the first medium-range missiles in Western Europe and Turkey. These were Jupiters and Thors, with the Pershing I following in the 1960s. After the Cuban missile crisis (1962) the United States increased its reliance on submarine-launched (as distinct from land-based) missiles, with first the Polaris class and in the 1970s the Poseidons. Throughout the 1950s and 1960s the US also stockpiled several thousand small nuclear weapons in Europe. These were for use on the battlefield, and included atomic artillery and weapons mounted on tanks. By 1961 America may have had as many as 20,000 nuclear weapons of all types, stockpiled mainly in the United States and Western Europe. The Russians attempted to keep up, and responded to the Thors and Jupiters by deploying SS–4 and SS–5 missiles. They built up a stockpile of battlefield weapons as well, and by the end of the 1960s were closing the gap in some (not all) types of weapons.

Sometimes the Soviet Union took the lead in specific weapons systems, as in August 1957 when Moscow announced the testing of the first operational ICBM. By launching the world's first earth satellite in October the Russians again demonstrated their superiority in heavy rockets. The ICBMs were based inside Russia itself but were capable of reaching the United States. Before the year was out, however, the United States conducted a test of the Atlas, which had a range of 5,000 miles, and also launched an earth satellite early in 1958. Despite the Russians' initial lead it took some years before the Soviet ICBM arsenal became a credible force – the USSR probably had no more than ten operational ICBMs in 1961, and American intelligence knew this (thanks to U–2 spy flights over Russia between 1956 and 1960).

The US soon took the lead in ICBMs away from the USSR, and kept it until the very end of the 1960s. In the meantime the Russians attempted to redress the balance by taking what proved to be an unacceptable risk: they prevailed upon Castro to permit the construction of missile-launching sites in Cuba. Moscow planned to deploy missiles with a range of only 1,100 to 2,200 miles, but this was enough to threaten most of the continental USA. Instead the result was the Cuban missile crisis of 1962 and a major defeat for Soviet foreign policy – the Russians failed to obtain a nuclear-missile base near American borders. Moreover, the crisis exposed their strategic weakness to the entire world. As a consequence Moscow decided that its best bet was to launch a major build-up to achieve parity with the Americans (especially on ICBMs and submarine-launched ballistic missiles, or SLBMs), while engaging in negotiations to avoid a nuclear confrontation in the future. The build-up would provide the margin of security that they lacked, and also assure the success of talks by persuading the Americans to bargain seriously. The United States could not count on being ahead for ever. This was a telling point, especially as Vietnam drained the coffers of the Defence Department. The US was not able to match every Russian gain in the late 1960s and the 1970s, though the Minuteman ICBM was being deployed in this period.

By the early 1970s the Soviet Union had closed the numerical gap in some categories of weapons and forged ahead in others. The Russians equalled and then surpassed the West in the number of ICBMs and SLBMs, and were deploying the first anti-ballistic missiles (ABMs). The latter were a new weapons system designed to shoot down incoming missiles. Their purpose was to prevent enemy missiles from landing, thereby protecting at least a small part of the Soviet nuclear arsenal and preserving the capacity to respond, even in the event of a first strike by the US. The US had been working on ABMs in the 1960s, but the Russians were ahead in deployment. The Soviet Union also expanded its navy on an unprecedented scale, although it did not have as many refuelling stations around the world as the US Navy. The Americans could keep more of their naval forces at sea for longer periods of time, but the growth of the Russian navy represented a new and destabilizing element in the arms race. The US had the advantage in other categories, such as long-range bombers, aircraft carriers (the Soviets had only two Kiev-class carriers in 1980) and, most importantly, the MIRV, or 'multiple independently targetable re-entry vehicle'. This was a single missile with several warheads, each of which could be directed to a different target.

In 1977, however, Moscow installed its first SS–20. This was a new intermediate-range weapon based initially in the USSR itself and designed to threaten Western Europe (and also China). It was mobile (i.e. moveable from one launching site to another), and had a longer range than the old SS–4 and SS–5 missiles. More importantly it was an MIRV with three warheads, and represented an important break-through for the USSR. Neither this nor the Russian lead in ICBMs, however, was enough to cancel the Americans' lead in MIRV technology. While the USA had fewer missiles, it seemed to have more warheads: American MIRVs carried from three to fourteen nuclear devices. The Americans were also ahead in the race for accuracy, and in the late 1970s Washington was preparing new intermediate-range weapons of its own, the cruise missile (e.g. the Tomahawk) and the Pershing II. Cruise missiles flew at low levels and followed the contours of the land, so as to elude enemy radar. They were well adapted to a surprise attack and therefore to a possible first strike. Many critics of US policy regarded them as the type of technological innovation bound to cause a significant escalation in the arms race, as they gave the Russians a reason to press ahead with their own innovations, which in turn justified renewed American efforts.

Furthermore, America's allies also had land-based and submarine-based missiles, as well as bomber forces. Neither the British nor the French maintained large arsenals, and instead calculated that it would take only a few bombs to make the Russians wary, not several thousand – there were only about 150 warheads between the two countries. On the other side, none of the Soviet Union's allies had developed an independent nuclear capability. Nor did Moscow want them to. The turmoil in Eastern Europe and the Sino-Soviet split were enough to make the Kremlin very cautious about deploying nuclear weapons outside the USSR itself, much less encouraging its allies to develop their own atomic weapons programmes.

Arms Control

None the less, for a time in the 1970s, negotiations towards a strategic arms limitations treaty (SALT) seemed to hold out the promise that both sides might settle for some sort of rough parity. There had been earlier efforts to initiate talks, and though limits were placed on testing and on proliferation, there had been no agreement to reduce the number of arms already in existence. In 1955 Eisenhower proposed his 'open skies' plan for mutual aerial inspection, while the Russians called for a complete ban on atomic weapons, though without inspection. Neither side accepted the other's proposal. The US, the USSR and the UK did agree to suspend nuclear tests in 1958, and at the United Nations in 1959 Khrushchev again called for complete disarmament. As East–West relations deteriorated in 1961 over Berlin and other issues, however, the Russians resumed testing. Only after the world came to the brink of atomic war during the Cuban missile crisis was there a breakthrough. Though the USSR embarked on a programme to achieve nuclear parity with the USA, it also negotiated in order to reduce the risk of war. Along with London, Moscow and Washington signed the test-ban treaty in 1963, barring nuclear testing in the atmosphere or oceans. Another agreement in 1967 banned nuclear weapons in outer space. In 1968 the members of the nuclear club (except France and China) agreed to the Non-Proliferation Treaty. This prohibited the transfer of nuclear-arms technology to other countries, but lacked effective enforcement mechanisms. There was also no way to compel a country to sign the treaty in the first place. None of the above agreements ended the arms race as such: there was no reduction in the quantity of weapons already available, and stockpiling continued, as did the quest for new and better weapons systems.

Conditions in the 1970s turned out to be more favourable to some sort of agreement on controlling the number of nuclear delivery systems, though not the number of weapons. As we have noted, the Russians needed to concentrate on the internal crises of the Eastern Bloc. Moscow was also worried about the *rapprochement* between the United States and the People's Republic of China, dating from 1972 and the visit of Nixon to Beijing. Settling with the Americans would enable them to look to their security needs on the USSR–PRC frontier. Probably the key difference between the 1970s and earlier attempts to negotiate arms reduction, though, was that the Russians were catching up with the Americans and in some cases even surpassing them, so that Moscow could negotiate from a position of strength. For their part the Americans also seemed to become more interested in arms talks as the Russians closed the gap. At the same time the United States needed a breathing spell, to rebuild its conventional military capability after the Vietnam war and to press ahead with new weapons systems.

In 1972 Richard Nixon and Soviet leader Leonid Brezhnev signed SALT I, which established parity on the number of ABMs, while allowing the Russians to expand its lead in the number of ICBMs and to keep its advantage in SLBMs. Yet SALT I was silent on the number of MIRVs, so that in fact the Russian advantage in delivery systems was offset by the American advantage in developing multiple-warhead technology. SALT I thus allowed the arms race to continue in a different form – technological virtuosity rather than the number of delivery systems became the new game. The agreement did not cover bombers and medium-range and intermediate-range missiles, and new talks on the reduction of military forces (beginning in Vienna in 1973) did not produce results. Even so, SALT I was an unprecedented first step, and both sides regarded it as a prelude to further talks. The risk was that it would turn out to be only a temporary reprieve from the arms race.

That the issue of superiority versus parity was still unresolved became apparent from the failure of SALT II. United States president Gerald Ford and Brezhnev reached a tentative understanding at Vladivostok in 1974, but five more years elapsed before a new agreement was signed in 1979, this time by Jimmy Carter and Brezhnev. It conceded the principle of parity on the total number of delivery vehicles (2,250 each), including MIRV-type missiles (1,320 each). The Americans, however, failed to ratify the agreement. President Carter adopted a hard line towards the USSR when it invaded Afghanistan at the end of the year (see Chapter 12), and arms limitations became one of the casualties. Soviet activity in

Africa and other parts of the Third World also soured Russian–American relations.

The treaty, however, faced serious trouble in the US Senate even before Afghanistan. (The Senate had to approve all treaties before they could go into effect.) The rise of the militant right was in full swing. Before signing SALT II, Carter had approved the development of a new type of ICBM as a concession to the hawks. This was the MX, and was supposed to be invulnerable to an enemy first strike. The right nevertheless objected that SALT II contained too many concessions. The doves protested that there were too few, and that the treaty was defective precisely because it did not explicitly limit the race in new technologies. With Afghanistan, the right wing carried the day, and it became politically impossible to win ratification. In January 1980 Carter himself requested that a vote be delayed. Although in May the President committed the USA to observe SALT II as long as the Russians did (despite the lack of Senate ratification), the Afghanistan invasion and the failure of SALT II marked the definitive end of *détente*.

By the autumn of 1980 the most important factor in the possibility of new arms talks was the election of Ronald Reagan. His administration made various proposals as the basis for negotiations, and participated in talks (at Geneva) on both intermediate-range nuclear forces and strategic weapons. Yet it also committed the United States to a major arms build-up and to the principle of superiority. The president played on the fear that the United States was far behind the Soviet Union in order to win support for increased defence appropriations. In reality, though, the number of warheads on each side was for all practical purposes comparable. The Russians had far more ICBMs, but the Americans had forged ahead in SLBMs and air-launched missiles capable of hitting Soviet territory. Reagan also raised the level of anti-Soviet rhetoric in the USA, referring to the USSR as the 'evil empire'. The result was another turn for the worse in Russian–American relations, so that some political commentators began to speak of a 'New' or a 'Second' Cold War. Research began on space weapons, including laser beams, and some administration supporters debated the possibility that a nuclear war might be 'winnable'.

To summarize, the 1970s drift towards arms control was always conditional and at best tentative. Neither side was ever going to accept a treaty which left it in the inferior position, and there were even difficulties about conceding parity as long as new technologies promised to upset the balance. A pattern emerged in which the bargaining focused mainly on existing technologies, because the best chance of staying ahead was in developing new weapons systems. The Americans in particular seemed to follow this strategy, so that they could deploy their technological virtuosity to good effect – it was their trump card. For most of the period after the Second World War the Russians were in the position of having to catch up, and as the number two power the USSR dedicated itself to matching every American advance. Rarely were the Russians the first to innovate, but they were invariably prepared to reciprocate. If they could close the gap and bargain from a position of strength, they would talk, and by the 1970s their lead in certain categories of weapons meant that there was some movement. Yet there were always new weapons and new technologies to master, so the end of the race was nowhere in sight.

Proliferation

Moreover, there were other runners. Besides Britain and France, the People's Republic of China had the bomb, and was also working on intercontinental missiles. For example, in May 1980 Beijing reported the successful testing of an ICBM, the CSSX–4. Other countries were possibly interested in building bombs and delivery systems as well. It was likely that Israel and South Africa had the technical capacity to do so, and perhaps Pakistan, Brazil and Argentina as well. On 18 May 1974 India exploded an underground nuclear device about the size of the bomb dropped on Nagasaki. The Indian experiment clearly illustrated the inadequacy of safeguards on proliferation, despite the 1968 treaty banning the transfer of nuclear-weapons technology. New Delhi had acquired research reactors from Canada, although India's nuclear development programme concentrated mainly on power reactors for generating electricity. It thus gained access to the technology it needed for an experimental weapons programme. The Canadians did not have a bomb of their own, but they were a major exporter of power reactors. By 1980 they had attempted to sell reactors and uranium to about twenty-five different countries. Most of these were in the Third World, because other industrial nations had their own reactors and in fact were also competing to sell overseas.

The United States played the most important role in promoting power reactor sales. In 1946 the McMahon Act placed restrictions on the dissemination of nuclear technology, an idea which had wide public support as the dangers of the atomic age became more and more apparent. Yet there was more to the McMahon Act than met the eye. By inhibiting acquisition of reactor technology by other countries, it helped secure American pre-eminence in the field of power reactors. Once their leadership was assured, the Americans began promoting the new technology. In 1953 President Dwight Eisenhower presented his 'Atoms for Peace' programme to the United Nations. In due course this led to the establishment of the International Atomic Energy Agency (IAEA), the main task of which, it turned out, was to regulate the expansion of the nuclear power reactor industry. Eisenhower's initiative thus facilitated rather than limited the spread of nuclear technology. This was indeed the intention. In a related move the US Atomic Energy Act of 1954 eased the restrictions of the McMahon Act, in order to permit the sale of power reactors.

American policy-makers believed that nuclear reactors could be sold as long as there were sufficient guarantees to assure that they would be used only for peaceful purposes. The promotion of sales, however, soon triumphed over the imposition of safeguards, and both the enforcement powers and the funding of the IAEA were inadequate to its task. The world was hungry for energy, and the nuclear-power industry welcomed the opportunity to respond. In the US the construction of power reactors was mainly in the hands of private enterprise, and the potential for profit would be higher if the industry could move beyond the domestic market. The same argument prevailed in Canada, where the nuclear industry had been heavily subsidized by the government – export sales might help recoup this investment. The USSR took a much more cautious approach, particularly in the case of exports to the Third World, so that the spread of this technology was mainly the responsibility of the West.

The 1974 Indian explosion demonstrated that existing safeguards were inadequate to prevent the use of research and power reactors for weapons production. Yet once the shock of the Indian test passed, the issue barely received any attention. Indeed the Non-Proliferation Treaty in 1968 may have exacerbated the problem by creating the illusion that sufficient safeguards were in place. The failure to confront this problem was every bit as important as the failure of SALT II. Moreover, although the superpowers dominated the talks on arms control and at times achieved a degree of agreement, the risk of a nuclear war in the Third World was not to be discounted.

11

THE SUPERPOWERS AND THE THIRD WORLD: THE MIDDLE EAST AND LATIN AMERICA

It was not just the arms race and nuclear proliferation which threatened the prospects for global peace – so did competition between the United States and the Soviet Union in the Third World. In the post-Missile Crisis era such competition became keener than ever, though it varied from region to region. It was still the case that the Russians presented a concerted challenge to the Americans only in certain areas, not everywhere, so that East–West rivalry affected some parts of the Third World more than others.

The Middle East and Latin America provided contrasting examples. In the first, US–USSR competition had a fundamental impact on regional politics. Both superpowers played a major role, even to the point of threatening direct intervention with their own armies. Eventually Washington scored a diplomatic coup by mediating a series of accords between Israel and Egypt, although only after they had gone to war in 1967 and again in 1973. Yet the chances for peace depended on Russian policy as well. Moscow's aid to Egypt and other Arab states had contributed to the escalation of the Arab–Israeli crisis. By the early 1970s, however, the Soviet Union was more interested in *détente* with the United States than in supporting Egypt's ambitions, and was prepared to sacrifice the latter in favour of the former. As a result the Egyptians moved into the American orbit and looked to Washington as the one country with enough influence over Israel to bring about some sort of accommodation between Cairo and Jerusalem. Washington thus assumed the initiative in the peace process, while Moscow acquiesced, and the first faltering steps towards a settlement were taken. None the less the USSR continued to provide assistance to various clients in the region, and remained a factor in Middle Eastern affairs.

In the second example, Latin America, the United States was the main external influence. After the Missile Crisis the Russians did not risk another head-on collision with Washington in the Western Hemisphere, despite their stake in Cuba and despite the spread of revolution in Central America. The Soviet government was certainly committed to economic and military aid for Havana, but elsewhere in Latin America it was hardly able to equal the role of the United States. The effect was to leave the field mainly to the USA. It was not to be assumed, however, that even a comparatively low level of East–West rivalry assured stability. The reason was clear enough. As we have often observed, influence in the Third World depended on contingencies defined by local forces beyond the ability of either Washington or Moscow to control. It was simply not possible for the superpowers to have their way on everything. This applied whether a particular region was the object of intense East–West competition or under the virtual hegemony of a single power.

THE ARAB–ISRAELI CRISIS AFTER SUEZ

The Middle East was the site of perhaps the sharpest superpower rivalry in the Third World. Egypt had been the target of the Russians' first concerted programme of economic and military aid to a non-communist country, beginning in the mid-1950s (see Chapter 5). At the same time the United States also sought the favour of the Arabs, a policy which tended to undermine Israel's security. The hope was to marshal an anti-Soviet bloc among the states of the region. Like Moscow, Washington regarded Egypt as the key to influence, because President Gamal Abdel Nasser seemed to be emerging as leader of much of the Arab world. The 1956 Suez war, however, discredited the West and drove Egypt closer to the Russians. In the early 1960s the Americans responded by approving the sale of US arms to Israel for the first time. Yet Washington still retained many friends in the Arab world, and was unwilling to concede them to Nasser or the Russians. Indeed it remained alert to any sign that Egypt itself might come around.

In March 1957 Congress passed the 'Eisenhower Doctrine'. This authorized the president to send US military forces to any Middle East country which called for help against communist aggression. Eisenhower invoked the new policy the very next month when a power struggle developed in Jordan between pro-Nasser forces and the country's ruler, King Hussein. Washington dispatched the US Sixth Fleet to the eastern Mediterranean in a show of support for the king, and Iraq (the leading Arab state in the Baghdad Pact) mobilized its troops in case neighbouring Syria attempted to intervene. As a recipient of Soviet arms and an ally of Egypt, Syria posed a threat. Checked by Iraq, it stood aside, and King Hussein weathered the storm. Saudi Arabia was also ready to make troops available to the king.

Any cause for euphoria quickly evaporated. Later in the year the Syrians foiled a conspiracy to overthrow their government, amid accusations that American and other pro-Western intelligence agents were involved. Whatever the US role, Washington would certainly have welcomed a change of government in Damascus, but it was not to be. Instead Syria joined with Egypt in February 1958 to form the United Arab Republic. Because Damascus was definitely the junior partner, the creation of the UAR represented a major extension of Nasser's influence. Moreover, further Egyptian gains seemed likely. In July 1958 General Abdel Karim Kassem led a successful coup against the government of Iraq. He had the support of Iraqi communists, and America was about to see one of its most important allies in the Arab world move into the Soviet orbit. Washington's response was to land marines on the beaches of Lebanon (where the government was also threatened). This was done after arranging for Beirut to request help under the terms of the Eisenhower Doctrine. At the same time the British dispatched paratroopers to Jordan. The goal was to safeguard two pro-Western governments against the spreading turmoil, and to station fighting forces near Iraq in case there was an opportunity to intervene. The latter contingency never arose, however, because Kassem quickly took effective control of the country. There were no pro-Western forces left in Iraq to invoke the Eisenhower Doctrine, and US and British troops withdrew from the area.

Yet events soon played into Washington's hands. As expected, Nasser attempted to draw Iraq into the United Arab Republic, but it turned out that he had little chance of success. Kassem feared that joining the UAR would turn Baghdad into an Egyptian puppet. He therefore remained aloof. For its part the Kremlin welcomed the changes in Iraq, yet this meant more trouble for Nasser. The UAR was no longer Moscow's only important client in the Middle East. With the Iraqis on their side the Russians need not respond to Nasser's every whim, particularly his demands for more and more weapons. Instead they diverted substantial amounts of military and economic aid to the new regime in Baghdad. While the USSR maintained its ties to Egypt and continued to provide aid, the effect was to drive Nasser back towards the West. He became openly critical of the Russians, and moderated his anti-Western rhetoric. The Americans thus gained an opportunity to influence the situation, and offered limited economic assistance to Egypt in the early 1960s (balanced by assistance to Israel). Perhaps they could drive a wedge between Cairo and Moscow, especially since Nasser was in trouble elsewhere besides Iraq. Damascus was restless under his tutelage. In the autumn of 1961 a military coup took place in Syria, and the new regime seceded from the UAR.

The 1967 War

Washington knew perfectly well that helping Egypt was a gamble. The odds were against success, because Nasser was not about to give up his quest for regional hegemony. Relations between the United States and Egypt took a turn for the worse in 1962, when he intervened in a civil war in Yemen after army officers overthrew the imam (i.e. the country's Muslim leader), and proclaimed the Yemen Arab Republic (later called North Yemen). Because Saudi Arabia was backing the royalists, the Egyptians conducted air raids into its territory as well. Given the American stake in Saudi oil, Washington sided with Riyadh. Yet other developments were about to alter the whole strategic situation in the Middle East. The next year, 1963, a military coup in Iraq brought Kassem's rule to an end. The new regime in Baghdad was anti-Soviet, thus forcing the USSR back into the arms of Cairo. Now Nasser was in a position to demand large amounts of aid, especially because the war in Yemen was becoming stalemated, and he launched a build-up of the Egyptian armed forces. The problem was that this also affected the balance of power relative to Israel. A new arms race began, with the Russians supplying Egypt and the Americans matching them on the Israeli side.

Even more destabilizing than Egypt's adventures in Yemen were Soviet efforts to make up for the loss of Iraq. The lesson the Russians drew from the 1963 Iraqi coup was to avoid becoming entangled in intra-regional rivalries. Even before the fall of Kassem their gains in Baghdad had been offset by strains with Cairo. Then the coup in Baghdad increased Nasser's bargaining power, making him too independent for Russian tastes. The need, therefore, was to promote coalitions of Arab states and also of communists and nationalists within these states, not to play favourites. A coalition strategy might avoid the kind of squabbles which had paralysed the Arab world in the past, and might also dilute Nasser's influence. The way to draw the Arabs together was to exploit the spectre of a common enemy, namely Zionism backed by Western imperialism. This was the constant theme of a new and massive Russian diplomatic and propaganda campaign beginning in the mid-1960s. The Russians also hoped to mediate a reconciliation between Egypt and Syria. Of course, all this had the effect of increasing the commitment of the United States to Israel, and of dashing American hopes for nurturing Nasser's friendship by means of economic assistance. In 1965 Washington ended all aid to Egypt.

It turned out that the Russians were playing a dangerous game. Rabid anti-Zionism might promote the unity of the Arab side, but it also increased the chances of war. The Arabs just might decide to take advantage of their Soviet connections to do something about Israel. An opportunity soon presented itself. In 1964–5 Israel and its neighbours became entangled in disputes over dividing the waters of the Jordan River. For Moscow the issue was simply another occasion to score points in the East–West struggle, but the Arab states placed a much higher value on the question. Water is a precious commodity in the Middle East. The Arabs even held summit meetings to plan for war, though these proved premature. More importantly, Moscow had created the impression that it was ready to support the Arabs on this and any other questions which they regarded as vital.

Russian expressions of support no doubt helped keep the crisis going. The Syrians attempted to divert the waters of the Jordan, and Israel tried to stop them with force. The result was a series of border clashes leading to all-out war in 1967. With Moscow's encouragement Cairo and Damascus had signed a defence agreement in November 1966. All the while, the Russians kept up their anti-Israeli propaganda, and seemed to be inviting the Arab side to do something. On 13 May 1967 the USSR relayed one of its many intelligence reports to Cairo, which apparently indicated that Israel was preparing a major attack on Syria. Although the Israelis were not in fact mobilizing, Nasser decided to use the report as an excuse to act. He could have selected some other time, but Russia's apparent encouragement probably played a role in his decision. Both he and the Kremlin soon got more than they had bargained for.

It was unlikely that Nasser contemplated a full-scale war, at least at the beginning. His goal was to improve his strategic position, enhance his prestige in the Arab world, and make enough trouble for the Americans perhaps to consider seeking his favour again. The problem was that one thing led to another. Initial probes evoked timid responses from the other side, so he kept raising the stakes. On 14 May Nasser warned Israel to leave Syria alone, and backed up his threat by sending troops into the

Sinai. The Israeli–Syrian confrontation thus became more of an Israeli–Egyptian confrontation.

The Israelis drew back from any precipitate action, but this only encouraged Nasser to press on. Within days Cairo ordered a United Nations peacekeeping force to leave Egyptian territory; it had been monitoring the frontier with Israel. On 22 May Nasser closed the Straits of Tiran and thus the Gulf of Aqaba to Israeli shipping; the gulf was Israel's link to the Red Sea and thence the Indian Ocean. Yet the Israeli prime minister, Levi Eshkol, responded weakly, and in the Israeli parliament (the Knesset) simply denied any war-like intent. His government was a delicate coalition of several parties, so it took some time for a consensus to emerge. For its part the United States urged caution, while attempting to organize a consortium of Western maritime powers to keep the Gulf of Aqaba open. In other words, the US did not seem eager for a fight any more than Israel. Nasser was beginning to conclude that he might hope for more. It was at this point that the Russians made a false move, and with disastrous results.

On 28 May the Russian premier, Aleksei Kosygin, assured Nasser that the USSR would check the USA should war break out, though exactly how was not specified.* It was probable that Moscow, like Cairo, had been intrigued by the cautious response of both the Johnson administration and the Eshkol government. The Kremlin did not seem to think that a direct confrontation with the United States was in the offing. In other words, Kosygin could extend support to the Egyptians in the expectation that he probably would not have to follow through. There was also the prospect of tremendous strategic gains for the Soviet side. It was all very tempting, and the Russian show of support was probably the major reason why Nasser decided to escalate the crisis again. On 29 May he raised the stakes to include the Palestinian question. This implied that he was out to destroy Israel altogether. Sensing the ultimate crisis, every Arab state rallied to his side. On 30 May King Hussein placed his military under Egyptian command. Iraq followed suit on 4 June, and Kuwaiti troops reached Egypt the same day. Other countries were also readying their forces. It seemed that the elusive goal of Arab unity was finally at hand, and the Middle East moved rapidly towards war.

Surrounded by a potentially much more powerful coalition, the Israelis decided to strike first and gain the advantage. They did so on 5

* Nadav Safran, *Israel: The Embattled Ally* (London: 1981), 399–401.

June 1967, first attacking Egypt with everything they had and then engaging the Jordanians and Syrians later in the day. Nasser was not really caught by surprise. An Israeli first strike was probably what he wanted, and his military had prepared to ride out the initial wave. If Egypt were to make the first move, the result would be to rally the Western world to Israel's side, in which case the balance of power might well turn against the Arabs and their Russian allies. With Israel as the aggressor, however, the response of the West would be confused, and in the meantime Nasser could seize the initiative. The Russians would presumably intimidate the Americans. Indeed, the USSR was moving additional warships into the Mediterranean, though it turned out that these were only token forces and hardly enough to challenge the US Sixth Fleet. In this scenario, by the time the West decided what to do, it would be too late.

The only flaw in the plan was that Israel's initial strike devastated Egypt's air force. Without air cover for the Arab side the war was over on all fronts (Egyptian, Syrian and Jordanian) within six days. Egypt never had the opportunity to take the offensive. Accordingly the USSR acted quickly to have the United Nations Security Council declare a cease-fire, because its side was losing. This would at least limit the losses. When the Israelis ignored the UN and launched a new offensive against Syria, the Russians threatened to intervene unilaterally. They even implied that rockets might be sent against Britain and France. Yet Israel's victory was already assured, so Moscow's threats proved empty. The Kremlin had been unable to lend any practical assistance to its Arab allies, and its tough talk was just a way of saving face. Israel took all of the Sinai peninsula and the Gaza Strip (from Egypt), the West Bank Territories along the Jordan River (previously controlled by Amman) and the strategically important Golan Heights (on the border with Syria).

Stalemate

The outcome of the 1967 war was to give the Israelis some bargaining power over the Arabs for the first time since 1948, at least in theory. Israel had taken control of vast territories, and these might provide the basis for a negotiated settlement of the Arab–Israeli conflict. Egypt, Jordan and Syria wanted their lands back. In order to obtain them, perhaps they would concede Israel's right to exist. Washington also understood this, and therefore did not press for the immediate return of the conquered territories, as it had in 1956. As long as Israel held them, it was in a position to demand something from the other side. Yet a peace agreement was hardly so simple as making a trade. The Arabs regarded the conquered territories as theirs by right. Also, a peace which recognized Israel meant solving the Palestinian question within the Arab world itself, not at Israel's expense, and this too militated against an early settlement. So did Russian efforts to rearm the Egyptian and Syrian military – within months Cairo and Damascus were well on the way to rebuilding their armies. Many Arabs wondered why they should talk, when instead they might return to the battlefield and deal with Israel once and for all. In reply the Americans extended more aid to the Israelis, and the arms race began all over again. Despite (or perhaps because of) Israel's newly found bargaining power, the Middle East soon returned to a stalemate.

Although the Soviet Union replenished the Arab arsenal, Nasser was convinced that the 1967 war contained an important lesson for his side. He seemed to conclude that by themselves the Arabs could not defeat Israel, and that a military solution depended on drawing the USSR into the actual fighting. In the immediate aftermath of the war he suggested that Cairo sign a defence treaty with the Russians, or at least have them take command of the Egyptian air force. Moscow rejected both propositions without hesitation. It was obvious that Nasser's idea was to draw the USSR so far into the defence of the Arabs that it would have no choice except to fight in the event of a new crisis. The Kremlin certainly wanted to rearm the Arab side, but it did not want to be dragged into a Middle Eastern war, because this was likely to mean a direct confrontation with the United States. The Russians had fallen for Nasser's *ad hoc* strategy in the weeks before the Six Day War, and they did not want it to happen again. At least, they hoped not. In other words, Moscow's objectives were beginning to diverge from those of its Arab allies.

Russian military assistance was intended to achieve several goals short of a new war. First, aid would help refurbish the Kremlin's battered image as a friend of the Arab world. The USSR had simply not been prepared to go to war on behalf of its allies in 1967, despite tough talk against the West. Its credibility among the Arabs had fallen accordingly. Second, Russian assistance would help restore the prestige of Nasser himself, and thus head off criticism inside Egypt and among the Arab states. His policies had led to disaster, yet he was still the Soviets' principal partner in the Middle East. Third, guns might enable Nasser to bargain from a position of strength and thus avoid a dictated peace. Moscow repeatedly insisted that negotiations be a condition of additional aid. It should be noted, however, that Nasser consented to talks only with reluctance, because he was under great pressure at home and abroad to do something about Israel. Fourth, aid would keep Nasser from turning to the United States in the hope that Washington could induce the Israelis to compromise.

To sum up, Russian military aid was not for the purpose of renewing the war, but to restore the Soviet Union's strategic position in the Middle East and to prepare the way for negotiations on terms which would protect the interests of its allies. For Moscow the need was to give enough aid to make the Israelis listen, but not so much that Nasser might return to the battlefield and possibly drag them into a war. The problem was that the more weapons the Russians supplied, even while insisting on talks, the greater the risk that Nasser might spurn negotiations. Yet failing to provide arms would leave the Arab side without much bargaining power in any talks which might take place, so that Russian policy was caught in a vicious circle. The stronger the Arabs became, the more Israel insisted that a peace agreement provide it with defensible boundaries – it became more and more committed to keeping at least a small part of the conquered territories on a permanent basis, in order to achieve military security. This was unacceptable to the Arabs, and stood in the way of negotiations. In November 1967 UN Security Council Resolution 242 called upon Israel to withdraw from the conquered territories, and urged all parties to acknowledge the independence and territorial integrity of every country in the region. Instead of leading to talks, however, Resolution 242 really only defined the differences.

Hence there was little movement during the following year and a half, and in the spring of 1969 Nasser abrogated the cease-fire arranged in 1967. A sporadic war of attrition had already begun, but escalated at this point. For a time it seemed that the Egyptians had found the way to defeat Israel. The apparent strategy was not to attempt one grand Armageddon, but to exhaust the other side gradually over a long period. The new Nixon administration (elected in the autumn of 1968) had opened talks with the USSR on the Arab–Israeli crisis, but Nasser's successes on the battlefield did not incline him to compromise. The war of attrition soon turned against him, however, and when the Israelis went on the offensive in July 1969 the Egyptians lost much of their newly replaced air defences and artillery, including aircraft and Russian-made SAMs (surface-to-air missiles). This placed Israel in a mood to insist on new boundaries. Efforts by the great powers to mediate did not succeed, and Nasser set out on a trip to Moscow to ask for more weapons. Events had seemed to confirm his earlier conclusion that the Arab side could not win without a lot more help from the Russians.

Nasser travelled secretly to the Soviet capital in January 1970, but the Russians initially refused his overtures. They only relented when he threatened to resign as president of Egypt. Nasser warned that if the USSR would not provide support, then Egypt would seek American help in negotiating with Israel. By stepping aside, he would clear the way for a new leader to do precisely this. Rather than risk such a prospect, Moscow decided to provide modern, sophisticated weapons to Cairo, especially to upgrade its air defences. This also meant sending advisers to provide training and sometimes to operate the new weapons systems themselves. By March 1970 there were over 10,000 Russian advisers in Egypt (the number soon doubled), and Soviet pilots began flying for the Egyptian air force. At first they defended the interior, so as to free Egyptians for duty over the front, though later they extended their coverage nearer to the war zone.

Soviet aid was again conditional on Nasser's seeking a political solution once his military position had been restored. As the war of attrition worsened, and as Russians edged closer and closer to a combat role, the Kremlin pressed him to honour his commitment. Something similar was happening on the other side. The domestic political crisis over Nixon's decision to invade Cambodia in 1970 delayed an effective American response to the Russian–Egyptian build-up. After the anti-war protests at home Washington was not keen to pursue an adventurous policy in the Middle East. The Nixon administration urged Israel to negotiate. Russian assistance to Egypt was making a difference in the war, and Israel became interested in ending the conflict. In August both sides agreed to a cease-fire and peace talks.

It was not to be so simple. Immediately after the cease-fire the Egyptians and Russians attempted to move their air defence system to more forward positions and thus gain a tactical advantage. This clearly violated the cease-fire and created a new crisis. As a result the Americans decided to send more military aid to Israel. The attempt to dupe the US only increased Washington's commitment to Israel, so the other side lost any advantage it might have gained by violating the cease-fire. Even as this crisis unfolded, however, fast-breaking events in Jordan nearly led to a direct US–USSR confrontation. It was there that the Palestinian Liberation Organization (PLO) had its headquarters, and a faction within it was about to take things into its own hands.

The PLO and Jordan

The PLO consisted of several groups working to establish a homeland for Arabs displaced by the creation of the state of Israel and scattered in refugee camps throughout Jordan and other parts of the Middle East. It opposed any peace agreement which recognized the legitimacy of Israel. Its policies thus ran directly counter to those of King Hussein, who as one of the weaker powers in the region favoured a negotiated settlement. The PLO was becoming much too powerful for him, in effect a state within a state. As the war of attrition between Egypt and Israel wound down, a group within the PLO – the Popular Front for the Liberation of Palestine – decided to act. The idea was to sabotage any negotiations, lest they lead to a compromise with Israel at the Palestinians' expense, and the method was terrorism. Early in September 1970 the Front hijacked four large passenger aircraft owned by Western airline companies. It tried but failed to take control of another owned by Israel. One of the planes was directed to Cairo, where it was blown up after the passengers were released. The other three landed in Amman, and suffered the same fate.

Hussein's response was to declare martial law and move against the Palestinians. It was a question of whether the king or the PLO controlled Jordan's affairs. The result was a war between Amman and Palestinian guerrillas inside the country. The crisis threatened to engulf the whole region when Syria intervened on the side of the PLO, and sent tanks against Hussein's army. If Syria succeeded, Jordan would fall into the hands of the guerrillas, and Israel would be completely surrounded by countries allied with the USSR. Remember also that, while Egypt had just agreed to a cease-fire, Cairo had also immediately violated it. It was therefore unclear at this point whether the truce on the Egyptian–Israeli front would last.

Syrian forces entered Jordan on 19 September 1970. The Americans issued a warning to Moscow, and the US military went on a partial alert. Israel also prepared for war. The crunch came when King Hussein requested the United States to arrange for the intervention of the Israeli air force, which of course meant widening the conflict and risking Egyptian and possibly Russian intervention. Hussein asked for British and American assistance as well. On 21 September Nixon consulted with the Israelis and committed the United States to participate in the fighting if the Jordanians could not halt the Syrians by themselves. He also undertook to act against both Egypt and the USSR should they come to Syria's assistance.* The Russians were in fact trying to restrain Damascus, but Washington could not be certain whether a wider war might force them to intervene militarily to keep their side from being defeated. Even as Washington made contingency plans, however, Hussein succeeded in stopping the Syrian drive. The invaders were in retreat by 22 September. Shortly thereafter the king moved against the Palestinians, driving them from the country. Thus the Jordanian crisis passed, but not before the world had come very close to a direct Soviet–American confrontation. The effect on the superpowers was to solidify Washington's support for Israel while making Moscow even more wary of its clients in the Middle East.

Sadat

Hardly had the dust settled when Nasser died of a heart attack on 28 September 1970. His successor was the vice-president, Anwar Sadat. Sadat concluded that some sort of peace agreement was unavoidable, and therefore was tempted to go directly to the Americans rather than have the Russians act as intermediaries. He also purged several pro-Soviet officials in the Egyptian government. In May 1971, therefore, the Russians insisted that Sadat sign a fifteen-year treaty of friendship and co-operation, not out of adventurism but because they doubted his loyalty. In other words, the treaty was anything but a vote of confidence – they were trying to bind Sadat to their strategy. The Egyptian president had little choice except to agree. If Moscow were to cut off its arms aid, Sadat would be in trouble with his own military. His hold on power was none too secure, so he could not take the chance. He signed. To the West, however, the treaty seemed to imply that the USSR was interested in assuming a much more aggressive stance in the Middle East. Its actual meaning did not come out until some time later.

The treaty did not stem the deterioration in Russian–Egyptian re-lations. Moscow wanted Cairo to accept its guidance, but seemed to have no way of breaking the deadlock with Israel. At the same time the Kremlin would not give Sadat the arms necessary to bargain from strength and thus force the Israelis to settle. The Russians were wary lest he go to war instead. Indeed, during Nixon's visit to Moscow in June 1972, the US and the USSR concluded an agreement (one of several) on the importance of preventing a military confrontation in the Middle East. The Russians seemed to have decided that *détente* with the United

* *Ibid.*, 454.

States was more important than Egypt's needs, but the effect was to turn Sadat against his patrons in the Kremlin.

In a dramatic bid to break the deadlock Sadat sent the Soviets packing in July 1972. He ordered virtually all Russian advisers out of Egypt, and revoked their right to use military bases in the country. The aim was to win the Americans to the Arab camp, so that the lure of more influence in the Middle East might induce Washington to force a settlement on Israel. The Israelis, however, concluded that keeping up the pressure would force Sadat to agree to talks with no prior conditions. The expulsion of the Russians seemed to suggest that the Egyptians were on the verge of giving in, so Israel stood its ground and refused concessions. The Americans tended to agree with this strategy, and for them there was an additional consideration as well. By expelling the Soviets, Cairo had given up its trump card. The US wanted to reduce the influence of the USSR, but with the departure of the Russians from Egypt this was well in hand.

The 1973 War

In short, Sadat's strategy did not work. He therefore back-tracked and sought the favour of Moscow once again, in the autumn of 1972, and the Russians supplied more military equipment. The deadlock with Israel continued, but this was no more acceptable than before. Therefore, after a year of frustration, Sadat decided to force the issue once and for all. He invoked the war option as the only alternative guaranteed to make the superpowers act, and particularly to make the United States press Israel for a settlement. The balance of military power was against him, but outright victory was not essential to his goal. All the Arabs had to do was to demonstrate that they could still threaten the life of Israel, and that the West could not count on the deadlock to protect its friends for ever. Even if they lost, the Arabs could hurt Israel badly. They could also hurt the West. Before Sadat went to war, he obtained the support of the Saudis for an oil embargo against the United States and its allies, and other Arab producers followed suit in due course. There was another consideration as well, one linked to Sadat's political future. Even if the outcome were unfavourable, it was necessary to make one last bid to destroy Israel before surrendering. Otherwise Sadat would be finished politically at home. Though the odds were against an Egyptian victory, his decision to go to war was by no means totally irrational.

Egypt and Syria acted in concert, and attacked on 6 October 1973, during Yom Kippur. To the surprise of both Moscow and Washington, the Arabs did well in the first days of battle, at least on the Egyptian front. Syria took heavy losses, however, so the USSR decided to ship more arms. At the same time the Russians pressed Sadat to seek a truce while he was ahead, but backed up their commitment to the Arab side by placing three airborne divisions on alert. Sadat did not desist, but instead pressed his advantage. Accordingly, on 12 October, the Israeli prime minister, Golda Meir, notified Nixon that the very survival of Israel was at stake. The US must send weapons. Meir also stated her determination to use whatever means were required to win. In Washington this was taken possibly to mean deploying an atomic bomb. The Israelis seemed to have the technical capacity to build a bomb, and some experts believed that everything was in place to assemble an operational weapon for use in case of an ultimate crisis. Hard evidence as to Israel's nuclear capability was uncertain, but the Americans decided to send more weapons rather than contemplate the possibility.*

By mid-month the tide turned. In a flanking operation Israeli forces crossed to the west bank of the Suez Canal, thus surrounding the Egyptian Third Army in the Sinai. This was a disastrous turn of fortune for Cairo, and the Kremlin concluded that its friends were facing total defeat. Soviet premier Aleksei Kosygin secretly flew to Cairo to persuade Sadat to seek a cease-fire. He succeeded, and on 20 October Nixon's security adviser, Henry Kissinger, and Russian party head Leonid Brezhnev met in Moscow to arrange the specifics. They reached a tentative agreement to draft UN Resolution 338 in favour of a cease-fire and peace-talks. It was adopted on 22 October, but the Israelis continued to fight. Sadat had accepted Kosygin's advice on condition that Moscow guarantee its observance, but events seemed to indicate that the Russians could not deliver. Sadat therefore turned to the Americans, who by then were proposing that a new cease-fire be negotiated. An appeal from Sadat was precisely what Kissinger had hoped for. The Egyptians were again losing faith in the USSR. This time the Americans acted quickly to take advantage of the opportunity. At Kissinger's direction Nixon secretly notified Cairo that the US would not permit Israel to destroy the Egyptian Third Army.

The Americans thus were about to gain a considerable increase in influence in the Middle East, but not before a final crisis unfolded. Although the US and the USSR combined their influence in the UN to

* *Ibid.*, 482–3, 489.

obtain a new cease-fire resolution on 24 October (UN Resolution 339), the Israelis still refused to desist. The Russians therefore placed all their airborne divisions on alert. At the same time Sadat requested that both superpowers send troops to the region to enforce the cease-fire. The Russians agreed, and moreover threatened to act unilaterally if the US did not join with them. If Washington agreed to a joint intervention, however, it would lose its role as the one player with influence on both sides (at least, since Sadat had appealed for help). Washington therefore responded with a global alert, including its nuclear forces, while urging Israel to observe the cease-fire. United States intelligence soon learned that a Russian ship with radioactive material aboard had arrived in Egypt, but in fact the cease-fire was on the verge of becoming effective.* Besides, superpower confrontation was to no one's gain, and both Moscow and Washington knew it. On 25 October the USSR supported US proposals for a United Nations peacekeeping force of 7,000 personnel.

Truce

The 1973 war thus altered the strategic situation and at last motivated the superpowers to become directly involved in the peace process, which was precisely Sadat's objective. Given that Egypt was clearly turning towards the United States, it was in the American interest to press Israel for concessions. Sensing the opportunity, Kissinger acted as broker between the two sides. The first step was to arrange for opening a line of supply to the still-beleaguered Egyptian Third Army. Unless this were done, Sadat threatened to turn back to the Russians and call upon them to break the Israeli siege. The Israelis expected a renewal of the fighting to occur at any moment, and therefore were reluctant to surrender their trump card without firm guarantees. The problem was that they feared the United States was prepared to sacrifice their interests in order to win influence with the Arabs and thus outflank the Russians. On the other hand, Israeli forces were over-extended. They could not stand a long war of attrition, and were dependent on American arms supplies. Prime Minister Meir was also keenly aware of Israel's diplomatic isolation. The oil embargo had driven Western Europe and Japan to the Arab side. She therefore consented to Kissinger's strategy, and military officers from Egypt and Israel signed an agreement on 11 November 1973, thus assuring a cessation of hostilities. The signing also had the effect of

* *Ibid.*, 494–5.

affirming the American role as mediator in the Middle East, the friend of both Egypt and Israel.

The Russians, of course, were eager to play a part in the peace process. Precisely because the initiative had passed to the United States, they wanted to find some way of regaining a modicum of prestige in the Middle East. At first Kissinger welcomed the idea of a role for the Kremlin, in order to co-opt Moscow into his plans. Any peace conference would take place more on his terms than the Kremlin's. The course of the war had assured this. Besides, the Americans could hardly exclude Moscow, as it still had the power to act unilaterally. The Kremlin could always offer more aid to Sadat in the hope of luring him away from Washington, and given the twists and turns of the Arab–Israeli crisis anything was possible. The United States was therefore agreeable to a Soviet role, and the superpowers co-sponsored an international conference at Geneva. In December 1973 Israel, Egypt, Jordan, the United States and the Soviet Union met to open discussions, although Syria refused to attend. Then the conference adjourned for the Israeli elections, which had been delayed by the war.

Despite an auspicious beginning at Geneva, it was none the less the case that Kissinger wanted to dominate any negotiations and limit the Russian role. An opportunity soon presented itself to do exactly this, leaving the Geneva conference in limbo. Early in 1974, before Geneva reconvened, the Israelis proposed that Kissinger mediate directly between themselves and the Egyptians. Israel was over-extended militarily and wanted a speedy agreement on disengagement. The Geneva forum brought together too many parties with disparate interests for there to be a quick settlement. Also, the participation of the two superpowers meant that East–West issues would complicate the resolution of regional problems. Hence the Israelis suggested that Kissinger mediate between Jerusalem and Cairo. Sadat proved agreeable, and for many of the same reasons. Kissinger therefore flew to Egypt in January 1974. Because of Israel's co-operation he was able to offer attractive terms to the Egyptian president. Sadat consequently decided that it might be better for him to continue dealing directly with the Americans, rather than at Geneva, where he would have to pay deference to the views of the Soviets. In other words, he offered to bypass the Geneva conference in exchange for Kissinger's continued help in bargaining with Israel. Of course, Sadat's decision to work through Kissinger meant snubbing the Russians. As Egypt could not go to war without Soviet aid, this in effect committed Sadat to a negotiated settlement. It was therefore a significant development. It was also a logical move for Egypt. Russian aid and support had never been sufficient to assure an Arab victory in the past, so the American card was the best one to play.

Moscow was not pleased to see the US secretary of state take charge, but did not interfere. The Russians apparently concluded that there was more to be gained by ending the constant state of crisis. This would lessen the chances of war and the risk of another superpower confrontation. It would also give *détente* a chance. In this respect peace in the Middle East depended on the Kremlin as much as Kissinger. The Russians could have interfered at any time, but instead they stood aside.

Kissinger therefore moved to centre-stage, as much remained to be done. The signing of an Egyptian–Israeli disengagement agreement took place on 18 January 1974, and was explicitly accepted by both sides as the first step towards a more comprehensive agreement, presumably at Geneva. The US also joined in exchanging letters of understanding on matters of strategic concern, with continued military support for Israel and some economic help for Egypt. The Americans thus assumed a *de facto* role as guarantor of the agreement. Kissinger then attempted to arrange a similar truce between Israel and Syria, and after many months of mediation succeeded in May. Along the way the Arabs ended their oil embargo. The formal signing between Syria and Israel took place at Geneva, thus allowing the Russians a symbolic presence and apparently keeping the Geneva option alive. In fact, though, the Americans continued as the principal mediator, and the Geneva conference became dormant.

Kissinger was unable to arrange a disengagement agreement with Jordan. The Jordanian–Israeli front was secure, so neither side was under pressure to bargain. On the contrary, many Israelis regarded the West Bank (occupied in 1967) as rightfully part of their country, because it included the ancient Judea and Samaria, and were not of a mind to give it back. Hussein wanted peace, but this became a problem. Fearing that the king was too eager to settle, an Arab conference at Rabat, in Morocco, in the autumn of 1974 designated the PLO as the only authority the Arabs would recognize as speaking for the Palestinians. The occupied West Bank was a likely site for a Palestinian homeland, and the more hard-line Arab states wanted to keep Hussein from bargaining any of it away. The PLO, however, was dedicated to the destruction of Israel, and some of its factions had resorted to terrorism. The Israelis would not negotiate with the Palestinians, whether in Geneva or some other forum.

In 1974 a new government took charge in Israel, and Yitzhak Rabin succeeded Meir. But the government was divided, torn between factions of doves and hawks. There were always factions, yet the situation by 1974 was that further peace-talks became more difficult for Jerusalem. At the same time uncertainty about American policy damaged Kissinger's ability to make credible commitments. Richard Nixon had resigned as US president in the summer over the Watergate scandal, though Kissinger remained as secretary of state under the new president, Gerald Ford. A presidential election was about two years away, again raising doubts about who would be in charge of future US policy. In brief, the opportunity for bargaining was fast fading.

A stalemate meant running the risk of a new outbreak of hostilities – somehow the momentum had to be maintained. Geneva was not an option, because the Palestinians were seeking representation there. The best chance was for another limited agreement on the Egyptian–Israeli front, as Sadat was willing to co-operate despite the opposition of the Rabat summit. Reconstruction was advancing in the canal zone on the basis of the first Sinai agreement, and refugees were returning to the area. Sadat therefore needed to make the frontier more secure by further dealings with Israel. His option to go to war was receding as reconstruction advanced. This was Kissinger's chance to arrange a second agreement on the Sinai. He succeeded, but only after months of flying from capital to capital ('shuttle diplomacy').

In September 1975 Egypt, Israel and the United States signed a series of agreements and memoranda. Though Geneva was the setting for the formal signing, the agreement was the result of Kissinger's mediation and not the Geneva conference as such. The Israelis drew farther back from the canal to create a new buffer zone, and surrendered the strategically important Gidi and Mitla passes and the oil fields at Abu Rodeis. This still left most of the Sinai in their hands, so that a final peace remained to be concluded. For their part the Egyptians agreed not to resort to force in the future, and to continue negotiating towards a definitive settlement. The Americans committed themselves to man an electronic surveillance system to watch for violations of the truce boundaries, while reaffirming their willingness to boost Israel's military capacity. Washington also assured Jerusalem that it would support Israel if it were threatened by the USSR. The Americans agreed to co-ordinate their strategy with Israel at a future Geneva conference, and to ostracize the PLO unless it conceded Israel's right to exist. The US thus assumed an even larger responsibility for guaranteeing the agreement than before.

The Egyptian–Israeli accord alienated the hardline Arab states even more. So did Sadat's decision in March 1976 to abrogate the 1971 Soviet–Egyptian treaty of friendship. Egypt had received over 30 per cent of all Soviet aid in the period 1954–72, but the Kremlin had nothing left to show for it. (The Russians, however, had naval facilities at Aden in South Yemen, and sought military bases in Somalia and then Ethiopia in the 1970s. Their Cuban allies were also present in South Yemen and Ethiopia.) Cairo's alignment with the West therefore drew the condemnation of much of the Arab world, but in 1976 the Americans agreed to sell arms to Egypt for the first time since the early 1950s, in the hope of fending off Sadat's critics and showing that Washington would stand by its new-found friend. Though an important symbolic act, US arms sales did nothing to end Egypt's isolation among Muslim countries. Egyptian–Syrian relations were particularly strained. Damascus saw the Egyptian–Israeli agreement as a sell-out, and favoured a return to war if necessary. Unable to count on Cairo as an ally in any future military confrontation with Israel, Damascus sought closer ties to the Palestinian Liberation Organization.

The PLO and Lebanon

The PLO remained the most outspoken opponent of Israel, and was supported by Syria. By the mid-1970s the PLO was headquartered in Lebanon and controlled the most important military forces there. The Palestinian presence threatened the stability of the country's official government, so that a Jordanian-style showdown seemed likely. As a patron of the PLO, Syria soon became entangled in Lebanon's factional conflicts. Damascus found it difficult to control the Palestinians, however, and the result was factional fighting inside Lebanon and a spreading civil war. The Israelis threatened to intervene, and Damascus itself was worried about its ability to contain the violence. Accordingly Syria backed down, and during the summer of 1976 sent troops into Lebanon in order to discipline the PLO (i.e. to discipline its ally) and contain the fighting. Because of the chaos the other Arab states authorized Syrian troops to remain as a peacekeeping force, despite the fear of some Arab capitals that the pro-Soviet government in Damascus would impose hegemony on Lebanon. Yet hegemony seemed to be exactly what Syria had in mind. Thus, while the Israelis were more secure on their southern flanks, the danger in the north was increasing. Syria and the PLO had raised the stakes, and Israel was not about to relax its vigilance. The overall effect was to block further movement towards a general peace for the region during 1976 and into 1977.

Camp David

The 1976 US presidential election also temporarily diverted the peace process. Jimmy Carter won, but then proceeded to depart from Kissinger's proven step-by-step approach. Instead, he wanted to go for a comprehensive peace treaty, and settle the whole Arab–Israeli crisis once and for all. Carter therefore suggested reconvening the Geneva conference and involving the Soviets. He also wanted more of a role for the Palestinians than the Israelis were prepared to concede. It was not to be so simple. Carter's approach failed to take account of the complexities of the situation. The Geneva forum was unattractive to Israel, because the Soviets were represented there and would surely support the claims of the Palestinians to participate. United States–Israeli relations deteriorated, and a stalemate threatened once again. This was precisely what every American administration wished to avoid. Without peace-talks, differences were likely to be resolved by war.

In Cairo, Sadat watched with dismay as Carter floundered. The Egyptian president believed that the step-by-step approach to peace was the only one with a chance of success. It was up to him to act, because by this time Egypt could not afford to see another major war break out in the Middle East. The hard-line Arab states might want to destroy Israel, but this was simply not an option as far as Sadat was concerned. In an ultimate showdown the Arabs might discover whether rumours of a secret Israeli nuclear bomb were true or not. Sadat was not eager to find out. In any case, American support for Israel gave it the advantage militarily. There was much to be gained from attempting further talks, even if it required Sadat to make a dramatic gesture.

Though Sadat's next move caught the whole world by surprise and seemed impulsive, it was in fact the result of careful calculation. Secret contacts with the Israelis suggested that new talks might be possible. In November 1977, therefore, Sadat offered to go to Jerusalem and address the Knesset in person.* Given the threat from Syria and the PLO, plus the general strain of years of conflict, the Israelis were prepared to receive him. Also, dealing directly with Sadat would sidetrack Carter's proposals for reconvening the Geneva conference, a net gain for Israel.

* *Ibid.*, 602–6.

Sadat's visit would also again divide the radical Arab states from the moderates, another advantage for Israel. Another consideration was that the new Israeli prime minister, Menachem Begin, had a slim majority in the national assembly. He was thus under pressure to show some results quickly. Everything recommended welcoming Sadat.

While the new American administration had a broader approach in mind, it settled for what was possible. The spreading crisis in Iran was another consideration, and inspired Washington to act in the hope of stabilizing developments in other parts of the Middle East (see Chapter 12). Taking advantage of the momentum created by Sadat's visit to Jerusalem, Carter turned away from the idea of a comprehensive peace treaty, and worked for more limited goals, which required almost a year of manoeuvring and bargaining. Along the way, PLO terrorist attacks caused Israel to invade southern Lebanon in the spring of 1978. Sadat was convinced that the Lebanon crisis was just another compelling reason to continue the peace process, before a wider war broke out. After Israeli troops left Lebanon in June, Carter eventually persuaded Sadat and Begin to come to the United States for face-to-face negotiations. The president at last came into his own as a skilful mediator, and in September 1978 they agreed to the Camp David Accords. These provided for immediate negotiations on a general Egyptian–Israeli peace treaty. In return Israel would turn over the rest of the Sinai in stages (this was completed in 1982). Israel could also use the Suez Canal and the Gulf of Aqaba. The future of the Gaza Strip and the West Bank was left unclear, but limited self-rule (i.e. a concession to Palestinian autonomy) was to be introduced in these areas while still under Israeli control. Their ultimate status would be negotiated. In other words, the West Bank and Gaza were not allowed to prevent general peace between Egypt and Israel. Egypt agreed to grant diplomatic recognition to Israel, and the two sides exchanged ambassadors early in 1980. For the first time in history an Arab state had formally acknowledged Israel's right to exist. It took further negotiation and shuttle diplomacy by Carter himself to finalize the peace treaty, but it was officially signed on 26 March 1979.

Retreat

Although the Accords were an important step, they did not lead to peace for the entire Middle East. Most Muslim countries condemned Sadat for recognizing Israel, and he was assassinated in October 1981. Furthermore, the Camp David Accords were only between Egypt and Israel. The Golan Heights (annexed by Israel in 1981) remained a grievance for

Syria, and the talks on Palestinian autonomy ran into trouble. Consequently Begin set up new Israeli settlements on the West Bank, affirming his determination to establish defensible boundaries, by unilateral action if necessary. In 1980 the government declared an undivided Jerusalem to be the permanent capital of Israel. Palestinian attacks on Israeli territory continued, with Syrian support and with Lebanon as the base of operations.

In reply Israel bombarded the headquarters of the PLO in Beirut in 1981, and then invaded southern Lebanon once again, in 1982. This time the Israelis also engaged the Syrians, as Damascus still maintained troops in the country and was supporting PLO forays against Israel. The Israelis inflicted severe losses, destroying nearly 50 per cent of Syria's complement of Soviet-supplied MIG fighters and making Damascus much more circumspect. They also committed atrocities against the Palestinian population. The PLO was forced to leave Lebanon in August. Syrian troops remained in the north of the country, so that despite Israeli gains the threat from Damascus could not be discounted. Of course, none of these developments solved the question of a homeland for the nearly three million Palestinians. The Palestinians therefore resorted to terrorism more and more, under the protection of such countries as Syria and Libya. Terrorism introduced an unpredictable element into the situation, and even the superpowers could do little to control it. America had succeeded in expanding its influence at the expense of the Russians, and for a time had been able to advance the peace process. Without the prospect of new peace-talks in the early 1980s, however, the danger of war in the Middle East remained.

ALLENDE'S CHILE

In Latin America the United States was the most important outside influence. There was very little competition from the Soviet Union, yet there were still problems. Chile was a case in point. There the Marxist Salvador Allende Gossens was elected president in 1970. Washington was not pleased, but it had reason to believe that the tide might turn in its favour. After all, Allende had won largely because of the disunity of the opposition, and he did not have the support of the majority of the electorate. His election owed much to the structure of the political system itself, which permitted him to become president with only 36.2 per cent of the popular vote. His plurality was greater than any other candidate's, but still formed a minority of the total. Even so, there was nothing unusual in how he came to power. A multitude of political parties normally contested elections in Chile. It was therefore common for no presidential candidate to win an absolute majority, in which case the constitution authorized the congress to make the choice. The practice was to take the candidate with the largest plurality, though only after a period of bargaining in which the president-elect would have to make concessions to the other parties in accordance with their strength in the legislature. This allowed Allende to assume office, but the congress remained in the hands of the opposition. It would be difficult for the new president to enact his programme, or so the United States hoped.

Allende faced other obstacles as well. The country's social structure included significant numbers of small-business operators, white-collar employees and professionals, and this too worked to Washington's advantage. According to the 1970 census the total number of self-employed and white-collar workers was 1,236,500, or 48.2 per cent of a workforce of 2,564,400. Of course, many of these people were on the fringes of the economy, but others constituted a significant middle-class element in Chilean society. By comparison, the number of blue-collar workers stood at 1,092,500, or 42.6 per cent of the total. The number of employers was 80,900, or 3.2 per cent. (The census did not categorize the remaining 154,500, or 6 per cent.) The combination of employers, self-employed and white-collar workers thus constituted more than half the workforce (51.4 per cent), though the statistics do not distinguish between rich and poor within their ranks or indicate how they might vote.

Obviously enough people had supported Allende for him to win, though blue-collar workers provided his largest following. Those small-business owners and white-collar workers who voted for Allende probably did so because of the failings of previous governments, but in many cases their material interests also made them receptive to appeals from the political right. Their long-term allegiance could be doubted. The right played on their fears that the government was about to seize all private property, and Allende's conduct sometimes seemed to give substance to the charge. As we shall see presently, he proceeded to nationalize key sectors of the economy, despite opposition from the congress. Although the president pledged to leave the small-business sector alone, the right wing asked where it would all end. Indeed, sometimes workers and peasants took events into their own hands and seized control of factories and estates without waiting for authorization from Santiago. Small property owners began to turn against the government. In sum, the balance of class forces in Chile was such as to give the political right an opportunity to mobilize the centre against Allende.

While Allende's opponents hardly needed any encouragement from the United States, the situation was ripe for Washington to interfere. As we shall see presently, it did so in three ways: it brought economic pressure to bear on the regime; it provided secret financial assistance to the opposition; and it continued military aid to the army. Although the Chilean president made mistakes of his own, the US campaign helped create economic chaos while strengthening the political right. Yet, because Washington operated for much of the time behind the scenes, its role was invisible to most of the population. The electorate tended to blame its troubles on Allende. As the country's woes increased, the right was able to win over more and more of the people. By the time the army staged a bloody coup in 1973 perhaps a majority of Chileans were prepared to accept its decision to act, and Allende and thousands of followers met their deaths.

The Rise of the Left

Allende's election was the result of developments in the 1950s and 1960s. The country's persistent problems pushed the electorate from the right to the centre and then to the left, as different remedies were tried but invariably seemed to fail. For most of the period Chile was plagued by rampant inflation, foreign debt, dependency on expensive imported foodstuffs and manufactures, and lagging investment in the mining sector. The last was particularly worrisome, because copper accounted for about 80 per cent of the country's export earnings. Wealth was highly concentrated as well: in the industrial sector 80 per cent of assets were controlled by 27 per cent of the corporations in the late 1960s. Large estates constituted under 0.3 per cent of all agricultural units, but these averaged 23,000 hectares each and occupied 55 per cent of the country's total arable land in 1965. Half of the total number of farm units were at the opposite pole, averaging 1.7 hectares each and occupying less than 1 per cent of the country's land.

Jorge Alessandri won the 1958 election for the right wing with 31.2 per cent of the popular vote. Allende headed a coalition of the left known as the *Frente de Acción Popular*, or FRAP, and received 28.6 per cent. The centrist Christian Democrat Eduardo Frei Montalva won 20.5 per cent. Once in power, Alessandri's solution was unfettered free enterprise, an austerity programme to limit government expenditures, lower tariffs to force Chilean industry to become more competitive, and more investment from abroad. His policies thus offered a clear-cut alternative to his predecessors. Ever since the late 1930s the role of the state in the economy had been increasing, but Alessandri attempted to halt the trend (even so, government enterprises accounted for more than 40 per cent of the gross domestic product in the late 1960s). His policies also polarized the electorate. The copper sector provided the best example. The US Anaconda and Kennecott corporations already controlled all the largest mines, but Alessandri wanted such companies to expand. On the other side, a growing nationalist opposition advocated various forms of expropriation, in order to take control of the country's most valuable resource. United States interests were also significant in other industries, particularly the fastest-growing sectors, and in commerce and banking. The question of foreign ownership was becoming increasingly sensitive. Moreover, despite Alessandri's faith, a heavy dose of austerity proved insufficient to generate sustained growth. The result was rising support for the FRAP and Allende.

Rather than risk a leftist victory in the 1964 presidential election, the right-wing parties (mainly the Liberals and the Conservatives) compromised and allied themselves with the centre. They backed the Christian Democrat Frei as a moderate reformer, but one committed to the capitalist system. United States interests reputedly contributed $20 million to the election, or about half of Frei's campaign funds. He became the first Chilean president in the twentieth century to receive an absolute majority of the popular vote, 55.7 per cent. Allende won 38.6 per cent, with the balance going to other candidates. Frei had condemned Allende as a tool of Moscow, and the campaign was notable for red-baiting. Foreign control of the economy was also a major issue, and Frei pledged to increase Chile's control of the copper sector. He also promised to open the political system to groups formerly excluded, such as the rural poor.

As Chile's most important export, copper became the test of Frei's middle-of-the-road approach. Both the left and many business leaders wished to see Chileans have a larger say in running their own economy. The only issue was how far to go with nationalization. Frei struck a compromise, and opted for buying a share of the industry. For example, the government bought a 51 per cent interest in the El Teniente mine (owned by the US multinational Kennecott), but paid more than double its book value. Kennecott also received tax concessions and remained in control of management. Similar deals were made in other cases. In return the private companies agreed to expand their investment, but for the most part reneged on their promises. Neither the left nor the right was satisfied, so that the 'Chileanization' question once again would be an issue in the 1970 election, as would land reform and political power for the poor. Frei inaugurated a programme for distributing land to peasants and creating co-operatives, his aim being to pre-empt the left, which was also promoting peasant unions and mobilizing the rural poor. Frei's land reform was too limited to have much impact, but there was more political activity in the countryside than ever before. Frei also organized new federations of labour unions to compete with those controlled by the left, again in the hope of dividing the working class.

The opportunity for the left to win came about in 1970 as the result of a split between the Christian Democrats and the parties of the right. The latter were unhappy with Frei's reforms, however mild, and feared the rising power of leftist sympathizers within the Christian Democratic Party itself. Indeed, the leader of the party's left-wing faction, Radomiro Tomic, became its candidate in the election. Alarmed by this prospect, the right nominated a candidate of its own, running under the banner of the National Party. This split the winning coalition of 1964, and Allende took the lead with 36.2 per cent. He headed a new alliance called *Unidad Popular* (UP), which brought together socialists, communists, and some white-collar and small-business interests. His percentage of the vote in 1970 was less than in 1964, but more than the right's 34.9 per cent and the Christian Democrats' 27.8 per cent. Washington provided financing to Allende's opponents, though not on the scale of 1964. The Central Intelligence Agency allocated only $1 million for the period 1969–70 (though private US companies and other government offices probably contributed to Allende's opponents as well). This was because the US Embassy expected Alessandri to win easily, and concluded that vast sums of money were not needed. The results took Washington by surprise, and it needed some weeks to decide how to respond. Initially Washington hoped the Chilean military might prevent Allende from assuming office, as did the US multinational International Telephone and Telegraph (ITT), who offered funds to the US government to help finance such an effort. The State Department did not accept. There was one attempt (by Chileans) to stage a coup, but it proved abortive. By then, however, Washington had concluded that a waiting game was best. The Chilean congress selected Allende in the customary fashion, and he was inaugurated in November 1970.

Decline and Fall

Allende's election meant that representatives of the working class gained access to a number of key positions in government for the first time in Chilean history. They received not only the labour ministry, but also the ministries of finance and public works. In due course Allende appointed the secretary-general of the *Central Unica de Trabajadores*, or CUT (Chile's principal labour organization), to the ministry of the interior. Other CUT leaders were given offices in the country's most important policy-making bodies: the state development corporation and various planning agencies, and the government steel, electrical and oil companies. They also had a role in recommending government wage policy. Allende's first order of business was to negotiate a series of agreements increasing the minimum wage in industry by 66.7 per cent for 1971 and giving workers a role in managing state-owned enterprises, both on the shop floor and at the highest levels. Lesser increases (though still high in percentage terms) were also scheduled for several other categories of employees. The effect was to fuel a boom in consumer spending, but also to contribute to rising inflation and shortages of both consumer and producer goods. Inflation led to further demands for wage and salary increases.

There was more to come. Allende's campaign had promised to move Chile towards socialism, and the government proceeded to divide the economy into three sectors: a nationalized 'Social' area made up of the largest enterprises and landed estates; a 'Mixed' area with shared public–foreign ownership of enterprises particularly dependent on imported technology and thus likely targets for foreign takeovers; and a 'Private' area composed mainly of small enterprises and constituting the greatest number of owners. The Private area was not subject to any expropriation, but the government wanted to include about 250 of the biggest domestic and foreign-owned corporations in the Social and Mixed areas. The congress attempted to block this by passing an alternative programme which required its approval for each case of nationalization (rather than giving Allende blanket authorization to expropriate). Moreover, it incorporated its plan into a constitutional amendment, which Allende vetoed. The congress overrode the veto by a simple majority, but then a dispute arose as to whether a two-thirds majority was required as in the case of an ordinary piece of legislation. The question became deadlocked, but in the meantime the government was proceeding with expropriations. Allende invoked emergency powers dating from the 1930s. In February 1972 the Allende government announced that it would take over ninety-one enterprises, though by then it already had taken charge of 150, with more to come.

The copper sector was not the subject of disagreement between Allende and his opposition, because of the disappointing results of Frei's programme. Congress unanimously passed a constitutional amendment to nationalize the copper companies in July 1971. It also provided for compensation, but only after any excess profits earned during the preceding fifteen years were deducted. Allende subsequently invoked the last clause to declare that Kennecott, Anaconda and other companies were entitled to nothing. United States president Richard Nixon responded in January 1972 by announcing that the US would not extend further economic aid to Chile because of its failure to pay compensation. It was a fact, however, that the US government had already stopped new loans and investment guarantees, though funds already allocated for 1970 were turned over. While the International Monetary Fund allowed Chile to draw upon credits it was automatically entitled to under IMF rules, the World Bank did not grant new funds. The Inter-American Development Bank granted only two small loans, in contrast to massive credits in previous years. Washington also pressed private US and foreign banks to reduce their loans, though it had little choice except to agree to a rescheduling of Chile's existing debts. Santiago had been one of the largest beneficiaries of US assistance in the past, so Washington's retrenchment was a serious blow to the economy. It created problems for the government, and was one factor in mobilizing Allende's opposition.

At the same time a split developed within the ranks of *Unidad Popular*. Allende's faction of the socialist party and also the communists wanted to slow down and consolidate existing programmes, while more radical factions among the ranks of the socialists wanted to speed things up. Working-class militancy was on the rise as well. Workers in both city and country took direct action, and seized control of factories and estates, including many small operations not scheduled for integration into the Social or Mixed areas. The first spontaneous seizure of a factory by workers occurred in April 1971. Allende attempted to discourage such takeovers, but sometimes went along with them where they were an accomplished fact. Property-holders were alarmed indeed, as even small businesses became the target of worker action. The majority were not affected, but the threat none the less seemed ominous.

The combined effect of the above developments was to draw the upper and middle classes into an alliance against the government. In fact the various right-wing parties had started co-operating with the Christian Democrats in congress from at least the summer of 1971. Allende therefore proposed a constitutional amendment to set up a new popular assembly, to replace the existing legislature, and in effect bypassing it. The catch was that Congress had to approve any such amendment, and of course it refused (in 1972). Allende threatened to proceed anyway, by placing the matter before the people themselves in a referendum. This was probably unconstitutional, and was never actually attempted. In the meantime other problems overwhelmed the government.

As the economy declined, the political opposition grew bolder. In the summer and autumn of 1972 major demonstrations (including a general strike) were launched against the government, with small-business owners, professionals and white-collar workers in the lead. Upper-class and corporate representatives tended to remain in the background, although they provided material aid and support. The US Central Intelligence Agency also had a fund of $8 million in the period 1971–3 to assist opposition forces, and much of this money went to support strikes. Moreover, Washington increased its aid to the Chilean military during Allende's tenure, and the president permitted this rather than risk alienating the army. It was likely that private US sources again helped his opponents as well. Pro-Allende workers responded to the anti-government demonstrations by occupying many factories during October, and working voluntarily to keep as much of the economy going as possible. Rather than rely on them and escalate the conflict with the right, however, Allende decided to appease the opposition. In November 1972 he brought three military officers into the cabinet, including the army commander-in-chief, General Carlos Prats. Their mission was to restore order. Having forced Allende to admit rightist sympathizers into the cabinet, the demonstrators and strikers immediately obeyed the army's call to return to work.

The final act opened with the congressional elections of March 1973. The right mobilized in an effort to win a two-thirds majority, the majority needed to impeach Allende. It failed, and the UP increased its representation, winning almost 44 per cent of the vote. The proletarian core of Allende's support was holding, however much the more radical workers might denounce his desire to pause and consolidate. It was thus clear that no legal way remained for rightists to dispose of Allende until the next presidential election (in 1976). The time had come for more dramatic action, and there was an unsuccessful effort to launch a coup in June. In reply Allende called upon his supporters to mobilize, and for a time even considered arming them. Workers took over hundreds of factories. But business and professional elements inspired another general strike in July, and the turmoil continued throughout the summer.

The president therefore chose once again to restore order by appeasing his opposition, as he had done the year before. He feared that arming the workers would result in all-out war with the right, but his reluctance to rely on his principal supporters meant that the military became the key factor in events. Unlike Castro in Cuba, however, Allende had not succeeded in taking charge of the army. Right-wing officers soon forced the relatively moderate defence minister (General Prats) to resign, and General Augusto Pinochet Ugarte took his place. The military was plotting to violate Chile's long tradition of constitutionalism. Allende died in a bloody coup on 11 September 1973. The United States played no direct role in his death, though it had certainly helped prepare the way for the Chilean military to act. Thousands of people were killed or simply disappeared.

No doubt the Christian Democrats and the right-wing parties expected the period of army rule to be brief, and hence supported dramatic action – surely the military would turn over power to the civilian authorities once the left was disposed of. Given the character of the remaining political parties, it would be safe to do so. Yet they were in for a surprise. Instead of transferring power to them, Pinochet emerged as head of the military government the next year, and invoked the spectre of global communism to establish what became known in Chile and elsewhere as a 'national security state'. In other words, he used the threat of the left to justify the imposition of a dictatorship and the suspension of basic human rights. The tide of global communism was presumably so powerful as to require ending democracy and creating a disciplined society able to resist the threat from within and without. The outcome was thus considerably more than rightist politicians had bargained for. The congress was dissolved, and all political parties were outlawed. Most industries and about half of the expropriated agricultural lands were returned to their former owners or sold, though the copper sector remained in government hands. On the whole, however, Pinochet reduced the role of the state in the economy and once again encouraged foreign investment. Many of his economic policies followed the prescriptions of the US free-market economist Professor Milton Friedman. In response to condemnation by the United Nations General Assembly for violations of human rights, Pinochet held a referendum in January

1978, in which he received the endorsement of 75 per cent of the voters. Whether the electorate had a free choice may be doubted. A new constitution was promulgated in March 1981, but to take full effect only by 1989. By the mid-1980s there were increasing demonstrations against the regime, yet it remained to be seen whether they could move the government.

A NOTE ON ARGENTINA AND THE GENERALS

Developments in Argentina also reached crisis proportions in the 1960s and 1970s, although the United States did not play a role in events. It did not need to, because the Argentinian military was quite willing to act against the *Peronistas* and the left (see Chapter 7). The problem was that the army's efforts to establish order and revive the economy proved no more effective than those of civilian governments. From time to time, therefore, it returned power to the latter, only to take it back in the face of the continuing strength of the *Peronistas*. Much of the working class remained committed to Perón, and pressed for his return. Thus a series of alternating civilian and military governments characterized the period, with the army acting as the final arbiter. Yet the military was often divided on how to proceed, and this too contributed to the vacillation. After expelling Perón in 1955, the army ruled until 1958, when it restored civilian government. Thereafter it intervened periodically to effect changes of policy and personnel, and once again took full power in 1966. This time army rule lasted until 1973, when economic conditions and worsening guerrilla activity in both city and country prepared the way for the return of Juan Perón as president.

The main obstacle to the hegemony of the right was that a large part of the working class remained loyal to Perón. To deny *Peronista* aspirations was to risk violence, as the incidence of guerrilla activity attested. The guerrillas were a tiny minority of Argentinian society, however, and involved no more than a few thousand activists. Nevertheless kidnappings and murders graphically illustrated the potential for disorder, as did labour agitation and troubles at the universities. Argentina reached a new stage, however, in 1971, when General Alejandro Lanusse assumed the presidency. He took over at a time when the army was deeply divided, and concluded that social order depended on winning the co-operation of the *Peronistas*. He therefore scheduled a presidential election for March 1973, and allowed the *Peronistas* to participate. Lanusse even invited Perón to return from exile in Spain and visit the country, which he did in late 1972. Perón did not immediately assume the leadership of his party (by then known as the *Frente Justicialista de Liberación*), but endorsed Héctor Cámpora as its presidential candidate and went back to Spain. Cámpora in effect acted as a stalking-horse for Perón. He won the 1973 election, and in an effort to create national unity proposed extensive concessions to the left. But then Perón returned permanently to Argentina in June, and forced Cámpora to resign. The army had been unhappy with Cámpora's election, so this played into Perón's hands. Moreover, it turned out that the ageing Perón was not prepared to oversee a move to the left. Still, he was a legend in Argentina, and won an easy victory in the presidential election of September. His wife Isabel ran as vice-president, and when Perón died the next year succeeded him in office. The new government was no more successful than its predecessors in solving the country's problems. Inflation was rampant, social disorder worsened, and political violence seemed endemic.

In March 1976, therefore, the military intervened once again, arresting *La Presidenta* and installing General Jorge Videla in power. He moved swiftly and brutally against the left, and thousands of people were killed under mysterious circumstances, never to be seen again. The missing were variously estimated at between 6,000 and 15,000 persons, and were described as the 'disappeared'. General Roberto Viola succeeded Videla in 1981. He initiated discussions with the leaders of the various political parties with a view to holding elections, only to be forced out of office by ill health. The army commander-in-chief therefore took over later the same year, General Leopoldo Galtieri. He allowed the political parties to become more active, but the economy showed little sign of recovery. Like Pinochet in Chile, the military leaders followed free-market prescriptions, with no better result. High military spending and corruption in the government also burdened the economy. And the working class remained militant, so that Argentina was a long way from achieving a stable political system.

The biggest mistake of the regime, however, was to seek refuge in patriotism and nationalism. Hoping to distract the population from its domestic troubles, the generals launched an invasion of the Falkland Islands, called the Islas Malvinas by the Argentinians. This was in April 1982. Great Britain had occupied them since the nineteenth century, though Argentina had long disputed the British claim. The UK won them back after a short war. The Argentinian forces surrendered in June, with 750 killed. The British dead numbered 255 persons.

Equally important for Argentina, the defeat discredited the military, and forced it to move towards civilian rule once again, though only after a series of general strikes in 1982 and 1983. There were widespread demands that the generals explain what happened to the disappeared after the 1976 coup. A military commission blamed the ruling junta for the Falklands defeat, and took the unprecedented act of recommending that the junta stand trial. In August 1983 the government, still under the control of a president appointed by the military (Reynaldo Bignone), granted immunity to the police and the military for their anti-leftist activities. Having acted to protect its interests, the military permitted elections in October 1983, and a new civilian government came to power. Raúl Alfonsín became the new president, running as the candidate of the *Unión Cívica Radical*, but also with substantial *Peronista* support. Alfonsín committed his government to human rights and to an investigation of military crimes, recent legislation notwithstanding. To sum up, the results of the Falklands/Malvinas war seemed to hold out the possibility of civilian rule once again, and that the military would be held to account. Indeed, Videla, Viola and others were eventually imprisoned, though whether the army would reassert itself in the future only time would tell.

EL SALVADOR

While political developments on the continent of South America inspired Washington to provide help to its friends, the United States did not resort to direct military intervention. Nor did the policy-makers want to. It would be far better for South Americans to solve their own problems with minimal outside interference, lest the charge of Yankee imperialism justify reprisals against US interests. Events in Santiago and Buenos Aires suggested that staying in the background could be effective. Indigenous forces were strong enough to achieve solutions compatible with Washington's interests. In Central America and the Caribbean, however, the United States traditionally had assumed a much more direct role. Along with Mexico this region was the site of every US military intervention in the Western Hemisphere.

Geographical proximity meant that the area was important more for its strategic than its economic value (although the United States did have substantial investments). It guarded the southern flank of the US itself and was therefore integral to the Pentagon's defence planning. It was the location of the Panama Canal, the approaches to which needed protecting. It was also the site of a possible second canal route through Nicaragua. Most importantly, it was poor and therefore in constant turmoil. A key factor in shaping the social context was the local oligarchy in each country, whose virtual monopoly of land and wealth inspired movements of resistance, so that crises of largely internal origins impinged upon US strategic calculations. The danger of social revolution on its doorstep recommended that Washington undertake a more active role than in other parts of the Western Hemisphere. By the 1970s El Salvador and Nicaragua seemed to pose the most serious problems.

El Salvador provided a particularly clear example of the role of the local oligarchy. The latter used its control of the political system to legalize the seizure of Indian and *mestizo* lands, the goal being to clear the way for the establishment of new plantations. The process began with decrees in 1881–2 defining private property as the only legal form of land tenure, thereby effectively abolishing the traditional village and communal holdings which had persisted since Spanish times. The oligarchy then claimed title to these lands. In law they were defined as unoccupied and therefore available. The rationale for the government's policy was that communal farming stood in the way of what the oligarchy defined as economic development, because the country's traditional agriculture was mainly for subsistence. By contrast, the plantations produced commodities for export, beginning with coffee in the nineteenth century and adding sugar and cotton later. This enriched the oligarchy, but also spurred its model of development. In time export crops produced enough revenue to begin diversifying the economy, and even to establish a small industrial sector in the capital city of San Salvador.

The oligarchy's control of the state thus enabled it to force much of the rural population from their homes in order to take over the best lands. The dispossessed had to seek work on the new plantations or make tenancy agreements. Alternatively they might flee to less desirable and therefore still undeveloped areas, but where legally they were only squatters. The oligarchy took control of more than 25 per cent of the country's territory in this fashion. As the economy continued to grow throughout the twentieth century there were successive waves of dispossession. These added to the surplus of labour, which in turn helped keep wages depressed. Increasing mechanization on the large estates compounded the problem by reducing the number of employees required. In sum, the oligarchy's development strategy deprived the rural population of land, income and then even work.

The result was a series of uprisings in protest. The worst of these was the rebellion of 1932, when the army took reprisals and slaughtered between 10,000 and 50,000 peasants. (The most authoritative estimate of the dead is probably 30,000.) Many of those killed were women and children, and most were defenceless. The entire system thus required the backing of the army as guarantor. The military became the real centre of power, with army officers almost always assuming the presidency. The seizure of peasant lands continued after the Second World War, so that there was a direct link between the process of dispossession and the rise of guerrilla movements in the 1970s. The families in the rural labour force who owned no land numbered 30,451 in 1961 and 166,922 in 1975.

The event which precipitated the crises of the 1970s and 1980s was the so-called 'Soccer War' between Honduras and El Salvador in July 1969. It lasted just four days, shortly after qualifying games for the World Cup, but had little to do with sport. The real issue was the fate of 300,000 Salvadoran migrants who had moved to Honduras. Honduras was much less densely populated than El Salvador, and was also less developed, but by the 1950s and 1960s a familiar pattern of dispossession was beginning to emerge. There the similarity ended. The Honduran peasantry formed several organizations to resist, and the courts provided greater protection for peasant titles. The peasants even reclaimed some lands. Part of the oligarchy's counter-attack was to blame the Salvadorans for increasing the pressure on Honduran land, and to call for their expulsion. As a result of a series of border incidents and the Soccer War about 130,000 Salvadorans were forced to return home.

The return of so many people exacerbated the land crisis for the government in San Salvador. It was impossible to put off the question of land reform (i.e. redistribution) any longer. Moreover, it came at a time when the political opposition was organizing. In the post-Second World War period the growth of the urban sector had contributed to the expansion of the small working and middle classes. These people expected to have a say in governance. In the 1960s the regime made an attempt to win their support, in the hope of heading off trouble. Washington applauded these efforts, as it wanted to avoid other Cubas. The regime achieved a certain amount of success, and many people joined the government party, which by the mid-1960s was known as the *Partido de Conciliación Nacional,* or PCN. The PCN government even spent money on social programmes. It used patronage to good effect, and set up a national labour organization, with assistance from the American Federation of Labour–Congress of Industrial Organizations (AFL–CIO). The AFL–CIO was the principal federation of labour organizations in the United States, and helped organize anti-communist trade unions in many countries. The government strategy was to co-opt or at least divide the independent labour movement. Despite the political opening, however, the regime continued to apply repression, though more selectively than in the past. Virtually no political concessions were extended to the countryside, but were mainly an urban development.

The government did make room for other political parties, as this was an essential part of gaining a modicum of legitimacy for the regime, and felt confident enough to permit relatively free elections in 1964. The Christian Democratic Party (founded in 1960) won a number of municipal offices and several seats in the legislative assembly, but not a majority. José Napoleón Duarte became the Christian Democratic mayor of the capital city. The PCN candidate won the 1967 presidential election, suggesting that the governing party could hold its own. That the government was playing a risky game, however, became apparent in 1968, when the Christian Democrats increased their representation in the legislative assembly. Smaller opposition parties won seats as well. As a result the PCN government controlled the assembly by only two votes. This represented enough of a crisis by itself, but then the return of the refugees forced the land question into the open. The scene was set for a confrontation between the opposition and the representatives of the PCN oligarchy.

The government decided to seize the initiative and propose a land reform programme on its own terms. The problem was that this also provided the opposition with the opportunity to address the question in the legislature, and to propose alternatives. The government hoped to create a façade of reform while still protecting the large landowners. After all, a real programme would probably benefit the Christian Democrats more than the PCN, by creating a large number of smallholders who might vote for the opposition, and it would erode the power of the oligarchy. As the debate gained momentum, independent labour and student groups came out in favour of land reform as did the Catholic Church, after a long history of siding with the oligarchs. In sum, the forces were gathering which would challenge the government in the 1972 presidential election.

The 1972 election result was probably a victory for Duarte, running on behalf of an opposition coalition. The government, however, declared its own candidate to be the winner. This in turn led to a coup attempt by some opposition forces, with Duarte joining in after others had made the first move, but it was too late. The country's National Guard and a shadowy paramilitary organization known as ORDEN (*Organización*

Democrática Nacionalista) defeated the rebels. Duarte was taken prisoner, tortured, and then exiled to Guatemala. The outcome made it quite clear that the government was willing to tolerate an opposition only so long as the latter had no chance of winning. If its opponents became too strong, then it was time for the government to change the rules. There were still elections, but the limits of democracy were drawn. The effect was that it became all the more difficult to resolve the country's social and economic problems. The conflict in the countryside thus deepened, and various peasant organizations and the Church mobilized the population. During the 1970s several groups came into being, both as political bodies and as guerrilla units. In 1980 most of these would coalesce into the FDR (*Frente Democrático Revolucionario*) and its military arm, the FMLN (*Farabundo Martí de Liberación Nacional*).

Washington therefore welcomed a Salvadoran *coup d'état* in October 1979 and the establishment of what appeared to be a moderate military–civilian junta. The Carter administration hoped this would lead to a lessening of conflict, but it turned out that the military soon emerged as the dominant faction in the new government. Accordingly a number of civilian members of the junta resigned during the next months. Duarte agreed to become provisional president in 1980 (serving until 1982), but there was little he could do to control the army. Repression continued, the FDR–FMLN coalition came together, and the guerrilla war worsened. The provisional government launched a programme of land reform, but it did not include the majority of peasants and was never fully implemented anyway. Some of the same US experts who had set up the pacification programme in Vietnam in the late 1960s shaped the Salvadoran plan, and with hardly better results. And throughout there was the violence. Opposition leaders were regularly murdered, some dropping out of sight without any evidence of exactly what had happened to them (the 'disappeared'). In 1980 the archbishop of San Salvador, Oscar Romero, was shot dead in his cathedral. Despite the continuing unrest Carter restored US military aid before he left office (it had been suspended earlier to protest at the murder of four US churchwomen). Apparently right-wing junta terrorism was preferable to a guerrilla victory. The new Reagan administration increased US military aid from $35.5 million in 1981 to $196.6 million in 1984. It also charged that the rebels were receiving weapons from Cuba (through Nicaragua). Although token contributions did arrive, the allegations of substantial amounts of aid were simply not borne out. Aid from Havana to the guerrillas was in no way comparable to US aid for the government. The guerrillas bought most of their weapons on the black market or captured them from the other side.

At least 45,000 people (mainly civilians) had been killed by the mid-1980s, while 750,000 were refugees abroad, with a greater number displaced at home. (The total population was only 4,800,000.) The US wanted stability, but it wanted to avoid the possibility of a leftist revolution even more, and this forced it to the government's side. Elections for a constituent assembly were held in 1982 and for the presidency in 1984 (Duarte won), but the FDR–FMLN dared not participate. Despite the elections the army remained the dominant force in Salvadoran politics. Thanks to US aid the government had the advantage against the guerrillas, at least in material terms. The Americans also provided small numbers of military advisers, but made only token efforts to persuade San Salvador to stop pro-government death squads from marauding the countryside and attacking peasants accused of supporting the guerrillas. Thus the repression continued, and no doubt helped generate support for the rebels. Yet Washington did not have to assume a direct role in the fighting, as in Vietnam, and to this extent it could be satisfied.

NICARAGUA

For Washington, Nicaragua represented a far worse outcome. In July 1979 social revolutionaries took charge of the government. Moreover, they did so with the support of most of the population, including the country's business and professional classes. The paradox was that US policy had helped drive political moderates into the arms of the revolutionaries, though eventually many in the centre and on the right turned against the new regime. Washington's own mistakes thus played an important role in events.

The US interest in Nicaragua dated from the mid nineteenth century, when Cornelius Vanderbilt's Accessory Transit Company constructed a transportation route across Central America. Overland segments were linked by Nicaragua's system of natural waterways. The latter also made the country a likely site for a trans-isthmian canal. In due course, however, Panama became Washington's choice for a canal. From this point on the US interest was to prevent the construction of another and competing canal. When Nicaraguan president José Santos Zelaya invited German and Japanese interests to consider doing so, Washington came to the support of an uprising against his government. United States

Marines were dispatched in December 1909. A new leader was installed as president, and US banks took over the financial administration of the country. Another rebellion took place in 1912. Again the Marines landed, this time to stay. In the 1914 Bryan–Chamorro Treaty the US acquired sovereignty over any Nicaraguan territory needed for a possible second canal, thus heading off its competitors.

For all practical purposes Nicaragua became a United States protectorate. Washington kept troops in the country continuously from 1912 to 1925 and, after a brief respite, from 1926 to 1933. In the second period a force of 6,000 US Marines became entangled in a fierce guerrilla war. As in El Salvador, a coffee boom beginning in the late nineteenth century had led to the expropriation of peasant lands, and by essentially the same means. Indian uprisings occurred again and again, as did factional conflicts among the oligarchy. In 1927 US troops became involved in a war against Augusto César Sandino, the leader of a small band of guerrillas seeking land for their people and refusing to accept the jurisdiction of the central government. By 1933, however, the Marines withdrew in a strategy which anticipated the Vietnamization programme attempted by the Nixon administration in South-East Asia decades later. Instead of taking permanent responsibility for the country's internal affairs, the United States trained a new National Guard, and turned the war over to Nicaraguan clients. Unlike in Vietnam, the policy worked.

In theory the withdrawal of the US Marines assured the formal independence of the country, which had a very important effect on the guerrillas. Disagreements developed over what to do next. Should they compromise and work with the regime, especially as the National Guard was proving a very effective fighting force? Or should they continue the war? Various factions began to break away from Sandino. He therefore attempted to negotiate with the regime, but there was treachery on the other side. Sandino was lured into the capital of Managua and assassinated on 21 February 1934. The leader of the National Guard, Anastasio Somoza García, gave the order. The US ambassador was implicated as well, and had close ties to Somoza. A gambler, counterfeiter and unsuccessful businessman, Somoza had been educated in the United States and then managed to marry into one of Nicaragua's leading families. He took over the presidency in 1936, inaugurating a dynasty which endured for forty-three years. The family observed the forms of democracy, and so sometimes transferred the presidency to various puppets in a practice known as *continuismo*. More to the point, strategic considerations assured the Somozas of Washington's constant support. Armed with US military aid, they overawed any potential opposition.

The Somozas used the state to advance their personal fortunes, while taking care to provide opportunities for the officers and men of the National Guard to do likewise. Still, the Somozas did not monopolize the entire economy, and there was a sizeable class of independent business and professional people (foreign enterprise did not play a large part in the economy). Because they often competed with the Somozas in business, the members of the upper and middle classes might have constituted an opposition force on the political right but none the less against the government (what we shall call the 'moderates'), but they feared the National Guard. At the same time they were reluctant to join forces with the small radical factions among the peasantry and urban workers – the radicals were likely to attack all business interests, not just those of the Somozas. The only choice left was to bargain with the Somozas at election time for a few seats in the legislature. Somoza was happy to oblige, to keep them quiet. Only after decades of stalemate did events force the moderates to assume a more active role.

On 23 December 1972 an earthquake devastated the capital city of Managua, killing 10,000 people, injuring another 50,000, and leaving 200,000 homeless. The world provided $600 million in reconstruction assistance, and President Anastasio Somoza Debayle (son of Somoza García) took charge of the aid. Not surprisingly the Somoza clan won most of the contracts and arranged most of the financing (the total value of family assets at home and abroad may have reached $1,000 million), the effect of which was to crowd out the rest of the economic elite – who in reply organized the first effective opposition. Moreover, they did so in a context of rising popular resistance to the regime. The earthquake had disrupted the entire economy, including the marketing of export crops. It worsened conditions in the countryside as well as in the city. There was also trouble because of a new cycle of expropriation in the 1950s and 1960s, as Nicaragua began producing cotton on a large scale. Indian communities in the north-west zones of the country, for example, lost 100,000 hectares between 1950 and 1955. The process of dispossession was by no means a distant memory. There was a communist party in Nicaragua, but it followed the Moscow line of collaborating with the existing governments in Latin America, and did not play a role in the events which were about to unfold. As we have noted, the Soviet Union for all practical purposes conceded the Western Hemisphere as a United States sphere of influence, except for Cuba. The USSR certainly welcomed successful anti-capitalist revolutions, but it did not try to initiate them. Hence the countryside would be organized by others.

For the time being, however, the moderates had the initiative. The prime mover was Pedro Joaquín Chamorro, editor of *La Prensa* and a member of one of the country's founding families. In December 1974 the moderates coalesced to form the *Union Democrática Liberación*, or UDEL, which thereby became the principal opposition coalition. Shortly thereafter an obscure group of guerrillas gained national attention. This was the *Frente Sandinista de Liberación Nacional* (FSLN), founded in 1962 and named after Sandino. The FSLN took the Cuban revolution as a guide to strategy, but its early efforts to organize resistance proved unsuccessful. Then, just after the formation of UDEL, twenty-five Sandinistas staged a dramatic raid in Managua and took a dozen prominent political and business leaders as hostages. These were exchanged for the release of several political prisoners and safe passage to Cuba, and the FSLN dropped out of sight.

The raid, however, provided Somoza with an excuse to act. Invoking the guerrilla threat, he declared a state of emergency, instituted martial law, and imposed censorship. The last, of course, also affected the UDEL. In the countryside the National Guard launched a series of forays against alleged FSLN strongholds. The attacks were intended to provide a graphic example of what would happen to anyone who supported the guerrillas. Possibly 80 per cent of the peasantry in the provinces of Zelaya, Matagalpa and Segovia were moved into resettlement camps. Thereafter the region was considered a 'free-fire' zone. The term recalled similar tactics in Vietnam, and meant that anyone found in the area after it had been cleared was presumed to be a guerrilla and liable to be shot on sight. The administration of Gerald Ford almost doubled its military aid to Somoza, but when Jimmy Carter became president in 1977 aid was reduced because of the government's human-rights violations. Washington did not consider the FSLN to be a substantial threat to Somoza, and concluded that cuts would not affect US strategic interests. After all, the FSLN had virtually disappeared after the 1974 raid, and the National Guard had taught a lesson to potential FSLN recruits. Reducing military aid would boost the US image as a defender of human rights. Besides, Argentina and Israel sold arms to Somoza, and helped offset the reduction of US aid.

After years of silence, however, the Sandinistas re-emerged and launched a series of attacks on five cities in October 1977, thus demonstrating that they were still a factor in developments. At the same time a group of exiles in Costa Rica called for including the FSLN in any new alliance of opposition forces. This was the first step towards creating a broad coalition of everyone opposed to Somoza. Yet such a coalition was many months off. More time passed before the moderates and the Sandinistas joined forces. The moderates did so only when it became clear that electoral politics could not bring about a transfer of power. For their part the Sandinistas were also slow to act. They were divided into different factions, some of which feared the consequences of joining with other classes whose interests might be opposed to those of the rural poor. Much of what might happen, therefore, was up to Somoza. The longer the stalemate, the more likely would his opponents be to coalesce.

The problem was that Somoza seemed bent on eliminating his opponents, not on compromising. Chamorro was assassinated on 10 January 1978, unleashing weeks of rioting and a new series of FSLN attacks on the National Guard. The moderates demanded Somoza's resignation, and backed this up by calling for a general strike. Most people complied, and the trouble lasted into February. Yet by 6 February the UDEL and other centrist groups were urging a return to work. They were concerned whether the rising tide of violence would permit the FSLN to take over, and the moderates did not wish to defeat Somoza only to see the Sandinistas assume power. The strike ended, and Somoza survived.

As the stand-off continued, however, the much-heralded grand coalition of all opposition groups finally came together, in the organization of the *Frente Amplio de Oposición*, or FAO, in July, which included the Sandinistas. The moderates wanted to mobilize the masses, so FSLN participation was essential. Until July they had hoped that Washington would press Somoza to compromise. The moderates interpreted a compromise to mean that he would give up the presidency, and that they would inherit power, in which case they need not cater to the FSLN. It was significant that few moderates contemplated disbanding the National Guard. In the absence of compromise, though, the moderates needed the Sandinistas. Hence the formation of the FAO.

The rising power of the Sandinistas became evident the next month, August. Guerrillas from the FSLN entered the National Palace during a session of the legislature and took about 1,500 people hostage. These were exchanged for fifty-nine political prisoners. More importantly, the guerrillas were cheered by masses of people when leaving Managua. The incident also led to uprisings in several provinces, indicating substantial support for the Sandinistas. About 3,000 people were killed in the next three weeks, as the National Guard took reprisals. These events persuaded the Carter administration that a Sandinista victory was quite possible. It was therefore finally time to press Somoza to share power with the moderates. Washington urged the Organization of American States (OAS) to act as mediator, and talks were soon under way. The US goal was to organize a transitional government made up of the FAO and also Somoza's National Liberal Party. The FSLN was not to be included, and Somoza's National Guard would remain in place. The US objective was to ensure that the moderates and not the FSLN took charge of any new government.

United States pressure on the FAO to negotiate with Somoza, however, split the coalition and thus undermined its capacity to assume a share in power. Many of the organizations in the FAO wanted Somoza to resign outright. The US initiative soon proved irrelevant, however, because in January 1979 Somoza announced he would not yield. Washington threatened to invoke sanctions against his government, but in fact engaged in only token actions: the embassy reduced its staff by 50 per cent, while a four-person military mission returned to the United States. And with the FAO beginning to fall apart, the US had decided to accept Somoza's decision to remain in office. The divisions in the ranks of the moderates meant that in Washington's view Somoza was still the only alternative to the guerrillas.

Given Washington's reluctance to act against Somoza, however, the moderates were driven into the arms of the FSLN. In effect the future of Nicaragua was put to the test of battle. While the National Guard had more fire-power than the other side, its brutality also alienated large parts of the population, so that the course of the war moved rapidly in favour of the Sandinistas. The final FSLN offensive began in June 1979. Before the end of the month the Sandinistas controlled most of the country. On 16 June they organized a junta of five people which included representatives of both the left and the moderates. Chamorro's widow was a member, as was one of the country's most important business leaders. There was only one representative from the FSLN, Daniel Ortega Saavedra. The junta appointed a cabinet of eighteen people, again with a large representation of moderates. Despite the formal make-up of the provisional government, though, real power had shifted to the Sandinistas. They were doing the fighting, and, more importantly, they had the support of the peasantry.

The formation of a provisional government that controlled most of the country finally persuaded Washington to abandon Somoza. On 22 June, at the Organization of American States, the United States came out in favour of his resignation. Ignoring the existence of the junta, the US secretary of state called for a new government and an OAS peacekeeping force to enforce a cease-fire. Many OAS members branded the latter as simply a disguised US military intervention, and it was rejected out of hand. But the OAS did endorse US efforts to mediate among the parties. Washington therefore again suggested that Somoza resign, but that his Liberal Party, the National Guard and the opposition share power in a transitional government, with elections to follow in 1981. The problem was that the FSLN had already won the war. The US was simply too late. Finally realizing that it could not hope to exclude the Sandinistas from the government altogether, Washington made one last effort to dilute their influence, by offering substantial economic aid in exchange for the entry of two additional moderates to the junta and a commitment not to disband the National Guard or the National Liberal Party. Again, this failed to take account of the effective victory of the FSLN, and suggested that even the most sophisticated political analysts were capable of losing touch with reality. Somoza fled to Miami on 17 July 1979, but was assassinated in Asunción, Paraguay, on 17 September 1980. The cost of overthrowing the dictatorship was between 40,000 and 50,000 lives, and was only one measure of the devastation caused by the Somozas. The Sandinistas were left with an inheritance of poverty and illiteracy, and faced a formidable task in rebuilding society.

A NOTE ON JAMAICA

Clearly the Sandinista victory of 1979 showed that there were limits to US hegemony in Central America. The same year, a revolutionary regime also seized power on the small Caribbean island of Grenada, eventually leading to an invasion by US forces in 1983 (see Chapter 12). All of Central America, the Caribbean and the Caribbean Common-wealth, however, did not follow the same course. Jamaica provides an example. There, in 1980, the People's National Party (PNP) of Michael Manley was voted out of power. Manley had been prime minister since 1972, winning re-election in 1976. Throughout he campaigned on a platform of anti-imperialism and social democracy (i.e. the gradual introduction of some socialist measures via parliamentary rather than revolutionary means). After eight years of Manley the voters turned to the Jamaica Labour Party (JLP) of Edward Seaga. The JLP stood for more foreign investment, anti-communism and pro-business policies on the home front. The theory was that a friendly policy towards business would result in new investment and jobs.

Washington viewed Manley much like Allende. Once in power he established close relations with Havana, and welcomed Cuban advisers. His government inaugurated a literacy campaign, free secondary education and a programme of land reform. The last, however, was very limited, and did not significantly alter the concentration of land holding. Manley also nationalized foreign-owned public utilities, specifically the telephone, electric and bus companies, although he compensated the owners. He dramatically increased taxes on the bauxite mining and alumina industry, which was 100 per cent foreign-owned. He also undertook negotiations to buy majority control. The industry accounted for 29 per cent of the value of Jamaica's exports in 1968, more than each of the next three sectors: agriculture, tourism and manufactures. It had grown rapidly from the 1950s on, led by US and Canadian aluminium companies. The companies fought Manley's policies by shifting production to other countries. In 1975 the US companies cut their imports of Jamaican bauxite by 30 per cent, while doubling those from Guinea. Bauxite sales were declining throughout the world in this period, but Jamaica experienced disproportionate losses. Other foreign investors besides the aluminium companies cut back as well. Although a global recession no doubt accounted for some of the decline, the inflow of foreign capital fell drastically from US $254 million to $115 million between 1973 and 1975, with a net outflow in 1976.

Much of Manley's programme, however, was *ad hoc* rather than the result of a coherent economic plan, despite policy statements issued by the PNP. Given Jamaica's dependency on foreign credit and investment, there was only so much he could do. The problem was that his socialist and anti-Yankee rhetoric suggested otherwise, and sounded the alarm in Washington. The US government rallied to the aluminium companies' side in 1975 and 1976 by refusing loans to Jamaica and attacking its credit-rating. In the same period the unfavourable press resulted in significantly fewer tourists from the United States. Even so, Manley was re-elected in 1976, suggesting that his policies were popular, and despite alleged CIA activity in the campaign. The outcome seemed to confirm Washington's gloomiest estimates of the situation. In 1977 Manley defied the International Monetary Fund, refusing to accept its austerity programme as a condition of credit. He also raised taxes on high-income groups, imposed restrictions on foreign exchange, established the State

Trading Corporation, and nationalized the Jamaican branch of Barclay's Bank. The latter was to be compensated.

The problem was that the island needed credit and foreign-controlled jobs. Within months of snubbing the IMF the prime minister accepted a loan (US $74 million) with some of the same strings attached as before. The IMF insisted on a drastic devaluation of the currency, a reduction in government spending and a wage freeze. Manley retreated in other areas as well, and sought better relations with the aluminium companies. In other words, there were more than a few difficulties in attempting to break away from a dependency on foreign capital, especially while at the same time promising costly social reform at home.

The overall problem was that the 1970s global recession made it relatively easy for the aluminium companies and credit agencies to bring pressure to bear on the government. Falling revenues made it impossible for the prime minister to fulfil his promises of domestic reform, and affected his chances of winning re-election. The economic down-swing also created hardship for many classes of people in Jamaica, so that they began turning to Seaga. Many thought that his pro-business policies would create jobs and bring relief. Manley himself was retreating from his anti-foreign policies by 1977, but the effect of this was to alienate his more radical supporters. The formula for his defeat at the polls in 1980 was working itself out, as he was losing support across the political spectrum. Although Manley repeated his earlier promises in the election campaign, his government was voted down. Seaga came to power with the biggest majority in Jamaican history: the JLP won fifty-two seats to the PNP's eight. The IMF acted quickly to extend a major loan (US $698 million in April 1981), once again illustrating the political character of IMF economic policy. From Washington's point of view the outcome was satisfactory indeed, because it was the result of the will of the people as expressed at the polls. There was no need for a coup, though there were charges that Manley's opponents received financial help from US sources.

To summarize, although US–USSR rivalry was not as intense in the Western Hemisphere as in the Middle East, Washington none the less faced a series of crises. The limited influence of the Soviet Union by no means assured US hegemony, and sometimes indigenous forces in the hemisphere proved capable of challenging Washington's sway, as in Nicaragua. Yet the record was mixed. The United States was indeed able to influence the outcome in many situations, with the fall of Allende and the electoral defeat of Manley as perhaps the clearest examples. The question, however, was whether pro-US regimes would reform, or whether the conditions which generated support for radical political alternatives in the first place would be perpetuated. It thus remained to be seen whether US hemispheric hegemony would be secure.

12

TRENDS

We have hardly scratched the surface of contemporary history – that is, the history which blends into our own times and affects outcomes today. Yet we have certainly done enough to begin drawing some conclusions. It is apparent, for example, that the United States and the developed Western countries still retain more influence globally than the Soviet Union and its allies, despite a significant increase in the power of the latter since the Second World War. While the Russians achieved approximate parity in nuclear arms and rocketry by the 1970s, after decades in which the Americans enjoyed superiority, we need to remember that influence depends on more than weapons alone – non-military forms of power, particularly economic, are just as important, and in this respect the West remains far ahead. Recall that the gross national product of the Soviet Union was generally half or less that of the United States in the 1980s, and that the total GNP of the Warsaw Pact countries was probably only one-third that of the industrialized Western Bloc countries (i.e. the members of the Organization for Economic Co-operation and Development).

On the other hand, it is also a fact that the Eastern Bloc came into existence mainly during and after the Second World War. Whereas the USSR and the Mongolian People's Republic were the only communist governments on the eve of the war, there were many more such regimes by the 1980s. Yet it is important to retain a sense of proportion. Marxist states (of widely varying degrees of ideological consistency) remained in a distinct minority, and in the 1980s numbered at most thirty out of 170 governments in the world. Thus, while the expansion of the Eastern Bloc has been a major trend in post-1945 history, the main point still holds – most countries are part of or linked to the Western Bloc, even allowing for those which have attempted to remain neutral in the East–West conflict (e.g. India). Moreover, other factors affect the Soviets' ability to act globally. The rise of Solidarity in Poland shows that the industrialized nations of Eastern Europe are as prone to internal crises as ever. This has a direct influence on Moscow's global strategies. The Soviets need to keep watch over their immediate neighbours, and this imposes constraints on their freedom of action elsewhere. Again, this works to the advantage of the West. Of course, the industrialized countries of the Western Bloc have their own internal problems, but their greater economic power still enables them to maintain the preponderance of influence globally.

The scope of Western influence thus makes it difficult to blame the spread of social revolution in the Third World entirely on Soviet expansionism, however much the USSR might gain by the establishment of anti-Western governments. We have emphasized the history of the Third World and its relations with the superpowers because about three-quarters of the world's population live there. The point is, however, that social revolution in the Third World has arisen in a context of mainly Western and not Soviet hegemony. The colonial world was largely in the West's orbit at the end of the Second World War. Moreover, while decolonization subsequently diminished the influence of the West, it hardly eliminated it. Instead, the influence of the former imperial powers assumed a new form, neo-colonialism. The problem was that Western influence was not always benign. The terms of trade between the First World and the Third World were often unfavourable to the latter, thus spurring anti-Western feeling. Furthermore, the Western powers too often supported authoritarian regimes, albeit in the name of anti-communism, and provided material assistance to them. The effect was to turn many Third World people against the West, and the Soviets profited accordingly.

Moscow therefore had an interest in encouraging anti-Western forces in the Third World, although its motives were usually more pragmatic than ideological, having more to do with the national security and self-interest of the USSR than with its mission to spread social revolution, and were calculated to gain strategic advantages by winning allies in the East–West struggle. The extent to which the Soviets are willing to foment (or initiate) revolution for the sake of revolution and consequently risk reprisals from the West remains a question. Moscow ought to do so if ideology dictates its policy, but the record shows that its foreign policies are often opportunistic. It is more likely to take advantage of existing revolutionary movements in the Third World after the fact than to try and create them itself. The legacy of Western colonialism and neo-colonialism is more commonly at the root of revolution in the Third World than the policies of the USSR. It is clear, for example, that the Soviets were not the cause of the 1979 revolution in Nicaragua. Among outside influences, US support for the Somoza dictatorship had much more to do with the outcome, although subsequently the USSR provided small amounts of assistance to the Sandinistas.

It is also clear that military force plays a large role in contemporary history, despite the importance of other, non-military forms of competition. Vietnam showed this perhaps most emphatically, though several other examples could be cited. After 1945 the Western powers deployed armies in many parts of the Third World. For their part the Russians did not hesitate to act in Eastern Europe, but the record shows that the USSR was less likely than the West to send its own troops to fight elsewhere (i.e. in the less-developed world). On the other hand, in 1979 Moscow did intervene militarily in Afghanistan, as we shall see presently. And although the superpowers have never gone to war directly against each other since 1945, they came dangerously close during the Cuban Missile Crisis. The rise of the militant right in the United States suggests that the Americans are likely to pursue tough policies towards Moscow, while the Soviets' overall inferiority (except for certain categories of arms) has steeled their determination to catch up. In most types of East–West competition the USSR has not usually been in the lead, but it is certainly willing to try to match and then surpass the USA.

Nevertheless it is a fact that the Third World, and not the developed centres, has been the site of most of the world's military conflicts since 1945. Barring a direct Soviet–American nuclear confrontation (which is by no means an impossible eventuality), this is likely to remain the case for the indefinite future. Hence it is still important to give a high priority to Third World affairs in estimating the probable course of future global history. There are other trends which might also provide the basis for projecting contemporary developments, but the risk of war in the Third World is certainly one of the most important. Always remember that the underdeveloped countries are home to most of the people on earth. Their problems deserve our particular attention. War in the Third World, of course, may be the result of either Western or Eastern intervention, or may arise from mainly indigenous roots. Events in Southern Africa, the Middle East, South-East Asia, and Central America and the Caribbean confirm the variety of possible outcomes.

WESTERN COLONIALISM AND REVOLUTION:
MOZAMBIQUE
In the 1970s and 1980s the legacy of Western colonialism was perhaps
nowhere clearer than in Southern Africa, and led to a series of violent
crises. Portugal's role in Mozambique provides a telling example. The
Soviets were not the cause of the revolutionary movements which
emerged there or elsewhere in the region, although they provided aid to
various participants once a revolutionary situation began to unfold.
Overall, Western influences were more salient in explaining the origins
of revolution.

Of all the European powers in Africa, Lisbon held on the longest and
maintained the most backward empire, at least as measured by the
degree of political participation permitted its subject peoples and by the
forms of economic exploitation practised. In law, any African who spoke
Portuguese fluently, adopted European ways, completed military duty,
and met a means test (i.e. who became assimilated) was eligible for
Portuguese citizenship and might enjoy the same rights as Europeans.
But the catch was that by 1950, when Lisbon incorporated its African
colonies as overseas provinces of Portugal itself, hardly any blacks were
accepted (indeed, considerably less than 1 per cent). Thus, in practice,
brute repression remained the main instrument of Portuguese
hegemony. This simply bred an opposition which became more and
more radicalized. Anti-colonial organizations took shape in the mid-
1950s and early 1960s, first in Guinea-Bissau and Angola under the
inspiration of the social revolutionary Amilcar Cabral, and then in
Mozambique. These gained momentum over the next decade, so that by
the mid-1970s, when the right-wing dictatorship of Marcello Caetano
(the successor of the infamous Antonio de Oliveira Salazar) fell to a
military coup in Lisbon, they were ready to assume power.

Portugal's neglect was the product of weakness, specifically its own
economic underdevelopment. The Portuguese lacked the resources to
exploit the territories they controlled, and before the Second World War
maintained a minimal presence in Africa. Mozambique may serve to
illustrate the problem. Lisbon provided a skeleton government, but one
hardly able to do more than police the country. In the private sector
Portuguese entrepreneurs had little wealth to invest compared to their
counterparts in the colonies of Britain and France. Hence they relied on
the cheapest and therefore the crudest forms of exploitation, including a
system of forced labour.

Various forms of compulsory labour had been established by all the European powers at one time or another, but in the case of Portugal such a system remained part of the formal corpus of law until 1962, and in practice for a few years after that – it was not something associated with the distant past. It went without saying, of course, that criminals were subjected to a system of prison labour. But, in addition, all indigenous peoples were required to work at least six months of each year on terms specified by the colonial bureaucracy. Moreover, the law provided that, if they did not do so, 'the public authorities will force them to comply'.* In most cases the choice was to seek wage labour in foreign-owned enterprises or to produce crops for export brokers. Traditional, tribal patterns of work were not what colonial officials had in mind as meeting the requirements of the law. Further, the colonial authorities could sell the services of the unemployed to private business under a system of contract labour, or could require such people to work for the state itself. In agriculture Africans were required to produce for European exporters, in accordance with quotas assigned by the government. They were thus not always free to choose which crops to grow on their own lands, and received less than world prices for their produce. For all practical purposes they were in the employ of Portuguese and other foreign interests, like it or not.

Yet even the labour system was insufficient for the Portuguese to monopolize their own territories, so that an important source of revenue for the colonial regime came from granting leases on possibly two-thirds of Mozambique to private companies owned by the citizens of other colonial powers. Most of these were controlled by British businessmen, and leases included the right to impose taxes, to apply the forced labour system, to sublet land, and to do their own policing. A major source of revenue for the Portuguese administration came from the provision of transportation services, again mainly to the entrepreneurs of other imperial powers. Mozambican ports provided shipping facilities for gold mines in the northern reaches of the Union of South Africa (later the Republic of South Africa, or RSA), as well as for land-locked Rhodesia. The rail and port system, in fact, had been largely financed by British capital. Finally the colonial authorities derived revenue from contracting out labour to the gold industry in South Africa. The Portuguese received

* Cited in David Wield, 'Mozambique – Late Colonialism and Early Problems of Transition', Gordon White et al. (eds), *Revolutionary Socialist Development in the Third World* (Lexington: 1983), 77.

a fee for each person recruited, and many Africans were desperate enough to volunteer for the work. Given the post-war context of decolonization, probably the most notable feature of Portuguese rule was that it lasted as long as it did.

Only by the mid-1940s did the Portuguese presence in Mozambique begin to increase relative to that of other foreigners, as businessmen in Portugal itself drew more and more upon colonial resources to support the development of their home economy. Thus the rise of a small textile industry in Portugal made the system of acreage quotas all the more important, so that in 1944 possibly one-third of all Mozambicans were forced to grow cotton in order to meet the needs of industry in the metropolis. Portugal's role in other sectors of Mozambique's economy increased as well, particularly banking, coffee, tea, cashew nuts, sisal and copra. Hence the colonial authorities intensified the system of forced labour and forced cropping, so that, rather than passing out of existence as an anachronism, the system gained a new lease on life. Moreover, the subordination of agriculture to the needs of Portuguese business often occurred at the expense of food production for the local population, and once self-sufficient regions experienced more and more shortages. It should be noted, though, that in overall terms Mozambique remained mainly a service economy for the Union of South Africa and Rhodesia. The importance of a larger Portuguese stake in the country was that internal development led to shortages of workers in some areas, and helped prolong the system of forced labour.

In sum, while colonial powers such as Britain and France eventually invoked the neo-colonial solution (though sometimes only after resisting to the point of war) and worked to groom successors who were nationalists but not revolutionaries, Portugal refused any meaningful political concessions. A tiny number of blacks were to be found in the Mozambican civil service, but invariably in the lowest postings. One authority, in fact, estimates that by 1970 only fifty of these people had earned secondary school credentials. Data for 1974 suggest that probably only a few hundred blacks had some (but incomplete) secondary education, so that the Portuguese record in Mozambique was comparable to that of the Belgians in the Congo, and probably worse.

The outcome, however, was different from that in the Congo, where foreign interests took advantage of the disarray of the indigenous political class. As we have seen (Chapter 6), the price was civil war, but the defeat of radicals like Lumumba was an important gain for the West. By contrast, the result in Mozambique worked against Western interests.

It also showed that every situation was unique, because in this case the persistence of Portuguese repression had the effect of offsetting the Africans' political inexperience and mobilizing them into action. By the late 1960s and early 1970s revolutionary organization was far more advanced than in the Congo earlier. It was precisely because Portugal refused to make any concessions and held on considerably longer than Belgium that these organizations had time to grow and mature. The problem for the West, though, was that the longer Lisbon's colonial wars dragged on, the more radical the opposition became. The goals of anti-capitalist revolutionaries thus became part and parcel of the independence struggle.

In Mozambique the most important organization was FRELIMO (the *Frente de Libertação de Moçambique*, or Mozambique Liberation Front). Its founders were students, young teachers and skilled workers who had fled to Tanzania, where they regrouped and prepared to return. A few of these people had studied in Lisbon, and were versed in Marxist thought, but adapted their strategies to the needs of African society. The result was that they built a movement based on peasant support and firmly rooted in the countryside, so that they soon became capable of waging guerrilla warfare. Furthermore, by the 1960s and 1970s the Soviet Union and China were in direct competition for the favour of Third World revolutionaries, and wooed them with economic and military aid. FRELIMO benefited accordingly. On the other side, the West provided assistance to Portugal. Besides their stake in supporting a government fighting social revolutionaries, the United States and other Western powers all had military bases on Portuguese-controlled territory, and so wanted to maintain friendly relations with Lisbon.

Thus, by the late 1960s, it was clear that Portugal faced the prospect of a long drawn-out battle. In the case of Mozambique, Lisbon was compelled to dispatch 70,000 troops to the colony, but the army was ill-equipped and ill-paid and achieved few military successes. Moreover, because armed anti-colonial and revolutionary organizations were making progress in Angola and Guinea-Bissau as well, it had to fight three wars at once. Accordingly FRELIMO was able to take control of about one-quarter of Mozambique's territory by the early 1970s, and began asserting its claim to legitimacy by setting up its own political and economic institutions in the conquered areas. At first the specific structures varied widely, but in time collective forms became common, so that FRELIMO's success in the anti-colonial struggle culminated in the establishment of a type of Marxist regime. The commitment to

Marxism came only after heated disputes (and even assassinations) in the late 1960s over not only political strategies (such as private versus collective ownership of land) but such traditional issues as polygamy, child marriage and the sale of brides, as well as tribal rivalries and the role of chiefs and elders in the new order. Further, some FRELIMO leaders profited personally from co-operative projects organized in the liberated zones, so that the problem of corruption had to be dealt with. But, owing to the popular identification of private production with Portuguese exploitation, collectivist solutions tended to win out.

Just as important, the colonial wars demoralized the Portuguese army. Officers and men were asked to make successive tours of duty, but in the absence of a clear military victory they received little more than criticism at home. By the early 1970s military expenditures constituted 40 per cent of the national budget, yet it was still not enough. Lisbon simply did not have the resources to do the job, no matter how they were divided between domestic and colonial priorities. The army had neither the numbers nor the equipment to bring the conflict to a resolution. Among others, university students were drafted into service, but many of these people were sympathetic to the guerrilla cause and sowed dissension in the ranks. They were not keen to sacrifice their lives to preserve the profits of entrepreneurs who not only exploited Africa but opposed democracy for Portugal itself. Both career officers and draftees therefore thought they were being badly used, and even befriended Mozambican captives, who of course reinforced the soldiers' sense of alienation.

The result was an army coup against Caetano on 25 April 1974 and the assumption of power in Lisbon by General Antonio de Spinola. Spinola favoured an end to both the war and the dictatorship, but the new regime was not completely united. While it had come to power largely because of the initiative of junior officers who had been radicalized by their experiences in Africa, it also included a number of older, right-wing officers whose goal was simply to vindicate the army. Indeed there were strict limits to Spinola's reformism. The more radical officers thought his prestige would assist their cause, and so supported him to lead an interim government until they had time to consolidate a power base of their own. But Spinola shared few of their views, and hardly sympathized with their links to radicals and communists in both Portugal and Africa. On the contrary, he had once been military governor of Guinea-Bissau and was regarded as the chief conspirator behind the assassination of Amilcar Cabral. He favoured the end of the colonial wars only because he saw that Portugal could not win militarily. He did not want immediate independence for all the colonies, but some new form of federation between them and Portugal. His preference thus was for a neo-colonial solution. On the home front he did favour dismantling the old political order, but because it was incapable of responding to the needs of modern industry and not because he was a democrat. Spinola was a director of one of the country's leading monopolies, the Champalimaud group, which had considerable interests in Africa. The result was a falling-out with the more radical officers, and Spinola was forced to resign as president in September. With his departure the radicals were in the ascendancy, though only for the next year. This, however, was long enough to assure the demise of the Portuguese empire.

The fall of the Caetano government enabled FRELIMO to make rapid gains on the battlefield, so that Lisbon promised full autonomy later in 1974. Mozambique became legally independent in November 1975. Moreover, the terms of independence recognized FRELIMO as the sole political party in the new nation. The outcome, however, was complicated by the departure of virtually all the white settlers. Of the 250,000 Portuguese in Mozambique at the beginning of the 1970s, only about 100,000 were still in the country by the time of independence, and most of these left shortly thereafter. Settler farms and plantations were simply abandoned, as were the few industries in the cities. Indeed the whites destroyed capital goods and machinery as they withdrew, in an attempt to take what reprisals they could. Because the Portuguese had run the most-developed sectors of the economy and monopolized the skills to administer the economy, Mozambique was thrown into even more chaos. Both the domestic and export sectors broke down, and massive unemployment ensued. Blacks as a result continued to seek work in the Republic of South Africa, just as in colonial times, though the decline in world demand associated with the late 1970s economic recession meant that there were fewer jobs to be had there as well.

The country thus faced a monumental task, the building of a new nation virtually whole and entire. The departure of practically all the Portuguese meant that the people most likely to support counter-revolution were gone, but the total collapse of the colonial order meant that FRELIMO had to move rapidly to assert its authority. Building on its experiences during the war, it organized *grupos dinamizadores*, or 'dynamizing groups', to generate support for the regime. These consisted of eight to ten elected community or workplace leaders, and were set up in villages, schools, factories or whatever institutional setting was practical. Their job was to mobilize the people behind the government and to hold weekly assemblies at the 'grass roots' level. In addition the government took possession of abandoned Portuguese property in both city and country, and this became the core of a publicly owned sector. Industry was partly nationalized (just under 50 per cent of enterprises remained in private hands), while in the countryside FRELIMO set up co-operatives and state farms. The plan was eventually to organize the rural population into communal villages, but by the end of the 1970s most land was still farmed individually. The government also took over social services such as education and medicine. In colonial times these had been almost entirely for the benefit of Europeans, but independence by itself did not immediately resolve the problems created by the flight of the Portuguese. For example, while there were 550 medical doctors in the country in 1974, only eighty were left at the end of 1975, for a total population approaching 12 million. The reorganization of society and the economy was thus a massive undertaking, and the new nation clearly needed time to see whether it could be done.

Of equal import for the future, Mozambique was dependent on its immediate neighbours, white-ruled Rhodesia and the Republic of South Africa, for trade and jobs. But they had a considerable stake in undermining the new regime, lest such a revolutionary idea as majority rule spread to their territories. Hence the number of Mozambicans recruited for work in South Africa dropped from 115,000 in 1975 to only 45,000 in 1976, though this was in part caused by the global recession and the falling demand for South African output. In Mozambique, where the earnings of migrant workers constituted about 35 per cent of the country's foreign exchange for 1975, the effects were devastating. And in 1976 the Mozambique–Rhodesia border was closed. The major Mozambican port of Beira thus lost a considerable transport business, as Rhodesia had accounted for about half of Mozambique's port and railway earnings. South African troops also operated inside Mozambique's borders, and sometimes even raided the capital of Maputo itself in the early 1980s. South Africa also provided the backing for anti-government guerrillas operating inside Mozambique, the *Movimento Nacional da Resistencia de Moçambique*, or MNR (Mozambique National Resistance). FRELIMO gave sanctuary to organizations such as the African National Congress (fighting white rule in South Africa), but it had to act with circumspection given its problems at home.

For the Western powers Lisbon's defeat had demonstrated the futility of resisting change. Indeed, the Portuguese collapse was so sudden that there was little to do but accept the outcome. The only choice was to rely on indirect forms of influence. Yet in the long run these promised the greatest dividends, as the West had the resources to outbid the Soviets. Thus, in the years after independence, it turned out that the industrial nations of the Organization for Economic Co-operation and Development provided considerably more economic and technical assistance to Mozambique than did the Eastern Bloc. The effect was to give the new regime time to consolidate its rule, and hence to survive. It also gave the West a chance to influence the future, but with what results remained to be seen.

ELSEWHERE IN SOUTHERN AFRICA

The situation in other areas of Southern Africa was rather similar to that in Mozambique, and the intervention of outside powers was equally overt. Angola's leading exports were oil, coffee and diamonds. The country bordered on Namibia (formerly South-West Africa), which was controlled by the Republic of South Africa. The RSA thus had a particular interest in what was happening in Angola, and was prepared to act militarily to influence developments. After the 1974 coup in Lisbon it offered assistance to one of the three principal anti-Portuguese guerrilla movements in Angola, the *União Nacional para a Independência Total de Angola* (UNITA). By supporting UNITA, Pretoria hoped to prevent more radical nationalists from seizing power. For a time the United States, Zaïre and some of the countries of Western Europe also provided small amounts of aid to the *Frente Nacional de Libertação de Angola* (FNLA), with the same goal in mind. Resistance in the US Congress, however, constrained the American role, especially after it was discovered that the Ford administration had secretly gone ahead and provided a small amount of aid without congressional authorization. The backlash against this, plus memories of defeat in Vietnam, prevented the United States from becoming a major factor in events, and Congress refused to appropriate money for further assistance. On the other side, Cuba intervened with troops at the behest of the Russians, while Moscow sent arms aid, advisers and economic assistance. They supported the *Movimento Popular de Libertação de Angola* (MPLA). For the Eastern Bloc, Angola presented a golden opportunity to capitalize on the mistakes of the West, in the form of Portugal's uncompromising record of colonial repression.

Angolan resistance to Portuguese rule had begun long before the April 1974 coup in Lisbon. The MPLA organized in 1956, the FNLA in

1962, and UNITA in 1966. Guerrilla fighting increased in the late 1960s, but as in Mozambique it was the coup in Lisbon which clinched independence. The problem then became which set of nationalist leaders would take charge of the government. A provisional government including representatives from the MPLA, FNLA and UNITA functioned briefly in 1975, but a struggle for power soon began among the various guerrilla organizations. At the same time the 300,000 European settlers sabotaged the economy as they left, just as in Mozambique.

The FNLA and UNITA formed an alliance against the MPLA, but the dispute had not been resolved by the time Lisbon bestowed formal independence on 11 November 1975. The Portuguese were in no position to delay, however, so they withdrew. In effect they washed their hands of the situation Thereupon each side proclaimed its own government. The MPLA set up the People's Republic of Angola at the capital of Luanda, and the FNLA–UNITA coalition created the People's Democratic Republic of Angola. It turned out, however, that the presence of Cuban troops made the difference, though South Africa had also sent in forces of its own to help FNLA–UNITA. By February–March 1976 the MPLA had succeeded in establishing its authority throughout most of Angola. The South Africans withdrew, though they would conduct forays into the country from time to time. About 20,000 Cubans remained. The Russians continued their arms aid, and provided military advisers. Moscow also signed a treaty of friendship and co-operation with Luanda on 8 October 1976. Yet it turned out that the war was not over. UNITA regrouped and launched new guerrilla actions. The war thus never quite came to a resolution, no doubt because UNITA received aid from South Africa and (in the mid-1980s) the Reagan administration.

Moreover, the crisis became entangled with events in Namibia, to Angola's immediate south. This was because the RSA sent troops into Angola in hot pursuit of nationalist guerrillas fleeing from Namibia, and attacked their bases inside Luanda's territory. Namibia was about three-quarters the size of the Republic of South Africa. More importantly, it was a great storehouse of diamonds, uranium, copper and other ores, and was the fourth largest exporter of minerals in Africa. Its location also made it a front line of defence for the Republic against the spread of revolution. Namibia had been a German colony, but was seized by South Africa during the First World War. After the war, in 1920, South Africa took charge of the colony under a League of Nations mandate. In other words, South Africa assumed guardianship of the region until such time as it was ready for independence. In 1946, however, Pretoria sought authority from the United Nations (as the successor of the League) to annex the territory, but was refused. It ignored the UN, and in 1949 proceeded to grant the white residents of Namibia representation in the South African parliament. In 1950 the International Court of Justice at the Hague ordered South Africa to accept UN jurisdiction, but Pretoria refused. In 1966 it applied its own racial and security laws to the country. The UN General Assembly cancelled the South African mandate over Namibia the same year. After efforts to negotiate a settlement failed in 1972–3, the General Assembly declared the principal guerrilla organization, the South West Africa People's Organization (SWAPO), to be the legitimate representative of the native population. A few years later, in 1976, the UN Security Council again demanded that South Africa remove its military and make way for elections.

Despite its rejection of UN jurisdiction Pretoria was not oblivious to the impact of decolonization on the region. Beginning in the early 1970s, it took steps to create a façade of self-government, but all subsequent concessions still left Pretoria with the real power. Despite Western efforts in the late 1970s and the 1980s to achieve a negotiated settlement, South Africa resisted granting full independence. Moreover, it made the removal of Cuban troops from Angola a condition of withdrawing its own forces from Namibia. Pretoria knew perfectly well that this was unacceptable to Luanda. The Reagan administration in the United States supported South Africa on the question of Cuban troops, even though US businessmen had significant investments in Angolan oil. But Luanda was not prepared to let its guard down, and the United Nations took its side in the dispute. Western efforts to mediate thus achieved little. Given South Africa's security needs, as well as its economic interests in Namibia, Pretoria seemed prepared to fund the opponents of the MPLA and SWAPO for as long as necessary. In the early 1980s there were probably 50,000 South African and South African-trained troops in Namibia, and forays into Angola continued. Moreover, as the memory of the American defeat in Vietnam faded, the Reagan administration attempted to bolster US support for South Africa, though the congressional opinion remained deeply divided. The battle for both Angola and Namibia was by no means over.

Developments in Rhodesia also persuaded Pretoria to take a hard line towards its neighbours. There the efforts of the white minority to establish an independent state had failed. The government of Ian Smith had broken away from Britain and proclaimed its Unilateral Declaration of Independence (UDI) in 1965, but after a decade and a half of guerrilla warfare finally submitted to outside pressure in favour of majority rule. Smith first attempted to implement his own plan, but then submitted to British mediation in 1979 at the Rhodesian Constitutional Conference, held at Lancaster House in London.

Even the Republic of South Africa reluctantly supported a compromise in the hope of seeing moderate blacks come to power, such as Bishop Abel Muzorewa. It did not want more radical leaders to take office, such as the self-proclaimed Marxist–Leninist Robert Mugabe of the Zimbabwe African National Union (ZANU), or Joshua Nkomo of the Zimbabwe African People's Union (ZAPU). ZANU and ZAPU joined forces in the late 1970s as the Patriotic Front. But the white strategy failed, no doubt because the long period of civil war did much to win the black population over to ZANU and ZAPU. The war cost about 27,000 lives. Elections held under British auspices in 1980 brought Mugabe to power with fifty-seven of the eighty seats reserved for blacks in the new parliament. Nkomo's party won twenty seats, while Muzorewa's took three. The Smith group won all twenty of the seats guaranteed to the whites under the terms of the Lancaster Conference. The country adopted the traditional name of Zimbabwe. Britain accorded it official independence on 18 April 1980, and eventually Mugabe proclaimed a one-party Marxist–Leninist state. For Pretoria the outcome was not such as to recommend compromise in the future.

INTERNAL COLONIALISM: THE REPUBLIC OF SOUTH AFRICA

The Republic of South Africa included the largest group of white settlers on the continent. Established in 1910 as the Union of South Africa after the British expanded northward from the Cape Colony and conquered the Afrikaners (the descendants of earlier Dutch settlers), it became a self-governing dominion under the British crown. It assumed full autonomy over its external affairs in 1934, and became a republic in 1960. The next year South Africa left the British Commonwealth because of protests from other member nations against its racial policies. The organization of government was divided, with Pretoria as the administrative capital, Cape Town the legislative capital, and Bloemfontein the judicial capital.

South Africa thus was a former Western colony, yet it was also one which perpetuated a colonial relationship towards the majority Bantu or Africans within its boundaries (see Chapter 6). The result was a regime which deployed the power of the state against large numbers of its own people, resulting in a record of violence comparable to many examples from the colonial past.

The whites enjoyed political rights, whereas those of Africans and other racial groups were virtually non-existent. The latter included the 'coloureds' (people of mixed race) and also the Asians (mainly Indians), but it was black labour which provided the mainstay of the economy. In the early days of the Union, Africans were particularly important in gold-mining and diamond-mining and also agriculture. The price of gold, however, tended to remain stable for long periods of time and was fixed by international agreement, while the cost of capital outlays kept rising. This left labour as the one cost which the industry could control, so that wages became the main focus of attention. At the same time the expansion of agriculture also depended on cheap labour. The problem was that both mining and agriculture needed a low-wage workforce, but competing for it would force labour costs beyond what either sector could pay. Hence the need for legal devices to increase the labour supply and thus control wages.

The solution was to establish native reserves. Unlike the Indian reservations of North America, which permitted little interaction with the rest of society, the Bantu reserves were intended to serve as a labour pool for white South Africa. Of course, the law had been used to control native labour throughout the history of white settlement, first with the Afrikaners and then the British, but the system increased in complexity as the economy grew and diversified. The most important innovation of the twentieth century was the Natives Land Act of 1913, which restricted the ownership of land by Africans to a group of reserves and prohibited them from owning land elsewhere. Just over 7 per cent of the country's entire territory was allotted to the indigenous peoples, which at the time constituted well over 70 per cent of the total population. In the 1930s the government increased the total available to about 13 per cent.

The white ruling group did not really intend that every African be confined on the reserves. The reserves were incapable of supporting the entire native population, and it was not the case that all Africans were literally herded into tribal compounds. Many were long-time residents of urban areas, or were workers or tenants on white estates. Because of their role in the workforce many would never return to their homelands. The important point about the reserves was that they restricted the Africans' access to income-producing land of their own, and made them depen-dent on white employment. The inadequacy of reserve lands meant that Africans had little choice except to take jobs in mines, commercial agriculture and (increasingly after the Second World War) manufactur-ing, and to do so on white terms. This was precisely the government's intention.

The reserve system had other functions as well. It absorbed the expense of nurturing the African young and preparing them for a lifetime of toil. In this way the reserves provided a subsidy to white capital by assuming much of the cost of reproducing the workforce. They also provided a safety-valve, in that the unemployed, the disabled or the old could always be sent back once white society was finished with them, as could trouble-makers. The movement of people, of course, was carefully regulated. A system of labour codes required that Africans obtain passes to leave the reserves or to reside in cities, thereby allowing the state to direct the flow of labour to where it was needed. Special legislation defined Africans as transients in urban areas, so that they could be ordered back to the reserves when necessary. Blacks from nearby countries also participated in the migrancy system, which further depressed wages and cut costs for South African capital.

There were more than a few contradictions in the policy of forced migrancy. The most blatant was that the poverty of the reserves was so severe that there was no other option but to allow large numbers of Africans to remain in the cities permanently. By the 1940s, therefore, the reserves' function as a safety-valve was breaking down. The problem became even more complicated with the development of secondary industry, because manufacturers began to train a semi-skilled black workforce. This was to have a significant impact on demographic patterns.

Secondary industry had become more important than mining or agriculture by the mid-1940s. South Africa was changing – it was no longer only a resource-based economy. To compete with cheaper imported manufactures, however, domestic industry needed to rational-ize its operations. The so-called 'Civilized Labour Policy' protected the wage levels of white workers, but it also increased costs for South African industry. Manufacturers therefore wanted to replace high-wage, skilled white labour with lower-wage, semi-skilled black labour. The introduc-tion of new technology would permit the substitution – machines could take over tasks formerly performed by master craftsmen, and permit the employment of people with a lower level of skill. The Africans still had to be trained, however, so that secondary industry acquired a stake in stabilizing the workforce, in order to protect its investment in human resources. This meant allowing increasing numbers of Africans to settle permanently in urban areas.

The growth of the urbanized native workforce thus exacerbated race relations and hurt white labour, especially Afrikaners. As a group the latter were lower on the social and economic scale than the British. Although state-owned industries had provided some capital-poor Afrikaners with opportunities for upward social mobility, the private economy was dominant, and there the British were in control. Not all Afrikaners were members of the working class, but the Afrikaner bourgeoisie tended to be more rural than urban. Its stake was in agriculture, and it feared the consequences of industry's competition for cheap black labour. The countryside was also the stronghold of Afrikaner nationalism, a fact of considerable politicial importance given that the Afrikaners were an absolute majority of the total white population. Decades of resentment against the conquering British thus united Afrikaners of many different classes. By the time of the 1948 election the lines were clearly drawn. British interests had dominated the political system for most of the twentieth century, and the ruling United Party still hoped to reconcile the diverse needs of white capital and labour. On the other side, the Afrikaners were represented by the National Party, but it was not interested in compromise.

The National Party promised to revitalize the migrancy system rather than permit Africans to become permanent residents in the urban areas. It proposed to abolish all representation of Africans in the national parliament, where three seats were reserved for white representatives to speak on their behalf. In due course the indigenous population would enjoy political rights only on the reserves. The party also promised to strengthen the existing system of controls on the right of Africans to reside and work in urban areas, and it played on the fears of the white working class. Even so, the vote was very close. The results suggested that deep divisions remained in white society, with some of the most important manufacturing interests opposed to the new government's programme. Nevertheless it turned out that the 1948 election marked the beginning of long-term National Party hegemony.

Once in office the new government dictated that the reserves should gradually assume a degree of internal self-rule. The policy was to create a series of competing Bantu states, each jealously guarding its own authority. In other words, the policy was one of divide and rule. The

African population was defined as eight and subsequently ten ethnic groups, and assigned territories according to their presumed tribal origins. The goal was to offset the unifying trends resulting from the urbanization and proletarianization of the black workforce, which had become manifest in the form of illegal workers' organizations and unions, and in the rising frequency of strikes and demonstrations. The Bantu Authorities Act of 1951 therefore provided a framework for ending direct white rule on the reserves, and substituting tribal, regional and territorial political institutions instead. The new system relied on the traditional chiefs at all levels of reserve government, and gave them a stake in the success of separate development. The Bantu states became known as 'Bantustans', or 'homelands'.

The next step was to create legislative assemblies for the Bantustans, made up of appointed and elected members. The government began with Transkei in 1963, and moved on to the other nine in the 1970s. The assemblies created an opportunity for the tribal bourgeoisie to play a part in government, however few in number and poor in capital they were. Once again, the black elite acquired a vested interest in the success of their competing homelands, thereby entrenching the strategy of divide and rule and playing into Pretoria's hands. There was another catch as well. The law bestowing internal self-rule on Transkei also dealt with citizenship. All persons of Transkeian origin ceased to be citizens of South Africa, even if they had been born there, and instead became citizens of their homeland. Equally important, Transkei served as the model for the rest of the Bantustans, so that in due course the overwhelming majority of South Africans suffered the same fate.

Pretoria also acted to revive the economic foundation of the home-lands by launching programmes to revitalize agriculture, to help such local entrepreneurs as existed, and after 1968 even to encourage white investment in the native territories. The idea was to restore the function of the Bantustans as a safety-valve by enhancing their ability to support the local population. Yet Pretoria never really provided enough money to revitalize agriculture or develop industry, nor was private investment sufficient to do so. The cost of making the Bantustan strategy work was simply beyond the government's means or will. Whites were not eager to pay high taxes in order to develop the tribal territories. The result was that the homelands remained over-populated relative to their capacity to sustain life. Furthermore, the issue of manufacturing's need for a permanent and semi-skilled African population in the cities would not go

away. Many industrialists even advocated developing the native population as a more substantial market. This would again mean allowing
Africans access to better jobs, in order to acquire the income to become
consumers. Yet new black jobs were likely to come at the expense of
white workers. All in all, the Bantustan strategy did little to resolve the
differences between whites and blacks or among the whites themselves.
This was hardly surprising, in that the government's policy was to avoid
fundamental change, not to encourage it.

The Africans, of course, resisted. There were white critics of the
government, but it was the native population itself which took the lead. In
the absence of free expression and the right to organize politically,
however, the result was violence. One of the worst examples occurred at
Sharpeville on 21 March 1960. Police fired on a crowd of 10,000
Africans, killing about seventy and wounding almost 200 more. The
demonstrators were protesting at the pass laws, but the killings only
induced further trouble. The next month Pretoria outlawed the two most
important native organizations, the African National Congress and the
Pan Africanist Congress, and both were forced underground. For the
time being the government succeeded in restoring order, but the spectre
of race war haunted South Africa's future. Government repression was
bound to evoke more resistance, and another major crisis occurred in
1976 at Soweto (near Johannesburg and the largest black township in
South Africa). There students and others protested against the compulsory teaching of the Afrikaner language (Afrikaans). The demonstrations
spread, and hundreds were killed before the crisis ended. Once again the
government imposed a semblance of order by brute force, but this did
nothing to address the fundamental grievances of the Africans.

On the contrary, the threat of internal turmoil and the spectre of
revolution in nearby countries (Mozambique and Angola) persuaded
Pretoria to carry the strategy of divide and rule to its logical conclusion.
The hope was to create at least the façade of reform, in order to stem
criticism from abroad, but without sacrificing the essential principle of
white rule within the boundaries of the Republic. Pretoria therefore
decreed that it was time for some of the Bantustans to become legally
independent states. The first to do so was Transkei, in October
1976. Others followed: Bophuthatswana (December 1977), Venda
(September 1979) and Ciskei (December 1981). The government thus
resorted to a neo-colonial strategy of substituting indirect influence
for direct rule. Though it invoked the rhetoric of decolonization,
the rest of the world did not regard the new states as genuinely

independent nations. Only South Africa itself accorded them diplomatic recognition.

Furthermore, most of the homelands and new states were completely surrounded by the Republic, and made up of fragments scattered throughout its territory. One of them (Bophuthatswana) consisted of six geographically separate units, while another (Kwazulu) was made up of ten separate areas. The states were still too poor to support their own populations, so that migrants had to seek work in the Republic just as before. In 1983 there were possibly nine million urban blacks in South Africa. While some of the independent homelands had vital resources, outside interests generally controlled them. Bophuthatswana accounted for 42 per cent of the world production of platinum in 1982, but about 65 per cent of its labour force still had to seek work in South Africa. Similarly, migrants to South Africa accounted for 65 per cent of Ciskei's national income.

The establishment of formally independent native states thus did not have the effect of freeing the Africans but of guaranteeing that they would remain dependent on white South Africa and subject to its will. They had few legal rights in the Republic, and as non-citizens they could be deported to their homelands at any time. In 1983 urban blacks resident in South Africa were allowed to vote for their own town councils, but few were willing to accept tokenism in lieu of full political rights. The turn-out for the elections averaged 20 per cent of the eligible voters. It was less than 11 per cent in Soweto. Most Africans saw the scheme as a form of collaboration. That the government was not really prepared to surrender power nationally was evident from its programme of constitutional reform. In the early 1980s it presented a plan to create a national parliament of three chambers, one each for whites, coloureds and Asians. As non-citizens, the Africans were not given a share of power, while the coloureds and Asians were fewer in number than the whites and had no hope of dominating the political process. The whites thus retained their monopoly on power, and in the mid-1980s the killing of African protestors was an almost daily occurrence. Because of investments in the RSA many countries in the developed West were reluctant to impose sanctions against Pretoria, despite pressure to do so from many anti-apartheid groups at home and abroad. The result was that the official policies of many Western countries placed them on the side of apartheid, and once again turned Third World peoples against the West.

THE SHAH AND THE AYATOLLAH

In many places Western influences altered the very structure of Third World society, and unleashed fundamental changes. The effects were usually very difficult to reverse – this was certainly the case in Southern Africa. Yet sometimes such a possibility did exist, at least up to a point, and Iran provides an excellent example. There a priestly caste assumed leadership of the opposition, and eventually took charge of the government. While Iran had never been colonized, both the Shah and his father had launched a headlong rush into Westernization, with massive implications for traditional society. The *ulama* were by no means entirely anti-modern, yet they succeeded in mobilizing an opposition based on a return to the principles of Islam.

After Mosaddeq's fall in 1953, Mohammad Reza Shah Pahlavi emerged as the real centre of power in Iran (see Chapter 5). Moreover, despite his increasingly repressive rule, he enjoyed the steadfast confidence of Britain and the United States, who after the Mosaddeq affair preferred strong government to the turmoil of the *majles*. Mosaddeq's ties to the left had spread alarm in Western capitals, whereas the anti-communist credentials of the Shah were impeccable. The rise of Nasser in Egypt and Iraq's withdrawal from the Baghdad Pact made Iran increasingly important in Western strategic thinking, as did oil.

For his part the Shah wanted to regain Iran's share of the world oil market. The British had offset the loss of Iranian oil during the Mosaddeq crisis by turning to Kuwait and Iraq. Western oil companies dominated production and pricing, and the Shah needed their goodwill in order to restore his revenues. It turned out that this worked more to the advantage of Washington than London. The British were reducing their strategic role in the region, which created more room for the Americans. Further, the Shah regarded Western technology as the key to Iran's economic development. Although British technicians continued to help build new industries, based on imported technology and financed by a combination of oil revenues and US economic aid, the Americans soon became the Shah's most important advisers on economic development. Iranian purchases of sophisticated armaments also played into Washington's hands. Teheran became a major military power, enhancing the Shah's prestige (at least in his own mind) and providing the United States with a powerful ally in the Middle East.

The overthrow of Mosaddeq did not end all opposition to the regime. The Shah attempted to contain this in two ways, co-optation and outright repression. Oil money provided the basis for industrial diversification, so that the state sector grew rapidly, and thoroughly dominated the country's economic development. There were plenty of technical and administrative jobs for those educated in the skills of the West, and who would co-operate with the regime. Yet these people were also politically articulate. The Shah's concessions did not extend into the realm of politics, and for this reason co-optation was only partly successful. For those who would not work with the regime, there was SAVAK. This was the Shah's infamous secret police, formed in 1957 and tutored in the arts of repression by the US Central Intelligence Agency. The Shah established other security agencies as well, plus a network of informers, who were successful in infiltrating the opposition, including groups that had gone underground or into exile. The co-optation and repression of the Westernized elite (the reformers as well as the more radical leftists) partly explained why the clerics rather than secular leaders eventually led the uprising against the Shah. SAVAK also attacked the Shah's religious critics, but the *ulama* proved to be a far more significant group. They had widespread support in a country where most people were committed to Islamic rather than Western or secular traditions.

Major political troubles occurred in the early 1960s, but were temporarily contained by a programme of reform called the 'White Revolution' and later the 'Shah–People Revolution'. The Kennedy administration in the United States also urged the Shah to adopt reforms, in order to defuse the opposition. Yet he was hardly an American puppet, and the changes only went so far. Probably the return of prosperity did more to salve the country's problems, at least for the time being, and SAVAK also played a role. None the less the White Revolution had important implications for the future. It built upon programmes of land reform launched in 1960 and 1962, and even included women's suffrage. More importantly it accelerated the process of Westernization. The latter had a devastating impact on society, and in the long run generated massive opposition to the government in Teheran.

While many villagers benefited from land reform, many others were left out. The latter included a large class of labourers who traditionally had worked for wages or goods in kind. But the new smallholders were less likely than the large landowners to make use of hired labour, so land reform spurred the movement of people to the cities. The government also preferred large-scale operations modelled on Western agribusinesses. Therefore some peasant owners were forced to exchange their holdings for shares in farm corporations based in the villages but modelled on Western-style agribusinesses. Perhaps a hundred such corporations had been organized by the end of the 1970s. In addition to the farm corporations the government invited multinational corporations to share in the ownership and operation of additional large-scale farming ventures. Again they imitated Western models, and usually ranged between 5,000 and 25,000 hectares in size. They utilized expensive imported farm machinery, and further reduced employment opportunities in the countryside. They also turned out not to be as productive as traditional agriculture, necessitating the importation of expensive foodstuffs from abroad. Agricultural development also encroached on pasture lands (which were nationalized), to the disadvantage of the country's still numerous nomadic-pastoral population. In sum, the Shah's policies affected the very structure of rural society.

In the urban sector new industries were being established, but there too the Shah's preference for capital-intensive rather than labour-intensive projects meant that not enough new jobs were created relative to the need, and they went to the skilled, not the refugees from the countryside. In fact tens of thousands of foreign technicians had to be called in to run the new enterprises, mainly from the United States and Western Europe. Outsiders were not allowed to buy a majority interest in Iranian industry, yet production still depended heavily on the importation of expensive foreign technology and components. Further, many of the new industries produced costly consumer goods available only to a limited clientele. Large-scale ventures in both country and city remained a minority of the total number of enterprises in Iran, but the policies of the state favoured them to the detriment of other interests in Iranian society. Rapid expansion also provided ample opportunities for corruption, which reached into the Shah's own entourage. The country also experienced inflation and shortages, and the total effect of the Shah's policies was to widen the relative gap between rich and poor.

The Americans and Europeans encouraged the Shah's expenditures as a means of recycling the profits of rising oil prices. During and after the 1973 Arab–Israeli war the price of oil had quadrupled, and the West hoped to recoup its losses partly by the sale of technology. Arms sales would help accomplish the same goal, while improving the Western strategic position in the Middle East. Both the Americans and British profited. And so did the Western oil companies – as operators of the oil sector they shared in Iran's revenues, and thus gained from rising oil prices. In short, Western capitals were not inclined to press for changes in the Shah's developmental strategy. And most of the time they also refrained from criticizing his use of repression to quell dissent.

Sooner or later the policies of the Shah would have mobilized the opposition, but events quickened in 1977. An inflationary spiral forced the government to institute cut-backs. Sporadic guerrilla attacks also showed that the Shah's repression was inspiring popular resistance. In addition the inauguration of the Carter administration in the United States influenced the timing of events. In 1977 the new president unveiled his human-rights policy. To the opposition in Iran this suggested that Washington's willingness to tolerate repression was waning, and that the Americans wanted a government with a broader base of support. In the US view this would make the regime more secure, and thus perpetuate Washington's influence in the region. The Shah apparently drew the same conclusion about Washington's intentions as did his opponents – perhaps it was time to permit a certain amount of dissent. The effect, however, was to inspire the Shah's opponents (especially intellectuals, professionals, students and clerics) to press for more tolerance, as did Amnesty International and similar groups. Television reporting of hostile demonstrations against the Shah during his visit to Washington in the autumn of 1977 encouraged his critics as well. There may also have been a personal reason for the Shah's change of heart. He was suffering from cancer, and in the event of his death had arranged for the Queen to act as regent until his young son could assume the throne. He may have believed that concessions might win a reprieve during a period of transition, but it was not to be. Besides, SAVAK still defined the limits of toleration.

It was the religious opposition which proved to be the most important. The *ulama* had the confidence of far more people than the secular leaders, because Iran was a strongly religious society. Even many Westernized and leftist critics of the regime justified their opposition by the principles of Islam. The clergy had many grievances against the Shah. His father had secularized education and the law. The Shah himself had attempted to undermine the authority of the *ulama* by organizing theological schools in the state-run universities and by sending his own instructors into the villages to teach religion. He also introduced major changes in family law and women's rights. In 1977 the government reduced its subsidies to the clergy, which had been used for a variety of purposes, such as maintaining mosques and religious schools. Land reform also hurt many of the *ulama's* followers. The Shah's policies injured the *bazaaris*, another bastion of clerical support. The *ulama* and others, furthermore, objected to the Shah's close ties to the United States, and blamed rampant Westernization for corrupting Iran.

By the late 1970s the most important clerical critic of the regime was the Islamic leader, the Ayatollah Ruhollah Khomaini. Exiled in 1964 from the holy city of Qom, he fled first to Turkey and then to Iraq, where he remained until Baghdad sent him away in the autumn of 1978. This time Khomaini left the Muslim world and travelled to France. There he was much freer to voice his criticisms of the Pahlavi Dynasty, and attracted the attention of the Western media. He used television coverage to good effect. He also continued his practice of recording speeches on tape cassettes to be smuggled into Iran, along with his writings. That the regime appreciated Khomaini's importance had become apparent earlier in the year (January), when it instigated a newspaper attack against him. Theology students at Qom demonstrated in protest. The result was violence, and a minimum of seventy people were killed. The significance of the incident was that it confirmed Khomaini's role as the key figure. The effect was to place an exiled religious leader at the head of the opposition movement just as the Shah's hold on power was weakening. Though the religious opposition was likely to dominate in any event, because of the influence of the *ulama* over the masses, the events of January assured that the initiative would quickly pass to Khomaini's supporters rather than to the secular opposition. Indeed, the latter rallied to Khomaini's banner. Events would soon pave the way for his return from abroad.

The *ulama* organized memorial services for those killed at Qom. Because these were religious events, the Shah could hardly prohibit them, but they were easily turned into anti-government demonstrations. The tradition of mourning was turned to a political purpose, with telling effect, as were religious holidays. Soon most of the country was involved. The *bazaaris* provided crucial support. Although overshadowed by the Shah's showy new industries, it was a fact that they remained a significant force in the economy. The *bazaar* still controlled at least two-thirds of wholesale trade in Iran and almost one-third of the trade in imported goods. Students, women and the urban poor (particularly those who had recently left the countryside) also provided vital support. The cycle of religious mourning and religious holidays kept the population in a constant state of mobilization, and the protests escalated over the next several months.

As in 1963 and the White Revolution the Shah attempted to manage the crisis with a façade of reform. He changed the leadership of the government, eased restrictions on the press and on debate in the *majles*, allowed political organizations to regroup, and permitted peaceful demonstrations. There was even an order shutting down the casinos. The catch was that SAVAK and other security agencies were given a free rein at the same time. Massive demonstrations occurred, and so in September 1978 martial law was declared. Unable to control the situation, the Shah had decided to revert to full-scale repression. New demonstrations resulted in more killings. The government closed all schools and universities. Newspapers were ordered to cease publishing. In Teheran public meetings of more than three persons were proscribed. The Shah appointed a general as prime minister. Yet strikes and demonstrations spread, almost completely closing the oil sector and bringing the economy to a halt. Khomaini, still in exile, rejected any possibility of compromising, and this proved to be the most effective tactic. By allowing the two sides to polarize, the ayatollah became the clear alternative to the Shah. Secular opponents of the regime were swept along in the belief that Khomaini would retreat into the background and turn to them when it came time to form a government.

On 11 December 1978 the opposition was able to organize demonstrations in several cities. There were over a million participants in Teheran. These resulted in a resolution asking Khomaini to return from exile and lead the country. In the face of this the Shah appointed a moderate reformer as prime minister, Shahpour Bakhtiar. But Khomaini remained aloof. Throughout, the Americans were in disarray. Near the end they worked behind the scenes for a secular-religious government, with the Shah abdicating. Their goal was to assure that more moderate leaders might dominate any new government, rather than the outspokenly anti-American Khomaini. The Carter administration also hoped to protect the interests of the military – this was one of the few potentially pro-US centres of power in Iran, though Khomaini had many supporters in the ranks. But the US soon discovered the limits of its power. The situation was long past saving, and the Americans had no real links to the religious opposition. The clerics soon took over, and without Washington's mediation.

On 16 January 1979 the Shah fled, leaving Bakhtiar in charge. The prime minister had little choice except to allow Khomaini to return, which he did on 1 February. Within days the ayatollah appointed his own prime minister, ignoring Bakhtiar altogether. A short period of violent confrontation ensued, but a coalition of clerical and secular leaders took power on 11 February. At the end of March a popular referendum resulted in the proclamation of an Islamic Republic, under the leadership of Ayatollah Khomaini. The ascendancy of the *ulama* over their secular allies thus seemed assured, although the latter remained part of the new regime. The United States was to learn the depth of anti-Americanism in Iran when university students seized control of the US embassy on 4 November 1979, taking sixty hostages. They were not released until 20 January 1981, and then only after a bungled rescue attempt by the Carter administration in April 1980. A force of ninety men landed on Iranian territory, but aborted the mission after mechanical trouble developed in three out of eight helicopters; an accident claimed eight lives. And time caught up with Mohammad Reza Shah Pahlavi as well. He died in exile on 27 July 1980.

The rule of the clerics was troubled, yet it endured. They applied Islamic law to all aspects of Iranian life, and even resurrected a SAVAK-like security agency (SAVAMA). In the autumn of 1980 Iraqi president Saddam Hussein launched an invasion of Iran. Hussein had several objectives. One was to assert Iraq's claim to full control of the Shatt al-Arab, a waterway vital to the port facilities, oil depots and refineries of both countries. Another was to contain the spread of the Iranian Revolution and its Shi'i Muslim followers. The latter belonged to a separate Muslim tradition than the mainly Sunni population of Iraq. There was an important Shi'i minority in Iraq, so Hussein regarded Khomaini as a subversive influence, fearing that the Shi'as might mobilize against his government. Baghdad also wished to enhance its prestige as a leader of the Islamic world. The Iranian Revolution had severely damaged Teheran's military preparedness, so perhaps the moment was ripe for a strike. The result was a protracted war which drained both Iraq and Iran. On the other hand, the war helped steel the resolve of the Iranians. It reinforced their fervour in the defence of Islam, so that Khomaini and the revolution retained widespread support at home. The great question was what would happen after his death, for he had already exceeded the life expectancy of most Westerners.

AFGHANISTAN AND THE RUSSIAN INVASION

Iran was not the only Middle Eastern country to experience a revolution in the late 1970s. Afghanistan did as well. Moreover, the revolution was largely indigenous in origin, at least compared with many Third World situations. Yet the result was to create such internal unrest that in December 1979 the Russians invaded in the futile hope of restoring some semblance of order. Their objective was to sustain a pro-Soviet regime, but the decision to act represented a major turning-point in their relations with the Third World. It was the first time since 1945 that the Russians sent armies of their own to fight a war in an underdeveloped country, a record which contrasted dramatically with that of the West. Of course, there had been border skirmishes with the People's Republic of China, but these had been of short duration and involved disputes over the frontiers of the Soviet Union itself. Most importantly, instead of supporting a popular revolution in Afghanistan, the USSR defied the clearly expressed wishes of the majority of the population and moved to sustain a regime which had lost virtually all credibility with its own people. The result was another terrible war in the Middle East.

No doubt the end of American influence in Iran (to the west of Afghanistan) and the instability of the pro-Western military dictatorship of General Zia ul-Haq in Pakistan (to the south and east) simplified the Russian decision to intervene. The diminution of US power in the region made it easier for the USSR to proceed. The likelihood of major counter-moves by the West was small. Besides, Afghanistan had generally been more in the Russian than the Western orbit since 1945, though the line was not so clearly drawn as in Eastern Europe. Both Washington and Moscow had provided aid to various Afghani governments, but the Russians were more active. After all, there were 45 million Muslims in Russia, or about 18 per cent of the total population of the USSR. Afghanistan bordered on the three Soviet republics of Turkmen, Uzbek and Tadzhik, and included some of the same ethnic groups. Moscow for this reason always maintained a lively interest in what was happening to its immediate south, and was alert to any opportunities to change the East–West balance of power in the region.

The Russian invasion came as a surprise to Western capitals, precisely because it was out of character for Moscow to risk becoming involved in a Vietnam-style war, though as we shall see presently there were significant differences between the Afghanistan adventure and the US role in Indo-China. Moreover, Afghanistan had never yielded to outright colonization in the past. It was a dry, mountainous country, and the meeting-ground for several peoples for whom Afghani nationalism had been an amorphous idea at best. Much of the history of Afghanistan before the late nineteenth century was the story of efforts to unify the diverse ethnic and linguistic groups: those of Indo-European origins, the Tadzhik (or Parziwan), Pushtun, Nuristani (or Kafir) and Baluchi peoples; and those of Turco-Mongolian origin, the Hazara, Uzbek,

Turkomen, Aimaq and Khirgiz peoples; as well as others. The formation of modern Afghanistan with approximately its present borders took place only by the early twentieth century.

In the nineteenth century the British established a sphere of influence in Afghanistan. The goal was to create a buffer zone for heading off the expansion of Czarist influence from the north and thus protecting Britain's control over India. After the First World War the ruler of Afghanistan proclaimed his country's full independence, with Britain acquiescing after a brief war. Treaties recognizing Kabul's autonomy soon followed with Russia in 1920, with Turkey and Iran in 1921, and in due course with other countries. A 1921 treaty with Britain fixed the border with British India (i.e. the zone which subsequently became Pakistan).

Afghanistan remained economically and socially backward despite the efforts of various rulers to promote development. The country maintained a balance in its relations with Russia and Britain before the Second World War, though in the late 1930s Nazi Germany was probably becoming the most important outside influence. After 1945 Moscow and Washington competed for influence, but the fortunes of the West were hurt when the British withdrew from the Indian subcontinent. The establishment of Pakistan meant that Islamabad had an interest in revising the boundary settlement made by Britain in 1921, and in asserting its territorial claims along the frontier with Afghanistan. Disputes thus existed between Kabul and the capital of a pro-Western country, and the Russians were prepared to take advantage of these. They made a trade agreement in 1950, but Soviet economic and military aid did not commence until 1955. Recall that it was only in the mid-1950s that Moscow instituted a major programme of assistance to court the non-communist nations of the Third World. But the West answered this challenge, and the US provided aid. Before the fall of the Shah, Washington also encouraged Iran to provide financial assistance to Afghanistan and to mediate in Kabul's disputes with Pakistan. Money came from Saudi Arabia as well. When it came to financial and economic aid, however, the Russians maintained the lead over the USA in the post-1945 period.

Ultimately it was not foreign affairs but internal developments which led to the Russian invasion of 1979. Although there were some gestures towards parliamentary democracy and a free press in the late 1940s, it was not until 1973 that the constitutional monarch was overthrown and a republic established. Even then it was the king's cousin Mohammad

Daud Khan who took charge of the new regime, and so 1973 was a personalist coup, not the establishment of genuine republicanism. Daud had been prime minister from 1953 to 1963, and during that time had demonstrated his capacity for autocratic rule. Between 1963 and 1973, however, reform had opened up the political system more than ever before, but factionalism resulted in a deadlock between the parliament and the king's government. It was this that inspired Daud to act.

Before Daud's 1973 coup the main leftist opposition group was the People's Democratic Party of Afghanistan (PDPA). It had been founded in 1965, but split into two factions by 1967, the Khalq and the Parcham. The left, however, tended to be an urban movement and had comparatively few members. Afghanistan was mainly a traditional rural society, and even in Kabul there barely existed a class which could be described as an industrial proletariat. The PDPA was important among university students, but their numbers were small indeed, again because the country was so underdeveloped. The result was that a traditional elite and not the left dominated parliamentary politics, including the anti-government opposition. The Parcham and Khalq factions each won only a single seat in the 1969 parliamentary elections.

One of the issues which divided the Parcham and the Khalq was the question of collaborating with other political forces in order to bring about change. The Parcham faction of Babrak Karmal regarded collaboration as a practical strategy for making at least some gains. It stood for democratic reforms and possibly, but not inevitably, socialism. The Khalq was not prepared to compromise on the latter. There were also distinctions of social class between the two PDPA groups, with Parchami coming from a somewhat more urban and establishment background than Khalq. The social distinctions between the two groups were also reflected in linguistic and cultural differences. Accordingly, when Daud proclaimed his republic in 1973, he did so with the support of the Parcham faction of the PDPA. The more radical Khalq remained aloof, and its leader, Hafizullah Amin, secretly began recruiting support in the army.

Once in power Daud set up what really amounted to a dictatorship. He pressed ahead with economic development, particularly railways and mining. Yet Daud's undoing was his willingness to resort to repression. By about 1975 he had purged the left from government, and attacked Islamic fundamentalists and other opposition forces both left and right. He also moved Afghanistan closer to the pro-American Shah of Iran and to Saudi Arabia, a change which no doubt worried the Russians. Daud was definitely interested in reducing his dependency on the USSR. The left therefore could expect trouble, and by 1977 the two PDPA factions came together again, though they were not fully reconciled.

Events quickened once Daud decided to begin arresting members of the PDPA in the spring of 1978. Anti-government demonstrations occurred when Mir Akbar Khyber was assassinated; he had been a member of the PDPA central committee and editor of the Parcham newspaper. Daud ordered the arrest of PDPA leaders on 26 April, and though Amin of the Khalq faction was among them he succeeded in alerting supporters in the army before being taken away. The result was *coup d'état* on 27–8 April and the release of the PDPA leadership. Daud, most of his family and his top government ministers were all killed. The secretary-general of the PDPA, Nur Mohammad Taraki, became president of a Revolutionary Council and prime minister. Taraki was identified with the Khalq faction, which was the dominant force in the PDPA coalition, but Karmal of the Parcham was given the vice-presidency.

Two developments affected the fortunes of the new regime. First, it launched a programme of radical reform which alienated the population. Second, it remained afflicted by internal squabbling. Beginning in May, the government announced a series of reforms aimed against 'feudalism' and cancelled the debts of the poorest peasants. Later it would cancel the debts of all peasants. There were also reforms of traditional social customs, such as arranged marriages and dowries. The PDPA had not really sorted out its position on many of these questions before the coup, and it soon became apparent that there were more than a few pitfalls in promoting rapid social and economic change. The test case was land reform, and on this the urban roots of the PDPA did not serve it well.

The PDPA outlined its programme in September. Peasant holdings were limited to six hectares of fertile (i.e. irrigated) land, and up to sixty of unirrigated land. In Afghanistan the key to productivity was water, and so it was the first category that counted. The difficulty was that the government's plans bypassed many questions relating to water rights and land surveys, as well as riding rough-shod over the complex set of traditional customs relating to the ownership of land. Further, the government needed to provide the inputs required, such as seed and animals, before landless peasants could join the ranks of owners. Perhaps most important, it was simply not the case that the countryside was monopolized by a few large owners. Holdings of over 100 hectares were uncommon, and owning ten hectares was often enough to classify a peasant as rich. A majority of peasants probably had two to four hectares, though the landless group was known to be 25 per cent of the peasantry in many places. In other words, the owners of small properties were perhaps more numerous than the landless.

The problem in Afghanistan was that there was not enough irrigated land to go around, so that a reform programme really required increasing the total amount of such land, not just redistributing what already existed. This was beyond the resources of the government. Moreover, it often happened that those who had been required to give up land took it back, and formerly landless peasants were unable to prevent this. Indeed there were problems in even taking control of land. For example, it was sometimes the case that peasants were simply not prepared to seize the lands of village headmen. The practices of traditional society did not encourage attacking the respected authorities of the community. Some new owners surrendered their lands to former owners in return for seed and other necessities. Even abolishing peasant debts had a negative side, as many smallholders were creditors as well as debtors. Cancelling debts cut two ways. In brief, the regime soon faced a massive tide of opposition in virtually every province of the country, but it did not have the wit to yield. Instead it sent the army.

Compounding the crisis in the countryside was the personal and factional competition which persisted in the PDPA. Almost from the first the Khalq began squeezing Parcham leaders out of the government. In August several were placed under arrest. Karmal was sent to Prague as ambassador (in effect he was exiled), but then ordered home. He discreetly decided not to go back, and instead remained in Eastern Europe. He would return somewhat more than a year later, with the Russians. Yet the triumph of the Khalq over the Parcham simply meant that conflicts developed within its ranks, especially as the civil war spread in 1979. The chief rivals were Amin and Taraki. Amin took over the prime ministership in March and the defence ministry and PDPA secretaryship in July. Taraki was still president, and with Russian advice came to favour compromising with the Parchami and the opposition forces in the countryside. Such a course of action would no doubt have required replacing Amin, but before this could happen he learned of Taraki's collaboration with the Russians. Amin therefore arrested Taraki and assumed the presidency. These events took place in September, and Taraki was executed early the next month.

The death of Taraki was the last straw for the Russians. Amin's intransigence was only leading to greater and greater turmoil. The

Kremlin did not want to see a potential satellite slip from its hands, and therefore invaded on 27 December. Amin was killed, and Babrak Karmal took over as the Russians' choice. Karmal reduced the factionalism in the government, but was unable to settle the civil war (he would be replaced in 1986). By the time of the Russian invasion the PDPA was thoroughly discredited, and the rebels were unwilling to compromise with a former colleague of Amin and Taraki. That Karmal owed his power to foreigners was no help either.

The Russians thus intervened to save a client state purportedly committed to socialist revolution. Indeed, they claimed that Kabul had requested their assistance, though this was scarcely credible. In the West some analysts speculated that Moscow may have acted lest the unrest in Afghanistan spill over into the Muslim republics of the USSR. It was indeed the case that the Afghani rebels sometimes preached the kind of Islamic fundamentalism that had contributed to the crisis in Iran, and which helped inspire their own struggles. The danger to the Soviets thus was real. On the other hand, the Muslim areas of the USSR had remained quiet throughout the turmoil. They were considerably more developed than Afghanistan, so that the social context was quite different. It was therefore more likely that Moscow's principal motive was to secure a permanent satellite in the Middle East and thus to make strategic gains in the region. Once the Russians intervened, their presence altered the balance of power. Their new satellite bordered directly on Iran and Pakistan, and this at a time when American influence had suffered a major setback with the fall of the Shah. To protect this strategic advantage, however, the Russians had to deal with the civil war, and this did not come to an end. Yet it was unlikely that Moscow expected it to.

The Russians seemed prepared for a long drawn-out battle. They banked on the situation being different from Vietnam. In the latter the Americans had faced a united opposition. Furthermore, the other side had received material aid from both the USSR and the People's Republic of China (i.e. two major powers in the world). But the Afghani rebels were anything but united, and even by the mid-1980s the amount of outside aid reaching them through Pakistan was hardly enough to turn the tide. Despite the presence of a repressive government in Kabul and foreign troops on their soil, the resistance remained fragmented and localized. The goals of the various rebel groups tended to be mainly regional. Afghanistan's roots were still too close to the tribal past to have achieved the kind of nationalist sense which might have united diverse ethnic, linguistic and religious groups into one cohesive force. The longer the struggle went on, the more likely this became, but in the meantime rebel disunity was the Russians' secret weapon. It gave them staying-power.

The Soviets' decision to wait it out was reflected in their military strategy. They made regular forays into the countryside, but usually did not attempt to hold it. They did not try to occupy all of Afghanistan, but concentrated their forces in key bases. Their operations were less costly than the American role in Vietnam, involving fewer troops (probably about 115,000 in the early 1980s). To sum up, Moscow wanted to rescue a client state, no matter how unattractive, as there were strategic advantages to be gained. They seemed prepared to do whatever was necessary to accomplish their objectives, and rebel disunity made a waiting game feasible. What all this had to do with the cause of social revolution, however, remained to be seen. It certainly did not reflect the wishes of the population. Afghanistan showed that there might be little to choose between Soviet and Western intervention in the Third World.

SOUTH-EAST ASIA

Cambodia and Pol Pot

Events in South-East Asia also bore witness to the appalling cost of military action in the Third World. The aftermath of the Vietnam war did not lead to peace in the region. On the contrary, the fortunes of various factions in neighbouring countries were vitally affected by the fighting in Vietnam, so that the war there had ramifications elsewhere. Cambodia provides the most extreme example.

Recall that during the Vietnam war Hanoi's support for the Cambodian communists, the Khmer Rouge, threatened the government of Lon Nol. Lon Nol had overthrown the neutralist Prince Norodom Sihanouk and taken charge of the capital, Phnom Penh, in 1970 (see Chapter 8). He had then pursued a pro-Western policy. As the war between the Khmer Rouge and Lon Nol spread, it created a flow of refugees from the countryside to the towns and cities, just as in the rest of Indo-China. Also recall that the United States secretly began bombing Vietminh sanctuaries in Cambodia in 1969, that it invaded in 1970, and that at various times it renewed the air war – that is, until Congress ordered the White House to stop by mid-August 1973. The result was a rain of devastation that compounded the country's refugee problem. The combined effect of the Khmer Rouge's actions and the American bombing was that roughly half the rural population became refugees in the early 1970s. The population of Phnom Penh rose more than threefold in the period 1970–75. Because the capital and many other towns were controlled by the pro-American Lon Nol, the Khmer Rouge tended to identify a good many refugees as enemy sympathizers. They attacked anyone suspected of supporting Lon Nol, though in fact most refugees were simply seeking safety from the bombing and the ground war, and were probably indifferent to politics. The problem for the refugees was that eventually the Khmer Rouge won the war in Cambodia.

The Khmer Rouge had led a shadowy existence in recent Cambodian history, as did their leader, Pol Pot. The organization emerged from a number of scattered nationalist and revolutionary groups after the division of the old Indo-Chinese Communist Party into three parts after the Second World War, one for each of the constituent states of the region. Yet the communists of Cambodia were not at all comparable to the Vietminh in Vietnam, being much weaker. It was not until about 1970–71 that Pol Pot emerged as a force in the country's politics, with Hanoi's help and also with the support of the country's former ruler, Prince Sihanouk. To Sihanouk, the main task was to avenge the Lon Nol coup of 1970. Phnom Penh fell in 1975, and Pol Pot formally became prime minister of the new Cambodia (called Democratic Kampuchea) in 1976. But Sihanouk soon found himself under house arrest. Once in power the Khmer Rouge no longer valued his endorsement, and even proceeded to murder several members of the prince's family.

Yet the turmoil did not come to an end. Upon taking the capital, the Khmer Rouge ordered all foreigners to leave, and the country was effectively sealed off from the rest of the world. Anything Western was condemned. Intellectuals and professionals (teachers, writers, doctors and others) were also vulnerable, as the Khmer Rouge attacked them as part of the old establishment, and their fate was often execution. The most dramatic change, however, was the relocation of most of the urban population.

The Khmer Rouge ordered everyone out of Phnom Penh and also the country's other cities and towns. Because years of war and the American bombing had driven much of the peasantry (i.e. the producers of food) into the cities, the country faced starvation. Therefore everyone was ordered to the fields in a crash programme to plant crops. This was particularly important because famine relief was not forthcoming from the outside world, a fact which may also have accounted for some of the

Khmer Rouge's ruthlessness. They faced an emergency, although they hardly needed tutoring in the techniques of repression. Long lines of people were forced to march to the countryside, where they were put to work under youthful and often arbitrary peasant guards who lorded it over their elders and the city people. Wanton violence was the result. A secret Khmer Rouge terrorist organization called the *Angkar* acted as enforcer and executioner. The *Angkar* meted out punishment and even death for minor or imaginary offences. Exhaustion and starvation also took their toll in lives. Despite Vietnam's help in the past, some of the worst atrocities eventually were meted out to Khmer Rouge cadres suspected of sympathizing with Hanoi. Pol Pot had never forgotten Cambodia's traditional fear of Vietnamese regional hegemonism, and towards the end of his regime thousands of Khmer Rouge fled to Vietnam.

Not much news leaked out of the country. The Khmer Rouge had sealed the borders, and only a few refugees escaped to tell their stories. At first they were accorded little credibility, as many of the interested parties had their reasons for playing down the rumours. Hanoi still wanted to keep Kampuchea friendly so as to draw Phnom Penh into a new alliance, and therefore denied the occurrence of atrocities, at least for the time being. The United States government had washed its hands of the whole area and did not pursue the issue. Even reporters posted in neighbouring Thailand at first failed to give much credit to the rumours. Some of them had witnessed the devastation caused by the American bombing of Cambodia, and were not favourably disposed towards the US. Finally, in many parts of the world, members of the political left condemned any questioning of Khmer Rouge policies as a plot to defame a much-needed social revolution in the country.

The evidence that something incredible was happening kept mounting, however, so that by the late 1970s it became too great to ignore. Just as important, relations between Hanoi and Phnom Penh finally broke down in 1978, and Vietnam invaded later in the year. Its motive was mainly strategic, not humanitarian. Hanoi, as a consequence, no longer had a stake in covering up news of the persecution, and in fact did all it could to condemn Pol Pot and his government. It was at this point that the West became fully alerted to the Khmer Rouge atrocities. The Vietnamese army captured Phnom Penh on 7 January 1979, and established control of much (not all) of the country in the following months. Pol Pot fled towards the mountains on the border with Thailand, where eventually he established new bases. And just before the Vietnamese arrived in Phnom Penh, Chinese agents helped Sihanouk escape from the country.

Hanoi proceeded to establish a puppet government (the People's Republic of Kampuchea) under Heng Samrin, a former member of the Khmer Rouge who had fled the country when Pol Pot instituted his purge of pro-Vietnam cadres. Hanoi also allowed selected Western journalists into the country, though its motive was not entirely altruistic. By highlighting (and in the judgement of some authorities exaggerating) the Khmer Rouge atrocities, Hanoi hoped to discredit Pol Pot, who after all had opposed their plans for an Indo-Chinese alliance or federation. Furthermore, by emphasizing Pol Pot's central role and blaming the killings on him personally, they hoped to deflect criticism away from communism as such and blame it on a single individual. It was not the system that was brutal, but one man. They charged Pol Pot with genocide, and soon the world was comparing what had happened in Kampuchea with the Holocaust. For example, the Vietnamese and Heng Samrin set up a museum at the Tuol Sleng, which had once been a high school in Phnom Penh, but had been converted into an interrogation and execution centre where perhaps 16,000 people (mainly suspect party cadres) were sent to their deaths. The displays included grisly photographs of the victims, taken by the Khmer Rouge, along with written confessions extracted under torture. Skulls and bones were stacked in great heaps. Elsewhere the Vietnamese discovered mass graves. Sometimes the bodies were found in craters left by B–52 bombs, a grim reminder of the American role in events. By 1978–9 estimates of the dead ranged between one and three million people, with Hanoi suggesting that the latter figure was closer to the mark. Three million dead would have been approximately 40 per cent of the total population of Cambodia.

Even so, the United States and many of its allies in South-East Asia chose to regard the 200,000 Vietnamese troops in Cambodia not as liberators but as aggressors. After all, the Americans had a vested interest in condemning anything the Vietnamese did. Hanoi had defeated the USA in Vietnam, and there was no love lost between the two capitals. Furthermore, Moscow had become Hanoi's principal patron by the late 1970s, i.e. at a time when relations between the United States and the Soviet Union had cooled. China was a factor in American attitudes as well. Beijing was no longer on good terms with Hanoi. Both had designs on Indo-China, and once the Americans left, they soon fell out. (Indeed China invaded the northern reaches of Vietnam for a four-week period beginning in mid-February 1979. It hoped to force Hanoi to leave Cambodia, but was unsuccessful.) The Chinese therefore supported the Khmer Rouge government against Vietnamese regional imperialism, and this at a time when Washington's relations with Beijing were improving. Washington therefore gave some credit to Beijing's views. Thailand too worried about Vietnamese expansionism, and the Americans had regard for its opinion as well. Even Prince Sihanouk once again endorsed the Khmer Rouge, at the urging of his Chinese patrons and with considerable ambiguity. He accepted the argument that anything was better than having Vietnamese invaders in Phnom Penh.

Accordingly, when Pol Pot's delegates arrived at the United Nations in September 1979, they were allowed to take their seats as the legitimate representatives of Cambodia. A delegation from Heng Samrin was turned away. Instead of supporting a Vietnamese puppet government, many Western powers sided with the unattractive Pol Pot. Perhaps the only consolation for Cambodia was that the number of dead was probably fewer than originally estimated. As the result of relief activities in the early 1980s it was discovered that the country's population was considerably larger than expected. Given the number of people who had to be fed, it appeared that the population decline under Pol Pot was between 500,000 and one million. In addition to Khmer Rouge atrocities, of course, the causes of death included disease and famine. And after 1979 there were further losses because the organization of Western relief was delayed by political considerations (Vietnam's presence in the country), though the Eastern Bloc provided some assistance, albeit inadequate. All this was in addition to the losses which had occurred before Pol Pot. Between 1970 and 1975 the presence of Vietminh sanctuaries, the Lon Nol–Khmer Rouge war, invasion by the South Vietnamese and Americans and the B–52 bombings also may have cost 500,000 to one million lives. Once again, conflict in the Third World exacted a terrible toll.

The Repercussions of War

It was not only the rise of the Khmer Rouge which traumatized South-East Asia. Decades of war had driven masses of people from their homes. The result was to have an impact on virtually every country in the region. Before the fall of Saigon in 1975 American officials were predicting mass murder if and when the Vietminh took over South Vietnam – the communists could be expected to exact reprisals against their enemies. As it turned out, the predicted bloodbath did not occur, though members of the old order were treated harshly. Some authorities estimate that the Vietminh imprisoned 200,000 people or more without trial in the first three or four years after 1975. Still, the main flow of refugees did not come from Vietnam until mid-1978. Until then the largest numbers came instead from Laos and Cambodia. The Laotians went mainly to Thailand, and began arriving immediately after the Pathet Lao established their rule at Vientiane in 1975. Perhaps 150,000 Laotians arrived during a two-year period. And tens of thousands more left Cambodia after the fall of Phnom Penh. Most of these were ethnic Chinese or Vietnamese and went to Vietnam, but some arrived in Thailand. The largest movement of Cambodians, however, did not begin until 1978, when border clashes increased between Kampuchea and Vietnam and when internal strife developed inside the Khmer Rouge itself. Eventually hundreds of thousands of people fled. All this imposed a tremendous burden on Thailand and Vietnam, as there was no way they could avoid assuming responsibility for feeding and housing the massive influx of people.

For the most part, however, the rest of the world ignored the refugee problem until the 'boat people' began arriving in the other countries of South-East Asia. The main movement (a small number left earlier) began in mid-1978 and came mainly from Vietnam. While around 160,000 ethnic Chinese went overland to China in the summer of 1978, others escaped on boats and ships of all kinds, and turned up on the shores of southern Thailand, Indonesia, the Philippine Islands, Singapore, Hong Kong, Macao and, in a few cases, even South Korea, Japan and Australia. Sailing in rickety, overloaded craft, and without sufficient food and water, they were stalked by disease and death. They also encountered pirates. And when they arrived, they were hardly welcomed by the host nations. The latter simply could not afford to take care of them all. At one point a minister of the Thai government even suggested shooting any new arrivals. This was no idle threat, as the Thais forcibly repatriated tens of thousands who had arrived by land from Cambodia. In a single incident in 1979, for example, about 45,000 were forced to return home against their will at the border point of Preah Vihear.

The legacy of war, the impact of famine and political reprisals were the main reasons for fleeing. In the case of Vietnam the exodus was also related to persecution of the country's Chinese residents, and particularly to the government's decision of March 1978 to close down privately run businesses. This was a move to accelerate the socialization of the economy, but it affected the ethnic Chinese (or Hoa) the most, as so many of them were in trade and commerce, mainly in the cities of the south. Accordingly most decided to depart rather than lose their livelihood and property. Many refugees thus were people of means, and could afford to buy boats and to bribe Vietnamese officials to permit their departure. Yet there was official complicity, for such a massive migration of people could not have taken place without at least tacit permission from the communist government. Itself a recipient of refugees from Cambodia, Vietnam had an interest in expelling others it considered undesirable, including Vietnamese who had collaborated with the Americans or who resisted integration into the new order. It was also a fact that the Vietminh had inherited terrible social problems in the south. The presence of vast numbers of US troops had turned Saigon into what US senator William Fulbright called 'an American brothel', and drug trafficking had also grown by leaps and bounds.* The government of Vietnam therefore was under considerable pressure, and was not of a mind to tolerate anyone who did not fit into its plans for the political and economic rehabilitation of the south.

Between 1975 and the early 1980s more than a million people left Vietnam, Cambodia and Laos and were permanently resettled abroad, while untold numbers remained in refugee camps. The United States accepted over 600,000 people (mainly Vietnamese), and the People's Republic of China more than 260,000 (mainly ethnic Chinese). Thousands found their way to France. The rest were distributed throughout South-East Asia, though many were held in camps. Wherever they went, the refugees encountered discrimination and experienced problems of adjustment. In South-East Asia, particularly Malaysia and Indonesia, the arrival of the ethnic Chinese upset delicate ethnic balances. As in Vietnam, well-established Chinese minorities already existed in these countries and had an important place in commerce. Despite living and working for generations in their adopted homelands, the established Chinese were still stereotyped as outsiders and exploiters. The arrival of the refugees compounded the problem. In the United States cultural and language barriers served to isolate the Indo-Chinese, and affected their economic opportunities. Of those admitted, approximately 420,000 were Vietnamese, 100,000 were Laotians, and 78,000 were Cambodians. Still, relief and resettlement were remedies for only the symptoms of South-East Asia's refugee crisis. By

---

* Cited in Frances FitzGerald, *Fire in the Lake: The Vietnamese and the Americans in Vietnam* (Boston: 1972), 351.

the 1980s it was too late to cure the causes of the region's ills. The tragedy wrought by generations of foreign intervention and civil war was likely to endure for many years to come.

Yet the foreign stake in South-East Asia had not come to an end. The Philippines, for example, still remained in a neo-colonial relationship with the United States. The Islands also had strategic importance for the Americans, and were the site of some of the largest US naval and air bases in the world (e.g. Subic Bay and Clark Air Field). They were vital to American strategic interests in the region, and had played a role in US military operations in Vietnam. Moreover, the country's leaders were reliable allies. The landowning and commercial elite was a bastion of anti-communism, and kept a firm grip on the country. Poverty was widespread, and despite democratic forms the political system remained unresponsive to popular demands for change. Yet Washington was not about to criticize. In South-East Asia anti-communism and strategic factors were more important. It thus supported Ferdinand Marcos after his election in 1965, and despite his subsequent moves to impose dictatorial rule. Eventually, in 1986, he was forced to flee the country, but it remained to be seen whether his successor, Corazon Aquino, would succeed in solving the country's problems. Washington welcomed the new president as a moderate – she was a member of the landowning class, and hardly a communist. The question was whether her brand of reform would be enough, or whether revolutionary guerrillas would continue to press for more radical changes. The US public, poorly informed about Washington's role in supporting Marcos in the past, celebrated his fall, and the Reagan administration's timely change of sides enabled it to escape the repercussions of decades of American collaboration with a dictatorial regime. Crises closer to home in the Western Hemisphere, however, were of even higher priority to the USA than events in the Philippines.

CENTRAL AMERICA AND THE CARIBBEAN

In the Western Hemisphere, Central America and the Caribbean were the trouble-spots most likely to witness foreign military intervention. In Nicaragua the United States was determined to see a government installed in Managua which was friendly to American interests, but the Sandinistas were unwilling to recognize Washington's claim to pre-eminent influence in the region. On the contrary, they acted quickly to dismantle the work of its client, the dictator Anastasio Somoza Debayle.

Once in power (see Chapter 11) the junta abrogated the constitution (prepared by Somoza in 1974), and dissolved both the legislature and the National Guard. Shortly thereafter it proclaimed the 'Statute on Rights and Guarantees for the Citizens of Nicaragua', including freedom of the press. The junta did not opt for immediate elections, given the need to restore order in the aftermath of war, but it did proclaim a 'Basic Statute' establishing an appointed legislative body to act in the interim. The junta constituted the executive for all practical purposes. Though the anti-Somoza moderates were represented in the government, the FSLN was clearly the dominant faction. A Sandinista People's Army took over the defence of the country, complemented by a popular militia. The junta inaugurated a literacy campaign as part of its goal of raising the political awareness of the people, and by most accounts it was highly successful. The government left about 50 per cent of the country's economy in private hands. Key areas (such as banking, insurance, mining, fishing and forestry) were nationalized. The junta seized all Somoza family holdings, and these constituted by far the majority of properties in the state sector. In the countryside a programme of land reform was instituted, with peasants receiving individual titles, participating in co-operatives, or going to work on state farms.

As we have noted earlier, the moderate anti-Somoza opposition was never comfortable with the FSLN. By 1981 it protested at the lack of elections, and moved more to the political right. It wanted an opportunity to increase its role in the new order, and feared the consequences of allowing the Sandinistas to remain the dominant faction in the government. The Sandinistas, however, faced a spreading counter-revolutionary war, and therefore were not prepared to hold elections just then. By late 1981 possibly 2,000 former members of Somoza's National Guard were launching raids against Nicaragua from Honduras. They and their recruits would soon be known as '*contras*'. There was also trouble with Miskito and other Indian groups on the Atlantic coast, who wanted Managua to recognize their long-standing aspirations for regional autonomy. An uprising against the Sandinistas in 1981 led to the forced resettlement of possibly 10,000 people. Many fled to Honduras as well. The effect was to turn many of the Indians against the government and towards the *contras*.

Yet the brutality of the *contras* far exceeded the abuses of the Sandinistas, and overall support for the latter remained strong. This meant, however, that the *contras* did not gain the kind of support among the majority of the people which had sustained Sandinista guerrillas earlier.

To succeed, they required outside assistance. Not surprisingly it turned out that the administration of Ronald Reagan was more than willing to provide it. About $10 million went to the counter-revolutionaries in 1981, while $19 million was provided in 1982 for the Central Intelligence Agency to finance covert activities. The CIA arranged for attacks on infrastructures such as bridges or fuel depots, in order to undermine the Nicaraguan economy, and also mined harbours. But the CIA role raised the spectre of a new Vietnam, and in 1984 Congress prohibited further aid to the *contras*. The *contras'* reputation for human-rights violations was also a factor in the ending of assistance. After two years of deliberation the World Court at the Hague ruled in 1986 that the American mining of Nicaraguan harbours had violated international law, but Washington refused to accept its jurisdiction.

As the US spurred the campaign against Nicaragua, the Sandinistas proclaimed a state of emergency in March 1982. They subsequently extended it again and again. A virtual state of war was developing, and civil rights and freedom of the press were limited in the name of national security. Faced with all-out war, many governments (even in the West) have done the same thing, to protect themselves against internal subversion. (For example, the United States and Canada interned citizens of Japanese descent during the Second World War.) Washington's support for an unofficial and undeclared war induced the Sandinistas to limit the right of dissent, but of course this enabled the Reagan administration to condemn their policies as repressive.

The government in Managua expected an invasion by the United States at any moment, but Washington preferred the *contras* to wage a war of attrition. Public-opinion polls in the United States indicated little enthusiasm for direct military intervention, especially after Vietnam. The strategy of the Reagan administration therefore became one of unrelenting but indirect pressure on the Sandinistas. United States aircraft conducted flights over Nicaraguan territory in order to gather intelligence. Washington also permitted anti-FSLN rebels to set up training-camps in the US. United States troops staged manoeuvres in Honduras, and also constructed air strips (for possible use in the event of military intervention in the future). Ships of the fleet were stationed off Nicaragua's shores on both the Atlantic and Pacific sides. Private citizens in the United States raised funds for the *contras* much as they might for charity, while the administration increased its aid to other countries in the area in order to strengthen friendly governments.

Determined to fight the reluctance of Congress to widen the US role,

Reagan went to the public, condemning the Sandinistas as the advance agents of Soviet imperialism in the Western Hemisphere and portraying the *contras* as 'freedom fighters'. The US government also exerted economic pressure by embargoing trade with Nicaragua and lobbying international credit agencies to restrict funds to Managua. The US president alleged that Cuba had thousands of advisers in Nicaragua, though the Sandinistas disputed the numbers and described the personnel who were present as mainly medical, technical and educational aides. Outside observers have estimated the number of Cuban military experts in Nicaragua to be only a small percentage of the total number of advisers. One authority sets the number at about one hundred for late 1982, certainly insufficient to determine the outcome. The Soviet Union also sent advisers and medical officials, and although the specific numbers were hotly disputed, most non-administration authorities agreed they were very few. Again, their numbers were hardly enough to affect the tide of events in the region. Despite its access to Cuba, the USSR was in no position to attempt a major military operation so far from its shores and so deep inside the American sphere of influence. Nor was Cuba strong enough to stand up to the United States. On the other side, there was no disputing that Reagan wanted to see the Sandinistas turned out.

The Sandinistas held elections for a constituent assembly and the presidency on 4 November 1984, just two days before Ronald Reagan was re-elected president of the United States for a second term. Washington denounced the resulting Sandinista victory, but other outside observers claimed the Nicaraguan elections were fairer than those held in El Salvador earlier in the year. Indeed, the Sandinistas won 67 per cent of the vote for the presidency and 61 out of 96 seats in the assembly, attesting to the existence of an active opposition able to function in the country's political system. Six other political parties besides the Sandinistas were in the running, and represented alternatives both to the left and the right. Pro-US opponents of the regime refused to participate, despite the Sandinistas' efforts to negotiate with them and to win their co-operation. But in the face of the Sandinistas' popularity in the countryside, the political party favoured by the US could hardly expect to win. No doubt its leaders hoped to discredit the results by refusing to contest the election.

Still, even after the voting the continuing war persuaded the government in Managua that it could not permit unfettered dissent, despite protests from Amnesty International. It restricted political-party and trade union activity, and resorted to censorship. There were instances of incommunicado detention, torture and killings, though not on the scale of the *contras'* abuses. All this rallied the opposition. The hierarchy of the Roman Catholic Church joined in criticizing the government, though many parish priests disagreed. Washington favoured a negotiated settlement in principle, but talks rarely moved beyond the preliminaries. The so-called '*Contadora*' group (Colombia, Mexico, Venezuela and Panama) tried to initiate discussions, but had little success. Given the Reagan administration's support for the *contras*, it was quite possible that Washington preferred to see the conflict settled by force rather than negotiation. This would, after all, have the advantage of obviating the need for compromise. Washington's words bespoke an interest in negotiation, but its actions suggested otherwise. The Sandinistas had reason to be worried.

The willingness of the United States to deploy direct military force in the region was confirmed in the autumn of 1983, when on 25 October, 6,000 American troops landed on the small Caribbean island of Grenada. Although a brief engagement, the invasion of Grenada requires more than passing mention, precisely because of the American decision to dispatch troops rather than rely on *contra*-style surrogates. The objective was to overthrow a leftist regime. In the context of Washington's inconclusive struggle with the Sandinistas the decisiveness of the US action in Grenada was a pledge of America's determination to preserve its influence in the Western Hemisphere, and was immensely popular in the United States. Of course, Grenada was an easy target. Its regular army numbered only 1,000. Even so, on the home front in the USA the invasion represented a political coup for the Reagan administration.

The leftist New Jewel Movement (NJM) of Maurice Bishop had seized power in March 1979, in the face of an alleged plot by the government of Sir Eric Gairy to assassinate the opposition leadership. The problem was that afterwards the NJM never felt secure enough to seek a mandate from the people by going to the polls, even though the easy-going Bishop remained very popular. For Washington, though, Grenada's foreign rather than domestic policies were of greater import. Bishop sought aid and advice from Cuba and the Soviet Union. Havana longed to end its isolation in the Western Hemisphere, and welcomed any opportunity to court a client. Grenada was far more peripheral for Moscow, but the USSR had an interest in annoying the Americans. Eastern Bloc aid, however, consisted mostly of small arms. The type of weapons involved would not have permitted aggression beyond the shores of Grenada itself.

Among the outside powers Cuba played the largest role in Grenada, mainly by helping to build a new airport at Point Salines. This had also been the pet project of Bishop's predecessor, and was supposed to boost the tourist trade by allowing large passenger aircraft to land on Grenada. The problem was that the U S State Department feared that Point Salines might become a staging-area for Havana, or even Moscow, in the event of trouble in the Western Hemisphere. For this reason Washington regarded Grenada as a security threat to the United States itself. In the autumn of 1983 there were 784 Cubans on the island. While most had militia training, only forty-three were full-fledged military advisers. In addition a small number of Russian, East German, North Korean and Libyan military personnel were in the country, but the largest contingent was from Cuba.

The opportunity for the Americans to intervene came as a result of internal feuding in the NJM itself, which resulted in the assassination of Bishop and the threat of internal chaos. Washington lobbied the Caribbean states for support, and succeeded in persuading seven of them to request US military intervention. The initiative thus came from the US government, and invasion followed. The official rationale for the American action was twofold. First, Reagan wanted to protect the 1,000 Americans resident in Grenada. The administration feared they might be taken hostage by the rebel government. Second, Washington cited the alleged strategic threat, specifically the Point Salines airport. Back in the United States the president was a hero, so that to many students of US politics Grenada raised the spectre of direct military strikes elsewhere, e.g. in Central America, Cuba or Libya. In short, the invasion boosted the militant right, and portended dangerous times ahead. While the American invasion of Grenada was hardly on the scale of the Soviet invasion of Afghanistan, it was notable that Washington, like Moscow, did not attempt to negotiate before invoking the military option. Again, the result was war in the Third World, however brief.

CONCLUSION

Conclusions about the post-1945 period must remain tentative because contemporary history has not come to an end, at least not yet. Of course, it could at any moment. While the Third World has been the site of most military conflicts since 1945 and has therefore required extended treatment in these pages, the possibility of nuclear war between the superpowers can hardly be dismissed. The threat of nuclear holocaust makes contemporary history more conditional than ever before. Other people in other times have no doubt feared for the survival of the human race, but today we really do have the power to destroy mankind.

The failure to limit the arms race attests to the danger. As we have seen, such agreements as have been concluded deal mainly with existing and even obsolescent technology, while superpower competition continues in the realm of research and development. This is likely to be the pattern in the future as well. Moreover, the treaties which have received the assent of the United States and the Soviet Union have not always involved the participation of other atomic powers (such as France or the People's Republic of China). There are many players besides the superpowers in the nuclear contest. The effect is to compound the problem of controlling the arms race. Indeed, the West in particular has promoted the sale of nuclear technology (for research and power reactors) to dozens of countries, including many in politically volatile regions of the Third World. This simply magnifies the threat from nuclear proliferation. Such sales have often been accompanied by aid programmes to assist in financing, suggesting that government support for the nuclear industry in the West is strong indeed. This aid represents a subsidy to the nuclear establishment in the donor country as much as to the country receiving assistance. In developed countries like Canada the nuclear industry could conceivably go into a major decline without foreign sales financed by loans and credits from Ottawa. Soviet attitudes towards the proliferation of nuclear technology in the Third World have been considerably more circumspect by comparison.

Obviously many recipients of nuclear technology are in a position to use their new knowledge to develop atomic weapons of their own. India's test in 1974 was public, but other countries have worked in secret. Certainly Israel has the scientific and technical capacity to build a bomb, as may Argentina, South Africa and others. Among developed Western nations profits from the sale of power and research reactors seem to have taken precedence over the need to control proliferation, so that there were hundreds of nuclear power plants around the world by the 1980s (in both industrially developed and underdeveloped countries). No doubt the world is hungry for energy, yet the dilemma remains. The nuclear threat arises not simply from the arms race, but from the sale of power technology as well. And even the strictly peaceful application of the technology is problematical, as major nuclear accidents at Three Mile

Island in the USA (1979) and at Chernobyl in the USSR (1986) attest.

Yet the dynamics of recent global change are affected by still other factors besides the possibility of nuclear holocaust. The decline of Western Europe as the arbiter of global affairs and the emergence of two superpowers also shapes the course of world history. The resultant two-way competition, between the USA and the USSR, defines much of world politics since 1945. It virtually guarantees that many local conflicts will take on global significance, as the superpowers come to the defence of their client states, and local or regional crises become caught up in the East–West struggle. Perhaps the most dangerous example is the Arab–Israeli crisis, which on more than one occasion has threatened to involve the United States and the Soviet Union in direct military confrontation. Although the People's Republic of China is the world's most populous nation and potentially a dominant player on the world stage, it is also preoccupied mainly with internal problems. Washington and Moscow have a much greater impact globally, and the effects are apparent.

World history, however, encompasses much more than diplomacy or politics, whether between the two superpowers or among other nations. Global crises have social and economic dimensions as well, and we have seen that these too play a large role in determining outcomes. The legacy of colonialism provides perhaps the clearest example. Recall the devastating impact of Japanese imperialism on society in Korea, or the role of the French in Indo-China and Algeria, or the incredibly repressive policies of the Portuguese in Africa. Colonialism reorganized the societies it affected. It altered their internal class structures, their economic life and their customs, as well as their political institutions. In some colonies even systems of forced labour were established. No wonder the outcome was nationalist or socialist revolution. The actions of local oligarchies also provide an example of how economic and social changes are reflected in politics. We have seen how their expropriation of Indian lands in El Salvador and Nicaragua disrupted traditional society and contributed to peasant uprisings in Central America. Throughout the Third World colonial warfare had a social impact as well, politicizing and often radicalizing the local population. Certainly this was the case in Vietnam and Mozambique. War uproots people, destroys homes, creates refugees, and thus polarizes politics. Of course, there is no clear line demarcating social, economic and political forces in history. They are inextricably linked, however convenient it is to treat them separately for analytical purposes. In the real world they are all of a piece, so that, although our analysis has emphasized diplomacy and politics, we have nevertheless often been drawn into an examination of social history as well.

The study of world history also seems to confirm that almost anything is possible today. Even genocide has not been banished from the face of the earth – remember Pol Pot. Also remember that many Western nations preferred to see Khmer Rouge delegates seated at the United Nations rather than those of a Vietnamese puppet government in Cambodia, even though it was Hanoi that ended Pol Pot's tyranny. The Western position was more than a little Machiavellian, and made for strange bedfellows indeed. Apparently it was more important to isolate Vietnam diplomatically than to banish the representatives of a genocidal regime.

The contemporary world is witness to other barbarities as well. Again, there are apparently few limits to the possibilities, so that many examples could be cited. These are as likely to represent the choices of policy-makers in the developed world as the underdeveloped world. Thus science and technology have been called into the service of war, and have helped make it more brutal than ever. An example is the use of chemical defoliants in Vietnam. It was impractical to deploy these weapons exclusively against enemy military targets. By their very nature they blanketed large areas and even entire regions, not only destroying forest cover and crops needed by the Vietcong, but damaging the civilian food supply as well. Moreover, defoliants poisoned innocent bystanders and guerrillas alike. Years later many of the victims (and also some of those who spread the chemicals) died of cancer from the after-effects. And then there was napalm, not a brand-new weapon by any means, yet one particularly injurious when deployed in populated areas, as it was. Of course, war itself is an extreme act. Yet it is distinctly not the case that the great powers (in the West or the East) resort to force only after all other means of resolving conflicts have been exhausted. When faced with what he perceived to be a crisis in the Dominican Republic in 1965, Lyndon Johnson immediately ordered an invasion. Similarly Washington would not negotiate with Maurice Bishop in the months before his murder, but landed troops in Grenada once its government had disintegrated in chaos. While not a belligerent itself, Moscow did its best to fan the Arab–Israeli crisis in 1967, encouraging Nasser's sabre-rattling and thus contributing to the outbreak of the Six Day War.

The list of atrocities is lengthy, and they are hardly the monopoly of any one people or nation. The Cultural Revolution in China witnessed notable crimes, as mob action was deployed against alleged enemies of Mao Zedong. The cult of Mao, indeed, illustrated the potential for manipulating masses of people, much as Hitler did in a very different situation and for very different purposes. Even religion is still called into the service of politics. Note the Moral Majority and the radical right in the United States. Elsewhere sectarian violence remains part of contemporary history, as events in India, Sri Lanka and Iran attest. Tens of thousands have paid with their lives because of their religious beliefs, not generations ago but in the 1970s and the 1980s. And it hardly needs repeating here that specifically political repression is part of everyday life in today's world. Witness the fate of the 'disappeared' in Argentina and Chile, the *apartheid* regime in the Republic of South Africa or the dictatorial regimes in both North and South Korea. One has only to read the annual reports of Amnesty International for a mind-numbing list, hundreds of pages long, of atrocities against political prisoners and prisoners of conscience. Racism is alive and well too. Even in the United States, one of the richest countries in the world by any standard, vast economic inequalities exist, and are correlated with race. Yet perhaps the greatest atrocity of all is that possibly 25 million persons have been killed in war and conflict in the Third World since 1945.

Our study also makes it clear that there are more than a few contradictions in history. History is not a subject that reconciles the irreconcilable, but follows the facts wherever they lead. Examples abound. Western nations often condemn the Eastern Bloc for failing to live up to its treaty obligations, yet the West itself is capable of violating treaties. Thus Washington has accused Moscow of ignoring some of the terms of the Strategic Arms Limitation Treaties, but, on the other hand, Lyndon Johnson's 1965 invasion of the Dominican Republic was in direct contravention of treaty obligations (the Charter of the Organization of American States) against unilateral intervention in the affairs of Western Hemispheric states. Washington's support for the *contras* in Nicaragua was also of dubious legality.

Perhaps some of the most important contradictions, however, are to be found in superpower support for authoritarian regimes. For the West such policies often spur the spread of anti-capitalist revolution and create opportunities for the Eastern Bloc to expand its influence. Yet many dictators continue to receive financial and military aid. The effect seems quite counter-productive to the goal of heading off revolutionary crises. The Soviets are equally misguided. In Afghanistan they intervened militarily on behalf of a government which had clearly alienated a majority of the population. The result was that the USSR soon found itself entangled in a major war. But whether this would further the cause of social revolution remained to be seen.

There are even conspiracies in contemporary history. Consider the role of the United States in the fall of the Arbenz government in Guatemala (1954). Recall how Britain, France and Israel plotted in secret to invade Egypt in 1956. The death of Ngo Dinh Diem in 1963 was the result of a conspiracy, and again one in which the highest officials of the US government were implicated. Surely the sequence of events which culminated in the Gulf of Tonkin incident (1964) had a conspiratorial dimension, as the Johnson administration prepared the way for a congressional resolution authorizing it to expand the war in Vietnam. Furthermore, the administration's explanation of the facts as given at the time was less than candid. Remember the alleged plot of Lin Biao against Mao Zedong in 1971, or the possibility that the Maoists had conspired against Lin. So too, the Soviets engaged in a conspiracy when they arranged to install Babrak Karmal as their puppet before invading Afghanistan in 1979.

Many things are done under cover. This means, of course, that the facts of recent history may be difficult to trace because of deliberate efforts to hide them, perhaps on grounds of national security. Until the US Congress investigated, this was true of various alleged US assassination attempts against Castro, Lumumba and others. Sometimes policymakers simply lie in the hope of protecting their political careers. This too distorts the record, although many times the facts ultimately come out – Richard Nixon apparently did his best to cover up the Watergate incident. In other cases the facts themselves may simply be obscure. The role of the United States in the fall of Allende provides an example, because it was so indirect. Congressional investigations were once again necessary before the full story came to light. Similarly the USSR certainly acted in secret when it attempted to install offensive missiles in Cuba in 1962, though it was soon caught in the act by American intelligence. Later the Soviet Union relied on Cuban troops to act as its surrogates in Africa in the 1970s and 1980s, while Moscow itself attempted to remain in the background.

It is thus often difficult to explain the real causes of events in contemporary history, and indeed for many reasons besides secrecy. Sometimes the problem is that we may be reluctant to face unpleasant facts. On the other hand, there are usually at least a few historians willing to pursue politically sensitive or embarrassing issues. The story of Cambodia is a case in point. Some authors argue that the US bombing in the early 1970s contributed to the conditions which made it possible for the Khmer Rouge to topple the Lon Nol government. This is an interpretation that many Americans would prefer to discredit, for obvious reasons. Nevertheless it is a possibility that historians must consider. Did Washington play an indirect and no doubt unwitting role in the assumption of power by the murderous Pol Pot?

Similarly myth and ideology can also obscure the facts. Recall our study of the economic 'miracle' in Japan and South Korea. Western analysts commonly ascribe the success of these economies to specific national characteristics (Japanese traditions of hard work, respect for authority and loyalty) or to the virtues of enlightened private enterprise (in Japan, for example, programmes of 'lifetime' employment). Yet the reality was that cheap labour policies had much to do with Japan's post-1945 recovery, and that lifetime employment was an important weapon for dividing the workforce and undermining its militancy. There was less to lifetime employment than many Westerners realized, and thus more compulsion behind the country's economic success. So too a repressive state, not simply private capital, helped account for South Korea's rapid economic development. Seoul's strategies for demobilizing the labour movement and its special tax and other concessions were designed to create a favourable investment climate for foreign enterprise. These policies often resulted in strikes and other forms of popular resistance, so that the regime deployed police and military force against dissidents and opposition political leaders. In both Japan and Korea the economic miracle was quite explicable once we moved beyond the mythology and propaganda. Whatever the intricacies of tracing the facts, historians often succeed in doing so, though it takes more than a little effort. The study of contemporary history is not a casual undertaking, nor can we really know the facts simply by living through the events of our own times. We need to go behind events, subjecting them to searching inquiry, before we can make sense of the contemporary world.

We have thus explored some important trends in this and preceding chapters, but there is much debate about their relative significance. In the West, of course, opinion-leaders are fond of pointing out the foibles and crimes of the East, while in the East policy-makers impugn the motives and methods of the West. The troubles of the world always seem to be the fault of the other side. This is not to say that there is no capacity for self-criticism anywhere. On the contrary, the opportunities for free and independent expression serve the developed countries of the First World very well indeed. On this score the developed countries of the Second World do not compare favourably – consider the fate of dissidents in the USSR, such as Alexander Solzhenitsyn or Andrei Sakharov. On the other hand, some Western clients in the Third World systematically curb freedom of expression, so that the Western Bloc, like the Eastern, is linked to several countries with a penchant for authoritarianism – consider Chile, South Korea, the Republic of South Africa, Indonesia and others. Moreover, it is still the case that the West exercises more influence in the Third World than the Soviet Union, so that it is in a strong position to persuade its clients to change. But it does not always do so.

Of course, it is not invariably within the power of the United States and its allies to dictate outcomes anywhere in the world. Local conditions impose limits on the possibilities, and dictators are more than a little resistant to reform. Nor does the United States, the Soviet Union or some other country necessarily have the right to intervene and impose a solution. The reality, however, is that both superpowers do not merely tolerate repressive regimes which they are unable to influence. Instead they often provide positive support for them in the form of economic and military aid. While most developed nations in the First World enjoy democracy at home, they are deeply implicated in dictatorship in the Third World – as are the Soviets. Moreover, the USSR has yet to achieve democracy for its own people, much less end repression in Eastern Europe or among its Third World friends. The one-party state remains the norm for communism, as the fate of Solidarity suggests. The same is true in China. How all these factors are likely to affect the future, only time will tell.

To sum up, while we may not be able to draw definitive conclusions about every aspect of world history since 1945, we have certainly succeeded in identifying some of the root causes of global change. This is no small achievement. It means that we can begin to explain the world around us. As a result we may even be able to influence the course of future events, although it is still a question whether the vested interests which gain from the *status quo* can be induced to change their ways. In many countries of the world the odds are very much against reform, however it may be defined in any particular place. Accordingly, new crises will emerge in both East and West, and all under the shadow of a possible nuclear catastrophe. Yet the prerequisite for action or even debate is to understand the dynamics which shape the world of today, and we are well on the way to doing precisely this.

BIBLIOGRAPHICAL NOTE

The following titles include the studies which most influenced my interpretation, provided vital data, or shaped the narrative. I am pleased to acknowledge their contribution to my work, though their authors may not always agree with my interpretation of events or how I have deployed their findings. In addition I identify a limited selection of titles which provide alternative points of view or which may serve as references for readers who wish to pursue specific subjects.

Two books were of particular importance in developing my overall view of world history: L. S. Stavrianos, *Global Rift: The Third World Comes of Age* (1981); and James Petras, *Critical Perspectives on Imperialism and Social Class in the Third World* (1978). *Global Rift* is without doubt the best comprehensive history of the Third World. Petras develops a model of First World–Third World relations which also comprehends the specific features of each local situation. Another valuable survey is Ian Roxborough, *Theories of Underdevelopment* (1979). A general study of capitalist development is Michel Beaud, *A History of Capitalism: 1500– 1980* (1983). Adam Westoby's *Communism since World War II* (1981) has had an important influence on how I interpret the history of the Eastern Bloc, as have Chris Harman's *Class Struggles in Eastern Europe, 1945–1983* (1983); Ernest Mandel's *From Stalinism to Eurocommunism: The Bitter Fruits of 'Socialism in One Country'* (1978); and Paul Sweezy's *Post-Revolutionary Society* (1980). My own thoughts on recent world history were first summarized in an article published at Queen's University in Canada, 'World History since 1945: An Interpretation', *Queen's Quarterly*, 88 (Autumn 1981).

Useful reference works include *The Europa Year Book: A World Survey*, published annually, and the yearly *World Development Report* of the World Bank. Europa Publications also issues more detailed references for specific areas of the world. See *The Far East and Australasia*; *The Middle*

East and North Africa; and *Africa South of the Sahara.* The *Statistical Abstract of the United States* (annual) is also a mine of information, as is *World Armaments and Disarmament: SIPRI Yearbook* (annual), published by the Stockholm International Peace Research Institute. See Alan Palmer's handy *Penguin Dictionary of Twentieth Century History* (1979) as well. In addition readers should note the *Amnesty International Report* (annual). This summarizes the record of human-rights violations around the world. The state of democracy is such that hardly any country escapes review. There are numerous regional histories for readers who wish to look up specific points or study a particular area. Examples which I have found to be reliable include Felix Gilbert, *The End of the European Era: 1890 to the Present* (1984); Walter Laqueur, *Europe since Hitler* (1982); Roland Oliver and J. D. Fage, *A Short History of Africa* (1978); Robert Shafer, *A History of Latin America* (1978); John Fairbank, Edwin Reischauer and Albert Craig, *East Asia: Tradition and Transformation* (1978); and Henry Wilson, *The Imperial Experience in Sub-Saharan Africa since 1870* (1977). There are many others as well, too numerous to list here. Surveys of national histories also abound, such as Basil Dmytryshyn, *USSR: A Concise History* (1978); Gordon Wright, *France in Modern Times* (1981); and William Chafe, *The Unfinished Journey: America since World War II* (1986). Alternative approaches to many of the issues discussed in these pages may be found in William Keylor's survey of global diplomacy, *The Twentieth-Century World: An International History* (1984); the fifth edition of Walter LaFeber's study of USA–USSR relations, *America, Russia, and the Cold War: 1945–1984* (1985); and several recent books on the colonial world: R. F. Holland, *European Decolonization, 1918–1981: An Introductory Survey* (1985); Raymond Betts, *Uncertain Dimensions: Western Overseas Empires in The Twentieth Century* (1985); and W. David McIntyre, *The Commonwealth of Nations: Origins and Impact, 1869–1971* (1977).

The United States and the Origins of the Cold War: 1941–1947 (1972) by John Lewis Gaddis; *The Politics of War: The World and United States Foreign Policy, 1943–1945* (1968) by Gabriel Kolko; *Power and Culture: The Japanese–American War, 1941–1945* (1981) by Akira Iriye; *Churchill, Roosevelt, Stalin: The War They Waged and the Peace They Sought* by Herbert Feis (1967); *The Meaning of Yalta: Big Three Diplomacy and the New Balance of Power* (1956), edited by John Snell; *The Limits of Power: The World and United States Foreign Policy, 1945–1954* (1972) by Joyce and Gabriel Kolko; and particularly *Soviet–American Confrontation: Postwar Reconstruction and the Origins of the Cold War* (1973) by Thomas

Paterson shaped my view of the Second World War and the early Cold War (Chapters 1 and 2). Paterson was also my main source for the economic content of US policy after the Second World War, as well as for many statistics. Jon Halliday's *A Political History of Japanese Capitalism* (1975) provided a guide through the many myths surrounding Japan's rehabilitation after the Second World War, and also for the discussion of Japan later in Chapter 9. A picture of the struggle inside the Truman administration over the international control of atomic energy can be found in Jordan Schwarz, *The Speculator: Bernard M. Baruch in Washington, 1917–1965* (1981).

Stavrianos was an important help for introducing the history of the Third World in Chapter 3. Although dealing with specific regions or themes, Jon Halliday along with Basil Davidson, *Africa in Modern History: The Search for a New Society* (1978); John R. Hanson II, *Trade in Transition: Exports from the Third World, 1840–1900* (1980); and Michael Klare and Cynthia Arnson, *Supplying Repression: US Support for Authoritarian Regimes Abroad* (1981) also provided ideas and data on the same subject, as did the essayists in Robin Jeffrey (ed.), *Asia–The Winning of Independence* (1981), and particularly Lee Kam Hing on Malaya. A valuable survey of the era of decolonization is Stewart Easton, *The Rise and Fall of Western Colonialism: A Historical Survey from the Early Nineteenth Century to the Present* (1964). Also see Stanley Wolpert, *A New History of India* (1982), and Michael Kidron, *Foreign Investments in India* (1965), although the relevant sections of *Global Rift* had a major impact on my interpretation of Gandhi and the Congress Party. The most useful book on the Chinese revolution is Maurice Meisner, *Mao's China and After: A History of the People's Republic* (1986), while C. P. FitzGerald's succinct account, *Mao Tse-tung and China* (1977), is especially clear about military developments during the Chinese civil war. See also Lucien Bianco, *Origins of the Chinese Revolution, 1915–1949* (1971), and Harold Isaacs, *The Tragedy of the Chinese Revolution* (1961). Meisner, however, was my principal source, and also shaped my account of the Great Leap Forward and the Cultural Revolution in Chapters 4 and 9. I found Nadav Safran to be the most helpful on the Arab–Israeli crisis: *Israel: The Embattled Ally* (1981). Safran's strength is to explain issues from the viewpoint of the various contenders, so that the logic of each position (however contradictory in the overall pattern of events) becomes apparent. His work also guided my subsequent treatment in later chapters.

The most valuable studies of Korea (Chapter 4) were Bruce Cumings,

The Origins of the Korean War: Liberation and the Emergence of Separate Regimes, 1945–1947 (1981); the essays in his edited collection entitled *Child of Conflict: The Korean–American Relationship, 1943–1953* (1983); and Joyce and Gabriel Kolko, *The Limits of Power*. Frances FitzGerald, *Fire in the Lake: The Vietnamese and the Americans in Vietnam* (1972), and John Prados, *The Sky Would Fall: Operation Vulture: The US Bombing Mission in Indochina, 1954* (1983), inspired my treatment of early Vietnamese history and the role of the French. In my view, however, the best single-volume account of the Vietnam War is Stanley Karnow, *Vietnam: A History* (1984). Karnow was especially valuable for the narrative presented in Chapter 8 and dealing with the American role in Indo-China. Jean Chesneaux, *China: The People's Republic, 1949–1976* (1979), provided insight into the early history of the People's Republic of China and particularly the Maoists, though *Mao's China* by Meisner was still my most important source.

As noted previously, Westoby and Harman influenced my interpretation of the Soviet Bloc, and Chapter 5 reflects their contribution. The following works were also significant: Julius Braunthal, *History of the International*; Vol. 3: *1943–1968* (1980); François Fejtö, *A History of the People's Democracies: Eastern Europe since Stalin* (1971); and Fernando Claudin, *The Communist Movement: From Comintern to Cominform* (1975). Braunthal was the source for the narrative of the events of 1956 in Poland and Hungary. Also see Bogdan Szajkowski (ed.), *Marxist Governments: A World Survey* (1981), 3 vols. The essays included in Szajkowski cover almost every Marxian regime in the world. A fine example is his own contribution on Albania. An important perspective on Hungary is to be found in Bill Lomax, 'The Working Class in the Hungarian Revolution of 1956', *Critique*, 12 (Autumn–Winter 1979–80). A comparative study of income distribution is to be found in Montek Ahluwalia, 'Inequality, Poverty, and Development', *Journal of Development Economics*, 3 (1976). Ahluwalia's data sample First, Second and Third World countries, and have had a bearing on my views of development in both East and West. For the industrialized Western powers, particularly European economic integration and German rearmament, I relied on Richard Barnet, *The Alliance: America, Europe, Japan, Makers of the Post-War World* (1983). For Iran I found Nikkie Keddie's *Roots of Revolution: An Interpretive History of Modern Iran* (1981) to be the most helpful, while Safran offered guidance through the Suez crisis.

Basil Davidson's *Africa in Modern History* shaped my view of the history of Africa in the era of decolonization (Chapter 6). There are several useful surveys, in particular Roland Oliver and Anthony Atmore, *Africa since 1800* (1972), and Oliver and J. D. Fage, *A Short History of Africa* (cited above), but Davidson most influenced the interpretation presented here and provided important data. An excellent source is vol. 8 of *The Cambridge History of Africa* (1984), edited by Michael Crowder and covering 1940–75. Gordon Wright's survey, *France in Modern Times*, includes an outline of French affairs during the post-war era, and in the present context during the Algerian crisis. My view of post-independence Algeria was influenced mainly by Michael Löwy's *The Politics of Combined and Uneven Development: The Theory of Permanent Revolution* (1981). Also see John Saul, *The State and Revolution in Eastern Africa* (1979), and J. Forbes Munro, *Africa and the International Economy, 1800–1960: An Introduction to the Modern Economic History of Africa South of the Sahara* (1976). The essays in Walter Laqueur (ed.), *The Pattern of Soviet Conduct in the Third World* (1983), include information on the Soviet role in Africa and elsewhere. *The Past Has Another Pattern: Memoirs* (1982) by George Ball gives a detailed review of the Congo crisis and American policy. For this and other crises see US Senate, 94th Congress, 1st Session, *Alleged Assassination Plots involving Foreign Leaders*, Report No. 94–465 (Washington, D.C.: 20 November 1975).

Several studies influenced my treatment of Latin America as an essentially neo-colonial area (Chapter 7): Petras, *Critical Perspectives*, noted above; Stanley Stein and Barbara Stein, *The Colonial Heritage of Latin America: Essays on Economic Dependence in Perspective* (1970); Michael Conniff (ed.), *Latin American Populism in Comparative Perspective* (1982); and Claudio Véliz, *The Centralist Tradition in Latin America* (1980). Thomas Skidmore and Peter Smith's survey, *Modern Latin America* (1984), and Shafer's *History of Latin America* are reliable references. For specific subjects see Klare and Arnson (cited above); Robert Alexander's clear and accessible *Juan Domingo Perón: A History* (1979); Walter LaFeber's *Inevitable Revolutions: The United States in Central America* (1983); and particularly Cole Blasier, *The Hovering Giant: US Responses to Revolutionary Change in Latin America* (1976). Blasier influenced my treatment of Guatemala and Cuba the most. George Ball's memoirs provide an insightful account of the Americans' strategy in the Cuban missile crisis, and I have drawn upon his outline of events. Westoby's *Communism since World War II* provides an assessment of the importance of the Cuban revolution for Latin America generally, as does Gérard Chaliand's *Revolution in the Third World* (1978). Additional data on the missile crisis and its aftermath came from Barnet (cited above) and also from E. P. Thompson and Dan Smith (eds.), *Protest and Survive* (1981).

As noted above, I have followed Karnow's *Vietnam* for the narrative of the American role in Indo-China, though my interpretation and conclusions reflect a broad sampling of historical literature (Chapter 8). The work of William Shawcross also influenced my account: *Sideshow: Kissinger, Nixon and the Destruction of Cambodia* (1979) and *The Quality of Mercy: Cambodia, Holocaust and Modern Conscience* (1984). Howard Zinn's survey of American history, *A People's History of the United States* (1980), includes a brief appreciation of the spirit of the anti-war movement during the Indo-China crisis, as well as a critical review of other aspects of life in the USA. Readers will also wish to refer to the appropriate essays in Szajkowski. Also see Christine White, 'Recent Debates in Vietnamese Development Policy', in Gordon White et al. (eds.), *Revolutionary Socialist Development in the Third World* (1983). A defence of US policy can be found in Guenter Lewy, *America in Vietnam* (1978).

For Chapter 9 Meisner provides an excellent account of the Cultural Revolution and after. Immanuel C. Y. Hsü's survey, *The Rise of Modern China* (1983), also carries through to the era of Deng Xiaoping. Hsü tends to reflect a Dengist interpretation of recent events. A report on Deng's reforms is Donald S. Zagoria, 'China's Quiet Revolution', *Foreign Affairs*, 62 (Spring 1984). For an interpretation of recent Japanese history see Jon Halliday, 'Capitalism and Socialism in East Asia', *New Left Review*, 124 (November–December 1980); F. Quei Quo, 'Japan's Role in Asia: A United States Surrogate?', *International Journal*, 38 (Spring 1983); and Jon Halliday and Gavan McCormack, *Japanese Imperialism Today: 'Co-Prosperity in Greater East Asia'* (1973). On the Koreas see the essays in Gavan McCormack and Mark Selden (eds.), *Korea, North and South: The Deepening Crisis* (1978). The history of North Korea after the 1950s war is also traced in Cumings, 'Democratic People's Republic of Korea', in Szajkowski, vol. 2, and Jon Halliday, 'The North Korean Enigma', in White et al. or his earlier version in *New Left Review*, 127 (May–June 1981). Halliday includes data on Japanese colonialism relevant to the history of both South and North Korea. Also see Ellen Brun and Jacques Hersh, *Socialist Korea: A Case Study in the Strategy of Economic Development* (1976). Noam Chomsky and Edward Herman review the American role in Indonesia in *The Political Economy of Human Rights*; Vol. 1: *The Washington Connection and Third World Fascism* (1979), while Westoby discusses the importance of the communist party.

The relevant Europa yearbooks are valuable for very recent statistics and factual information on these and other subjects in later chapters.

Several studies have influenced my treatment in Chapter 10 of the United States during the 1970s and 1980s: Fred Halliday, *The Making of the Second Cold War* (1983); and a series of articles by Mike Davis, in particular 'The New Right's Road to Power', *New Left Review*, 128 (July–August 1981), 'The Political Economy of Late Imperial America', *ibid.*, 143 (January–February 1984) and 'Reaganomics' Magical Mystery Tour', *ibid.*, 149 (January–February 1985). For Eastern Europe in the same period, besides Westoby and Braunthal, see Daniel Singer, *The Road to Gdansk: Poland and the USSR* (1982), and Lawrence Weschler, *Solidarity: Poland in the Season of Its Passion* (1982). There are dozens of other books available on the Polish crisis, but I found Singer particularly strong on the social forces behind political change in both the USSR and Poland. Also see William Korey, 'The Future of Soviet Jewry: Emigration and Assimilation', *Foreign Affairs*, 58 (Fall 1979). Surveys of the arms race are the relevant sections of Halliday on the 'Second' Cold War; Robert Malcolmson, *Nuclear Fallacies: How We Have Been Misguided since Hiroshima* (1985); Thompson and Smith, *Protest and Survive*; and the New Left Books edition of *Exterminism and Cold War* (1982). An excellent study of nuclear proliferation is Ron Finch's *Exporting Danger: A History of the Canadian Nuclear Energy Export Programme* (1986).

Safran's *Israel* again made the most sense in sorting out the complexities of the 1967 and 1973 wars in the Middle East and the role of the great powers (Chapter 11). His is certainly one of the best accounts. A very critical treatment of Israel and the United States is Noam Chomsky, *The Fateful Triangle: Israel, the United States and the Palestinians* (1984). For Latin America in the 1970s and after several studies shaped my narrative. See Barbara Stallings, *Class Conflict and Economic Development in Chile, 1958–1973* (1978); James Petras and Morris Morley, *The United States and Chile: Imperialism and the Overthrow of the Allende Government* (1975); Gabriel Smirnow, *The Revolution Disarmed: Chile, 1970–1973* (1979); Liisa North, *Bitter Grounds: Roots of Revolt in El Salvador* (1985); William LeoGrande, 'The Revolution in Nicaragua: Another Cuba?', *Foreign Affairs*, 58 (Fall 1979); Henri Weber, *Nicaragua: The Sandinist Revolution* (1981); Carlos Vilas, *The Sandinista Revolution: National Liberation and Social Transformation in Central America* (1986); Roger Burbach and Patricia Flynn, *Agribusiness in the Americas* (1980); and the essays in Fitzroy Ambursley and Robin Cohen (eds.), *Crisis in the Caribbean* (1983). Also see Ambursley's 'Jamaica: The Demise of

"Democratic Socialism"', *New Left Review*, 128 (July–August 1981). Note too Aaron Klieman's *Israel's Global Reach: Arms Sales as Diplomacy* (1985).

The concluding chapter (Chapter 12) surveys a broad spectrum of contemporary crises, and therefore brings together a variety of sources, with the Europa yearbooks helpful for the most recent data. The following guided my interpretations: David Wield, 'Mozambique–Late Colonialism and Early Problems of Transition', in White et al.; Stavrianos, also for Mozambique; Saul, *The State and Revolution*; Shawcross, *The Quality of Mercy*; Summers, 'Democratic Kampuchea', and 'Lao People's Democratic Republic', both in Szajkowski, *Marxist Governments*, Vol. 2; Barry Wain, 'The Indo-China Refugee Crisis', *Foreign Affairs*, 58 (Fall 1979); Keddie, *Roots of Revolution*; Fred Halliday, *Iran: Dictatorship and Development* (1979); Shaul Bakhash, *The Reign of the Ayatollahs: Iran and the Islamic Revolution* (1984); John Saul and Stephen Gelb, *The Crisis in South Africa: Class Defence, Class Revolution* (1981); Roger Southall, *South Africa's Transkei: The Political Economy of an 'Independent' Bantustan* (1983); Gérard Chaliand, *Report from Afghanistan* (1982); and Hugh O'Shaughnessy, *Grenada: Revolution, Invasion and Aftermath* (1984).

There are, of course, literally tens of thousands of books and articles relevant to recent world history. Government documents, the publications of international organizations and memoirs provide an additional storehouse of information. However restricted a sampling, the above titles are testimony to the quality of research on contemporary history, and I have drawn upon them accordingly. It is notable how much can be learned about very recent events, even though many countries withhold sensitive or controversial source materials on grounds of national security.

CHRONOLOGICAL TABLE

See the definitions of First, Second and Third Worlds in Chapter 3.

THE SECOND WORLD WAR

First World	Second World	Third World
	1939	
□	Nazi–Soviet Non-Aggression Pact □	□ Nomonhan
□	War in Europe □	□ White Paper on Palestine
	1940	
□ France surrenders		□ Japan stations troops in Indo-China
□ Tripartite Pact		
	1941	
□	Japan–USSR Neutrality Pact □	□ Yangtze River
□	Nazis invade USSR □	incident in China
□ US sanctions against Japan		□ Vietminh organized in Vietnam
□ Atlantic Charter		□ Japan invades
□ Pearl Harbor		South-East Asia
	1942	
□	British–Soviet Alliance Treaty □	□ Coral Sea and Midway
□ Dieppe		□ Western Allies invade North Africa
		□ 'Quit India' Resolution
	1943	
□ Casablanca Conference	□ Stalingrad	□ Greater East Asia Conference in Tokyo
□ Invasion of Sicily and Italy		
□	Teheran Conference □	

First World	Second World	Third World

——————————————————— 1944 ———————————————————

First World	Second World	Third World
□ Rome falls □ D-Day □ Bretton Woods Conference		□ US landings in Philippines

——————————————————— 1945 ———————————————————

First World	Second World	Third World
□	Yalta Conference (Churchill, Roosevelt, Stalin)	□ □ Korea divided □ Western powers
□	Germany surrenders	□ return to
□	Potsdam Conference (Churchill/Attlee, Truman, Stalin)	□ Japanese-occupied colonies
□	USSR requests US credits	□ □ Dutch colonial war in Indonesia □ Hukbalahap uprising in Philippines
□ Alamogordo □ Hiroshima–Nagasaki □ Japan surrenders □ US loan to Britain	□ Soong–Stalin Agreement □	□ Uprisings in Algeria □ Jewish refugees go to Palestine □ Korean People's Republic proclaimed □ Marshall Mission to China

THE WORLD SINCE 1945

——————————————————— 1946 ———————————————————

First World	Second World	Third World
□ Greek civil war spreads □ Baruch Plan	□ Polish resistance to Russian hegemony	□ Perón elected in Argentina □ Philippine independence □ French–Vietminh war □Civil war renewed in China □ Iran–Turkish crises

——————————————————— 1947 ———————————————————

First World	Second World	Third World
□ GATT □ Truman Doctrine □ Marshall Plan □ Japanese Constitution	□ Cominform □ Molotov Plan	□ Rio Pact □ Indian–Pakistani independence □ Civil war in South Korea

——————————————————— 1948 ———————————————————

First World	Second World	Third World
□	Berlin Blockade	□ □ OAS formed

First World	*Second World*	*Third World*
	——— 1948 ———	
	□ Tito–Stalin Break	□ War in Malaya
		□ Gandhi assassinated
		□ Israel proclaimed
		□ *Apartheid*
	——— 1949 ———	
□ Federal Republic of Germany	□ German Democratic Republic	□ People's Republic of China
□ NATO	□ COMECON	□ Indonesian independence
	□ Soviet A-bomb	
□	US aid to Yugoslavia □	
	——— 1950 ———	
□ NSC–68		□ War in Korea
□ Pleven Plan (EDC)		□ Agrarian reform in China
	——— 1951 ———	
□ US–Japan peace and security treaties		□ Mau Mau uprising in Kenya
	——— 1952 ———	
□ ECSC		□ Egyptian Revolution
□ US hydrogen bomb		
□ UK tests A-bomb		
	——— 1953 ———	
□ 'Atoms for Peace'	□ Stalin dies	□ Castro attacks Moncada Barracks
	□ Khrushchev USSR party secretary	□ Korean armistice
	□ East Berlin riots	□ First Five Year Plan in People's Republic of China
		□ Anti-Mosaddeq coup in Iran
		□ Central African Federation
	——— 1954 ———	
□ France rejects EDC	□ USSR launches concerted aid programme for non-communist Third World	□ Coup in Guatemala
□ New US Atomic Energy Act		□ Dien Bien Phu
		□ Geneva Conference on Indo-China
		□ War in Algeria
		□ SEATO
	——— 1955 ———	
□	East–West summit at Geneva □	□ Péron falls
□ Germany enters NATO	□ Warsaw Pact	□ Diem cancels elections in Vietnam

First World	*Second World*	*Third World*
	1955	
		□ Baghdad Pact □ Eastern Bloc arms aid for Egypt
	1956	
	□ Twentieth Party Congress, USSR □ Cominform dissolved □ Polish crisis □ Hungarian revolution	□ Hundred Flowers Campaign, China □ Suez crisis
	1957	
□ Treaty of Rome (EEC) □ Eisenhower Doctrine □ USA tests Atlas ICBM	□ USSR announces world's first operational ICBM	□ Ghanaian independence □ Malayan independence
	1958	
□ Fifth Republic in France	□ Khrushchev consolidates power in USSR	□ Great Leap Forward, China □ United Arab Republic formed □ Iraqi coup □ Algeria: Committee of Public Safety
	1959	
		□ Cuban Revolution □ Liu Shaoqi head of People's Republic of China □ Tibetan uprising
	1960	
□ France detonates A-bomb □ US sugar and trade embargoes against Cuba □ New US–Japan security treaty	□ Soviet–Cuban aid agreements □	□ Sino-Soviet split □ National Liberation Front organized in South Vietnam □ Full independence for French colonies in Africa

First World	Second World	Third World
	1960	
		□ Congolese independence; Katanga secedes □ Sharpeville Massacre
	1961	
□ John F. Kennedy assumes US presidency	□ Berlin Wall □ USSR places first man in earth orbit □ USSR explodes 50-megaton H-bomb	□ Lumumba murdered □ Bay of Pigs □ Castro declares he is a Marxist–Leninist □ Geneva agreement on Laos □ Syria leaves UAR
	1962	
□ Missile crisis over Cuba □ □ *One Day in the Life of Ivan Denisovich*		Himalayan war: China–India □ Algerian independence
	1963	
□ Test-Ban treaty □ □ Kennedy assassinated; Lyndon Johnson his successor		□ Buddhist crisis in Vietnam □ Diem assassinated □ Kenyan independence □ Malaysia formed
	1964	
□ Student demonstrations in USA; anti-war movement spreads	□ Khrushchev falls; Brezhnev and Kosygin succeed	□ Gulf of Tonkin incident □ China detonates A-bomb
	1965	
□ Watts race riots in Los Angeles		□ US invades Dominican Republic □ Coup in Indonesia □ Rhodesian UDI
	1966	
□ French forces withdrawn from NATO command		□ Indira Gandhi prime minister of India □ Cultural Revolution in China

First World	Second World	Third World

——————————————— 1967 ———————————————

First World	Second World	Third World
□ Detroit and Newark race riots		□ Shanghai People's Commune □ Six-Day War in Middle East □ Ché Guevara killed

——————————————— 1968 ———————————————

First World	Second World	Third World
□ Non-Proliferation Treaty		□ □ Tet offensive in
□ Paris student–worker strikes □ Martin Luther King assassinated, USA	□ Warsaw Pact invades Czechoslovakia	South Vietnam

——————————————— 1969 ———————————————

First World	Second World	Third World
□ Nixon assumes US presidency □ De Gaulle resigns as president of France		□ Ussuri River battle, China v. USSR □Ho Chi Minh dies □Gadhafi seizes power in Libya

——————————————— 1970 ———————————————

First World	Second World	Third World
□ Kent State killings in USA	□ Strikes and killings in Poland	□ US and South Vietnam invade Cambodia
□ West Germany signs non-aggression pacts with USSR and Poland		□ □ Hussein expels PLO from Jordan □ Nasser dies; Sadat his successor □ Allende elected president of Chile

——————————————— 1971 ———————————————

First World	Second World	Third World
	□ USSR–Egyptian treaty of friendship □	
□ East–West treaty on Berlin		□ □ Bangladesh Republic proclaimed □ South Vietnamese ground forces invade Laos □ Lin Biao killed

——————————————— 1972 ———————————————

First World	Second World	Third World
□ SALT I: USA–USSR		□ □ Nixon visits Beijing
□ Watergate burglary in USA		□ Tanaka visits Beijing □ Sadat expels Russians from Egypt □ Managua earthquake

First World	*Second World*	*Third World*

_____ 1973 _____

First World	*Second World*	*Third World*
□ UK enters Common Market		□ US troops withdraw from Vietnam □ US bombing of Cambodia ends □ October (Yom Kippur) War in Middle East

_____ 1974 _____

□ Coup in Portugal □ Nixon resigns US presidency	□ Alexander Solzhenitsyn exiled from USSR	□ India detonates nuclear device □ Ethiopian Revolution

_____ 1975 _____

□ Helsinki Conference on European Security □

		□ South Vietnam and Cambodia fall □ Communist government in Laos □ Indonesia invades East Timor □ 'State of Emergency' in India □ Portugal's African colonies independent

_____ 1976 _____

□ Carter elected US president	□ New strikes in Poland	□ Zhou Enlai dies □ Mao Zedong dies □ Gang of Four arrested □ Sadat abrogates 1971 USSR treaty □ Military coup in Argentina □ Soweto riots, South Africa

_____ 1977 _____

□ Carter pardons US Vietnam draft dodgers		□ Sadat visits Jerusalem □ Deng Xiaoping re-emerges in China

_____ 1978 _____

□ Militant right in USA		□ Camp David Accords

First World	Second World	Third World
	1978	
		□ Vietnam invades Cambodia □ Coup in Afghanistan
	1979	
□ SALT II signed □ US accords diplomatic recognition to People's Republic of China □ Three Mile Island nuclear accident in USA	□	□ Shah flees Iran □ Grenadian Revolution □ Sandinista Revolution in Nicaragua □ Coup in El Salvador □ USSR invades Afghanistan
	1980	
□ Ronald Reagan elected US president	□ Gdansk Accords in Poland □ Solidarity formed	□ Gang of Four on trial □ Egypt and Israel exchange ambassadors □ Zimbabwean independence
	1981	
	□ Martial law in Poland	□ Sadat assassinated
	1982	
□ Equal Rights Amendment defeated in USA	□ Leonid Brezhnev dies	□ Israel invades Lebanon □ Falklands/Malvinas War
	1983	
□ American cruise missiles arrive in UK		□ US invades Grenada
	1984	
□ Reagan re-elected president in USA	□ USSR tests cruise-type missile	□ Indira Gandhi assassinated
	1985	
□ Reagan opposes sanctions against South Africa		□ US trade embargo against Nicaragua
	1986	
□ US extends new military aid to *contras*	□ Chernobyl nuclear accident in USSR	□ Marcos flees Philippines □ State of emergency in Republic of South Africa

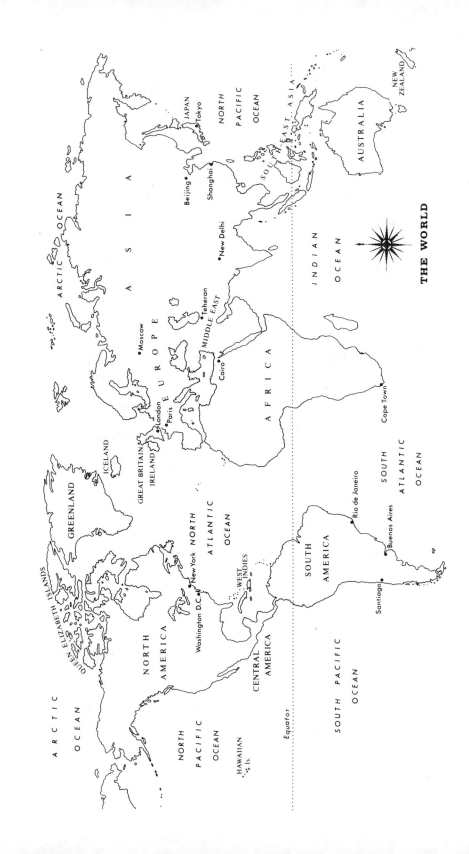

THE WORLD

MIDDLE EAST AND SOUTH ASIA

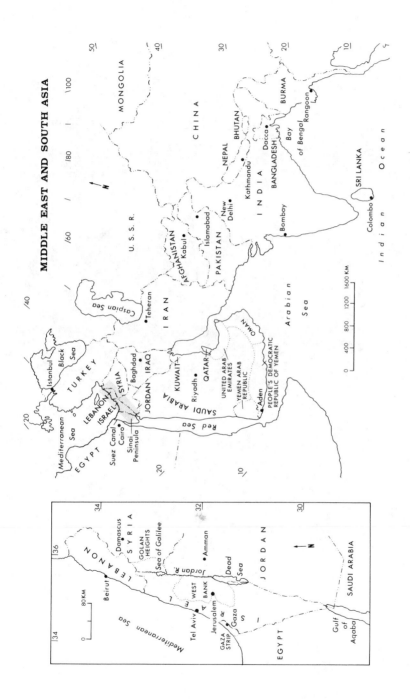

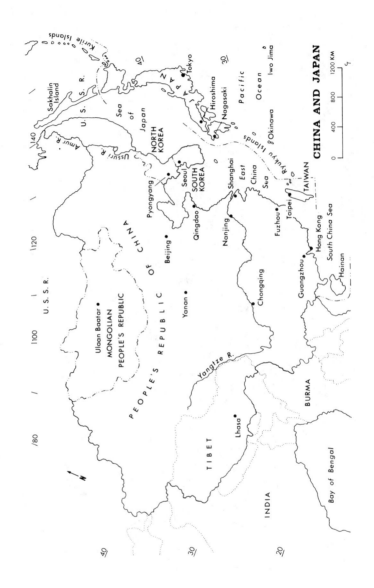

CHINA AND JAPAN

0   400   800   1200 KM

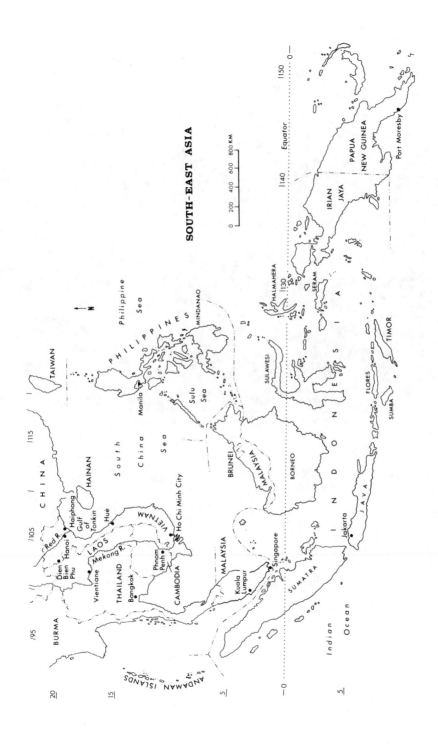

SOUTH-EAST ASIA

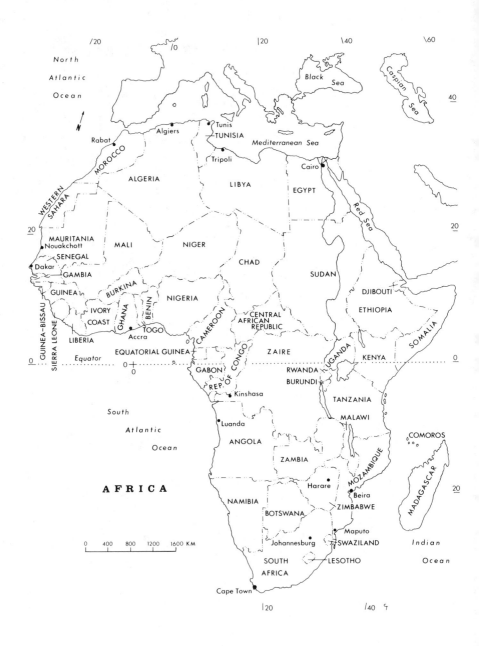

Caribbean Sea

|70

TOBAGO
TRINIDAD

|50

North Atlantic
Ocean

N

Panamá

Caracas

VENEZUELA

Georgetown

SURINAME

PANAMA

Bogatá

COLOMBIA

FRENCH GUIANA
Cayenne

GUYANA

Equator

0

0

Quito

Galapagos Is.

ECUADOR

Amazon R.

PERU

Lima

BRAZIL

La Paz

BOLIVIA

Brasilia

20

20

South Pacific

Ocean

PARAGUAY

Rio de Janeiro

São Paulo

CHILE

Asunción

ARGENTINA

URUGUAY

40

Santiago

Montevideo

Buenos Aires

South Atlantic

Ocean

SOUTH AMERICA

0   200   600   1000 KM

Falkland Is.

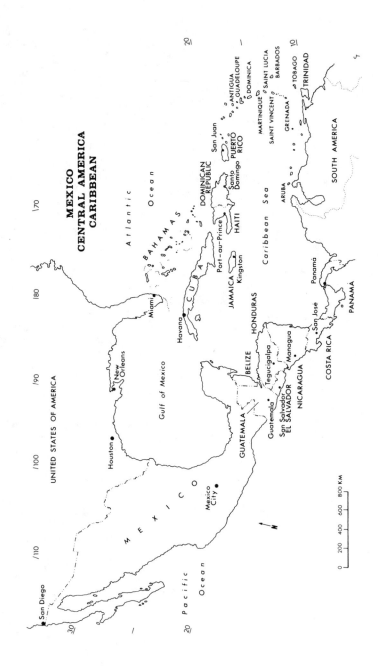

MEXICO
CENTRAL AMERICA
CARIBBEAN

INDEX

David Carter 4/91 (Roskie) 5-